HOMILIES

By

Thomas Cranmer

Contents

PRELIMINARIES

CERTAIN SERMONS OR HOMILIES

appointed to be read in
CHURCHES,
In the time of the late Queen Elizabeth
of famous memory.

And now thought fit to be reprinted by
Authority from the KINGS most
Excellent Majesty.

THE PREFACE

AS it was published in the year 1562.

Considering how necessary it is, that the word of GOD, which is the only food of the soul, and that most excellent light that we must walk by, in this our most dangerous pilgrimage, should at all convenient times be preached unto the people, that thereby they may both learn their duty towards God, their Prince, and their neighbors, according to the mind of the holy Ghost, expressed in the Scriptures: And also to avoid the manifold enormities which heretofore by false doctrine have crept into the Church of God: and how that all they which are appointed Ministers, have not the gift of preaching sufficiently to instruct the people, which is committed unto them, whereof great inconveniences might rise, and ignorance still be maintained, if some honest remedy be not speedily found and provided. The Queens most Excellent Majesty, tendering the soul health of her loving Subjects, and the quieting of their consciences, in the chief and principle points of Christian Religion, and willing also by the true setting forth, and pure declaring of Gods word, which is the principle guide and leader unto all godliness and virtue, to expel and drive away as well all corrupt, vicious, and ungodly living, as also erroneous and poisoned doctrines, tending to superstition and idolatry: hath by the advice of her most Honorable Counselors, for her discharge in this behalf, caused a Book of Homilies, which heretofore was set forth by her most loving brother, a Prince of most worthy memory, EDWARD the sixth, to be Printed anew, wherein are contained certain wholesome and godly exhortations, to move the people to honor and worship Almighty God, and diligently to serve him, every one according to their degree, state and vocation. All which Homilies, her Majesty commands, and straitly charges all Parsons, Vicars, Curates, and all other having spiritual cure, every Sunday and Holyday in the year, at the ministering of the holy Communion, or if there be no Communion ministered that day, yet after the Gospel and Creed, in such order and place as is appointed in the Book of Common Prayers, to read and declare to their Parishioners plainly and distinctly one of the said Homilies, in such order as they stand in the Book, except there be a Sermon, according as it is enjoined in the Injunctions Book of her Highness Injunctions, and then for that cause only, and for none other, the reading of the said Homily to be deferred unto the next Sunday, or Holyday following. And when the aforesaid Book of Homilies is read over, her Majesties pleasure is, that the same be repeated and read again, in such like sort as was before prescribed. Furthermore, her Highness commands, that notwithstanding this order, the said Ecclesiastical persons shall read her Majesties Injunctions, as such times, and in such order, as is in the book thereof appointed. And that the Lords Prayer, the Articles of the faith, and the ten Commandments, be openly read unto the people, as in the said Injunctions is specified, that all her people, of what degree or condition soever they be, may learn how to invoke and call upon the name of God, and know what duty they owe both to God and man: so that they may pray, believe, and work according to knowledge, while they shall live here, and after this life be with him that with his blood hath bought vs all. To whom with the Father and the holy Ghost, be all honor and glory forever. Amen.

HOMILY ON THE READING OF SCRIPTURE

A FRVITFVLL EXHORTATION TO
the reading and knowledge of holy Scripture.

The prayse of holy Scripture. TO a Christian man there can bee nothing either more necessarie or profitable, then the knowledge of holy Scripture, forasmuch as in it is conteyned GODS true word, setting foorth his glory, and also mans duety.

The Perfection of Holy Scripture: And there is no trueth nor doctrine necessarie for our iustification and euerlasting saluation, but that is (or may bee) drawne out of that fountaine and Well of trueth.

The knowledge of holy Scripture is necessary. Therefore as many as bee desirous to enter into the right and perfect way vnto GOD, must applie their mindes to know holy Scripture, without the which, they can neither sufficiently know GOD and his will, neither their office and duty.

To whom the knowledge of holy Scripture is sweet and pleasant. Who be enemies to holy Scripture. And as drinke is pleasant to them that bee drie, and meate to them that be hungrie: so is the reading, hearing, searching, and studying of holy Scripture, to them that bee desirous to know GOD or themselues, and to doe his will. And their stomackes onely doe loathe and abhorre the heauenly knowledge and food of GODS word, that be so drowned in worldly vanities, that they neither fauour GOD, nor any godlinesse: for that is the cause why they desire such vanities, rather then the true knowledge of GOD.

An apt similitude, declaring of whom the Scripture is abhorred. As they that are sicke of an ague, whatsoeuer they eate and drinke (though it bee never so pleasant) yet it is as bitter to them as wormewood, not for the bitternesse of the meate, but for the corrupt and bitter humour that is in their own tongue and mouth: euen so is the sweetnesse of GODS word bitter, not of it selfe, but onely vnto them that haue their mindes corrupted with long custome of sinne and loue of this world.

THE I. PART OF THE EXHORTATION

An exhortation vnto the diligent reading and searching of the holy Scripture. Therefore forsaking the corrupt iudgement of fleshly men, which care not but for their carkasse: let vs reuerently heare and read holy Scriptures, which is the foode of the soule (Matthew 4.4). Let vs diligently search for the Well of Life in the bookes of the New and Old Testament, and not runne to the stinking puddles of mens traditions (deuised by mens imagination) for our iustification and saluation.

The holy Scripture is a sufficient doctrine for our saluation.What things we may learne in the holy Scripture. For in holy Scripture is fully contayned what we ought to doe, and what to eschew; what to beleeue, what to loue, and what to looke for at GODS hands at length. In these Books we shall finde the father from whom, the sonne by whom, and the holy Ghost, in whom all things haue their being and keeping vp, and these three persons to be but one GOD, and one substance. In these books we may learne to know our selues, how vile and miserable we be, and and also to know GOD, how good he is of himselfe, and how hee maketh vs and all creatures partakers of his goodnesse. We may learne also in these Bookes to know GODS will and pleasure, as much as (for this present time) is conuenient for vs to know. And (as the great Clerke and godly Preacher Saint Iohn Chrysostome sayth) whatsoeuer is required to saluation of man, is fully contayned in the Scripture of GOD. He that is ignorant, may there learne and haue knowledge. He that is hard hearted, and an obstinate sinner, shall there finde euerlasting torments (prepared of GODS iustice) to make him afrayd, and to mollifie or soften him. He that is oppressed with misery in this world, shall there finde releefe in the promises of euerlasting life, to his great consolation and comfort. He that is wounded by the Diuell onto death, shall finde there medicine whereby he may bee restored againe vnto health.

Holy Scripture ministreth sufficient doctrinev for all degrees and ages. What commodities and profits, the knowledge of holy Scripture bringeth. If it shall require to teach any trueth, or reprooue false doctrine, to rebuke any vice, to commend any vertue, to giue good counsell, to comfort or to exhort, or to doe any other thing requisite for our saluation, all those things (sayth Saint Chrysostome) we may learne plentifully of the Scripture. There is (sayth Fulgentius) abundantly enough, both for men to eat, and children to sucke. There is, whatsoeuer is meet for all ages, and for all degrees and sorts of men. These Bookes therefore ought to bee much in our hands, in our eyes, in our eares, in our mouthes, but most of all in our hearts. For the Scripture of GOD is the heauenly meat of our soules (Matthew 4.4), the hearing and keeping of it maketh vs blessed (Luke 11.28), sanctifieth vs (John 17.17), and maketh vs holy, it turneth our soules (Psalms 19.7-10), it is a light lanterne to our feet (Psalms 119.105), it is a sure, stedfast, and euerlasting instrument of saluation, it giueth wisedome to the humble and lowly hearts, it comforteth, maketh glad, cheereth, and cherisheth our conscience: it is a more excellent iewell or treasure, then any gold or precious stone, it is more sweet then hony, or hony combe, it is called the best part, which Mary did choose, for it hath in it euerlasting comfort (Luke 10.42). The wordes of holy Scripture be called words of euerlasting life (John 6.68): for they bee GODS instrument, ordayned for the same purpose. They haue power to turne through GODS promise, and they be effectuall through GODS assistance, and (being receiued in a faithfull heart) they haue euer an heauenly spirituall working in them: they are liuely, quicke, and mighty in operation, and sharper then any two edged sword, and entreth thorow, euen vnto the diuiding asunder of the soule and the spirit, of the ioynts and the marrow (Hebrews 4.12). Christ calleth him a wise builder, that buildeth vpon his word, vpon his sure and substantiall foundation (Matthew 7.24). By this word of GOD, wee shall bee iudged: for the word that I speake (sayth Christ) is it, that shall iudge in the last day (John 12.48). Hee that keepeth the word of Christ, is promised the loue and fauour of GOD, and that hee shall bee the dwelling place or temple of the blessed Trinity (John 14.23). This word, whosoeuer is diligent to read, and in his heart to print that he readeth, the great affection to the transitory things of this world, shall be minished in him, and the great desire of heauenly things (that be therein promised of GOD) shall increase in him. And there is nothing that so much strengtheneth our faith and trust in GOD, that so much keepeth vp innocency and purenesse of the heart, and also of outward godly life and conuersation, as continuall reading and recording of GODS word. For that thing, which (by continuall vse of reading of holy Scripture, and diligent searching of the same) is deepely printed and grauen in the heart, at length turneth almost into nature. And moreouer, the effect and vertue of GODS word is, to illuminate the ignorant, and to giue more light vnto them, that faithfully and diligently read it, to comfort their hearts, and to encourage them to performe that, which of GOD is commanded. It teacheth patience in all aduersity, in prosperity, humblenesse: what honour is due vnto GOD, what, mercy and charity to our neighbor. It giueth good counsell in all doubtfull things. It sheweth of whom wee shall looke for ayde and helpe in all perils, and that GOD is the onely giuer of victory, in all battels and temptations of our enemies, bodily and ghostly (1 Sam 14.4-23, 2 Chronicles 20.7, 17, 29, 1 Corinthians 15.57, 1 John 5.4).

Who profit most in reading GODS word. And in reading of GODS word, hee most profiteth not alwayes, that is most ready in turning of the booke, or in saying of it without the booke, but hee that is most turned into it, that is most inspired with the holy Ghost, most in his heart and life altered and changed into that thing which hee readeth: he that is dayly lesse and lesse proud, lesse wrathfull, lesse couetous, and lesse desirous of worldly and vaine pleasures: he that dayly (forsaking his old vicious life) increaseth in vertue more and more. And to bee short, there is nothing that more maintayneth godlinesse of the minde, and drieth away vngodlinesse, then doeth the continuall reading or hearing of GODS word, if it be ioyned with a godly minde, and a good affection, to know and follow GODS will.

What discommodities the ignorante of GODS word bringeth. For without a single eye, pure intent, and good minde, nothing is allowed for good before GOD. And on the other side, nothing more darkeneth Christ, and the glory of GOD, nor bringeth in more blindnesse, and all kindes of vices, then doeth the ignorance of GODS word (Isaiah 5.13, 24, Matthew 22.29, 1 Corinthians 14.20, 37-38).

THE SECOND PART OF THE SERMON OF THE KNOWLEDGE OF HOLY SCRIPTURE.

The first part of this Sermon, which exhorteth to the knowledge of holy Scripture, was declared wherefore the knowledge of the same is necessary and profitable to all men, and that by the true knowledge and vnderstanding of Scripture, the most necessary points of our duty towards GOD and our neighbours are also knowne. Now as concerning the same matter, you shall heare what followeth. If we professe Christ, why be we not ashamed to be ignorant in his doctrine? Seeing that euery man is ashamed to bee ignorant in that learning which he professeth.

GODS word excelleth all sciences. That man is ashamed to bee called a Philosopher, which readeth not the bookes of Philosophie, and to be called a Lawyer, and Astronomer, or Physition, that is ignorant in the bookes of Law, Astronomie, and Physicke. Now can any man then say that he professeth Christ and his religion, if hee will not applie himselfe (as far foorth as he can or may conueniently) to read and heare, and so to know the bookes of Christes Gospell and doctrine? Although other sciences be good, and to be learned, yet no man can denie, but this is the chiefe, and passeth all other incomparably. What excuse shall wee therefore make (at the last day before Christ) that delight to read or heare mens fantasies and inuentions, more then his most holy Gospell? And will finde no time to doe that which chiefly (aboue all things) wee should doe, and will rather read other things then that, for the which we ought rather to leaue reading of all other things. Let vs therefore applie ourselues, as far forth as we can haue time and leasure, to know GODS word, by diligent hearing and reading thereof, as many as professe GOD, and haue faith and trust in him.

Vaine excuses disswading from the knowledge of Christes word. The first. The second. But they that haue no good affection to GODS word (to colour this their fault) alledge commonly two vaine and feyned excuses. Some goe about to excuse them by their owne frailenesse and fearefulnesse, saying that they dare not reade holy Scripture, least through their ignorance, they should fall into any errour. Other pretend that the difficulty to vnderstand it, and the hardnesse thereof is so great, that it is meet to be read only of Clarkes and learned men.

As touching the first: Ignorance of GODS word, is the cause of all errour, as Christ himselfe affirmed to the Saduces, saying that they erred, because they knew not the Scripture (Matthew 22.29). How should they then eschew errour, that will be still ignorant ? And how should they come out of ignorance, that will not reade nor heare that thing which should giue them knowledge? He that now hath most knowledge, was at the first ignorant, yet he forbare not to reade, for feare hee should fall into errour: but he diligently read, lest he should remaine in ignorance, and through ignorance in error. And if you will not know the truth of GOD (a thing most necessary for you) lest you fall into errour, by the same reason you may then lie still, and neuer goe, lest (if you goe) you fall in the mire: nor eat any good meat, lest you take a surfet, nor sow your corne, nor labour in your occupation, nor vse your merchandise, for feare you lose your seed, your labour, your stocke, and so by that reason, it should be best for you to liue idly, and neuer to take in hand to doe any manner of good thing, lest peraduenture some euill thing may chance thereof. And if you be afrayd to fall into errour, by reading of holy Scripture: I shall shew you how you may read it without danger of error.

How most commodiouslie and without all perill the holy Scripture is to bee read. Read it humbly with a meeke and lowly heart, to the intent you may glorifie GOD, and not your selfe, with the knowledge of it: and read it not without dayly praying to GOD, that he would direct your reading to good effect: and take vpon you to expound it no further, then you can plainely vnderstand it. For (as Saint Augustine sayth) the knowledge of holy Scripture, is a great, large, and a high place, but the doore is very low, so that the high & arrogant man cannot run in: but he must stoope low, and humble himselfe, that shall enter into it. Presumption and arrogancy is the mother of all error: and humility nedeth to feare no error. For humility will only search to know the truth, it will search, and will bring together one place with another, and where it cannot finde out the meaning, it will pray, it will aske of other that know, and will not presumptuously and rashly define any thing, which it knoweth not. Therefore the humble man may search any trueth boldly in the Scripture, without any danger of errour. And if he be ignorant, he ought the more to read and to search holy Scripture, to bring him out of ignorance. I say not nay, but a man may prosper with onely hearing, but hee may much more prosper, with both hearing and reading.

Scripture in some places is easie, and in some places hard to bee vnderstood. This haue I sayd, as touching the feare to reade, thorow ignorance of the person. And concerning the hardnesse of Scripture, he that is so weake that he is not able to brooke strong meat, yet he may sucke the sweet and tender milke, and deferre the rest, vntill he wax stronger, and come to more knowledge. For GOD receiueth the learned and vnlearned, and casteth away none, but is indifferent vnto all. And the Scripture is full, as well of low valleyes, plaine wayes, and easie for euery man to vse, and to walke in: as also of high hilles & mountaynes, which few men can climbe vnto.

GOD leaueth no man vntaught, that hath good will to know his word. And whosoeuer giueth his minde to holy Scriptures, with diligent study and burning desire, it can not bee (saith Saint Chrysostome) that hee should bee left without helpe. For either GOD Almighty will send him some godly doctour, to teach him, as hee did to instruct Eunuchus, a noble man of Aethiope, and Treasurer vnto Queene Candace, who hauing affection to reade the Scripture (although hee vnderstoode it not) yet for the desire that hee had vnto GODS word, GOD sent his Apostle Philip to declare vnto him the true sense of the Scripture that he read: or else, if we lacke a learned man to instruct and teach vs, yet GOD himselfe from aboue, will giue light vnto our mindes, and teach vs those things which are necessary for vs, & wherin we be ignorant.

How the knowledge of the Scripture may be attayned vnto. And in another place Chrysostome sayth, that mans humane and worldly wisedome or science, needeth not to the vnderstanding of Scripture, but the reuelation of the holy Ghost, who inspireth the true meaning vnto them, that with humility and diligence doe search therefore. He that asketh, shall haue, and he that seeketh shall finde, and he that knocketh, shall haue the doore open (Matthew 7.7-8).

A good rule for the vnderstanding of Scripture. If wee reade once, twice, or thrice, and vnderstand not, let vs not cease so, but still continue reading, praying, asking of other, and so by still knocking (at the last) the doore shall be opened (as Saint Augustine sayth.) Although many things in the Scripture be spoken in obscure mysteries, yet there is nothing spoken vnder darke mysteries in one place, but the selfe same thing in other places, is spoken more familiarly and plainly, to the capacity both of learned and vnlearned.

No man is excepted from the knowledge of Christes will. And those things in the Scripture that be plaine to vnderstand, and necessary for saluation, euery mans duty is to learne them, to print them in memory, and effectually to exercise them. And as for the darke mysteries, to bee contented to bee ignorant in them, vntill such time as it shall please GOD to open those things vnto him. In the meane season, if he lacke either aptnesse or opportunity, GOD will not impute it to his folly: but yet it behoueth not, that such as bee apt, should set aside reading, because some other be vnapt to read: neuerthelesse, for the hardnesse of such places, the reading of the whole ought not to be set apart.

What persons would haue ignorance to continue. And briefly to conclude, (as Saint Augustine sayth) by the Scripture, all men be amended, weake men bee strengthened, and strong men be comforted. So that surely, none bee enemies to the reading of GODS word, but such as either bee so ignorant, that they know not how wholesome a thing it is: or else be so sicke, that they hate the most comfortable medicine that should heale them: or so vngodly, that they would wish the people still to continue in blindnesse and ignorance of GOD.

The holy Scripture is one of GODS chiefe benefits. Thus wee haue briefly touched some part of the commodities of GODS holy word, which is one of GODS chiefe and principall benefits, giuen and declared to mankinde heere in earth. Let vs thanke GOD heartily, for this his great and speciall gift, beneficiall fauor, and fatherly prouidence.

The right reading, vse, and fruitfull studying in holy Scripture. Let vs bee glad to reuiue this precious gift of our heauenly Father. Let vs heare, reade, and know these holy rules, iniunctions, and statutes of our Christian religion, and vpon that we haue made profession to GOD at our baptisme. Let vs with feare and reuerence lay vp (in the chest of our hearts) these necessary and fruitfull lessons. Let vs night and day muse, and haue meditation and contemplation in them. Let vs ruminate, and (as it were) chew the cudde, that we may haue the sweet iuice, spirituall effect, marrow, hony, kirnell, taste, comfort and consolation of them (Psalms 56.4). Let vs stay, quiet, and certifie our consciences, with the most infallible certainty, trueth, and perpetuall assurance of them. Let vs pray to GOD (the onely authour of these heauenly studies) that wee may speake, thinke, beleeue, liue and depart hence, according to the wholesome doctrine, and verities of them.

And by that meanes, in this world we shall haue GODS defence, fauour, and grace, with the vnspeakeable solace of peace, and quietnesse of conscience, and after this miserable life, we shall enioy the endlesse blisse and glory of heauen: which he grant vs all that died for vs all, Iesus Christ, to whom with the Father and the holy Ghost, bee all honour and glory, both now and euerlastingly.

HOMILY ON THE MISERY OF MANKIND

A SERMON OF THE misery of all mankinde,
and of his condemnation to death euerlasting, by his owne sinne.

THE Holy Ghost, in writing the holy Scripture, is in nothing more diligent then to pull downe mans vaine glory and pride, which of all vices is most vniuersally grafted in all mankinde, euen from the first infection of our first father Adam. And therefore wee reade in many places of Scripture, many notable lessons against this old rooted vice, to teach vs the most commendable vertue of humility, how to know our selues, and to remember what wee bee of our selues.

In the booke of Genesis, Almighty GOD giueth vs all a title and name in our great grandfather Adam, which ought to warne vs all to consider what wee bee, whereof wee bee, from whence we came, and whither we shall, saying thus, In the sweat of thy face shalt thou eat thy bread, till thou bee turned againe into the ground, for out of it wast thou taken, in as much as thou art dust, into dust shalt thou be turned againe (Genesis 3.19). Heere (as it were in a glasse) wee may learne to know our selues to be but ground, earth, and ashes, and that to earth and ashes we shall returne.

Also, the holy Patriarch Abraham did well remember this name and title, dust, earth, and ashes, appointed and assigned by GOD to all mankinde: and therefore he calleth himselfe by that name, when hee maketh his earnest prayer for Sodome & Gomorre. And wee read that Iudith, Esther, Iob, Ieremy, with other holy men and women in the old Testament, did vse sackcloth, and to cast dust and ashes vpon their heads, when they be wayled their sinfull liuing (Judith 4.10-11, Job 42.6, Jeremiah 6.26). They called and cried to GOD, for helpe and mercy, with such a ceremony of sackcloth, dust, and ashes, that thereby they might declare to the whole world, what an humble and lowly estimation they had of themselues, and how well they remembred their name and title aforesayd, their vile corrupt fraile nature, dust, earth, and ashes. The booke of Wisedome also willing to pull downe our proud stomaches, moueth vs diligently to remember our mortall and earthly generation, which we haue all of him that was first made (Wisdom 7.1): and that all men, as well kings as subiects, come into this world, and goe out of the same in like sort: that is, as of our selues full miserable, as wee may dayly see. And Almighty GOD commanded his Prophet Esay to make a Proclamation, and crie to the whole world: and Esay asking, what shall I crie? The Lord answered, Crie, that all flesh is grasse, and that all the glory thereof, is but as the flowre of the field, when the grasse is withered, the flowre falleth away, when the winde of the Lord bloweth vpon it. The people surely is grasse, the which drieth vp, and the flowre fadeth away (Isaiah 40.6-7). And the holy man Iob, hauing in himselfe great experience of the miserable and sinfull estate of man, doeth open the same to the world in these words; Man (sayth he) that is borne of a woman, liuing but a short time, is full of manifold miseries, hee springeth vp like a flowre, and fadeth againe, vanisheth away as it were a shadow, and neuer continueth in one state. And doest thou iudge it meet (O Lord) to open thine eyes vpon such a one, and to bring him to iudgement with thee? Who can make him cleane, that is conceiued of an vncleane seede (Job 14.1-4), and all men of their euilnesse, and naturall pronenesse, be so vniuersally giuen to sinne, that (as the Scripture sayth) GOD repented that euer he made man (Genesis 6.6). And by sin his indignation was so much prouoked against, the world, that he drowned all the world with Noes floud (except Noe himselfe, and his little houshold, Genesis 7.11-24). It is not without great cause, that the Scripture of GOD doeth so many times call all men heere in this world by this word, earth, O thou earth, earth, earth, sayth Ieremy, heare the word of the Lord (Jeremiah 22.29). This our right name, calling, and title, earth, earth, earth, pronounced by the Prophet, sheweth what wee bee indeed, by whatsoeuer other stile, title, or dignity, men doe call vs. Thus hee plainely named vs, who knoweth best, both what we be, and what wee ought of right to be called. And thus hee setteth vs foorth, speaking by his faithfull Apostle Saint Paul, All men, Iewes and Gentiles, are vnder sinne, there is none righteous, no not one: there is none that vnderstandeth, there is none that seeketh after GOD, they are all gone out of the way, they are all vnprofitable, there is none that doeth good, no not one: their throat is an open sepulchre, with their tongues they haue vsed craft and deceit, the poyson of serpents is vnder their lippes, their mouth is full of curling and bitternesse, their feet are swift to shed blood, destruction and wretchednesse are in their wayes, and the way of peace haue they not knowen: there is no feare of GOD before their eyes. And in another place, Saint Paul writeth thus, GOD hath wrapped all nations in vnbeleefe, that hee might haue mercy on all (Romans 11.32). The Scripture shutteth vp all vnder sinne, that the promise by the fayth of Iesus Christ, should bee giuen vnto them that beleeue (Galatians 3.22). Saint Paul in many places painteth vs out in our colours, calling vs the children of the wrath of GOD (Ephesians 2.3), when wee bee borne: saying also that wee cannot thinke a good thought of our selues, much lesse can we say well, or do well of our selues.

And the Wise man sayth in the booke of Prouerbes, The iust man falleth seuen times a day (Proverbs 24.16). The most tried and approoued man Iob, feared all his workes. Saint Iohn the Baptist being sanctified in his mothers wombe, and praised before he was borne, being called an Angel, and great before the Lord, filled euen from his birth with the holy Ghost, the preparer of the way for our Sauiour Christ (Luke 1.15, 76), and commended of our Sauiour Christ to bee more then a Prophet, and the greatest that euer was borne of a woman: yet he plainely granteth, that he had need to bee washed of Christ, he worthily extolleth and glorifieth his Lord and master Christ, and humbleth himselfe as vnworthy to vnbuckle his shoes (Matthew 3.11, 14), and giueth all honour and glory to GOD. So doth Saint Paul both oft and euidently confesse himselfe, that he was of himselfe, euer giuing (as a most faithfull seruant) all prayse to his master and Sauiour. So doth blessed Saint Iohn the Euangelist, in the name of himselfe, and of all other holy men (bee they neuer so iust) make this open confession: If wee say wee haue no sinne, wee deceiue our selues, and the trueth is not in vs: If we acknowledge our sinnes, GOD is faithfull and iust to forgiue our sinnes and to cleanse vs from all vnrighteousness: If wee say we haue not sinned, we make him a lyer, and his word is not in vs (1 John 1.8-10). Wherefore, the wise man in the booke called Ecclesiastes, maketh this true and generall confession, There is not one iust man vpon the earth that doeth good, and sinneth not (Ecclesiastes

7.20). And Dauid is ashamed of his sin, but not to confesse his sin (Psalms 51).

How oft, how earnestly, and lamentably doth hee desire GODS great mercy for his great offences, and that GOD should not enter into iudgement with him (Psalms 143.2)? And againe, how well weigheth this holy man his sinnes, when hee confesseth that they be so many in number, and so hid, and hard to vnderstand, that it is in a maner vnpossible to know, vtter, or number them? Wherefore, hee hauing a true, earnest, and deepe contemplation and consideration of his sinnes, and yet not comming to the bottome of them, he maketh supplication to GOD, to forgiue him his priuy, secret, hid sinnes: to the knowledge of which we cannot attaine vnto (Psalms 19.12, 40.12). Hee weigheth rightly his sins from the originall roote and spring head, perceiuing inclinations, prouocations, stirrings, stingings, buds, branches, dregges, infections, tastes, feelings, and sents of them to continue in him still. Wherefore hee sayth, Marke, and behold, I was conceiued in sinnes (Psalms 51.5): Hee sayth not sinne, but in the plurall number, sins, for as much as out of one (as a fountaine) springeth all the rest.

Our Sauiour Christ sayth, There is none good, but GOD (Mark 10.18, Luke 18.19): and that we can doe nothing that is good without him, nor no man can come to the father but by him (John 15.5, 14.6). Hee commandeth vs also to say, that wee be vnprofitable seruants, when wee haue done all that wee can doe (Luke 17.10). Hee preferreth the penitent Publicane, before the proude, holy, and glorious Pharisee (Luke 18.14). Hee calleth himselfe a Physition, but not to them that bee whole, but to them that bee sicke (Matthew 9.12), and haue neede of his salue for their sore. Hee teacheth vs in our prayers, to reknowledge our selues sinners, and to aske righteousnesse and deliuerance from all euils, at our heauenly Fathers hand. He declareth that the sinnes of our owne hearts, doe defile our owne selues. Hee teacheth that an euill word or thought deserueth condemnation, affirming that wee shall giue account for euery idle word (Matthew 12.36). He saith, He came not to saue, but the sheepe that were vtterly lost, and cast away (Matthew 15.24). Therefore few of the proude, iust, learned, wise, perfect, and holy Pharisees, were saued by him, because they iustified themselues by their counterfeite holynesse before men. Wherefore (good people) let vs beware of such hypocrisie, vaine glory, and iustifying of ourselues.

FOrasmuch as the true knowledge of our selues is very necessary, to come to the right knowledge of God, yee haue heard in the last reading, how humbly all godly men alwaies haue thought of themselues, and so to thinke and iudge of themselues, are taught of GOD their Creator, by his holy word. For of our selues wee bee crabtrees, that can bring foorth no apples. We be of our selues of such earth, as can bring foorth but weedes, netles, brambles, briers, cockle, and darnel. Our fruits be declared in the fifth chapter to the Galathians. We haue neither fayth, charitie, hope, patience, chastitie, nor any thing else that good is, but of GOD, and therefore these vertues bee called there, the fruits of the holy ghost, and not the fruits of man (Galatians 5.19-23). Let vs therefore acknowledge our selues before GOD (as wee bee indeede) miserable and wretched sinners. And let vs earnestly repent, and humble our selues heartily, and cry to God for mercy. Let vs all confesse with mouth and heart, that we be full of imperfections: Let vs know our owne workes, of what imperfection they be, and then wee shall not stand foolishly and arrogantly in our owne conceits, nor challenge any part of iustification by our merites or workes. For truely there be imperfections in our best workes: wee doe not loue GOD so much as wee are bound to doe, with all our heart, minde, and power: we doe not feare GOD so much as wee ought to doe: we doe not pray to GOD, but with great and many imperfections: we giue, forgiue, beleeue, liue, and hope vnperfectly: we speake, thinke, and doe imperfectly: we fight against the deuill, the world, and the flesh imperfectly: Let vs therefore not be ashamed to confesse plainely our state of imperfection: yea, let vs not bee ashamed to confesse imperfection, euen in all our best workes. Let none of vs be ashamed to say with holy Saint Peter, I am a sinfull man (Luke 5.8). Let vs say with the holy Prophet Dauid, We haue sinned with our fathers, we haue done amisse and dealt wickedly (Psalms 106.6), Let vs all make open confession with the prodigall sonne to our father, and say with him, We haue sinned against heauen, and before thee (O Father) wee are not worthy to be called thy sonnes (Luke 15.18). Let vs all say with holy Baruch, O Lord our GOD, to vs is worthily ascribed shame and confusion, and to thee righteousnesse: Wee haue sinned, wee haue done wickedly, wee haue behaued our selues vngodly in all thy righteousnes (Baruch 2.6, 12). Let vs all say with the holy Prophet Daniel, O Lord, righteousnesse belongeth to thee, vnto vs belongeth confusion. Wee haue sinned, wee haue beene naughtie, wee haue offended, wee haue fled from thee, wee haue gone backe from all thy precepts and iudgements

(Daniel 9.7, 5). So we learne of all good men in holy Scriptures, to humble our selues, and to exalt, extoll, praise, magnifie, and glorifie GOD.

Thus we haue heard how euill we be of our selues, how of our selues, and by our selues, we haue no goodnes, helpe nor saluation, but contrariwise, sinne, damnation, and death euerlasting: which if we deeply weigh and consider, we shall the better vnderstand the great mercie of GOD, and how our saluation commeth onely by Christ. For in our selues (as of our selues) we find nothing (2 Corinthians 3.5), whereby we may be deliuered from this miserable captiuitie, into the which we were cast, through the enuie of the deuill, by breaking of GODS commandement, in our first parent Adam. We are all become vncleane, but we all are not able to cleanse our selues, nor to make one another of vs cleane (Psalms 51.1-10). Wee are by nature the children of GODS wrath (Ephesians 2.3), but we are not able to make our selues the children and inheritours of GODS glorie. Wee are sheepe that runne astray (1 Peter 2.25), but we can not of our owne power come againe to the sheepfold, so great is our imperfection and weakenes. In our selues therefore may we not glorie, which (of our selues) are nothing but sinfull: neither may we reioyce in any works that we do, which all be so vnperfect and vnpure, that they are not able to stand before the righteous iudgement seat of GOD, as the holy Prophet Dauid saith, Enter not into iudgement with thy seruant (O Lord:) for no man that liueth shall be found righteous in thy sight (Psalms 143.2). To God therefore must we flee, or else shall we neuer finde peace, rest and quietnes of conscience in our hearts. For he is the Father of mercies, and GOD of all consolation (2 Corinthians 1.3). Hee is the Lord, with whom is plenteous redemption (Psalms 130.7): Hee is the GOD which of his owne mercie saueth vs, and setteth out his charitie and exceeding loue towards vs, in that of his owne voluntarie goodnes, when we were perished, he saued vs, and prouided an euerlasting Kingdome for vs. And all these heauenly treasures are giuen vs, not for our owne deserts, merits, or good deeds, (which of our selues we haue none) but of his meere mercy freely. And for whose sake? Truely for Iesus Christes sake, that pure and vndefiled lamb of GOD. He is that dearely beloued Sonne, for whose sake GOD is fully pacified, satisfied, and set at one with man. He is the Lambe of GOD, which taketh away the sinnes of the world (John 1.29), of whome onely it may be truely spoken, that he did all things well, and in his mouth was found no craft nor subtiltie (1 Peter 2.22). None but he alone may say, The prince of the world came, and in mee he hath nothing (John 14.30). And he alone may also say, Which of you shall reprooue me of any fault (John 8.46)? He is the high and euerlasting Priest, which hath offered himselfe once for all vpon the altar of the crosse, and with that one oblation hath made perfect for euermore them that are sanctified (Hebrews 7.27 and 10.14). He is the alone mediatour betweene GOD and man, which paid our ransome to GOD with his owne blood, and with that hath he cleansed vs all from sinne. Hee is the Phisition which healeth all our diseases. He is that Sauiour which saueth his people from all their sinnes (Matthew 1.21): To be short, he is that flowing and most plenteous fountaine, of whose fulnesse all wee haue receiued. For in him alone are all the treasures of the wisedom and knowledge of GOD hidden. And in him, and by him, haue wee from GOD the Father all good things, pertaining either to the body or to the soule. O how much are we bound to this our heauenly Father for his great mercies, which he hath so plenteously declared vnto vs in Christ Iesu our Lord and Sauiour! What thanks worthie and sufficient can we giue to him? Let vs all with one accord burst out with ioyfull voyce, euer praising and magnifying this LORD of mercie, for his tender kindnes shewed vnto vs in his dearly beloued Sonne Iesus Christ our Lord.

Hitherto haue we heard what we are of our selues: very sinfull, wretched, and damnable. Againe, wee haue heard how that of our selues, and by our selues, wee are not able either to thinke a good thought, or worke a good deed, so that wee can finde in our selues no hope of saluation, but rather whatsoeuer maketh vnto our destruction. Again, we haue heard the tender kindnesse and great mercy of GOD the Father towards vs, and how beneficiall he is to vs for Christs sake, without our merits or deserts, euen of his owne meere mercy & tender goodnes. Now, how these exceeding great mercies of GOD, set abroad in Christ Iesu for vs, be obtayned, and how we be deliuered from the captiuity of sinne, death, and hell, it shall more at large (with GODS helpe) bee declared in the next Sermon. In the meane season, yea, and at all times let vs learne to know our selues, our frailty and weakenesse, without any craking or boasting of our owne good deedes and merits. Let vs also knowledge the exceeding mercy of GOD towards vs, and confesse, that as of our selues commeth all euill and damnation: so likewise of him commeth all goodnesse and saluation, as GOD himselfe sayth by the Prophet Osee, O Israel, thy destruction commeth of thy selfe, but in me only is thy helpe and comfort (Hosea

13.9). If we thus humbly submit our selues in the sight of GOD, we may be sure that in the time of his visitation, hee will lift vs vp vnto the kingdome of his dearely beloued sonne Christ Iesu our Lord: To whom, with the Father, and the holy Ghost, bee all honour and glory for euer. Amen.

HOMILY ON THE SALVATION OF MANKIND

A SERMON OF THE salvation of mankind,
by only Christ our Savior from sin and death everlasting.

Because all men be sinners and offenders against GOD, and breakers of his law and commandments, therefore can no man by his own acts, works, & deeds (seem they never so good) be justified, and made righteous before GOD: but every man of necessity is constrained to seek for another righteousness or justification, to be received at GOD'S own hands, that is to say, the forgiveness of his sins and trespasses, in such things as he hath offended. And this justification or righteousness, which we so receive of GOD'S mercy and Christ's merits. embraced by faith, is taken, accepted and allowed of GOD, for our perfect and full justification. For the more full understanding hereof, it is our parts and duties ever to remember the great mercy of GOD, how that (all the world being wrapped in sin by breaking of the Law) GOD sent his only son our Savior Christ into this world, to fulfill the Law for us, and by shedding of his most precious blood, to make a sacrifice and satisfaction, or (as it may be called) amends to his Father for our sins, to assuage his wrath and indignation conceived against us for the same.

The efficacy of Christ's passion & oblation. In so much that infants, being baptized and dying in their infancy, are by this sacrifice washed from their sins, brought to GODS favor, and made his children, and inheritors of his kingdom of heaven. And they which in act or deed do sin after their baptism, when they turn again to GOD unfeignedly, they are likewise washed by this sacrifice from their sins, in such sort, that there remains not any spot of sin, that shall be imputed to their damnation. This is that justification or righteousness which S. Paul speaks of, when hee saith, No man is justified by the works of the Law, but freely by faith in Jesus Christ. And again he saith, We believe in Jesus Christ, that we be justified freely by the faith of Christ, and not by the works of the Law, Because that no man shall be justified by the works of the Law (Galatians 2.16). And although this justification be free unto us, yet it cometh not so freely unto us, that there is no ransom paid therefore at all.

Objection. But here may mans reason be astonied, reasoning after this fashion. If a ransom be paid for our redemption, then is it not given us freely. For a prisoner that payed his ransom, is not let go freely, for if he go freely, then he goes without ransom: for what is it else to go freely, then to be set at liberty without paying of ransom?

Answer. This reason is satisfied by the great wisdom of GOD in this mystery of our redemption, who hath so tempered his justice & mercy together, that he would neither by his justice condemn us unto the everlasting captivity of the devil, & his prison of Hell, remediless for ever without mercy, nor by his mercy deliver us clearly, without justice or payment of a just ransom: but with his endless mercy he joined his most upright and equal justice. His great mercy he showed unto us in delivering us from our former captivity, without requiring of any ransom to be paid, or amends to be made upon our parts, which thing by us had been impossible to be done. And where as it lay not in us that to do, he provided a ransom for us, that was, the most precious body and blood of his own most dear and best beloved Son Jesus Christ, who besides this ransom, fulfilled the law for us perfectly. And so the justice of GOD & his mercy did embrace together, & fulfilled the mystery of our redemption. And of this justice and mercy of GOD knit together, speaks S. Paul in the third Chap. to the Romans, All have offended, & have need of the glory of GOD, but are justified freely by his grace, by redemption which is in Jesus Christ, whom GOD hath sent forth to us for a reconciler & peace maker, through faith in his blood, to shew his righteousness (Romans 3.23-25). And in the tenth Chap. Christ is the end of the law unto righteousness, to every man that believeth (Romans 10.4). And in the 8. Chap. That which was impossible by the law, in as much as it was weak by the flesh, GOD sending his own Son, in the similitude of sinful flesh, by sin damned sin in the flesh, that the righteousness of the law might be fulfilled in us, which walk not after the flesh, but after the spirit (Romans 8.3-4).

Three things must go together in our justification. In these aforesaid places, the Apostle touches specially three things, which must go together in our justification. Upon GODS part, his great mercy and grace: upon Christ's part, justice, that is, the satisfaction of GODS justice, or the price of our redemption, by the offering of his body, and shedding of his blood, with fulfilling of the law perfectly & throughly; and upon our part true & lively faith in the merits of Jesus Christ, which yet is not ours, but by GODS working in us: so that in our justification, is not only Gods mercy & grace, but also his justice, which the Apostle calls the justice of GOD, & it consists in paying our ransom, & fulfilling of the law: & so the grace of God doth not shut out the justice of God in our justification, but only shuts out the justice of, that is to say, the justice of our works, as to be merits of deserving our justification. And therefore S. Paul declares here nothing upon the behalf of man, concerning his justification, but only a true & lively faith, which nevertheless is the gift of GOD, and not mans only work, without GOD: And yet that faith doth not shut out repentance, hope, love, dread, & the fear of God, to be joined with faith in every man that is justified, but it shuts them out fro the office of justifying.

<u>How it is to be understood, justifies without works.</u> So that although they be all present together in him that is justified, yet they justify not all together: Nor the faith also does not shut out the justice of our good works, necessarily to be done afterwards of duty towards GOD (for we are most bounden to serve GOD, in doing good deeds, commanded by him in his holy Scripture, all the days of our life:) But it excludes them, so that we may not do them to this intent, to be made good by doing of them. For all the good works that we can do, be imperfect, and therefore not able to deserve our justification: but our justification doth come freely by the mere mercy of GOD, and of so great and free mercy, that whereas all the world was not able of their selves to pay any part towards their ransom, it pleased our heavenly Father of his infinite mercy, without any our desert or deserving, to prepare for us the most precious jewels of Christ's body and blood, whereby our ransom might be fully paid, the law fulfilled, and his justice fully satisfied. So that Christ is now the righteousness of all them that truly do believe in him. Hee for them paid their ransom by his

death. Hee for them fulfilled the Law in his life. So that now in him, and by him, every true Christian man may be called a fulfiller of the Law, forasmuch as that which their infirmity lacked, Christ's justice hath supplied.

THE SECOND PART OF THE SERMON OF SALVATION.

YE have heard of whom all me ought to seek their justification and righteousness, and how also this righteousness cometh unto men by Christ's death and merits: ye heard also how that three things are required to the obtaining of our righteousness, that is, GODS mercy, Christ's justice, and a true and a lively faith, out of the which faith springs good works. Also before was declared at large, that no man can be justified by his own good works, that no man fulfills the Law, according to the full request of the Law.

And S. Paul in his Epistle to the Galatians proves the same, saying thus, If there had been any law given which could have justified, verily righteousness should have been by the law. And again he saith, If righteousness be by the Law, then Christ died in vain (Galatians 2.21). And again he saith, You that are justified by the law, are fallen away from grace. And furthermore he writes to the Ephesians on this wise, By grace are ye saved through faith, and that not of your selves, for it is the gift of GOD, and not of works, lest any man should glory (Ephesians 2.8-9). And to be short, the sum of all Paul's disputation is this: that if justice come of works, then it cometh not of grace: and if it come of grace, then it cometh not of works. And to this end tend all the Prophets, as Saint Peter saith in the tenth of the Acts. Of Christ al the Prophets (faith S. Peter) do witness that through his name, all they that believe in him, shall receive the remission of sins (Acts 10.43).

Faith only justifies, is the doctrine of old Doctors. And after this wise to be justified only by this true and lively faith in Christ, speaks all the old and ancient Authors, both Greeks and Latins. Of whom I will specially rehearse three, Hilary, Basil, and Ambrose. Saint Hilary saith these words plainly in the ix. Canon upon Matthew, Faith only justifies. And Saint Basil a Greek author writes thus, This is a perfect and whole rejoicing in GOD when a man advances not himself for his own righteousness, but acknowledges himself to lack true justice and righteousness, and to be justified by the only faith in Christ. And Paul (saith hee) doth glory in the contempt of his own righteousness, and that he looks for the righteousness of GOD, by faith (Philipp. 3.9).

These be the very words of Saint Basil. And Saint Ambrose, a Latin Author, saith these words, This is the ordinance of GOD, that they which believe in Christ, should be saved without works, by faith only, freely receiving remission of their sins. Consider diligently these words, Without works by faith only, freely we receive remission of our sins. What can be spoken more plainly, then to say, That freely without works, by faith only we obtain remission of our sins? These and other like sentences, that we be justified by faith only, freely, and without works, we do read oft times in the most best and ancient writers. As beside Hilary, Basil, and Saint Ambrose before rehearsed, we read the same in Origen, Saint Chrisostome, Saint Cyprian, Saint Augustine, Prosper, Oecumenius, Phocius, Bernardus, Anselme, and many other Authors, Greek, and Latin.

<u>Faith alone, how it is to be understood.</u> Nevertheless, this sentence, that we be justified by faith only, is not so meant of them, that the said justifying faith is alone in man, without true repentance, hope, charity, dread, and the fear of GOD, at any time and season. Nor when they say, That we be justified freely, they mean not that we should or might afterward be idle, and that nothing should be required on our parts afterward: Neither they mean not so to be justified without good works, that we should do no good works at all, like as shall be more expressed at large hereafter. But this saying, That we be justified by faith only, freely and without works, is spoken for to take away clearly all merit of our works, as being unable to deserve our justification at GODS hands, and thereby most plainly to express the weakness of man, and the goodness of GOD, the great infirmity of our selves, and the might and power of GOD, the imperfectness of our own works, and the most abundant grace of our Savior Christ, and therefore wholly to ascribe the merit and deserving of our justification unto Christ only, and his most precious blood shedding.

<u>The profit of the doctrine of faith only justifies.</u> This faith the holy Scripture teaches us, this is the strong Rock and foundation of Christian Religion, this doctrine all old and ancient Authors of Christ's

Church do approve, this doctrine advances and sets forth the true glory of Christ, and beats down the vain glory of man, this whosoever denies, is not to be accounted for a Christian man, nor for a setter forth of Christ's glory, but for an adversary to Christ and his Gospel, and for a setter forth of mens vain glory.

<u>What they be that impugn the doctrine of Faith only justifies.</u> And although this doctrine be never so true (as it is most true indeed) that we be justified freely without all merit of our own good works (as Saint Paul doth express it) and freely by this lively and perfect faith in Christ only (as the ancient authors used to speak it) yet this true doctrine must be also truly understood and most plainly declared, lest carnal men should take unjustly occasion thereby to live carnally, after the appetite and will of the world, the flesh and the devil.

<u>A declaration of this doctrine of faith without works justifies.</u> And Because no man should err by mistaking of this doctrine, I shall plainly and shortly so declare the right understanding of the same, that no man shall justly think that hee may thereby take any occasion of carnal liberty, to follow the desires of the flesh, or that thereby any kind of sin shall be committed, or any ungodly living the more used.

First, you shall understand, that in our justification by Christ, it is not all one thing, the office of GOD unto man, and the office of man unto GOD. Justification is not the office of man, but of GOD, or man cannot make himself righteous by his own works, neither in part, nor in the whole, for that were the greatest arrogance and presumption of man, that Antichrist could set up against GOD, to affirm that a man might by his own works, take away and purge his own sins, and so justify himself.

<u>Justification is the office of God only.</u> But justification is the office of GOD only, and is not a thing which we render unto him, but which we receive of him: not which we give to him, but which we take of him, by his free mercy, and by the only merits of his most dearly beloved Son, our only Redeemer, Savior, and Justifier Jesus Christ: so that the true understanding of this doctrine, We be justified freely by faith without works, or that we be justified by faith in Christ only, is not, that this our own act, to believe in Christ, or this our faith in Christ, which is within us, doth justify us, and deserve our justification unto us (for that were to count our selves to be justified by some act or virtue that is within our selves) but the true understanding and mean-

ing thereof is, that although we hear GODS word, and believe it, although we have faith, hope, charity, repentance, dread, and fear of GOD within us, and do never so many works thereunto: yet we must renounce the merit of all our said virtues, of faith, hope, charity, and all other virtues and good deeds, which we either have done, shall do, or can do, as things that be far too weak and insufficient, and imperfect, to deserve remission of our sins, and our justification, and therefore we must trust only in GODS mercy, and that sacrifice which our high Priest and Savior Christ Jesus the son of GOD once offered for us upon the Crosse, to obtain thereby GODS grace, and remission, as well of our original sin in Baptism, as of all actual sin committed by us after our Baptism, if we truly repent, and turn unfeignedly to him again. So that as S. John Baptist, although he were never so virtuous and godly a man, yet in this matter of forgiving of sin, he did put the people from him, & appointed them unto Christ, saying thus unto them, Behold, yonder is the lamb of GOD, which taketh away the sins of the world (John 1.29): even so, as great and as godly a virtue as the lively faith is, yet it puts us from it self, and remits or appoints us unto Christ, for to have only by him remission of our sins, or justification. So that our faith in Christ (as it were) saith unto us thus, It is not I that take away your sins, but it is Christ only, and to him only I send your for that purpose, forsaking therein all your good virtues, words, thoughts, and works, and only putting your trust in Christ.

THE THIRD PART OF THE SERMON OF SALVATION

IT hath been manifestly declared unto you, that no man can fulfill the Law of GOD, and therefore by the law all men are condemned: whereupon it follows necessarily, that some other thing should be required for our salvation then the law: and that is, a true and a lively faith in Christ: bringing forth good works, and a life according to GODS commandments. And also you heard the ancient authors minds of this saying, Faith in Christ only justifies man, so plainly declared, that you see, that the very true meaning of this proposition or saying, We be justified by faith in Christ only, (according to the meaning of the old ancient authors) is this: We put our faith in Christ, that we be justified by him only, that we be justified by GODS free mercy, and the merits of our Savior Christ only, and by no virtue or good works of our own, that is in us, or that we can be able to have or to do, for to deserve the same: Christ himself only being the cause meritorious thereof.

Here you perceive many words to be used to avoid contention in words with them that delight to brawl about words, and also to show the true meaning to avoid evil taking and misunderstanding, and yet peradventure all will not serve with them that be contentious: but contenders will ever forge matters of contention, even when they have none occasion thereto. Not withstanding, such be the less to be passed upon, so that the rest may profit, which will be the most desirous to know the truth, then (when it is plain enough) to contend about it, and with contentious and captious caviling, to obscure and darken it. Truth it is, that our own works do not justify us, to speak properly of our justification, (that is to say) our works do not merit or deserve remission of our sins, and make us of unjust, just before GOD: but GOD of his own mercy, through the only merits and deservings of his son Jesus Christ, does justify us. Nevertheless, Because faith does directly send us to Christ for remission of our sins, and that by faith given us of GOD, we embrace the promise of GODS mercy, and of the remission of our sins, (which thing none other of our virtues or works properly does) therefore Scripture uses to say, that faith without works doth justify. And forasmuch that it is all one sentence in effect, to say, faith without works, and only faith doth justify us, therefore the old ancient Fathers of the Church from time to time, have uttered our justification with this speech, Only faith justifies us: meaning none other thing then Saint Paul meant, when he said, Faith without works justifies us. And Because all this brought to passe through the only merits and deservings of our Savior Christ, and not through our merits, or through the merit of any virtue that we have within us, or of any work that cometh from us: therefore in that respect of merit and deserving, we forsake (as it were) altogether again, faith, works, and all other virtues. For our own imperfection is so great, through the corruption of original sin, that all is imperfect that is within us, faith, charity, hope, dread, thoughts, words, and works, and therefore not apt to merit and discern any part of our justification for us. And this form of speaking used we, in the humbling of our selves to GOD, and to give all the glory to our Savior Christ, which is best worthy to have it.

Here you have heard the office of GOD in our justification, and how we receive it of him freely, by his mercy, without our deserts, through true and lively faith.

They that preach faith only justifies, do not teach carnal liberty, or that we should do no good works. Now you shall hear the office and duty of a Christian man unto GOD, what we ought on our part to render unto GOD again, for his great mercy and goodness. Our office is, not to passe the time of this present life unfruitfully, and idly, after that we are baptized or justified, not caring how few good works we do, to the glory of GOD, and profit of our neighbors: Much less is it our office, after that we be once made Christ's members, to live contrary to the same, making our selves members of the devil, walking after his incitements, and after the suggestions of the world and the flesh, whereby we know that we do serve the world and the devil, and not GOD.

The devils have faith, but not the true faith. For that faith which brings forth (without repentance) either evil works, or no good works, is not a right, pure, and lively faith, but a dead, devilish, counterfeit and feigned faith, as Saint Paul and Saint James call it. For even the devils know and believe that Christ was borne of a virgin, that he fasted forty days and forty nights without meat and drink, that he wrought all kind of miracles, declaring himself very GOD: They believe also, that Christ for our sakes suffered most painful death, to redeem from everlasting death, and that hee rose again from death the third day: They believe that hee ascended into heaven, and that he sits on the right hand of the Father, and at the last end of this world shall come again, and judge both the quick and the dead. These articles of our faith the Devils believe, and so they believe all things that be written in the new and old Testament to be true: and yet for all this faith, they be but Devils, remaining still in their damnable estate, lacking the very true Christian faith.

What is the true and justifying faith. For the right and true Christian faith is, not only to believe that holy Scripture, and all the aforesaid articles of our faith are true, but also to have a sure trust and confidence in GODS merciful promises, to be saved from everlasting damnation by Christ: whereof doth follow a loving heart to obey his commandments. And this true Christian faith neither any devil hath, nor yet any man, which in the outward profession of his mouth, and in his outward receiving of the Sacraments, in coming to the Church, and in all other outward appearances, seems to be a Christian man, and yet in his living and deeds shows the contrary.

They that continue in evil living, have not true faith. For how can a man have this true faith, this sure trust and confidence in GOD, that by the merits of Christ, his sins be forgiven, and be reconciled to the favor of GOD, and to be partaker of the kingdom of heaven by Christ, when he lives ungodly, and denies Christ in his deeds? Surely no such ungodly man can have this faith and trust in GOD. For as they know Christ to be the only savior of the world: so they know also that wicked men shall not enjoy the kingdom of GOD. They know that GOD hates unrighteousness (Psalms 5.5-6), that he will destroy all those that speak untruly, that those which have done good works (which cannot be done without a lively faith in Christ) shall come forth into the resurrection of life, and those that have done evil, shall come unto the resurrection of judgement: very well they know also, that to them that be contentious, and to them that will not be obedient unto the truth, but will obey unrighteousness, shall come indignation, wrath, and affliction, &c.

Therefore to conclude, considering the infinite benefits of GOD, showed and given unto us, mercifully without our deserts, who hath not only created us of nothing; and from a piece of vile clay, of his infinite goodness, hath exalted us (as touching our soul) unto his own similitude and likeness: but also whereas we were condemned to hell, and death everlasting, hath given his own natural Son, being GOD eternal, immortal, and equal unto himself, in power and glory, to be incarnated, and to take our mortal nature upon him, with the infirmities of the same, and in the same nature to suffer most shameful and painful death for our offences, to the intent to justify us, and to restore us to life everlasting: so making us also his dear children, brethren unto his only son our Savior Christ, and inheritors for ever with him of his eternal kingdom of heaven.

These great and merciful benefits of GOD (if they be well considered) do neither minister unto us occasion to be idle, and to live without doing any good works, neither yet stirs us up by any means to do evil things: but contrariwise, if we be not desperate persons, and our hearts harder then stones, they move us to render our selves unto GOD wholly with all our will, hearts, might, and power, to serve him in all good deeds, obeying his commandments during our lives, to seek in all things his glory and honor, not our sensual pleasures and vain glory, evermore dreading willingly to offend such a merciful GOD, and loving redeemer, in word, thought, or deed. And the said benefits of GOD deeply considered, move us for his sake also to be ever ready to give our selves to our neighbors, and as much as lies in us, to study with all our endeavor, to do good to every man. These be the fruits of true faith, to do good as much as lies in us to every man, and above all things, and in all things to advance the glory of GOD, of whom only we have our sanctification, justification, salvation, and redemption: to whom be ever glory, praise, and honor, world without end. Amen.

HOMILY ON THE TRUE AND LIVELY FAITH

A SHORT DECLARATION
of the true, liuely, and Christian Faith.

Faith. THE first comming vnto GOD (good Christian people) is through Faith, whereby (as it is declared in the last Sermon) we be iustified before GOD. And lest any man should be deceiued, for lacke of right vnderstanding thereof, it is diligently to bee noted, that Faith is taken in the Scripture two manner of wayes.

A Dead Faith. There is one fayth, which in Scripture is called a dead fayth, which bringeth foorth no good workes, but is idle, barren, and vnfruitfull. And this faith, by the holy Apostle Saint Iames, is compared to the fayth of Diuels, which beleeue GOD to bee true and iust, and tremble for feare, yet they doe nothing well, but all euill (James 2.17, 19). And such a manner of fayth haue the wicked and naughty Christian people, which confesse GOD, (as S. Paul sayth) in their mouth, but denie him in their deeds, being abominable, and without the right fayth, and to all good workes reproouable (Titus 1.16). And this faith is a perswasion and beleefe in mans heart, whereby hee knoweth that there is a GOD, and agreeth vnto all trueth of GOD'S most holy word, conteyned in the holy Scripture. So that it consisteth onely in beleeuing in the word of GOD, that it is true. And this is not properly called faith. But as hee that readeth C'sars Commentaries, beleeuing the same to bee true, hath thereby a knowledge of C'sars life, and notable acts, because hee beleeueth the history of C'sar: yet it is not properly sayd that hee beleeueth in C'sar, of whom he looketh for no helpe nor benefit. Euen so, he that beleeueth that all that is spoken of GOD in the Bible is true, and yet liueth so vngodly, that he cannot looke to enioy the promises and benefits of GOD: although it may be sayd, that such a man hath a fayth and beleefe to the words of GOD, yet it is not properly sayd that hee beleeueth in GOD, or hath such a fayth and trust in GOD, whereby hee may surely looke for grace, mercy, and euerlasting life at GOD'S hand, but rather for indignation and punishment, according to the merits of his wicked life. For as it is written in a booke, intituled to be of Didymus Alexandrinus, Forasmuch as faith without workes is dead, it is not now faith, as a dead man, is not a man.

A Liuely Faith. This dead faith therefore is not the sure and substantiall faith, which saueth sinners. Another faith there is in Scripture, which is not (as the foresaid faith) idle, vnfruitfull, and dead, but worketh by charity (as S. Paul declareth, Galatians 5.6) Which as the other vaine faith is called a dead faith, so may this be called a quick or liuely faith. And this is not onely the common beleefe of the Articles of our faith, but it is also a true trust and confidence of the mercy of GOD through or Lord Iesus Christ, and a stedfast hope of all good things to be receiued at GOD'S hand: and that although wee, through infirmitie or temptation of our ghostly enimie, doe fall from him by sin, yet if we returne againe vnto him by true repentance, that he will forgiue, and forget our offences for his Sonnes sake our Sauiour Iesus Christ, and will make vs inheritours with him of his euerlasting Kingdome, and that in the meane time vntill that kingdome come, he will be our protectour and defendour in all perils and dangers, whatsoeuer do chance: and that though sometime he doeth send vs sharp aduersitie, yet that euermore hee will be a louing Father vnto vs, correcting vs for our sinne, but not withdrawing his mercie finally from vs, if we trust in him, and commit our selues wholy vnto him, hang onely vpon him, and call vpon him, ready to obey and serue him. This is the true, liuely, and vnfeigned Christian faith, and is not in the mouth and outward profession onely: but it liueth, and stirreth inwardly, in the heart. And this faith is not without hope and trust in GOD, nor without the loue of GOD and of our neighbours, nor without the feare of GOD, nor without the desire to heare GOD'S word, and to follow the same in eschewing euill, and doing gladly all good workes.

This faith (as Saint Paul describeth it) is the sure ground and foundation of the benefites which wee ought to looke for, and trust to receiue of GOD, a certificate and sure looking for them, although they yet sensibly appeare not vnto vs. And after hee saith, Hee that commeth to GOD, must beleeue, both that he is, and that he is a mercifull rewarder of well doers. And nothing commendeth good men vnto GOD, so much as this assured faith and trust in him (Hebrews 11.1, 6).

Three Things Are to Be Noted of Faith. Of this faith, three things are specially to be noted. First, that this faith doth not lie dead in the heart, but is liuely and fruitefull in bringing forth good workes. Second, that without it, can no good workes be done, that shall be acceptable and pleasant to GOD. Third, what maner of good workes they be, that this faith doth bring forth.

Faith Is Full of Good Workes. For the first, that the light can not be hid, but will shew forth it selfe at one place or other: So a true faith can not be kept secret, but when occasion is offered, it will breake out, and shew it selfe by good workes. And as the liuing bodie of a man euer exerciseth such things as belong to a naturall and liuing bodie, for nourishment and preseruation of the same, as it hath need, opportunity, and occasion: euen so the soule that hath a liuely fayth in it, will bee doing alway some good worke, which shall declare that it is liuing, and will not be vnoccupied. Therfore when men heare in the Scriptures so high commendations of fayth, that it maketh vs to please GOD, to liue with GOD, and to be the children of GOD: if then they phantasie that they bee set at liberty from doing all good workes, and may liue as they lust, they trifle with GOD and deceiue themselues. And it is a manifest token; that they bee farre from hauing the true and liuely fayth, and also farre from knowledge, what true fayth meaneth. For the very sure and liuely Christian fayth is, not onely to beleeue all things of GOD, which are contayned in holy Scripture, but also is an earnest trust, and confidence in GOD, that he doeth regard vs, and that he is carefull ouer vs, as the father is ouer the Childe whom hee doth loue, and that hee will bee mercifull vnto vs for his onely sonnes sake, and that wee haue our Sauiour Christ our perpetuall aduocate, and Priest, in whose onely merits, oblation, and suffering, wee doe trust that our offences bee continually washed and purged, whensoeuer wee (repenting truely) doe returne to him, with our whole heart, stedfastly determining with our selues, through his grace, to obey and serue him in keeping his commandements, and neuer to turne backe againe to sinne. Such is the true faith, that the Scripture doeth so much commend, the which when it seeth and considereth what GOD hath done for vs, is also mooued through continuall assistance of the Spirit of

GOD, to serue and please him, to keepe his fauour, to feare his displeasure, to continue his obedient children, shewing thankefulnesse againe by obseruing or keeping his commandements, and that freely, for true loue chiefly, and not for dread of punishment, or loue of temporall reward, considering how cleerely, without deseruings wee haue receiued his mercy and pardon freely.

This true faith will shew foorth it selfe, and cannot long bee idle: For as it is written, The iust man doeth liue by his faith (Habakkuk 2.4). Hee neuer sleepeth nor is idle, when hee would wake, and be well occupied. And GOD by his Prophet Ieremie saith, that hee is a happy and blessed man, which hath faith and confidence in GOD (Jeremiah 17.7-8). For he is like a tree set by the water side, and spreadeth his roots abroad toward the moysture, and feareth not heate when it commeth, his leafe will bee greene, and will not cease to bring foorth his fruit: euen so, faithfull men (putting away all feare of aduersitie) will shew foorth the fruit of their good workes, as occasion is offered to doe them.

THE SECOND PART OF THE SERMON OF FAITH.

YE haue heard in the first part of this Sermon, that there be two kindes of fayth, a dead and an vnfruitfull fayth, and a fayth liuely that worketh by charity. The first to be vnprofitable, the second, necessary for the obtayning of our saluation: the which faith hath charity alwaies ioyned vnto it, and is fruitfull, and bringeth foorth all good workes. Now as concerning the same matter, you shall heare what followeth. The wise man sayth, He that beleeueth in GOD, will hearken vnto his commandements (Sirach 32.24). For if wee doe not shew our selues faythfull in our conuersation, the fayth which we pretend to haue, is but a fayned faith: because the true Christian faith is manifestly shewed by good liuing, and not by words onely, as S. Augustine saith, (Augustine, De Fide et Operibus 23, 42 (PL 40. 224), Libro de fide & operibus) Good liuing cannot be separated from true faith, which worketh by loue.

And S. Chrysostome sayth (Pseudo-Chrysostom, De Fide et Lege Naturae 1 [PG 48.1081], Sermo. de lege & fide.), Faith of it selfe is full of good works: as soone as a man doth beleeue, he shall be garnished with them. How plentifull this fayth is of good workes, and how it maketh the worke of one man more acceptable to GOD, then of another, S. Paul teacheth at large in the xi. Chapter to the Heb. saying, That fayth made the oblation of Abel, better then the oblation of Cain. This made Noah to build the Arke. This made Abraham to forsake his Country, and all his friends, and to goe into a far Country, there to dwell among strangers. So did also Isaac and Iacob, depending or hanging onely of the helpe and trust that they had in GOD. And when they came to the country which GOD promised them, they would build no Cities, Townes, nor Houses, but liued like strangers in Tents, that might euery day be remooued (Hebrews 11.4-38, Genesis 4.4-5, Genesis 6.22, Sir 44.17, Genesis 11.31, 12.1-5). Their trust was so much in GOD, that they set but little by any worldly thing, for that GOD had prepared for them better dwelling places in heauen of his owne foundation and building. This faith made Abraham ready at GOD'S commandement, to offer his owne sonne and heire Isaac, whom hee loued so well, and by whom he was promised to haue innumerable issue, among the which, one should bee borne, in whom all nations should bee blessed, trusting so much in GOD, that though he were slaine, yet that GOD was able by his omnipotent power to rayse him from death, and performe his promise (Genesis 22.1-18, 26.1-35, Sirach 44.20). He mistrusted not the promise of GOD, although vnto his reason euery thing seemed contrary. He beleeued verily that GOD would not forsake him in death and famine that was in the country. And in all other dangers that hee was brought vnto, hee trusted euer that GOD should be his GOD, and his protectour and defender, whatsoeuer he saw to the contrary. This faith wrought so in the heart of Moses, that he refused to be taken for King Pharao his daughters sonne, and to haue great inheritance in Egypt, thinking it better with the people of God to haue affliction and sorrow, then with naughty men, in sinne to liue pleasantly for a time (Exodus 2.11). By faith hee cared not for the threatning of king Pharao: for his trust was so in GOD, that hee passed not of the felicitie of this world, but looked for the reward to come in heauen, setting his heart vpon the inuisible GOD, as if he had seene him euer present before his eyes. By faith, the children of Israel passed through the red sea (Exodus 14.22). By faith, the walles of Hierico fell downe without stroke, and many other wonderfull miracles haue beene wrought (Joshua 6.20). In all good men that heretofore haue beene, faith hath brought forth their good workes, and obteined the promises of GOD. Faith hath stopped the Lions mouthes (Daniel 6.16-23): faith hath quenched the force of fire (Daniel 3.13-28): faith hath escaped the swords edges: faith hath giuen weake men strength, victorie in battaile, ouerthrowen the armies of Infidels, raysed the dead to life: faith hath made good men to take aduersitie in good part, some haue beene mocked and whipped, bound, and cast in prison, some haue lost all their goods, and liued in great pouertie, some haue wandered in mountaines, hilles, and wildernesse, some haue bene racked, some slaine, some stoned, some sawen, some rent in pieces, some beheaded, some brent without mercy, and would not be deliuered, because they looked to rise againe to a better state (Hebrews 11.36-38).

All these Fathers, Martyrs, and other holy men, (whom Saint Paul spake of) had their faith surely fixed on GOD, when all the world was against them. They did not onely know GOD to bee the Lord, maker, and gouernour of all men in the world: but also they had a speciall confidence and trust, that he was and would bee their GOD, their comforter, ayder, helper, maintainer, and defender. This is the Christian faith which these holy men had, and wee also ought to haue. And although they were not named Christian men, yet was it a Christian faith that they had, for they looked for all benefites of GOD the Father, through the merites of his Sonne Iesu Christ, as wee now doe. This difference is betweene them and vs, that they looked when Christ should come, and we bee in the time when hee is come. Therefore faith S. Augustine (Augustine, In Ioannis Evangelium Tract. 45 10, 9 [PL 35: 1722]), The time is altered and changed, but not the faith. For wee haue both one faith in one Christ. The same holy ghost also that wee haue, had they, saith S. Paul (2 Corinthians 4.13). For as the holy Ghost doeth teach vs to trust in GOD, and to call vpon him as our Father: so did he teach them to say, as it is written, Thou Lord art our Father and Redeemer, and they Name is without beginning and euerlasting. GOD gaue them then grace to bee his children, as hee doth vs now (Isaiah 63.10-11). But now by the comming of our Sauiour Christ, we haue receiued more aboundantly the spirit of GOD in our hearts, whereby we may conceiue a greater faith, and a surer trust then many of them had. But in effect they and we be all one: we haue the same faith that they had in GOD, and they the same that wee haue And Saint Paul so much extolleth their faith, because we should no lesse, but rather more, giue our selues wholy vnto Christ, both in profession and liuing, now when Christ is come, then the olde fathers did before his comming. And by all the declaration of S. Paul, it is euident, that the true, liuely, and Christian faith, is no dead, vaine, or vnfruitfull thing, but a thing of perfect vertue, of wonderfull operation or working, and strength, bringing foorth all good motions, and good workes.

All holy Scripture agreeably beareth witnesse, that a true liuely faith in Christ, doeth bring foorth good workes: and therefore euery man must examine and trye himselfe diligently, to know whether hee haue the same true liuely faith in his heart vnfeignedly, or not, which hee shall know by the fruits thereof. Many that professed the faith of Christ, were in this errour, that they thought they knew GOD, and beleeued in him, when in their life they declared the contrary: Which errour Saint Iohn in his first Epistle confuting, writeth in this wise, Hereby wee are certified that we know GOD, if we obserue his commandements. He that sayth, he knoweth GOD, and obserueth not his commandements, is a lyar, and the trueth is not in him (1 John 2.3-4). And againe hee sayth, Whosoeuer sinneth, doeth not see GOD, nor know him: let no man deceiue you, welbeloued children (1 John 3.6-7). And moreouer hee sayeth, Hereby we know that we be of the trueth, and so we shall perswade our hearts, before him (1 John 3.19-22).

For if our owne hearts reproue vs, GOD is aboue our hearts, & knoweth all things. Welbeloued, if our hearts reproue vs not, then haue wee confidence in GOD, and shall haue of him whatsoeuer we aske, because wee keepe his Commandements, and doe those things that please him. And yet further hee sayeth, Euery man that beleeueth that Iesus is Christ, is borne of GOD, and wee know that whosoeuer is borne of GOD, doeth not sinne: but hee that is begotten of God, purgeth himselfe, and the deuill doeth not touch him (1 John 5.1, 18). And finally he concludeth, and sheweth the cause why he wrote this Epistle, saying, For this cause haue I thus written vnto you, that you may know that you haue euerlasting life, which doe beleeue in the Sonne of GOD (1 John 5.13). And in his iii. Epistle he confirmeth the whole matter of faith and workes, in few wordes, saying, Hee that doeth well, is of GOD, and hee that doeth euill, knoweth not God (3 John 11). And as S. Iohn saith, That as the liuely knowledge and faith of GOD bringeth foorth good workes: so sayth he likewise of hope and charitie, that they cannot stand with euill liuing. Of hope he writeth thus, We know that when GOD shall appeare, we shall be like vnto him, for we shall see him, euen as hee is: and whosoeuer hath this hope in him, doeth purifie himselfe, like as GOD is pure (1 John 3.2-3). And of charitie hee sayth these wordes, Hee that doeth keepe

Gods word and commandement, in him is truely the perfect loue of GOD (1 John 2.5). And againe hee sayth, This is the loue of GOD, that wee should keepe his Commandements (1 John 5.3). And S. Iohn wrote not this, as a subtill saying, deuised of his owne fantasie, but as a most certaine and necessary trueth, taught vnto him by Christ himselfe, the eternall and infallible veritie, who in many places doth most clearely affirme, that faith, hope and charitie, can not consist or stand without good and godly workes. Of faith, he saith, He that beleeueth in the Sonne, hath euerlasting life: but hee that beleeueth not in the Sonne, shall not see that life, but the wrath of GOD remaineth vpon him. And the same hee confirmeth with a double othe, saying, Verily, verily I say vnto you, Hee that beleeueth in mee, hath euerlasting life (John 6.47).

Now forasmuch as he that beleeueth in Christ, hath euerlasting life: it must needes consequently follow, that he that hath this faith, must haue also good workes, and be studious to obserue Gods commandements obediently. For to them that haue euill workes, and leade their life in disobedience, and transgression or breaking of Gods commandements, without repentance, perteineth not euerlasting life but euerlasting death, as Christ himselfe saith, They that doe well, shall goe into life eternall, but they that doe euill, shall goe into euerlasting fire (Matthew 25.46). And againe he sayth, I am the first letter, and the last, the beginning and the ending: to him that is athirst, I will giue of the well of the water of life freely: he that hath the victorie, shall haue all things, and I will be his GOD, and he shall be my sonne: but they that be fearefull, mistrusting GOD, and lacking faith, they that be cursed people, and murtherers, and fornicators and sorcerers, and all lyers, shall haue their portion in the lake that burneth with fire and brimstone, which is the second death (Revelations 21.6-8).

Charitie Bringeth Foorth Good Workes. And as Christ vndoubtedly affirmeth, that true faith bringeth forth good works, so doeth hee say likewise of Charitie. Whosoeuer hath my commandements and keepeth them, that is he that loueth me. And after he sayth, He that loueth me, will keepe my word, and hee that loueth me not, keepeth not my wordes. And as the loue of GOD is tryed by good workes, so is the feare of GOD also, as the wise man saith, The dread of GOD putteth away sinne. And also he saith, Hee that feareth GOD, will doe good workes (John 14.21-24, Sir 1.21, Sir 15.1).

THE THIRD PART OF THE SERMON OF FAITH.

YOu haue heard in the second part of this Sermon, that no man should thinke that hee hath that liuely faith which Scripture commandeth, when he liueth not obediently to Gods lawes, for all good workes spring out of that faith: And also it hath beene declared vnto you by examples, that faith maketh men stedfast, quiet, and patient in all affliction. Now as concerning the same matter, you shall heare what followeth. A man may soone deceiue himselfe, and thinke in his owne phantasie that he by faith knoweth GOD, loueth him, feareth him, and belongeth to him, when in very deede he doeth nothing lesse. For the triall of all these things is a very godly and Christian life. He that feeleth his heart set to seeke Gods honour, and studieth to know the will & commandements of GOD, and to frame himselfe thereunto, and leadeth not his life after the desire of his owne flesh, to serue the deuill by sinne, but setteth his mind to serue GOD for his owne sake, and for his sake also to loue all his neighbours, whether they be friends or aduersaries, doing good to euery man (as opportunitie serueth) and willingly hurting no man: such a man may well reioice in GOD, perceiuing by the trade of his life, that hee vnfeignedly hath the right knowledge of GOD, a liuely faith, a stedfast hope, a true and vnfeigned loue, and feare of GOD. But he that casteth away the yoke of GOD'S commandements from his necke, and giueth himselfe to liue without true repentance, after his owne sensuall minde and pleasure, not regarding to know GOD'S word, and much lesse to liue according thereunto: such a man clearely deceiueth himselfe, and seeth not his owne heart, if hee thinketh that hee either knoweth GOD, loueth him, feareth him, or trusteth in him. Some peraduenture fantasie in themselues, that they belong to GOD, although they liue in sinne, and so they come to the Church, and shew themselues as GOD'S deare children. But S. Iohn saith plainely, If wee say that wee haue any company with GOD, and walke in darkenesse, we doe lie (1 John 1.6). Other doe vainely thinke that they know and loue GOD, although they passe not of the commandements. But S. Iohn saith clearely, Hee that saith I know GOD, and keepeth not his commandements, he is a lyer (1 John 2.4). Some falsely perswade themselues, that they loue GOD, when they hate their neighbours. But S. Iohn saith manifestly, If any man say I loue GOD, and yet hateth his brother, he is a lyer (1 John 4.20). He that sayth that he is in the light, and hateth his brother, he is still in darkenesse. He that loueth his brother, dwelleth in the light, but he that hateth his brother, is in darknesse, and walketh in darkenesse, and knoweth not whither hee goeth: For darkenesse hat blinded his eyes (1 John 2.9-11). And moreouer hee sayeth, Hereby wee manifestly know the children of GOD from the children of the deuill. Hee that doeth not righteously, is not the childe of GOD, nor he that hateth his brother (1 John 3.10). Deceiue not your selues therefore, thinking that you haue faith in GOD, or that you loue GOD, or doe trust in him, or doe feare him, when you liue in sinne: for then your vngodly and sinfull life declareth the contrary, whatsoeuer you say or thinke. It perteineth to a Christian man to haue this true Christian faith, and to trie himselfe whether he hath it or no, and to know what belongeth to it, and how it doth worke in him. It is not the world that wee can trust to, the world and all that is therein, is but vanitie. It is GOD that must bee our defence, and protection against all temptation of wickednesse and sinne, errours, superstition, idolatrie, and all euill. If all the world were on our side, and GOD against vs, what could the world auaile vs? Therefore let vs set our whole faith and trust in GOD, and neither the world, the deuill, nor all the power of them shall preuaile against vs. Let vs therefore (good Christian people) trie and examine our faith, what it is: let vs not flatter our selues, but looke vpon our works, and so iudge of our faith what it is. Christ himselfe speaketh of this matter, and saith, The tree is knowen by the fruit (Luke 6.44, Matthew 12.33). Therefore let vs doe good workes, and thereby declare our faith to bee the liuely Christian faith. Let vs by such vertues as ought to spring out of faith, shew our election to bee sure and stable, as S. Peter teacheth, Endeuour your selues to make your calling & election certaine by good works. And also hee saith, Minister or declare in your faith vertue, in vertue knowledge, in knowledge, in temperance patience, in patience godlines, in godlinesse brotherly charity, in brotherly charity loue (2 Peter 1.5-7): so shall we shew in deed that we haue the very liuely Christian fayth, and may so both certifie our conscience the better that we be in the right fayth, and also by these meanes confirme other men. If these fruites doe not follow, we do but mocke with GOD, deceiue our selues, and also other men. Well may wee beare the name of Christian men, but wee doe lacke the true fayth that doeth belong thereunto: for true fayth doeth euer bring foorth good workes, as S. Iames sayth: Shew me thy fayth by thy deeds (James 2.18). Thy deeds and workes must be an open testimoniall of thy fayth: otherwise thy fayth (being without good works) is but the Diuels fayth, the faith of the wicked, a fantasie of fayth, and not a true Christian fayth. And like as the Diuels and euill people bee nothing the better for their counterfait fayth, but it is vnto them the more cause of damnation: so they that be Christians and haue receiued knowledge of GOD and of Christ's merits, and yet of a set purpose doe liue idlely, without good workes, thinking the name of a naked fayth to bee either sufficient for them, or else setting their mindes vpon vaine pleasures of this world, doe liue in sinne without repentance, not vttering the fruites that doe belong to such an high profession, vpon such presumptuous persons, and wilfull sinners, must needs remayne the great vengeance of GOD, and eternall punishment in hell, prepared for the vniust and wicked liuers. Therfore as you professe the name of Christ (good Christian people) let no such phantasie and imagination of fayth at any time beguile you: but be sure of your fayth, trie it by your liuing, looke vpon the fruites that commeth of it, marke the increase of loue and charity by it towards GOD and your neighbour, and so shall you perceiue it to bee a true liuely fayth. If you feele and perceiue such a fayth in you, reioyce in it: and be diligent to maintaine it, and keepe it still in you, let it be dayly increasing, and more and more by well working, and so shall you bee sure that you shall please GOD by this fayth, and at the length (as other faithfull men haue done before) so shall you (when his will is) come to him, and receiue the end and finall reward of your fayth (as S. Peter nameth it) the saluation of your soules (1 Peter 1.9): the which GOD grant vs, that hath promised the same vnto his faithfull, to whom be all honour and glory, world without end. Amen.

HOMILY ON GOOD WORKS

A SERMON OF GOOD
workes annexed vnto Faith.

No good workes can bee done without faith. IN the last Sermon was declared vnto you, what the liuely and true fayth of a Christian man is, that it causeth not a man to bee idle, but to bee occupied in bringing foorth good workes, as occasion serueth. Now by GOD'S grace shall bee declared the second thing that before was noted of fayth, that without it can no good worke bee done, accepted and pleasant vnto GOD. For as a branch can not beare fruite of it selfe (sayth our Sauiour Christ) except it abide in the Vine: so can not you, except you abide in me. I am the Vine, and you bee the branches, he that abideth in me, and I in him, he bringeth foorth much fruit: for without me, you can doe nothing (John 15.4-5). And S. Paul prouueth that the Eunuch had fayth, because he pleased GOD. For without fayth (sayth he) it is not possible to please GOD (Hebrews 11.6). And againe to the Romans he sayth, whatsoeuer worke is done without fayth, it is sinne (Romans 14.23). Faith giueth life to the soule, and they be as much dead to GOD that lacke fayth, as they be to the world, whose bodies lacke soules. Without fayth all that is done of vs, is but dead before GOD, although the worke seeme neuer so gay and glorious before man. Euen as the picture grauen or painted, is but a dead representation of the thing it selfe, and is without life, or any maner of moouing: so be the workes of all vnfaythfull persons before GOD. They doe appeare to bee liuely workes, and indeed they bee but dead, not auayling to the euerlasting life. They be but shadowes and shewes of liuely and good things, and not good and liuely things indeed. For true fayth, doth giue life to the workes, and out of such fayth come good works, that be very good workes indeed, & without fayth, no worke is good before GOD, as sayth S. Augustine (Enarratio in Psalm. 31 2, 4 [PL 36.259]). We must let no good works before fayth, nor think that before fayth a man many doe any good works: for such workes, although they seeme vnto men to be prayse worthy, yet indeed they be but vaine, and not allowed before GOD. They bee as the course of an Horse that runneth out of the way, which taketh great labour, but to no purpose. Let no man therefore (sayth he) reckon vpon his good workes before his fayth: Where as fayth was not, good workes were not. The intent (sayth hee) maketh the good workes, but fayth must guide and order the intent of man. And Christ sayth, If thine eye be naught, thy whole body is full of darkenesse (Matthew 6.23). The eye doeth signifie the intent (sayth S. Augustine) wherewith a man doeth a thing. So that he which doth not his good works with a godly intent, and a true fayth, that worketh by loue: the whole body beside (that is to say) all the whole number of his workes, is darke, and there is no light in them. For good deedes bee not measured by the facts themselues, and so discerned from vices, but by the ends and intents for the which they were done. If a Heathen man clothe the naked, feed the hungrie, and doe such other like workes: yet because he doeth them not in fayth, for the honour and loue of GOD, they be but dead, vaine, and fruitlesse workes to him. Fayth is it that doeth commend the worke to GOD: for (as S. Augustine saith) whether thou wilt or no, that work that commeth not of faith, is naught: where the fayth of Christ is not the foundation, there is no good worke, what building so euer we make. There is one worke, in the which be all good workes, that is, faith, which worketh by charity: if thou haue it, thou hast the ground of all good workes. For the vertues of strength, wisedome, temperance, and iustice, be all referred vnto this same faith. Without this faith we haue not them, but onely the names and shadowes of them (as Saint Augustine sayth,) All the life of them that lacke the true faith, is sinne, and nothing is good, without him, that is the authour of goodnesse: where hee is not, there is but fained vertue, although it be in the best workes. And S. Augustine, declaring this verse of the Psalme, The turtle hath found a nest where shee may keepe her yong birds, saith, that Iewes, Heretickes, and Pagans doe good workes, they cloath the naked, feede the poore, and doe other good workes of mercy: but because they bee not done in the true faith, therefore the birdes bee lost. But if they remaine in faith, then faith is the nest and safegard of their birdes, that is to say, safegard of their good workes, that the reward of them be not vtterly lost. And this matter (which Saint Augustine at large in many bookes disputeth) (Ambrosiaster, De Vocatione Gentium 1, 3 [PL 17.1078], De vocatione gentium, lib.cap.). Saint Ambrose concludeth in few wordes saysaying, Hee that by nature would withstand vice, either by naturall will, or reason, hee doeth in vaine garnish the time of this life and attaineth not the verie true vertues: for without the worshipping of the true GOD, that which seemeth to bee vertue, is vice. And yet most plainely to this purpose writeth Saint Chrysostome in this wise, (Pseudo-Chrysostom, De Fide et Lege Naturae 1 [PG 48. 1081-82], In sermone de fide, lege, & spiritu sancto). You shall finde manie which haue not the true faith, and bee not of the flocke of Christ , and yet (as it appeareth) they flourish in good workes of mercy: you shall finde them full of pitie, compassion, and giuen to iustice, and yet for all that they haue no fruit of their workes, because the chiefe worke lacketh. For when the Iewes asked of Christ what they should doe to worke good workes: hee answered, This is the worke of GOD, to beleeue in him whom hee sent (John 6.29): so that hee called faith the worke of GOD. And assoone as a man hath faith, anone hee shall florish in good workes: for faith of it selfe is full of good workes, and nothing is good without faith. And for a similitude, he saith that they which glister and shine in good workes without fayth in GOD, bee like dead men, which haue godly and precious tombes, and yet it auayleth them nothing. Faith may not bee naked without good workes, for then it is no true faith: and when it is adioyned to workes, yet it is aboue the workes. For as men that be verie men indeed, first haue life, and after bee nourished: so must our faith in Christ goe before, and after bee nourished with good workes. And life may bee without nourishment, but nourishment cannot bee without life. A man must needes bee nourished by good workes, but first hee must haue faith. Hee that doeth good deedes, yet without faith hee hath no life. I can shew a man that by faith without workes liued, and came to heauen: but without faith, neuer man had life. The thiefe that was hanged, when Christ suffered, did beleeue onely, and the most mercifull GOD iustified him. And because no man shall say againe that hee lacked time to doe good workes, for else he would haue done them: trueth it is, and I will not contend therein, but this I will surely affirme, that faith onely saued him. If hee had liued and not regarded faith and the workes thereof, hee should haue lost his saluation againe. But this is the effect that I say, that faith by it selfe saued him, but workes by themselues neuer iustified any man. Here yee haue heard the minde of Saint Chrysostome, whereby you may perceiue, that neither faith is without workes (hauing opportunity thereto) nor workes can auaile to euerlasting life, without faith.

THE SECOND PART OF THE SERMON OF GOOD WORKES

OF three things which were in the former Sermon especially noted of liuely faith, two bee declared vnto you.

What works they are that spring out of faith. The first was, that faith is neuer idle, without good workes when occasion serueth. The second, that good workes, acceptable to GOD, cannot bee done without faith. Now to goe forward to the third part, that is, What maner of workes they be which spring out of true faith, and leade faithfull men vnto euerlasting life. This cannot bee knowen so well, as by our Sauiour Christ himselfe who was asked of a certain great man the same question;, What works shall I do (said a prince) to come to euerlasting life? To whom Iesus answered, if thou wilt come to euerlasting life, keepe the Commandements (Matthew 19.16-17). But the prince not satisfied herewith, asked farther, Which commandements? The Scribes and Pharisees had made so many of their owne lawes and traditions, to bring men to heauen, besides GOD'S commandements, that this man was in doubt whether he should come to heauen by those lawes and traditions or by the law of GOD, and therefore he asked Christ which commandements hee meant.

The workes that leade to heauen, bee workes of Gods commandements. Whereunto Christ made him a plaine answere, rehearsing the commandements of GOD, saying, Thou shalt not kill, Thou shalt not commit adulterie, Thou shalt not steale, Thou shalt not beare false witnesse, Honour thy father and thy mother, and loue thy neighbour as thy selfe (Matthew 19.18-19). By which wordes Christ declared that the lawes of GOD bee the very way that doeth leade to euerlasting life, and not the traditions and lawes of men. So that this is to be taken for a most true lesson taught by Christ's owne mouth, that the workes of the morrall commandements of GOD bee the very true workes of faith, which leade to the blessed life to come. But the blindnesse and malice of man, euen from the beginning, hath euer beene readie to fall from GOD'S Commandements.

Man from his first falling from Gods commandements hath euer beene ready to doe the like, and doeth deuise workes of his owne phantasy to please God withall. As Adam the first man, hauing but one commandement, that hee should not eate of the fruit forbidden: not withstanding GOD'S Commandement, hee gaue credit vnto the woman, seduced by the subtill perswasion of the Serpent, and so followed his owne will, and left GOD'S commandement. And euer since that time all that came of him, haue beene so blinded through originall sinne, that they haue beene euer readie to fall from GOD and his law, and to inuent a new way vnto saluation by workes of their owne deuice: so much that almost all the world, forsaking the true honour of the onely eternall liuing GOD, wandered about their owne phantasies, worshipping some the Sonne, the Moone, the Starres, some Iupiter, Iuno, Diana, Saturnus, Apollo, Neptunus, Ceres, Bacchus, and other dead men and women. Some therewith not satisfied, worshipped diuerse kindes of beastes, birdes, fish, foule, and serpents, euery countrie, town, and house in manner being diuided, and setting vp images of such things as they liked, and worshipping the same. Such was the rudenesse of the people, after they fell to their owne phantasies, and left the eternall liuing GOD and his commandements, that they deuised innumerable Images and gods. In which errour and blindnesse they did remaine, vntill such time as Almighty GOD, pitying the blindnesse of man, sent his true Prophet Moses into the world, to reprooue and rebuke this extreme madnesse, and to teach the people to know the onely liuing GOD and his true honour and worshippe. But the corrupt inclination of man, was so much giuen to follow his owne phantasie, and (as you would say) to fauour his owne byrde, that hee brought vp himselfe, that all the admonitions, exhortations, benefites, and threatenings of GOD, could not keep him from such his inuentions.

The deuises and idolatries of the Israelites. For not withstanding all the benefits of GOD shewed vnto the people of Israel, yet when Moses went vp into the mountaine to speake with Almighty GOD, he had taried there but a few dayes, when the people began to inuent new Gods. And as it came in their heads, they made a calfe of gold, & kneeled downe, & worshipped it (Exodus 32.1-6). And after that, they followed the Moabites, & worshipped Beelphegor the Moabits God. Read the book of Iudges, the book of the Kings, & the Prophets, and there you shall finde how vnstedfast the people were, how full of inuentions, and more ready to runne after their owne phantasies, then

GOD'S most holy commandements. There shall you reade of Baal, Moloch, Chamos, Melchom, Baalpeor, Astaroth, Bell, the Dragon, Priapus, the brasen Serpent, the twelue signes, and many other vnto whose images the people with great deuotion inuented Pilgrimages, precious decking and sensing them, kneeling downe, and offering to them, thinking that an high merit before God, and to bee esteemed aboue the precepts and commandements of GOD, And where at that time GOD commanded no Sacrifice to be made but in Ierusalem only, they did cleane contrary, making Altars and sacrifices euery where, in hilles, in woodes, and in houses, not regarding GOD'S commandements, but esteeming their owne phantasies, and deuotions to bee better then they. And the error hereof was so spread abroad, that not only the vnlearned people, but also the Priestes, and teachers of the people, partly by glory and couetousnesse were corrupted, and partly by ignorance blindly deceiued with the same abominations. So much, that king Achab hauing but only Helias a true teacher and minister of God, there were eight hundred and fiftie Priestes, that perswaded him to honour Baal, and to doe sacrifice in the woods or groues. And so continued that horrible error, vntill the three noble Kings, as Iosaphat, Ezechias, and Iosias, GOD'S chosen Ministers, destroyed the same clearely, and brought againe the people from such their faigned inuentions, vnto the very commandements of GOD: for the which thing their immortall reward and glory, doeth, and shall remaine with GOD for euer.

<u>Religions and sectes among the Iewes.</u> And beside the foresaid inuentions, the inclination of man to haue his owne holy deuotions, deuised new sects, and religions, called Pharisees, Sadduces, and Scribes, with many holy and godly traditions and ordinances (as it seemed by the outward appearance, and goodly glistering of the workes) but in very deede all tending to idolatrie, superstition, & hypocrisie: their hearts within being full of malice, pride, couetousnesse, & all wickednesse. Against which sectes, and their pretended holinesse Christ cried out more vehemently, then hee did against any other persons, saying, and often rehearsing these wordes, Woe bee to you Scribes and Pharisees, yee hypocrites, for you make cleane the vessell without, but within yee bee full of rauine and filthinesse: thou blinde Pharisee, and hypocrite, first make the inward part cleane (Matthew 23.25-26). For not withstanding all the goodly traditions and outward shewes of good workes, deuised of their owne imagination, whereby they appeared to the world most religious and holy of all

men, yet Christ (who saw their hearts) knew that they were inwardly in the sight of GOD, most vnholy, most abominable, and farthest from GOD of all men. Therefore sayd hee vnto them, Hypocrites, the Prophet Esai spake full truely of you, when hee sayd, This people honour mee with their lips, but their heart is farre from mee. They worship mee in vaine, that teach doctrines and commandements of men: for you leaue the commandements of GOD, to keepe your owne traditions (Matthew 15.7-9, Isaiah 29.13-14).

Mans lawes must be obserued and kept, but not as Gods Lawes. And though Christ sayd, They worship GOD in vaine, that teach doctrines and commandements of men: yet hee meant not thereby to ouerthrow all mens commandements, for he himselfe was euer obedient to the Princes and their lawes, made for good order and gouernance of the people, but hee reprooued the lawes and traditions made by the Scribes and Pharisees: which were not made onely for good order of the people, (as the Ciuill lawes were) but they were (set vp so high, that they were made to be right and pure worshipping of GOD, as they had beene equall with GOD'S Lawes, or aboue them: for many of Gods Lawes could not bee kept, but were faine to giue place vnto them. This arrogancie GOD detested, that man should so aduance his lawes, to make them equall with GOD'S Lawes, wherein the true honouring and right worshipping of GOD standeth, and to make his Lawes for them to be left off. GOD hath appointed his Lawes, whereby his pleasure is to be honoured. His pleasure is also, that all mens lawes, not being contrary vnto his Lawes, shalbe obeyed and kept, as good and necessary for euery Common-weale, but not as things wherein principally his honour resteth: and all Ciuill and mans lawes, either bee, or should be made, to bring men the better to keepe GOD'S Lawes, that consequently, or followingly, GOD should bee the better honoured by them.

Holy traditions were esteemed as Gods Lawes. Howbeit, the Scribes and Pharisees were not content that their lawes should bee no higher esteemed then other positiue and Ciuill lawes, nor would not haue them called by the name of other Temporall lawes: but called them holy and godly traditions, and would haue them esteemed not onely for a right and true worshipping of GOD (as GOD'S Lawes be in deede) but also for the most high honouring of GOD, to the which the commandements of GOD should giue place.

Holinesse of mans deuise, is commonly occasion that God is offended. And for this cause did Christ so vehemently speake against them, saying, Your traditions which men esteeme so high, be abomination before GOD. For commonly of such traditions, followeth the transgression or breaking of GOD'S commandements, and a more deuotion in keeping of such things, and a greater conscience in breaking of them, then of the commandements of GOD. As the Scribes and Pharises so superstitiously, and scrupulously kept the Sabboth, that they were offended with Christ , because he healed sicke men, and with his Apostles, because they being sore hungry, gathered the eares of corne to eate vpon that day, and because his disciples washed not their handes, so often as the traditions required: the Scribes and Pharises quarrelled with Christ, saying, Why doe they disciples breake the traditions of the Seigniours (Matthew 12.1-14)? But Christ layd to their charge, that they for to keepe their owne traditions, did teach men to breake the very commandements of GOD (Matthew 15.2). For they taught the people such a deuotion, that they offered their goods into the treasure house of the Temple, vnder the pretence of GOD'S honour, leauing their fathers and mothers (to whom they were chiefly bound) vnholpen, and so they brake the commandements of GOD, to keepe their owne traditions. They esteemed more an othe made by the golde or oblation in the Temple, then an othe made in the Name of GOD himselfe, or of the Temple. They were more studious to pay their tithes of small things, then to doe the greater things commanded of GOD, as works of mercy, or to doe iustice, or to deale sincerely, vprightly, and faithfully with GOD and man. These (saith Christ) ought to bee done, and the other not left vndone. And to bee short, they were of so blinde iudgement, that they stumbled at a straw, and leaped ouer a blocke. They would (as it were) nicely take a flie out of their cup, and drinke downe a whole Camell (Matthew 23.16-24). And therefore Christ called them blinde guides, warning his disciples from time to time to eschew their doctrine. For although they seemed to the world to bee most perfect men, both in liuing and teaching, yet was their life but hypocrisie, and their doctrine sowre leauen, mingled with superstition, idolatry, and ouerthwart iudgement, setting vp the traditions and ordinances of man, in stead of GOD'S commandements.

THE THIRD PART OF THE SERMON OF GOOD WORKES.

THat all men might rightly iudge of good workes, it hath beene declared in the second part of this Sermon, what kinde of good workes they bee that GOD would haue his people to walke in, namely such as he hath commanded in his holy Scripture, and not such workes as men haue studied out of their owne braine, of a blind zeale and deuotion, without the word of GOD: And by mistaking the nature of good workes, man hath most highly displeased GOD, and hath gone from his will and commandements. So that thus you haue heard how much the world from the beginning vntill Christes time, was euer ready to fall from the commandements of GOD, and to seeke other meanes to honour and serue him, after a deuotion found out of their own heads: and how they did set vp their owne traditions, as high or aboue GOD'S commandements, which hath happened also in our times (the more it is to be lamented) no lesse then it did among the Iewes, and that by the corruption, or at least by the negligence of them that chiefly ought to haue preserued the pure and heauenly doctrine left by Christ . What man hauing any iudgement or learning, ioyned with a true zeale vnto GOD, doeth not see, and lament, to haue entred into Christes religion, such false doctrine, superstition idolatry, hypocrisie, and other enormities and abuses, so as by little and little, through the sowre leauen thereof, the sweete bread of GOD'S holy word hath bene much hindred and layed apart?

Sectes and religion amongst Christian men. Neuer had the Iewes in their most blindnesse, so many Pilgrimages vnto Images, nor vsed so much kneeling, kissing, and sensing of them, as hath bene vsed in our time. Sects and feigned religions were neither the fourtieth part so many among the Iewes, nor more superstitiously and vngodly abused, then of late dayes they haue been among vs. Which sects and religions, had so many hypocriticall and feigned workes in their state of religion (as they arrogantly named it) that their lampes (as they said) ran alwayes ouer, able to satisfie, not onely for their owne sinnes, but also for all other their benefactors, brothers, and sisters of religion, as most vngodly and craftily they had perswaded the multitude of ignorant people: keeping in diuers places (as it were) marts or markets of merites, being full of their holy reliques, images, shrines, and workes of ouerflowing abundance ready to be solde. And all things which they had were called holy, holy cowles, holy girdles, holy pardons, beades, holy shooes, holy rules, and all full of holinesse. And what thing can be more foolish, more superstitious, or vngodly, then that men, women, and children, should weare a Friers coat, to deliuer them from agues, or pestilence? or when they die, or when they be buried, cause it to be cast vpon them, in hope thereby to be saued? Which superstition, although (thankes bee to GOD) it hath beene little vsed in this Realme, yet in diuers other Realmes, it hath beene, and yet it is vsed among many both learned and vnlearned. But to passe ouer the innumerable superstitiousnes that hath bene in strange apparel, in silence, in Dormitory, in Cloyster, in Chapter, in choise of meates, and drinkes, and in such like things, let vs consider what enormities & abuses haue been in the three chiefe principall points, which they called the three essentials, or three chiefe foundations of religion, that is to say, obedience, chastitie, and wilfull pouertie.

The three chiefe vowes of religion. First, vnder pretence or colour of obedience to their Father in religion (which obedience they made themselues) they were made free by their rule and Canons, from the obedience of their natural father and mother, and from the obedience of Emperour and King, and all temporall power, whom of very duetie by GOD'S lawes they were bound to obey. And so the profession of their obedience not due, was a forsaking of their due obedience. And how their profession of chastitie was kept, it is more honestly to passe ouer in silence, and let the world iudge of that which is well knowen, then with vnchaste wordes, by expressing of their vnchaste life, to offend chaste and godly eares. And as for their wilfull pouertie, it was such, that when in possessions, iewels, plate, and riches, they were equall or aboue merchants, gentlemen, Barons, Earles, and Dukes: yet by this subtill sophisticall terme, *Proprium in commune,* that is to say, Proper in common, they mocked the world, perswading, that not withstanding all their possessions, and riches, yet they kept their vow, and were in wilfull pouertie. But for all their riches, they might neuer helpe father nor mother, nor other that were in deede very needy and poore, without the licence of their father Abbot, Prior, or Warden, and yet they might take of euery man, but they might not giue ought to any man, no not to them whom the lawes of GOD bound them to helpe. And so through their traditions and rules, the lawes of GOD could beare no rule with them. And therefore of them might be most truely sayd, that which Christ spake vnto the Pharisees, You breake the commandements of GOD by your traditions: you honour GOD with your lips, but your hearts be farre from him (Matthew 15.3, 8). And the longer prayers they vsed by day and by night, vnder pretence or colour of such holinesse, to get the fauour of widowes, and other simple folkes, that they might sing Trentalles and seruice for their husbands and friends, and admit or receiue them into their prayers: the more truely is verified of them the saying of Christ, Woe bee vnto you Scribes and Pharisees, hypocrites, for you deuoure widowes houses, vnder colour of long prayers, therefore your damnation shall bee the greater (Matthew 23.14-15). Woe bee to you Scribes and Pharisees hypocrites, for you goe about by sea and by land to make moe Nouices, and new brethren, and when they be let in, or receiued of your sect, you make them the children of hell, worse then your selues bee. Honour bee to GOD, who did put light in the heart of his faithfull and true minister, of most famous memorie King Henry the eight, and gaue him the knowledge of his word, and an earnest affection to seeke his glory, and to put away all such superstitious, and Pharisaicall sectes by Antichrist inuented, and set vp against the true word of GOD, and glory of his most blessed Name, as he gaue the like spirit vnto the most noble and famous Princes, Iosaphat, Iosias, and Ezechias. GOD grant all vs the Kings Highnesse faithfull and true Subiects, to feed of the sweete and sauoury bread of GOD'S owne worde, and (as Christ commanded) to eschew all our Pharisaicall and Papisticall leauen of mans fained religion. Which, although it were before GOD most abominable, and contrary to Gods commandements, and Christ's pure Religion, yet it was praysed to be a most godly life, and highest state of perfection: as though a man might bee more godly, and more perfect by keeping the rules, traditions, and professions of men, then by keeping the holy commandements of GOD.

<u>Other deuises and superstitions.</u> And briefly to passe ouer the vngodly and counterfait religion, let vs rehearse some other kindes of Papisticall superstitions & abuses, as of Beades, of Lady Psalters, and Rosaries, of fifteene Oes, of Saint Barnards verses, of Saint Agathes letters, of Purgatorie, of Masses satisfactory, of Stations, and Iubilees, of fained Reliques, or hallowed Beades, Belles, Bread, Water, Psalmes, Candels, Fire, and such other: of superstitious fastings, of fraternities or brotherheads, of pardons, with such like merchandise, which were so esteemed and abused to the great preiudice of Gods glory and Commaundements, that they were made most high and most

holy things, whereby to attaine to the euerlasting life, or remission of sinne:

Decrees and decretals. Yea also vaine inuentions, vnfruitfull ceremonies, and vngodly lawes, decrees, and councels of Rome, were in such wise aduanced, that nothing was thought comparable in authoritie, wisedome, learning, and godlinesse vnto them. So that the lawes of Rome, (as they sayd) were to be receiued of all men, as the foure Euangelists, to the which all lawes of Princes must giue place. And the lawes of GOD also partly were left off, and lesse esteemed, that the said lawes, decrees and councels, with their traditions and ceremonies, might be more duely kept, and had in greater reuerence. Thus was the people through ignorance so blinded, with the godly shew and appearance of those things, that they thought the keeping of them to be a more holinesse, a more perfect seruice and honouring of GOD, and more pleasing to GOD, then the keeping of Gods commandements. Such hath bene the corrupt inclination of man, euer superstitiously giuen to make new honouring of GOD of his owne head, and then to haue more affection and deuotion to keepe that, then to search out Gods holy commandements, and to keepe them. And furthermore, to take GOD'S commandements for mens commandements, and mens commandements for Gods commandements, yea, and for the highest and most perfect and holy of all GOD'S commandements. And so was all confused, that scant well learned men, and but a small number of them knew, or at the least would know, and durst affirme the trueth, to separate or seuer GOD'S Commandements from the commandements of men. Whereupon did grow much errour, superstition, idolatrie, vaine religion, ouerthwart iudgement, great contention, with all vngodly liuing.

An exhortation to the keeping of Gods commandements. Wherefore, as you haue any zeale to the right and pure honouring of GOD, as you haue any regard to your owne soules, and to the life that is to come, which is both without paine, and without ende, apply your selues chiefly aboue all things, to reade and heare GOD'S worde, marke diligently therein what his will is you shal doe, and with all your endeuour apply your selues to follow the same.

A briefe rehearsall of Gods commandements. First you must haue an assured faith in GOD, and giue your selues wholly vnto him, loue him in prosperitie and aduersitie, and dread to offend him euermore. Then for his sake loue all men, friends and foes, because they bee his creation and image, and redeemed by Christ , as ye are. Cast in your mindes, how you may doe good vnto all men, vnto your powers, and hurt no man. Obey all your superiours, and gouernours, serue your Masters faithfully and diligently, as well in their absence, as in their presence, not for dread of punishment onely, but for conscience sake, knowing that you are bound so to doe by Gods Commandements. Disobey not your Fathers and Mothers, but honour them, helpe them, and please them to your power. Oppresse not, kill not, beate not, neither slaunder, nor hate any man: but loue all men, speake well of all men, helpe and succour euery man, as you may, yea, euen your enemies that hate you, that speake euill of you, and that doe hurt you. Take no mans goods, nor couet your neighbours goods wrongfully, but content your selues with that which yee get truely, and also bestow your owne goods charitably, as neede and case requireth. Flee all idolatrie, witchcraft, and periury, commit no maner of adulterie, fornication, or other vnchastnesse, in will, nor in deede, with any other mans wife, widdow, or mayde, or otherwise. And trauayling continually, (during this life) thus in keeping the commandements of GOD (wherein standeth the pure, principall, and right honour of GOD, and which wrought in faith, GOD hath ordeined to bee the right trade and path way vnto heauen) you shall not faile, as Christ hath promised, to come to that blessed and euerlasting life, where you shall liue in glory and ioy with GOD for euer: to whom be praise, honour and emperie, for euer and euer. Amen.

HOMILY ON CHRISTIAN LOVE AND CHARITY

A SERMON OF CHRIstian loue and charity.

OF all things that be good to bee taught vnto Christian people, there is nothing more necessary to be spoken of, and dayly called vpon, then charity: aswell for that all maner of workes of righteousnesse bee contayned in it, as also that the decay thereof is the ruine or fall of the world, the banishment of vertue, and the cause of all vice. And for so much as almost euery man, maketh and frameth to himselfe charity after his own appetite, and how detestable soeuer his life bee, both vnto GOD and man, yet hee perswadeth himselfe still that he hath charity: therfore you shall heare now a true and plaine description or setting foorth of charity, not of mens imagination, but of the very wordes and example of our Sauiour Iesus Christ. In which description or setting foorth, euery man (as it were in a glasse) may consider himselfe, and see plainely without errour, whether hee bee in the true charity, or not.

<u>What charitie is. The loue of God.</u> Charity is, to loue GOD with all our heart, all our soule, and all our powers and strength. With all our heart: That is to say, that our heart, minde, and study be set to beleeue his word, to trust in him, and to loue him aboue all other things that wee loue best in heauen or in earth. With all our life: that is to say, that our chiefe ioy and delight be set vpon him and his honour, and our whole life giuen vnto the seruice of him aboue all things, with him to liue and die, and to forsake all other things, rather then him. For he that loueth his father or mother, sonne or daughter, house, or land, more then me (sayth Christ) is not woorthy to haue me (Matthew

10.37). With all our power, that is to say, that with our hands and feete, with our eyes and eares, our mouthes and tongues, and with all our parts and powers, both of body and soule, we should be giuen to the keeping and fulfilling of his commandements.

The loue of thy neighbor. This is the first and principall part of charity, but it is not the whole: for charity is also to loue euery man, good and euill, friend and foe, and whatsoeuer cause be giuen to the contrary, yet neuerthelesse to beare good will and heart vnto euery man, to vse our selues well vnto them, aswell in wordes and countenances, as in all our outward actes and deedes: for so Christ himselfe taught, and so also hee performed indeed. Of the loue of GOD hee taught in this wise vnto a doctour of the law, that asked him which was the great and chiefe commandement in the Law, Loue thy Lord GOD, (sayd Christ) with all thy heart, with all thy soule, and with all thy mind (Matthew 22.37). And of the loue, that wee ought to haue among our selues each to other, he teacheth vs thus, You haue heard it taught in times past, Thou shalt loue thy friend, and hate thy foe: But I tell you, Loue your enemies, speake well of them that defame and speake euill of you, doe well to them that hate you, pray for them that vexe and persecute you, that you may be the children of your father that is in heauen. For he maketh his Sunne to rise both vpon the euill and good, and sendeth raine to the iust and vniust. For if you loue them that loue you, what reward shall you haue? Doe not the Publicanes likewise? And if you speake well onely of them that be your brethren and deare beloued friends, what great matter is that? Doe not the Heathen the same also (Matthew 5.43-47)? These bee the very wordes of our Sauiour Christ himselfe, touching the loue of our neighbour. And forasmuch as the Pharisees (with their most pestilent traditions, and false interpretations, and glosses) had corrupted, and almost clearly stopped vp this pure Well of GODS liuely word, teaching that this loue and charity pertayned onely to a mans friends, and that it was sufficient for a man to loue them which doe loue him, and hate his foes: therefore Christ opened this Well againe, purged it and scoured it by giuing vnto his godly law of charitie, a true and cleare interpretation, which is this: that we ought to loue euery man, both friend and foe, adding thereto what commodity we shall haue therby, and what incommodity by doing the contrary. What thing can we wish so good for vs, as the eternall heauenly father, to reckon, and take vs for his children? And this shall we be sure of (sayth Christ) if we loue euery man without exception. And if we doe otherwise (sayth he) we be no better then the Pharisees, Publicanes, and Heathen, and shall haue our reward with them, that is, to be shut out from the number of GOD'S chosen children, and from his euerlasting inheritance in heauen.

Thus of true charitie, Christ taught that euery man is bound to loue GOD aboue all things, and to loue euery man, friend and foe. And this likewise hee did vse himselfe, exhorting his aduersaries, rebuking the faults of his aduersaries, and when hee could not amend them, yet hee prayed for them. First hee loued GOD his Father aboue all things, so much that hee sought not his owne glorie and will, but the glorie and will of his Father. I seeke not (sayd hee) mine owne will, but the will of him that sent mee (John 5.30). Nor hee refused not to die, to satisfie his Fathers will, saying, If it may bee, let this cuppe of death passe from mee: if not, thy will bee done, and not mine (Matthew 26.39, 42). Hee loued not onely his friends, but also his enemies, which (in their heartes) bare exceeding great hatred against him, and with their tongues spake all euill of him, and in their actes and deedes pursued him with all their might and power, euen vnto death, yet all this notwithstanding, hee withdrew not his fauour from them, but still loued them, preached vnto them in loue, rebuked their false doctrine, their wicked liuing, and did good vnto them, patiently taking whatsoeuer they spake or did against him. When they gaue him euill wordes, hee gaue none euill againe. When they did strike him, hee did not smite him againe: and when hee suffred death, hee did not slay them, nor threaten them, but prayed for them, and did put all things to his fathers will. And as a sheepe that is lead vnto the shambles to be slaine, and as a lambe that is shorne of his fleece, maketh no noyse nor resistance, euen so hee went to his death, without any repugnance, or opening of his mouth to say any euill. Thus haue I set foorth vnto you what charity is, aswell by the doctrine, as by the examples of Christ himselfe, whereby also euery man may without errour know himselfe, what state and condition hee standeth in, whether he bee in charity, (and so the child of the father in heauen) or not. For although almost euery man perswadeth himselfe to be in charity, yet let him examine none other man, but his owne heart, his life and conuersation, and he shall not be deceiued, but truely discerne and iudge whether hee bee in perfect charity or not. For hee that followeth not his owne appetite and will, but giueth himselfe earnestly to GOD, to doe all his will and commandements, hee may bee sure that hee loueth GOD aboue all things, and else surely hee loueth him not, whatsoeuer hee pretend: as Christ sayd, If yee loue mee, keepe my commandements. For hee that knoweth my commandements, and keepeth them, he it is (sayth Christ) that loueth mee (John 14.15, 21). And againe he sayth, Hee that loueth me, will keepe my word, and my Father will loue him, and we will both come to him, and dwell with him: and hee that loueth mee not, will not keepe my words. And likewise hee that beareth a good heart and minde, and vseth well his tongue and deeds vnto euery man, friend and foe, he may know thereby that he hath charitie. And when hee is sure that Almighty GOD taketh him for his deare beloued sonne, as S. Iohn sayth, Heereby manifestly are knowne the children of GOD, from the children of the Diuell: for whosoeuer doeth not loue his brother, belongeth not vnto GOD (1 John 3.10).

THE SECOND PART OF THE SERMON OF CHARITIE.

YOU haue heard a plaine and a fruitfull setting foorth of charity, and how profitable and necessary a thing charitie is: how charitie stretcheth it selfe both to GOD and man, friend and foe, and that by the doctrine and example of Christ: and also who may certifie himselfe whether he be in perfect charity, or not. Now as concerning the same matter, it followeth.

Against carnall men that will not forgiue their enemies. The peruerse nature of man, corrupt with sinne, and destitute of GOD'S word and grace, thinketh it against all reason, that a man should loue his enemie, and hath many perswasions which bring him to the contrary. Against all which reasons, wee ought aswell to set the teaching, as the liuing of our Sauiour Christ, who louing vs (when we were his enemies) doeth teach vs to loue our enemies. He did patiently take for vs many reproches, suffered beating, and most cruell death. Therefore wee be no members of him, if we will not follow him. Christ (saith S. Peter) suffered for vs, leauing an example that we should follow him (1 Peter 2.21).

Furthermore, wee must consider, that to loue our friends, is no more but that which theeues, adulterers, homicides, and all wicked persons doe: in so much that Iewes, Turkes, Infidels, and all bruite beasts, doe loue them that be their friends, of whom they haue their liuing, or any other benefites. But to loue enemies, is the proper condition of them that bee the children of GOD, the disciples and followers of Christ. Notwithstanding, mans froward and corrupt nature weigheth ouer deepely many times, the offence and displeasure done vnto him by enemies, and thinketh it a burden intolerable, to bee bound to loue them that hate him. But the burden should be easie ynough, if (on the other side) euery man would consider, what displeasure hee hath done to his enemie againe, and what pleasure hee hath receiued of his enemie. And if we finde no equall or euen recompence, neither in receiuing pleasures of our enemie, nor in requiting displeasures vnto him againe: then let vs ponder the displeasures which we haue done vnto Almightie GOD, how often and how grieuously wee haue offended him, whereof if wee will haue of GOD forgiuenesse, there is none other remedy, but to forgiue the offences done vnto vs, which be very small, in comparison of our offences done against GOD. And if we consider that he which hath offended vs, deserueth not to bee forgiuen of vs, let vs consider againe, that we much lesse deserue to bee forgiuen of GOD. And although our enemie deserue not to be forgiuen for his owne sake, yet we ought to forgiue him for GOD'S loue, considering how great and many benefits we haue receiued of him, without our desertes, and that Christ hath deserued of vs, that for his sake wee should forgiue them their trespasses committed against vs.

A question. But heere may rise a necessary question to bee dissolued. If charitie require to thinke, speake, and doe well vnto euery man, both good and euill: how can Magistrates execute iustice vpon malefactors or euill doers with charitie? How can they cast euill men in prison, take away their goods, and sometime their liues, according to lawes, if charitie will not suffer them so to doe?

Answere. Hereunto is a plaine and a briefe answer, that plagues and punishments be not euill of themselues, if they be well taken of the harmelesse. And to an euill man they are both good and necessarie, and may bee executed according to charity, and with charitie should be executed.

Charity hath two offices. For declaration whereof, you shall vnderstand that charitie hath two offices, the one contrary to the other, and yet both necessary to bee vsed vpon men of contrary sort and disposition. The one office of charitie is, to cherish good and harmelesse men, not to oppresse them with false accusations, but to encourage them with rewards to doe well, and to continue in well doing, defending them with the sword from their aduersaries: as the office of Bishopes and Pastours is, to praise good men for well doing, that they may continue therein, and to rebuke and correct by the word of GOD, the offences and crimes of all euill disposed persons. The other office of charity is, to rebuke, correct, and punish vice, without regard of persons, and is to be vsed against them onely that be euill men, and malefactours or euill doers. And that it is aswell the office of charitie to rebuke, punish, and correct them that bee euill, as it is to cherish and reward them that bee good and harmelesse. S. Paul declareth (writing to the Romans) saying, That the high powers are ordeined of GOD, not to be dreadfull to them that doe well, but vnto malefactors, to draw the sword to take vengeance of him that committeth the sinne (Romans 13.1, 4). And S. Paul biddeth Timothy stoutly and earnestly to rebuke sinne by the word of GOD (1 Timothy 5.20). So that both offices should be diligently executed, to fight against the kingdome of the Diuell, the Preacher with the word, and the Gouernours with the sword. Else they neither loue GOD, nor them whom they gouerne, if (for lacke of correction) they wilfully suffer GOD to be offended, and them whom they gouerne, to perish. For as euery louing father correcteth his naturall sonne when he doeth amisse, or else he loueth him not: so all gouernours of Realmes, Countreys, Townes, and Houses, should louingly correct them which bee offendours, vnder their gouernance, and cherish them which liue innocently, if they haue any respect either vnto GOD and their office, or loue vnto them of whom they haue gouernance. And such rebukes and punishments of them that offend, must be done in due time, lest by delay, the offenders fall headlong into all manner of mischiefe, and not onely be euill themselues, but also doe hurt vnto many men, drawing other by their euill example, to sinne and outrage after them. As one theefe may both robbe many men, and also make many theeues: and one seditious person may allure many, and annoye a whole Towne or Countrie. And such euill persons that bee so great offenders to GOD, and the common weale, charitie requireth to bee cut from the body of the common weale, least they corrupt other good and honest persons: like as a good Surgion cutteth away a rotten and festered member, for loue he hath to the whole body, lest it infect other members adioyning vnto it. Thus it is declared vnto you what true charitie or Christian loue is, so plainely, that no man neede to be deceiued. Which loue, whosoeuer keepeth, not onely towards GOD (whom he is bound to loue aboue all things) but also toward his neighbour, as well friend as foe, it shall surely keepe him from all offence of GOD, and iust offence of man. Therefore bears well away this one short lesson, that by true Christian charitie, GOD ought to be loued, good, and euill, friend, and foe, and to all such, wee ought (as wee may) to doe good: those that be good, of loue to encourage and cherish, because they be good: and those that be euill, of loue to procure and seeke their correction and due punishment, that they may thereby either bee brought to goodnesse, or at the least that GOD and the common wealth may be lesse hurt and offended. And if we thus direct our life, by Christian loue and charitie, then Christ doeth promise and assure vs that hee loueth vs, that we be the children of our heauenly Father, reconciled to his fauour, very members of Christ, and that after this short time of this present and mortall life, wee shall haue with him euerlasting life in his euerlasting kingdome of heauen. Therefore to him with the Father and the holy Ghost, be all honour and glory, now and for euer. Amen.

HOMILY ON SWEARING AND PERJURY

A SERMON AGAINST Swearing and Periury.

ALmighty GOD, to the intent his most holy Name should be had in honour, and euermore be magnified of the people, commandeth that no man should take his Name vainely in his mouth, threatning punishment vnto him that vnreuerently abuseth it by swearing, forswearing, and blasphemie.

How and in what causes it is lawfull to sweare. To the intent therefore that this commandement may be the better knowen and kept, it shall bee declared vnto you, both how it is lawfull for Christian people to sweare, and also what perill and danger it is vainely to sweare, or to be forsworne. First, when Iudges require othes of the people for declaration or opening of the trueth, or for execution of iustice, this manner of swearing is lawfull. Also when men make faithfull promises with calling to witnesse of the Name of GOD, to keepe couenants, honest promises, statutes, lawes and good customes, as Christian Princes doe in their conclusions of peace, for conseruation of common wealths, and priuate persons promise their fidelitie in Matrimony, or one to another in honestie and true friendship: and all men when they doe sweare to keepe common lawes, and locall statutes, and good customes, for due order to be had and continued among men, when Subiects doe sweare to be true and faithfull to their King and Soueraigne Lord, and when Iudges, Magistrates, and Officers sweare truely to execute their Offices, and when a man would affirme the trueth to the setting foorth of Gods glorie (for the saluation of the people) in open preaching of the Gospel, or in giuing of good counsell priuately for their soules health: all these maner of swearing, for causes necessary and honest, be lawfull. But when men doe sweare of custome, in reasoning, buying and selling, or other daily communications (as many be common and great swearers) such kind of swearing is vngodly, vnlawfull, and forbidden by the commandement of GOD. For such swearing is nothing els, but taking of GOD'S holy name in vaine. And here is to be noted, that lawfull swearing is not forbidden, but commanded by Almighty GOD. For we haue examples of Christ, and godly men, in holy Scripture, that did sweare themselues, and required othes of others likewise. And GOD'S Commandement is, Thou shalt dread thy Lord GOD, and shalt sweare by his Name (Deuteronomy 6.13). And Almightie GOD by his Prophet Dauid saith, All men shall be praised that sweare by him (Psalms 63.11).

Thus did our Sauiour Christ sweare diuers times, saying, Verily, verily (John 3.3). And S. Paul sweareth thus, I call GOD to witnesse (2 Corinthians 1.23). And Abraham (waxing old) required an oath of his seruant, that he should procure a wife for his sonne Isahac, which should come of his owne kinred (Genesis 24.3): and the seruant did sweare that he would performe his masters will. Abraham also being required, did sweare vnto Abimelech the king of Geraris, that hee should not hurt him, nor his posteritie (Genesis 21.23), and likewise did Abimelech sweare vnto Abraham. And Dauid did sweare to be and continue a faithfull friend to Ionathan, and Ionathan did sweare to become a faithfull friend vnto Dauid.

Also God once commanded, that if a thing were laide to pledge to any man, or left with him to keepe, if the same thing were stollen, or lost, that the keeper thereof should be sworne before Iudges, that hee did not conueigh it away, nor vsed any deceit in causing the same to bee conueied away, by his consent or knowledge. And Saint Paul saith, that in all matters of controuersie betweene two persons, whereas one sayth, Yea, and the other, Nay, so as no due proofe can be had of the truth, the end of euery such controuersie must be an oath ministred by a Iudge (Hebrews 6.16). And moreouer GOD by the Prophet Ieremy sayth, Thou shalt sweare, The Lord liueth, in trueth, in iudgement, in righteousnesse (Jeremiah 4.2). So that whosoeuer sweareth when hee is required of a Iudge, let him bee sure in his conscience that his oath haue three conditions, and he shall neuer need to be afrayd of periurie.

<u>What condition an oath ought to haue.</u> First, he that sweareth, may sweare truely, that is, hee must (setting apart all fauour and affection to the parties) haue the trueth onely before his eyes, and for loue

thereof, say and speake that which hee knoweth to be trueth, and no further.

The second. The second is, he that taketh an oath, must doe it with iudgement, not rashly and vnaduisedly, but soberly, considering what an oath is.

The third. The third is, hee that Sweareth, must sweare in righteousnesse: that is, for the very zeale and loue which hee beareth to the defence of innocencie, to the maintenance of the trueth, and of the righteousnesse of the matter or cause: all profit, disprofit, all loue and fauour vnto the person for friendship or kinred layd apart.

Why wee bee willed in scripture to sweare by the Name of God. Thus an oath (if it haue with it these three conditions) is a part of GOD'S glory, which we are bound by his commandements to giue vnto him. For hee willeth that wee shall sweare onely by his name, not that hee hath pleasure in oathes, but like as hee commanded the Iewes to offer sacrifices vnto him, not for any delight that he had in them, but to keep the Iewes from committing of idolatrie: so he commanding vs to sweare by his holy name, doeth not teach vs that he delighteth in swearing, but he thereby forbiddeth all men to giue his glory to any creature in heauen, earth, or water (Isaiah 42.8). Hitherto you see, that oathes lawfull are commanded of GOD, vsed of Patriarches and Prophets, of Christ himselfe, and of his Apostle Paul. Therefore Christian people must thinke lawfull oathes, both godly and necessary.

Commodities had by lawfull oths made and obserued. For by lawfull promise and couenants confirmed by oathes, Princes and their Countries are confirmed in common tranquillity & peace. By holy promises with calling the name of GOD to witnesse, we be made liuely members of Christ, when wee professe his Religion receiuing the Sacrament of Baptisme. By like holy promise the Sacrament of Matrimonie knitteth man and wife in perpetuall loue, that they desire not to be separated for any displeasure or aduersity that shall after happen. By lawfull oathes, which Kings, Princes, Iudges, and Magistrates doe sweare, common lawes are kept inuiolate, Iustice is indifferently ministred, harmelesse persons, fatherlesse children, widowes, and poore men, are defended from murderers, oppressours, and theeues, that they suffer no wrong, nor take any harme. By lawfull oathes, mutuall society, amity, and good order is kept continually in all cominalties, as Boroughes, Cities, Townes, and Villages. And by lawfull oathes, malefactors are searched out, wrong doers are punished, and they which sustaine wrong, are restored to their right. Therefore lawfull swearing can not be euill, which bringeth vnto vs so many godly, good, and necessary commodities.

Vaine swearing is forbidden. Wherfore when Christ so earnestly forbad swearing, it may not be vnderstood, as though hee did forbid all maner of oathes: but he forbiddeth all vaine swearing and forswearing both by GOD, and by his creatures, as the common vse of swearing in buying, selling, and in our dayly communication, to the intent euery Christian mans word should be aswell regarded in such matters, as if he should confirme his communication with an oath. For euery Christian mans word (sayth S. Hierome) should be so true, that it should bee regarded as an oath. And Chrysostome witnessing the same, sayth, It is not conuenient to sweare: for what needeth vs to sweare, when it is not lawfull for one of vs to make a lie vnto another?

An obiection. Peraduenture some will say, I am compelled to sweare, for else men that doe commune with me, or do buy and sell with me will not beleeue me.

An answer. To this, answereth S. Chrysostome, that he that thus sayth, sheweth himselfe to be an vniust and a deceitfull person. For if hee were a trustie man, and his deedes taken to agree with his words, he should not need to sweare at all. For he that vseth trueth and plainenesse in his bargayning and communication, he shall haue no need by such vaine swearing, to bring himselfe in credence with his neighbours, nor his neighbours will not mistrust his sayings. And if his credence be so much lost indeed, that hee thinketh no man will beleeue him without he sweare, then hee may well thinke his credence is cleane gone. For trueth it is (as Theophylactus writeth) that no man is lesse trusted, then he that vseth much to sweare. And Almighty GOD by the Wise man sayth, That man which sweareth much shall bee full of sinne, and the scourge of GOD shall not depart from his house (Ecclesiasticus 23.11).

Another obiection. But heere some men will say, for excusing of their many oathes in their dayly talke: Why should I not sweare, when I sweare truely?

An answer. To such men it may be sayd, that though they sweare truly, yet in swearing often vnaduisedly, for trifles, without necessity, and when they should not sweare, they be not without fault, but doe take GOD'S most holy name in vaine. Much more vngodly and vnwise men are they, that abuse GOD'S most holy name, not onely in buying and selling of small things dayly in all places, but also in eating, drinking, playing, communing and reasoning. As if none of these things might be done, except in doing of them, the most holy name of GOD bee commonly vsed and abused, vainely and vnreuerently talked of, sworne by, and forsworne, to the breaking of GOD'S commandement, and procurement of his indignation.

THE SECOND PART OF THE SERMON OF SWEARING.

YOu haue beene taught in the first part of this Sermon against swearing and periurie, what great danger it is to vse the name of GOD in vaine. And that all kinde of swearing is not vnlawfull, neither against GOD'S commandement, and that there be three things required in a lawfull oath. First, that it bee made for the maintenance of the trueth. Secondly, that it bee made with iudgement, not rashly and vnaduisedly. Thirdly, for the zeale and loue of Iustice. Ye heard also what commodities commeth of lawfull oathes, and what danger commeth of rash and vnlawfull oathes.

Lawfull oths and promises would be better regarded. Now as concerning the rest of the same matter, you shall vnderstand, that aswell they vse the name of GOD in vaine, that by an oath make vnlawfull promises of good and honest things, and performe them not: as they which doe promise euill and vnlawfull things, and doe performe the same. Of such men that regard not their godly promises bound by an oath, but wittingly and wilfully breaketh them, wee doe reade in holy Scripture two notable punishments. First, Iosua and the people of Israel made a league and faithfull promise of perpetuall amitie and friendship with the Gabaonites (Joshua 9.15): not withstanding afterward in the dayes of wicked Saul, many of these Gabaonites were murdered, contrary to the sayde faithfull promise made. Wherewith Almighty GOD was sore displeased that hee sent an vniuersall hunger vpon the whole countrey, which continued by the space of three yeeres. And GOD would not withdraw his punishment, vntill the sayd offence was reuenged by the death of seuen sonnes, or next kinsmen of king Saul. And whereas Zedekias king of Hierusalem, had promised fidelitie to the king of Chaldea, afterwarde when Zedechias contrarie to his oath and allegiance, did rebell against K. Nabuchodonosor: this heathen king by GOD'S permission and sufferance, inuading the land of Iurie, and besieging the citie of Hierusalem, compelled the sayd king Zedechias to flee, and in fleeing, tooke him prisoner, slewe his sonnes before his face, and put out both his eyes: and binding him with chaines, led him prisoner miserablie into Babylon (2 Kings 24.17, 20, 2 Kings 25.1-7).

Vnlawfull oathes and promises are not bee kept. Thus doeth GOD shew plainely how much hee abhorreth breakers of honest promises bound by an oath made in his Name. And of them that make wicked promises by an oath, and will performe the same, wee haue example in the Scriptures, chiefely of Herod, of the wicked Iewes, and of Iephtah. Herode promised by an oath vnto the Damosell which danced before him, to giue vnto her whatsoeuer shee would aske (Matthew 14.7-11): when shee was instructed before of her wicked mother to aske the head of Saint Iohn Baptist, Herod as hee tooke a wicked oath, so hee more wickedly performed the same, and cruelly slewe the most holy Prophet. Likewise did the malicious Iewes make an oath, cursing themselues if they did either eate or drinke, vntill they had slaine Saint Paul (Acts 23.14). And Iephtah when GOD had giuen to him victorie of the children of Ammon, promised (of a foolish deuotion) vnto GOD, to offer for a sacrifice vnto him, that person which of his owne house should first meete with him after his returne home. By force of which fonde and vnaduised oath, hee did slay his owne and onely daughter, which came out of his house with mirth and ioy to welcome him home (Judges 11.30-39). Thus the promise which hee made (most foolishly) to GOD, against GOD'S euerlasting will, and the law of nature, most cruelly hee performed, so committing against GOD a double offence. Therefore, whosoeuer maketh any promise, binding himselfe thereunto by an oath: let him foresee that the thing which hee promiseth, bee good, and honest, and not against the commandement of GOD, and that it bee in his owne power to performe it iustly. And such good promises must all men keepe euermore assuredly. But if a man at any time shall, either of ignorance, or of malice, promise and sweare to doe any thing which is either against the law of Almighty GOD, or not in his power to performe: let him take it for an vnlawfull and vngodly oath.

<u>Against periurie.</u> Now something to speake of periurie, to the intent you should know how great and grieuous an offence against GOD this wilfull periurie is, I will shew you what it is to take an oath before a Iudge vpon a booke.

<u>An oath before a Iudge.</u> First, when they laying their hands vpon the Gospell booke, doe sweare truely to enquire, and to make a true presentment of things wherewith they be charged, and not to let from saying the trueth, and doing truely, for fauour, loue, dread, or malice of any person, as GOD may helpe them, and the holy contents of that booke: They must consider, that in that booke is contayned GOD'S euerlasting truth, his most holy and eternall word, whereby we haue forgiuenesse of our sinnes, and be made inheritours of heauen, to liue for euer with GOD'S Angels and Saints, in ioy and gladnesse. In the Gospell booke is contayned also GOD'S terrible threats to obstinate sinners, that will not amend their liues, nor beleeue the trueth of GOD his holy word, and the euerlasting paine prepared in hell for Idolaters, hypocrites, for false and vaine swearers, for periured men, for false witnesse bearers, for false condemners of innocent and guiltlesse men, and for them which for fauour, hide the crimes of euill doers, that they should not bee punished. So that whosoeuer wilfully forsweare themselues vpon Christs holy Euangelie, they vtterly forsake GOD'S mercy, goodnesse, and trueth, the merits of our Sauiour Christs natiuity, life, passion, death, resurrection and ascension, they refuse the forgiuenesse of sinnes, promised to all penitent sinners, the ioyes of heauen, the company with Angels and Saints for euer. All which benefits and comforts are promised vnto true Christian persons in the Gospell. And they, so being forsworne vpon the Gospell, doe betake themselues to the Diuels seruice, the master of all lies, falshood, deceit, and periurie, prouoking the great indignation and curse of GOD against them in this life, and the terrible wrath and iudgement of our Sauiour Christ, at the great day of the last iudgement, when hee shall iustly iudge both the quicke and the dead, according to their workes. For whosoeuer forsaketh the trueth, for loue of displeasure of any man, or for lucre and profit to himselfe, doeth forsake Christ, and with Iudas betray him.

<u>Though periurie doe escape heerevn spied and vnpunished, it shall not doe so euer.</u> And although such periured mens falshood bee now kept secret, yet it shall bee opened at the last day, when the se-

crets of all mens hearts shall bee manifest to all the world. And then the trueth shall appeare, and accuse them: and their owne conscience, with all the blessed company of Heauen, shall beare witnesse truely against them. And Christ the righteous Iudge shall then iustly condemne them to euerlasting shame and death. This sinne of periurie, Almighty GOD by the Prophet Malachie doeth threaten to punish sore, saying vnto the Iewes, I will come to you in iudgement, and I will bee a swift witnesse and a sharpe Iudge vpon sorcerers, adulterers, and periured persons (Malachai 3.5). Which thing to the Prophet Zachary GOD declareth in a vision, wherein the Prophet saw a booke fleeing, which was twenty cubites long, and ten cubites broad, GOD saying then vnto him, this is the curse that shall goe foorth vpon the face of the earth, for falsehood, falseswearing, and periurie. And this curse shall enter into the house of the false man and into the house of the periured man, and it shall remaine in the middest of his house, consume him, and the timber and stones of his house (Zachariah 5.1-4). Thus you see how much GOD doth hate periurie, and what punishment GOD hath prepared for false swearers, and periured persons.

Thus you haue heard, how and in what causes it is lawfull for a Christian man to sweare: yee haue heard what properties and conditions a lawfull oath must haue, and also how such lawfull oathes are both godly and necessary to be obserued: yee haue heard, that it is not lawfull to sweare vainely, (that is) other wayes then in such causes, and after such sort as is declared. And finally, yee haue heard how damnable a thing it is, either to forsweare ourselues, or to keepe an vnlawfull, and an vnaduised oath. Wherefore let vs earnestly call for grace, that all vaine swearing and periurie set apart, wee may onely vse such oathes as be lawfull and godly, and that wee may truely without all fraud keepe the same, according to GOD'S will and pleasure. To whom with the Sonne, and the holy Ghost, be all honour and glory. AMEN.

HOMILY ON THE DECLINING FROM GOD

A SERMON HOW dangerous a thing it is to fall from God.

OF our going from GOD, the wise man saith, that pride was the first beginning: for by it mans heart was turned from GOD his maker. For pride (saith hee) is the fountaine of all sinne: he that hath it, shall be full of cursings, and at the end it shall ouerthrow him (Ecclesiasticus 10.13). And as by pride and sinne wee goe from GOD, so shall GOD and all goodnesse with him goe from vs. And the Prophet Osee doth plainely affirme, that they which goe away still from GOD by vicious liuing, and yet would goe about to pacifie him otherwise by sacrifice, and entertaine him thereby, they labour in vaine. For, notwithstanding all their sacrifice, yet hee goeth still away from them. For so much (saith the Prophet) as they doe not apply their minds to returne to GOD, although they goe about with whole flockes and heards to seeke the Lord, yet they shall not find him: for he is gone away from them (Hosea 5.5-6, 6.6, 8.13). But as touching our turning to GOD, or from GOD, you shall vnderstand, that it may bee done diuers wayes. Sometimes directly by Idolatry, as Israel and Iuda then did: sometimes men goe from GOD by lacke of Fayth, and mistrusting of GOD, whereof Esay speaketh in this wise, Woe to them that goe downe into Egypt to seeke for helpe, trusting in horses, & hauing confidence in the number of chariots, and puisance or power of horsemen. They haue no confidence in the holy GOD of Israel, nor seeke for the Lord (Isaiah 31.1-3). But what followeth? The Lord shall let his hand fall vpon them, and downe shall come both the helper, and hee that is holpen: they shall bee destroyed altogether. Sometime men goe from GOD by the neglecting of his Commandements concerning their neighbours, which commandeth them to expresse hearty loue towards euery man, as Zacharie said vnto the people in GOD'S behalfe. Giue true iudgement, shew mercy and compassion euery one to his brother, imagine no deceit towards widowes, or children fatherlesse and motherlesse, toward strangers, or the poore, let no man forge euill in his heart against his brother (Zechariah 7.9-10). But these things they passed not off, they turned their backes, and went their way, they stopped their eares that they might not heare, they hardened their hearts as an Adamant stone, that they might not listen to the Law, and the wordes that the Lord had sent through his holy Spirit, by his ancient Prophets. Wherefore the Lord shewed his great indignation vpon them. It came to passe (saith the Prophet) euen as I told them: as they would not heare, so when they cryed, they were not heard, but were scattered into all kingdomes which they neuer knew, and their land was made desolate. And to be short, all they that may not abide the word of GOD, but following the perswasions and stubbornnesse of their owne hearts, goe backeward and not forward (as it is said in Ieremie, Jeremiah 7.24) They goe and turne a way from GOD. Insomuch that Origen saith, Hee that with mind, with study, with deedes, with thought, and care applyeth and giueth himselfe to GOD'S word, and thinketh vpon his Lawes day and night, giueth himselfe wholly to GOD, and in his precepts and Commandements is exercised: this is hee that is turned to GOD. And on the other part hee sayth, Whosoeuer is occupied with Fables and Tales, when the worde of GOD is rehearsed, hee is turned from GOD. Whosoeuer in time of reading GOD'S word, is carefull in his minde of worldly businesse, of money, or of lucre, hee is turned from GOD: whosoeuer is intangled with the cares of possessions, filled with couetousnesse of riches, whosoeuer studieth for the glory and honour of this world, hee is turned from GOD. So that after his minde, whosoeuer hath not a speciall minde to that thing that is commanded or taught of GOD, hee that doeth not listen vnto it, embrace, and print it in his heart, to the intent that hee may duely fashion his life thereafter, hee is plainely turned from GOD, although hee doe other things of his owne deuotion and mind, which to him seeme better, and more to GOD'S honour. Which thing to be true, wee bee taught and admonished in the holy Scripture by the example of king Saul, who being commanded of GOD by Samuel, that he should kill all the Amalekites, and destroy them clearely with their goods and cattel (1 Samuel 15.3): yet hee, being mooued partly with pitie, and partly (as he thought) with deuotion vnto GOD, saued Agag the King, and all the chiefe of their cattell, therewith to make sacrifice vnto GOD. Wherewithall GOD being displeased highly, sayd vnto the Prophet Samuel, I repent that euer I made Saul King, for hee hath forsaken me, and not followed my words, and so he commanded Samuel to shew him, and when Samuel asked wherefore (contrary to GOD'S word) he had saued the cattel, he excused the matter, partly, by feare, saying, hee durst doe none other, for that the people would haue it so, partly, for that they were goodly beastes, hee thought GOD would bee content, seeing it was done of a good intent and deuotion, to honour GOD with the sacrifice of them.

But Samuel reproouing all such intents and deuotions (seeme they neuer so much to GOD'S honour, if they stand not with his word, whereby wee may be assured of his pleasure) said in this wise, Would GOD haue sacrifices and offerings? Or rather that his word should be obeyed? To obey him, is better then offerings, and to listen to him is better then to offer the fat of Rammes: yea, to repugne against his voyce is as euill as the sinne of soothsaying: and not to agree to it is like abominable Idolatrie. And now forasmuch as thou hast cast away the word of the Lord, he hath cast away thee, that thou shouldest not be king.

The turning of God from man. By all these examples of holy Scripture, we may know, that as wee forsake GOD, so shall hee euer forsake vs. And what miserable state doeth consequently and necessarily follow thereupon, a man may easily consider by the terrible threatnings of GOD. And although hee consider not all the sayd miserie to the vttermost, being so great that it passeth any mans capacitie in this life sufficiently to consider the same: yet hee shall soone perceiue so much thereof, that if his heart bee not more then stonie, or harder then the Adamant, he shall feare, tremble, and quake, to call the same to his remembrance. First the displeasure of GOD towards vs is commonly expressed in the Scripture by these two things: by shewing his fearefull countenance vpon vs, and by turning his face, or hiding it from vs. By shewing his dreadfull countenance, is signified his great wrath: but by turning his face or hiding thereof is many times more signified, that is to say, that he cleerely forsaketh vs, and giueth vs ouer. The which significations bee taken of the properties of mens manners. For men towards them whom they fauour, commonly beare a good, a chearefull, and a louing countenance: so that by the face or countenance of a man, it doeth commonly appeare what will or minde hee beareth towards other. So when GOD doeth shew his dreadfull countenance towards vs, that is to say, doeth send dreadfull plagues of Sword, famine, or pestilence vpon vs, it appeareth that hee is greatly wroth with vs. But when he withdraweth from vs his Word, the right doctrine of Christ, his gracious assistance and ayde (which is euer ioyned to his word) and leaueth vs to our own wit, our owne will and strength: he declareth then, that he beginneth to forsake vs. For whereas GOD hath shewed to all them that truely beleeue his Gospel, his face of mercie in Iesus Christ, which doeth so lighten their hearts, that they (if they behold it as they ought to doe) be transformed to his Image, be made partakers of the heauenly light, and of his holy Spirit, and bee fashioned to him in all goodnesse requisite to the children of GOD: so, if they after doe neglect the same, if they bee vnthankefull vnto him, if they order not their liues according to his example and doctrine, and to the setting forth of his glory, he will take away from them his Kingdome, his holy word, whereby hee should reigne in them, because they bring not foorth the fruit thereof that he looketh for. Neuerthelesse, his is so mercifull, and of so long sufferance, that he doeth not shew vpon vs that great wrath suddenly. But when we begin to shrinke from his word, not beleeuing it, or not expressing it in our liuings: first hee doeth send his messengers, the true preachers of his word, to admonish and warne vs of our duetie: that as hee for his part, for the great loue hee bare vnto vs, deliuered his owne Sonne to suffer death, that wee by his death might be deliuered from death, and be restored to the life euerlasting, euermore to dwell with him, and to bee partakers and inheritours with him, of his euerlasting glory and kingdome of heauen: so againe, that we for our parts should walke in a godly life, as becommeth his children to doe. And if this will not serue, but still we remaine disobedient to his word and wil, not knowing him, nor louing him, not fearing him, not putting our whole trust and confidence in him: and on the other side, to our neighbours behauing our selues vncharitably, by disdaine, enuie, malice, or by committing murder, robbery, adultery, gluttony, deceit, lying, swearing, or other like detestable workes, and vngodly behauiour, then he threatneth vs by terrible comminations, swearing in great anger, that whosoeuer doth these workes, shall neuer enter into his rest, which is the kingdome of heauen. (Hebrews 3.11, Psalms 15, 1 Corinthians 6).

THE SECOND PART OF THE SERMON OF FALLING FROM GOD.

IN the former part of this sermon, yee haue learned how many manner of wayes men fall from GOD: some by idolatrie, some for lacke of faith, some by neglecting of their neighbors, some by not hearing of GOD'S word, some by the pleasure they take in the vanities of worldly things. Yee haue also learned in what misery that man is, which is gone from GOD: and how that GOD yet of his infinite goodnesse to call againe man from that his miserie vseth first gentle admonitions by his Preachers, after he layeth on terrible threatnings. Now if this gentle monition and threatning together doe not serue, then GOD will shew his terrible countenance vpon vs, hee will powre intolerable plagues vpon our heads, and after he will take away from vs all his ayde and assistance, wherewith before hee did defend vs from all such manner of calamitie. As the Euangelicall prophet Esay agreeing with Christ's parable doeth teach vs, saying, That GOD had made a goodly vineyard for his beloued children, hee hedged it, he walled it round about, he planted it with chosen vines, and made a Turret in the middest thereof, and therein also a vine-presse. And when he looked that it should bring him foorth good grapes, it brought forth wild graps (Isaiah 5.1-2, Matthew 21.33): and after it followeth, Now shall I shew you (saith GOD) what I wil doe with my vineyard: I will plucke downe the hedges, that it may perish: I will breake downe the walles that it may bee troden vnder foot: I will let it lie wast, it shall not be cut, it shall not bee digged, but briers and thornes shall ouergrowe it, and I shall command the cloudes that they shall no more raine vpon it.

By these threatnings we are monished and warned, that if we which are the chosen vineyard of GOD, bring not foorth good grapes, that is to say, good workes that may bee delectable and pleasant in his sight, when hee looketh for them, when he sendeth his messengers to call vpon vs for them, but rather bring foorth wild grapes, that is to say, sowre workes, vnsauery, and vnfruitfull: then will hee plucke away all desence, and suffer grieuous plagues of famine, battell, dearth, and death, to light vpon vs. Finally, if these serue not, he will let vs lie waste, he will giue vs ouer, he will turne away from vs, he will dig and delue no more about vs, hee will let vs alone, and suffer vs to bring foorth euen such fruite as wee will, to bring foorth brambles, bryers, and thornes, all naughtinesse, all vice, and that so abundantly, that they shall cleane ouergrow vs, choke, strangle, and vtterly destroy vs. But they that in this world liue not after GOD, but after their owne carnall libertie, perceiue not this great wrath of GOD towards them, that he will not digge, nor delue any more about them, that hee doeth let them alone euen to themselues. But they take this for a great benefit of GOD, to haue all their owne libertie: and so they liue, as if carnall libertie were the true libertie of the Gospel. But GOD forbid (good people) that euer we should desire such libertie. For although GOD suffer sometimes the wicked to haue their pleasure in this world, yet the ende of vngodly liuing is at length endlesse destruction. The murmuring Israelites had that they longed for, they had Quailes ynough, yea, till they were weary of them. But what was the end thereof? Their sweete meate had sowre sauce: euen whiles the meate was in their mouthes, the plague of GOD lighted vpon them, and suddenly they died (Numbers 11.31-33). So, if wee liue vngodly, and GOD suffereth vs to follow our owne willes, to haue our owne delightes and pleasures, and correcteth vs not with some plague: it is no doubt but hee is almost vtterly displeased with vs. And although hee be long ere he strike, yet many times when he striketh such persons, hee striketh them at once for euer. So that when he doeth not strike vs, when he ceaseth to afflict vs, to punish or beat vs, and suffereth vs to runne headlong into all vngodlinesse, and pleasures of this world that wee delight in, without punishment and aduersity, it is a dreadfull token that hee loueth vs no longer, that he careth no longer for vs, but hath giuen vs ouer to our owne selues. As long as a man doeth prune his vines, doeth dig at the rootes, and doeth lay fresh earth to them, hee hath a mind to them, he perceiueth some token of fruitfulnes that may be recouered in them, but when hee will bestow no more such cost and labour about them, then it is a signe that hee thinketh they will neuer bee good. And the father, as long as he loueth his childe, he loketh angerly, he correcteth him when hee doeth amisse: but when that serueth not, and vpon that he ceaseth from correction of him, and suffereth him to do what he list himselfe, it is a signe that he intendeth to disinherit him and to cast him away for euer. So surely nothing should pearce our heart so sore, and put vs in such horrible feare, as when wee know in our conscience, that we haue greeuously offended GOD, and doe so continue, and that yet he striketh not, but quietly suffereth vs in the naughtines that wee haue delight in. Then specially it is time to cry, and to cry againe, as Dauid did: Cast mee not away from thy face, and take not away thy holy spirit from mee

(Psalms 51.11). Lord turne not away thy face from mee, cast not thy seruant away in displeasure. Hide not thy face from mee, least I bee like vnto them that goe downe to hell. The which lamentable prayers of him, as they doe certifie vs what horrible danger they be in, from whom GOD turneth his face (for the time, and as long as he so doth:) so should they mooue and stirre vs to cry vpon GOD with all our heart, that wee may not bee brought into that state, which doubtlesse is so sorrowfull, so miserable, and so dreadfull, as no tongue canne sufficiently expresse, nor any heart canne thinke. For what deadly greefe may a man suppose it is to bee vnder the wrath of GOD, to bee forsaken of him, to haue his holy spirit the authour of all goodnesse to bee taken from him, to bee brought to so vile a condition, that hee shall bee left meete for no better purpose, then to bee for euer condemned in hell? For not onely such places of Dauid doe shew, that vpon the turning of GOD'S face from any persons, they shall bee left bare from all goodnesse, and farre from hope of remedie: but also the place rehearsed last before of Esay, doeth meane the same, which sheweth, that GOD at length doeth so forsake his vnfruitfull vineyard, that hee will not onely suffer it to bring foorth weedes, bryers, and thornes, but also further to punish the vnfruitfulnesse of it. Hee saith hee will not cut it, hee will not delue it, and hee will commaund the cloudes that they shall not raine vpon it: whereby is signified the teaching of his holy word, which Saint Paul, after a like manner, expressed by planting and watering, meaning that hee will take that away from them, so that they shall bee no longer of his kingdome, they shall bee no longer gouerned by his holy Spirit, they shall bee put from the grace and benefits that they had, and euer might haue enioyed through Christ, they shall bee depriued of the heauenly light, and life which they had in Christ, whiles they abode in him: they shall bee (as they were once) as men without GOD in this world, or rather in worse taking. And to be short, they shall bee giuen into the power of the deuill, which beareth the rule in all them that be cast away from GOD, as hee did in Saul and Iudas (1 Samuel 15.23, 16.14), and generally in all such, as worke after their owne willes, the children of mistrust and vnbeliefe. Let vs beware therefore (good Christian people) least that wee reiecting or casting away GOD'S word (by the which we obtaine and retaine true faith in GOD) bee not at length cast of so farre, that wee become as the children of vnbeleefe, which bee of two sortes, farre diuerse, yea, almost cleane contrarie, & yet both be very farre from returning to GOD; the one sort, onely weighing their sinfull and detestable liuing, with the right iudgement and straightnesse of GOD'S righteousnesse, bee so without counsaile, and bee so comfortlesse (as they all must needes bee from whom the spirit of counsell and comfort is gone) that they will not bee perswaded in their heartes, but &that; either GOD can not, or else that hee will not take them againe to his fauour and mercie. The other, hearing the louing and large promises of GOD'S mercie, and so not conceiuing a right faith thereof, make those promises larger then euer GOD did, trusting, that although they continue in their sinfull and detestable lyuing neuer so long, yet that GOD at the end of their life, will shew his mercie vpon them, and that then they will returne. And both these two sortes of men be in a damnable state, and yet neuerthelesse, GOD (who willeth not the death of the wicked) hath shewed meanes, whereby both the same (if they take heede in season) may escape (Ezekiel 18.32, 33.11).

Against desperation. The first, as they doe dread GOD'S rightfull iustice in punishing sinners (whereby they should bee dismayed, and should despaire in deede, as touching any hope that may be in themselues) so if thy would constantly or stedfastly beleeue, that GOD'S mercy is the remedy appointed against such despaire and distrust, not onely for them, but generally for all that bee sorry & truely repentant, and will therewithall sticke to GOD'S mercie, they may be sure they shall obtaine mercie, and enter into the port or hauen of safegard, into the which whosoeuer doth come, bee they before time neuer so wicked, they shall be out of danger of euerlasting damnation, as GOD by Ezechiel saith, what time soeuer a sinner doth returne, and take earnest and true repentance, I will forget all his wickednesse (Ezekiel 33.19).

Against presumption. The other, as they be ready to beleeue GOD'S promises, so they should bee as ready to beleeue the threatnings of GOD: as well they should beleeue the law, as the Gospel: as well that there is an hell & euerlasting fire, as that there is an heauen, and euerlasting ioy: as well they should beleeue damnation to be threatned to the wicked and euill doers, as saluation to be promised to the faithfull in word and workes, aswell they should beleeue GOD to be true in the one, as in the other. And the sinners that continue in their wicked liuing, ought to thinke, that the promises of GOD'S mercy, and the Gospell, pertaine not vnto them being in that state, but only the law, and those Scriptures which contayne the wrath and indignation of GOD, and his threatnings, which should certifie them, that as they doe ouer boldly presume of Gods mercy, and liue dissolutely: so doth GOD still more and more withdraw his mercy from them, and he is so prouoked thereby to wrath at length, that he destroyeth such presumers many times suddenly. For of such S. Paul sayd thus, When they shall say it is peace, there is no danger, then shall sudden destruction come vpon them (1 Thessalonians 5.3). Let vs beware therefore of such naughty boldnesse to sinne. For GOD, which hath promised his mercie to them that bee truely repentant (although it bee at the latter ende) hath not promised to the presumptuous sinner, either that he shall haue long life, or that he shall haue true repentance at the last end. But for that purpose hath hee made euery mans death vncertaine, that hee should not put his hope in the ende, and in the meane season (to GOD'S high displeasure) liue vngodly. Wherefore, let vs follow the counsell of the wise man, let vs make no tarrying to turne vnto the Lord: let vs not put off from day to day, for suddainly shall his wrath come, and in time of vengeance hee will destroy the wicked. Let vs therefore turne betimes, and when wee turne let vs pray to GOD, as Ose teacheth, saying, Forgiue all our sinnes, receiue vs gratiously (Hosea 14.2). And if wee turne to him with an humble and a very penitent heart, hee will receiue vs to his fauour and grace for his holy Names sake, for his promise sake, for his trueth and mercies sake, promised to all faithfull beleeuers in Iesus Christ his onely naturall Sonne: to whom the onely Sauiour of the world with the Father and the holy Ghost, be all honour, glory, and power, world without end. Amen.

HOMILY ON THE FEAR OF DEATH

AN EXHORTATION against the feare of Death.

IT is not to bee maruelled that worldly men doe feare to die. For death depriueth them of all worldly honors, riches, and possessions, in the fruition whereof, the worldly man counteth himselfe happy, so long as hee may enioy them as his owne pleasure: and otherwise, if he bee dispossessed of the same, without hope of recouery, then he can none otherwise thinke of himselfe, but that hee is vnhappy, because he hath lost his worldly ioy and pleasure. Alas thinketh this carnall man, shall I now depart for euer from all my honours, all my treasure, from my countrie, friends, riches, possessions, and worldly pleasures, which are my ioy and heartes delight? Alas that euer that day shall come, when all these I must bid farewell at once, and neuer to enioy any of them after. Wherefore it is not without great cause spoken of the Wise man, O death, how bitter and sowre is the remembrance of thee to a man that liueth in peace and prosperitie in his substance, to a man liuing at ease, leading his life after his owne minde without trouble, and is therewithall well pampered and fedde (Ecclesiasticus 41.1)? There bee other men, whom this world doeth not so greatly laugh vpon, but rather vexe and oppresse with pouertie, sickenesse, or some other aduersitie, yet they doe feare death, partly because the flesh abhorreth naturally his owne sorrowfull dissolution, which death doeth threaten vnto them, and partly by reason of sickenesses and painefull diseases, which be most strong pangues and agonies in the flesh, and vse commonly to come to sicke men before death, or at the least accompanie death, whensoeuer it commeth.

Although these two causes seeme great and weightie to a worldly man, whereupon hee is mooued to feare death, yet there is an other cause much greater then any of these afore rehearsed, for which indeede he hath iust cause to feare death, and that is the state and condition wherevnto at the last end death bringeth all them that haue their hearts fixed vpon this world, without repentance and amendment. This state and condition is called the second death, which vnto all such shall ensue after this bodily death. And this is that death, which indeed ought to be dread and feared: for it is an euerlasting losse without remedy of the grace and fauour of GOD, and of euerlasting ioy, pleasure, and felicitie. And it is not onely the losse for euer of all these eternall pleasures, but also it is the condemnation both of body and soule (without either appellation, or hope of redemption) vnto euerlasting paines in hell. Vnto this state death sent the vnmercifull and the vngodly rich man (that Luke speaketh of in his Gospel, Luke 16.19-23) who liuing in all wealth and pleasure in this world, and cherishing himselfe dayly with dainty fare, and gorgious apparell, despised poore Lazarus that lay pitifull at his gate, miserably plagued and full of sores, and also grieuously pined with hunger. Both these two were arrested of death, which sent Lazarus the poore miserable man by Angels anon vnto Abraham's bosome, a place of rest, pleasure, and consolation: but the vnmercifull rich man descended downe into hell, and being in torments, he cryed for comfort, complaining of the intolerable paine that he suffered in that flame of fire, but it was too late. So vnto this place bodily death sendeth all them that in this world haue their ioy and felicity, all them that in this world be vnfaithfull vnto GOD, and vncharitable vnto their neighbours, so dying without repentance and hope of GOD'S mercy. Wherefore it is no maruaile, that the worldly man feareth death, for hee hath much more cause so to doe, then he himselfe doeth consider.

The first. Thus wee see three causes why worldly men feare death. One, because they shall loose thereby their worldly honours, riches, possessions, and all their hearts desires:

Second. Another, because of the painefull diseases, and bitter pangs, which commonly men suffer, either before, or at the time of death:

Third. but the chiefe cause aboue all other, is the dread of the miserable state of eternall damnation both of body and soule, which they feare shall follow, after their departing from the worldly pleasures of this present life.

For these causes be all mortall men, (which be giuen to the loue of this world) both in feare, and state of death, through sin (as the holy Apostle saith, Hebrews 2.15) so long as they liue here in this world: But (euerlasting thankes be to Almightie GOD for euer) there is neuer a one of all these causes, no nor yet them altogether, that can make a true Christian man afraid to die (who is the very member of Christ, the Temple of the holy Ghost, 1 Corinthians 3.16, the sonne of God, and the very inheritour of the euerlasting kingdome of heauen:) but plainely contrary, hee conceiueth great and many causes vndoubtedly grounded vpon the infallible and euerlasting trueth of the word of GOD, which mooueth him not onely to put away the feare of bodily death, but also for the manifold benefits and singular commodities which ensue vnto euery faithfull person by reason of the same, to wish, desire, and long heartily for it. For death shall bee to him no death at all, but a very deliuerance from death, from all paines, cares, and sorrowes, miseries, and wretchednesse of this world, and the very entry into rest, and a beginning of euerlasting ioy, a tasting of heauenly pleasures, so great, that neither tongue is able to expresse, neither eye to see, nor eare to heare them: nor any earthly mans heart to conceiue them. So exceeding great benefits they be, which GOD our heauenly Father by his meere mercy, and for the loue of his Sonne Iesus Christ, hath laid vp in store, and prepared for them that humbly submit themselues to GOD'S, and euermore vnfainedly loue him from the bottome of their hearts. And wee ought to beleeue that death being slaine by Christ, cannot keepe any man that stedfastly trusteth in Christ, vnder his perpetuall tyrranie and subiection: but that hee shall rise from death againe vnto glory at the last day, appointed by Almightie GOD, like as Christ our head did rise againe, according to GOD'S appointment, the thirde day. For S. Augustine saith, The head going before, the members trust to follow and come after. And S. Paul sayth, If Christ be risen from the dead, we shall rise also from the same. And to comfort all Christian persons herein, holy Scripture calleth this bodily death a sleepe, wherein mannes senses be (as it were) taken from him for a season, and yet when hee awaketh, he is more fresh then he was when he went to bed. So although we haue our soules separated from our bodies for a season, yet at the generall Resurrection we shall be more fresh, beautifull, and perfect then we be now. For now we be mortall, then shall we be immortall: now infected with diuers infirmities, then clearely void of all mortall infirmities: now we be subiect to all carnall desires, then we shall be all Spirituall, desiring nothing but GOD'S glory, and things eternall. Thus is this bodily death a doore or entring vnto life, and therefore not so much dreadfull (if it be rightly considered) as it is comfortable, not a mischiefe, but a remedy for all mischiefe, no enemy, but a friend, not a cruell tyrant, but a gentle guide leading vs not to mortality, but to immortality, not to sorrow and paine, but to ioy and pleasure, and that to endure for euer, if it be thankefully taken and accepted as GOD'S messenger, and patiently borne of vs for Christ's loue, that suffered most painefull death for our loue, to redeeme vs from death eternall. According hereunto S. Paul saith, our life is hid with Christ in GOD (Colossians 3.3-4): but when our life shall appeare, then shall we also appeare with him in glory. Why then shall we feare to die, considering the manifold and comfortable promises of the Gospel, and of holy Scriptures? GOD the Father hath giuen vs euerlasting life (saith S. Iohn) to you that beleeue in the Name of the Sonne of GOD, that you may know that you haue euerlasting life (1 John 5.11-13) and that you doe beleeue vpon the Name of the Sonne of GOD. And our Sauiour Christ saith, He that beleeueth in me hath life euerlasting, and I will raise him from death to life at the last day (John 6.40): S. Paul also saith, that Christ is ordained and made of GOD our righteousnesse, or holinesse and redemption, to the intent that he which will glory should glory in the Lord (1 Corinthians 1.30-31). S. Paul did contemne and set little by all other things, esteeming them as doung which before he had in very great price, that he might be found in Christ, to haue euerlasting life, true holinesse, righteousnesse, and redemption (Philippians 3.8-9). Finally, S. Paul maketh a plaine argument in this wise. If our heauenly Father would not spare his owne naturall Sonne, but did giue him to death for vs: how can it bee, that with him hee should not giue vs all things (Romans 8.32)? Therefore if we haue Christ, then haue we with him, and by him, all good things whatsoeuer wee can in our hearts wish or desire, as victorie ouer death, sinne, and hell: wee haue the fauour of GOD, peace with him, holinesse, wisedome, iustice, power, life, and redemption, wee haue by him perpetuall health, wealth, ioy, and blisse euerlasting.

THE SECOND PART OF THE SERMON AGAINST THE FEARE OF DEATH.

IT hath beene heretofore shewed you, that there be three causes wherefore men doe commonly feare death. First, the sorrowfull departing from worldly goods and pleasures. The second, the feare of the pangs and paines that come with death. Last and principall cause is, the horrible feare of extreame misery, and perpetuall damnation in time to come. And yet none of these three causes troubleth good men, because they stay themselues by true Faith, perfect Charitie, and sure Hope of the endlesse ioy and blisse euerlasting.

All those therefore haue great cause to be full of ioy that be ioyned to Christ with true Faith, stedfast Hope, and perfect Charitie, and not to feare death nor euerlasting damnation. For death cannot depriue them of Iesu Christ, nor any sin can condemne them that are graffed surely in him, which is their onely ioy, treasure, and life. Let vs repent our sinnes, amend our liues, trust in his mercy and satisfaction, and death can neither take him from vs, nor vs from him. For then (as Saint Paul saith) whether we liue or die, we be the Lords own. And againe he saith, Christ did die, and rose againe, because hee should be Lord both of the dead and quicke. Then if we be the Lords owne when we be dead, it must needs follow that such temporall death, not onely cannot harme vs, but also that it shall be much to our profite, and ioyne vs vnto GOD more perfectly. And thereof the Christian heart may surely be certified by the infallible or vndeceiuable trueth of holy Scripture. It is GOD (saith S. Paul) which hath prepared vs vnto immortalitie, and the same is hee which hath giuen vs an earnest of the Spirit (2 Corinthians 5.5). Therefore let vs be alwayes of good comfort, for we know that so long as we be in the body, we be (as it were) far from GOD in a strange countrey, subiect to many perils, walking without perfect sight and knowledge of Almightie GOD, only seeing him by Faith in holy Scriptures. But we haue a courage and desire rather to be at home with GOD and our Sauiour Christ, farre from the body, where we may behold his Godhead as he is, face to face, to our euerlasting comfort. These be S. Paul's words in effect, whereby we may perceiue, that the life in this world, is resembled and likened to a Pilgrimage in a strange countrey, farre from GOD, and that death, deliuering vs from our bodies, doth send vs straight home into our owne countrey, and maketh vs to dwell presently with GOD for euer, in euerlasting rest and quietnesse: So that to die, is no losse, but profit and winning to all true Christian people. What lost the theefe that hanged on the Crosse with Christ, by his bodily death? yea, how much did he gaine by it? Did not our Sauiour say vnto him, This day thou shalt be with me in Paradise? And Lazarus that pitifull person, that lay before the rich mans gate, pained with sores, and pined with hunger, did not death highly profit and promote him, which by the ministery of Angels sent him vnto Abraham's bosome, a place of rest, ioy, and heauenly consolation (Luke 16.22)? Let vs thinke none other (good Christian people) but Christ hath prepared and made ready before, the same ioy and felicitie for vs, that he prepared for Lazarus and the theefe. Wherefore, let vs sticke vnto his saluation, and gracious redemption, and beleeue his word, serue him from our hearts, loue and obey him, and whatsoeuer we haue done heretofore contrary to his most holy will, now let vs repent in time, and heereafter study to correct our life: and doubt not, but we shall find him as mercifull vnto vs, as he was either to Lazarus, or to the theefe, whose examples are written in holy Scripture for the comfort of them that be sinners, and subiect to sorrowes, miseries, and calamities in this world, that they should not despaire in GOD'S mercy, but euer trust thereby to haue forgiuenesse of their sinnes, and life euerlasting, as Lazarus and the thiefe had. Thus I trust euery Christian man perceiueth by the infallible or vndeceiueable word of GOD, that bodily death cannot harme nor hinder them that truely beleeue in Christ, but contrarily shall profit and promote the Christian soules, which being truely penitent for their offences depart hence in perfect Charitie, and in sure trust, that GOD is mercifull to them, forgiuing their sinnes, for the merits of Iesus Christ his onely naturall Sonne.

The second cause why some doe feare death. The second cause why some doe feare death, is sore sickenesse and grieuous paines, which partly come before death, and partly accompanie or come with death, whensoeuer it commeth. This feare is the feare of the fraile flesh, and a naturall passion belonging vnto the nature of a mortall man. But true faith in GOD'S promises, and regard of the paines and pangs which Christ vpon the crosse suffered for vs miserable sinners, with consideration of the ioy and euerlasting life to come in heauen, will mitigate and asswage lesse those paines, and moderate or bring into a meane this feare, that it shall neuer bee able to ouerthrow the hearty desire and gladnesse, that the Christian soule hath to be separated from this corrupt body, that it may come to the gracious presence of our Sauiour Iesus Christ. If we beleeue stedfastly the word of GOD, we shall perceiue that such bodily sickenesse, pangs of death, or whatsoeuer dolorous pangs we suffer, either before or with death bee nothing else in Christian men, but the rod of our heauenly and louing Father, wherewith hee mercifully correcteth vs, either to trye and declare the faith of his patient children, that they may bee found laudable, glorious, and honourable in his sight, when Iesus Christ shall be openly shewed to bee the Iudge of all the world, or else to chastice and amend in them whatsoeuer offendeth his Fatherly and gracious goodnesse, lest they should perish euerlastingly. And this his correcting rodde is common to all men that bee truely his. Therefore let vs cast away the burden of sinne that lieth too heauie in our neckes, and returne vnto GOD by true penance and amendment of our liues, let vs with patience runne this course that is appoynted, suffering (for his sake that dyed for our saluation) all sorrowes and pangs of death, and death it selfe ioyfully, when GOD sendeth it to vs, hauing our eyes fixed and set fast euer vpon the head and Captaine of our faith, Iesus Christ: who (considering the ioy that hee should come vnto) cared neither for the shame nor paine of death, but willingly conforming and framing his will to his Fathers will, most patiently suffered the most shamefull and painefull death of the crosse, being innocent and harmelesse (Philippians 2.8). And now therefore hee is exalted in heauen, and euerlastingly sitteth on the right hand of the throne of GOD the Father. Let vs call to our remembrance therefore the life and ioyes of heauen, that are kept for all them that patiently doe suffer here with Christ, and consider that Christ suffered all his painefull passion by sinners, and for sinners: and then wee shall with patience, and the more easily suffer such sorrowes and paines, when they come. Let vs not set at light the chastising of the Lord, nor grudge at him, nor fall from him, when of him wee bee corrected: for the Lord loueth them whom he doeth correct, and beateth euery one whom he taketh to his childe. What childe is that (sayth S. Paul) whom the Father loueth, and doeth not chastice? If ye be without GOD'S correction (which all his welbeloued and true children haue) then bee you but bastards, smally regarded of GOD, and not his true children (Hebrews 12.6, 8).

Therefore seeing that when we haue in earth our carnall fathers to be our correctours, we doe feare them, and reuerently take their correction: shall we not much more be in subiection to GOD our spirituall Father, by whom we shall haue euerlasting life? And our carnall fathers sometime correct vs euen as it pleaseth them, without cause: but this Father iustly correcteth vs, either for our sinne, to the intent wee should amend, or for our commoditie and wealth, to make vs thereby partakers of his holinesse. Furthermore, all correction which GOD sendeth vs in this present time, seemeth to haue no ioy and comfort, but sorrow and paine, yet it bringeth with it a taste of GOD'S mercy and goodnesse, towards them that be so corrected, and a sure hope of GOD'S euerlasting consolation in heauen. If then these sorrowes, diseases, and sickenesses, and also death it selfe bee nothing els but our heauenly Fathers rod, whereby hee certifieth vs of his loue and gracious fauour, whereby hee trieth and purifieth vs, whereby hee giueth vnto vs holinesse, and certifieth vs that we be his children, and he our mercifull Father: shall not wee then with all humilitie, as obedient and louing children, ioyfully kisse our heauenly Fathers rod, and euer say in our heart, with our Sauiour Iesus Christ, Father, if this anguish and sorrow which I feele, and death which I see approch may not passe, but that thy will is that I must suffer them, thy will bee done.

THE THIRD PART OF THE SERMON OF THE FEARE OF DEATH.

IN this Sermon against the feare of death, two causes were declared, which commonly mooue worldly men to be in much feare to die, and yet the same do nothing trouble the faithfull and good liuers when death commeth, but rather giueth them occasion greatly to reioyce, considering that they shalbe deliuered from the sorrow and miserie of this world, and be brought to the great ioy and felicitie of the life to come.

<u>The third cause why death is to be feared.</u> Now the third and speciall cause why death in deede is to bee feared, is the miserable state of the worldly and vngodly people after their death: but this is no cause at all, why the godly and faithfull people should feare death, but rather contrariwise, their godly conuersation in this life, and beliefe in Christ, cleauing continually to his mercies, should make them to long sore after that life, that remaineth for them vndoubtedly after this bodily death. Of this immortall state, (after this transitory life) where wee shall liue euermore in the presence of GOD, in ioy, and rest, after victorie ouer all sicknesse, sorrowes, sinne, and death: there be many

plaine places of holy Scripture, which confirme the weake conscience against the feare of all such dolours, sickenesses, sinne, and bodily death, to asswage such trembling and vngodly feare, and to encourage vs with comfort and hope of a blessed state after this life. S. Paul wisheth vnto the Ephesians, that GOD the Father of glory would giue vnto them the Spirit of wisedome and reuelation, that the eyes of their hearts might giue life to know him, and to perceiue how great things he had called them vnto, and how rich inheritance hee hath prepared after this life, for them that pertaine vnto him (Ephesians 1.17-18). And S. Paul himselfe declareth the desire of his heart, which was to bee dissolued and loosed from his body, and to be with Christ, which (as hee said, was much better for him, although to them it was more necessary that hee should liue, which he refused not, for their sakes, Philippians 1.23-24). Euen like as S. Martin said, Good Lord, if I be necessary for thy people to doe good vnto them, I will refuse no labour: but els for mine owne selfe, I beseech thee to take my soule.

Now the holy Fathers of the olde law, and all faithfull and righteous men which departed before our Sauiour Christes ascension into heauen, did by death depart from troubles vnto rest, from the handes of their enemies, into the handes of GOD, from sorrowes and sicknesses, vnto ioyfull refreshing in Abraham's bosome, a place of all comfort and consolation, as the Scriptures doe plainely by manifest words testifie. The booke of wisedome saith, that the righteous mens soules bee in the hand of GOD, and no torment shall touch them (Wisdom 3.1, 3). They seemed to the eyes of foolish men to die, and their death was counted miserable, and their departing out of this world wretched, but they be in rest. And an other place sayth, That the righteous shall liue for euer, and their reward is with the Lord, and their mindes bee with GOD, who is aboue all: therefore they shall receiue a glorious Kingdome, and a beautifull crowne at the Lords hand. And in another place the same booke sayth, The righteous, though hee bee preuented with sodaine death, neuerthelesse hee shall bee there where hee shall bee refreshed (Wisdom 4.7). Of Abraham's bosome, Christs wordes bee so plaine, that a Christian man needeth no more proofe of it. Now then, if this were the state of the holy Fathers and righteous men, before the comming of our Sauiour, and before hee was glorified: how much more then ought all we to haue a stedfast faith, and a sure hope of this blessed state & condition, after our death? seeing that our Sauiour now hath performed the whole worke of our redemption, and is gloriously ascended into heauen, to prepare our dwelling places with him, and said vnto his Father, Father, I will that where I am, my seruants shall bee with mee (John 17.24). And we know, that whatsoeuer Christ will, his Father will the same, wherefore it cannot bee, but if wee bee his faithfull seruants, our soules shall be with him, after our departure out of this present life. Saint Steuen when he was stoned to death, euen in the middest of his torments, what was his minde most vpon? when hee was full of the holy Ghost (sayth holy Scripture) hauing his eyes lifted vp into heauen, hee saw the glory of GOD, and Iesus standing on the right hand of GOD. The which trueth, after hee had confessed boldly before the enemies of Christ, they drew him out of the Citie, and there they stoned him, who cryed vnto GOD, saying, Lord Iesu Christ, take my spirit (Acts 7.55, 59). And doeth not our Sauiour say plainely in Saint Iohns Gospell, Verily, verily I say vnto you, Hee that heareth my word, and beleeueth on him that sent mee, hath euerlasting life, and commeth not into iudgement, but shall passe from death to life (John 5.24)? Shall wee not then thinke that death to bee precious, by the which we passe vnto life?

Therefore it is a true saying of the Prophet, The death of the holy and righteous men, is precious in the Lords sight (Psalms 116.15). Holy Simeon, after that he had his hearts desire in seeing our Sauiour, that he euer longed for in his life, hee imbraced, and tooke him in his armes, and sayd, Now Lord, let mee depart in peace, for mine eyes haue beholden that Sauiour, which thou hast prepared for all Nations (Luke 2.29, 31).

It is trueth therefore, that the death of the righteous is called peace, and the benefite of the Lord, as the Church sayth, in the name of the righteous departed out of this world: My soule turne thee to thy rest, for the Lord hath beene good to thee, and rewarded thee (Psalms 116.7). And wee see by holy Scripture, and other ancient hystories of Martyrs, that the holy, faithfull, and righteous, euer since Christes ascension, or going vp, in their death did not doubt, but that they went to Christ in Spirit, which is our life, health, wealth, and saluation. Iohn in his holy Reuelation, saw an hundred forty and foure thousand virgins and innocentes, of whom he sayd, These follow the Lambe Iesu Christ wheresoeuer hee goeth. And shortly after in the same place hee sayth, I heard a voyce from heauen, saying vnto mee, Write, happy and blessed are the dead, which die in the Lord: from henceforth (surely sayth the spirit) they shall rest from their paines and labours, for their works doe follow them (Revelations 14.4, 13): so that then they shall reape with ioy and comfort, that which they sowed with labours and paines.

They that sowe in the spirit, of the spirit shall reape euerlasting life. Let vs therefore neuer bee weary of well doing, for when the time of reaping or reward commeth, wee shall reape without any wearinesse euerlasting ioy. Therefore while wee haue time (as Saint Paul exhorteth vs) let vs doe good to all men (Galatians 6.8-10), and not lay vp our treasures in earth, where rust and mothes corrupt it, which rust (Matthew 6.19) (as Saint Iames saith) shall beare witnesse against vs at the great day, condemne vs, and shall (like most burning fire) torment our flesh (James 5.3). Let vs beware therefore (as wee tender our owne wealth) that wee bee not in the number of those miserable, couetous, and wretched men, which Saint Iames biddeth mourne and lament for their greedy gathering, and vngodly keeping of goods. Let vs bee wise in time, and learne to follow the wise example of the wicked Steward. Let vs so wisely order our goods and possessions, committed vnto vs here by GOD for a season, that wee may truely heare and obey this commandement of our Sauiour Christ: I say vnto you (saith hee) make you friendes of the wicked Mammon, that they may receiue you into euerlasting tabernacles, or dwellings (Luke 16.9). Riches bee called wicked, because the world abuseth them vnto all wickednesse, which are otherwise the good gifts of GOD, and the instruments wherby GOD'S seruants doe truely serue him in vsing of the same. Hee commanded them not to make them rich friends, to get high dignities and worldly promotions, to giue great gifts to rich men that haue no neede thereof, but to make them friends of poore and miserable men, vnto whom, whatsoeuer they giue, Christ taketh it as giuen to himselfe. And to these friends Christ in the Gospel giueth so great honour and preheminence, that he sayth, They shall receiue them that doe good vnto them into euerlasting houses: not that men shall bee our rewarders for our well doing, but that Christ will reward vs, and take it to bee done vnto himselfe, whatsoeuer is done to such friends.

Thus making poore wretches our friends, wee make our Sauiour Christ our friend, whose members they are: whose misery as hee taketh for his owne misery, so their releefe, succour, and helpe, he taketh for his succour, releefe, and helpe, and will as much thanke vs and reward vs for our goodnesse shewed to them, as if he himselfe had receiued like benefit at our hands, as he witnesseth in the Gospell, saying, Whatsoeuer yee haue done to any of these simple persons, which doe beleeue in mee, that haue ye done to my selfe (Matthew 25.40). Therefore let vs diligently foresee, that our fayth and hope which we haue conceiued in Almighty GOD, and in our Sauior Christ waxe not faint, nor that the loue which we beare in hand to beare to him, waxe not cold: but let vs study dayly and diligently to shew our selues to be the true honourers and louers of GOD, by keeping of his commandements, by doing of good deedes vnto our needy neighbours, releeuing by all meanes that wee can their pouerty with our abundance and plenty, their ignorance with our wisedome and learning, and comfort their weakenesse with our strength and authority, calling all men backe from euill doing by godly counsaile and good example, perseuering still in well doing, so long as we liue: so shall wee not neede to feare death for any of those three causes afore mentioned, nor yet for any other cause that can be imagined: but contrarily, considering the manifold sicknesses, troubles, and sorrowes of this present life, the dangers of this perillous pilgrimage, and the great encumbrance which our Spirit hath by this sinfull flesh and frayle body subiect to death: considering also the manifold sorrowes and dangerous deceits of this world on euery side, the intolerable pride, couetousnesse, and lechery, in time of prosperity, the impatient murmuring of them that bee worldly, in time of aduersity, which cease not to withdraw and plucke vs from GOD, our Sauiour Christ, from our life, wealth, or euerlasting ioy and saluation: considering also the innumerable assaults of our Ghostly enemy the Diuell, with all his fierie darts of ambition, pride, lechery, vaine glory, enuie, malice, detraction, or backbiting, with other his innumerable deceits, engines, and snares, whereby he goeth busily about to catch all men vnder his dominion, euer like a roaring Lion, by all meanes searching whom hee may deuour (1 Peter 5.8). The faythfull Christian man which considereth all these miseries, perils, and incommodities (whereunto he is subiect so long as he heere liueth vpon earth) and on the other part considereth that blessed and comfortable state of the heauenly life to come, and the sweet condition of them that depart in the Lord, how they are deliuered from the continuall encumbrances of their mortall and sinnefull body, from all the malice, crafts, and deceits of this world, from all the assaults of their Ghostly enemy the Diuell, to liue in peace, rest, and endlesse quietnesse, to liue in the fellowship of innumerable Angels, and with the congregation of perfect iust men, as Patriarches, Prophets, Martyrs, and Confessours, and finally vnto the presence of Almighty GOD, and our Sauiour Iesus Christ. Hee that doeth consider all these things, and beleeueth them assuredly, as they are to be beleeued, euen from the bottome of his heart, being established in GOD in this true fayth, hauing a quiet conscience in Christ, a firme hope, and assured trust in GOD'S mercy, through the merits of Iesu Christ to obtayne this quietnesse, rest, and euerlasting ioy, shall not onely bee without feare of bodily death, when it commeth, but certainely (as S. Paul did) so shall hee gladly (according to GOD'S will, and when it pleaseth GOD to call him out of this life) greatly desire in his heart, that he may be rid from all these occasions of euill, and liue euer to GOD'S pleasure (Philippians 1.23), in perfect obedience of his will, with our Sauiour Iesus Christ, to whose gracious presence the Lord of his infinite mercy and grace bring vs, to raigne with him in life euerlasting: to whom with our heauenly Father, and the holy Ghost, be glory in worldes without end. Amen.

HOMILY ON OBEDIENCE

AN EXHORTATION
concerning good Order, and obedience
to Rulers and Magistrates.

ALmighty GOD hath created and appointed all things in heauen, earth, and waters, in a most excellent and perfect order. In Heauen, hee hath appointed distinct and seuerall orders and states of Archangels and Angels. In earth hee hath assigned and appointed Kings, Princes, with other gouernours vnder them, in all good and necessary order. The water aboue is kept, and rayneth downe in due time and season. The Sun, Moone, Starres, Rainebow, Thunder, Lightning, Clouds, and all Birdes of the ayre, doe keepe their order. The Earth, Trees, Seedes, Plants, Hearbes, Corne, Grasse, and all maner of Beasts keepe themselues in order: all the parts of the whole yeare, as Winter, Summer, Moneths, Nights and Dayes, continue in their order: all kindes of Fishes in the Sea, Riuers, and Waters, with all Fountaines, Springs, yea, the Seas themselues keepe their comely course and order: and man himselfe also hath all his parts both within and without, as soule, heart, minde, memory, vnderstanding, reason, speech, with all and singular corporall members of his body in a profitable, necessarie, and pleasant order: euery degree of people in their vocation, calling and office, hath appointed to them their duty and order: some are in high degree, some in low, some Kings and Princes, some inferiours and subiects, Priests, and lay men, masters and seruants, fathers, and children, husbands and wiues, rich and poore, and euery one haue neede of other, so that in all things is to bee lauded and praised the goodly order of GOD, without the which no house, no Citie, no Commonwealth can continue and endure, or last. For where there is no right order, there reigneth all abuse, carnall liberty, enormitie, sinne, and Babylonicall confusion.

Take away Kings Princes, Rulers, Magistrates, Iudges, and such estates of GODS order, no man shall ride or goe by the high way vnrobbed, no man shall sleepe in his owne house or bedde vnkilled, no man shall keepe his wife, children, and possession in quietnesse, all things shall bee common, and there must needes follow all mischiefe, and vtter destruction both of soules, bodies, goodes, and common wealthes. But blessed bee GOD, that wee in this Realme of England, feele not the horrible calamities, miseries, and wretchednesse, which all they vndoubtedly feele and suffer, that lacke this godly order: and praysed bee GOD, that wee know the great excellent benefit of GOD shewed towards vs in this behalfe, GOD hath sent vs his high gift, our most deare Soueraigne Lord King IAMES, with a godly, wise, and honourable Counsell, with other superiours and inferiours, in a beautifull order, and godly.

Wherefore, let vs subiectes doe our bounden dueties, giuing hearty thankes to GOD, and praying for the preseruation of this godly order. Let vs all obey euen from the bottome of our heartes, all their godly proceedings, lawes, statutes, proclamations, and iniunctions, with all other godly orders. Let vs consider the Scriptures of the holy Ghost, which perswade and command vs all obediently to bee subiect, first and chiefely to the Kings Maiestie, supreme gouernour ouer all, and the next to his honourable counsell, and to all other noble men, Magistrates, and officers, which by GODS goodnesse, be placed and ordered.

For Almighty GOD is the onely authour and prouider for this forenamed state and order, as it is written of GOD, in the booke of the Prouerbs: Thorow mee kings doe raigne, thorow mee counsellers make iust lawes, thorow mee doe princes beare rule, and all iudges of the earth execute iudgement, I am louing to them that loue mee (Proverbs 8.15, 17).

Here let vs marke well, and remember that the high power and authoritie of Kinges, with their making of lawes, iudgements and offices, are the ordinances not of man, but of GOD: and therefore is this word (through mee) so many times repeated. Here is also well to bee considered and remembred, that this good order is appointed by GODS wisedome, fauour, and loue, especially for them that loue GOD, and therefore hee sayth, I loue them that loue mee. Also in the booke of wisedome wee may euidently learne, that a kinges power, authoritie, and strength, is a great benefite of GOD, giuen of his great mercie, to the comfort of our great miserie. For thus wee reade there spoken to kinges, Heare O yee Kinges, and vnderstand, learne yee that bee Iudges of the endes of the earth, giue eare yee that rule the multitudes: for the power giuen you of the Lord, and the strength, from the highest (Wisdom 6.1-3). Let vs learne also here by the infallible and vndeceiueable word of GOD, that kinges and other supreme and higher officers, are ordeined of GOD, who is most highest: and therefore they are here taught diligently to apply and giue themselues to knowledge and wisedome, necessary for the ordering of GODS people to their gouernance committed, or whom to gouerne they are charged of GOD.

And they bee here also taught by Almighty GOD, that they should acknowledge themselues to haue all their power and strength not from Rome, but immediatly of GOD most Highest. Wee reade in the booke of Deuteronomie, that all punishment pertaineth to GOD, by this sentence, Vengeance is mine, and I will reward (Deuteronomy 32.35). But this sentence wee must vnderstand to pertaine also vnto the Magistrates which doe exercise GODS roome in iudgement, and punishing by good and godly lawes, here in earth. And the places of Scripture, which seeme to remooue from among all christian men, iudgement, punishment, or killing, ought to be vnderstood, that no man (of his owne priuate authority) may bee iudge ouer other, may punish, or may kill. But we must referre all iudgement to GOD, to Kings, and Rulers, Iudges vnder them, which be GODS officers to execute iustice, and by plaine wordes of Scripture, haue their authoritie and vse of the sword graunted from GOD, as we are taught by Saint Paul, that deare and chosen Apostle of our Sauiour Christ, whom wee ought diligently to obey, euen as we would obey our Sauiour Christ if hee were present.

Thus Saint Paul writeth to the Romanes, Let euery soule submit himselfe vnto the authority of the higher powers, for there is no power but of GOD. The powers that bee, be ordained of GOD. Whosoeuer therefore withstandeth the power, withstandeth the ordinance of GOD: but they that resist, or are against it, shall receiue to themselues damnation. For rulers are not fearefull to them that doe good, but to them that doe euill. Wilt thou bee without feare of that power? Doe well them, and so shalt thou bee praysed of the same, for he is the minister of GOD, for thy wealth. But and if thou doe that which is euil, then feare, for he beareth not the sword for nought, for he is the minister of GOD, to take vengeance on him that doeth euill. Wherefore ye must needes obey, not onely for feare of vengeance, but also, because of conscience, and euen for this cause pay yee tribute, for they are GODS ministers seruing for the same purpose (Romans 13.1-6).

Here let vs learne of Saint Paul the chosen vessell of GOD, that all persons hauing soules (hee excepteth none, nor exempteth none, neither Priest, Apostle, nor Prophet, saith S. Chrysostome) do owe of bounden duty, and euen in conscience, obedience, submission, and subiection to the high powers, which bee set in authority by GOD, for as much as they bee GODS Lieuetenants, GODS Presidentes, GODS Officers, GODS Commissioners, GODS Iudges, ordained of GOD himselfe, of whom onely they haue all their power, and all their authority. And the same Saint Paul threatneth no lesse paine, then euerlasting damnation to all disobedient persons, to all resisters against this generall, and common authority, for as much as they resist not man, but GOD.

THE SECOND PART OF THE SERMON OF OBEDIENCE.

Not Mans Deuice and Inuention, but Gods Wisedome, Gods Order, Power, and Authority. Or as much as GOD hath created and disposed all things in a comely order, we haue beene taught in the first part of the Sermon, concerning good order and obedience, that we also ought in all common weales, to obserue and keepe a due order, and to bee obedient to the powers, their ordinances, and lawes, and that all rulers are appointed of GOD, for a goodly order to bee kept in the world: and also how the Magistrates ought to learne how to rule and gouerne according to GODS Lawes: and that all Subiects are bound to obey them as GODS ministers, yea, although they be euill, not onely for feare, but also for conscience sake. And here (good people) let vs all marke diligently, that it is not lawfull for inferiors and Subiects, in any case to resist and stand against the superiour powers: for Saint Pauls wordes be plaine, that whosoeuer withstandeth, shall get to themselues damnation: for whosoeuer withstandeth, withstandeth the ordinance of GOD. Our Sauiour Christ himselfe, and his Apostles, receiued many and diuers iniuries of the vnfaithfull and wicked men in authoritie: yet wee neuer reade, that they, or any of them, caused any sedition or rebellion against authoritie. We reade oft, that they patiently suffered all troubles, vexations, slaunders, pangs, and paines, and death it selfe obediently without tumult or resistance. They committed their cause to him that iudgeth righteously, and prayed for their enemies heartily and earnestly. They knew that the authoritie of the powers, was GODS ordinance, and therefore both in their words and deedes, they taught euer obedience to it, and neuer taught nor did the contrary.

The wicked Iudge Pilate, sayd to Christ, Knowest thou not that I haue power to crucifie thee, and haue power also to loose thee? Iesus answered, Thou couldest haue no power at all against me, except it were giuen thee from aboue. Whereby Christ taught vs plainely, that euen the wicked rulers haue their power and authoritie from GOD, and therefore it is not lawfull for their Subiects to withstand them, although they abuse their power: much lesse then it is lawfull for subiects, to withstand their godly and Christian Princes, which doe not abuse their authoritie, but vse the same to GODS glory, and to the profite and commoditie of GODS people. The holy Apostle Peter commandeth seruants to be obedient to their masters, not onely if they be good and gentle, but also if they be euill and froward: affirming that the vocation and calling of GODS people is to bee patient, and of the suffering sides. And there he bringeth in the patience of our Sauiour Christ, to perswade obedience to gouernours, yea, although they bee wicked and wrong doers.

But let vs now heare S. Peter himselfe speake, for his wordes certifie best our conscience. Thus he vttereth them in his first Epistle, Seruants, obey your masters with feare, not onely if they bee good and gentle, but also if they be froward. For it is thanke worthy, if a man for conscience toward GOD, endureth griefe, and suffer wrong vndeserued: for what prayse is it, when ye be beaten for your faults, if ye take it patiently? but when ye doe well, if you then suffer wrong, and take it patiently, then is there cause to haue thanke of GOD, for hereunto verily were yee called: for so did Christ suffer for vs, leauing vs an example, that we should follow his steps (1 Peter 2.18-21). All these bee the very wordes of S. Peter.

Holy Dauid also teacheth vs a good lesson in this behalfe, who was many times most cruelly and wrongfully persecuted of king Saul, and many times also put in ieopardie and danger of his life by king Saul and his people, yet hee neither withstood, neither vsed any force or violence against king Saul his mortall and deadly enemie, but did euer to his liege Lord and Master king Saul, most true, most diligent, and most faithfull seruice (1 Samuel 18.11, 14, 30, 19.10-11; 20.31; 24.2-7). Insomuch that when the Lord GOD had giuen king Saul into Dauids handes in his owne Caue, hee would not hurt him, when hee might without all bodily perill easily haue slaine him, no he would not suffer any of his seruants once to lay their hand vpon king Saul, but prayed to GOD in this wise, Lord keepe me from doing that thing vnto my Master, the Lords anoynted, keepe me that I lay not my hand vpon him, seeing he is the anoynted of the Lord: for as truely as the Lord liueth (except the Lord smite him, or except his day come, or that he goe downe to warre, and perish in battaile) the Lord be mercifull vnto me, that I lay not my hand vpon the Lords anoynted.

And that Dauid might haue killed his enemie king Saul, it is euidently prooued in the first booke of the Kings, both by the cutting off the lap of Sauls garment, and also by plaine confession of king Saul. Also another time, as is mentioned in the same booke, when the most vnmercifull and most vnkinde King Saul did persecute poore Dauid, GOD did againe giue king Saul into Dauids handes, by casting of king Saul and his whole armie into a dead sleepe, so that Dauid, and one Abisai with him, came in the night into Sauls host, where Saul lay sleeping, and his speare stacke in the ground at his head: then said Abisai vnto Dauid, GOD hath deliuered thine enemie into thy hands at this time, now therefore let me smite him once with my speare to the earth, and I will not smite him againe the second time: meaning thereby to haue killed him with one stroke, and to haue made him sure for euer. And Dauid answered and said to Abisai, Destroy him not, for who can lay his hands on the Lords anointed, and be guiltlesse? And Dauid sayd furthermore, As sure as the Lord liueth, the Lord shall smite him, or his day shall come to die, or he shall descend or goe downe into battaile, and there perish, the Lord keepe me from laying my handes vpon the Lords anoynted. But take thou now the speare that is at his head, and the cruse of water, and let vs goe: and so he did. Here is euidently prooued that we may not withstand, nor in any wise hurt an anointed King, which is GODS lieftenant, vice-gerent, and highest minister in that countrey where he is King.

An obiection. But peraduenture some heere would say, that Dauid in his owne defence might haue killed King Saul lawfully, and with a safe conscience.

An answere. But holy Dauid did knowe that hee might in no wise withstand, hurt, or kill his Soueraigne lord and King: hee did know that hee was but king Sauls subiect, though he were in great fauour with GOD, and his enemy king Saul out of Gods fauour. Therefore though he were neuer so much prouoked, yet he refused vtterly to hurt the Lords anoynted. He durst not for offending GOD & his own conscience (although he had occasion and opportunity) once lay his hands vpon Gods high officer the king, whom he did know to be a person reserued & kept (for his office sake) onely to GODS punishment and iudgement.

Therefore hee prayeth so oft, and so earnestly, that hee lay not his handes vpon the Lords annointed. And by these two examples, Saint Dauid (being named in Scripture a man after GODS owne heart) giueth a generall rule and lesson to all subiectes in the world, not to withstand their liege lord and king, not to take a sword by their priuate authority against their king, GODS annointed (1 Samuel 26.11; Psal.88.), who onely beareth the sword by GODS authority for the maintenance of the good, and for the punishment of the euill, who only by GODS Law hath the vse of the sword at his command, and also hath all power, iurisdiction, regiment, correction and punishment, as supreme gouernour of all his Realmes & Dominions, and that euen by the authority of GOD, and by GODS ordinances.

Yet another notable story and doctrine is in the second booke of the kinges, that maketh also for this purpose. When an Amalekite, by king Saules owne consent and commandement, had killed king Saul (2 Samuel 1.8-10), hee went to Dauid, supposing to haue had great thankes for his message that hee had killed Dauids deadly enemy, and therefore hee made great haste to tell to Dauid the chaunce, bringing with him king Saules crowne that was vpon his head, and his bracelet that was vpon his arme, to perswade his tidings to bee true. But godly Dauid was so farre from reioycing at this newes, that immediatly and foorthwith hee rent his clothes off his backe, hee mourned and wept, and said to the messenger, How is it that thou wast not afraid to lay thy hands on the Lords annointed to destroy him? And by and by Dauid made one of his seruants to kill the messenger, saying, Thy blood bee on thine owne head, for thine owne mouth hath testified and witnessed against thee, granting that thou hast slaine the Lords annointed.

These examples being so manifest and euident, it is an intolerable ignorance, madnesse, and wickednesse for subiects to make any murmuring, rebellion, resistance, or withstanding, commotion, or insurrection against their most deare and most dread Soueraigne Lord and King, ordeined and appointed of GODS goodnes for their commodity, peace, and quietnesse.

Yet let vs beleeue vndoubtedly, (good Christian people) that we may not obey Kings, Magistrates, or any other, (though they bee our owne fathers) if they would command vs to doe any thing contrary to GODS commandements. In such a case wee ought to say with the Apostle, Wee must rather obey GOD then man (Acts 5.29). But neuerthelesse in that case wee may not in any wise withstand (violenly) violently, or rebell against rulers, or make any insurrection sedition, or tumults, either by force of armes (or otherwise) against the annointed of the Lord, or any of his officers: But wee must in such case patiently suffer all wrongs, and iniuries, referring the iudgement of our cause onely to GOD (Acts 7). Let vs feare the terrible punishment of Almighty GOD against traytors and rebellious persons, by the example of Chore, Dathan, and Abiron, which hee repugned and grudged against GODS Magistrates and officers, and therefore the earth opened and swallowed them vp aliue. Other for their wicked murmuring and rebellion, were by a sudden fire sent of GOD, vtterly consumed. Other for their froward behauiour to their rulers and gouernours, GODS ministers, were suddenly stricken with a foule leprosie. Other were stinged to death, with wonderfull strange fiery serpents. Other were sore plagued, so that there was killed in one day, the number of foureteene thousand and seuen hundred, for rebellion against them whom GOD had appointed to bee in authority.

Absalon also rebelling against his father King Dauid, was punished with a strange and notable death (2 Samuel 18.9-10).

THE THIRD PART OF THE SERMON OF OBEDIENCE.

YEe haue heard before in this Sermon of good order and obedience, manifestly proued both by the Scriptures and examples, that all subiects are boden to obey their Magistrates, and for no cause to resist, or withstand, or rebell, or make any sedition against them, yea, although they bee wicked men. And let no man thinke that hee can escape vnpunished, that committeth treason, conspiracy, or rebellion against his soueraigne Lord the King, though hee commit the same neuer so secretly, either in thought, word, or deede, neuer so priuily, in his priuie chamber by himselfe, or openly communicating, and consulting with others. For treason will not bee hid, treason will out at length. GOD will haue that most detestable vice both opened and punished, for that it is so directly against his ordinance, and against his high principall iudge, and anoynted in earth. The violence and iniury that is committed against authoritie, is committed against GOD, the common weale, and the whole Realme, which GOD will haue knowen, and condignly or worthily punished one way or other. For it is notably written of the wise man in Scripture, in the booke called Ecclesiastes: With the King no euill in thy thought, nor speake no hurt of him in thy priuie chamber: for the bird of the ayre shall betray thy voyce, and with her fethers shall bewray thy words (Ecclesiastes 10.20). These lessons and examples are written for our learning.

Therefore let vs all feare the most detestable vice of rebellion, euer knowing and remembring, that he that resisteth or withstandeth common authority, resisteth or withstandeth GOD and his ordenance, as it may bee proued by many other moe places of holy Scripture. And here let vs take heede that we vnderstand not these or such other like places (which so straitly command obedience to superiours, and so straitly punished rebellion, and disobedience to the same) to bee meant in any condition of the pretensed or coloured power of the Bishop of Rome. For truely the Scripture of GOD alloweth no such vsurped power, full of enormities, abusions, and blasphemies. But the true meaning of these and such places, bee to extoll and set forth GODS true ordinance, and the authoritie of GODS anoynted Kings, and of their officers appoynted vnder them. And concerning the vsurped power of the Bishop of Rome, which he most wrongfully challengeth, as the successor of Christ and Peter: we may easily perceiue how false, fained, and forged it is, not onely in that it hath no sufficient ground in holy Scripture, but also by the fruites and doctrine thereof.

For our Sauiour Christ, and S. Peter, teacheth most earnestly and agreeably obedience to Kings, as to the chiefe and supreme rulers in this world, next vnder GOD: but the Bishop of Rome teacheth, that they that are vnder him, are free from all burdens and charges of the common wealth, and obedience toward their Prince, most clearely against Christs doctrine and S. Peters. He ought therefore rather to be called Antichrist, and the successour of the Scribes and Pharises, then Christs vicar, or S. Peters successour: seeing that not onely in this point, but also in other weighty matters of Christian religion, in matters of remission and forgiuenesse of sinnes, and of saluation, hee heacheth so directly against both S. Peter, and against our Sauiour Christ, who not onely taught obedience to Kings, but also practised obedience in their conuersation and liuing: For we reade that they both payd tribute to the king (Matthew 17.27): And also we reade that the holy virgin Mary, mother to our Sauiour Christ, and Ioseph, who was taken for his father, at the Emperours commandement, went to the citie of Dauid, named Bethlehem, to be taxed among other, and to declare their obedience to the Magistrates, for GODS ordinances sake (Luke 2.4-5). And heere let vs not forget the blessed virgin Maries obedience: for although she was highly in GODS fauour, and Christs naturall mother, and was also great with childe at the same time, and so nigh her trauaile, that shee was deliuered in her iourney, yet shee gladly without any excuse or grudging (for conscience sake) did take that cold and foule winter iourney, being in the meane season so poore, that she lay in a stable, and there shee was deliuered of Christ.

And according to the same, loe how S. Peter agreeth, writing by expresse words in his first Epistle: Submit your selues, and bee subiect (saith hee) vnto kings, as vnto the chiefe heads, and vnto rulers, as vnto them that are sent of him for the punishment of euill doers, and for the prayse of them that doe well, for so is the will of GOD (1 Peter 2.13-15). I neede not to expound these wordes, they be so plaine of themselues. S. Peter doth not say, Submit your selues vnto mee, as supreme head of the Church: neither sayth hee, Submit your selues from time to time to my successours in Rome: but he saith, Submit your selues vnto your King, your supreme head, and vnto those that he appointeth in authoritie vnder him, for that you shall so shew your obedience, it is the will of GOD. GOD will that you be in subiection to your head and king.

This is GODS ordinance, GODS commandement, and GODS holy will, that the whole body of euery Realme, and all the members and parts of the same, shall be subiect to their head, their king, and that (as S. Peter writeth) for the Lords sake (1 Peter 2.13): and (as S. Paul writeth) for conscience sake, and not for feare onely (Romans 13.5). Thus we learne by the word of GOD, to yeeld to our king, that is due to our king: that is, honour, obedience, payments of due taxes, customes, tributes, subsidies, loue and feare (Matthew 22.21, Romans 13). Thus wee know partly our bounden duties to common authority, now let vs learne to accomplish the same. And let vs most instantly and heartily pray to GOD, the onely authour of all authority, for all them that be in authority, according as S. Paul willeth, writing thus to Timothie in his first Epistle: I exhort therefore, that aboue all things, prayers, supplications, intercessions, and giuing of thankes be done for all men: for kings, and for all that be in authority, that wee may liue a quiet and a peaceable life, with all godlinesse and honesty: for that is good and accepted or allowable in the sight of GOD our Sauiour (1 Timothy 2.1-3). Heere S. Paul maketh an earnest and an especiall exhortation, concerning giuing of thankes, and prayer for kings and rulers, saying, Aboue all things, as he might say, in any wise principally and chiefly, let prayer bee made for kings.

Let vs heartily thanke GOD for his great and excellent benefit and prouidence concerning the state of kings. Let vs pray for them, that they may haue GODS fauour and GODS protection. Let vs pray that they may euer in all things haue GOD before their eyes. Let vs pray, that they may haue wisedome, strength, iustice, clemency, & zeale to GODS glory, to GODS verity, to Christian soules, and to the common wealth. Let vs pray, that they may rightly vse their sword and authority, for the maintenance and defence of the Catholike fayth conteyned in holy Scripture, and of their good and honest subiects, for the feare and punishment of the euill and vicious people. Let vs pray, that they may most faythfully follow the Kings and Captaines in the Bible, Dauid, Ezekias, Iosias, and Moses, with such other. And let vs pray for our selues, that we may liue godly in holy and Christian conuersation: so shall wee haue GOD on our side, and then let vs not feare what man can doe against vs: so we shall liue in true obedience, both to our most mercifull King in Heauen, and to our most Christian King in Earth: so shall wee please GOD and haue the exceeding benefit, peace of conscience, rest and quietnesse heere in this world, and after this life, wee shall enioy a better life, rest, peace, and the euerlasting blisse of heauen, which hee grant vs all, that was obedient for vs all, euen to the death of the crosse, Iesus Christ: to whom with the Father and the Holy Ghost, be all honour and glory, both now and euer. Amen.

HOMILY AGAINST WHOREDOM AND ADULTERY

A SERMON AGAINST
whoredom and uncleanness.

Although there want not (good Christian people) great swarms of vices worthy to be rebuked (unto such decay is true Godliness and virtuous living now come:) yet above other vices, the outrageous seas of adultery (or breaking of wedlock) whoredom, fornication and uncleanness, have not only burst in, but also overflowed almost the whole world, unto the great dishonor of GOD, the exceeding infamy of the name of Christ, the notable decay of true Religion, and the utter destruction of the public wealth, and that so abundantly, that through the customary use thereof, this vice is grown into such an height, that in a manner among many, it is counted no sin at all, but rather a pastime, a dalliance, and but a touch of youth: not rebuked, but winked at: not punished, but laughed at.

Wherefore it is necessary at this present, to entreat of the sin of whoredom and fornication, declaring unto you the greatness of this sin, and how odious, hateful, and abominable it is, and hath always been reputed before GOD and all good men, and how grievously it hath been punished both by the law of GOD, and the laws of diverse Princes.

Again, to shew you certain remedies, whereby you may (through the grace of GOD) eschew this most detestable sin of whoredom and fornication, and lead your lives in all honesty and cleanness, and that you may perceive that fornication and whoredom are (in the sight of GOD) most abominable sins, you shall call to remembrance this commandment of GOD, Thou shalt not commit adultery (Exodus 20.14): by the which word, adultery, although it be properly understood of the unlawful commixtion or joining together of a married man with any woman beside his wife, or of a wife with any man beside her husband: yet thereby is signified also all unlawful use of those parts, which be ordained for generation. And this one commandment (forbidding adultery) doth sufficiently paint and set out before our eyes the greatness of this sin of whoredom, and manifestly declares how greatly it ought to be abhorred of all honest and faithful persons. And that none of us all shall think himself excepted from this commandment, whether we be old or yong, married, or unmarried, man or woman, hear what GOD the Father saith by his most excellent Prophet Moses: There shall be no whore among the daughters of Israel, nor no whoremonger among the sons of Israel (Deuteronomy 23.17).

Here is whoredom, fornication, and all other uncleanness forbidden to all kinds of people, all degrees, and all ages without exception. And that we shall not doubt, but that this precept or commandment pertains to us indeed, hear what Christ (the perfect teacher of all truth) saith in the new Testament, You have heard (saith Christ) that it was said to them of old time, Thou shalt not commit adultery: but I say unto you, Whosoever sees a Woman, to have his lust of her, hath committed adultery with her already in his heart (Matthew 5.27-28). Hear our Savior Christ doth not only confirm and establish the law against adultery, given in the old Testament of GOD the Father by his servant Moses, and make it of full strength, continually to remain among the professors of his Name in the new law: but he also (condemning the grosse interpretation of the Scribes and Pharisees, which taught that the aforesaid commandment only required to abstain from the outward adultery, and not from the filthy desires and impure lusts,) teaches us an exact and full perfection of purity and cleanness of life, both to keep our bodies undefiled, and our hearts pure and free from all evil thoughts, carnal desires, and fleshly consents. How can we then be free from this commandment, where so great charge is laid upon us?

May a servant do what he will in any thing, having commandment of his master to the contrary? Is not Christ our Master? Are not we his servants? How then may we neglect our Masters will and pleasure, and follow our own will and fantasy? You are my friends (saith Christ) if you keep those things that I command you (John 15.14).

Now hath Christ our Master commanded us that we should forsake all uncleanness and filthiness both in body and spirit: this therefore must we do, if we look to please GOD. In the Gospel of Saint Matthew we read, that the Scribes and Pharisees were grievously offended with Christ, because his disciples did not keep the traditions of the forefathers, for they washed not their hands when they went to dinner or supper (Matthew 15.1-2): And among other things, Christ answered and said, Hear and understand; Not that thing which enters into the mouth defiles the man, but that which cometh out of the mouth defiles the man (Matthew 15.10-11). For those things which proceed out of the mouth, come forth from the heart, and they defile the man. For out of the heart proceed evil thoughts, murders, breaking of wedlock, whoredom, thefts, false witness, blasphemies: these are the things which defile a man (Matthew 15.19-20, Mark 7.21). Here may we see, that not only murder, theft, false witless, and blasphemy, defile men, but also evil thoughts, breaking of wedlock, fornication, and whoredom. Who is now of so little wit, that he will esteem whoredom and fornication to be things of small importance, and of no weight before GOD? Christ (who is the trueth, and can not lie) saith that euill thoughts, breaking of wedlocke, whoredome, and fornication defile a man, that is to say, corrupt both the body and soul of man, and make them, of the temples of the holy Ghost, the filthy dunghill, or dungeon of all unclean spirits, of the house of GOD, the dwelling place of Satan (Titus 1.15).

Again in the Gospel of Saint John, when the woman taken in adultery, was brought unto Christ, said not he unto her, Go thy way, and sin no more (John 8.11)? Doth not he here call whoredom sin? And what is the reward of sin, but everlasting death (Romans 6.23)? If whoredom be sin, then it is not lawful for us to commit it. For Saint John saith, He that commits sin is of the devil (1 John 3.8). And our Savior saith, Every one that commits sin, is the servant of sin (John 8.34). If whoredom had not been sin, Surely Saint John Baptist would never have rebuked king Herod for taking his brothers wife, but he told him plainly, that it was not lawful for him to take his brothers wife. He winked not at the whoredom of Herod, although he were a king of power, but boldly reproved him for his wicked and abominable living (Mark 6.18), although for the same he lost his head. But he would rather suffer death (then see GOD so dishonored, by the breaking of his holy precept and commandment) then to suffer whoredom to be unrebuked, even in a king. If whoredom had been but a pastime, a dalliance, & not to be passed off, (as many count it now a days) truly John had been more then twice mad, if he would have had the displeasure of a king, if he would have been cast in prison, and lost his head for a trifle. But John knew right well how filthy, and stinking, and abominable the sin of whoredom is in the sight of GOD, therefore would not he leave it unrebuked, no not in a king, If whoredom be not lawful in a king, neither is it lawful in a subject. If whoredom be not lawful in a public or common officer, neither is it lawful in a private person. If it be not lawful neither in king, nor subject, neither in common officer, nor private person, truly then it is lawful in no man nor woman of whatsoever degree or age they be.

Furthermore in the Acts of the Apostles we read that when the Apostles & Elders with the whole Congregation, were gathered together to pacify the hearts of the faithful dwelling at Antioch, (which were disquieted through the false doctrine of certain Jewish preachers) they sent word to the brethren, that it seemed good to the holy Ghost, and to them, to charge them with no more then with necessary things: among other, they willed them to abstain from idolatry and fornication, from which (said they) if ye keep your selves, ye shall do well (Acts 15.28-29). Note here, how these holy and blessed Fathers of Christ's Church, would charge the congregation with no more things then were necessary. Mark also how among those things, from the which they commanded the brethren of Antioch to abstain, fornication and whoredom is numbered. It is therefore necessary, by the determination and consent of the holy Ghost, and the Apostles and Elders, with the whole Congregation that as from idolatry and superstition, so likewise we must abstain from fornication and whoredom. It is necessary unto salvation to abstain from idolatry: So is it to abstain from whoredom. Is there any nigher way to lead unto damnation, then to be an idolater? No. Even so, neither is there any nearer way to damnation, then to be a fornicator and a whoremonger. Now where are those people, which so lightly esteem breaking of wedlock, whoredom, fornication and adultery. It is necessary, saith the holy Ghost, the blessed Apostles, the Elders, with the whole Congregation of Christ, it is necessary to salvation (say they) to abstain from whoredom. If it be necessary unto salvation, then woe be to them which neglecting their salvation, give their minds to so filthy and stinking sin, to so wicked vice, and to such detestable abomination.

THE SECOND PART OF THE SERMON AGAINST ADULTERY.

YOU have been taught in the first part of this Sermon against Adultery, how that vice at this day reigns most above all other vices, and what is meant by this word (Adultery) and how holy Scripture dissuades or discounsaileth (dis-counsels) from doing that filthy sin, and finally what corruption cometh to mans soul through the sin of Adultery. Now to proceed further, let us hear what the blessed Apostle Saint Paul saith to this matter, writing to the Romans he hath these words. Let us cast away the works of darkness, and put on the armor of light. Let us walk honestly as it were in the day time, not in eating and drinking, neither in chambering and wantonness, neither in strife and envying, but put you on the Lord Jesus Christ, and make not provision for the flesh to fulfill the lusts of it (Romans 13.12-14). Here the holy Apostle exhorts us to cast away the works of darkness, which (among other) he calls gluttonous eating, drinking, chambering, and wantonness, which are all ministers unto that vice, and preparations to induce and bring in the filthy sin of the flesh.

He calls them the deeds and works of darkness, not only because they are customary in darkness, or in the night time (for every one that doth evil, hates the light, neither cometh he to the light, lest his works should be reproved, John 3.20) but that they lead the right way unto that utter darkness, where weeping and gnashing of teeth shall be (Matthew 25.30). And he saith in an other place of the same Epistle, They that are in the flesh, cannot please GOD: We are debtors, not to the flesh, that we should live after the flesh, for if you live after the flesh, ye shall die (Romans 8.8, 12-13). Again he saith, Flee from whoredom, for every sin that a man commits, is without his body: but whosoever commits whoredom, sins against his own body. Do ye not know, that your members are the Temple of the holy Ghost which is in you, whom also ye have of GOD, and you are not your own? For you are dearly bought: glorify God in your bodies, &c. And a little before he saith, Do you not know that your bodies are the members of Christ: Shall I then take the members of Christ, and make them the members of a whore? GOD forbid. Do ye not know, that he which cleaves to a whore, is made one body with her? There shall be two in one flesh (saith he) but he that cleaves to the Lord, is one spirit (1 Corinthians 6.15-17). What godly words doth the blessed Apostle Saint Paul bring forth here, to dissuade and discounsell (dis-counsel, or counsel against) us from whoredom and all uncleanness? Your members (saith he) are the Temple of the holy Ghost, which whosoever doth defile, GOD will destroy him, as saith Saint Paul. If we be the Temple of the holy Ghost, how unfitting then is it, to drive that holy Spirit from us through whoredom, and in his place to set the wicked spirits of uncleanness and fornication, and to be joined, and do service to them?

Ye are dearly bought (saith he) therefore glorify GOD in your bodies. Christ that innocent Lamb of GOD, hath bought us from the servitude of the devil, not with corruptible gold & silver, but with his most precious and dear heart blood (1 Peter 1.18-19). To what intent? That we should fall again into our old uncleanness and abominable living? Nay verily: but that we should serve him all the days of our life (Isaiah 38.20, Luke 1.74-75), in holiness and righteousness, that we should glorify him in our bodies, by purity and cleanness of life. He declares also that our bodies are the members of Christ: How unseemly a thing is it then to cease to be incorporate or embodied and made one with Christ, and through whoredom to be enjoined and made all one with a whore? What greater dishonor or injury can we do to Christ, then to take away from him the members of his body, and to join them to whores, devils, and wicked spirits? And what more dishonor can we do to our selves, then through uncleanness, to loose so excellent a dignity and freedom, and to become bondslaves, and miserable captives to the spirits of darkness? Let us therefore consider, first the glory of Christ, then our estate, our dignity, and freedom, wherein GOD hath set us, by giving us his holy Spirit, and let us valiantly defend the same against Satan, and al his crafty assaults, that Christ may be honored, and that we loose not our liberty or freedom, but still remain in one Spirit with him.

Moreover, in his Epistle to the Ephesians, the blessed Apostle wills us to be so pure and free from adultery, fornication, and all uncleanness, that we not once name them among us (as it becomes Saints) nor filthiness, nor foolish talking, nor jesting, which are not comely, but rather giving of thanks: for this you know (saith he) that no whoremonger, neither unclean person, or covetous person (which is an idolater) hath any inheritance in the kingdom of Christ and of GOD

(Ephesians 5.3-5, 1 Corinthians 6.9-10). And that we should remember to be holy, pure, and free from all uncleanness, the holy Apostle calls us Saints, because we are sanctified and made holy by the blood of Christ, through the holy ghost.

Now if we be Saints, what have we to do with the manners of the Heathen? Saint Peter saith, as he which called you is holy, even so be ye holy also in your conversation, because it is written, Be ye holy, for I am holy (1 Peter 1.15-16, Leviticus 19.4, 19.2). Hitherto have we heard how grievous a sin fornication and whoredom is, and how greatly GOD doth abhor it throughout the whole Scripture: How can it any otherwise be then a sin of most abomination, seeing it may not once be named among the Christians, much less it may in any point be committed. And surely if we would weigh the greatness of this sin, and consider it in the right kind, we should find the sin of whoredom, to be that most filthy lake, soul puddle, and stinking sink, whereunto all kinds of sins and evils flow, where also they have their resting place and abiding.

For hath not the adulterer a pride in his whoredom? As the Wise man saith, They are glad when they have done evil, and rejoice in things that are stark naught. Is not the adulterer also idle, and delights in no godly exercise, but only in that his most filthy and beastly pleasure? Is not his mind plucked, and utterly drawn away from all virtuous studies, and fruitful labors, and only given to carnal and fleshly imagination? Doth not the whoremonger give his mind to gluttony, that he may be the more apt to serve his lusts and carnal pleasures? Doth not the adulterer give his mind to covetousness, and to polling and pilling of other, that he may be the more able to maintain his harlots and whores, and to continue in his filthy and unlawful love? Swells he not also with envy against other, fearing that his pray should be allured and taken away from him? Again is he not ireful, and replenished with wrath and displeasure, even against his best beloved, if at any time his beastly and devilish request be letted (permitted)? What sin, or kind of sin is it that is not joined with fornication and whoredom? It is a monster of many heads: it receives all kinds of vices, and refuses all kinds of virtues. If one several sins bring damnation, what is to be thought of that sinne, which is accompanied with all euils, and hath waiting on it whatsoeuer is hateful to GOD, damnable to man, and pleasant to Satan.

Great is the damnation that hangs over the heads of fornicators and adulterers. What shall I speak of other discommodities, which issue and flow out of this stinking puddle of whoredom? is not that treatreasure, which before all other is most regarded of honest persons, the good fame and name of man and woman, lost through whoredom? What patrimony or livelode (livelihood), what substance, what goods, what riches doth whoredome shortly consume and bring to nought? What valiantness and strength is many times made weak, and destroyed with whoredom? What wit is so fine, that is not besotted and defaced through whoredom? What beauty (although it were never so excellent,) is not disfigured through whoredom? Is not whoredom an enemy to the pleasant flower of youth, & bring it not gray hairs and old age before the time? What gift of nature (although it were never so precious) is not corrupted with whoredom? Come not many foul and most loathsome diseases of whoredome? From whence come so many bastards and misbegotten children, to the high displeasure of GOD, and dishonor of holy wedlock, but of whoredom? How many consume all their substance and goods, and at the last fall into such extreme poverty, that afterward they steal, and so are hanged, through whoredom? What contention and manslaughter cometh of whoredom? How many maidens be deflowered, how many wives corrupted, how many widows defiled through whoredom? How much is the public and common weal (commonwealth) impoverished, and troubled through whoredom? How much is GODS word contemned and depraved through whoredom & whore mongers? Of this vice cometh a great part of the divorces which (nowadays) be so commonly accustomed and used by mens private authority, to the great displeasure of GOD, and the breach of the most holy knot and bond of matrimony. For when this most detestable sin is once crept into the breast of the adulterer, so that he is entangled with unlawful and unchaste love, straightway his true and lawful wife is despised, her presence is abhorred, her company stinks, and is loathsome, whatsoever she doth is dispraised: there is no quietness in the house, so long as she is in sight: therefore to make short work, she must away, for her husband can brook her no longer. Thus through whoredom, is the honest and harmless wife put away, and an harlot received in her stead: and in like sort, it happens many times in the wife towards her husband. O abomination! Christ our Savior, very GOD and man, coming to restore the Law of his heavenly Father, unto the right sense, understanding, and meaning (among other things) reformed the abuse of this Law of GOD. For where as the Jews used a long sufferance, by custom, to put away their wives, at their pleasure, for every cause, Christ correcting that evil custom, did teach, that if any man put away his wife, and marries another, for any cause, except only for adultery, (which then was death by the law) he was an adulterer (Matthew 19.9), and forced also his wife so divorced, to commit adultery, if she were joined to any other man, and the man also so joined with her, to commit adultery.

In what case then are these adulterers, which for the love of an whore put away their true and lawful wife, against all law, right, reason and conscience? O how damnable is the estate wherein they stand! Swift destruction shall fall on them, if they repent not, and amend not: For GOD will not suffer holy wedlock thus to be dishonored, hated and despised. He will once punish this fleshly and licentious manner of living, and cause that this holy ordinance shall be had in reverence and honor. For surely wedlock (as the Apostle saith) is honorable among all men, and the bed undefiled: But whore mongers and fornicators God will judge, that is to say, punish and condemn (Hebrews 13.4). But to what purpose is this labor taken, to describe and set forth the greatness of the sin of whoredom, and the discommodities that issue & flow out of it, seeing that breath and tongue shall sooner fail any man, then he shall or may be able to set it out according to the abomination and heinousness thereof? Notwithstanding this is spoken to the intent that all men should flee whoredom, and live in the fear of GOD: GOD grant that it may not be spoken in vain.

THE THIRD PART OF THE SERMON AGAINST ADULTERY.

IN the second part of this Sermon against adultery that was last read, you have learned how earnestly the Scripture warns us to avoid the sin of adultery, and to embrace cleanness of life: and that through adultery, we fall into all kinds of sin, and are made bond-slaves to the devil: through cleanness of life we are made members of Christ: and finally, how far adultery bring a man from all goodness, and drives him headlong into all vices, mischief, and misery. Now will I declare unto you in order, with what grievous punishments GOD in times past plagued adultery, and how certain worldly Princes also did punish it, that you may perceive that whoredom and fornication be sins no less detestable in the sight of GOD, to all good men, then I have hitherto uttered. In the first book of Moses, we read that when mankind began to be multiplied upon the earth, the men and women gave their minds so greatly to fleshly delight, and filthy pleasure, that they lived without all fear of GOD. GOD seeing this their beastly and abominable living and perceiving that they amended not, but rather increased daily more and more in their sinful and unclean manners, repented that ever he had made man: and to shew how greatly he abhors adultery, whoredom, fornication, and all uncleanness, he made all the fountains of the deep earth to burst out, and the sluices of heaven to be opened, so that the rain came down upon the earth by the space of forty days and forty nights, and by this means destroyed the whole world, and all mankind, eight persons only excepted, that is to say, Noah the preacher of righteousness, (as S. Peter calls him) and his wife, his three sons and their wives. O what a grievous plague did GOD cast here upon all living creatures for the sin of whoredom! For the which GOD, took vengeance, not only of man, but of all beasts, fowls, and all living creatures. Manslaughter was committed before (Genesis 4.8), yet was not the world destroyed for that: but for whoredom all the world (few only except) was overflowed with waters, and so perished. An example worthy to be remembered, that ye may learn to fear GOD.

We read again, that for the filthy sin of uncleanness, Sodom and Gomorrah, and the other Cities nigh unto them, were destroyed by fire and brimstone from heaven (Genesis 19.24), so that there was neither man, woman, child, nor beast, nor yet any thing that grew upon the earth there left undestroyed. Whose heart trembles not at the hearing of this history? Who is so drowned in whoredom and uncleanness, that will not now for ever after leave this abominable living, seeing that GOD so grievously punishes uncleanness, to rain fire and brimstone from heaven, to destroy whole Cities, to kill man, woman, and child, and all other living creatures there abiding, to consume with fire all that ever grew? What can be more manifest tokens of GODS wrath and vengeance against uncleanness and impurity of life? Mark this history (good people) and fear the vengeance of GOD. Do you not read also, that GOD did smite Pharaoh and his house with great plagues, because that he ungodly desired Sara the wife of Abraham (Genesis 12.17)? Likewise read we of Abimelech king of Gerar, although he touched her not by carnal knowledge (Genesis 20.4). These plagues and punishments did GOD cast on upon filthy and unclean persons, before the Law was given (the law of nature only reigning in the hearts of men) to declare how great love he had to Matrimony and wedlock, and again, how much he abhorred adultery, fornication, and all uncleanness. And when the Law that forbade whoredom was given by Moses to the Jews, did not GOD command that the breakers thereof should be put to death? The words of the law be these: Who so commits adultery with any mans wife, shall die the death, both the man and the woman, because he hath broken wedlock with his neighbors wife (Leviticus 20.10). In the Law also it was commanded, that a damsel and a man taken together in whoredom should be both stoned to death. In another place we also read, that GOD commanded Moses to take all the head Rulers, and Princes of the people, and to hang them upon gibbets openly, that every man might see them, because they either committed, or did not punish whoredom (Numbers 25.4). Again, did not GOD send such a plague among the people for fornication, and uncleanness, that they dyed in one day three and twenty thousand? I passe over for lack of time many other histories of the holy Bible, which declare the grievous vengeance, and heavy displeasure of GOD against whore mongers and adulterers. Certainly this extreme punishment appointed of GOD, shows evidently how greatly GOD hates whoredom. And let us not doubt, but that GOD at this present abhors all manner of uncleanness, no less then he did in the old law, and will undoubtedly punish it, both in this world, and in the world to come. For he is a GOD that can abide no wickedness: therefore ought it to be eschewed of all that tender the glory of GOD, and the salvation of their own souls (Psalms 5.4).

Saint Paul saith, All these things are written for our example, and to teach us the fear of GOD, and the obedience to his holy Law (1 Corinthians 10.11). For if GOD spared not the natural branches, neither will he spare us that be but grafts, if we commit like offence. If GOD destroyed many thousands of people, many cities, yea the whole, world for whoredom, let us not flatter our selves, and think we shall escape free, and without punishment. For he hath promised in his holy Law, to send most grievous plagues upon them that transgress, or break his holy commandments. Thus have we heard, how GOD punishes the sin of adultery: let us now hear certain laws, which the Civil Magistrates devised in their countries, for the punishment thereof, that we may learn how uncleanness hath ever been detested in all well ordered cities and commonwealths, and among all honest persons.

Lawes deuised for the punishment of whoredome. The law among the Lepreians was this, that when any were taken in adultery, they were bound and carried three days through the city, and afterward as long as they lived, were they despised, and with shame and confusion counted as persons void of all honesty. Among the Locrensians the adulterers have both their eyes thrust out. The Romans in times past, punished whoredom, sometime by fire, sometime by sword. If any man among the Egyptians had bene taken in adultery, the law was, that he should openly in the presence of all the people be scourged naked with whips, unto the number of a thousand stripes, the woman was then taken with him, had her nose cut off, whereby she was known ever after, to be a whore, and therefore to be abhorred of all men. Among the Arabians, they that were taken in adultery, had their heads struck from their bodies. The Athenians punished whoredom by death in like manner. So likewise, did the barbarous Tartarians. Among the Turks even at this day, they that be taken in adultery, both man and woman are stoned straightway to death, without mercy. Thus we see what godly acts were devised in times past of the high powers, for the putting away of whoredom, and for the maintaining of holy Matrimony, or wedlock, and pure conversation. And the authors of these acts were no Christians, but the Heathen: yet were they so inflamed with the love of honesty and pureness of life, that for the maintenance and conservation or keeping up of that, they made godly Statutes, suffering neither fornication or adultery to reign in their Realms unpunished. Christ said to the people, The Ninevites shall rise at the judgement with this Nation (meaning the unfaithful Jews) and shall condemn them: for they repented at the preaching of Jonas, but behold (saith he) a greater then Jonas is here, (meaning him self) and yet they repent not (Matthew 12.41). Shall not (think you) likewise the Locrensians, Arabians, Athenians, with such other, rise up in the judgement, and condemn us, for as much as they ceased from the whoredom at the commandment of man, and we have the Law, and manifest precepts and commandments of GOD, and yet forsake we not our filthy conversation? truly, truly, it shall be easier at the day of judgement, to these Heathen, then to us, except we repent and amend. For though death of body seems to us a grievous punishment in this world for whoredom: yet is that pain nothing in comparison of the grievous torments which adulterers, fornicators, and all unclean persons shall suffer after this life. For all such shall be excluded and shut out of the Kingdom of heaven, as S. Paul saith, Be not deceived, for neither whore mongers, nor worshipers of Images, nor adulterers, nor effeminate persons, nor Sodomites, nor thieves, nor covetous persons, nor drunkards, nor cursed speakers, nor pillers (swindlers), shall inherit the Kingdome of GOD (I Corinthians 6.9-10, Galatians 5.19, Ephesians 5.5). And S. Iohn in his Revelation saith, That whore mongers shall have their part with murderers, sorcerers, enchanters, liars, idolaters, and such other, in the lake which burns with fire and brimstone, which is the second death (Revelations 21.8). The punishment of the body, although it be death, hath an end: but the punishment of the soul, which S. John calls the second death, is everlasting, there shall be fire and brimstone, there shall be weeping and gnashing of teeth, the worm that there shall gnaw the conscience of the damned, shall never die (Matthew 13.42, Mark 9.44). O whose heart distills not even drops of blood, to hear and consider these things? If we tremble and shake at the hearing and naming of these pains, oh what shall they do that shall feel them, that shall suffer them, yea, and ever shall suffer, worlds without end: GOD have mercy upon us. Who is now so drowned in sin, and past all godliness, that he will set more by filthy and stinking pleasure, (which soon passes away) then by the loss of everlasting glory? Again, who will so give himself to the lusts of the flesh, that he fears nothing at all the pain of hell fire? But let us hear how we may eschew the sin of whoredom, and adultery, that we may walks in the fear of GOD, and be free from those most grievous and intolerable torments, which abide all unclean persons.

<u>Remedies whereby to avoid fornication and adultery.</u> Now to auoide fornication, adultery, and all vncleannesse, let us provide that aboue all things, we may keep our hearts pure and clean, from all evil thoughts and carnal lusts: for if that be once infected and corrupt, we fall headlong into all kind of ungodliness. This shall we easily do, if when we feel inwardly, that Satan our old enemy tempts us unto whoredom, we by no means consent to his crafty suggestions, but valiantly resist and withstand him by strong faith in the word of GOD, alleging against him always in our heart, this commandment of GOD: *Scriptum est, non mœchaberis.* It is written, Thou shalt not commit whoredom. It shall be good also for us, ever to live in the fear of GOD, and to set before our eyes the grievous threats of GOD against all ungodly sinners, and to consider in our mind, how filthy, beastly, and short that pleasure is, whereunto Satan continually stirs and moves us: And again, how the pain appointed for that sin is intolerable and everlasting. Moreover, to use a temperance and sobriety in eating and drinking, to eschew unclean communication, to avoid all filthy company, to flee idleness, to delight in reading the holy Scriptures, to watch in godly prayers and virtuous meditation, and at all times, to

exercise some godly travails, shall help greatly unto the eschewing of whoredom.

And here are all degrees to be admonished, whether they be married or unmarried, to love chastity and cleanness of life. For the married are bound by the law of GOD so purely to love one another, that neither of them seek any strange love. The man must only cleave to his wife, and the wife again only to her husband: they must so delight one in another's company, that none of them covet any other. And as they are bound thus to liue together in all godlinesse and honesty, so likewise it is their duty, virtuously to bring up their children, and provide, that they fall not into Satan's snare, nor into any uncleanness, but that they come pure and honest vnto holy wedlocke, when time requires. So likewise ought all masters, and rulers to provide that no whoredom, nor any point of uncleanness be used among their servants. And again, they that are single, and feel in themselves that they cannot live without the company of a woman, let them get wives of their own, and so live godly together: For it is better to marry then to burn (1 Corinthians 7.9).

And to avoid fornication, saith the Apostle, let every man have his own wife, and every woman her own husband. Finally, all such as feel in themselves a sufficiency and ability (through the working of GODS Spirit) to lead a sole and continent life, let them praise GOD for his gift, and seek all means possible to maintain the same: as by reading of holy Scriptures, by godly meditations, by continual prayers, and such other virtuous exercises. If we all on this wise will endeavor our selves to eschew fornication, adultery, and all uncleanness, and lead our lives in all godliness and honesty, serving GOD with a pure and clean heart, and glorifying him in our bodies by the leading an innocent and harmless life, we may be sure to be in the number of those, of whom our Savior Christ speaks in the Gospel on this manner, Blessed are the pure in heart, for they shall see GOD (Matthew 5.8): to whom alone be all glory, honor, rule, and power, worlds without end. Amen.

THE SECOND TOME

OF HOMILIES,

OF SUCH MATTERS AS WERE PROMISED, and entitled in the former part of Homilies.

AN ADMONITION TO all Ministers Ecclesiastical.

FOR that the Lord doth require of his servant, whom he hath set over his household, to show both faithfulness and prudence in his office: it shall be necessary that ye above all other doe behave yourselves most faithfully and diligently in your so high a function: that is, aptly, plainly, and distinctly to read the sacred Scriptures, diligently to instruct the youth in their Catechism, gravely and reverently to minister his most holy Sacraments, prudently also to choose out such Homilies as be most meet for the time, and for the more agreeable instruction of the people committed to your charge, with such discretion, that where the Homily may appear too long for one reading, to divide the same to be read part in the forenoon, and part in the afternoon. And where it may so chance some one or other Chapter of the Old Testament to fall in order to be read upon the Sundays or Holy days, which were better to be changed with some other of the New Testament of more edification, it shall be well done to spend your time to consider well of such Chapters before hand, whereby your prudence and diligence in your office may appear, so that your people may have cause to glorify God for you, and be the readier to embrace your labors, to your better commendation, to the discharge of your consciences and their own.

HOMILY ON THE RIGHT USE OF THE CHURCH

AN HOMILIE OF THE RIGHT VSE OF
the Church or Temple of GOD, and of the reuerence due vnto the same.

THE FIRST CHAPTER.

WHERE there appeareth at these dayes great slackenesse and negligence of a great sort of people, in resorting to the Church, there to serue GOD their heauenly Father, according to their most bounden duety, as also much vncomely and vnreuerent behauiour of many persons in the same when they be there assembled, and therby may iust feare arise of the wrath of GOD, and his dreadful plagues hanging ouer our heads for our grieuous offences in this behalfe, amongst other many and great sinnes which wee dayly and hourely commit before the Lord. Therefore for the discharge of all our consciences, and for the auoyding of the common perill and plague hanging ouer vs, let vs consider what may be sayd out of GODS holy booke concerning this matter, whereunto I pray you giue good audience, for that it is of great weight, and concerneth you all. Although the eternall and incomprehensible Maiestie of GOD, the Lord of heauen and earth, whose feat is heauen, and the earth his footstoole, cannot bee inclosed in temples or houses made with mans hand, as in dwelling places able to receiue or conteyne his Maiestie, according as is euidently declared by the Prophet Esaias (Isaiah 66.1), and by the doctrine of S. Steuen, and S. Paul in the Actes of the Apostles (Acts 17.24). And where King Solomon (who builded vnto the Lord, the most glorious Temple that euer was made) saith, Who shal be able to build a meet or worthy house for him? if heauen, and the heauen aboue all heauens cannot conteine him: how much lesse can that which I haue builded (1 Kings 8.27)? And further confesseth: What am I, that I should bee able to build thee an house, O Lord? But yet for this purpose onely it is made, that thou mayest regard the prayer of thy seruant, and his humble supplication. (2 Chronicles 2.6, 2 Chronicles 6.18) Much lesse then be our Churches meet dwelling places to receiue the incomprehensible Maiestie of GOD. And indeed, the chiefe and speciall Temples of GOD, wherein hee hath greatest pleasure, and most delighteth to dwell and continue in are the bodies and minds of true Christians, and the chosen people of GOD, according to the doctrine of the holy Scripture, declared in the first Epistle to the Corinthians. Know yee not (saith Saint Paul) that ye be the Temple of GOD, and that the spirit of GOD dwelleth in you? If any man defile the temple of GOD, him wil GOD destroy. For the temple of GOD is holy, which ye are (1 Corinthians 3.16-17). And againe in the same Epistle: Know yee not that your body is the Temple of the holy Ghost dwelling in you, whom yee haue giuen you of GOD, and that yee be not your owne? For yee are dearely bought. Glorifie yee now therefore GOD in your body, and in your Spirit, which are GODS (1 Corinthians 6.19-20). And therefore as our Sauiour Christ teacheth in the Gospel of Saint Iohn, they that worship GOD the Father in spirit and trueth, in what place soeuer they doe it, worship him a right: for such worshippers doth GOD the Father looke for. For GOD is a Spirit, and those that worship him, must worship him in spirit and trueth (John 4.23-24), saith our Sauiour Christ. Yet all this notwithstanding, the materiall Church or Temple is a place appointed aswell by the vsage and continuall examples expressed in the olde Testament, as in the New, for the people of GOD to resort together vnto, there to heare GODS holy Word, to call vpon his holy Name, to giue him thankes for his innumerable and vnspeakeable benefits bestowed vpon vs, and duely and truely to celebrate his holy Sacraments: (In the vnfained doing and accomplishing of the which, standeth that true and right worshipping of GOD afore mentioned) and the same Church or Temple, is by the holy Scriptures both of the Olde Testament and New, called the House and Temple of the Lord, for the peculiar seruice there done to his Maiestie by his people, and for the effectuous presence of his heauenly Grace, wherewith hee by his sayd holy Word endueth his people so there assembled. And to the said house or Temple of GOD, at all times, by common order appointed, are all people that be godly indeed, bound with all diligence in resort, vnlesse by sickenesse, or other most vrgent causes they bee letted therefro. And all the same so resorting thither, ought with all quietnesse and reuerence there to behaue themselues, in doing their bounden duetie and seruice to Almightie GOD, in the Congregation of his Saints. All which things are euident to bee prooued by GODS holy word, as hereafter shall plainely appeare.

And first of all, I will declare by the Scriptures, that it is called (as it is in deede) the house of GOD (John 2.16), and Temple of the Lord. Hee that sweareth by the Temple (saith our Sauiour Christ) sweareth by it, and him that dwelleth therein (Matthew 23.21), meaning GOD the father, which hee also expresseth plainely in the Gospel of Saint Iohn, saying: Do not make the house of my father, the house of merchandize (John 2.16). And in the booke of the Psalmes, the Prophet Dauid saith, I will enter into thine house, I will worship in thy holy Temple, in thy feare (Psalms 5.7). And it is almost in infinite places of the Scripture, specially in the Prophets and booke of Psalmes, called the house of GOD, or house of the Lord. Sometime it is named the Tabernacle of the Lord, and sometime the Sanctuary, that is to say, the holy place or house of the Lord (Exodus 25.8-9, Leviticus 19.30). And it is likewise called the house of prayer, as Solomon, who builded the Temple of the Lord at Ierusalem, doth oft call it the house of the Lord, in the which the Lords Name should be called vpon (1 Kings 8.43, 2 Chronicles 6.10). And Esaias in the 56. Chapter, My house shall be called the house of prayer amongst all nations (Isaiah 56.7). Which text our Sauiour Christ alleadgeth in the new Testament, as doth appeare in three of the Euangelists (Matthew 12.4, Matthew 21.13, Mark 11.17, Luke 19.46), and in the parable of the Pharisee and the Publicane which went to pray, in which parable our Sauiour Christ saith, They went vp into the Temple to pray (Luke 18.10). And Anna the holy widow and prophetisse, serued the Lord in fasting and prayer in the Temple, night and day (Luke 2.37). And in the story of the Acts it is mentioned, how that Peter and Iohn went vp into the Temple at the houre of prayer (Acts 3.1). And S. Paul praying in the Temple at Ierusalem, was rapt in the Spirit, and did see Iesus speaking vnto him. And as in all conuenient places, prayer may be vsed of the godly priuately: so it is most certaine, that the Church or Temple is the due and appointed place for common and publike prayer. Now that it is likewise the place of thankesgiuing vnto the Lord for his innumerable and vnspeakeable benefits bestowed vpon vs, appeareth notably in the latter end of the Gospel of S. Luke (Luke 24.53), and the beginning of the story of the Acts, where it is written that the Apostles & Disciples after the ascension of the Lord, continued with one accord dayly in the Temple, alwaies praising, and blessing GOD (Acts 2.46-47). And it is likewise declared in the first Epistle to the Corinthians, that the Church is the due place appointed for the vse of the Sacraments (1 Corinthians 11.18). It remaineth now to be declared, that the Church or Temple is the place where the liuely word of GOD (and not mans inuentions) ought to be read and taught, & that the people are bound thither with all diligence to resort: and this proofe likewise to be made by the Scriptures, as hereafter shall appeare.

In the story of the Acts of the Apostles, we read that Paul and Barnabas preached the word of GOD in the Temples of the Iewes at Salamine. And when they came to Antiochia, they entered on the Sabbath day into the Synagogue or Church, and sate downe, & after the Lesson or reading of the Law and the Prophets, the ruler of the temple sent vnto them, saying: Ye men & brethren, if any of you haue any exhortation to make vnto the people, say it. And so Paul standing vp, and making silence with his hand, said: Ye me that be Israelites, & ye that feare God, giue eare, &c. preaching to them a sermon out of the Scriptures, as there at large appeareth (Acts 13.14-16). And in the same Storie of the Acts, the seuenteenth Chapter is testified, how Paul preached Christ out of the Scriptures at Thessalonica (Acts 17.1-2). And in the fifteenth Chapter, Iames the Apostle in that holy Counsell and Assembly of his fellow Apostles saith, Moses of old time hath in euery city certaine that preach him in the Synagogues or Temples, where he is read euery Sabboth day (Acts 15.21). By these places ye may see the vsage of reading the Scriptures of the old Testament among the Iewes in their Synagogues euery Sabboth day, and Sermons vsually made vpon the same. How much more then is it conuenient that the Scriptures of GOD, and specially the Gospel of our Sauiour Christ should bee read and expounded to vs that be Christians in our Churches, specially our Sauiour Christ and his Apostles allowing this most godly and necessary vsage, and by their examples confirme the same?

It is written in the Stories of the Gospels in diuers places, that Iesus went round about all Galile, teaching in their Synagogues, and preaching the Gospel of the kingdome (Matthew 4.23, Mark 1.14, Luke 4.15, Matthew 13.54, Mark 6.1-2, Luke 13.10): In which places is his great diligence in continual preaching and teaching of the people most euidently set forth.

In Luke ye read, how Iesus according to his accustomed vse came into the Temple, and how the booke of Esaias the Prophet was deliuered him, how he read a text therein, and made a Sermon vpon the same.

And in the xix. is expressed how hee taught dayly in the Temple (Luke 19.47). And it is thus written in the viii. of Iohn: Iesus came againe early in the morning into the Temple, and all the people came vnto him, and he sate downe and taught them (John 8.1-2). And in the xviii. of Iohn, our Sauiour testifieth before Pilate, that he spake openly vnto the world, and that hee alwayes taught in the Synagogue and in the Temple, whither all the Iewes resorted, and that secretly hee spake nothing (John 18.20). And in Saint Luke Iesus taught in the Temple, and all the people came early in the morning vnto him, that they might heare him in the Temple (Luke 21.37-38).

Here ye see aswell the diligence of our Sauiour in teaching the word of GOD in the Temple daily, and specially on the Sabboth dayes, as also the readinesse of the people resorting altogether, and that earely in the morning, into the Temple to heare him.

The same example of diligence in preaching the word of GOD in the Temple, shall ye find in the Apostles, and the people resorting vnto them. Acts the fift., where the Apostles, although they had beene whipped and scourged the day before, and by the high Priest commanded that they should preach no more in the Name of Iesus, yet the day following they entred earely in the morning into the Temple, and did not cease to teach and declare Iesus Christ (Acts 5.21, 42). And in sundry other places of the storie of the Actes, ye shall finde like diligence both in the Apostles in teaching, and in the people in comming to the Temple to heare GODS word (Acts 13.15, 17). And it is testified in the first of Luke, that when Zacharie the holy Priest, and father to Iohn Baptist, did sacrifice within the Temple, all the people stoode without a long time praying, such was their zeale and feruencie at that time (Luke 1.9-10). And in the second of Luke appeareth what great iourneyes men, women, yea and children tooke, to come to the Temple on the Feast day, there to serue the Lord, and specially the example of Ioseph, the blessed virgin Marie, mother to our Sauiour, and of our

Sauiour Christ himselfe, being yet but a child, whose examples are worthy for vs to follow (Luke 2.41, 46). So that if wee would compare our negligence in resorting to the house of the Lord there to serue him, with the diligence of the Iewes in comming daily very early, sometime by great iourneys to their Temple, and when the multitude could not be receiued within the Temple, the feruent zeale that they had, declared in standing long without and praying: we may iustly in this comparison condemne our slouthfulnesse and negligence, yea plaine contempt, in comming to the Lords house, standing so neere vnto vs, so seldome, and scarcely at any time. So farre is it from a great many of vs to come early in the morning, or giue attendance without, who disdain to come into the Temple: and yet we abhorre the very name of the Iewes when wee heare it, as of a most wicked and vngodly people. But it is to bee feared, that in this point wee be farre worse then the Iewes, and that they shall rise at the day of Iudgement, to our condemnation, who in comparison to them, shew such slackenesse and contempt in resorting to the house of the Lord, there to serue him, according as we are of duety most bound. And besides this most horrible dread of GODS iust Iudgement in the great day, wee shall not in this life escape his heauy hand and vengeance for this contempt of the house of the Lord, and his due seruice in the same, according as the Lord himselfe threatneth in the first Chapter of the Prophet Aggeus, after this sort: Because you haue left my House desert and without company (saith the Lord) and ye haue made hast euery man to his owne house, for this cause are the heauens stayed ouer you, that they should giue no deaw, and the earth is forbidden that it shall bring foorth her fruit, and I haue called drought vpon the earth, and vpon the mountaines, and vpon corne, and vpon wine, and vpon oyle, and vpon all things that the earth bringeth foorth, and vpon men, and vpon beasts, and vpon all things that mens hands labour for (Haggai 1.9-11). Behold, if wee bee such worldlings that wee care not for the eternall Iudgements of GOD (which yet of all other are most dreadfull, and horrible) we shall not escape the punishment of GOD in this world by drought and famine, and the taking away of all worldly commodities, which we as worldlings seeme onely to regarde and care for. Whereas on the contrary part, if we would amend this fault, or negligence, slouthfulnesse and contempt of the house of the Lord, and his due Seruice there, and with diligence resort thither together, to serue the Lord with one accord and consent, in all holinesse and righteousnesse before him, wee haue promises of benefits both heauenly and worldly. Wheresoeuer two or three bee gathered in my Name (sayth our Sauiour Christ) there am I in the middest of them (Matthew 18.20). And what can be more blessed, then to haue our Sauiour Christ among vs? Or what againe can bee more vnhappy or mischieuous then to driue our Sauiour Christ from amongst vs, to leaue a place for his and our most ancient and mortall enemy the old Dragon and serpent Satan the diuel in the middest of vs? In the second of Luke it is written, how that the mother of Christ and Ioseph, when they had long sought Christ, whom they had lost, and could find him no where, that at the last they found him in the Temple, sitting in the middest of the Doctors (Luke 2.46). So if wee lacke Iesus Christ, that is to say, the Sauiour of our soules and bodies, wee shall not find him in the Market-place, or in the Guild-hall, much lesse in the Ale-house or Tauerne, amongst good fellowes (as they call them) so soone as wee shall find him in the Temple, the Lords house, amongst the Teachers & Preachers of his Word, where indeed hee is to be found. And as concerning worldly commodities, wee haue a sure promise of our Sauiour Christ: Seeke ye first the kingdome of GOD, and the righteousnesse thereof, and all these things shall withall be giuen vnto you. And thus we haue in the first part of this Homily declared by GODS word, that the Temple or Church is the house of the Lord, for that the Seruice of the Lord (as teaching and hearing of his holy Word, calling vpon his holy Name, giuing thankes to him for his great and innumerable benefits, and due ministring of his Sacraments) is there vsed. And it is likewise declared by the Scriptures, how all godly and Christian men and women ought at times appointed, with diligence to resort vnto the house of the Lord, there to serue him, and to glorifie him, as he is most worthy, and wee most bound, to whom bee all glorie and honour world without end. Amen.

THE SECOND PART OF THE HOMILY OF THE RIGHT VSE OF THE CHURCH.

IT was declared in the first part of this Homily, by GODS word, that the Temple or Church is the house of the Lord, for that the Seruice of the Lord (as teaching and hearing of his holy Word, calling vpon his holy Name, giuing thankes to him, for his great and innumerable benefits, and due ministring of the Sacraments) is there vsed. And it is likewise already declared by the Scriptures, how all godly and Christian men and women, ought at times appointed, with diligence to resort vnto the house of the Lord, there to serue him, and to glorifie him, as he is most worthy, and we most bounden.

Now it remaineth in this second part of the Homilie concerning the right vse of the Temple of GOD, to be likewise declared by GODS word, with what quietnesse, silence, and reuerence, those that resort to the house of the Lord, ought there to vse and behaue themselues.

It may teach vs sufficiently how well it doeth become vs Christian men reuerently to vse the Church and holy house of our prayers, by considering in how great reuerence and veneration in the Iewes in the olde law had their Temple, which appeareth by sundry places, whereof I will note vnto you certaine. In the xxvi. of Matthew, it is laid to our Sauiour Christs charge before a Temporall Iudge, as a matter worthy death, by the two false witnesses, that he had said, hee could destroy the Temple of GOD, and in three dayes build it againe, not doubting but if they might make men to beleeue that hee had sayde any thing against the honour and maiestie of the Temple, he should seeme to all men most worthy of death. And in the xxi. of the Actes, when the Iewes found Paul in the Temple, they layd hands vpon him, crying, Yee men Israelites helpe, this is that man who teacheth all men euery where against the people and the law, and against this place: besides that, hee hath brought the Gentiles into the Temple, and hath prophaned this holy place (Acts 21.27-28). Behold how they tooke it for a like offence to speake against the Temple of GOD, as to speake against the Law of GOD, and how they iudged it conuenient, that none but godly persons and the true worshippers of GOD, should enter into the Temple of GOD (Acts 24.6). And the same fault is layd to Pauls charge by Tertullus an eloquent man, and by the Iewes in the xxiiii. of the Actes, before a temporall Iudge, as a matter worthy of death, that hee went about to pollute the Temple of GOD. And in the xxuii. of Matthew, when the chiefe Priests had receiued againe the pieces of siluer as Iudas hand, they said, It is not lawfull to put them into Corban (which was the treasure house of the Temple) because it is the price of blood (Matthew 27.6). So that they could not abide that not onely any vncleane person, but also any other dead thing that was iudged vncleane, should once come into the Temple, or any place thereto belonging. And to this end is S. Pauls saying in the second Epistle to the Corinthians the vi. Chapter to bee applied: What fellowship is there betwixt righteousnesse, and vnrighteousnesse? or what communion betweene light and darkenesse? or what concorde betweene Christ, and Belial? or what part can the faithfull haue with the vnfaithfull? or what agreement can there be betweene theTemple of GOD and images (2 Corinthians 6.14-16)? Which sentence, although it be chiefely referred to the temple of the minde of the godly: yet seeing that the simisimilitude and pith of the argument is taken from the materiall Temple, it enforceth that no vngodlinesse, specially of images or idols, may be suffered in the Temple of GOD, which is the place of worshipping GOD: and therefore can no more bee suffered to stand there, then light can agree with darkenesse, or Christ with Belial: for that the true worshipping of GOD, and the worshipping of images, are most contrary. And the setting of them vp in the place of worshipping, may giue great occasion to the worshipping of them. But to turne to the reuerence that the Iewes had to their Temple. You will say that they honoured it superstitiously, and a great deale too much, crying out, The Temple of the Lord, the Temple of the Lord (Jeremiah 7.4), being notwithstanding most wicked in life, and be therefore most iustly reproued of Ieremie the Prophet of the Lord. Trueth it is that they were superstitiously giuen to the honouring of their Temple. But I would wee were not as farre too short from the due reuerence of the Lords house, as they ouershot themselues therein. And if the Prophet iustly reprehended them, hearken also what the Lord requireth at our hands, that we may know whether we be blame-worthy or no. It is written in Ecclesiastes the fourth Chapter: When thou doest enter into the house of GOD (saith he) take heede to thy feete, draw neere that thou mayest heare: for obedience is much more worth then the sacrifice of fooles, which know not what euill they doe. Speake nothing rashly there, neither let thine heart be swift to vtter words before GOD. For GOD is in heauen, and thou art vpon the earth, therefore let thy wordes be few (Ecclesiastes 5.1-2). Note (welbeloued) what quietnesse in gesture and behauiour, what silence in talke and wordes, is required in the house of GOD; for so he calleth it, See whether they take heede to their feete, as they be here warned, which neuer cease from vncomely walking and ietting vp and downe, and ouerthwart the Church, shewing an euident signification of notable contempt, both of GOD, and all good men there present: and what heede they take to their tongues, and speech, which doe not onely speake wordes swiftly and rashly before the Lord (which they be here forbidden) but also oftentimes speake filthily, couetously, and vngodly, talking of matters scarce honest or fitte for the Ale-house or Tauerne, in the house of the Lord, little considering that they speake before GOD, who dwelleth in heauen, (as is here declared) when they be but vermins here creeping vpon the earth, in comparison to his eternall Maiestie, and lesse regarding that they must giue an account at the great day, of euery idle worde wheresoeuer it bee spoken (Matthew 12.36), much more of filthy, vncleane, or wicked wordes spoken in the Lords house, to the great dishonour of his Maiestie, and offence of all that heare them. And indeede concerning the people and multitude, the Temple is prepared for them to bee hearers, rather then speakers, considering that aswell the word of GOD is there read or taught, whereunto they are bound to giue diligent eare, with all reuerence and silence, as also that common prayer and thankesgiuing are rehearsed and sayd by the publique Minister in the name of the people and the whole multitude present, whereunto they giuing their ready audience, should assent and say, Amen, as S. Paul teacheth in the first Epistle to the Corinthians (1 Corinthians 14.16). And in another place, glorifiing GOD with one spirit and mouth: which cannot bee when euery man and woman in seuerall pretence of deuotion prayeth priuately, one asking, another giuing thankes, another reading doctrine, and not regarding to heare the common prayer of the Minister. And peculiarly, what due reuerence is to bee vsed in the ministring of the Sacraments in the Temple, the same S. Paul teacheth to the Corinthians, rebuking such as did vnreuerently vse themselues in that behalfe. Haue ye not houses to eate and drinke in (sayth he?) Doe ye despise the Church or congregation of GOD? What shall I say to you? Shall I prayse you? In this I prayse you not (1 Corinthians 11.22). And GOD requireth not onely this outward reuerence of behauiour and silence in his house, but all inward reuerence in cleansing of the thoughts of our hearts, threatning by his Prophet Osee in the ix. Chapter, that for the malice of the inuentions and deuices of the people, he will cast them out of his house: whereby is also signified the eternall casting of them out of his heauenly house and kingdome, which is most horrible (Hosea 9.15). And therefore in the xix. of Leuiticus GOD saith, Feare you with reuerence my Sanctuary, for I am the Lord (Leviticus 19.30). And according to the same the Prophet Dauid sayth, I will enter into thine house. I will worship in thy holy Temple in thy feare (Psalms 5.7): shewing what inward reuerence and humblenesse of minde the godly men ought to haue in the house of the Lord. And to alleadge somewhat concerning this matter out of the new Testament, in what honour GOD would haue his house or Temple kept, and that by the example of our Sauiour Christ. whose authoritie ought of good reason with all true Christians to bee of most weight and estimation. It is written of all the foure Euangelists. as a notable act, and worthy to be testified by many holy witnesses, how that our Sauiour Iesus Christ, that mercifull and milde Lord, compared for his meekenesse to a sheepe, suffering with silence his fleece to bee shorne from him, and to a Lambe led without resistance to the slaughter, which gaue his body to them that did smite him, answered not him that reuiled, nor turned away his face from them that did reproch him and spit vpon him, and according to his owne example, gaue precepts of mildnesse and sufferance to his disciples (Isaiah 53.7, Acts 8.32, Isaiah 50.6, Matthew 5.39-48): Yet when hee seeth the Temple and holy house of his heauenly Father misordered, polluted, and prophaned, vseth great seuerity and sharpenesse, ouerturneth the tables of the exchanges, subuerteth the feates of them that sold doues, maketh a whip of cordes, and scourgeth out those wicked abusers and prophaners of the Temple of GOD, saying, My house shalbe called the house of prayer, but yee haue made it a denne of theeues (Matthew 21.12, Mark 11.15, Luke 19.45, John 2.14), And in the second of Iohn, Doe not ye make the house of my Father, the house of merchandize (John 2.16). For as it is the house of GOD, when GODS seruice is duely done in it: So when wee wickedly abuse it with wicked talke or couetous bargaining, wee make it a denne of theeues, or an house of merchandize. Yea, and such reuerence would Christ should bee therein, that hee would not suffer any vessell to bee caryed through the Temple (Mark 11.16). And whereas our Sauiour Christ (as is before mentioned) could bee found no where (when he was sought) but only in the; Temple amongst the doctors (Luke 2.46), and now againe hee exerciseth his authoritie and iurisdiction, not in castles and princely palaces amongst souldiers, but in the Temple: Ye may hereby vnderstand in what place his spirituall Kingdome (which he denyeth to be of this world) is soonest to be found, and best to be knowen of Chrysost all places in this world. And according to this example of our Sauiour Christ in the primitiue Church, which was most holy and godly, and in the which due discipline with seueritie was vsed against the wicked, open offenders were not suffered once to enter into the house of the Lord, nor admitted to common prayer, and the vse of the holy Sacraments with other true Christians, vntill they had done open penance before the whole Church.

The peoples fault was most grieuous: the sentence executed otherwise and more cruell then it should. He was only dehorted from receiuing the Sacrament, vntil by Repentance he might be better prepared. And this was practised, not onely vpon meane persons, but also vpon the rich, noble, and mighty persons, yea, vpon Theodosius that puissant and mighty Emperour, whom for committing a grieuous and wilfull murder, S. Ambrose Bishop of Millaine reprooued sharpely, and did also excommunicate the sayd Emperour, and brought him to open penance. And they that were so iustly exempted and banished (as it were) from the house of the Lord, were taken (as they be indeede) for men deuided & separated from Christes Church, and in most dangerous estate, yea as S. Paul saith, euen giuen vnto Satan the deuill for a time (1 Corinthians 5.5), and their company was shunned & auoyded of all godly men and women, vntill such time as they by repentance & publike penance were reconciled. Such was the honour of the Lords house in mens hearts, and outward reuerence also at that time, and so horrible a thing was it to bee shut out of the Church and house of the Lord in those dayes, when religion was most pure, and nothing so corrupt as it hath beene of late dayes. And yet wee willingly, either by absenting our selues from the house of the Lord, doe (as it were) excommunicate our selues from the Church and fellowship of the Saintes of GOD, or else comming thither, by vncomely and vnreuerent behauiour there, by hastie, rash, yea vncleane and wicked thoughts and wordes before the Lord our GOD, horribly dishonour his holy house the Church of GOD, and his holy Name and Maiestie, to the great danger of our soules, yea and certaine damnation also, if we do not speedily and earnestly repent vs of this wickednesse.

Thus ye haue heard (dearely beloued) out of GODS word, what reuerence is due to the holy house of the Lord, how all godly persons ought with diligence at times appointed thither to repayre, how they ought to behaue themselues there, with reuerence and dread before the Lord, what plagues and punishments, aswell temporall, as eternall, the Lord in his holy word threatneth, as well to such as neglect to come to his holy house, as also to such, who comming thither, doe vnreuerently by gesture or talke there behaue themselues. Wherefore if wee desire to haue seasonable weather, and thereby to enioy the good fruites of the earth, if wee will auoyd drought and barrennesse, thirste and hunger, which are plagues threatned vnto such as make haste to goe to their owne houses, to alehouses and tauerns, and leaue the house of the Lord empty and desolate, if wee abhorre to bee scourged, not with whips made of cordes, out of the materiall Temple onely (as our Sauiour Christ serued the defilers of the house of GOD in Hierusalem) but also to bee beaten and driuen out of the eternall temple and house of the Lord (which is his heauenly kingdome) with the yron rodde of euer lasting damnation, and cast into vtter darkenesse, where is weeping and gnashing of teeth, if we feare, dread and abhorre this (I say) as wee haue most iust cause to doe: then let vs amend this our negligence and contempt in comming to the house of the Lord, this our vnreuerent behauiour in the house of the Lord, and resorting thither diligently together, let vs there with reuerent hearing of the Lords holy word, calling on the Lords holy Name, giuing of hearty thankes vnto the Lord for his manifold and inestimable benefits dayly and hourely bestowed vpon vs, celebrating also reuerently the Lords holy Sacraments, serue the Lord in his holy house, as becommeth the seruants of the Lord, in holinesse and righteousnesse before him all the dayes of our life, and then we shall bee assured, after this life, to rest in his holy hill, and to dwell in his Tabernacle, there to prayse and magnifie his holy Name in the congregation of his Saints, in the holy house of his eternall kingdome of heauen, which hee hath purchased for vs, by the death and shedding of the precious blood of his Sonne our Sauiour Iesus Christ, to whom with the Father and the Holy Ghost, one immortall GOD, bee all honour, glory, praise, and thankesgiuing, world without end. Amen.

HOMILY AGAINST PERIL OF IDOLATRY

AN HOMILIE AGAINST
perill of Idolatrie, and superfluous decking
of Churches.

The first part. IN what points the true ornaments of the Church or Temple of GOD do consist and stand, hath beene declared in the two last Homilies, entreating of the right vse of the Temple or house of GOD, and of the due reuerence that all true Christian people are bound to giue vnto the same. The summe whereof is, that the Church or house of GOD, is a place appointed by the holy Scriptures, where the liuely word of GOD ought to bee read, taught, and heard, the Lords holy name called vpon by publike prayer, hearty thankes giuen to his Maiestie for his infinite and vnspeakable benefits bestowed vpon vs, his holy Sacraments duely and reuerently ministred, and that therefore all that be godly indeed, ought both with diligence at times appointed, to repayre together to the sayd Church, and there with all reuerence to vse and behaue themselues before the Lord. And that the sayd Church thus godly vsed by the seruants of the Lord, in the Lords true seruice, for the effectuall presence of GODS grace, wherewith he doeth by his holy word and promises, endue his people there present and assembled, to the attainement, aswell of commodities worldly, necessary for vs, as also of all heauenly gifts, and life euerlasting, is called by the word of GOD (as it is indeed) the Temple of the Lord, and the house of GOD, and that therefore the due reuerence thereof, is stirred vp in the hearts of the godly, by the consideration of these true ornaments of the sayd house of GOD, and not by any outward ceremonies or costly and glorious decking of the sayd house or Temple of the Lord, contrary to the which most manifest doctrine of the Scriptures, and contrary to the vsage of the Primitiue Church, which was most pure and vncorrupt, and contrary to the sentences and iudgements of the most ancient, learned and godly Doctours of the Church (as heereafter shall appeare) the corruption of these latter dayes, hath brought into the Church infinite multitudes of images, and the same, with other parts of the Temple also, haue decked with gold and siluer, painted with colours, set them with stone and pearle, clothed them with silkes and precious vestures, fancying vntruely that to be the chiefe decking and adorning of the Temple or house of GOD, and that all people should bee the more mooued to the due reuerence of the same, if all corners thereof were glorious, and glistering with gold and precious stones. Whereas indeed they by the sayd images, and such glorious decking of the Temple, haue nothing at all profited such as were wise and of vnderstanding: but haue thereby greatly hurt the simple and vnwise, occasioning them thereby to commit most horrible idolatrie. And the couetous persons, by the same occasion, seeming to worship, and peraduenture worshipping indeed, not onely the images, but also the matter of them, gold and siluer, as that vice is of all others in the Scriptures peculiarly called idolatrie or worshipping of images (Ephesians 5.5, Colossians 3.5). Against the which foule abuses and great enormities shall be alleadged vnto you: First, the authority of GODS holy word, aswell out of the old Testament, as of the new. And secondly, the testimonies of the holy and ancient learned Fathers and Doctours, out of their owne workes and ancient histories Ecclesiasticall, both that you may at once know their iudgements, and withall vnderstand what maner of ornaments were in the Temples in the Primitiue Church in those times, which were most pure and syncere. Thirdly, the reasons and arguments made for the defence of images or idols, and the outragious decking of Temples and Churches, with gold, siluer, pearle, and precious stone, shall be confuted, and so this whole matter concluded. But lest any should take occasion by the way, of doubting by wordes or names, it is thought good heere to note first of all, that although in common speech we vse to call the likenesse or similitudes of men or other things images, and not idols: yet the Scriptures vse the sayd two words (idols and images) indifferently for one thing alway. They be words of diuers tongues and sounds, but one in sense and signification in the Scriptures. The one is taken of the Greeke word (ed. note: probably *eikwn*), an Idol, and the other of the Latine word *Imago*, an Image, and so both vsed as English termes in the translating of Scriptures indifferently, according as the Septuaginta haue in their translation in Greeke, (ed. note: probably *eidwlon*), and S. Ierome in his translation of the same places in Latin hath *Simulachra*, in English, Images. And in the new Testament, that which S. Iohn calleth *eidwlon*, S. Ierome likewise translateth *Simulachrum*, as in all other like places of Scripture vsually hee doeth so translate (1 John 5.21). And S. Ierome, a most ancient Doctor, and well learned in both the tongues, Greeke and Latine, interpreting this place of S. Iohn, Beware of Idols, that is to say (sayth S. Ierome) of the images themselues: the Latin words which he vseth, be *Effigies* and *Imago*, to say, an Image (S. Ierome, Liber de Corona Militis). And therefore it skilleth not, whether in this processe wee vse the one terme or the other, or both together, seeing they both (though not in common English speech, yet in Scripture) signifie one thing. And though some to blinde mens eyes, haue heretofore craftily gone about to make them to be taken for words of diuers signification in matters of Religion, and haue therefore vsually named the likenesse or similitude of a thing set vp amongst the Heathen in their Temples or other places to bee worshipped, an Idoll. But the like similitude with vs, set vp in the Church, the place of worshipping, they call an Image, as though these two words (Idoll and Image) in Scripture, did differ in proprietie and sense, which as is aforesaid) differ onely in sound and language, and in meaning bee in deed all one, specially in the Scriptures and matters of Religion. And our Images also haue beene, and bee, and if they bee publikely suffered in Churches and Temples, euer will bee also worshipped, and so Idolatrie committed to them, as in the last part of this Homilie shall at large bee declared and prooued. Wherefore our Images in Temples and Churches, bee in deed none other but Idoles, as vnto the which Idolatrie hath beene, is, and euer will be committed.

And first of all, the Scriptures of the olde Testament, condemning and abhorring aswell all Idolatrie or worshipping of Images, as also the very Idoles or Images themselues, specially in Temples, are so many and plentifull; that it weere almost an infinite worke, and to bee conteined in no small volume, to record all the places concerning the same. For when GOD had chosen to himselfe a peculiar and speciall people from amongst all other Nations that knew not GOD, but worshipped Idols and false gods, he gaue vnto them certaine ordinances and Lawes to bee kept and obserued of his said people. But concerning none other matter did hee giue either moe, or more earnest and expresse Lawes to his said people, then those that concerned the true worshipping of him, and the auoyding and fleeing of Idols and

Images, and Idolatrie: for that, both the said Idolatrie is most repugnant to the right worshipping of him and his true glorie, aboue all other vices, and that hee knew the pronenesse and inclination of mans corrupt kinde and nature, to that most odious and abominable vice. Of the which ordinances and Lawes, so giuen by the Lord to his people concerning that matter, I will rehearse and alleadge some that bee most speciall for this purpose, that you by them may iudge of the rest.

In the fourth Chapter of the Booke named, is a notable place, and most worthy with all diligence to be marked, which beginneth thus: And now Israel heare the Commandements and Iudgements which I teach thee (saith the Lord) that thou doing them, maist liue, and enter and possesse the land which the Lord GOD of your Fathers will giue you. Yee shall put nothing to the word which I speake to you, neither shall ye take any thing from it. Keepe yee the Commandements of the Lord your GOD, which I commaund you (Deuteronomy 4.1-2, Numbers 22.18, 35, 38). And by and by after hee repeateth the same sentence three or foure times, before hee come to the matter that hee would speacially warne them of, as it were for a Preface, to make them to take the better heed vnto it. Take heed to thy selfe (saith he) and to thy soule, with all carefulnesse, lest thou forgettest the things which thine eyes haue seene, and that they goe not out of thine heart all the dayes of thy life, thou shalt teach them to thy children and nephewes, or posteritie. And shortly after, The Lord spake vnto you out of the middle of fire, but you heard the voyce or sound of his words, but you did see no forme or shape at all. And by and by followeth, Take heed therefore diligently vnto your soules, you saw no manner of Image in the day in the which the Lord spake vnto you in Horeb, out of the middest of the fire, lest peraduenture, you being deceiued, should make to your selues any grauen Image, or likenesse of man or woman, or the likenesse of any beast which is vpon the earth, or of the birds that flee vnder heauen, or of any creeping thing that is mooued on the earth, or of the fishes that doe continue in the waters: least peraduenture thou lifting vp thine eyes to heauen, doe see the Sunne and the Moone, and the Starres of heauen, and so thou, being deceiued by errour, shouldest honour, and worship them which the Lord thy GOD hath created to serue all Nations that be vnder heauen. And againe: Beware that thou forget not the couenant of the Lord thy GOD, which hee made with thee, and so make to thy selfe any carued Image of them which the Lord hath forbidden to bee made: for the Lord thy GOD is a consuming fire, and a iealous GOD.

If thou haue children and nephewes, and doe tarry in the land, and being deceiued doe make to your selues and similitude, doing euill before the Lord your GOD, and prouoke him to anger: I doe this day call vpon heauen and earth to witnesse, that ye shall quickly perish out of hte land which you shall possesse, you shall not dwell in it any long time, but the Lord will destroy you, and will scatter you amongst all Nations, and ye shall remaine but a very few amongst the Nations, whither the Lord will leade you away, and then shall you serue gods which are made with mans hands, of wood and stone, which see not, and heare not, neither eat nor smell, and so foorth. This is a notable chapter, and entreateth almost altogether of this matter. But because it is too long to write out the whole, I haue noted you certaine principall points out of it. First, how earnestly and oft he calleth vpon them to marke and to take heed, and that vpon the perill of their soules, to the charge which he giueth them. Then how he forbiddeth by a solemne and long rehearsall of all things in heauen, in earth, and in the water, any Image or likenesse of any thing at all to be made. Thirdly, what penaltie and horrible destruction, he solemnely, with inuocation of heauen and earth, for record, denounceth and threatneth to them, their children and posteritie, if they contrary to this Commandement, do make or worship any Images or similitude, which he so straightly hath forbidden. And when they, this notwithstanding, partly by inclination of mans corrupt nature most prone to Idolatry, and partly occasioned by the Gentiles and heathen people dwelling about them, who were Idolaters, did fall to the making and worshipping of Images: GOD according to his word, brought vpon them all those plagues which hee threatned them with, as appeareth in the bookes of the Kings and the Chronicles, in sundry places at large. And agreeable hereunto are many other notable places in the old Testament, (Deuteronomy 27) "Cursed be he that maketh a carued Image, or a cast or molten Image, which is abomination before the Lord, the worke of the artificers hand, and setteth it vp in a secret corner, and all the people shall say, Amen."

Read the thirteene and fourteene Chapters of the booke of Wisedome, concerning Idoles or Images, how they be made, set vp, called vpon, and offered vnto, and how he praiseth the tree whereof the gibbet is made, as happy, in comparison to the tree that an Image or Idoll is made of, euen by these very words, Happy is the tree wherethrough righteousnesse commeth, (meaning the gibbet) but cursed is the Idoll that is made with hands, yea, both it, and hee that made it, and so foorth (Apocrypha. Wisdom 14.7-8). And by and by hee sheweth how that the things which were the good creatures of GOD before (as Trees or Stones) when they be once altered and fashioned into Images to bee worshipped, become abomination, a temptation vnto the soules of men, and a snare for the feet of the vnwise. And why? the seeking out of Images, is the beginning of whoredome (sayth hee) and the bringing vp of them, is the destruction of life: for they were not from the beginning, neither shall they continue for euer. The wealthy idlenes of men hath found them out vpon earth, therefore shall they come shortly to an end: and so foorth to the end of the Chapter, conteining these points, Now Idoles or Images were first inuented, and offered vnto, how by an vngracious custome they were established, how tyrants compell men to worship them, how the ignorant and the common people are deceiued by the cunning of the workeman, and the beautie of the Image, to doe honour vnto it, and so to erre from the knowledge of GOD, and of other great and many mischiefes that come by Images. And for a conclusion hee saith, that the honouring of abominable Images, is the cause, the beginning, and end of all euill, and that the worshippers of them be either mad, or most wicked. See and view the whole Chapter with diligence, for it is worthy to be well considered, specially that is written of the deceauing of the simple and vnwise common people by Idols and Images, and repeated twise or thrise lest it should be forgotten. And in the Chapter following be these words: The painting of the picture and carued Image with diuers colours, entiseth the ignorant so, that he honoureth and loueth the picture of a dead image that hath no soule (Apocrypha. Wisdom 15.4-5). Neuerthelesse, they that loue such euill things, they that trust in them, they that make them, they that fauour them, and they that honour them, are all worthy of death, and so foorth.

In the booke of Psalmes, the Prophet curseth the Image honourers, in diuers places. Confounded be all they that worship carued Images, and that delight or glory in them (Psalms 97.7, 96.5, 115.8). Like bee they vnto the Images that make them, and all they that put their trust in them (Psalms 135.15, 18). And in the Prophet Esai, sayth the Lord: Euen I am the Lord, and this is my Name, and my glory will I giue to none other, neither my honour to grauen Images (Isaiah 42.8). And by and by: Let them bee confounded with shame that trust in Idoles or Images, or say to them, you are our GODS, And in the xl. Chapter after he hath set foorth the incomprehensible Maiestie of GOD, he asketh, To whom then will yee make GOD like? Or what similitude will yee set vp vnto him (Isaiah 40.18)? Shall the caruer make him a carued Image? and shall the Goldsmith couer him with gold, and cast him into a forme of siluer plates? And for the poore man, shall the Image maker frame an Image of timber, that hee may haue somewhat to set vp also? And after this he cryeth out: O wretches, heard ye neuer of this? Hath it not beene preached vnto you since the beginning, and so foorth, how by the Creation of the world, and the greatnesse of the worke, they might vnderstand the Maiestie of GOD, the the Creatour and maker of all, to be greater then that it should be expressed, or set forth in any Image or bodily similitude? And besides this preaching, euen in the law of GOD written with his owne finger (as the Scripture speaketh) and that in the first Table, and the beginning thereof, is this doctrine aforesaid against Images (not briefly touched) but at large set foorth and preached, and that with denunciation of destruction to the contemners and breakers of this Law, and their posteritie after them (Exodus 20.4). And lest it should yet not be marked or not remembred, the same is written and reported not in one, but in sundry places of the Word of GOD, that by oft reading and hearing of it, wee might once learne and remember it, as you also heare daily read in the Church, GOD spake these words, and said, I am the Lord thy GOD. Thou shalt haue none other GODS but me. Thou shalt not make to thy selfe any grauen Image, nor the likenesse of any thing that is in Heauen aboue, nor in the Earth beneath, nor in the water vnder the Earth, Thou shalt not bowe downe to them, nor worship them: For I the Lord thy GOD am a iealous GOD, and visit the sinne of the fathers vpon the children, vnto the third and fourth generation of them that hate mee, and shew mercie vnto thousands in them that loue mee, and keepe my Commandements (Exodus 20.1-6, Leviticus 26.13, Deuteronomy 5.6-10). All this notwithstanding, neither could the notablenesse of the place, being the very beginning of the very louing Lords Law, make vs to marke it, nor the plaine declaration by recounting of all kind of similitudes, cause vs to vnderstand it, nor the oft repeating and reporting of it in diuers and sundry places, the oft reading and hearing of it, could cause vs to remember it, nor the dread of the horrible penaltie to our selues, our children, and posterity after vs, feare vs from transgressing of it, nor the greatnesse of the rewarde to vs and our children after vs, mooue vs any thing to obedience, and the obseruing of this the Lords great Law: But as though it had beene written in some corner, and not at large expressed, but briefely and obscurely touched, as though no penalty to the transgressours, nor reward to the obedient, had beene adioyned vnto it, like blind men without all knowledge and vnderstanding, like vnreasonable beastes, without dread of punishment or respect of reward, haue diminished and dishonoured the high Maiestie of the liuing GOD, by the basenesse and vilenesse of sundry and diuers images of dead stockes, stones, and metals.

Places of the Scripture against idoles or images. And as the Maiestie of GOD, whom we haue left, forsaken, and dishonoured, and therefore the greatnesse of our sinne and offence against his Maiestie, cannot bee expressed: So is the weakenesse, vilenesse, and foolishnesse, in deuice of the images (whereby wee haue dishonoured him) expressed at large in the Scriptures, namely the Psalmes, the booke of Wisedome, the Prophet Esaias, Ezekiel, and Baruch, specially in these places and Chapters of them: Psalms 115.8, 135.15, Apocrypha: Wisdom 13, 14, 15, Isaiah 40.18, 44.9, and Ezekiel 6.13. The which places, as I exhort you often and diligently to reade, so are they too long at this present to be rehearsed in an Homilie. Notwithstanding, I will make you certaine briefe or short notes out of them, what they say of these idoles or images. First, that they bee made but of small pieces of wood, stone, or mettall, and therefore they cannot be any similitudes of the great Maiestie of GOD, whose seate is heauen, and the earth his footestoole. Secondarily, that they bee dead, haue eyes and see not, hands and feele not, feete and cannot goe, & c. and therefore they cannot be fit similitudes of the liuing GOD. Thirdly, that they haue no power to doe good nor harme to others, though some of them haue an axe, some a sword, some a speare in their hands, yet doe theeues come into their Temples and robbe them, and they cannot once sturre to defend themselues from the thieues: nay, if the Temple or Church bee set afire, that their Priests can run away and saue themselues, but they cannot once mooue, but tary still like blockes as they are, and be burned, and therefore they can bee no meete figures of the puissant and mighty GOD, who alone is able both to saue his seruants, and to destroy his enemies euerlastingly. They bee trimly deckt in Golde, Siluer, and Stone, aswell the images of men, as of women, like wanton wenches (sayth the Prophet Baruch) that loue paramours, and therefore can they not teach vs, nor our wiues and daughters any sobernesse, modestie, and chastitie (Ezekiel 6.9-11). And therefore although it is now commonly sayd that they be the lay mens bookes, yet wee see they teach no good lesson, neither of GOD, nor godlinesse, but all errour and wickednesse. Therefore GOD by his word, as he forbiddeth any idoles or images to bee made or set vp: so doeth hee commaund such as wee finde made and set vp to bee pulled downe, broken, and destroyed.

And it is written in the booke of Numbers, the xxiii. Chapter, that there was no idole in Iacob, nor there was no image seene in Israel, and that the Lord GOD was with the people (Numbers 23.21, ed. note: the Hebrew word *'aven* means both trouble/sorrow and idolatry). Where note, that the true Israelites, that is, the people of GOD, haue no images among them, but that GOD was with them, and that therefore their enemies cannot hurt them, as appeareth in the processe of that Chapter. And as concerning Images already set vp, thus saith the Lord in Deuteronomie. Ouerturne their altars, and breake them to pieces, cut downe their groues, burne their images: for thou art an holy people vnto the Lord (Deuteronomy 7.5, 12.2-3). And the same is repeated more vehemently againe in the twelfth Chapter of the same booke. Here not, what the people of GOD ought to doe to images, where they finde them. But lest any priuate persons, vpon colour of destroying images, should make any stirre or disturbance in the common wealth, it must alwayes be remembred, that the redresse of such publique enormities perteineth to the Magistrates, and such as be in authoritie onely, and not to priuate persons, and therefore the good Kings of Iuda, Asa, Ezechias, Iosaphat, and Iosias, are highly commended for the breaking downe and destroying of the altars, idoles, and images. And the Scriptures declare that they, specially in that point, did that which was right before the Lord. And contrariwise, Hieroboam, Achab, Ioas, and other Princes, which either set vp, or suffered such altars or images vndestroyed, are by the word of GOD reported to haue done euill before the Lord (1 Kings 14.9, 2 Kings 13.11, 2 Chro.14, 15.31, 1 Kings 16.32). And if any, contrary to the commaundement of the Lord, will needes set vp such altars or images, or suffer them vndestroyed amongst them, the Lord himselfe threatneth in the first Chapter of the booke of Numbers, and by his holy Prophets, Ezechiel, Micheas, and Abacuc, that he will come himselfe and pull them downe. And how hee will handle, punish, and destroy the people that so set vp, or suffer such altars, images, or idoles vndestroyed, he denounceth by his Prophet Ezechiel on this manner:

> I my selfe (sayth the Lord) will bring a sward ouer you, to destroy your high places, I will cast downe your altars, and breake downe your images, your slaine men will I lay before your gods, and the dead carkases of the

> children of Israel will I cast before their idoles, your bones will I straw round about your altars and dwelling places, your Cities shall bee desolate, the hill Chappels layd waste, your altars destroyed and broken, your gods cast downe and taken away, your Temples layd euen with the ground, your owne workes cleane rooted out, your slayne men shall lye amongst you, that yee may learne to know how that I am the Lord (Ezekiel 6.3-7).

and so foorth to the Chapters ende, worthy with diligence to be read: that they that be neare, shall perish with the sword, they that bee farre off, with the pestilence, they that flee into holds or wildernesse, with hunger: and if any be yet left, that they shalbe caryed away prisoners to seruitude and bondage. So that if either the multitude, or plainnesse of the places might make vs to vnderstand, or the earnest charge that GOD giueth in the sayd places mooue vs to regard, or the horrible plagues, punishments, and dreadfull destruction, threatned to such worshippers of images or idoles, setters vp, or maintainers of them, might ingender any feare in our hearts, wee would once leaue and forsake this wickednesse, being in the Lords sight so great an offence and abomination. Infinite places almost might bee brought out of the Scriptures of the olde Testament concerning this matter, but these few at this time shall serue for all.

You will say peraduenture these things pertaine to the Iewes, what haue wee to doe with them? Indeed they pertaine no lesse to vs Christians, then to them. For if we be the people of GOD, how can the Word and Law of GOD not appertaine to vs? Saint Paul alleadging one text out of the old Testament, concludeth generally for other Scriptures of the old Testament as well as that, saying, Whatsoeuer is written before (meaning in the old Testament) is written for our instruction (Romans 15.4): which sentence is most specially true of such writings of the old Testament, as containe the immutable law and ordinances of GOD, in no age or time to be altered, nor of any persons of any nations or age to bee disobeyed, such as the aboue rehearsed places be. Notwithstanding, for your further satisfying herein, according to my promise, I will out of the Scriptures of the new Testament or Gospel of our Sauiour Christ, likewise make a confirmation of the said doctrine against Idoles or Images, and of our duetie concerning the same. First the Scriptures of the new Testament doe in sundry places make mention with reioycing, as for a most excellent benefit and gift of GOD, that they which receiued the Faith of Christ, were turned from their dumbe and dead Images, vnto the true and liuing GOD, who is to be blessed for euer: namely in these places, the xiiii. and xvii. of the Acts of the Apostles, the eleuenth to the Romanes, the first Epistle to the Corinthians, the twelfth Chapter, to the Galathians, the fourth, and the first to the Thessalonians the first Chapter.

And in likewise the said is Idoles, Images, and worshipping of them, are in the Scriptures of the new Testament by the spirit of GOD much abhorred and detested, and earnestly forbidden, as appeareth both in the forenamed places, and also many other besides, as in the seuen, and fifteenth of the Actes of the Apostles, the first to the Romanes, where is set foorth the horrible plague of Idolaters, giuen ouer by GOD into a reprobate sense to worke all wickednes and abominations not to be spoken, as vsually spirituall and carnall Fornication goe together.

In the first Epistle to the Corinthians the fifth Chapter, we are forbidden once to keepe company, or to eate and drinke with such as bee called brethren or Christians that doe worship Images. In Galatians 5.20, the worshipping of Images is numbred amongst the workes of the flesh. and in 1 Corinthians 10.19-20, it is called the seruice of deuils, and that such as vse it, shall be destroyed. And in 1 Corinthians 6.9, and Galatians 5.20-21, is denounced, that such Image worshippers shall neuer come into the inheritance of the Kingdome of heauen. And in sundry other places is threatned, that the wrath of GOD shall come vpon all such. And therefore Saint Iohn in 1 John 5.21 exhorteth vs as his deare children to beware of Images. And Saint Paul warneth vs to flee from the worshipping of them, if we be wise, that is to say, if wee care for health, and feare destruction, if we regard the Kingdome of GOD and life euerlasting, and dread the wrath of GOD, and euerlasting damnation (1 Corinthians 10.14). For it is not possible that wee should be worshippers of Images, and the true seruants of GOD also, as S. Paul teacheth, in 2 Corinthians 6.16, affirming expressely that there can bee no more consent or agreement betweene the Temple of GOD (which all true Christians be) and Images, then betweene righteousnesse and vnrighteousnesse, betweene light and darkenesse, betweene the faithfull and the vnfaithfull, or betweene Christ and the deuill. Which place enforceth both that wee should not worship Images, and that we should not haue Images in the Temple, for feare and occasion of worshipping them, though they be of themselues things indifferent: for the Christian is the holy Temple and liuely Image of GOD, as the place well declareth, to such as will reade and weigh it. And whereas all godly men did euer abhorre that any kneeling and worshipping or offering should bee vsed to themselues when they were aliue (for that it was the honour due to GOD only) as appeareth in the Acts of the Apostles by S. Peter forbidding it to Cornelius (Acts 10.25-26), and by S. Paul and Barnabas forbidding the same to the Citizens in Lystra (Acts 14.14-15): Yet wee like madde men fall downe before the dead idols or images of Peter and Paul, and giue that honour to stockes and stones, which they thought abominable to be giuen to themselues being aliue. And the good Angel of GOD, as appeareth in the booke of S. Iohns Reuelation, refused to bee kneeled vnto, when that honour was offered him of Iohn: Beware (sayth the Angel) that thou doe it not, for I am thy fellow seruant. But the euill angel Satan, desireth nothing so much as to bee kneeled vnto, and thereby at once both to robbe GOD of his due honour, and to worke the damnation of such as make him so low curtesie, as in the story of the Gospel appeareth in sundry places. Yea, and hee offered our Sauiour Christ all earthly goods, on the condition that he would kneele down & worship him (Matthew 4.9, Luke 4.7). But our Sauiour repelleth Satan by the Scriptures, saying, It is written, thou shalt worship thy Lord GOD, and him alone shalt thou serue. But we by not worshipping and seruing GOD alone (as the Scriptures teach vs) and by worshipping of images, contrary to the Scriptures, plucke Satan to vs, and are ready without reward to follow his desire: yea, rather then fayle, wee will offer him gifts and oblations to receiue our seruice. But let vs brethren, rather follow the counsell of the good Angel of GOD, then the suggestion of subtill Satan, that wicked angel and old Serpent: Who according to the pride whereby hee first fell, attempteth alway by such sacriledge to depriue GOD (whom he enuieth) of his due honour: and (because his owne face is horrible and vgly) to conuey it to himselfe by the mediation of gilt stockes and stones, and withall to make vs the enemies of GOD, and his own suppliants and slaues, and in the end to procure vs for a reward, euerlasting destruction and damnation. Therefore aboue all things, if wee take our selues to be Christians indeed (as we be named) let vs credit the word, obey the law, and follow the doctrine and example of our Sauiour and master Christ, repelling Satans suggestion to idolatrie, and worshipping of Images, according to the trueth alleadged and taught out of the Testament and Gospel of our sayd heauenly Doctour and Schoolemaster Iesus Christ, who is GOD to be blessed for euer, AMEN.

THE SECOND PART OF THE HOMILIE AGAINST PERILL OF IDOLATRY.

YOU haue heard (welbeloued) in the first part of this Homilie, the doctrine of the word of GOD against idols and images, against Idolatrie, and worshipping of images, taken out of the Scriptures of the old Testament & the New, & confirmed by the examples as well of the Apostles as of our Sauiour Christ himselfe. Now although our Sauiour Christ taketh not, or needeth not any testimony of men, and that which is once confirmed by the certainty of his eternall trueth, hath no more need of the confirmation of mans doctrine and writings, then the bright sunne at noonetide hath neede of the light of a little candle to put away darkenesse, and to increase his light: yet for your further contentation, it shall in this second part bee declared (as in the beginning of the first part was promised) that this trueth and doctrine concerning the forbidding of images and worshipping of them, taken out of the holy Scriptures, aswell of the old Testament as the new, was beleeued and taught of the old holy Fathers, and most ancient learned Doctours, and receiued in the old Primitiue Church, which was most vncorrupt and pure. And this declaration shall bee made out of the sayd holy Doctours owne writings, and out of the ancient histories Ecclesiasticall to the same belonging.

S. Ierome, a most ancient Writer and Doctour of the Church, who liued about one hundred and threescore yeeres after the death of our Sauiour Christ, both in sundry other places of his workes, and specially in his booke written against the maner of crowning, and in another little treatise entituled, Of the souldiers crowne or garland, doth most sharply and vehemently write and inueygh against images or idols (S. Ierome, Liber contra Coronandi Morem). And vpon S. Iohns words, the first Epistle and fifth Chapter, sayth thus, S. Iohn (sayth hee) deepely considering the matter, sayth: My little children, keepe your selues from images or idols (1 John 5.21). Hee sayth not now, keepe your selues from idolatrie, as it were from the seruice and worshipping of them: but from the images or idols themselues, that is, from the very shape and likenesse of them. For it were an vnworthy thing, that the image of the liuing GOD should become the image of a dead idoll. Doe you not thinke those persons which place images and idols in Churches and Temples, yea shrine them euen ouer the Lords table, euen as it were of purpose to the worshipping and honoring of them, take good heed to either of S. Iohns counsell, or S. Ieromes? For so to place images and idols is it to keepe themselues from them, or else to receiue and embrace them. Origenes in his booke against Celsus, sayth thus: Christian men and Iewes, when they heare these words of the Law (Thou shalt feare the Lord thy GOD, and shalt not make any image) doe not onely abhorre the Temples, Altars, and Images of the gods, but if need be, will rather die then they should defile themselues with any impiety. And shortly after he sayth: In the common wealth of the Iewes, the caruer of idols and image maker, was cast farre off and forbidden, lest they should haue any occasion to make images, which might plucke certain foolish persons from GOD, and turne the eyes of their soules to the contemplation of earthly things. And in another place of the same booke: It is not onely (sayth he) a mad and franticke part to worship images, but also once to dissemble or winke at it. And a man may know GOD and his onely son, and those which haue had such honour giuen them by GOD, that they be called gods: But it is not possible that any should by worshipping of images get any knowledge of GOD.

Athanasius in his booke against the Gentiles, hath these words: Let them tell, I pray you, how GOD may be knowen by an image. If it be by the matter of an image, then there needeth no shape or forme, seeing that GOD hath appeared in all materiall creatures which do testifie his glory. Now if they say he is knowen by the forme or fashion: Is he not better to be knowen by the liuing things themselues, whose fashions the images expresse? For of surety, the glory of GOD should bee more euidently knowen, if it were declared by reasonable and liuing creatures, rather then by dead and vnmooueable images. Therefore when yee doe graue or paint images, to the end to know GOD thereby, surely ye doe an vnworthy and vnfit thing. And in another place of the same booke he sayth, The inuention of images came of no good, but of euill, and whatsoeuer hath an euill beginning, can neuer in any thing bee iudged good, seeing it is altogether naught. Thus farre Athanasius, a very ancient, holy, and learned Bishop and Doctour, who iudgeth both the first beginning and the end, and altogether of images or idols, to be naught.

Lactantius likewise, an olde and learned writer, in his booke of the Origine of errour, hath these wordes, GOD is aboue man, and is not placed beneath, but is to bee sought in the highest region. Wherefore there is no doubt, but that no religion is in that place wheresoeuer any image is: For if religion stand in godly things, (and there is no godlinesse but in heauenly things) then be images without religion. These be Lactantius wordes, who was aboue xiii. hundred yeeres ago, and within three hundreth yeeres after our Sauiour Christ (Lactantius, Of the Origin of Error, Bk. 2, Chap. 16).

Cyrillus, an old and holy doctour, vpon the Gospel of Saint Iohn hath these wordes, Many haue left the creatour, and haue worshipped the creature, neither haue they beene abashed to say vnto a stocke: Thou art my father, and vnto a stone, Thou begottest me. For many, yea, almost all (alasse for sorrow) are fallen vnto such folly, that they haue giuen the glory of deity or Godhead, to things without sense or feeling.

Epiphanius Bishop of Salamine in Ciprus, a very holy and learned man, who liued in Theodosius the Emperours time, about three hundred and ninetie yeeres after our Sauiour Christs ascension, writeth this to Iohn Patriarch of Hierusalem: I entred (sayth Epiphanius) into a certaine Church to pray: I found there a linnen cloth hanging in the Church doore, paynted, and hauing in it the image of Christ, as it were, or of some other Saint, (for I remember not well whose image it was) therefore when I did see the image of a man hanging in the Church of Christ, contrary to the authoritie of the Scriptures, I did teare it, and gaue counsell to the keepers of the Church, that they should wind a poore man that was dead in the sayd cloth, and to bury him.

And afterwards the same Epiphanius sending another vnpaynted cloth, for that paynted one which hee had torne, to the sayd Patriarch, writeth thus, I pray you will the Elders of that place to receiue this cloth which I haue sent by this bearer, and commaund them that from hencefoorth no such painted clothes contrary to our religion, be hanged in the Church of Christ . For it becommeth your goodnesse rather to haue this care, that you take away such scrupulositie, which is vnfitting for the Church of Christ, and offensiue to the people committed to your charge. And this Epistle, as worthy to be read of many, did S. Ierome himselfe translate into the Latine tongue.

<u>All notable Bishops were then called Popes.</u> And that ye may know that S. Ierome had this holy and learned Bishop Epiphanius in most high estimation, and therefore did translate this Epistle, as a writing of authoritie: heare what a testimonie the said S. Ierome giueth him

in another place, in his Treatie against the errours of Iohn Bishop of Hierusalem, where hee hath these wordes: Thou hast (sayth Saint Ierome) Pope Epiphanius, which doeth openly in his letters call thee an heretike. Surely thou art not to be preferred before him, neither for age nor learning, nor godlinesse of life, nor by the testimonie of the whole world. And shortly after in the same treatie saith S. Ierome: Bishop Epiphanius was euer of so great veneration and estimation, that Valens the Emperour, who was a great persecutour, did not once touch him. For heretikes, being princes, thought it their shame if they should persecute such a notable man. And in the tripartite Ecclesiasticall historie, the ninth booke and xlviii. Chapter, is testified, that Epiphanius being yet aliue did worke miracles, and that after his death deuils, being expelled at his graue or tombe, did roare. Thus you see what authoritie S. Ierome and that most ancient historie giue vnto the holy and learned Bishop Epiphanius, whose iudgement of images in Churches and Temples, then beginning by stealth to creepe in, is worthy to be noted.

First, hee iudged it contrary to Christian religion and the authoritie of the Scriptures, to haue any images in Christs Church. Secondly, hee reiected not onely carued, grauen, and moulten images, but also paynted images, out of Christs Church. Thirdly, that hee regarded not whether it were the image of Christ, or of any other Saint, but being an image, would not suffer it in the Church. Fourthly, that hee did not onely remooue it out of the Church, but with a vehement zeale tare it in sunder and exhorted that a corse should bee wrapped and buried in it, iudging it meete for nothing but to rotte in the earth, following herein the example of the good king Ezechias, who brake the brasen Serpent to pieces, and burned it to ashes, for that idolatrie was committed to it. Last of all, that Epiphanius thinketh it the duetie of vigilant Bishops, to bee carefull that no images be permitted in the Church, for that they be occasion of scruple and offence to the people committed to their charge. Now whereas neither S. Ierome, who did translate the same Epistle, nor the authours of that most ancient historie Ecclesiasticall tripartite (who doe most highly commend Epiphanius, as is aforesayd) nor any other godly or learned Bishoppe at that time, or shortly after, haue written any thing against Epiphanius iudgement concerning images: it is an euident proofe, that in those dayes, which were about foure hundred yeeres after our Sauiour Christ, there were no images publiquely vsed and receiued in the Church of Christ, which was then much lesse corrupt, and more pure then now it is.

And whereas Images beganne at that time secretly and by stealth to creepe out of priuate mens houses into the Churches, and that first in paynted clothes and walles, such Byshops as were godly and vigilant, when they spyed them, remooued them away, as vnlawfull and contrary to Christian religion, as did heere Epiphanius, to whose iudgement you haue not onely Saint Ierome the translatour of his Epistle, and the writer of the historie tripartite, but also all the learned and godly Clarkes, yea and the whole Church of that age, and so vpward to our Sauiour Christes time, by the space of about foure hundred yeeres, consenting and agreeing. This is written the more largely of Epiphanius, for that our image maynteiners now a dayes, seeing themselues so pressed with this most plaine and earnest act and writing of Epiphanius, a Bishop and Doctour of such antiquity, and authoritie, labour by all meanes (but in vaine against the trueth) either to proue that this Epistle was neither of Epiphanius writing, nor Saint Ieromes translation: either if it bee, say they, it is of no great force: for this Epiphanius, say they, was a Iew, and being conuerted to the Christian faith, and made a Bishop, reteined the hatred which Iewes haue to images still in his minde, and so did and wrote against them as a Iew, rather then as a Christian. O Iewish impudencie and malice of such deuisers, it would be prooued, and not sayd onely, that Epiphanius was a Iewe. Furthermore, concerning the reason they make, I would admitte it gladly. For if Epiphanius iudgement against Images is not to bee admitted, for that hee was borne of a Iewe an enemie to Images, which bee GODS enemies, conuerted to Christes religion, then likewise followeth it, that no sentence in the olde Doctours and Fathers sounding for Images, ought to be of any authority: for that in the primitiue Church the most part of learned writers, as S. Ierome, Cyprian, Ambrose, Austen, and infinite others more, were of Gentiles (which bee fauourers and worshippers of Images) conuerted to the Christian faith, and so let somewhat slippe out of their pennes, sounding for Images, rather as Gentiles then Christians, as Eusebius in his Historie Ecclesiasticall, and Saint Ierome sayth plainely, that Images came first from the Gentiles to vs Christians. And much more doeth it follow, that the opinion of all the rablement of the Popish Church, maintaining Images, ought to be esteemed of small or no authority, for that it is no maruell that they which haue from their childhoode beene brought vp amongest Images and Idoles, and haue drunke in idolatry almost with their mothers milke, hold with Images and Idols, and speake and write for them. But in deede it would not bee so much marked whether hee were of a Iewe or a Gentile conuerted vnto Christes Religion, that writeth, as how agreeable or contrarie to GODS word hee doeth write, and so to credite or discredite him. Now what GODS worde sayth of Idoles and Images, and the worshipping of them, you heard at large in the first part of this Homilie.

Saint Ambrose in his treatie of the death of Theodosius the Emperour, saith, Helene found the Crosse and the title on it. Shee worshipped the King, and not the wood surely (for that is an heathenish errour, and the vanitie of the wicked) but shee worshipped him that hanged on the Crosse, and whose name was written in the title, and so foorth. See both the godly Empresse fact, and Saint Ambrose iudgement at once: They thought it had beene an heathenish errour and vanitie of the wicked, to haue worshipped the Crosse it selfe which was embrewed with our Sauiour Christs owne pretious blood. And wee fall downe before euery Crosse peece of timber, which is but an Image of that Crosse.

Saint Augustine, the best learned of all ancient doctours, in his xliiii. Epistle to Maximus sayth, know thou that none of the dead, nor anie thing that is made of GOD, is worshipped as GOD of the Catholique Christians, of whom there is a Church also in your Towne. Note that by Saint Augustine, such as worshipped the dead, or creatures, be not Catholique Christians.

The same Saint Augustine teacheth in the xii. booke of the Citie of God, the tenth Chapter, that neither Temples or Churches ought to bee builded or made for Martyrs or Saints, but to GOD alone: and that there ought no Priestes to bee appointed for Martyr or Saint, but to GOD only. The same Saint Augustine in his booke of the maners of the Catholique Church, hath these wordes: I know that many bee worshippers of tombes and pictures, I know that there bee many that banquet most riotously ouer the graus of the dead, and giuing meat to dead carkases, doe burie themselues vpon the buried, and attribute their gluttonie and drunkennesse to religion. See, hee esteemeth worshipping of Saints tombes, and pictures, as good religion as gluttonie and drunkennesse, and no better at all. Saint Augustine greatly alloweth Marcus Varro, affirming that religion is most pure without images, and saith himselfe: images be of more force to crooken an vnhappy soule, then to teach and instruct it. And saith further: Euery childe, yea euery beast knoweth that it is not GOD that they see. Wherefore then doeth the holy Ghost so often monish vs of that which all men know? Whereunto Saint Augustine himselfe answereth thus (Augustine, Liber de Civi. Deim Chap. 43; Psalms 36 and 113). For (saith hee) when images are placed in Temples, and set in honourable sublimity and begin once to bee worshipped, foorthwith breedeth the most vile affection of errour. This is Saint Augustines iudgement of Images in Churches; that by and by they breed errour and idolatrie. It would be tedious to rehearse all other places, which might bee brought out of the ancient Doctours against Images and idolatrie. Wherefore wee shall holde our selues contented with these fewe at this present. Now as concerning histories Ecclesiasticall, touching this matter, that yee may know why and when, and by whom Images were first vsed priuately, and afterwardes not onely receiued into the Christians Churches and Temples, but in conclusion worshipped also, and how the same was gaine-said, resisted, and forbidden, aswell by godly Bishoppes and learned Doctours, as also by sundry Christian Princes: I will briefely collect into a compendious history, that which is at large and in sundry places written by diuerse ancient writers and historiographers concerning this matter.

As the Iewes, hauing most plaine and expresse commaundement of GOD, that they should neither make nor worshippe any Image (as it is at large before declared) did notwithstanding, by the example of the Gentiles or Heathen people that dwelt about them, fall to the making of Images, and worshipping of them, and so to the committing of most abominable idolatrie, for the which GOD by his holy Prophets doeth most sharpely reprooue and threaten them, and afterwarde did accomplish his sayd threatnings by extreame punishing of them (as is also aboue specified:) Euen so some of the Christians in olde time, which were conuerted from worshipping of Idoles and false Gods, vnto the true liuing GOD, and to our Sauiour Iesus Christ, did of a certaine blinde zeale (as men long accustomed to Images) paynt or carue Images of our Sauiour Christ, his Mother Marie, and of the Apostles, thinking that this was a point of gratitude and kindnesse towards those, by whom they had receiued the true knowledge of GOD, and the doctrine of the Gospell. But these pictures or Images came not yet into Churches, nor were not yet worshipped of a long time after. And lest you should thinke that I doe say this of mine owne head onely without authoritie, I alleadge for mee Eusebius Bishoppe of Cesarea, and the most ancient Authour of the Ecclesiasticall historie, who liued about the three hundred and thirtieth yeere of our Lord in Constantinus Magnus dayes, and his sonne Constantius Emperours, in the seuenth booke of his history Ecclesiasticall, the xiiii Chapter, and Saint Ierome vpon the tenth Chapter of the Prophet Ieremie: who both expresly say, that the errours of Images (for so Saint Ierome calleth it) hath come in and passed to the Christians from the Gentiles, by an Heathenish vse and custome. The cause and meanes Eusebius sheweth, saying, It is no maruell if they which being Gentiles before, and did beleeue, seemed to offer this, as a gift to our Sauiour, for the benefites which they had receiued of him, Yea and wee doe see now that Images of Peter and Paul, and of our Sauiour himselfe be made, and tables to bee painted, which me thinke to haue beene obserued and kept indifferently by an Heathenish custome. For the Heathen are wont so to honour them whom they iudged honour worthy, for that some tokens of old men should bee kept. For the remembrance of posterity is a token of their honour that were before, and the loue of those that come after.

Thus farre I haue rehearsed Eusebius words. Where note ye, that both Saint Ierome and hee agreeth heerein, that these Images came in amongst Christian men by such as were Gentiles, and accustomed to idols, and being conuerted to the fayth of Christ, reteyned yet some remnants of Gentility not throughly purged: for Saint Ierome calleth it an errour manifestly. And the like example wee see in the Actes of the Apostles, of the Iewes, who when they were conuerted to Christ, would haue brought in their circumcision (whereunto they were so long accustomed) with them, into Christs Religion. With whom the Apostles (namely Saint Paul) had much adoe for the staying of that matter (Acts 15.5). But of Circumcision was lesse maruell, for that it came first in by GODS ordinance and commandement. A man may most iustly wonder of Images so directly against GODS holy word and straite commandement, how they should enter in. But Images were not yet worshipped in Eusebius time, nor publikely set vp in Churches and Temples, and they who priuately had them, did erre of a certaine zeale, and not by malice: but afterwards they crept out of priuate houses into Churches, and so bredde first superstition, and last of all Idolatrie amongst Christians, as heereafter shall appeare.

In the time of Theodosius and Martian, Emperours, who reigned about the yeere of our Lord 460, and 1117. yeeres agoe, when the people of the citie of Nola once a yeere did celebrate the birth day of Saint Felix in the Temple, and vsed to banquet there sumptuously, Pontius Paulinus Bishop of Nola caused the walles of the Temple to be painted with stories taken out of the old Testament, that the people beholding and considering those pictures, might the better abstaine from too much surfetting and riot. And about the same time Aurelius Prudentius, a very learned and Christian Poet, declareth how he did see painted in a Church, the history of the passion of Saint Cassian, a Schoolemaster and Martyr, whom his owne schollers at the commandement of the tyrant, tormented with the pricking or stabbing in front of their pointells or brasen pennes into his body, and so by a thousand wounds and moe (as sayth Prudentius) most cruelly slew him. And these were the first paintings in Churches that were notable of antiquity. And so by this example came in painting, and afterward Images of Timber and Stone, and other matter, into the Churches of Christians. Now and ye well consider this beginning, men are not so ready to worship a picture on a wall, or in a window, as an imbossed and gilt Image, set with pearle and stone. And a processe of a story, painted with the gestures and actions of many persons, and commonly the sum of the story written withall, hath another vse in it, then one dumbe idoll or image standing by it selfe. But from learning by painted stories, it came by little and little to idolatry. Which when godly men (aswell Emperours and learned Bishops as others) perceiued, they commanded that such pictures, images, or idols, should be vsed no more. And I will for a declaration thereof, begin with the decree of the ancient Christian Emperours, Valens and Theodosius the second, who raigned about foure hundred yeeres after our Sauiour Christs ascension, who forbad that any Images should be made or painted priuately: for certaine it is, that there was none in Temples publikely in their time. These Emperours did write vnto the captaine of the armie attending on the Emperours, after this sort, Valens and Theodosius Emperours, vnto the captaine of the armie: Whereas we haue a diligent care to maintaine the religion of GOD aboue, in all things, wee will grant to no man to set foorth, graue, carue, or paint the image of our Sauiour Christ in colours, stone, or any other matter, but in what place soeuer it shall be found, wee command that it be taken away, and that all such as shall attempt any thing contrary to our decrees or commandement heerein, shall bee most sharply punished. This decree is written in the bookes named Libri Augustales, the Emperiall bookes, gathered by Tribonianus, Basilides, Theophilus, Dioscorus, and Satira, men of great authority and learning, at the commandement of the Emperour Iustinian, and is alleadged by Petrus

Crinitus, a notable learned man, in the ix. booke and ix. Chapter of his worke, intituled, De honesta disciplina, that is to say, of honest learning. Heere you see what Christian Princes of most ancient times dedecreed against images, which then began to creepe in amongst the Christians. For it is certaine that by the space of three hundred yeeres and more, after the death of our Sauiour Christ, and before these godly Emperours raigned, there were no images publikely in Churches or Temples. How would the idolaters glory, if they had so much antiquity and authority for them, as is heere against them?

Now shortly after these dayes, the Gothes, Vandales, Hunnes, and other barbarous and wicked nations, burst into Italy, and all partes of the West countries of Europe, with huge and mighty armies, spoyled all places, destroyed Cities, and burned Libraries, so that learning and true Religion went to wracke, and decayed incrediblie. And so the Bishops of those latter dayes, being of lesse learning, and in the middest of the warres, taking lesse heede also then did the Bishops afore, by ignorance of GODS word, and negligence of Bishops, and specially barbarous Princes, not rightly instructed in true Religion bearing the rule, images came into the Church of Christ in the sayd West parts, where these barbarous people ruled, not now in painted clothes onely, but embossed in stone, timber, mettall, and other like matter, and were not only set vp, but began to be worshipped also. And therefore Serenus Bishop of Massile, the head Towne of Gallia Nabonensis (now called the Prouince) a godly and learned man, who was about sixe hundred yeeres after our Sauiour Christ, seeing the people by occasion of images fall to most abominable idolatrie, brake to pieces all the images of Christ and Saints which were in that City, and was therefore complayned vpon to Gregorie, the first of that name, Bishop of Rome, who was the first learned Bishop that did allow the open hauing of Images in Churches, that can be known by any writing or history of antiquity. And vpon this Gregorie doe all image-worshippers at this day ground their defence. But as all things that be amisse, haue from a tolerable beginning growen worse and worse, till they at the last became vntolerable: so did this matter of images. First, men vsed priuately stories painted in tables, clothes, and walles. Afterwards, grosse and embossed images priuately in their owne houses. Then afterwards, pictures first, and after them embossed images began to creepe into Churches, learned and godly men euer speaking against them. Then by vse it was openly maintayned that they might be in Churches, but yet forbidden that they should be worshipped. Of which opinion was Gregorie, as by the sayd Gregories Epistle to the forenamed Serenus Bishop of Massile, plainely appeareth. Which Epistle is to be found in the booke of Epistles of Gregorie, or Register, in the tenth part of the fourth Epistle, where hee hath these wordes: That thou didst forbid images to be worshipped, we prayse altogether, but that thou didst breake them, we blame. For it is one thing to worship the picture, and another thing by the picture of the story, to learne what is to be worshipped. For that which Scripture is to them that reade, the same doth picture performe vnto idiots or the vnlearned beholding, and so foorth. And after a few wordes: therefore it should not haue beene broken, which was set vp, not to be worshipped in Churches, but only to instruct the mindes of the ignorant. And a little after, thus thou shouldest haue sayd, If you will haue images in the Church for that instruction wherefore they were made in old time, I doe permit that they may bee made, and that you may haue them, and shew them, that not the sight of the story, which is opened by the picture: but that worshipping which was inconueniently giuen to the pictures, did mislike you. And if any would make images, not to forbid them, but auoyd by all meanes to worship any image. By these sentences taken heere and there out of Gregories Epistle to Serenus (for it were too long to rehearse the whole) ye may vnderstand whereunto the matter was now come sixe hundred yeeres after Christ : that the hauing of Images or pictures in the Churches, were then maintayned in the West part of the world (for they were not so forward yet in the East Church) but the worshipping of them was vtterly forbidden. And you may withall note, that seeing there is no ground for worshipping of Images in Gregories writing, but a plaine condemnation thereof, that such as doe worship Images, doe vniustly alleadge Gregorie for them. And further, if Images in the Church doe not teach men according to Gregories minde, but rather blinde them: it followeth, that Images should not be in the Church by his sentence, who onely would they should be placed there, to the end that they might teach the ignorant. Wherefore, if it bee declared that Images haue beene and be worshipped, and also that they teach nothing but errours and lies (which shall by GODS grace heereafter be done) I trust that then by Gregories owne determination, all images and image worshippers shall bee ouerthrowen. But in the meane season, Gregories authority was so great in all the West Church, that by his incouragement men set vp images in all places: but their iudgement was not so good to consider why hee would haue them set vp, but they fell all on heapes to manifest idolatrie by worshipping of them, which Bishop Serenus (not without iust cause) feared would come to passe. Now if Serenus his iudgement, thinking it meete that images, whereunto Idolatrie was committed, should be destroyed, had taken place, idolatrie had bin ouerthrowen: For to that which is not, no man committeth idolatrie. But of Gregories opinion, thinking that images might bee suffered in Churches, so it were taught that they should not bee worshipped: what ruine of religion, and what mischiefe ensued afterward to all Christendome, experience hath to our great hurt and sorrow proued. First, by the schisme rising betweene the East and the West Church about the sayd images. Next, by the deuision of the Empire into two partes by the same occasion of images, to the great weakening of all Christendome, whereby last of all, hath followed the vtter ouerthrow of the Christian religion and noble Empire in Greece and all the East partes of the world, and the encrease of Mahomets false religion, and the cruell dominion and tyranny of the Saracens and Turkes, who doe now hang ouer our neckes also & that; dwell in the West partes of the world, ready at all occasions to ouerrunne vs. And all this doe we owe vnto our idolles and images, and our idolatry in worshipping of them.

But now giue you eare a little to the processe of the history, wherein I doe much follow the histories of Paulus Diaconus, and others ioyned with Eutropius an olde writer (Eutropius, Liber de Rebus Rom., 23). For though some of the authours were fauourers of images: yet do they most plainely and at large prosecute the histories of those times whom Baptist Platina also in his historie of Popes (Baptist Platina, Lives of Constantine and Gregory II), as in the liues of Constantine, and Gregorie the second, Bishoppes of Rome, and other places (where hee intreateth of this matter) doeth chiefely follow. After Gregories time, Constantine Bishoppe of Rome assembled a councell of Bishoppes in the West Church, and did condemne Philippicus then Emperour, and Iohn Bishoppe of Constantinople of the heresie of the Monothelites, not without a cause in deede, but very iustly. When hee had so done, by the consent of the learned about him, the said Constantine Bishoppe of Rome, caused the images of the ancient fathers, which had beene at those sixe councels which were allowed and receiued of all men, to bee painted in the entrie of Saint Peters Church at Rome. When the Greekes had knowledge hereof, they beganne to dispute and reason the matter of images with the Latines, and held this opinion, that images could haue no place in Christes Church, and the Latines held the contrarie, and tooke part with the images. So the East and West Churches which agreed euill before, vpon this contention about images fell to vtter enmity, which was neuer well reconciled yet. But in the meane season Philippicus and Arthemius, or Anastatius, Emperours, commanded images and pictures to bee pulled downe, and rased out in euery place of their dominion. After them came Theodosius the third, hee commanded the defaced images to bee painted againe in their places: but this Theodosius raigned but one yeere. Leo the third of that name succeeded him, who was a Syrian borne, a very wise, godly, mercifull, and valiant prince. This Leo by proclamation commanded, that all images set vp in Churches to bee worshipped, should bee plucked downe and defaced: and required specially the Bishop of Romethat hee should doe the same, and himselfe in the meane season caused all images that were in the imperiall citie Constantinople, to be gathered on an heape in the middest of the citie, and there publiquely burned them to ashes, and whited ouer, and rased out all pictures painted vpon the walles of the Temples, and punished sharpely diuers maintainers of images. And when some did therefore report him to bee a tyrant, hee answered, that such of all other were most iustly punished, which neither worshipped GOD aright, nor regarded the imperiall Maiestie and authority, but maliciously rebelled against wholsome and profitable lawes. When Gregorius, the third of that name, Bishop of Rome, heard of the Emperours doings in Greece concerning the images, hee assembled a councell of Italian Bishoppes against him, and there made decrees for images, and that more reuerence and honour should yet be giuen to them then was before, and stirred vp the Italians against the Emperour, first at Rauenna, and moued them to rebellion.

Treason and rebellion for the defence of images. And as Vspurgensis and Anthonius Bishoppe of Florence testifie in their Chronicles, he caused Rome and all Italie, at the least to refuse their obedience and the payment of any more tribute to the Emperour: and so by treason and rebellion maintained their idolatry. Which example, other Bishops of Rome haue continually followed, and gone through withall most stoutly.

After this Leo, who raigned xxxiiii. yeeres, succeeded his sonne Constantine the fifth, who after his fathers example, kept images out of the Temples, and being moued with the councell which Gregorie had assembled in Italie for images against his father: he also assembled a councel of all the learned men and Bishops of Asia and

Greece, although some writers place this Councell in Leo Isauricus his fathers latter dayes.

A councell against images. In this great assembly they sate in councell from the fourth of & the; Idus of February, to the sixt of the Idus of August, and made concerning the vse of images this decree. It is not lawfull for them that beleeue in GOD through Iesus Christ, to haue any images, neither of the creator, nor of any creatures, set vp in Temples to bee worshipped: but rather & that; all things by the Law of GOD, and for the auoyding of offence, ought to bee taken out of the Churches. And this decree was executed in all places where any images were found in Asia or Greece. And the Emperour sent the determination of this councell holden at Constantinople, to Paul then Bishop of Rome, and commanded him to cast all images out of the Churches: which hee (trusting in the friendship of Pipine a mighty prince) refused to doe. And both hee and his successour Stephanus the third (who assembled another councell in Italie for images) condemned the Emperour and the councell of Constantinople of heresie, and made a decree that the holy images (for so they called them) of Christ the blessed Virgine, and other Saints, were in deede worthy honour and worshipping.

Or Eirene. When Constantine was dead, Leo the fourth his sonne raigned after him, who maried a woman of the citie of Athens, named Theodora, who also was called Irene, by whom hee had a sonne, named Constantine the sixt, and dying whilest his sonne was yet young, left the regiment of the Empire and gouernance of his yong sonne to his wife Irene. These things were done in the Church about the yeere of our Lord 760. Note here I pray you in this processe of the story, that in the Churches of Asia and Greece, there were no images publiquely by the space of almost seuen hundred yeeres. And there is no doubt but the primitiue Church next the Apostles time was most pure. Note also, that when the contention beganne about images, how of sixe Christian Emperours, who were the chiefe Magistrates by GODS law to bee obeyed, only one, which was Theodosius, who raigned but one yeere, held with images. All the other Emperours, and all the learned men and Bishoppes of the East Church, and that in assembled councels condemned them, besides the two Emperours before mentioned, Valence and Theodosius the second, who were long before these times, who straightly forbade that any images should be made. And vniuersally after this time, all the Emperours of Greece (onely

Theodosius excepted) destroyed continually all images. Now on the contrary part, note ye, that the Bishoppes of Rome, being no ordinary Magistrates appoynted of GOD, out ot their diocesse, but vsurpers of Princes authority contrary to GODS word, were the maintainers of images against GODS word, and stirrers vp of sedition and rebellion, and workers of continuall treason against their soueraigne Lords, contrary to GODS Law, and the ordinances of all humane lawes, being not onely enemies to GOD, but also rebelles and traitours against their Princes. These bee the first bringers in of images openly into Churches, These bee the mayntayners of them in the Churches, and these bee the meanes whereby they haue mayntayned them: to wit, conspiracie, treason, and rebellion against GOD and their Princes.

Now to proceede in the history, most worthy to bee knowen. In the nonage of Constantine the sixt, the Empresse Irene his mother, in whose handes the regiment of the Empire remained, was gouerned much by the aduise of Theodore Bishoppe, and Tharasius Patriarche of Constantinople, who practised and held with the Bishoppe of Rome in maintaining of images most earnestly. By whose counsell and intreatie, the Empresse first most wickedly digged vp the body of her father in law Constantine the fift, and commanded it to bee openly burned, and the ashes to be throwen into the sea. Which example (as the constant report goeth) had like to haue been put in practise with Princes corses in our dayes, had the authority of the holy father continued but a little longer. The cause why the Empresse Irene thus vsed her father in law, was, for that hee, when hee was aliue, had destroyed images, and had taken away the sumptuous ornaments of Churches, saying that Christ, whose Temples they were, allowed pouerty, and not pearles and pretious stones. Afterward the sayd Irene at the perswasion of Adrian Bishoppe of Rome, and Paul the Patriarch of Constantinople and his successour Tharasius, assembled a councell of the Bishoppes of Asia and Greece, at the Citie Nicea where the Bishop of Romes legates, being presidentes of the councell, and ordering all things as they listed, the councell which were assembled before vnder the Emperour Constantine the fifth, and had decreed that all images should bee destroyed, was condemned as an hereticall councell and assemblie: And a decree was made, that images should bee put vp in all the Churches of Greece, and that honour and worshippe also should bee giuen vnto the said images.

A decree that Images should bee worshipped. And so the Empresse sparing no diligence in setting vp of images, nor cost in decking them in all Churches, made Constantinople within a short time altogether like Rome it selfe. And now you may see that come to passe which Bishoppe Serenus feared, and Gregorie the first forbade in vaine: to wit, that images should in no wise bee worshipped. For now not onely the simple and vnwise (vnto whom images, as the Scriptures teach, bee specially a snare) but the Bishoppes and learned men also, fall to idolatrie by occasion of images, yea and make decrees and lawes for the maintenance of the same. So hard is it, and in deede impossible any long time to haue images publikelie in Churches and Temples without idolatrie, as by the space of little more then one hundred yeeres betwixt Gregory the first, forbidding most straightly the worshipping of images, and Gregory the third, Paul, and Leo the third, Bishoppes of Rome, with this councell commaunding and decreeing that images should bee worshipped, most euidently appeareth.

Now when Constantine the young Emperour came to the age of twentie yeeres, he was dayly in lesse and lesse estimation. For such as were about his mother, perswaded her, that it was GODS determination that she should reigne alone, and not her sonne with her. The ambitious woman beleeuing the same, depriued her sonne of all Imperiall dignitie, and compelled all the men of warre, with their Captaines, to sweare to her that they would not suffer her Sonne Constantine to reigne during her life. With which indignitie the young Prince being mooued, recouered the regiment of the Empire vnto himselfe by force, and being brought vp in true religion in his fathers time, seeing the superstition of his mother Irene, and the Idolatrie committed by images, cast downe, brake, and burned all the idoles and images that his mother had set vp. But within a few yeeres after, Irene the Empresse, taken againe into her sonnes fauour, after shee had perswaded him to put out Nicephorus his vncles eyes, and to cut out the tongues of his foure other vncles, and to forsake his wife, and by such meanes to bring him into hatred with all his subiects; now further to declare that shee was no changeling, but the same woman that had before digged vp and burned her father in lawes body, and that shee would be as naturall a Mother as shee had beene a kinde Daughter, seeing the images, which shee loued so well, and had with so great cost set vp dayly destroyed by her sonne the Emperour, by the helpe of certaine good companions depriued her Sonne of the Empire: And first, like a kinde and louing mother, put out both his eyes, and layd him in prison, where after long and many torments, she at the last most cruelly slew him.

In this historie, ioyned to Eutropius, it is written, that the Sunne was darkened by the space of xvii. dayes most strangely and dreadfully, and that all men sayd, that for the horriblenesse of that cruell and vnnaturall fact of Irene, and the putting out of the Emperours eyes, the Sunne had lost his light. But indeede, GOD would signifie by the darkenesse of the Sunne, into what darkenesse and blindesse of ignorance and idolatrie, Christendome should fall by the occasion of Images. The bright Sunne of his eternall trueth, and light of his holy worde, by the mystes and blacke cloudes of mens traditions being blemished and darkened, as by sundry most terrible earthquakes that happened about the same time, GOD signified, that the quiet estate of true religion, should by such idolatry be most horribly tossed and turmoyled. And here may you see what a gracious and vertuous Lady this Irene was, how louing a neece to her husbands vncles, how kinde a mother in law to her sonnes wife, how louing a daughter to her father in law, how naturall a mother to her owne sonne, and what a stout and valiant Captaine the Bishops of Rome had of her, for the setting vp and maintenance of their idoles or images. Surely, they could not haue found a meeter patrone for the maintenance of such a matter, then this Irene, whose ambition and desire of rule was insatiable, whose treason continually studied and wrought, was most abominable, whose wicked and vnnaturall crueltie passed Medea and Progne, whose detestable paracides haue ministred matter to Poets, to write their horrible tragedies.

And yet certaine Historiographers, who doe put in writing all these her horrible wickednesses, for loue they had to images, which the mainteyned, doe prayse her as a godly Empresse, and as sent from GOD. Such is the blindnesse of false superstition, if it once take possession in a mans minde, that it will both declare the vices of wicked princes, and also commend them. But not long after, the sayd Irene being suspected to the princes and Lords of Greece of treason, in alienating the Empire to Charles king of the Francons, and for practising a secret marriage betweene her selfe and the sayd king, and being conuicted of the same, was by the sayd Lords deposed and depriued againe of the Empire, and caried into exile into the Iland Lesbos, where she ended her lewde life.

Another councell against images. While these tragedies about images were thus working in Greece, the same question of the vse of images in Churches began to bee mooued in Spaine also. And at Eliberi, a notable citie, now called Granate, was a councell of Spanish Bishops and other learned men assembled, and there, after long deliberation and debating of the matter, it was concluded at length by the whole councell, after this sort, in the 36. article.

Doctours of the councell against images. Wee thinke that pictures ought not to bee in Churches, lest that which is honoured or worshipped be painted on walles. And in the xli. Canon of that councel it is thus written: Wee thought good to admonish the faithfull, that as much as in them lieth, they suffer no images to bee in their houses, but if they feare any violence of their seruants, at the lest let them keepe themselues cleane and pure from Images, if they doe not so, let them be accounted as none of the Church. Note here, I pray you, how a whole and great countrey in the West and South parts of Europe, neerer to Rome a greater deale then to Greece in situation of place, doe agree with the Greekes against Images, and doe not onely forbid them in Churches, but also in priuate houses, and doe excommucate them that doe the contrarie.

Yet another councell against images. And an other councell of the learned men of all Spaine also, called Concilium Toletanum Duodecimum, decreed and determined likewise against Images and Image worshippers. But when these decrees of the Spanish councell at Eliberi came to the knowledge of the Bishop of Rome and his adherents, they fearing lest all Germany also would decree against Images, and forsake them, thought to preuent the matter, and by the consent and helpe of the prince of Francons (whose power was then most great in the West parts of the world) assembled a councell of Germanes at Frankford, and there procured the Spanish councell against Images afore mentioned, to bee condemned by the name of the Foelician heresie, (for that Foelix Bishoppe of Aquitania was chiefe in that councell) and obtained that the actes of the second Nicene councell, assembled by Irene (the holy Empresse whom ye heard of before) and the sentence of the Bishop of Rome for images might be receiued. For much after this sort do the Papists report of the history of the councell of Frankford. Notwithstanding the booke of Carolus Magnus his owne writing, as the title sheweth, which is now put in print, and commonly in mens hands, sheweth the iudgement of that Prince, & of the whole councell of Frankford also, to be against Images, and against the second councell of Nice assembled by Irene for Images, and calleth it an arrogant, foolish, and vngodly councell, and declareth the assembly of the councell of Frankford, to haue beene directly made and gathered against that Nicene councell, and the errours of the same. So that it must needs follow, that either there were in one Princes time two councels assembled at Frankford, one contrary to the other, which by no history doth appeare, or els that after their custome, the Popes and Papistes haue most shamefully corrupted the councell, as their maner is to handle, not onely councels, but also all histories and writings of the olde Doctors, falsifying and corrupting them for the maintenance of their wicked and vngodly purposes, as hath in times of late come to light, and doth in our dayes more and more continually appeare most euidently.

The forged gift of Constantine.&c. Let the forged gift of Constantine, and the notable attempt to falsifie the first Nicene councell for the Popes Supremacie, practised by Popes in Saint Augustines time bee a witnesse hereof: which practise in deed had then taken effect, had not the diligence and wisedome of S. Augustine and other learned and godly Bishops in Affrik, by their great labour and charges also, resisted and stopped the same. Now to come towards and end of this history, and to shew you the principall point that came to passe by the maintenance of images.

Nicene councell like to be falsified. Whereas from Constantinus Magnus time, vntill this day, all authority imperiall and princely dominion of the Empire of Rome, remayned continually in the right and possession of the Emperours, who had their continuance and seate Imperiall at Constantinople the Citie royall. Leo the third, then Bishop of Rome, seeing the Greeke Emperours so bent against his gods of golde and siluer, timber and stone, and hauing the king of the Francons or Frenchmen, named Charles, whose power was exceeding great in the West Countreys, very applyable to his minde, for causes hereafter appearing, vnder the pretence that they of Constantinople were for that matter of images vnder the Popes ban and curse, and therefore vnworthy to bee Emperours, or to beare rule, and for that the Emperours of Greece being farre off, were not ready at a becke to defend the Pope against the Lumbardes his enemies, and other with whom hee had variance: this Leo the third, I say, attempted a thing exceeding strange and vnheard of before, and of vncredible boldnesse and presumption:

For he by his Papall authoritie doeth translate the gouernement of the Empire, and the crowne and name Imperiall, from the Greekes, and giueth it vnto Charles the great, King of the Francons, not without the consent of the forenamed Irene, Empresse of Greece, who also sought to be ioyned in mariage with the said Charles. For the which cause the said Irene was by the Lords of Greece deposed and banished, as one that had betrayed the Empire, as ye before haue heard.

These things were done about the 803 yeere of our Lord. And the said princes of Greece did, after the depriuation of the said Irene, by common consent, elect and create (as they alwayes had done) an Emperour, named Nicephorus, whom the Bishop of Rome and they of the West would not acknowledge for their Emperour; For they had already created them another: and so there became two Emperours. And the Empire which was before one, was diuided into two parts, vpon occasion of idols and images, and the worshipping of them: euen as the kingdome of the Israelites was in old time for the like cause of idolatrie diuided in King Roboam his time. And so the Bishop of Rome, hauing the fauour of Charles the great by this meanes assured to him, was wondrously enhanced in power and authority, and did in all the West Church (especially in Italy) what he lust, where images were set vp, garnished, and worshipped of all sorts of men.

Or, Stauratius. But Images were not to fast set vp, and so much honoured in Italie and the West: but Nicephorus Emperour of Constantinople, and his successours Scauratius, the two Michaels, Leo, Theophilus, and other Emperours their successours in the Empire of Greece, continually pulled them downe, brake them, burned them, and destroyed them as fast. And when Theodorus Emperour, would at the Councell of Lions haue agreed with the Bishop of Rome, and haue set vp images: he was by the Nobles of the Empire of Greece depriued, and another chosen in his place, and so rose a ielousie, suspicion, grudge, hatred, and enmity betweene the Christians and Empires of the East countries and West, which could neuer be quenched nor pacified. So that when the Saracens first, and afterward the Turkes, inuaded the Christians, the one part of Christendome would not helpe the other. By reason whereof at the last, the noble Empire of Greece, and the city imperiall Constantinople, was lost, and is come into the hands of the Infidels, who now haue ouerrunne almost all Christendome, and possessing past the middle of Hungary, which is part of the West Empire, doe hang ouer all our heads, to the vtter danger of all Christendome.

Thus wee see what a sea of mischiefes the maintenance of Images hath brought with it, what an horrible Schisme betweene the East and the West Church, what an hatred betweene one Christian and another, Councels against Councels, Church against Church, Christians against Christians, Princes against Princes, rebellions, treasons, vnnaturall and most cruell murders, the daughter digging vp & burning her father the Emperours body, the mother for loue of idols most abominably murdering her owne sonne, being an Emperour, at the last, the tearing in sunder of Christendome and the Empire into two pieces, till the Infidels, Saracens, and Turkes, common enemies to both parts, haue most cruelly vanquished, destroyed and subdued the one part, the whole Empire of Greece, Asia the lesse, Thracia, Macedonia, Epirus, and many other great and goodly countreyes and Prouinces, and haue wonne a great piece of the other Empire, and put the whole in dreadfull feare and most horrible danger. For it is not without a iust and great cause to bee dread, left as the Empire of Rome was euen for the like cause of Images and the worshipping of them torne in pieces and diuided, as was for Idolatrie the kingdome of Israel in old time diuided: so like punishment, as for the like offence fell vpon the Iewes, will also light vpon vs: that is, left the cruell tyrant and enemy of our common wealth and Religion the Turke, by GODS iust vengeance, in likewise partly murder, and partly leade away into captiuity vs Christians, as did the Assyrian and Babylonian Kings murder and leade away the Israelites, and left the Empire of Rome and Christian Religion be so vtterly brought vnder foot, as was then the kingdome of Israel and true Religion of GOD, whereunto the matter already (as I haue declared) shrewdly enclineth on our part, the greater part of Christendome within lesse then three hundred yeers space, being brought into captiuity and most miserable thraldome vnder the Turke, and the noble Empire of Greece cleane euerted. Whereas if the Christians, deuided by these Image matters, had holden together, no Infidels and miscreants could thus haue preuayled against Christendome. And all this mischiefe and misery, which we haue hitherto fallen into doe we owe to our mighty gods of gold and siluer, stocke and stone, in whose helpe and defence (where they can not helpe themselues) wee haue trusted so long, vntill our enemies the Infidels haue ouercome and ouerrunne vs almost altogether. A iust reward for those that haue left the mighty liuing GOD, the Lord of hosts, and haue stooped and giuen the honour due to him, to deade blockes and stockes, who haue eyes and see not, feet and cannot goe, and so foorth, and are cursed of

GOD, and all they that make them, and put their trust in them. Thus you vnderstand (welbeloued in our Sauiour Christ) by the iudgement of the old learned and godly Doctours of the Church, and by ancient histories Ecclesiasticall, agreeing to the verity of GODS word, al-leaged out of the old Testament and the new, that Images and Image worshipping were in the Primitiue Church (which was most pure and vncorrupt) abhorred and detested, as abominable and contrary to true Christian Religion. And that when Images began to creepe into the Church, they were not onely spoken and written against by godly and learned Bishops, Doctours, and Clarkes, but also condemned by whole Councels of Bishops and learned men assembled together, yea, the sayd Images by many Christian Emperours and Bishops were defaced, broken, and destroyed, and that aboue seuen hundred and eight hundred yeers agoe, and that therefore it is not of late dayes (as some would beare you in hand) that images and image worshipping haue beene spoken and written against. Finally, you haue heard what mischiefe and misery hath by the occasion of the said Images fallen vpon whole Christendome, besides the losse of infinite soules, which is most horrible of all. Wherefore let vs beseech GOD, that we, being warned by his holy word, forbidding all Idolatry, and by the writing of old godly Doctours and Ecclesiasticall histories written, and preserued by GODS ordinance for our admonition and warning, may flee from all Idolatry, and so escape the horrible punishment and plagues, aswell worldly, as euerlasting, threatned for the same, which GOD our heauenly Father graunt vs, for our onely Sauiour and Mediator Iesus Christs sake. Amen.

THE THIRD PART OF THE HOMILIE AGAINST IMAGES, AND THE WORSHIPPING OF THEM, CONTEYNING THE CONFUTATION OF THE PRINCIPALL ARGUMENTS WHICH ARE VSED TO BEE MADE FOR THE MAINTENANCE OF IMAGES. WHICH PART MAY SERUE TO INSTRUCT THE CURATES THEMSELUES, OR MEN OF GOOD VNDERSTANDING.

NOW ye haue heard how plainely, how vehemently, and that in many places, the word of GOD speaketh against not onely idolatrie and worshipping of images, but also against idols and images themselues: (I meane alwaies thus heerein, in that we be stirred and prouoked by them to worship them, and not as though they were simply forbidden by the New Testament, without such occasion and danger.) And ye haue heard likewise out of histories Ecclesiasticall, the beginning, proceeding, and successe of idolatrie by images, and the great contention in the Church of Christ about them: to the great trouble and decay of Christendome: and withall ye haue heard the sentences of old ancient Fathers and godly learned Doctours and Bishops, against images and idolatry, taken out of their owne writings. It remayneth, that such reasons as be made for the maintenance of images, and excessiue painting, gilding and decking, aswell of them, as of the Temples or Churches, also be answered and confuted, partly by application of some places before alleadged, to their reasons, and partly, by otherwise answering the same. Which part hath the last place in this Treatise, for that it cannot be well vnderstood of the meaner sort, nor the arguments of image maintayners, can without prolixitie too much tedious, bee answered without the knowledge of the Treatise going before. And although diuers things before mentioned, bee heere rehearsed againe: yet this repetition is not superfluous, but in a maner necessary, for that the simple sort cannot else vnderstand how the foresayd places are to be applied to the arguments of such as doe maintaine images, wherewith otherwise they might be abused.

First, it is alleadged by them that maintaine images, that all lawes, prohibitions, and curses, noted by vs out of the holy Scripture, and sentences of the Doctours also by vs alleadged, against images and the worshipping of them, appertaine to the idols of the Gentiles or Pagans, as the idoll of Iupiter, Mars, Mercury, etc. and not to our images of GOD, of Christ, and his Saints. But it shall be declared both by GODS word, and the sentences of the ancient Doctours, and iudgement of the Primitiue Church, that all images, aswell ours, as the idoles of the Gentiles, be forbidden and vnlawfull, namely in Churches and Temples. And first this is to be replied out of GODS word, that the images of GOD the Father, the Sonne, and the holy Ghost, either seuerally, or the images of the Trinitie, which we had in euery Church, be by the Scriptures expressely and directly forbidden, and condemned, as appeareth by these places: The Lord spake vnto you out of the middle of fire, you heard the voyce or sound of his wordes, but you did see no forme or shape at all, lest peraduenture you being deceiued, should make to your selfe any grauen image or likenesse (Deuteronomy 4.12, 16): and so foorth, as is at large rehearsed in the first part of this treatise against images. And therefore in the old Law, the middle of the propitiatorie, which presented GODS seate, was emptie, lest any should take occasion to make any similitude or likenesse of him. Esaias, after he hath set forth the incomprehensible Maiestie of GOD, he asketh, to whom then will ye make GOD like? or what similitude will yee set vp vnto him? Shall the caruer make him a carued image? and shall the goldsmith couer him with golde, or cast him into a forme of siluer plates (Isaiah 40.18-20)? And for the poore man, shall the image maker frame an image of timber, that hee may haue somewhat to set vp also? And after this hee cryeth out: O wretches, heard yee neuer of this? Hath it not beene preached to you since the beginning, how by the creation of the world, and the greatnesse of the worke, they might vnderstand the Maiestie of GOD, the maker and creatour of all, to bee greater then that it could bee expressed or set foorth in any image or bodily similitude? Thus farre the Prophet Esaias, who from the xliiii. Chapter, to the xlix. intreateth in a maner of no other thing. And S. Paul in the Acts of the Apostles euidently teacheth the same, that no similitude can be made vnto GOD, in gold, siluer, stone or any other matter (Acts 17.29). By these and many other places of Scripture it is euident, that no image either ought or can be made vnto GOD. For how can GOD, a most pure spirit, whom man neuer saw, be expressed by a grosse, bodily, and visible similitude? How can the infinite Maiestie and greatnesse of GOD, incomprehensible to mans minde, much more not able to be compassed with the sense, be expressed in a small and little image? How can a dead and dumbe image expresse the liuing GOD? What can an image, which when it is fallen, cannot rise vp againe, which can neither helpe his friends, nor hurt his enemies, expresse of the most puissant and mighty GOD, who alone is able to reward his friends, and to destroy his enemies euerlastingly? A man might iustly cry with the Prophet Habacuc, Shall such Images instruct or teach any thing right of GOD? or shall they become doctours? Wherefore men that haue made an image of GOD, whereby to honour him, haue thereby dishonoured him most highly, diminished his Maiestie, blemished his glory, and falsified his trueth (Habakkuk 2.18). And therefore S. Paul sayth, that such as haue framed any similitude or Image of GOD like a mortall man, or any other likenesse, in timber, stone, or other matter, haue changed his trueth into a lie (Romans 1.25). For both they thought it to bee no longer that which it was, a stocke or a stone, and tooke it to be that which it was not, as GOD, or an image of GOD. Wherefore an image of GOD, is not onely a lie, but a double lie also. But the deuill is a lier, and the father of lyes: wherefore the lying Images which bee made of GOD, to his great dishonour, and horrible danger of his people, came from the deuill (John 8.44).

Wherefore they be conuict of foolishnesse and wickednesse in making of images of GOD, or the Trinitie: for that no image of GOD ought or can bee made, as by the Scriptures and good reason euidently appeareth: yea, and once to desire an image of GOD commeth of infidelitie, thinking not GOD to bee present, except they might see some signe or image of him, as appeareth by the Hebrewes in the wildernesse willing Aaron to make them gods whom they might see goe before them. Where they obiect, that seeing in Esaias and Daniel bee certaine descriptions of GOD, as sitting on a high seate, etc. Why may not a painter likewise set him forth in colours to be seene, as it were a Iudge sitting in a throne, aswell as he is described in writing by the Prophets, seeing that Scripture or writing, and picture, differ but a little? First, it is to be answered, that things forbidden by GODS word, as painting of images of GOD, and things permitted of GOD, as such descriptions vsed of the Prophets, be not all one: neither ought, nor can mans reason (although it shew neuer so goodly) preuaile any thing against GODS expresse worde, and plaine statute Law, as I may well terme it. Furthermore, the Scripture although it haue certaine descriptions of GOD, yet if you reade on forth, it expoundeth it selfe, declaring that GOD is a pure spirit, infinite, who replenisheth heauen and earth, which the picture doeth not, nor expoundeth it selfe, but rather when it hath set GOD foorth in a bodily similitude, leaueth a man there, and will easily bring one into the heresie of the Anthropomorphites, thinking GOD to haue hands and feete, and to sit as a man doeth. which they that doe (saith S. Augustine in his booke de fide & symbolo cap.7.) fall into that sacriledge which the Apostle detesteth, in those, who haue changed the glory of the incorruptible GOD, into the similitude of a corruptible man. For it is wickednesse for a Christian to erect such an image to GOD in a Temple, and much more wickednes to erect such a one in his heart by beleeuing of it. But to this they reply, that this reason notwithstanding, Images of Christ may be made, for that he tooke vpon him flesh, and became man. It were well that they would first graunt, that they haue hitherto done most wickedly in making and mayntayning of Images of GOD, and of the Trinitie in euery place, whereof they are by force of GODS word and good reason conuicted: and then to descend to the triall for other images.

Now concerning their obiection, that an Image of Christ may bee made, the answer is easie. For in GODS word and religion, it is not only required whether a thing may be done or no: but also, whether it be lawfull and agreeable to GODS word to bee done, or no. For all wickednesse may be and is dayly done, which yet ought not to be done. And the words of the reasons aboue alleaged out of the Scriptures are, that Images neither ought, nor can be made vnto GOD. Wherefore to replie that Images of Christ may bee made, except withall it bee prooued, that it is lawfull for them to be made, is, rather then to hold ones peace, to say somewhat, but nothing to the purpose. And yet it appeareth that no Image can be made of Christ, but a lying image (as the Scripture peculiarly calleth Images lies) for Christ is GOD and man. Seeing therefore that for the Godhead, which is the most excellent part, no Images can be made, it is falsly called the image of Christ (Romans 1.23). Wherefore images of Christ be not onely defects, but also lies. Which reason serueth also for the Images of Saints, whose soules, the most excellent partes of them, can by no Images be presented and expressed. Wherefore, they bee no Images of Saints, whose soules reigne in ioy with GOD, but of the bodies of Saints, which as yet lie putrified in the graues. Furthermore, no true image can be made of Christs body, for it is vnknowen now of what forme and countenance he was. And there bee in Greece and at Rome, and in other places, diuers Images of Christ, and none of them like to other, and yet euery of them affirmeth, that theirs is the true and liuely image of Christ, which cannot possible be. Wherefore, as soon as an image of Christ is made, by and by is a lie made of him, which by GODS word is forbidden. Which also is true of the images of any Saints of antiquity, for that it is vnknowen of what forme and countenance they were. Wherefore seeing that Religion ought to be grounded vpon trueth, Images which cannot be without lies, ought not to bee made, or put to any vse of Religion, or to bee placed in Churches and Temples, places peculiarly appointed to true Religion and seruice of GOD. And thus much, that no true image of GOD, our Sauiour Christ, or his Saints can be made: wherewithall is also confuted that their allegation, that Images be the Lay mens bookes. For it is euident by that which is afore rehearsed, that they teach no things of GOD, or our Sauiour Christ, and of his Saints, but lies and errours. Wherefore either they be no bookes, or if they be, they be false and lying bookes, the teachers of all errour.

And now if it should be admitted and granted, that an image of Christ could truely bee made, yet it is vnlawfull that it should bee made, yea, or that the Image of any Saint should bee made, specially to bee set vp in Temples, to the great and vnauoydable danger of Idolatry, as heereafter shall be prooued. And first concerning the Image of Christ ; that though it might be had truely, yet it were vnlawfull to haue it in Churches publikely, is a notable place in Ireneus, who reprooued the Heretikes called Gnostici, for that they carried about the Image of Christ, made truely after his owne proportion in Pilates time (as they sayd) and therefore more to be esteemed, then those lying Images of him which we now haue (Irenaeus, Bk. 1, Chap. 24). The which Gnostici also vsed to set garlands vpon the head of the sayd Image, to shew their affection to it. But to goe to GODS word. Bee not, I pray you, the wordes of the Scripture plaine? Beware lest thou being deceiued, make to thy selfe (to say, to any vse of Religion) any grauen Image, or any similitude of any thing, etc (Leviticus 26.1, Deuteronomy 5.8, *Sculptile*, ed. note: original text also refers to *Fusile* and *Similitudo*). And cursed bee the man that maketh a grauen or molten Image, abomination before the Lord, etc (Deuteronomy 27.15). Be not our Images such? Be not our Images of Christ and his Saints, either carued or molten, or cast, or similitudes of men and women? It is happy that we haue not followed the Gentiles in making of Images of beasts, fishes, and vermines also. Notwithstanding, the Image of an Horse, as also the Image of the Asse that Christ rode on, haue in diuers places beene brought into the Church and Temple of GOD. And is not that which is written in the beginning of the Lords most holy Law, and dayly read vnto you, most euident also? Thou shalt not make any likenesse of any thing in heauen aboue, in earth beneath, or in the water vnder the earth, etc. Could any more bee forbidden, and sayd, then this? either of the kindes of Images, which bee either carued, molten or otherwise similitudes? or of things whereof images are forbidden to be made? Are not all things either in heauen, earth, or water vnder the earth (Exodus 20.4)? And be not our Images of Christ and his Saints, likenesses of things in heauen, earth, or in the water? If they continue in their former answer, that these prohibitions concerne the idols of the Gentiles, and not our Images: First that answer is already confuted, concerning the Images of GOD and the Trinity at large, & concerning the Images of Christ also, by Ireneus. And that the Law of GOD is likewise to bee vnderstood against all our Images, as well of Christ, as his Saints, in Temples and Churches, appeareth further by the iudgement of the old Doctours, and the Primitiue

Church. Epiphanius renting a painted cloth, wherein was the picture of Christ, or of some Saint, affirming it to bee against our Religion, that any such image should be had in the Temple or Church (as is before at large declared) iudged that not onely idols of the Gentiles, but that all Images of Christ and his Saints also, were forbidden by GODS word and our Religion. Lactantius affirming it to bee certaine that no true Religion can be where any Image or picture is (as is before declared) iudged, that aswell all Images and pictures, as the idols of the Gentiles were forbidden, else would he not so generally haue spoken and pronounced of them. And Saint Augustine (as is before alleaged) greatly alloweth M. Varro, affirming that Religion is most pure without Images: and sayth himselfe, Images be of more force to crooke an vnhappy soule, then to teach and instruct it (Augustine, De Civit. Dei, Bk. 4, Chap. 3, Psalms 36, 113). And hee sayth further, Euery childe, yea euery beast knoweth that it is not GOD that they see. Wherefore then doeth the holy Ghost so often monish vs of that which all men know? Whereunto Saint Augustine answereth thus. For (sayth he) when Images are placed in Temples, and set in honourable sublimity, and begin once to be worshipped, foorthwith breedeth the most vile affection of errour. This is Saint Augustines iudgement of Images in Churches, that by and by they breed errour and Idolatrie. The Christian Emperours, the learned Bishops, all the learned men of Asia, Greece, and Spaine, assembled in Councels at Constantinople and in Spaine, seuen and eight hundred yeeres agoe and more, condemning and destroying all Images, aswell of Christ, as of the Saints, set vp by the Christians (as is before at large declared) testifie, that they vnderstood GODS word so, that it forbad our Images, aswell as the idols of the Gentiles. And as it is written, Sap.14. that images were not from the beginning, neither shall they continue to the end (Apocrypha. Wisdom 14.13): so were they not in the beginning in the Primitiue Church, GOD grant they may in the end bee destroyed. For all Christians in the Primitiue Church, as Origen against Celsus (Origen, `Against Celsus', bks. 4, 8), Cyprian also and Arnobius doe testifie (Cyprian `Against Demetrium'), were sore charged and complayned on, that they had no Altars nor Images. Wherefore did they not (I pray you) conforme themselues to the Gentiles in making of Images, but for lacke of them sustayned their heauy displeasure, if they had taken it to bee lawfull by GODS word to haue Images? It is euident therefore that they tooke all Images to bee vnlawfull in the Church or Temple of GOD, and therefore had none (though the Gentiles there fore were most highly displeased) following this rule, Wee must obey GOD rather then men (Acts 5.29). And Zephirus in his notes vpon the Apologie of S. Ierome, gathereth, that all his vehement perswasion should bee but cold, except we know this once for all, that Christian men in his time did most hate Images, with their ornaments. And Iren'us (as is aboue declared) reprooueth the Heretikes called Gnostici, for that they carried about the image of Christ . And therefore the Primitiue Church, which is specially to be followed as most incorrupt and pure, had publikely in Churches neither idols of the Gentiles, nor any other Images, as things directly forbidden by GODS worde. And thus it is declared by GODS word, the sentences of the Doctours, and the iudgement of the Primitiue Church, which was most pure and syncere, that all Images, aswell ours, as the Idols of the Gentiles, bee by GODS word forbidden, and therefore vnlawfull, specially in Temples and Churches.

Now if they (as their custome is) flee to this answere, that GODS word forbiddeth not absolutely all Images to bee made, but that they should not bee made to bee worshipped, and that therefore wee may haue Images, so wee worship them not, for that they bee things indifferent, which may bee abused, or well vsed. Which seemeth also to be the iudgement of Damascene and Gregorie the first, as is aboue declared (Damascene, `De Fide Orth.', bk. 4, chap. 17, Gregory I, `Epistle to Serenum Massil.'). And this is one of their chiefe allegations for the maintenance of Images, which haue beene alleaged since Gregorie the first his time.

Well, then we bee come to their second allegation, which in part we would not sticke to grant them. For wee are not so superstitious or scrupulous, that wee doe abhorre either flowers wrought in carpets, hanginges, and other arasse, either Images of Princes printed or stamped in their coynes, which when Christ did see in a Romane Coyne, we reade not that hee reprehended it, neither doe wee condemne the artes of paynting and image making, as wicked of themselues. But we would admit and graunt them, that Images vsed for no religion, or superstition rather, we meane Images of none worshipped, nor in danger to bee worshipped of any, may be suffered. But Images placed publikely in Temples, cannot possibly bee without danger of worshipping and idolatrie, wherefore they are not publiquely to bee had or suffered in Temples and Churches. The Iewes, to whom this Law was first giuen (and yet being a morrall commandement, and not ceremoniall, as all Doctours interpret it, bindeth vs aswell as them) the Iewes I say, who should haue the true sense and meaning of GODS Law so peculiarly giuen vnto them, neither had in the beginning any Images publiquely in their Temple (as Origenes and Iosephus at large declareth, Origen `Against Celsus', bk. 4, Josephus, `Antiq.', bk. 17, chap. 8, bk. 18, chaps. 5, 15) neither after the restitution of the Temple, would by any meanes consent to Herode, Pilate or Petronius, that Images should bee placed onely in the Temple at Hierusalem, although no worshipping of Images was required at their hands: but rather offered themselues to the death, than to assent that Images should once bee placed in the Temple of GOD, neither would they suffer any Image-maker among them. And Origen added this cause, lest their mindes should bee plucked from GOD, to the contemplation of earthly things. And they are much commended for this earnest zeale, in maintaining of GODS honour and true religion. And trueth it is, that the Iewes and Turkes, who abhorre Images and Idoles as directly forbidden by GODS word, will neuer come to the trueth of our religion, whiles the stumbling blockes of Images remaine amongst vs, and lie in their way. If they obiect yet the brasen serpent which Moses did set vp, or the Images of the Cherubims, or any other Images which the Iewes had in their Temple, the answere is easie. Wee must in religion obey GODS generall Law, which bindeth all men, and not follow examples of particular dispensation, which bee no warrants for vs: els wee may by the same reason resume circumcision and sacrificing of beastes, and other rites permitted to the Iewes. Neither canne those Images of Cherubim, set in secret where no man might come nor behold, bee any example for our publique setting vp of Images in Churches and Temples. But to let the Iewes goe. Where they say that Images, so they be not worshipped, as things indifferent may bee tolerable in Temples and Churches: Wee inferre and say for the aduersatiue, that all our Images of GOD, our Sauiour Christ, and his Saints, publiquely set vp in Temples and Churches, places peculiarly appointed to the true worshipping of GOD, bee not things indifferent, nor tolerable: but against GODS Lawe and Commandement, taking their owne interpretation and exposition of it. First, for that all Images, so set vp publiquely, haue beene worshipped of the vnlearned and simple sort shortly after they haue beene publiquely so set vp, and in conclusion, of the wise and learned also. Secondly, for that they are worshipped in sundry places now in our time also. And thirdly, for that it is impossible that Images of GOD, Christ, or his Saints can be suffered (especially in Temples and Churches) any while or space, without worshipping of them: and that idolatry, which is most abominable before GOD, cannot possibly bee escaped and auoyded, without the abolishing and destruction of Images and pictures in Temples and Churches, for that idolatrie is to Images, specially in Temples and Churches, an inseparable accident (as they terme it) so that Images in Churches, and idolatrie, go alwayes both together, and that therefore the one cannot bee auoyded, except the other (specially in all publike places) bee destroyed. Wherefore, to make Images, and publikely to set them vp in the Temples and Churches, places appointed peculiarly to the seruice of GOD, is to make Images to the vse of religion, and not onely against this precept, Thou shalt make no maner of Images: but against this also, Thou shalt not bowe downe to them, nor worship them. For they being set vp, haue beene, bee, and euer will bee worshipped. And the full proofe of that which in the begining of the first part of this treatie was touched, is here to bee made and perfourmed: To wit, that our Images, and idoles of the Gentiles bee all one, aswell in the things themselues, as also in that our Images haue beene before, bee now, and euer will bee worshipped, in like fourme and maner, as the idoles of the Gentiles were worshipped, so long as they be suffered in Churches and Tempels. Whereupon it followeth, that our Images in Churches haue bene, be, and euer will be none other but abominable Idols, and bee therefore no things indifferent.

Simulachra gentium Argentum & aurum. Fusile. Similitudo, Sculptilo. Similachrum opera mannum hominum. And euery of these parts shall bee prooued in order, as hereafter followeth. And first, that our Images and the idols of the Gentiles bee all one concerning themselues, is most euident, the matter of them being gold, siluer, or other mettall, stone, wood, clay, or plaster, as were the idoles of the Gentiles, and so being either moulten or cast, either carued, grauen, hewen, or other wise formed and fashioned after the similitude and likenesse of man or woman, be dead and dumbe works of mans handes, hauing mouths and speake not, eyes and see not, handes and feele not, feete and goe not, and so aswell in forme as matter, bee altogether like the idoles of the Gentiles. Insomuch that all the titles which bee giuen to the idoles in the Scriptures, may bee verified of our Images. Wherefore, no doubt but the like curses which are mentioned in the Scriptures, will light vpon the makers and worshippers of them both. Secondly, that they haue beene and bee worshipped in our time, in like forme and manner as were the idoles of the Gentiles, is now to bee prooued.

Dii tutelares (ed. note: image maintainers?). And for that idolatrie standeth chiefely in the minde, it shall in this part first bee prooued, that our Image maintainers haue had, and haue the same opinions and iudgement of Saints, whose Images they haue made and worshipped, as Gentiles idolaters had of their Gods. And afterwards shall be declared, that our Image-maintainers and worshippers, haue vsed, and vse the same outward rites and maner of honouring and worshipping their Images, as the Gentiles did vse before their idoles, and that therefore they commit idolatrie, aswell inwardly and outwardly, as did the wicked Gentiles idolaters.

And concerning the first part of the idolatrous opinions of our Image maintainers. What I pray you bee such Saints with vs, to whom wee attribute the defence of certaine countreys, spoyling GOD of his due honour herein, but *Dii tutelares* of the Gentiles idolaters? Such as were Belus to the Babilonians and Assyrians, Osiris and Isis to the Egyptians: Vulcane to the Lemnians, and to such other.

Dii praesides (ed. note: image rulers/judges?, perhaps in this context, images considered rulers of a locale). What bee such Saints to whom the sauegard of certaine cities are appointed, but *Dii Pr'sides*, with the Gentiles idolaters? Such as were at Delphos Apollo, at Athens Minerua, at Carthage Iuno, at Rome Quirinus. & c.

Dij patroni. What be such Saints, to whom, contrary to the vse of the Primitiue Church, Temples and Churches bee builded, and Altars erected, but *Dij Patroni*, of the Gentiles idolaters? Such as were in the Capitoll Iupiter, in Paphus Temple Venus, in Ephesus Temple Diana, and such like. Alas, wee seeme in thus thinking and doing to haue learned our religion not out of GODS word, but out of the Pagan Poets, who say, *Excessere omnes adytis, arisque relictis, Dij quibus imperiu hoc steterat.* & c. That is to say, All the gods by whose defence this Empire stood, are gone out of the Temples, and haue forsaken their Altars. And where one Saint hath Images in diuers places, the same saint hath diuers names thereof, most like to the Gentiles. When you heare of our Lady of Walsingham, our Lady of Ipswich, our Lady of Wilsdon, and such other: what is it but an imitation of the Gentiles idolaters? Diana Agrotera, Diana Coriphea, Diana Ephesia. & c. Venus Cypria, Venus Paphia, Venus Gnidia. Whereby is euidently meant, that the Saint for the Image sake, should in those places, yea, in the Images themselues, haue a dwelling, which is the ground of their idolatrie. For where no Images bee, they haue no such meanes. Terentius Varro sheweth, that there were three hundred Iupiters in his time, there were no fewer Veneres and Dian', wee had no fewer Christophers, Ladies, and Marie Magdalenes, and other Saints. Oenomaus, and Hesiodus shew, that in their time there were thirtie thousand gods. I thinke wee had no fewer Saints, to whom wee gaue the honour due to GOD. And they haue not onely spoyled the true liuing GOD of his due honour, in Temples, Cities, Countreys, and lands, by such deuises and inuentions as the Gentiles idolaters haue done before them: but the Sea and waters haue aswell speciall Saints with them, as they had gods with the Gentiles, Neptune, Triton, Nereus, Castor, and Pollux, Venus, and such other. In whose places bee come Saint Christopher, Saint Clement, and diuers other, and specially our Lady, to whom shipmen sing *Aue maris stella.* Neither hath the fire scaped the idolatrous inuentions. For in stead of Vulcan and Vesta, the Gentiles gods of the fire, our men haue placed Saint Agatha, and make letters on her day for to quench fire with. Euery Artificer and profession hath his special Saint, as a peculiar god. As for example, Schollers haue Saint Nicholas and Saint Gregory, Painters Saint Luke, neither lacke souldiers their Mars, nor louers their Venus, amongst Christians. All diseases haue their speciall Saints, as gods the curers of them. The pockes Saint Roche, the falling euil Saint Cornelis, the tooth ache Saint Appolin, & c. Neither doe beastes and cattell lacke their gods with vs, for Saint Loy is the horseleach, and Saint Anthony the swineherd. &c. Where is GODS prouidence and due honour in the meane season? who sayth, The heauens be mine, and the earth is mine, the whole world and all that in it is, I doe giue victorie, and I put to flight, of mee bee all counsels and helpe.&c. Except I keepe the citie, in vaine doeth he watch that keepeth it, thou Lord shalt saue both men and beastes. But we haue left him neither heauen, nor earth, nor water, nor countrey, nor citie, peace nor warre to rule and gouerne, neither men, nor beastes, nor their diseases to cure, that a godly man might iustly for zealous indignation cry out, O heauen, O earth, and seas, what madnesse and wickednesse against GOD are men fallen into? What dishonour doe the creatures to their Creator and maker? And if we remember GOD sometime, yet because wee doubt of his abilitie or will to helpe, wee ioyne to him another helper, as hee were a nowne adiectiue, vsing these sayings: such as learne, GOD and Saint Nicholas be my speede: such as neese, GOD helpe and Saint Iohn: to the horse, GOD and Saint Loy saue thee. Thus are wee become like horses and Mules, which haue no vnderstanding. For, is there not one

GOD onely, who by his power and wisedome made all things, and by his prouidence gouerneth the same? and by his goodnesse mainteineth and saueth them? Bee not all things of him, by him, and through him? Why doest thou turne from the Creatour to the creatures? This is the manner of the Gentiles idolaters: but thou art a Christian, and therefore by Christ alone hast accesse to GOD the Father, and helpe of him onely. These things are not written to any reproch of the Saints themselues, who were the true seruants of GOD, and did giue all honour to him, taking none vnto themselues, and are blessed soules with GOD: but against our foolishnesse and wickednes, making of the true seruants of GOD, false gods, by attributing to them the power and honour which is GODS, and due to him onely. And for that wee haue such opinions of the power and ready helpe of Saints, all our Legends, Hymnes, Sequenses, and Masses, did conteine Stories, Laudes, and Prayses of them, and prayers to them: yea, and Sermons also altogether of them, and to their prayses, GODS word being cleane laid aside. And this wee doe altogether agreeable to the Saints, as did the Gentiles idolaters to their false gods. For these opinions which men haue had of mortall persons, were they neuer so holy, the old most godly & learned Christians haue written against the fained gods of the Gentiles, and Christian Princes haue destroyed their images, who if they were now liuing, would doubtlesse likewise both write against our false opinions of Saints, and also destroy their images. For it is euident, that our Image-mainteiners, haue the same opinion of Saintes, which the Gentiles had of their false gods, and thereby are mooued to make them images as the Gentiles did.

Medioximi Dij. If answere bee made, that they make Saints but intercessours to GOD, and meanes for such things as they would obteine of GOD: that is euen after the Gentiles idolatrous vsage, to make them of Saints, Gods, called *Dij Medioximi*, to be meane intercessours and helpers to GOD, as though he did not heare, or should bee weary if hee did all alone. So did the Gentiles teach, that there was one chiefe power working by other, as meanes, and so they made all gods subiect to fate or destinie: as Lucian in his dialogues faineth that Neptune made suite to Mercurie, that hee might speake with Iupiter. And therefore in this also, it is most euident that our Image mainteiners be all one in opinion with the Gentiles idolaters.

Now remaineth the third part, that their rites and ceremonies in honouring and worshipping of the Images or Saints bee all one with the rites which the Gentiles idolaters vsed in honouring their idoles. First, what meaneth it, that Christians, after the example of the Gentiles idolaters, goe on pilgrimage to visite Images, where they haue the like at home, but that they haue a more opinion of holinesse and vertue in some Images, then other some, like as the Gentiles idolaters had? which is the readiest way to bring them to idolatry by worshipping of them, and directly against GODS word, who saith, Seeke mee, and yee shall liue, and doe not seeke Bethel, enter not into Gilgal, neither goe to Bersheba (Amos 5.4-5). And against such as had any superstition in holinesse of the place, as though they should bee heard for the places sake, saying, Our fathers worshipped in this mountaine, and yee say, that at Hierusalem is the place where men should worshippe, our Sauiour Christ pronounceth, Beleeue mee, the houre commeth when you shall worship the father neither in this mountaine, nor at Hierusalem, but true worshippers shall worshippe the father in spirit and trueth (John 4.20-21). But it is too well knowen, that by such pilgrimage going, Lady Venus and her sonne Cupide, were rather worshipped wantonly in the fleshe, then God the Father and our Sauiour Christ his Sonne truely worshipped in the spirit.

And it was very agreeable (as Saint Paul teacheth) that they which fell to Idolatry, which is spirituall fornication, should also fall into carnall fornication, and all vncleannesse, by the iust iudgements of GOD, deliuering them ouer to abominable concupiscenses (Romans 1.24).

What meaneth it that Christian men, after the vse of the Gentiles Idolaters kneele before Images? which if they had any sense and gratitude, would kneele before men, Carpenters, Masons, Plasterers, Founders, and Goldsmithes, their makers and framers, by whose meanes they haue attained this honour, which else should haue beene euilfauoured and rude lumpes of clay, or plaster, pieces of timber, stone, or mettall. without shape or fashion, and so without all estimation and honour, as that Idole in the Pagane Poete confesseth (Horatius.), saying, I was once a vile blocke, but now I am become a GOD, etc.

Adorare, Genesis 23.7, 12 and 33.3, 7, 9, 10. What a fonde thing is it for man, who hath life and reason, to bow himselfe to a dead and vnsensible Image, the worke of his owne hand? is not this stouping and kneeling before them, adoration of them, which is forbidden so earnestly by GODS word? Let such as so fall downe before Images of Saintes, know and confesse that they exhibite that honour to dead stocks and stones, which the Saintes themselues, Peter, Paul, and Barnabas would not to be giuen them being aliue (Acts 10.25, 14.14): which the Angel of GOD forbiddeth to be giuen to him (Revelations 19.10). And if they say, they exhibite such honour not to the Image, but to the Saint whom it representeth, they are conuicted of folly, to beleeue that they please Saints with that honour, which they abhorre as a spoile of GODS honour: for they bee no changelings: but now both hauing greater vnderstanding, and more feruent loue of GOD, do more abhorre to depriue him of his due honor: & being now like vnto the Angels of GOD, do with angels flee to take vnto them by sacriledge the honour due to GOD, And herewithall is confuted their lewde distinction of *Latria* & *Dulia*, where it is euident, that the Saints of GOD can not abide, that as much as any outward worshipping bee done or exhibited to them. But Satan, GODS enemie, desiring to robbe GOD of his honor, desireth exceedingly that such honour might bee giuen to him (Matthew 4.9). Wherefore those which giue the honour due to the creator, to any creature, doe seruice acceptable to no Saintes, who bee the friends of GOD, but vnto Satan, GOD and mans mortall and sworne enemie. And to attribute such desire of diuine honour to Saintes, is to blot them with a most odious and diuelish ignominie and villanie, and in deede of Saintes, to make them Satans and very deuils, whose propertie is to challenge to themselues the honour which is due to GOD onely. And furthermore, in that they say that they doe not worship the Images, as the Gentiles did their Idoles, but GOD and the Saints whom the Images doe represent, and therefore that their doings before Images, be not like the Idolatrie of the Gentiles before their Idoles, Saint Augustine, Lactantius, and Clemens, doe prooue euidently, that by this their answere, they be al one with the Gentiles Idolaters. The Gentiles (saith S. Augustine) which seeme to be of the purer religion say, We worship not the Images, but by the corporall Image, we doe behold the signes of the things which wee ought to worship (Augustine, on Psalm (1)35). And Lactantius saith, The Gentiles say, wee feare not the Images, but them after whose likenesse the Images be made, and to whose names they bee consecrated (Lactantius `Insti.', bk. 2). Thus farre Lactantius. And Clemens saith, That serpent the deuill vttereth these words by the mouth of certaine men, Wee to the honour of the inuisible GOD, worship visible Images: Which surely is most false. See how in vsing the same excuses which the Gentiles Idolaters pretended, they shewe themselues to ioyne with them in Idolatery. For notwithstanding this excuse, Saint Augustine, Clemens, and Lactantius prooue them Idolaters. And Clemens saith, that the Serpent the deuill putteth such excuses in the mouth of Idolaters. And the scriptures say, they worship the stockes and stones (notwithstanding this excuse) euen as our Image mainteiners doe. And Ezekiel therefore calleth the GODS of the Assyrians, stockes and stones, although they were but Images of their GODS. So are our Images of GOD and the Saintes named by the names of GOD and his Saintes, after the vse of the Gentiles. And the same Clemens saith thus in the same booke, They dare not giue the name of the Emperour to any other, for hee punisheth his offendour and traytour by and by: but they dare giue the name of GOD to other, because hee for repentance suffereth his offendours. And euen so doe our Image worshippers giue both names of GOD and the Saintes, and also the honour due to GOD, to their Images, euen as did the Gentiles, Idolaters to their Idoles. What should it meane that they, according as did the Gentiles Idolaters, light candles at noone time, or at midnight, before them, but therewith to honour them? for other vse is there none in so doing. For in the day it needeth not, but was euer a prouerbe of foolishnes, to light a candle at noone time. And in the night, it auayleth not to light a candle before the blinde: and GOD hath neither vse nor honour thereof. And concerning this candle lighting, it is notable that Lactantius aboue a thousand yeeres agoe hath written, after this maner, If they would behold the heauenly light of the Sunne, then should they perceiue that GOD hath no neede of their candles, who for the vse of man hath made so goodly a light (Lactantius, `Instit.', bk. 6, chap. 2). And whereas in so little a circle of the Sunne, which for the great distance, seemeth to bee no greater then a mans head, there is so great brightnesse, that the sight of mans eye is not able to behold it, but if one stedfastly looke vpon it a while, his eyes will be dulled and blinded with darknesse. Now great light, how great clearenesse may wee thinke to bee with GOD, with whom is no night nor darkenesse? and so forth. And by and by he sayth, Seemeth hee therefore to bee in his right minde, who offereth vp to the giuer of light the light of a ware candle for a gift? He requireth another light of vs, which is not smokie, but bright and cleare, euen the light of the minde and vnderstanding. And shortly after he saith, But their goddes, because they bee earthly, haue neede of light, lest they remaine in darkenesse, whose worshippers, because they vnderstand no heauenly thing, doe drawe religion, which they vse, downe to the earth, in the which beeing darke of nature, is neede of light. Wherefore they giue to their goddes no heauenly, but the earthly vnderstanding of mortall men. And therefore they beleeue those things to bee necessary and pleasant vnto them, which are so to vs, who haue neede either of meate when wee bee hungrie, or drinke when wee be thirstie, or clothing when wee bee acolde, or when the Sunne is set, candle light, that wee may see. Thus farre Lactantius, and much more, too long heere to write, of candle lighting in Temples before Images and Idoles for religion: whereby appeareth both the foolishnesse thereof, and also, that in opinion and acte, wee doe agree altogether in our candle religion, with the Gentiles idolaters. What meaneth it that they, after the example of the Gentiles idolaters, burne incense offer vp golde to Images, hang vp crouches, chaines, and ships, legges, armes, and whole men and women of waxe, before images, as though by them, or Saints (as they say) they were deliuered from lamenesse, sicknesse, captiuity, or shipwracke? Is not this Colere imagines, to worship images, so earnestly forbidden in GODS word?

Colere. If they denie it, let them reade the xi. Chapter of Daniel the Prophet, who saith of Antichrist: He shall worship God whom his fathers knew not, with golde, siluer, and with precious stone, and other things of pleasure. in which place the Latine worde is *Colet.*

Cultus. And in the second of Paralipomenon the xxix. Chapter, all the outward rites and ceremonies, as burning of incense, and such other, wherewith GOD in the Temple was honoured, is called *Cultus* (to say) worshipping, which is forbidden straitly by GODS word to bee giuen to images.

Doe not all stories Ecclesiasticall declare, that our holy Martyrs, rather then they would bow and kneele, or offer vp one crumme of incense before an image or idole, haue suffered a thousand kinds of most horrible and dreadful death? And what excuses soeuer they make, yet that all this running on pilgrimage, burning of incense and candles, hanging vp of crouches, chaines, ships, armes, legges, and whole men and women of waxe, kneeling and holding vp of handes, is done to the Images, appeareth by this, that where no Images bee, or where they haue beene, and bee taken away, they doe no such things at all. But all the places frequented when the Images were there, now they be taken away, be forsaken and left desert, nay, now they hate and abhorre the place deadly, which is an euident proofe, that that which they did before, was done in respect of the Images. Wherefore, when we see men and women on heapes to goe on pilgrimage to images, kneele before them, hold vp their hands before them, set vp candles, burne incense before them, offer vp golde and siluer vnto them, hang vp ships, crouches,chaines, men and women of waxe before them, attributing health and safegard, the gifts of GOD, to them, or the Saintes whom they represent, as they rather would haue it: who I say, who can doubt, but that our Image mainteiners, agreeing in all idolatrous opinions, outward rites, and ceremonies with the Gentiles idolaters, agree also with them in committing most abominable idolatry? And to increase this madnesse, wicked men which haue the keeping of such Images, for their more lucre and aduantage, after the example of the Gentiles idolaters, haue reported and spread abroad, aswell by lying tales, as written fables, diuers miracles of Images. As that such an Image miraculously was sent from heauen, euen like Paladium, or magna Diana Ephesiorum. Such an other was as miraculously found in the earth, as the mans head was in Capitol, or the horse head in Capua. Such an Image was brought by Angels. Such an one came it selfe farre from the East to the West, as dame Fortune fledde to Rome. Such an Image of our Lady was painted by Saint Luke, whom of a Physicion they haue made a Painter for that purpose. Such an one an hundred yokes of oxen could not moue, like bona Dea, whom the ship could not carry, or Iupiter Olympius, which laught the artificers to scorne that went about to remoue him to Rome. Some images, though they were hard and stonie, yet for tender heart and pitie, wept. Some like Castor and Pollux, helping their friends in battaile, sweat, as marble pillars doe in dankish weather. Some spake more monstrously then euer did Balaams Asse, who had life and breath in him. Such a criple came and saluted this Saint of oke, and by and by he was made whole, and loe, here hangeth his crouch. Such an one in a tempest vowed to Saint Christopher, and scaped, and behold here is his ship of waxe. Such an one by S. Leonards helpe brake out of prison, and see where his fetters hang. And infinite thousands moe miracles, by like or more shamelesse lyes were reported. Thus doe our Image mainteiners, in earnest apply to their images, all such miracles as the Gentiles haue fained of their idoles. And if it were to bee admitted, that some miraculous actes were by illusion of the deuill done where Images bee: (For it is euident that the most part were fained lyes, and craftie iuglings of men) yet followeth it not therefore, that such images are either to bee honoured, or suffered to remaine, no more them Ezechias left the brasen Serpent vndestroyed, when it was worshipped, although it were both set vp by GODS commandement, and also approoued by a great and true miracle, for as many as beheld it, were by and by healed: neither ought miracles perswade vs to doe contrary to GODS worde. For the Scriptures haue for a warning hereof foreshewed, that the kingdome of Antichrist shall bee mighty in miracles and wonders, to the strong illusion of all the reprobate. But in this they passe the folly and wickednesse of the Gentiles, that they honour and worship the reliques and bones of our Saintes, which prooue that they bee mortall men and dead, and therefore no Gods to be worshipped, which the Gentiles would neuer confesse of their gods for very shame. But the reliques wee must kisse and offer vnto, specially on relique Sunday. And while wee offer (that wee should not bee weary or repent vs of our cost) the musicke and minstrelsie goeth merrily all the offertorie time, with praysing and calling vpon those Saints, whose reliques be then in presence. Yea, and the water also wherein those reliques haue beene dipped, must with great reuerence bee reserued, as very holy and effectuall. Is this agreeable to Saint Chrysostome, who writeth thus of reliques (Chrysostome, Homily of the Seven Machabees)? Doe not regard the ashes of the Saintes bodies, nor the reliques of their flesh and bones, consumed with time: but open the eyes of thy faith, and behold them clothed with heauenly vertue, and the grace of the holy Ghost, and shining with the brightnesse of the heauenly light. But our idolaters found too much vantage of reliques and relique water, to follow Saint Chrysostomes counsell. And because reliques were so gainefull, few places were there but they had reliques prouided for them. And for more plenty of reliques, some one Saint had many heads, one in one place, and another in another place. Some had sixe armes, and xxvi. fingers. And where our lord bare his crosse alone, if all the pieces of the reliques thereof were gathered together, the greatest ship in England would scarcely beare them, and yet the greatest part of it, they say, doeth yet remaine in the handes of Infidels, for the which they pray in their beades bidding, that they may get it also into their hands, for such godly vse and purpose. And not onely the bones of the Saints, but euery thing appertaining to them was an holy relique. In some place they offer a sword, in some the scabberd, in some a shooe, in some a saddle that had bene set vpon some holy horse, in some the coales wherewith Saint Laurence was rosted, in some place the taile of the Asse which our Lord Iesus Christ sate on, to bee kissed and offered vnto for a relique. For rather then they would lacke a relique, they would offer you a horse bone, in stead of a virgins arme, or the taile of the Asse to bee kissed and offered vnto for reliques. O wicked, impudent, and most shameles men, the deuisers of these things, O seely, foolish, and dastardly dawes, and more beastly then the Asse whose taile they kissed, that beleeue such things. Now GOD be mercifull to such miserable and seely Christians, who by the fraud and falshood of those which should haue taught them the way of trueth and life, haue beene made not onely more wicked then the Gentiles idolaters, but also no wiser then asses, horses, and mules, which haue no vnderstanding.

Of these thinges already rehearsed, it is euident, that our Imagemaintainers haue not onely made Images, and set them vp in Temples, as did the Gentiles idolaters their idoles: but also that they haue had the same idolatrous opinions of the Saints, to whom they haue made Images, which the Gentiles idolaters had of their false gods, and haue not onely worshipped their Images with the same rites, ceremonies, superstition, and all circumstances, as did the Gentiles Idolaters their Idoles: but in many poynts also haue farre exceeded them in all wickednesse, foolishnesse, and madnesse. And if this bee not sufficient to prooue them Image worshippers, that is to say, Idolaters: loe, you shall heare their owne open confession, I meane, not onely, the decrees of the second Nicene councell vnder Irene, the Romane councell vnder Gregorie the shipped, as is before declared: so yet doe they it warily and fearefully, in comparison to the blasphemous bolde blasing of manifest idolatry to bee done to Images, set foorth of late, euen in these our dayes, the light of GODS trueth so shining, that aboue other abominable doings, and writings, a man would marueile most at their impudent, shamelesse, and most shamefull blustering boldnesse, who would not at the least haue chosen them a time of more darkenesse, as meeter to vtter their horrible blasphemies in: but haue now taken an harlotes face, not purposed to blush, in setting abroad the furniture of their spirituall whoredome. And heare the plaine blasphemie of the reuerend father in GOD, Iames Naclantus Bishop of Clugium, written in his exposition of Saint Pauls Epistle to the Romanes and the first Chapter, and put in print now of late at Venice, may stand instead of all, whose words of image worshipping be these in Latine, as he did write them, not one syllable altered:

> *Ergo non solum fatendum est, fideles in Ecclesia adorare coram imagine (vt nonnulli ad cautelam forte loquuntur) sed & adorare imaginem, sine quo volueris scrupulo, quin & eo illam venerantur cultu, quo & prototypon eius propter quod si illud*

> *habet adorare latria, & illa latria: si dulia, vel hyper-dulia, & illa pariter eiusmodi cultu adoranda est.*

The sense whereof in English is this:

> Therefore it is not onely to bee confessed, that the faithfull in the Church do worshippe before an Image (as some peraduenture doe warily speake) but also doe worship the Image it selfe, without any scruple or doubt at all: Yea, and they worshippe the Image with the same kinde of worship, wherewith they worship the copy of the Image, or the thing whereafter the Image is made. Wherefore if the copie it selfe is to be worshipped with diuine honour (as is GOD the Father, Christ, and the holy Ghost) the Image of them is also to bee worshipped with diuine honour. If the copie ought to bee worshipped with inferiour honour, or higher worshippe: the Image also is to bee worshipped with the same honour or worshippe.

Thus farre hath Naclantus, whose blasphemies let Pope Gregorius the first confute, & by his authority damne them to hell, as his successours haue horribly thundred (Gregory). For although Gregorie permitteth Images to be had, yet he forbiddeth them by any meanes to be worshipped, and praiseth much Bishop Serenus for the forbidding the worshipping of them, and willeth him to teach the people to auoyde by all meanes to worship any Image (Gregory, `Epistle to Serenus Massil.').

Of Image worshipping. But Naclantus bloweth forth his blaphemous Idolatry, willing Images to be worshipped with the highest kinde of adoration & worship: and least such wholesome doctrine should lacke authoritie, he groundeth it vpon Aristotle, in his booke *de somno & vigilia*, that is, of sleeping and waking as by his printed Booke noted in the margin, is to bee seene: whose impudent wickednesse and idolatrous iudgement, I haue therefore more largely set foorth, that yee may (as Virgil speaketh of Simon) of one know all these Image - worshippers and idolaters, and vnderstande to what point in conclusion the publike hauing of Images in Temples and Churches hath brought vs: comparing the times and writings of Gregory the first, with our dayes, the blasphemies of such idolaters as this instrument of

Belial, named Naclantus, is. Wherefore, now it is by the testimony of the old godly Fathers and Doctours, by the open confession of Bishops assembled in Councels, by most euident signes and arguments, opinions, idolatrous actes, deedes, and worshipping done to their Images, and by their owne open confession and doctrine set foorth in their books, declared and shewed, that their Images haue beene, and bee commonly worshipped, yea, and that they ought so to bee: I will out of GODS word make this generall argument against all such makers, setters vp, and maintayners of Images in publike places. And first of all I will begin with the words of our Sauiour Christ, Woe bee to that man by whom an offence is giuen, woe be to him that offendeth one of these little ones, or weake ones: better were it for him, that a milstone were hanged about his necke, and hee cast into the middle of the sea and drowned, then he should offend one of these little ones, or weake ones(Matthew 18.6-7). And in Deut. GOD himselfe denounceth him accursed that maketh the blinde to wander in his way (Deuteronomy 27.18). And in Leuit. Thou shalt not lay a stumbling block or stone before the blinde (Leviticus 19.14). But images in Churches and Temples haue beene, and be, and (as afterward shall be prooued) euer will bee offences and stumbling blockes, specially to the weake, simple, and blinde common people, deceiuing their hearts by the cunning of the artificer (as the Scripture expresly in sundry places doeth testifie) and so bringing them to Idolatrie. Therefore woe be to the erecter, setter vp, and maintayner of Images in Churches and Temples, for a greater penalty remayneth for him then the death of the body (Apocrypha, Wisdom 13.10, 14.8).

If answer be yet made, that this offence may bee taken away by diligent and syncere doctrine and preaching of GODS word, as by other meanes: and that Images in Churches and Temples therfore bee not things absolutely euill to all men, although dangerous to some: and therefore that it were to bee holden, that the publike hauing of them in Churches and Temples, is not expedient, as a thing perillous, rather then vnlawfull, and a thing vtterly wicked. Then followeth the third article to be prooued, which is in this: That it is not possible, if Images be suffered in Churches and Temples, either by preaching of GODS word, or by any other meanes, to keepe the people from worshipping of them, and so to auoyd Idolatrie. And first concerning Preaching. If it should be admitted, that although Images were suffered in Churches, yet might Idolatrie by diligent and syncere preaching of GODS word be auoyded: It should follow of necessity, that syncere doctrine might alwayes be had and continue, aswell as Images, and so that wheresoeuer, to offence, were erected an Image, there also, of reason, a godly and syncere Preacher should and might bee continually maintayned. For it is reason, that the warning be as common as the stumbling blocke, the remedy as large as is the offence, the medicine as generall as the poyson: but that is not possible, as both reason and experience teacheth. Wherefore preaching cannot stay Idolatry, Images being publikely suffered. For an Image, which will last for many hundred yeeres, may for a little be bought: but a good Preacher cannot without much bee continually maintayned. Item, if the Prince will suffer it, there will bee by and by many, yea, infinite Images: but syncere Preachers were and euer shall be but a few in respect of the multitude to be taught. For our Sauiour Christ sayth, The haruest is plentifull, but the workemen bee but few: which hath beene hitherto continually true, and will bee to the worlds end: And in our time, and heere in our country so true, that euery Shire should scarcely haue one good Preacher, if they were diuided.

Now Images will continually to the beholders preach their doctrine, that is, the worshipping of Images and Idolatrie, to the which Preaching mankinde is exceeding prone, and enclined to giue eare and credit: as experience of all nations and ages doth too much prooue. But a true Preacher to stay this mischiefe, is in very many places scarcely heard once in a whole yeere, and some where not once in seuen yeeres, as is euident to bee prooued. And that euill opinion which hath beene long rooted in mens hearts, cannot suddenly by one Sermon be rooted out clean. And as few are enclined to credit sound doctrine: as many, and almost all, be prone to superstition and idolatry. So that heerein appeareth not onely a difficulty, but also an impossibility of the remedy. Further, it appeareth not by any story of credit, that true and syncere Preaching hath endured in any one place aboue one hundred yeeres: But it is euident, that Images, superstition, and worshipping of Images and idolatrie, haue continued many hundred yeeres. For all writings and experience doe testifie, that good things doe by little and little euer decay, vntill they be cleane banished: and contrariwise, euill things doe more and more increase, till they come to a full perfection and wickednesse. Neither neede wee to seeke examples farre off for a proofe heereof, our present matter is an example. For Preaching of GODS word (most syncere in the beginning) by processe of time, waxed lesse and lesse pure, and after corrupt, and last of all, altogether layd downe and left off, and other inuentions of men crept in place of it. And on the other part, Images among Christian men were first painted, and that in whole stories together, which had some signification in them: Afterwards, they were embossed, and made of timber, stone, playster, and mettall. And first they were onely kept priuately in priuate mens houses: And then after, they crept into Churches and Temples, but first by paynting, and after by embossing: and yet were they no where at the first worshipped. But shortly after, they began to be worshipped of the ignorant sort of men: as appeareth by the Epistle that Gregory the first of that name Bishop of Rome, did write to Serenus Bishop of Marcelles. Of the which two Bishops, Serenus for idolatrie committed to Images, brake them, and burned them, Gregory although he thought it tolerable to let them stand: yet he iudged it abominable that they should be worshipped, and thought (as is now alleaged) that the worshipping of them might be stayed, by teaching of GODS word, according as he exhorteth Serenus to teach the people, as in the same Epistle appeareth. But whether Gregories opinion, or Serenus iudgement were better heerein, consider ye, I pray you, for experience by and by confuteth Gregories opinion. For notwithstanding Gregories writing, and the Preaching of others, Images being once publikely set vp in Temples and Churches, simple men and women shortly after fell on heaps to worshipping of them: And at the last, the learned also were carried away with the publike errour, as with a violent streame or flood. And at the second Councell Nicene, the Bishops and Clergie decreed, that Images should bee worshipped: and so by occasion of these stumbling blockes, not only the vnlearned and simple, but the learned and wise, not the people onely, but the Bishops, not the sheepe, but also the shepheards themselues (who should haue beene guides in the right way, and light to shine in darkenesse) being blinded by the bewitching of Images, as blind guides of the blinde, fell both into the pit of damnable Idolatry. In the which all the world, as it were drowned, continued vntill our age, by the space of aboue eight hundred yeeres, vnspoken against in a manner. And this successe had Gregories order: which mischiefe had neuer come to passe, had Bishop Serenus way beene taken, and all idols and Images beene vtterly destroyed and abolished: for no man worshippeth that that is not. And thus you see, how from hauing of Images priuately, it came to publike setting of them vp in Churches and Temples, although without harme at the first, as was then of some wise and learned men iudged: and from simple hauing them there, it came at the last to worshipping of them. First, by the rude people, who specially (as the Scripture teacheth) are in danger of superstition and idolatry, and afterwards by the Bishops, the learned, and by the whole Clergie (Apocrypha. Wisdom 13.10, 14.16). So that Layty and Clergie, learned and vnlearned, all ages, sectes, and degrees of men, women, and children, of whole Christendome (an horrible and most dreadfull thing to think) haue beene at once drowned in abominable idolatrie, of all other vices most detested of GOD, and most damnable to man and that by the space of eight hundred yeeres and more. And to this end is come that beginning of setting vp of Images in Churches then iudged harmelesse, in experience prooued not onely harmfull, but exitious and pestilent, and to the destruction and subuersion of all good religion vniuersally. So that I conclude, as it may be possible in some one City or little Country, to haue Images set vp in Temples and Churches, and yet idolatry by earnest and continuall preaching of GODS true word, and the syncere Gospel of our Sauiour Christ, may be kept away for a short time: So is it impossible, that (Images once set vp and suffered in Temples and Churches) any great countreyes, much lesse the whole world, can any long time bee kept from idolatry. And the godly will respect, not onely their owne City, countrey and time, and the health of men of their age: but be carefull for all places and times, and the saluation of men of all ages. At the least, they will not lay such stumbling blockes and snares, for the feet of other countrymen and ages, which experience hath already prooued to haue beene the ruine of the world. Wherefore I make a generall conclusion of all that I haue hitherto sayd: If the stumbling blockes, and poysons of mens soules, by setting vp of Images, will bee many, yea, infinite if they be suffered, and the warnings of the same stumbling blockes, and remedies for the sayd poysons by preaching but few, as is already declared: if the stumbling blockes be easie to be layd, the poysons soone prouided, and the warnings and remedies hard to know or come by: if the stumbling blockes lie continually in the way, and poyson bee ready at hand euery where, and warnings and remedies but seldome giuen: and if all men be more ready of themselues to stumble and be offended, then to bee warned, all men more ready to drinke of the poyson, then to taste of the remedy (as is before partly, and shall heereafter more fully be declared) and so in fine, the poyson continually and deepely drunke of many, the remedy seldome and faintly tasted of a few: How can it be but that infinite of the weake and infirme shalbe offended, infinite by ruine shall breake their neckes, infinite by deadly venome by poysoned in their soules? And how is the charity of GOD, or loue of our neighbour in our hearts then, if when we may remooue such dangerous stumbling blockes, such pestilent poysons, we will not remooue them: What shall

I say of them which will lay stumbling blockes, where before there was none, and set snares for the feet, nay, for the soules of weake and simple ones, and worke the danger of their euerlasting destruction, for whom our Sauiour Christ shedde his most pretious blood, where better it were that the arts of painting, plaistering, caruing, grauing, and founding, had neuer beene found nor vsed, then one of them, whose soules in the sight of GOD are so pretious, should by occasion of image or picture perish and bee lost. And thus is it declared that Preaching cannot possibly stay Idolatry, if Images be set vp publikely in Temples and Churches. And as true is it, that no other remedy, as writing against idolatry, Councels assembled, Decrees made against it, seuere Lawes likewise and Proclamations of Princes and Emperours, neither extreme punishments and penalties, nor any other remedy could or can be possible deuised for the auoyding of idolatry, if Images bee publikely set vp and suffered. For concerning writing against Images, and Idolatrie to them committed, there hath beene alleaged vnto you in the second part of this Treatise a great many places, out of S. Ierome, Origen, Lactantius, S. Augustine, Epiphanius, S. Ambrose, Clemens, and diuers other learned and holy Bishops and Doctours of the Church. And besides these, all histories Ecclesiasticall, and books of other godly and learned Bishops and Doctours are full of notable examples and sentences against Images and the worshipping of them. And as they haue most earnestly written, so did they syncerely and most diligently in their time teach and preach, according to their writings and examples. For they were then Preaching Bishops, and more often seene in Pulpits, then in Princes palaces, more often occupied in his legacy, who sayd, Goe ye into the whole world, and preach the Gospel to all men, then in Embassages and affayres of Princes of this world. And as they were most zealous and diligent, so were they of excellent learning and godlinesse of life, and by both of great authority and credit with the people, and so of more force and likelihood to perswade the people, and the people more like to beleeue and follow their doctrine. But if their preachings could not helpe, much lesse could their writings, which doe but come to the knowledge of a few that be learned, in comparison to continual preaching, wherof the whole multitude is partaker. Neither did the old Fathers, Bishops, and Doctours, seuerally onely by preaching and writing, but also together, great numbers of them assembled in Synods and Councels, make Decrees and Ecclesiasticall Lawes against Images, and the worshipping of them, neither did they so once or twise, but diuers times, and in diuers ages and Countreyes, assembled Synodes and Councels, and made seuere Decrees against Images and worshipping of them, as hath beene at large in the second part of this Homilie before declared. But all their writing, preaching, assembling in Councels, decreeing and making of Lawes Ecclesiasticall, could nothing helpe, either to pull downe Images to whom Idolatrie was committed, or against Idolatrie whilest Images stood. For those blinde bookes and dumbe Schoolemasters, I meane Images and Idols (for they call them Lay mens books, and Schoolemasters) by their carued and painted writings, teaching and preaching Idolatry, preuayled against all their written bookes, and preaching with liuely voice, as they call it. Well, if preaching and writing could not keepe men from worshipping of Images and Idolatry, if pen and words could not doe it, you would thinke that penalty and sword might doe it, I meane, that Princes by seuere Lawes and punishments, might stay this vnbridled affection of all men to idolatry, though Images were set vp and suffered. But experience prooueth, that this can no more helpe against Idolatrie, then writing and preaching. For Christian Emperours (whose authoritie ought of reason, and by GODS Law, to be greatest) aboue eight in number, and sixe of them successiuely raigning one after another (as is in the histories before rehearsed) making most seuere Lawes and Proclamations against Idols, and Idolatry, Images, and the worshipping of Images, and executing most grieuous punishments, yea, the penalty of death, vpon the maintayners of Images, and vpon Idolaters and Image-worshippers: could not bring to passe, that either Images once set vp, might throughly be destroyed, or that men should refrayne from the worshipping of them, being set vp. And what thinke you then will come to passe, if men of learning should teach the people to make them, and should maintaine the setting vp of them, as things necessary in religion? To conclude, it appeareth euidently by all stories and writings, and experience in times past, that neither preaching, neither writing, neither the consent of the learned, nor authority of the godly, nor the decrees of Councels, neither the Lawes of Princes, nor extreme punishments of the offendours in that behalfe, nor any other remedy or meanes, can helpe against Idolatrie, if Images be suffered publikely. And it is truely sayd, that times past are Schoolemasters of wisedome to vs that follow and liue after. Therefore if in times past, the most vertuous and best learned, the most diligent also, and in number almost infinite, ancient Fathers, Bishops, and Doctors, with their writing, preaching, industry, earnestnesse, authority, assemblies and Councels could doe nothing against Images and Idolatry, to Images once set vp: what can we, neither in learning, nor holinesse of life, neither in diligence, neither authority, to bee compared with them, but men in contempt, and of no estimation (as the world goeth now) a few also in number, in so great a multitude and malice of men. What can we doe, I say, or bring to passe to the stay of Idolatrie or worshipping of Images, if they be allowed to stand publikely in Temples and Churches? And if so many, so mighty Emperours, by so seuere Lawes and Proclamations, so rigorous and extreme punishments and executions could not stay the people from setting vp and worshipping of Images: what will ensue, thinke you, when men shall commend them as necessary bookes of the lay men. Let vs therefore of these latter dayes learne this lesson of the experience of ancient antiquitie, that Idolatrie can not possibly bee separated from Images any long time: but that as an vnseparable accident, or as a shadow followeth the bodie when the Sunne shineth, so Idolatrie followeth and cleaueth to the publique hauing of Images in Temples and Churches. And finally, as Idolatrie is to be abhorred and auoyded, so are Images (which can not bee long without Idolatry) to be put away and destroyed. Besides the which experiments and proofe of times before, the very nature and origine of Images themselues draweth to Idolatry most violently, and mens nature and inclination also is bent to Idolatrie so vehemently, that it is not possible to seuer or part Images, nor to keepe men from Idolatrie, if Images bee suffered publikely. That I speake of the nature and origine of Images, is this: Euen as the first inuention of them is nought, and no good can come of that which had an euill beginning, for they bee altogether nought, as Athanasius in his booke against the Gentiles declareth, and Saint Ierome also vpon the prophet Ieremie the sixt Chapter, and Eusebius the seuenth booke of his Ecclesiasticall Historie the xviii. Chapter testifieth, that as they first came from the Gentiles, which were idolaters and worshippers of Images, vnto vs, and as the inuention of them was the beginning of spirituall fornication, as the word of GOD testifieth: (Apocrypha, Wisdom 14.12) So will they naturally (as it were of necessity) turne to their origine from whence they came, and draw vs with them most violently to Idolatrie, abominable to GOD and all godly men. For if the origine of Images, and worshipping of them, as it is recorded in the eight Chapter of the booke of Wisedome, began of a blinde loue of a fond father, framing for his comfort an Image of his sonne, being dead, and so at the last men fell to the worshipping of the Image of him whom they did know to bee dead: How much more will men and women fall to the worshipping of the Images of GOD, our Sauiour Christ, and his Saints, if they bee suffered to stand in Churches and Temples publiquely? For the greater the opinion is of the maiestie and holinesse of the person to whom an Image is made, the sooner will the people fall to the worshipping of the sayd Image. Wherefore the Images of GOD, our Sauiour Christ, the blessed virgin Marie, the Apostles, Martyrs, and other of notable holinesse, are of all other Images most dangerous for the perill of Idolatrie, and therefore greatest heede to bee taken that none of them bee suffered to stand publiquely in Churches and Temples. For there is no great dread lest any should fall to the worshipping of the images of Annas, Caiaphas, Pilate, or Iudas the traytor, if they were set vp. But to the other, it is already at full prooued, that Idolatrie hath beene, is, and is most like continually to bee committed. Now as was before touched, and is heere most largely to bee declared, the nature of man is none otherwise bent to worshipping of Images (if hee may haue them, and see them) then it is bent to whoredome and adulterie in the company of harlots. And as vnto a man giuen to the lust of the flesh, seeing a wanton harlot, sitting by her, and imbracing her, it profiteth little for one to say, Beware of fornication, GOD will condemne fornicatours and adulterers: for neither will hee, being ouercome with greater intisements of the strumpet giue eare or take heede to such godly admonitions, and when hee is left afterwardes alone with the harlotte, nothing can follow but wickednesse (1 Corinthians 6.9-10, 1 Thessalonians 4.3, 1.Cor. 5.1, Hebrews 13.4): euen so, suffer Images to bee set in the Churches and Temples, ye shall in vaine bid them beware of Images, as Saint Iohn doeth, and flee Idolatrie (1 John 5.21), as all the Scriptures warne vs, yee shall in vaine preach and teach them against Idolatry. For a number will notwithstanding fall headlong vnto it, what by the nature of Images, and what by the inclination of their owne corrupt nature.

Wherefore as for a man giuen to lust, to sit downe by a strumpet, is to tempt GOD: So is it likewise to erect an Idole in this pronenesse of mans nature to Idolatrie, nothing but a tempting. Now if any will say that this similitude prooueth nothing, yet I pray them let the word of GOD, out of the which the similitude is taken, prooue something. Doeth not the worde of GOD call Idolatrie spirituall fornication (Leviticus 17.7, 20.3, Numbers 25.2, Deuteronomy 31.16, Ezekiel 6.9)? Doeth it not call a gylte or painted Idole or Image, a strumpet with a painted face? Bee not the spirituall wickednesses of an Idols intising, like the flatteries of a wanton harlot? Bee not men and women as prone to spirituall fornication (I meane Idolatrie) as to carnall fornication? If this bee denyed, let all nations vpon the earth which haue beene Idolaters (as by all Stories appeareth) prooue it true. Let the Iewes and the people of GOD which were so often and so earnestly warned, so dreadfully threatned concerning images and idolatry, and so extremely punished therefore (and yet fell vnto it) prooue it to be true: as in almost all the bookes of the old Testament, namely the Kings and the Chronicles, and the Prophets, it appeareth most euidently. Let all ages and times, and men of all ages and times, of all degrees and conditions, wise men, learned men, Princes, Idiotes, vnlearned, and comminalty, proue it to be true. If you require examples: For wise men, ye haue the Egyptians, and the Indian Gymnosophistes, the wisest men of the world, you haue Solomon the wisest of all other. For learned men, the Greekes, and namely the Athenians, exceeding all other nations in superstition and idolatrie, as in the historie of the Actes of the Apostles S. Paul chargeth them (Acts 17.16, Romans 1.23). For Princes and gouernours, you haue the Romanes, the rulers of the rost, (as they say) you haue the same forenamed king Solomon, and all the kings of Israel and Iuda after him, sauing Dauid, Ezechias and Iosias, and one or two more. All these (I say) and infinite others, wise, learned, Princes, and Gouernours, being all Idolaters, haue you for examples and a proofe of mens inclination to idolatrie. That I may passe ouer with silence in the meane time, infinite multitudes and millions of Idiotes and vnlearned, the ignorant and grosse people, like vnto Horses and Mules in whom is no vnderstanding, whose perill and danger to fall on heapes to Idolatrie by occasion of Images, the Scriptures specially foreshew and giue warning of (Psalms 32.9). And indeede how should the vnlearned, simple, and foolish scape the nettes and snares of Idolles, and Images, in the which the wisest and the best learned haue beene so entangled, trapped, and wrapped (Apocrypha. Wisdom 13.17-19, 14.1, 27)? Wherefore the argument holdeth this ground sure, that men bee as inclined of their corrupt nature to spirituall fornication, as to carnall, which the wisedome of GOD foreseeing, to the generall prohibition, that none should make to themselues and Image or similitude, addeth a cause, depending of mans corrupt nature. Lest (sayeth GOD) thou being deceiued with errour, honour and worshippe them (Deuteronomy 4.16, 19). And of this ground of mans corrupt inclination, aswell to spirituall fornication, as to carnall, it must needes follow, tht as it is the duetie of the godly Magistrate, louing honestie, and hating whoredome, to remooue all strumpets and harlots, specially out of places notoriously suspected, or resorted vnto of naughty packes, for the auoyding of carnall fornication: so it is the duetie of the same godly

Magistrate, after the examples of the godly Kings, Ezechias and Iosias, to driue away all spirituall harlots, (I meane Idoles and Images) especially out of suspected places, Churches and Temples, daungerous for idolatry to bee committed to Images placed there, as it were in the appointed place and height of honour and worship (as Saint Augustine sayth) where the liuing GOD onely (and not dead stones and stockes) is to bee worshipped: It is (I say) the office of godly Magistrates likewise to auoide Images and Idoles out of Churches and Temples, as spirituall harlots out of suspected places for the auoyding of Idolatrie, which is spirituall Fornication (Augustine, on Psalms 36 and 113 in `De Civitatis Dei', Bk. 4, Chap. 3). And as he were the enemy of all honesty, that should bring strumpets and harlots out of their secret corners into the publique market place, there freely to dwell and practise their filthy Marchandise: So is the enemy of the true worshipping of GOD, that bringeth Idols and Images into the Temple and Church, the house of GOD, there openly to be worshipped, and to robbe the zealous GOD of his honour, who will not giue it to any other, nor his glory to carued Images, who is as much forsaken, and the bond of loue betweene man and him as much broken by Idolatry, which is spirituall Fornication, as is the knot and bond of marriage broken by carnall Fornication. Let all this be taken as a lie, if the word of GOD enforce it not to be true. Cursed be the man, saith GOD in Deuteronomie, that maketh a carued or molten Image, and placeth it in a secret corner: and all the people shall say, Amen (Deuteronomy 27.15). Thus saith GOD, for at that time no man durst haue or worship Images openly, but in corners onely: and the whole world being the great Temple of GOD, hee that in any corner thereof robbeth GOD of his glorie, and giueth it to stockes and stones, is pronounced by GODS word accursed. Now hee that will bring these spirituall harlots out of their lurking corners, into publique Churches and Temples, that spirituall Fornication may there openly of all men and women without shame be committed with them, no doubt that person is cursed of GOD, and twise cursed, and all good and godly men and women will say, Amen, and their Amen will take effect also. Yea, and furthermore the madnesse of all men professing the Religion of Christ, now by the space of a sort of hundred yeeres, and yet euen in our time in so great light of the Gospell, very many running on heapes by sea and land, to the great losse of their time, expence and waste of their goods, destitution of their Wiues, Children, and Families, and danger of their owne bodies and liues, to Compostella, Rome, Hierusalem, and other farre Countreys, to visite dumbe and dead stockes and stones, doeth sufficiently prooue the pronenesse of mans corrupt nature to the seeking of Idolles once set by, and the worshipping of them. And thus aswell by the origine and nature of Idolles and Images themselues, as by the pronepronenesse and inclination of mans corrupt nature to Idolatrie, it is euident, that neyther Images, if they bee publiquely set vp, can bee separated, nor men, if they see Images in Temples and Churches, can bee staide and kept from Idolatrie. Now whereas they yet alleadge, that howsoeuer the people, Princes, learned, and wise of olde time, haue fallen into Idolatrie by occasion of Images, that yet in our time the most part, specially the learned, wise, and of any authoritie, take no hurt nor offence by Idolles and Images, neyther doe runne into farre Countreys to them, and worship them: And that they know well what an Idoll or Image is, and how to bee vsed, and that therefore it followeth, Images in Churches and Temples to be an indifferent thing, as the which of some is not abused: and that therefore they may iustly hold (as was in the beginning of this part by them alleadged) that it is not vnlawfull or wicked absolutely to haue Images in Churches and Temples, though it may for the danger of the simple sort seeme to be not altogether expedient.

Whereunto may bee well replyed, that Solomon also the wisest of all men, did well know what an Idoll or Image was, and neither tooke any harme thereof a great while himselfe, and also with his godly writings armed others against the daunger of them. But yet afterward the same Solomon suffering his wanton Paramours to bring their Idolles into his Court and Palace, was by carnall harlots perswaded, and brought at the last to the committing of Spirituall Fornication with Idolles, and of the wisest and godliest Prince, became the most foolishest and wickeddest also (Apocrypha. Wisdom 13.14). Wherefore it is better euen for the wisest to regard this warning, Hee that loueth danger shall perish therein: and Let him that standeth, beware lest he fall, rather then wittingly and willingly to lay such a stumbling blocke for his owne feet and others, that may perhappes bring at last to breake necke (Apocrypha. Ecclesiasticus 3.26, 13.13, 1 Corinthians 10.12). The good King Ezechias did know well enough, that the brasen Serpent was but a dead Image, and therefore hee tooke no hurt himselfe thereby through Idolatrie to it (2 Kings 18.4): Did hee therefore let it stand, because himselfe tooke no hurte thereof? No not so: but beeing a good King, and therefore regarding the health of his seelie Subiects, deceiued by that Image, and committing Idolatrie thereto, hee did not onely take it downe, but also brake it to pieces. And this hee did to that Image that was set vp by the commandement of GOD, in the presence whereof great Myracles were wrought, as that which was a figure of our Sauiour Christ to come, who should deliuer vs from the mortall sting of the old Serpent Satan. Neither did hee spare it in respect of the ancientnesse or antiquity of it, which had continued aboue seuen hundreth yeeres, nor for that it had beene suffered, and preserued by so many godly Kings before his time. Now (thinke you) would that godly Prince (if hee were now liuing) handle our Idols, set vp against GODS commandement directly, and being figures of nothing but follie, and for fooles to gaze on, till they become as wise as the blockes themselues which they stare on, and so fall downe as dared Larkes in that gase, and being themselues aliue, worship a dead stocke or stone, gold or siluer, and so become Idolaters, abominable and cursed before the liuing GOD, giuing the honour due vnto him which made them when they were nothing, and to our Sauiour Christ who redeemed them being lost, to the dead and dumbe Idoll, the worke of mans hand, which neuer did nor can doe any thing for them, no, is not able to stirre nor once to mooue, and therefore worse then a vile worme which can mooue and creepe? The excellent King Iosias also did take himselfe no hurt of Images and Idols, for he did know well what they were: did hee therefore because of his owne knowledge let Idolles and Images stand? much lesse did he set any vp? Or rather did hee not by his knowledge and authoritie also succour the ignorance of such as did not know what they were, by vtter taking away of all such stumbling blockes as might be occasion of ruine to his people and Subiects? Will they because a few tooke no hurt by Images or Idols, breake the generall Law of GOD, Thou shalt make to thee no similitude, etc. They might aswell, because Moses was not seduced by Iethroes daughter, nor Boos by Ruth, being strangers, reason, that all the Iewes might breake the generall Law of GOD, forbidding his people to ioyne their children in marriage with strangers, lest they seduce their children that they should not follow GOD. Wherefore they which thus reason, thought it bee not expedient, yet it is lawfull to haue Images publikely, and doe proue that lawfulnesse by a few picked and chosen men: if they obiect that indifferently to all men, which a very few can haue without hurt and offence, they seeme to take the multitude for vile soules (as he saith in Virgil) of whose losse and safegard no reputation is to be had, for whom yet Christ paid as dearely as for the mightiest Prince, or the wisest and best learned in the earth. And they that will haue it generally to bee taken for indifferent, that a very few take no hurt of it, though infinite multitudes beside perish thereby, shew that they put little difference betweene the multitude of Christians and bruit beasts, whose danger they doe so little esteeme. Besides this, if they be Bishops or Parsons, or otherwise hauing charge of mens consciences that thus reason, It is lawfull to haue Images publikely, though it be not expedient, what manner of pastours shew they themselues to be to their flocke, which thrust vnto them that which they themselues confesse not to be expedient for them, but to the vtter ruine of the soules committed to their charge, for whom they shall giue a strait account before the Prince of Pastours at the last day? For indeede to obiect to the weake, and readie to fall of themselues, such stumbling blockes, is a thing not onely not expedient, but vnlawfull, yea, and most wicked also. Wherefore it is to be wondered how they can call Images, set vp in Churches and Temples to no profite or benefit of any, and to so great perill and daunger, yea hurt and destruction of many, or rather infinite, things indifferent. Is not the publike setting vp of them rather a snare for all men, and the tempting of GOD? I beseech these reasoners to call to minde their owne accustomed ordinance and Decree, whereby they determined that the Scripture, though by GOD himselfe commaunded to bee knowen of all men, women, and children, should not be read of the simple, nor had in the vulgar tongue, for that (as they said) it was dangerous, by bringing the simple people into errours (Deuteronomy 31.11-12). And will they not forbid Images to bee set vp in Churches and Temples, which are not commanded, but forbidden most straitly by GOD, but let them still be there, yea, and maintaine them also, seeing the people are brought, not in danger onely, but in deed into most abominable errours and detestable Idolatry thereby? Shall GODS word, by GOD commanded to be read vnto all, and knowen of all, for danger of Heresie (as they say) be shut vp? and Idols and Images, notwithstanding they be forbidden by GOD, and notwithstanding the danger of Idolatrie by them, shall they yet be set vp, suffered, and maintained in Churches and Temples? O worldly and fleshly wisedome, euen bent to maintaine the inuentions and traditions of men by carnall reason, and by the same to disanull or deface the holy ordinances, lawes, and honour of the Eternall GOD, who is to bee honoured and praised foreuer. Amen.

Now it remayneth for the conclusion of this Treatie, to declare aswell the abuse of Churches and Temples, by too costly and sumptuous decking and adorning of them, as also the lewde paynting, gilding, and clothing of Idoles and Images, and so to conclude the whole treatie.

In S. Ieromes time, an hundreth and threescore yeeres after Christ, Christians had none other Temples but common houses, whither they for the most part secretly resorted (S. Ierome, `Apolog.', chap. 39, Tertul.Apo). And so farre off was it that they had before his time any goodly or gorgious decked Temples, that lawes were made in Antonius, Verus and Commodus the Emperours times, that no Christians should dwell in houses, come in publique bathes, or bee seene in streetes, or any where abroad, and that if they were once accused to be Christians, they should by no meanes be suffered to escape (Eusebius, `Eccles. Hist.', bk. 5, Hieronymus). As was practised on Apolonius a noble Senatour of Rome, who being accused of his owne bondman and slaue that hee was a Christian, could neither by his defence and apologie learnedly and eloquently written and read publiquely in the Senate, nor in respect that hee was a Citizen, nor for the dignitie of his order, nor for the vilenesse and vnlawfulnesse of his accuser, being his owne slaue, by likelihood of malice mooued to forge lyes against his Lord, nor for no other respect or helpe, could be deliuered from death. So that Christians were then driuen to dwell in caues and dennes: so farre off was it that they had any publique Temples adorned and decked as they now be. Which is here rehearsed to the confutation of those, which report such glorious glosed fables, of the goodly and gorgious Temple, that Saint Peter, Linus, Cletus, and those thirtie Bishoppes their successours had at Rome, vntill the time of the Emperour Constantine, and which Saint Policarpe should haue in Asia, or Ireneus in France, by such lyes, contrary to all true Histories, to mayntaine the superfluous gilding and decking of Temples now a dayes, wherein they put almost the whole summe and pith of our religion. But in those times the world was wonne to Christendome, not by gorgious, gilded, and paynted Temples of Christians, which had scarcely houses to dwell in: but by the godly, and as it were golden mindes, and firme faith of such as in all aduersitie and persecution professed the trueth of our religion. And after these times in Maximinian and Constantius the Emperours proclamation, the places where Christians resorted to publique prayer, were called conuenticles (Eusebius, `Eccles. Hist.', bk. 8, chap. 19, and bk. 9. chap. 9). And in Galerius Maximinus the Emperours Epistle, they are called *Oratories* and *Dominicae*, to say, places dedicate to the seruice of the Lord. And heere by the way it is to bee noted, that at that time there were no Churches or Temples erected vnto any Saint, but to GOD onely, as Saint Augustine also recordeth, saying, Wee build no Temples vnto our Martyrs (Augustine, `De Civitate', bk. 8, chap. 1). And Eusebius himselfe calleth Churches, houses of prayer, and sheweth that in Constantine the Emperours time, all men reioyced, seeing in stead of low conuenticles, which tyrants had destroyed, high Temples to bee builded.

Crypt. Loe, vnto the time of Constantine, by the space of aboue three hundred yeeres after our Sauiour Christ, when Christian religion was most pure, and indeede golden, Christians had but low and poore conuenticles, and simple Oratories, yea caues vnder the ground, called Crypt', where they for feare of persecution assembled secretly together.

Basilic'. A figure whereof remayneth in the vaultes which yet are builded vnder great Churches, to put vs in remembrance of the olde state of the primitiue Church before Constantine, whereas in Constantines time, and after him, were builded great and goodly Temples for Christians, called Basilic', either for that the Greekes vsed to call all great and goodly places Basilicas, or for that the high and euerlasting King GOD and our Sauiour Christ was serued in them. But although Constantine, and other Princes, of good zeale to our religion, did sumptuously decke and adorne Christians Temples, ye did they dedicate at that time all Churches and Temples to GOD or our Sauiour Christ, and to no Saint, for that abuse began long after in Iustinians time. And that gorgiousnesse then vsed, as it was borne with, as rising of a good zeale: so was it signified of the godly learned euen at that time, that such cost might otherwise haue beene better bestowed (`Novel. Constit.', 3, 47). Let Saint Ierome (although otherwise too great a liker and allower of externall and outward things) bee a proofe hereof, who hath these wordes in his Epistle to Demetriades, Let other (sayth Saint Ierome) build Churches, couer walles with tables of Marble, carrie together huge pillars, and gild their tops or heads, which doe not feele or vnderstand their precious decking and adorning, let them decke the doores with Iuorie, and Siluer, and set the golden Altars with precious stones, I blame it not, let euery man abound in his owne sense, and better is it so to doe, then carefully to keepe their riches layd vp in store. But thou hast another way appoynted thee, to clothe Christ in the poore, to visit him in the sicke, feede him in the hungry, lodge him in those who doe lacke harbour, and especially such as bee of the houshold of faith.

And the same Saint Ierome toucheth the same matter somewhat more freely in his treatie of the life of Clerkes to Nepotian, saying thus, Many build walles, and erect pillars of Churchers, the smoothe Marbles doe glister, the roofe shineth with gold, the altar is set with precious stones: But of the ministers of Christ, there is no election or choyse. Neither let any man obiect and alleadge against mee the rich Temple that was in Iurie, the table, candlestickes, incense, shippes, platters, cups, morters, and other things all of golde. Then were these things allowed of the Lord, when the Priests offered sacrifices, and the blood of beastes was accounted the redemption of sinnes. Howbeit all these things went before in figure, and they were written for vs, vpon whom the end of the world is come. And now when that our Lord being poore, hath dedicate the pouerty of his house, let vs remember his crosse, & we shall esteeme riches as mire and dung. What do we maruell at that which Christ calleth wicked Mammon? Whereto do we so highly esteeme and loue that which S. Peter doeth for a glory testifie that he had not? Hitherto S. Ierome. Thus you see how S. Ierome teacheth the sumptuousnesse amongst the Iewes to bee a figure to signifie, and not an example to follow, and that those outward things were suffered for a time, vntill Christ our Lord came, who turned all those outward things into spirit, faith and trueth. And the same Saint Ierome vpon the seuenth Chapter of Ieremy saith, GOD commaunded both the Iewes at that time, and now vs who are placed in the Church, that wee haue no trust in the goodlinesse of building and guilt rooffes, and in walles couered with tables of marble, and say: the Temple of the Lord, the Temple of the Lord. For that is the Temple of the Lord, wherein dwelleth true faith, godly conuersation, and the company of all vertues. And vpon the Prophet Agge, hee describeth the true and right decking or ornaments of the Temple after this sort: I (saith Saint Ierome) doe thinke the Siluer wherewith the house of GOD is decked, to bee the doctrine of the Scriptures, of the which it is spoken, The doctrine of the Lord is a pure doctrine, Siluer tried in the fire, purged from drosse, purified seuen times. And I doe take gold to bee that which remaineth in the hid sence of the Saintes, and the secret of the heart, and shineth with the true light of GOD. Which is euident that the Apostle also meant of the Saints that build vpon the foundation of Christ, some siluer, some gold, some pretious stones: that by the gold, the hid sense, by siluer, godly vtterance, by pretious stones, workes which please God, might bee signified. With these metals, the Church of our Sauiour is made more goodly and gorgeous, then was the Synagogue in olde time. With these liuely stones, is the Church and house of Christ builded, and peace is giuen to it for euer. All these be Saint Ieromes sayings. No more did the old godly Bishopes and Doctours of the Church allow the ouersumptuous furniture of Temples and Churches, with plate, vessels of gold, siluer, and pretious vestments. S. Chrysostome saith, in the ministery of the holy Sacraments, there is no neede of golden vessels, but of golden mindes (Chrysostome, `2 Offi.', chap. 28'). And Saint Ambrose saith, Christ sent his Apostles without golde, and gathered his Church without gold. The Church hath gold, not to keepe it, but to bestow it on the necessities of the poore. The sacraments looke for no gold, neither doe they please GOD for the commendation of gold, which are not bought for golde. The adorning and decking of the Sacraments, is the redemption of Captiues. Thus much saith Saint Ambrose.

Saint Ierome commendeth Exuperius Bishop of Tolose, that he carried the Sacrament of the Lordes body in a wicker basket, and the Sacrament of his blood in a glasse, and so cast couetousnesse out of the Church (unidentified, Tit. de consecra. can. Triburien.). And Bonifacius Bishop and Martyr, as it is recorded in the decrees, testifieth, that in olde time the ministers vsed wodden, and not golden vessels. And Zepherinus the xvi. Bishop of Rome made a decree, that they should vse vessels of glasse. Likewise were the vestures vsed in the Church in olde time very plaine and single, and nothing costly (Lactantius? `Insti.', bk. 1, chap. 14). And Rabanus at large declareth, tht this costly and manifold furniture of vestments of late vsed in the Church, was set from the Iewish vsage, and agreeth with Aarons apparelling almost altogether. For the maintenance of the which Innocentius the Pope pronounceth boldly, that all the customes of the old Law bee not abolished, that wee might in such apparell, of Christians the more willingly become Iewish. This is noted, not against Churches and Temples, which are most necessary, and ought to haue their due vse and honour, as is in another Homily for that purpose declared, nor against the conuenient cleanesse & ornaments thereof: but against the sumptuousnesse and abuses of the Temples and Churches. For it is a Church or Temple also that glittereth with no marble, shineth with no Gold nor Siluer, glistereth with no Pearles nor pretious stones: but with plainenesse and frugality, signifieth no proud doctrine nor people, but humble, frugall, and nothing esteeming earthly and outward things, but gloriously decked with inward ornaments, according as the Prophet declareth, saying, The kings daughter is altogether glorious inwardly.

Now concerning excessiue decking of Images and Idoles, with painting, gilding, adorning, with pretious vestures, pearle, and stone, what is it else, but for the further prouocation and intisement to spirituall fornication, to decke spirituall harlots most costly and wantonly, which the idolatrous Church vnderstandeth well ynough. For shee being in deede not onely an harlot (as the Scripture calleth her) but also a foule, filthie, olde withered harlot (for she is indeede of ancient yeeres) and vnderstanding her lacke of nature and true beautie, and great lothsomenesse which of her selfe shee hath, doeth (after the custome of such harlots) paint her selfe, and decke and tyre her selfe with gold, pearle, stone, and all kinde of pretious iewells, that she shining with the outward beauty and glory of them, may please the foolish fantasie of fonde louers, and so entise them to spirituall fornication with her. Who, if they saw her (I will not say naked) but in simple apparell, would abhorre her, as the fowlest and filthiest harlot that euer was seene, According as appeareth by the discription of the garnishing of the great strumpet of all strumpets, the Mother of Whoredome, set foorth by Saint Iohn in Revelations 17.2, who by her glory prouoked the Princes of the earth to commit whoredome with her. Whereas on the contrary part, the true Church of GOD, as a chaste matron, espoused (as the Scripture teacheth) to one husband, our Sauiour Iesus Christ, whom alone shee is content onely to please and serue, and looketh not to delight the eyes or phantasies of any other strange louers, or wooers is content with her naturall ornaments, not doubting, by such sincere simplicitie, best to please him, who can well skill of the difference betweene a painted visage, and true naturall beauty. And concerning such glorious gilding and decking of Images, both GODS worde written in the tenth Chapter of the Prophet Ieremie, and Saint Hieroms commentaries vpon the same, are most worthy to bee noted. First, the wordes of the Scriptures bee these, The workeman with his axe hewed the timber out of the wood with the worke of his hands, he decked it with gold and siluer, he ioyned it with nayles and pinnes, and the stroke an hammer, that it might holde together. They bee made smoth as the Palme, and they can not speake: if they bee borne they remooue, for they cannot goe. Feare yee them not, for they can neither doe euill nor good: thus saith the Prophet (Jeremiah 10.3-5), Upon which text, Saint Hierome hath these words, This is the description of Idoles, which the Gentiles worship, their matter is vile and corruptible.

And whereas the Artificer is mortall, the things hee maketh must needs be corruptible: hee decketh it with siluer and gold, that with the glittering or shining of both mettals, hee may deceaue the simple. Which errour indeed hath passed ouer from the Gentiles, that we should iudge Religion to stand in riches. And by and by after hee saith, They haue the beautie of mettalles, and be beautified by the Arte of Painting, but good or profite is there none in them. And shortly after againe, They make great promises, and deuise an Image of vaine worshipping of their owne fantasies, they make great bragges to deceiue euery simple body, they dull and amaze the vnderstanding of the vnlearned, as it were with golden sentences, and eloquence, shining with the brightnes of siluer. And of their own deuisers and makers are these Images aduanced and magnified, in the which is no vtilitie nor profit at all, and the worshipping of the which, properly pertaineth to the Gentiles and Heathen, and such as know not GOD.

Thus farre of Saint Ieromes words. Whereupon you may note aswell his iudgement of Images themselues, as also of the painting, gilding, and decking of them: that it is an errour which came from the Gentiles, that it perswadeth Religion to remaine in riches, that it amazeth and deceiueth the simple and vnlearned with golden sentences, and siluer shining eloquence, and that it appertaineth properly to the Gentiles and Heathens, and such as know not GOD. Wherefore the hauing, paynting, gilding, and decking of Images, by Saint Ieromes iudgement, is erroneus, seducing and bringing into errour (specially the simple and vnlearned) Hethenish, and voyde of the knowledge of GOD.

Surely the Prophet Daniel in the eleuenth Chapter declareth such sumptuous decking of Images with gold, siluer, and precious stones, to be a token of Antichrists kingdome, who (as the Prophet foresheweth) shal worship GOD with such gorgeous things. Now vsually such excessiue adorning and decking of Images, hath risen and beene maintained, either of offerings prouoked by superstition and giuen in Idolatrie, or of spoyles, robberies, vsurie, or goods otherwise vniustly gotten, whereof wicked men haue giuen part to the Images or Saints, (as they call them) that they might be pardoned of the whole: as of diuers writings and old monuments concerning the cause and end of certaine great gifts, may well appeare. And in deed such money so wickedly gotten, is most meet to be put to so wicked a vse. And that which they take to bee amends for the whole before GOD, is more abominable in his sight, then both the wicked getting, and the more wicked spending of all the rest. For how the Lord alloweth such gifts, hee declareth euidently in the Prophet Esaias, saying, I (saith the Lord) doe loue iudgement, and I hate spoile and rauenie offered in Sacrifice: which the very Gentiles vnderstood. For Plato sheweth, that such men as suppose that GOD doeth pardon wicked men, if they giue part of their spoyles and rapine to him, take him to bee like a dogge, that would bee entreated and hired with part of the pray, to suffer the wolues to weary the sheepe (Plato, `De Legib.', 10). And in case the goods wherewith Images bee decked, were iustly gotten, yet it is extreme madnesse, so foolishly and wickedly to bestow goods purchased by wisedome and trueth. Of such leudnesse Lactantius writeth thus, Men doe in vaine decke Images of the Gods with gold, Iuorie, and precious stone, as though they could take any pleasure in those things (Lactantius, `Inst.', bk. 2, chap. 4). For what vse haue they of precious gifts, which vnderstand nor feele nothing? Euen the same that dead men haue. For with like reason doe they bury dead bodies, farced with spices and odours, and clothed with precious vestures, and decke images, which neither felt or knew when they were made, nor vnderstand when they bee honoured, for they get no sense and vnderstanding by their consecration. Thus farre Lactantius, and much more, too long here to rehearse, declaring, that as little girles play with little puppets, so be these decked images great puppets for old fooles to play with. And that wee may knowe what, not onely men of our religion, but Ethnikes also, iudge of such decking of dead images, it is not vnprofitable to heare what Seneca, a wise and excellent learned Senatour of Rome, and Philosopher, saith concerning the foolishnesse of ancient and graue men, vsed in his time in worshipping and decking of images: Wee (saith Seneca) bee not twise children (as the common saying is) but alwayes children: but this is the difference, that wee beeing elder, play the children: and in these playes they bring in before great and well decked puppets (for so hee calleth images) ointments, incense, and odours. To these puppets they offer up sacrifice, which haue a mouth, but not the vse of teeth. Upon these they put attiring and precious apparell, which haue no vse of clothes. To these they giue gold and siluer, which they who receiue it (meaning the images) lacke, as well as they that haue giuen it from them. And Seneca much commendeth Dionysius king of Sicile, for his merrie robbing of such decked and iewelled puppets. But you will aske, what doeth this appertaine to our Images, which is written against the Idoles of the Gentiles? Altogether surely. For what vse or pleasure haue our images of their decking and precious ornaments? Did our images vnderstand when they were made? or knowe when they bee so trimmed and decked? Bee not these things bestowed vpon them, as much in vaine, as vpon dead men which haue no sense? Wherefore it followeth, that there is like foolishnesse and lewdnesse in decking of our images, as great puppets for old fooles, like children, to play the wicked play of idolatry before, as was among the Ethnikes and Gentiles. Our Churches stand full of such great puppets, wonderously decked and adorned, Garlands and Coronets bee set on their heads, precious pearles hanging about their neckes, their fingers shine with rings, set with precious stones, their dead and stiffe bodies are clothed with garments stiffe with golde. You would beleeue that the images of our men Saints, were some Princes of Persia land with their proud apparell, and the idoles of our women Saints, were nice and well trimmed harlots, tempting their paramours to wantonnesse: Whereby the Saints of GOD are not honoured, but most dishonoured, and their godlinesse, sobernesse, chastitie, contempt of riches, and of the vanitie of the world, defaced and brought in doubt by such monstrous decking, most differing from their sober and godly liues. And because the whole pageant must throughly bee playd, it is not enough thus to decke idoles, but at the last come in the Priests themselues, likewise decked with gold and pearle, that they may be meete seruants for such Lords and Ladies, and fit worshippers of such gods and goddesses. And with a solemne pace they passe forth before these golden puppets, and fall downe to the ground on their marrow bones before these honourable idoles, and then rising vp againe, offer vp odours and incense vnto them, to giue the people and example of double idolatrie, by worshipping not onely the idole, but the gold also, and riches wherewith it is garnished. Which things, the most part of our olde Martyrs rather then they would doe, or once kneele, or offer vp one crumbe of incense before an image, suffered most cruell and terrible deaths, as the histories of them at large doe declare. And here againe their allegation out of Gregorie the first and Damascen, that images bee the Lay-mens Bookes, and that pictures are the Scripture of idiotes and simple persons, is worthy to bee considered (Gregory, `Epistle to Serenus Masile', Damascene, `De Fide Ortho.', bk. 4, chap. 17). For as it hath beene touched in diuers places before, how they bee bookes teaching nothing but lyes, as by Saint Paul in the first Chapter to the Romanes euidently appeareth, of the images of GOD: So what manner of bookes and Scripture these painted and gilt images of Saints be vnto the common people, note well I pray you. For after that our preachers shall haue instructed and exhorted the people to the following of the vertues of the Saints, as contempt of this world, pouerty, sobernesse, chastitie, and such like vertues, which vndoubtedly were in the Saints: Thinke you, assoone as they turne their faces from the Preacher, and looke vpon the grauen bookes and painted Scripture of the glorious gilt images and idoles, all shining and glittering with mettall and stone, and couered with precious vestures, or else with Choerea in Terence, behold a paynted table, wherein is set foorth by the arte of the painter, an image with a nice and wanton apparell and countenance, more like to Venus or Flora, then Mary Magdalen, or if like to Mary Magdalen, it is when she played the harlot, rather then when she wept for her sinnes. When I say they turne about from the preacher, to these bookes and schoolemasters and painted scriptures: shal they not find them lying books? teaching other maner of lessons, of esteeming of riches, of pride, and vanity in apparell, of nicenesse and wantonnesse, and peraduenture of whoredome, as Choerea of like pictures was taught. And to Lucian, one learned of Venus Gnidia a lesson, too abominable here to be remembered. Bee not these thinke you pretie bookes and scriptures for simple people, and especially for wiues and young maydens to looke in, reade on, and learne such lessons of? What will they thinke either of the preacher, who taught them contrary lessons of the Saints, and therefore by these carued doctours, are charged with a lye, or of the Saints themselues, if they beleeue these grauen bookes and painted scriptures of them, who make the Saintes now reigning in heauen with GOD, to their great dishonour, schoolemasters of such vanitie, which they in their life time most abhorred? For what lessons of contempt of riches and vanitie of this world, can such bookes, so besmeared with golde, set with precious stones, couered with silkes, teach? What lessons of sobernesse and chastitie, can our women learne of these pictured sons of sobernesse and chastitie, can our women learne of these pictured scriptures, with their nice apparell and wanton lookes? But a way for shame with these coloured clokes of Idolatrie, of the bookes and scriptures of Images and pictures, to teach idiots, nay to make idiots and starke fooles and beastes of Christians. Doe men, I pray you, when they haue the same bookes at home with them, runne on pilgrimage to seeke like bookes at Rome, Compostella, or Hierusalem, to be taught by them, when they haue the like to learne at home? Doe men reuerence some bookes, and despite and set light by other of the same sort? Doe men kneele before their bookes, light candles at noone time, burne incense, offer vp golde and siluer, and other giftes to their bookes? Doe men either feigne or beleeue miracles to be wrought by their bookes? I am sure that the new Testament of our Sauiour Iesus Christ, conteining the worde of life, is a more liuely, expresse, and true Image of our Sauiour, then all carued, grauen, moulten, and painted images in the world bee, and yet none of all these things be done to that booke or scripture of the Gospel of our Sauiour, which bee done to images and pictures, the bookes and scriptures of lay men and idiots, as they call them. Wherefore call them what they list, it is most euident by their deedes, that they make of them no other bookes nor scripture, then such as teach most filthy and horrible idolatry, as the vsers of such bookes dayly prooue by continuall practising the same. O bookes and scriptures, in the which the deuilish schoolemaster Sathan, hath penned the lewd lessons of wicked idolatry, for his dastardly disciples and schollers to behold, reade, and learne, to GODS most high dishonour, and their most horrible damnation. Haue not we beene much bound, thinke you, to those which should haue taught vs the trueth out of GODS booke and his holy Scripture, that they haue shut vp that booke and Scripture from vs, and none of vs so bolde as once to open it, or reade on it? and in stead thereof, to spread vs abroad these goodly, caruen, and gilten bookes and painted scriptures, to teach vs such good and godly lessons? Haue not they done well, after they ceased to stand in pulpets themselues, and to teach the people committed to their instruction, keeping silence of GODS word, and become dumbe dogs (as the Prophet calleth them) to set vp in their stead. on euery pillar and corner of the Church, such goodly doctours, as dumbe, but more wicked then themselues be? We neede not to complaine of the lacke of one dumbe Parson, hauing so many dumbe deuilish Vicars (I meane these idoles and painted puppets) to teach in their stead. Now in the meane season, whilest the dumbe and dead idoles stand thus decked and clothed, contrary to GODS law and commandement, the poore Christian people, the liuely images of GOD, commended to vs so tenderly by our Sauiour Christ as most deare to him, stand naked, shiuering for cold, and their teeth chattering in their heads, and no man couereth them, are pined with hunger and thirst, and no man giueth them a peny to refresh them, whereas pounds bee ready at all times (contrary to GODS will) to decke and trimme dead stockes and stones, which neither feele cold, hunger nor thirst.

Clemens hath a notable sentence concerning this matter, saying thus, That serpent the Diuell doth by the mouth of certaine men vtter these words: We for the honour of the inuisible GOD, doe worship visible images: which doubtlesse is most false. For if you will truely honour the image of GOD, you should by doing well to man, honour the true image of GOD in him. For the image of GOD is in euery man: But the likenesse of GOD is not in euery one, but in those only which haue a godly heart and pure minde. If you will therefore truely honour the Image of GOD, we doe declare to you the truth, that ye do well to man, who is made after the image of GOD, that you giue honour and reuerence to him, and refresh the hungry with meat, the thirsty with drinke, the naked with clothes, the sicke with attendance, the stranger harbourlesse with lodging, the prisoners with necessaries: and this shall bee accounted as truely bestowed vpon GOD. And these things are so directly appertayning to GODS honour, that whosoeuer doth not this, shal seeme to haue reproched and done villany to the image of GOD. For what honour of GOD is this, to runne to images of stocke and stone, and to honour vaine and dead figures of GOD, and to despise man, in whom is the true image of GOD? And by and by after he sayth, Understand ye therefore that this is the suggestion of the serpent Satan, lurking within you, which perswadeth you that you are godly, when you honour insensible and dead images, and that you be not vngodly, when you hurt or leaue vnsuccoured the liuely and reasonable creatures. All these bee the words of Clemens.

Note, I pray you, how this most ancient and learned Doctour, within one hundred yeeres of our Sauiour Christes time, most plainely teacheth, that no seruice of GOD, or Religion acceptable to him, can bee in honouring of dead images: but in succouring of the poore the liuely images of GOD, according to Saint Iames, who sayth, This is the pure and true Religion before GOD the Father, to succour fatherlesse and motherlesse children, and widowes in their affliction, and to keepe himselfe vndefiled from this world.

True Religion then and pleasing of GOD, standeth not in making, setting vp, painting, gilding, clothing and decking of dumbe and dead images (which bee but great puppets and babies for old fooles in dotage, and wicked idolatrie, to dally and play with) nor in kissing of them, capping, kneeling, offering to them, in sensing of them, setting vp of candles, hanging vp of legges, armes, or whole bodies of waxe before them, or praying, and asking of them or of Saints, things belonging onely to GOD to giue. But all these things bee vaine and abominable, and most damnable before GOD. Wherefore all such doe not onely bestow their money and labour in vaine: but with their paines and cost purchase to themselues GODS wrath and vtter indignation, and euerlasting damnation both of body and soule. For yee haue heard it euidently prooued in these Homilies against idolatrie, by GODS word, the Doctoures of the Church, Ecclesiasticall histories, reason, and experience, that Images haue beene and bee worshipped, and so idolatry committed to them by infinite multitudes, to the great offence of GODS Maiestie, and danger of infinite soules, and that idolatrie can not possibly bee separated from Images set vp in Churches and Temples, gilded and decked gloriously, and that therefore our Images bee in deede very Idoles, and so all the prohibitions, lawes, curses, threatnings of horrible plagues, aswell temporall as eternall, contained in the holy Scripture, concerning idoles, and the makers, and maintainers, and worshippers of them, appertaine also to our Images set vp in Churches and Temples, and to the makers, maintainers, and worshippers of them. And all those names of abomination, which GODS word in the holy Scriptures giueth to the idoles of the Gentiles, appertaine to our Images, being idoles like to them, and hauing like idolatry committed vnto them. And GODS owne mouth in the holy Scriptures calleth them vanities, lies, deceites, vncleannesse, filthinesse, dung, mischiefe, and abomination before the Lord. Wherefore GODS horrible wrath, and our most dreadfull danger can not bee auoided, without the destruction and vtter abolishing of all such Images and idoles out of the Church and Temple of GOD, which to accomplish, GOD put in the mindes of all Christian princes. And in the meane time, let vs take heede and be wise, O yee beloued of the Lord, and let vs haue no strange gods, but one onely GOD, who made vs when wee were nothing, the Father of our Lord Iesus Christ, who redeemed vs when wee were lost, and with his holy Spirit who doeth sanctifie vs. For this is life euerlasting, to know him to bee the onely true GOD, and Iesus Christ whom hee hath sent (John 17.3). Let vs honour and worship for Religions sake none but him, and him let vs worship and honour as he will himselfe, and hath declared by his worde, that hee will bee honoured and worshipped, not in, nor by Images or idoles, which he hath most straightly forbidden, neither in kneeling, lighting of candels, burning of incense, offering vp of gifts vnto Images and Idoles, to beleeue that wee shall please him, for all these bee abomination before GOD: but let vs honour and worshippe GOD in spirit and trueth, fearing and louing him aboue all things, trusting in him onely, calling vpon him, and praying to him onely, praising and lauding of him onely, and all other in him, and for him. For such worshippers doeth our heauenly Father loue, who is a most pure Spirit, and therefore will bee worshipped in spirit and trueth

(John 4.24). And such worshippers were Abraham, Moses, Dauid, Helias, Peter, Paul, Iohn, and all other the holy Patriarches, Prophets, Apostles, Martyrs, and all true Saints of GOD, who all, as the true friends of GOD, were enemies and destroyers of images and idols, as the enemies of GOD and his true Religion. Wherefore take heed and bee wise, O yee beloued of the Lord, and that which others, contrary to GODS word, bestow wickedly, and to their damnation, vpon dead stockes and stones, (no images, but enemies of GOD and his Saints) that bestow ye, as the faithfull seruants of GOD, according to GODS word, mercifully vpon poore men and women, fatherlesse children, widowes, sicke persons, strangers, prisoners, and such others that bee in any necessity, that ye may at that great day of the Lord, heare that most blessed and comfortable saying of our Sauiour Christ: Come yee blessed into the kingdome of my father, prepared for you before the beginning of the world. For I was hungrie, and ye gaue me meat, thirsty, and ye gaue me drinke, naked, and ye clothed me, harbourlesse, and ye lodged me, in prison, and ye visited me, sicke, and ye comforted me. For whatsoeuer yee haue done for the poore and needy in my name, and for my sake, that haue ye done for me. To the which his heauenly kingdome, GOD the Father of mercies bring vs, for Iesus Christs sake our onely Sauiour, Mediatour, and Aduocate, to whom with the holy Ghost, one immortall, inuisible and most glorious GOD, be all honour and thankesgiuing, and glory, world without end. Amen.

HOMILY ON REPAIRING AND KEEPING CLEAN THE CHURCH

AN HOMILIE FOR REpayring and keeping cleane, and comely adorning of Churches.

IT is a common custome vsed of all men, when they intend to haue their friends or neighbours to come to their houses to eat or drinke with them, or to haue any solemne assemblie to treat and talke of any matter, they will haue their houses, which they keepe in continuall reparations, to be cleane and fine, lest they should bee counted sluttish, or little to regard their friendes and neighbours. How much more then ought the house of GOD, which wee commonly call the Church, to be sufficiently repayred in all places, and to bee honourably adorned and garnished, and to be kept cleane and sweete, to the comfort of the people that shall resort thereunto.

It appeareth in the holy Scripture, how GODS house, which was called his holy Temple, and was the mother Church of all Iewrie, fell sometimes into decay, and was oftentimes prophaned and defiled, through the negligence and vngodlinesse of such as had the charge thereof. But when godly Kings and gouernours were in place, then commandement was giuen foorthwith, that the Church and Temple of GOD should be repayred, and the deuotion of the people to bee gathered, for the reparation of the same. We reade in the fourth Booke of the Kings, how that king Ioas, being a godly Prince, gaue commandement to the Priests, to conuert certaine offerings of the people, towards the reparation and amendment of GODS Temple (2 Kings 12.4-5).

Like commandement gaue that most godly King Iosias, concerning the reparation and reedification of GODS Temple, which in his time he found in sore decay (2 Kings 22.3-7). It hath pleased Almightie GOD, that these Histories touching the reedifying and repayring of his holy Temple, should be written at large, to the end wee should be taught thereby: First, that GOD is well pleased that his people should haue a conuenient place to resort vnto, and to come together, to praise and magnifie GODS holy Name. And secondly, hee is highly pleased with all those, which diligently and zealously goe about to amend and restore such places as are appointed for the Congregation of GODS people to resort vnto, and wherein they humbly and ioyntly render thankes to GOD for his benefits, and with one heart and voice praise his holy Name. Thirdly, GOD was sore displeased with his people, because they builded, decked, and trimmed vp their owne houses, and suffered GODS house to bee in ruine and decay, to lye vncomely and fulsomely. Wherefore GOD was sore grieued with them, and plagued them, as appeareth in the Prophet Aggeus. Thus saith the Lord: Is it time for you to dwell in your seeled houses, and the Lords house not regarded? Yee haue sowed much, and gathered in but little, your meat and your clothes haue neither filled you, nor made you warme, and hee that had his wages, put it in a bottomelesse purse (Haggai 1.4, 6). By these plagues which GOD laid vpon his people for neglecting of his Temple, it may euidently appeare & that; GOD will haue his Temple, his Church, the place where his Congregation shall resort to magnifie him, well edified, well repaired, and well maintained. Some neither regarding godlinesse, nor the place of godly exercise, will say, The Temple in the old Law was commaunded to bee built and repaired by GOD himselfe, because it had great promises annexed vnto it, and because it was a figure, a Sacrament, or a signification of Christ, and also of his Church. To this may bee easily answered: First, that our Churches are not destitute of promises, forasmuch as our Sauiour Christ saith, Where two or three are gathered together in my Name, there am I in the middest among them. A great number therefore comming to Church together in the Name of Christ, haue there, that is to say in the Church, their GOD and Sauiour Christ Iesus present among the Congregation of his faithfull people, by his grace, by his fauour and godly assistance, according to his most assured and comfortable promises. Why then ought not Christian people to build them Temples and Churches, hauing as great promises of the presence of GOD, as euer had Salomon for the materiall Temple which hee did build? As touching the other point, that Salomons Temple was a figure of Christ: we know that now in the time of the cleare light of Christ Iesus the Sonne of GOD, all shadowes, figures, and significations are vtterly gone, all vaine and vnprofitable ceremonies, both Iewish and Heathenish, fully abolished. And therefore our Churches are not set vp for figures, and significations of Messias and Christ to come, but for other godly and necessary purposes, that is to say, That like as euery man hath his owne house to abide in, to refresh himselfe in, to rest in, with such like commodities: So Almightie GOD will haue his house and place whither the whole Parish and Congregation shall resort, which is called the Church and Temple of GOD, for that the Church, which is the company of GODS people, doth there assemble and come together to serue him. Not meaning hereby, that the Lord whom the heauen of heauens is not able to holde or comprise, doth dwell in the Church of lime and stone, made with mans hands, as wholly and onely conteined there within, and no where els, for so he neuer dwelt in Salomons Temple. Moreouer, the Church or Temple is counted and called holy, yet not of it selfe, but because GODS people resorting thereunto, are holy, and exercise themselues in holy and heauenly things. And to the intent yee may vnderstand further, why Churches were built among Christian people, this was the greatest consideration: that GOD might haue his place, and that GOD might haue his time, duely to be honoured and serued of the whole multitude in the parish. First there to heare and learne the blessed word and will of the euerlasting GOD. Secondly, that there the blessed Sacraments, which our Lord and Sauiour Christ Iesus hath ordained and appointed, should be duely, reuerently, and decently ministred. Thirdly, that there the whole multitude of GODS people in the Parish, should with one voice and heart call vpon the Name of GOD, magnifie and praise the Name of GOD, render earnest and heartie thankes to our heauenly Father for his heape of benefits dayly and plentifully powred vpon vs, not forgetting to bestow our almes vpon GODS poore, to the intent GOD may blesse vs the more richly. Thus yee may well perceiue and vnderstand wherefore Churches were built and set vp amongst Christian people, and dedicated & appointed to these godly vses, and wholly exempted from all filthy, prophane, & worldly vses. Wherefore all they that haue little mind or deuotion to repaire and build GODS Temple, are to be counted people of much vngodlinesse, spurning against good order in Christes Church, despising the true honour of GOD, with euill example offending and hindering their neighbours otherwise well and godly disposed. The world thinketh it but a trifle to see their Church in ruine and decay. But who so doth not lay to their helping handes, they sinne against GOD & his holy congregation. For if it had not been sin to neglect & slightly regard the reedifying and building vp againe of his Temple, GOD would not haue been so much grieued, and so soone haue plagued his people, because they builded and decked their owne houses so gorgeously, and despised the house of GOD their Lord. It is sinne and shame to see so many Churches, so ruinous, and so fouly decayed, almost in euery corner. If a mans priuate house wherein hee dwelleth, bee decayed, he will neuer cease till it bee restored vp againe. Yea, if his barne where he keepeth his corne be out of reparations, what diligence vseth he to make it in perfect state againe? If his stable for his horse, yea, the stie for his swine, be not able to hold out water and wind, how carefull is he to doe cost thereon? And shall we be so mindfull of our common base houses, deputed to so vile employment, & be forgetfull toward that house of GOD, wherin be intreated the words of our eternall saluation, wherin be ministred the Sacraments and mysteries of our redemption? The fountaine of our regeneration is there presented vnto vs, the partaking of the Body and Blood of our Sauiour Christ, is there offered vnto vs: And shall we not esteeme the place where so heauenly things are handled? Wherefore if ye haue any reuerence to the seruice of GOD, if ye haue any common honesty, if ye haue any conscience in keeping of necessary and godly ordinances, keepe your Churches in good repaire, whereby ye shall not onely please GOD, and deserue his manifold blessings, but also deserue the good report of all godly people.

The second point, which appertaineth to the maintenance of GODS house, is, to haue it well adorned, & comely, and cleane kept. Which things may bee the more easily refourmed, when the Church is well repayred. For like as men are well refreshed and comforted, when they finde their houses hauing all things in good order, and all corners cleane and sweete: so when GODS house the Church is well adorned, with places conuenient to sit in, with the Pulpit for the preacher, with the Lords table, for the ministration of his holy supper, with the Font to Christen in, and also is kept cleane, comely, and sweetly, the people are more desirous, and the more comforted to resort thither, and to tarry there the whole time appointed them. With what earnestnesse, with what vehement zeale did our Sauiour Christ driue the buyers & sellers out of the temple of GOD, and hurled downe the tables of the changers of money, and the seates of the Doue-sellers, & could not abide any man to carry a vessell through the Temple (Matthew 21.12)? He told them that they had made his Fathers house a den of theeues, partly through their superstition, hypocrisie, false worship, false doctrine, and insatiable couetousnesse, and partly through contempt, abusing that place with walking and talking, with worldly matters without all feare of God, and due reuerence to that place. What dennes of theeues the Churches of England haue beene made by the blasphemous buying & selling the most precious body and blood of Christ in the Masse, as the world was made to beleeue, at diriges, at monthes minds, at trentalles, in abbeyes & chantries, beside other horrible abuses (GODS holy name be blessed for euer) which we now see & vnderstand. All these abominations, they that supplie the roome of Christ, haue cleansed and purged the Churches of England of, taking away all such fulsomnesse and filthinesse, as through blinde deuotion and ignorance hath crept into the Church these many hundred yeeres. Wherefore, O yee good Christian people, ye dearely beloued in Christ Iesu, yee that glory not in worldly and vaine religion, in phantasticall adorning and decking, but reioyce in heart to see the glory of GOD truly set foorth, and the Churches restored to their ancient and godly vse, render your hearty thankes to the goodnesse of Almighty GOD, who hath in our dayes stirred vp the hearts, not onely of his godly Preachers and Ministers, but also of his faithfull and most Christian magistrates and gouernours, to bring such godly things to passe.

And forasmuch as your Churches are scoured and swept from the sinfull and superstitious filthinesse wherewith they were defiled and disfigured: Doe yee your partes, good people to keepe your Churchs comely and cleane, suffer them not to bee defiled with raine and weather, with doung of doues, and owles, stares, and choughs, and other filthinesse, as it is foule and lamentable to behold in many places of this countrey. It is the house of prayer, not the house of talking, of walking, of brawling, of minstrelsie, of hawkes, of dogs. Prouoke not the displeasure and plagues of GOD, for despising & abusing his holy house, as the wicked Iewes did. But haue GOD in your heart, be obedient to his blessed will, bind your selues euery man and woman, to your power, toward the reparations and cleane keeping of the Church, to the intent that yee may be partakers of GODS manifold blessings, and that yee may be the better encouraged to resort to your parish Church, there to learne your duetie towards GOD and your neighbour, there to be present and partakers of Christs holy Sacraments, there to render thankes to your heauenly Father for the manifold benefits which hee daily powreth vpon you, there to pray together, and to call vpon GODS holy Name, which be blessed world without end. Amen.

HOMILY ON GOOD WORKS: AND FIRST OF FASTING

AN HOMILIE OF GOOD
Workes. And first of Fasting.

THE life which wee liue in this world (good Christian people) is of the free benefit of GOD lent vs, yet not to vse it at our pleasure, after our owne fleshly will: but to trade ouer the same in those works which are beseeming them that are become new creatures in Christ. These workes the Apostle calleth good workes, saying, We are GODS workemanship, created in Christ Iesu to good workes, which GOD hath ordained that wee should walke in them (Ephesians 2.10). And yet his meaning is not by these words, to induce vs, to haue any affiance, or to put any confidence in our workes, as by the merite and deseruing of them to purchase to our selues and others remission of sin, and so consequently euerlasting life, for that were mere blasphemie against GODS mercy, and great derogation to the bloodshedding of our Sauiour Iesus Christ. For it is of the free grace and mercie of GOD, by the meditation of the blood of his Sonne Iesus Christ, without merite or deseruing on our part, that our sinnes are forgiuen vs, that we are reconciled and brought againe into his fauour, and are made heires of his heauenly kingdome. Grace (saith S. Augustine) belonging to GOD, who doth call vs, and then hath hee good workes, whosoeuer receiued grace (Augustine, `*De Diver. Questio. ad Simpli.*', bk. 1, quest. 28). Good works then bring not forth grace: but are brought forth by grace. The wheele (saith he) turneth round, not to the end that it may be made round: but because it is first made round, therefore it turneth round. So, no man doth good works, to receiue grace by his goodworkes: but because hee hath first receiued grace, therefore consequently he doth good workes. And in another place hee saith (Augustine, *`De Fide et Operibus'*, chap. 4): good workes goe not before in him which shall afterward be iustified, but good works doe follow after when a man is first iustified. S. Paul therefore teacheth, that wee must doe good workes for diuers respects. First, to shew our selues obedient children vnto our heauenly Father, who hath ordained them, that we should walke in them. Secondly, for that they are good declarations and testimonies of our iustification. Thirdly, that others seeing our good workes, may the rather by them be stirred vp and excited to glorifie our Father which is in heauen. Let vs not therefore be slacke to doe good workes, seeing it is the will of GOD that we should walke in them, assuring our selues that at the last day, euery man shall receiue of God for his labour done in true faith, a greater reward then his workes haue deserued. And because somewhat shall now be spoken of one particular good worke, whose commendation is both in the Law and in the Gospel: thus much is said in the beginning generally of all good workes. First, to remoue out of the way of the simple and vnlearned, this dangerous stumbling blocke, that any man should goe about to purchase or buy heauen with his workes. Secondly, to take away (so much as may be) from enuious minds, and slanderous tongues, all iust occasion of slanderous speaking, as though good workes were reiected. This good worke which now shall be entreated of, is Fasting, which is found in the Scriptures to be of two sorts. The one outward, pertaining to the body, the other inward, in the heart and mind. This outward Fast, is an abstinence from meat, drinke, and all naturall food, yea, from all delicious pleasures and delectations worldly. When this outward Faste perteineth to one particular man, or to a fewe, and not the whole number of the people, for causes which hereafter shalbe declared, then it is called a priuate fast: But when the whole multitude of men, women and children, in a Towneshippe or citie, yea, though a whole countrey do fast, it is called a publique fast. Such was that fast which the whole multitude of the children of Israel were commanded to keepe the tenth day of the seuenth moneth, because almightie God appointed that day to bee a clensing day, a day of atonement, a time of reconciliation, a day wherein the people were cleansed from their sinnes. The order and manner how it was done, is written in the. xvi. and xxiii. Chapters of Leuiticus (Leviticus 16.29-30, 23.27-32).

That day the people did lament, mourne, weepe, and bewaile their former sins. And whosoeuer vpon that day did not humble his soule, be wailing his sinnes, as is said, abstaining from all bodily foode, vntill the euening, that soule, (saith the almightie GOD) should be destroyed from among his people. Wee doe not reade that Moses ordeined, by order of law, any dayes of publique fast throughout the whole yeere, more then that one day. The Iewes notwithstanding had more times of common fasting, which the Prophet Zacharie reciteth to bee the fast of the fourth, the fast of the fifth, the fast of the seuenth, and the fast of the tenth moneth (Zachariah 8.19). But for that it appeareth not in the Lawe when they were instituted, it is to bee iudged, that those other times of fasting, more then the fast of the seuenth moneth, were ordained among the Iewes by the appointment of their gouernours, rather of deuotion, then by any expresse commandement giuen from GOD. Upon the ordinance of this generall fast, good men tooke occasion to appoint to themselues priuate fastes, at such times as they did either earnestly lament and bewaile their sinfull liues, or did addict themselues to more feruent prayer, that it might please GOD to turne his wrath from them, when either they were admonished and brought to the consideration thereof by the preaching of the Prophets, or otherwise when they saw present danger to hang ouer their heades. This sorrowfulnesse of heart, ioyned with fasting, they vttered sometime by their outward behauiour and gesture of body, puting on sackecloth, sprinckeling themselues with ashes and dust, and sitting or lying vpon the earth. For when good men feele in themselues the heauie burden of sinne, see damnation to bee the reward of it, and behold with the eye of their minde the horrour of hell, they tremble, they quake, and are inwardly touched with sorrowfulnesse of heart for their offences, and cannot but accuse themselues & open this their griefe vnto Almighty GOD, and call vnto him for mercy. This being done seriously, their minde is so occupied, partly with sorrow and heauinesse, partly with earnest desire to bee deliuered from this danger of hell, and damnation, that all desire of meate and drinke is layd apart, and lothsomenesse of all worldly things and pleasures commeth in place, so that nothing then liketh them more, then to weepe, to lament, to mourne and both with wordes and behauiour of body, to shew themselues weary of this life. Thus did Dauid fast, when hee made intercession to Almighty GOD for the childes life, begotten in adultery of Bethsabe Vrias wife. King Achab fasted after this sort, when it repented him of murdering of Naboth, bewayling his owne sinfull doings. Such were the Nineuites fast, brought to repentance by Ionas preaching. When fourty thousand of the Israelites were slaine in battaile against the Beniamites, the scripture saith All the children of Israel, and the whole multitude of the people went to Bethel, and sate there weeping before the Lord, and fasted all that day till night (Judges 20.26). So did Daniel, Hester, Nehemias, and many others in the old Testament fast. But if any man will say, it is true, so they fasted in deede, but we are not now vnder that yoke of the law, we are set at liberty by the freedome of the Gospel: therefore those rites & customes of the old law bind not vs, except it can be shewed by the Scriptures of the new Testament, or by examples out of the same, the fasting now vnder the Gospel, is a restraint of meat, drink, and all bodily food and pleasures from the body, as before. First, that we ought to fast, is a truth more manifest, then that it should here neede to bee prooued, the Scriptures which teach the same, are euident. The doubt therefore that is, is whether when we fast, wee ought to withhold from our bodies all meate and drinke during the time of our fast, or no? That we ought so to doe, may bee well gathered vpon a question mooued by the Pharisees to Christ, and by his answere againe to the same. Why (say they) doe Iohns disciples fast often, and pray, & we likewise? but thy disciples eat and drinke, & fast not at all (Luke 5.33). In this smoothe question, they couch vp subtilly this argument or reason: Who so fasteth not, that man is not of GOD. For fasting and prayer are workes both commended and commanded of GOD in his Scriptures, and all good men, from Moses till this time, aswell the Prophets as others, haue exercised themselues in these workes. Iohn also and his disciples at this day doe fast oft, and pray much, and so doe we the Pharisees in like maner: But thy disciples fast not at all, which if thou wilt denie, wee can easily prooue it. For whosoeuer eateth and drinketh, fasteth not. Thy disciples eate and drinke, therefore they fast not. Of this we conclude (say they) necessarily, that neither art thou, nor yet thy disciples, of GOD. Christ maketh answere, saying, Can yee make that the children of the wedding shall fast, while the bridegrome is with them? The dayes shall come, when the bridegrome shall bee taken from them: In those dayes shall they fast. Our Sauiour Christ, like a good master, defendeth the innocencie of his disciples against the malice of the arrogant Pharisees, and prooueth that his disciples are not guilty of transgressing any iote of GODS Law, although as then they fasted, and in his answere reprooueth the Pharisees of superstition and ignorance. Superstition, because they put a religion in their doings, and ascribed holinesse to the outward worke wrought, not regarding to what end fasting is ordeined. Of ignorance, for that they could not discerne betweene time and time. They knew not that there is a time of reioycing and mirth, and a time againe of lamentation and mourning, which both he teacheth in his answere, as shalbe touched more largely hereafter, when we shall shew what time is most fit to fast in.

But here, beloued, let vs note, that our Sauiour Christ, in making his answere to their question, denied not, but confessed that his disciples fasted not, and therefore agreeth to the Pharisees in this, as vnto a manifest trueth: that who so eateth and drinketh, fasteth not. Fasting then, euen by Christs assent, is a withholding of meate, drinke, and all naturall foode from the body, for the determined time of fasting. And that it was vsed in the primitiue Church, appeareth most euidently by the Chalcedon councell, one of the foure first generall councels. The fathers assembled there, to the number of 630. considering with themselues how acceptable a thing fasting is to GOD, when it is vsed according to his word: Againe, hauing before their eyes also the great abuses of the same crept into the Church at those dayes, through the negligence of them which should haue taught the people the right vse thereof, and by vaine gloses, deuised of men: to reforme the sayd abuses, and to restore this so good and godly a worke, to the true vse thereof, decreed in that councell, that euery person aswell in his priuate as publique fast, should continue all the day without meate and drinke, till after the Euening prayer. And whosoeuer did eate or drinke before the Euening prayer was ended, should be accounted and reputed not to consider the puritie of his fast. This Canon teacheth so euidently how fasting was vsed in the primitiue Church, as by words it cannot be more plainely expressed.

Fasting then, by the decree of those sixe hundred and thirty fathers, grounding their determination in this matter vpon the sacred Scriptures, and long continued vsage or practise, both of the Prophets and other godly persons, before the comming of Christ, and also of the Apostles and other deuout men in the new Testament, is, a withholding of meate, drinke, and all naturall foode from the body, for the determined time of fasting. Thus much is spoken hitherto, to make plaine vnto you what fasting is. Now hereafter shall be shewed the true and right vse of fasting.

Good workes are not all of one sort. For some are of themselues and of their owne proper nature alwayes good: as to loue GOD aboue all things, to loue thy neighbour as thy selfe, to honour thy father and mother, to honour the higher powers, to giue to euery man that which is his due, and such like. Other workes there bee, which considered in themselues, without further respect, are of their owne nature meerly indifferent, that is, neither good nor euill, but take their denomination of the vse or ende whereunto they serue. Which workes hauing a good end, are called good workes, and are so in deede: but yet that commeth not of themselues, but of the good end whereunto they are referred. On the other side; if the end that they serue vnto, bee euill, it can not then otherwise bee, but that they must needes bee euill also. Of this sort of workes, is fasting, which of it selfe is a thing meerely indifferent: but it is made better or worse by the ende that it serueth vnto. For when it respecteth a good ende, it is a good worke: but the ende being euill, the worke it selfe is also euill. To fast then with this perswasion of minde, that our fasting, and our good workes, can make vs perfect and iust men, and finally, bring vs to heauen: this is a diuelish perswasion, and that fast is so far of from pleasing GOD, that it refuseth his mercy, and is altogether derogatory to the merites of Christs death, and his pretious bloodshedding. This doeth the parable of the Pharisee and the Publicane teach. Two men (sayth Christ) went vp together into the Temple to pray, the one a Pharisee, the other a Publicane: The Pharisee stood and prayed thus with himselfe: I thanke thee, O GOD, that I am not as other men are, extortioners, vniust, adulterers, and as this publicane is, I fast twise in the weeke, I giue tithes of all that I possesse. The Publicane stood a farre of, and would not lift vp his eyes to heauen, but smote his brest, and said, GOD bee mercifull to me a sinner (Luke 18.10-13). In the person of this Pharisee, our Sauiour Christ setteth out to the eye, and to the iudgement of the world, a perfect, iust, and righteous man, such a one as is not spotted with those vices that men commonly are infected with, extortion, bribery, polling and pilling their neighbour, robbers and spoylers of common weales, crafty, & subtile in chopping and changing, vsing false weightes, and detestable periury in their buying and selling, fornicators, adulterers, & vicious liuers. The Pharisee was no such man, neither faulty in any such like notorious crime. But where other transgressed by leauing things vndone, which yet the Lawe required: this man did more then was requisite by the Law. For hee fasted thrise in the weeke, and gaue tithes of all that hee had. What could the world then iustly blame in this man? yea, what outward thing more could bee desired to be in him, to make him a more perfect and a more iust man? Truely nothing by mans iudgement: And yet our Sauiour Christ preferreth the poore Publicane without fasting before him with his fast. The cause why hee doeth so, is manifest. For the publicane hauing no good workes at all to trust vnto, yeelded vp himselfe vnto GOD, confessing his sinnes, and hoped certainely to bee saued by GODS free mercie onely. The Pharisee gloried, and trusted so much to his workes, that he thought himselfe sure ynough without mercy, and that hee should come to heauen by his fasting and other deeds. To this end serueth that parable. For it is spoken to them that trusted in themselues, that they were righteous, and despised other. Now because the Pharisee directeth his worke to an euill ende, seeking by them iustification, which in deede is the proper worke of GOD, without our merites, his fasting twise in the weeke, and all his other workes, though they were neuer so many, and seemed to the world neuer so good and holy, yet in very deede before GOD they are altogether euill and abominable. The marke also that the Hypocrites shoote at with their fast, is, to appeare holy in the eye of the world, and so to winne commendation and praise of men. But our Sauiour Christ sayth of them, they haue their reward, that is, they haue prayse and commendation of men, but of GOD they haue none at all (Matthew 6.2). For whatsoeuer tendeth to an euill end, is it selfe, by that euill end, made euill also. Againe, so long as wee keepe vngodlinesse in our hearts, & suffer wicked thoughts to tarry there, though we fast as oft as did either S. Paul, or Iohn Baptist, and keepe it as straightly as did the Niniuites: yet shall it bee not only vnprofitable to vs, but also a thing that greatly displeaseth Almighty GOD. For he sayth, that his soule abhorreth and hateth such fastings, yea they are a burden vnto him, and he is weary of bearing them (Isaiah 1.13-14). And therefore hee enueieth most sharpely against them, saying by the mouth of the Prophet Esay, Behold, when you fast, your lust remaineth still, for doe ye no lesse violence to your debtters. Loe, ye fast to strife and debate, and to smite with the fist of wickednesse. Now ye shall not fast thus, that you may make your voice to be heard aboue. Thinke yee this fast pleaseth me, that a man should chasten himselfe for a day? should that bee called a fasting, or a day that pleaseth the Lord (Isaiah 58.3-5)? Now dearely beloued, seeing that Almighty GOD alloweth not our fast for the works sake, but chiefely respecteth our heart how it is affected, & then esteemeth our fast either good or euill by the end that it serueth for: it is our part to rent our hearts, & not our garments as we are aduertised by the Prophet Ioel, that is, our sorrow and mourning must bee inward in heart, and not in outward shew onely (Joel 2.12-13), yea, it is requisite that first before all thinges, wee cleanse our heartes from sinne, and then to direct our fast to such an end as GOD will allowe to be good.

There bee three endes, whereunto if our fast bee directed, it is then a worke profitable to vs, and accepted of GOD. The first is, to chastise the flesh, that it be not too wanton, but tamed and brought in subiection to the spirit. This respect had Saint Paul in his fast, when he sayd, I chastice my body, and bring it into subiection, lest by any meanes it commeth to passe, that when I haue preached to other, I my selfe be found a castaway (1 Corinthians 9.27).

The second, that the spirit may be more earnest and feruent to prayer. To this end fasted the Prophets and teachers that were at Antioch, before they sent foorth Paul and Barnabas to preach the Gospel (Acts 13.2-3). The same two Apostles fasted for the like purpose, when they commended to GOD, by their earnest prayers, the congregations that were at Antioch, Pvsidia, Iconium, and Lystra, as we read in the Acts of the Apostles (Acts 14.21-23).

The third, that our fast bee a testimonie and witnesse with vs before GOD, of our humble submission to his high maiesty, when we confesse and acknowledge our sinnes vnto him, and are inwardly touched with sorrowfulnesse of heart, bewayling the same in the affliction of our bodies. These are the three ends, or right vses of fasting. The first belongeth most properly to priuate fast. The other two are common, aswell to publike fast, as to priuate: and thus much for the vse of fasting. Lord haue mercy vpon vs, and giue vs grace, that while wee liue in this miserable world, we may through thy helpe bring forth this, and such other fruites of the spirit, commended and commanded in thy holy word, to the glory of thy Name, and to our comforts, that after the race of this wretched life, we may liue euerlastingly with thee in thy heauenly kingdome, not for the merits and worthinesse of our workes, but for thy mercies sake, and the merites of thy deare Sonne Iesus Christ, to whom with thee & the Holy Ghost, be all laud, honour, and glory, for euer and euer. Amen.

THE SECOND PART OF THE HOMILY OF FASTING.

IN the former Homilie (beloued) was shewed, that among the people of the Iewes, fasting as it was commanded them from God by

Moses, was to abstaine the whole day, from morning till night, from meat, drink, & all maner of food, that nourisheth the body, & that whoso tasted ought before the euening, on the day appointed to fasting, was accounted among them a breaker of his fast. Which order, though it seemeth strange to some in these our dayes, because it hath not been so generally vsed in this Realme of many yeeres past: yet that it was so among Gods people (I meane the Iewes) whom before the comming of our Sauiour Christ, GOD did vouchsafe to chuse vnto himselfe, a peculiar people aboue all other nations of the earth, and that our Sauiour Christ so vnderstood it, and the Apostles after Christs ascension did so vse it, was there sufficiently prooued by the testimonies and examples of the holy Scriptures, aswell of the new Testament, as of the old. The true vse of fasting was there also shewed. In this second part of this Homilie shalbe shewed, that no constitution or Law made by man, for things which of their owne proper nature be meere indifferent, can binde the conscience of Christian men to a perpetuall obseruation and keeping thereof, but that the higher powers haue full liberty to alter and change euery such law and ordinance, either Ecclesiasticall or Politicall, when time and place shall require. But first an answere shall be made to a question that some may make, demanding what iudgement wee ought to haue of such abstinences as are appointed by publike order and Lawes made by Princes, and by the authority of the Magistrates, vpon policy, not respecting any Religion at all in the same. As when any Realme in consideration of the maintayning of fisher townes bordering vpon the seas, and for the encrease of fisher men, of whom doe spring Mariners to goe vpon the sea, to the furnishing of the nauie of the Realme, whereby not onely commodities of other countries may bee transported, but also may be a necessary defence to resist the inuasion of the aduersary.

For the better vnderstanding of this question, it is necessary that wee make a difference betweene the policies of Princes, made for the ordering of their common weales, in prouision of things seruing to the most sure defence of their subiects and countreyes, and betweene Ecclesiasticall policies, in prescribing such workes, by which, as secondary meanes, GODS wrath may be pacified, and his mercy purchased. Positiue lawes made by Princes, for conseruation of their policie, not repugnant vnto GODS Law, ought of all Christian subiects with reuerence of the Magistrate to bee obeyed, not onely for feare of punishment, but also (as the Apostle saith) for conscience sake. Conscience I say, not of the thing which of it owne nature is indifferent:

but of our obedience, which by the Law of GOD wee owe vnto the Magistrate, as vnto GODS minister. By which positiue lawes, though wee subiects for certaine times and dayes appointed, bee restrained from some kindes of meates and drinke, which GOD by his holy word hath left free to bee taken and vsed of all men with thankesgiuing in all places, and at all times: yet for that such lawes of Princes and other Magistrates are not made to put holinesse in one kinde of meate and drinke more then another, to make one day more holy then another, but are grounded meerely vpon policie, all subiects are bound in conscience to keepe them by GODS commandement, who by the Apostle willeth all without exception, to submit themselues vnto the authority of the higher powers. And in this point concerning our dueties which be here dwelling in England, enuironed with the sea as we be, we haue great occasion in reason to take the commodities of the water, which almighty GOD by his diuine prouidence hath layd so nigh vnto vs, whereby the encrease of victuals vpon the land may the better be spared and cherished, to the sooner reducing of victuals to a more moderate price, to the better sustenance of the poore. And doubtlesse hee seemeth to be too dainty an Englishman, who considering the great commodities which may ensue, will not forbeare some piece of his licentious appetite vpon the ordinance of his Prince, with the consent of the wise of the Realme. What good English heart would not wish that the old ancient glory should returne to the Realme, wherein it hath with great commendations excelled before our dayes, in the furniture of the Nauie of the same? What will more daunt the hearts of the aduersaries, then to see vs well fenced and armed on the sea, as we be reported to be on the land? If the Prince requested our obedience to forbeare one day from flesh more then we doe, and to bee contented with one meale in the same day, should not our owne commodity thereby perswade vs to subiection? But now that two meales bee permitted on that day to bee vsed, which sometime our Elders in very great numbers in the Realme did vse with one onely spare meale, and that in fish onely: shall we thinke it so great a burthen that is prescribed?

Furthermore, consider the decay of the townes nigh the seas, which should be most ready by the number of the people there to repulse the enemie, and we which dwell further off vpon the land, hauing them as our buckler to defend vs, should bee the more in safetie. If they be our neighbours, why should we not wish them to prosper? If they be our defence as nighest at hand to repell the enemie, to keepe out the rage of the seas which els would breake vpon our faire pastures, why should we not cherish them? Neither doe we vrge that in the Ecclesiasticall policie, prescribing a fourme of Fasting, to humble our selues in the sight of almighty GOD, that that order which was vsed among the Iewes, and practised by Christes Apostles after his ascension, is of such force and necessitie, that that onely ought to bee vsed among Christians, and none other, for that were to binde GODS people vnto the yoke and burthen of Moses policie, yea, it were the very way to bring vs which are set at libertie by the freedome of Christs Gospel, into the bondage of the Law againe, which GOD forbid that any man should attempt or purpose. But to this end it serueth, to shew how farre the order of fasting now vsed in the Church at this day, differeth from that which then was vsed. GODS Church ought not, neither may it be so tyed to that or any other order now made, or hereafter to be made and deuised by the authoritie of man, but that it may lawfully for iust causes, alter, change, or mitigate those Ecclesiasticall decrees and orders, yea, recede wholy from them: and breake them, when they tend either to superstition, or to impietie, when they draw the people from GOD, rather then worke any edification in them. This authoritie Christ himselfe vsed, and left it to his Church. He vsed it I say: For the order or decree made by the Elders for washing oft times, which was diligently obserued of the Iewes, yet tending to superstition, our Sauiour Christ altered and changed the same in his Church, into a profitable Sacrament, the Sacrament of our regeneration or new birth. This authoritie to mitigate lawes and decrees Ecclesiasticall, the Apostles practised, when they, writing from Ierusalem vnto the congregation that was at Antioch, signified vnto them that they would not lay any further burthen vpon them, but these necessaries: that is, that they should abstaine from things offered vnto idoles, from blood, from that which is strangled, and from fornication, notwithstanding that Moses law required many other obseruances (Acts 15.20). This authoritie to change the orders, decrees, and constitutions of the Church, was after the Apostles time vsed of the Fathers about the manner of fasting, as it appeareth in the Tripartite history, where it is thus written (`Tripartite History,' bk. 9, chap. 38): Touching fasting, we finde that it was diuersly vsed in diuers places by diuers men. For they at Rome fast three weekes together before Easter, sauing vpon the Saturdayes and Sundayes, which fast they call Lent. And after a few lines in the same place, it followeth: They haue not all one vniforme order in fasting. For some doe fast and abstaine both from fish and flesh. Some when they fast, eate nothing but fish. Others there are, which when they fast, eate of all water foules, aswell as of fish, grounding themselues vpon Moses, that such foules haue their substance of the water, as the fishes haue. Some others when they fast, will neither eate hearbs nor egges. Some fasters there are, that eate nothing but drye bread. Others when they fast, eate nothing at all, no not so much as dry bread. Some fast from all maner of foode till night, and then eate, without making any choice or difference of meates. And a thousand such like diuers kindes of fasting may bee found in diuers places of the world, of diuers men diuersly vsed (Eusebius, bk. 5, chap. 24). And for all this great diuersitie in fasting, yet charitie the very true bond of Christian peace was not broken, neither did the diuersitie of fasting breake at any time their agreement and concord in faith. To abstaine somtime from certaine meates, not because the meates are euill, but because they are not necessary, this abstinence (saith Saint Augustine) is not euill (Augustine, *'Dogma. Ecclesiast.'*, chap. 66). And to restraine the vse of meates when necessary and time shall require, this (saith he) doth properly pertaine to Christian men.

Thus yee haue heard, good people, first that Christian subiectes are bound euen in conscience to obey princes lawes, which are not repugnant to the Lawes of GOD. Ye haue also heard that Christes Church is not so bound to obserue any order, law, or decree made by man, to prescribe a fourme in religion: but that the Church hath full power and authoritie from GOD, to change and alter the same, when neede shall require, which hath beene shewed you by the example of our Sauiour Christ, by the practise of the Apostles, and of the fathers since that time.

Now shall be shewed briefly what time is meete for fasting, for all times serue not for all things: but as the wise man saith, All things haue their times. There is a time to weepe, and a time againe to laugh, a time to mourne, and a time to reioyce. &c (Ecclesiastes 3.1, 4). Our Sauiour Christ excused his disciples, and reprooued the Pharisees, because they neither regarded the vse of fasting, nor considered what time was meete for the same. Which both he teacheth in his answere, saying, The children of the mariage cannot mourne, while the bridegrome is with them (Matthew 9.15). Their question was of fasting, his answere is of mourning, signifying vnto them plainely that the outward fast of the body, is no fast before GOD, except it be accompanied with the inward fast, which is a mourning and a lamentation of the heart, as is before declared. Concerning the time of fasting, he saith, The dayes will come, when the bridegrome shall be taken from them, in those dayes they shall fast. By this it is manifest, that it is no time of fasting while the mariage lasteth, and the bridegrome is there present. But when the mariage is ended, and the bridegrome gone, then is it a meete time to fast (Luke 5.34-35, Matthew 6). Now to make plaine vnto you what is the sense and meaning of these words, Wee are at the mariage, and againe, The bridegrome is taken from vs: Ye shall note, that so long as GOD reuealeth his mercy vnto vs, and giueth vs of his benefites, either spirituall or corporall, wee are sayd to be with the bridegrome at the mariage. So was that good olde father Iacob at the mariage, when hee vnderstood that his sonne Ioseph was aliue, and ruled all Egypt vnder king Pharao. So was Dauid in the mariage with the bridegrome, when he had gotten the victory of great Goliah, and had smitten off his head. Iudith and all the people of Bethulia were the children of the wedding, and had the bridegrome with them, when GOD had by the hand of a woman slaine Holofernes, the grand captaine of the Assyrians host, and discomfited all their enemies. Thus were the Apostles the children of the mariage while Christ was corporally present with them, and defended them from all dangers, both spirituall and corporall. But the mariage is said then to bee ended, and the bridegrome to be gone, when Almighty GOD smiteth vs with affliction, and seemeth to leaue vs in the middest of a number of aduersities. So GOD sometime striketh priuate men priuately with sundry aduersities, as trouble of mind, losse of friendes, losse of goods, long and dangerous sicknesses, &c. Then is it a fit time for that man to humble him selfe to Almighty GOD by fasting, and to mourne and to bewaile his sinnes with a sorrowfull heart, and to pray vnfainedly, saying with the Prophet Dauid, Turne away thy face, O Lord, from my sinnes, and blot out of thy remembrance all mine offences (Psalms 51.9). Againe, When GOD shall afflict a whole region or countrey with warres, with famine; with pestilence, with strange diseases and vnknowen sicknesses, and other such like calamities: then is it time for all states and sortes of people, high and low, men, women, and children, to humble themselues by fasting, and bewaile their sinfull liuing before GOD, and pray with one common voyce, saying thus, or some other such like prayer. Bee fauourable O Lord, be fauourable vnto thy people, which turneth vnto thee, in weeping, fasting, and praying, spare thy people whom thou hast redeemed with thy precious blood, and suffer not thine inheritance to bee destroyed and brought to confusion. Fasting thus vsed with prayer, is of great efficacie, and waigheth much with GOD. So the angel Raphael told Tobias. It also appeareth by that which our Sauiour Christ answeared to his disciples, demanding of him why they could not cast foorth the euill spirit out of him, that was brought vnto them. This kinde (saith hee) is not cast out but by fasting and prayer. How auaileable fasting is, how much it waieth with GOD, and what it is able to obtaine at his hand, can not better bee set foorth, then by opening vnto you, and laying before you some of those notable things that haue beene brought to passe by it. Fasting was one of the meanes whereby Almighty GOD was occasioned to alter the thing which hee had purposed concerning Ahab, for murdering the innocent man Naboth, to possesse his vineyard. GOD spake vnto Elia, saying: Goe thy way and say vnto Ahab, Hast thou killed, and also gotten possession? Thus sayth the Lord, In the place where dogges licked the bloud of Naboth, shall dogges euen licke thy bloud also. Behold, I will bring euill vpon thee, and will take away thy posteritie (1 Kings 21.27-29): Yea, the dogges shall eat him of Ahabs stocke that dieth in the city, and him that dieth in the field shall the foules of the ayre eate. This punishment had Almighty GOD determined for Ahab in this world, and to destroy all the male kinde that was begotten of Ahabs body, besides that punishment which should haue happened vnto him in the world to come. When Ahab heard this, he rent his clothes, and put sackecloth vpon him, and fasted, and lay in sackecloth, and went barefooted. Then the word of the Lord came to Elia, saying, seest thou how Ahab is humbled before me? Because he submitteth himselfe before me, I will not bring that euill in his dayes, but in his sonnes dayes will I bring it vpon his house. Although Ahab through the wicked counsell of Iesabel his wife had committed shamefull murder, and against all right disinherited and dispossessed for euer Nabothes stocke of that vineyard: yet vpon his humble submission in heart vnto GOD, which hee declared outwardly by putting on sackecloth and fasting, GOD changed his sentence, so that the punishment which hee had determined, fell not vpon Ahabs house in his time, but was deferred vnto the dayes of Ioram his sonne. Heere we may see of what force our outward fast is, when it is accompanied with the inward fast of the mind, which is (as is sayd) a sorrowfulnes of heart, detesting and bewayling our sinfull doings. The like is to be seene in the Nineuites: For when GOD had determined to destroy the whole city of Nineue, and the time which he had appointed, was euen now at hand, hee sent the Prophet Ionas to say vnto them: yet forty dayes, and Nineue shall be ouerthrowen. The people by and by beleeued GOD, and gaue themselues to fasting, yea, the King by the aduice of his counsell, caused to bee proclaimed saying, Let neither man nor beast, bullocke nor sheepe taste any thing, neither feed nor drinke water: But let man and beast put on sackecloth, and crie mightily vnto GOD, yea, let euery man turne from his euill way, and from the wickednesse that is in their hands. Who can tell if GOD will turne and repent, and turn away from his fierce wrath, that we perish not (Jonah 3.4-9)? And vpon this their hearty repentance, thus declared outwardly with fasting, renting of their clothes, putting on sackecloth, and sprinkling themselues with dust and ashes, the Scripture saith, God saw their works that they turned from their euill waies, & God repented of the euill that he had sayd that he would do vnto them, and he did it not. Now beloued, yee haue heard first what fasting is, aswell that which is outward in the body, as that which is inward in the heart. Ye haue heard also that there are three ends or purposes, whereunto if our outward fast be directed, it is a good worke that GOD is pleased with. Thirdly hath beene declared, what time is most meet for to fast, either priuately or publikely. Last of all, what things fasting hath obtayned of GOD, by the examples of Ahab and the Nineuites. Let vs therefore dearely beloued, seeing there are many more causes of fasting and mourning in these our dayes, then hath beene of many yeeres heeretofore in any one age, endeuour our selues both inwardly in our hearts, and also outwardly with our bodies, diligently to exercise this godly exercise of fasting, in such sort and manner, as the holy Prophets, the Apostles, and diuers other deuout persons for their time vsed the same. GOD is now the same GOD that he was then. GOD that loueth righteousnesse, and that hateth iniquity, GOD which willeth not the death of a sinner, but rather that he turne from his wickednesse and liue, GOD that hath promised to turne to vs, if we refuse not to turne to him: yea, if we turne our euill workes from before his eyes, cease to doe euill, learne to doe well, seeke to doe right, releeue the oppressed, be a right iudge to the fatherlesse, defend the widow, breake our bread to the hungry, bring the poore that wander into our house, clothe the naked, and despise not our brother which is our owne flesh: then shalt thou call (sayth the Prophet) and the Lord shall answer, thou shalt crie, and hee shall say, heere am I: Yea, GOD which heard Ahab and the Nineuites, and spared them, will also heare our prayers, and spare vs so, that we after their example, will vnfaynedly turne vnto him: yea, he will blesse vs, with his heauenly benedictions the time that we haue to tarrie in this world, and after the race of this mortall life, he will bring vs to his heauenly kingdome, where we shall reigne in euerlasting blessednes with our Sauiour Christ, to whom with the Father and the holy Ghost, bee all honour and glory for euer and euer, Amen.

HOMILY ON GLUTTONY AND DRUNKENNESS

AN HOMILIE AGAINST
Gluttony and Drunkennesse.

YE haue heard in the former Sermon, welbeloued, the description and the vertue of fasting, with the true vse of the same. Now yee shall heare how foule a thing gluttony and drunkennesse is before GOD, the rather to mooue you to vse fasting the more diligently. Understand yee therefore, that Almighty GOD (to the end that we might keep our selues vndefiled and serue him in holinesse and righteousnesse, according to his word) hath charged in his Scriptures so many as looke for the glorious appearing of our Sauiour Christ, to lead their liues in all sobriety, modesty, and temperancie (Titus 2.12-14). Whereby we may learne how necessary it is for euery Christian that will not be found vnready at the comming of our Sauiour Christ, to liue sober minded in this present world, forasmuch as otherwise being vnready, he cannot enter with Christ into glory: And being vnarmed in this behalfe, he must needes bee in continuall danger of that cruell aduersary the roaring Lion, against whom the Apostle Peter warneth vs to prepare our selues in continuall sobriety, that we may resist, being stedfast in fayth (1 Peter 5.8). To the intent therefore that this sobernesse may bee vsed in all our behauiour, it shall be expedient for vs to declare vnto you how much all kinde of excesse offendeth the maiestie of almightie GOD, and howe grieuously hee punisheth the immoderate abuse of those his creatures which he ordeineth to the maintenance of this our needy life, as meates, drinkes, and apparell. And againe, to shew the noysome diseases and great mischiefes that commonly doe follow them that inordinatly giue vp themselues to be caried headlong with such pleasures as are ioyned eyther with daintie and ouerlarge fare, or else with costly and sumptuour apparell.

And first, that ye may perceiue how detestable and hatefull all excesse in eating and drinking is before the face of almighty GOD, ye shall call to minde what is written by Saint Paul to the Galathians, where hee numbreth gluttonie and drunkennesse among those horrible crimes, with the which (as he saith) no man shall inherite the kingdome of heauen (Galatians 5.21). Hee reckoneth them among the deedes of the flesh, and coupleth them with idolatrie, whoredome, and murder, which are the greatest offences that can bee named among men. For the first spoyleth GOD of his honour, the second defileth his holy Temple, that is to wit, our owne bodies, the third maketh vs companions of Cayne in the slaughter of our brethren, and who so committeth them, as Saint Paul saith, cannot inherite the kingdome of GOD. Certainely, that sinne is very odious and lothsome before the face of GOD, which causeth him to turne his fauourable countenance so farre from vs, that hee should cleane barre vs out of the doores, and disherite vs of his heauenly kingdome. But hee so much abhorreth all beastly banquetting, that by his sonne our Sauiour Christ in the Gospel, hee declareth his terrible indignation against all belly gods, in that hee pronounceth them accursed, saying, Wo bee to you that are full, for yee shall hunger (Luke 6.25). And by the Prophet Esaias hee cryeth out, Wo be to you that rise vp early to giue your selues to drunkennes, & set all your mindes so on drinking, that you sit swilling thereat vntill it bee night (Isaiah 5.11-12). The Harpe, the Lute, the shalme, and plentie of wine are at your feastes, but the workes of the Lord yee doe not beholde, neither consider the workes of his hands. Woe bee vnto you that are strong to drinke wine, and are mighty to aduance drunkennesse. Heere the Prophet plainely teacheth, that fasting and banquetting maketh men forgetfull of their duty towards GOD, when they giue themselues to all kindes of pleasures, not considering nor regarding the workes of the Lord, who hath created meates and drinkes, as S. Paul sayth, to bee receiued thankefully of them that beleeue and know the trueth. So that the very beholding of these creatures (being the handy worke of Almighty God) might teach vs to vse them thankefully as God hath ordeyned (1 Timothy 4.3).

Therefore they are without excuse before God, which either filthily feede themselues, not respecting the sanctification which is by the word of God and prayer, or else vnthankefully abuse the good creatures of God by surfetting & drunkennes, forasmuch as Gods ordinances in his creatures plainely forbidde it. They that giue themse-themselues therefore to bibbing and banqueting, being without all consideration of Gods iudgements, are suddenly oppressed in the day of vengeance. Therefore Christ saith to his disciples, Take heede to your selues, least at any time your hearts bee ouercome with surfeting and drunkennesse, and cares of this world, and so that day come on you vnwares (Luke 21.34). Whosoeuer then will take warning at Christ, let him take heede to himselfe, least his heart being ouerwhelmed by surfeting and drowned in drunkennes, he be taken vnwares with that vnthrifty seruant, which, thinking not on his masters comming, began to smite his fellow seruants, & to eate, & to drinke, & to bee drunken, & being sudenly taken, hath his iust reward with vnbeleeuing hypocrites (Luke 12.45-46). They that vse to drink deeply, & to feed at ful (wallowing themselues in all kind of wickednes) are brought asleep in that slumbring forgetfulnesse of Gods holy will & commandements. Therefore almighty God cryeth by the Prophet Ioel : Awake ye drunkards, weepe and howle all ye drinkers of wine, because the new wine shalbe pulled from your mouth (Joel 1.5). Here the Lord terribly threatneth to withdraw his benefites from such as abuse them, and to pull the cup from the mouth of drunkards. Here we may learne, not to sleepe in drunkennesse and surfetting lest GOD depriue vs of the vse of his creatures, when we vnkindly abuse them. For certainly the Lord our GOD will not only take away his benefits when they are vnthankefully abused: but also in his wrath and heauie displeasure take vengeance on such as immoderately abuse them. If our first parents Adam and Eve had not obeyed their greedy appetite in eating the forbidden fruit, neither had they lost the fruition of GODS benefites which they then enioyed in paradise, neither had they brought so many mischiefs both to themselues, and to all their posteritie (Genesis 3.6). But when they passed the bonds that GOD had appointed them, as vnworthy of GODS benefits, they are expelled and driuen out of paradise, they may no longer eate the fruites of that garden, which by excesse they had so much abused. As transgressors of GODS commandement, they and their posterity are brought to a perpetuall shame and confusion, and as accursed of GOD, they must now sweate for their liuing, which before had abundance at their pleasure. Euen so, if we in eating and drinking exceede, when God of his large liberality sendeth plenty, he will soone change plenty into scarcenesse. And whereas we gloried in fulnesse, he will make vs emptie, and confound vs with penury, yea, we shalbe compelled to labour and trauaile with paines, in seeking for that which we sometime enioyed at ease. Thus the Lord will not leaue them vnpunished, who not regarding his works, follow the lusts and appetites of their owne hearts.

Noah. The Patriarch Noah, whom the Apostle calleth the preacher of righteousnes, a man exceedingly in GODS fauour, is in holy Scripture made an example, whereby we may learne to auoid drunkennesse (2 Peter 2.5). For when he had powred in wine more then was conuenient, in filthy maner hee lay naked in his tent, his priuities discouered. And whereas sometime hee was so much esteemed, he is now become a laughing stocke to his wicked sonne Cham, no small griefe to Sem and Iapeth his other two sonnes, which were ashamed of their fathers beastly behauiour. Heere wee may note that drunkennesse bringeth with it shame and derision, so that it neuer escapeth vnpunished.

Lot. Lot in like maner, being ouercome with wine, committed abominable incest with his owne daughters. So will almighty GOD giue ouer drunkards, to the shamefull lusts of their owne hearts. Heere is Lot by drinking fallen so farre beside himselfe, that hee knoweth not his owne daughters. Who would haue thought that an olde man in that heauie case, hauing lost his wife and all that he had, which had seene euen now GODS vengeance in fearefull maner declared on the fiue Cities for their vicious liuing, should be so farre past the remembrance of his duety? But men ouercome with drinke, are altogether madde as Seneca saith (Seneca, `*Epist.*', 84). He was deceiued by his daughters: but now many deceiue themselues, neuer thinking that GOD by his terrible punishments will bee auenged on them that offend by excesse. It is no small plague that Lot purchased by his drunkennesse. For he had copulation most filthily with his owne daughters, which conceiued thereby, so that the matter is brought to light, it can no longer bee hidde. Two incestuous children are borne, Ammon and Moab, of whom came two nations, the Ammonites and Moabites, abhorred of GOD, and cruell aduersares to his people the Israelites. Loe Lot hath gotten to himselfe by drinking, sorrow, and care, with perpetuall infamie and reproch vnto the worldes ende. If GOD spared not his seruant Lot, being otherwise a godly man, nephew vnto Abraham, one that entertained the Angels of GOD: What will he doe to these beastly belly slaues, which voide of all godlinesse or vertuous behauiour, not once, but continually day and night, giue themselues wholly to bibbing and banquetting?

Amnon. But let vs yet further behold the terrible examples of GODS indignation against such as greedily follow their vnsatiable lusts. Amnon the sonne of Dauid, feasting himselfe with his brother Absolom, is cruelly murdered of his owne brother (2 Samuel 13.28-29).

Holophernes, a valiant and mighty captaine, being ouerwhelmed with wine, had his head striken from his shoulders by that seely woman Iudith (Judith 13.2, 8). Simon the hie Priest, and his two sonnes Mattathias and Iudas, being entertained of Ptolomie the sonne of Abobus , who had before married Simons daughter, after much eating and drinking, were traiterously murdered of their owne kinseman. If the Israelites had not giuen themselues to belly cheare, they had neuer so often fallen to idolatrie (Exodus 32.6). Neither would wee at this day bee so addict to superstition, were it not that wee so much esteemed the filling of our bellies. The Israelites when they serued Idolles, sate downe to eate and drinke, and rose againe to play, as the Scripture reporteth (1 Corinthians 10.7). Therefore seeking to serue their bellies, they forsooke the seruice of the Lord their GOD. So are wee drawen to consent vnto wickednesse, when our hearts are ouerwhelmed by drunkennesse and feasting. So Herode set ting his minde on banquetting, was content to grant, that the holy man of GOD Iohn Baptist, should bee beheaded at the request of his whores daughter (Matthew 14.6-10). Had not the rich glutton bene so greedily giuen to the pampering of his belly, he would neuer haue beene so vnmercifull to the poore Lazarus, neither had he felt the torments of the vnquenchable fire (Luke 16.19-25).

What was the cause that GOD so horribly punished Sodom and Gomorrha? was it not their proud banquetting and continuall idlenesse, which caused them to bee so lewde of life, and so vnmercifull towards the poore (Ezekial 16.49)? What shall we now thinke of the horrible excesse, whereby so many haue perished, and bene brought to destruction?

Alexander. The great Alexander after that hee had conquered the whole world, was himselfe ouercome by drunkennesse, insomuch that being drunken, hee slew his faithfull friend Clitus, whereof when he was sober, he was so much ashamed, that for anguish of heart he wished death. Yet notwithstanding, after this hee left not his banquetting, but in one night swilled in so much wine, that hee fell into a feufeuer, and when as by no meanes hee would abstaine from wine, within few dayes after in miserable sort he ended his life. The conquerour of the whole world is made a slaue by excesse, and becommeth so madde that he murdereth his deare friend, hee is plagued with sorrow, shame, and griefe of heart for his intemperancie, yet can he not leaue it, hee is kept in captiuitie, and hee which sometime had subdued many, is become a subiect to the vile belly. So are drunkards and gluttons altogether without power of themselues, and the more they drinke, the dryer they waxe, one banquet prouoketh another, they studie to fill their greedie stomackes. Therefore it is commonly sayd, A drunken man is alwayes drie, and A gluttons gut is neuer filled. nsatiable truely are the affections and lustes of mans heart, and therefore wee must learne to bridle them with the feare of GOD, so that we yeeld not to our owne lustes, lest we kindle GODS indignation against our selues, when we seeke to satisfie our beastly appetite. Saint Paul teacheth vs, whether wee eate or drinke, or whatsoeuer wee doe, to doe all to the glory of GOD (1 Corinthians 10.31). Where hee appointeth, as it were by a measure, how much a man may eate and drinke: that is to wit, so much that the minde be not made sluggish by cramming in meate, and powring in drinke, so that it cannot lift vp it selfe to the glory and prayse of GOD. Whatsoeuer he be then, that by eating and drinking maketh himselfe vnfit to serue GOD, let him not thinke to escape vnpunished.

Yee haue heard how much almighty GOD detesteth the abuse of his creatures, as he himselfe declareth, aswell by his holy word, as also by the fearefull examples of his iust iudgement. Now if neither the word of GOD can restraine our raging lustes and greedy appetites, neither the manifest examples of GODS vengeance feare vs from riotous and excessiue eating and drinking, let vs yet consider the manifold mischiefes that proceede thereof, so shall wee know the tree by the fruits. It hurteth the body, it infecteth the minde, it wasteth the substance, and is noysome to the neighbours. But who is able to expresse the manifolde dangers and inconueniences that follow of intemperate diet? Oft commeth sodaine death by banquetting, sometime the members are dissolued, and so the whole body is brought into a miserable state. Hee that eateth and drinketh vnmeasurably, kindleth oft times such an vnnaturall heate in his body, that his appetite is prouoked thereby to desire more then it should, or else it ouercommeth his stomacke, and filleth all the body full of sluggishnesse, makes it vnable and vnfit to serue either GOD or man, not nourishing the body, but hurting it: and last of all, bringeth many kindes of incurable diseases, whereof ensueth sometimes desperate death. But what should I neede to say any more in this behalfe? For except GOD blesse our meates, and giue them strength to feede vs: againe, except GOD giue strength to nature to digest, so that we may take profit by them, either shall we filthily vomite them vp againe, or els shal they lie stinking in our bodies, as in a lothsome sinke or chanell, and so diuersely infect the whole body. And surely the blessing of GOD is so farre from such as vse riotous banquetting, that in their faces be sometimes seene the expresse tokens of this intemperancy: as Solomon noteth in his prouerbes. To whom is woe (sayth hee) to whom is sorrow? to whom is strife? to whom is brawling, to whom are wounds without cause? and for whom is the rednesse of eyes? euen to them that tarrie long at the wine (Proverbs 23.29-30). Marke (I beseech you) the terrible tokens of GODS indignation: Woe, and sorrow, strife, and brawling, wounds without cause, disfigured face, and rednesse of eyes are to bee looked for, when men set themselues to excesse and gurmandise, deuising all meanes to encrease their greedy appetites by tempering the wine, and sawcing in it such sort, that it may bee more delectable and pleasant vnto them. It were expedient, that such delicate persons should bee ruled by Solomon, who in consideration of the aforesayde inconueniences, forbiddeth the very sight of wine. Looke not vpon the wine (sayth hee) when it is red, and when it sheweth his colour in the cup, or goeth downe pleasantly: for in the ende thereof it will bite like a serpent, and hurt like a cockatrice. Thine eyes shall looke vpon strange women, and thine heart shall speake lewde things, and thou shalt bee as one that sleepeth in the middes of the sea, and as he that sleepeth in the toppe of the maste. They haue stricken mee (thou shalt say) but I was not sicke, they haue beaten mee, but I felt it not, therefore will I seeke it yet still. Certainely that must needes bee verie hurtfull which biteth and infecteth like a poysoned Serpent, whereby men are brought to filthy fornication, which causeth the heart to deuise mischiefe. Hee doubtlesse is in great danger that sleepeth in the middest of the sea, for soone hee is ouerwhelmed with waues. He is like to fall sodainely that sleepeth in the toppe of the maste. And surely hee hath lost his senses, that cannot feele when he is stricken, that knoweth not when he is beaten. So, surfetting and drunkennesse bites by the belly, and causeth continuall gnawing in the stomack, bringes men to whoredome and lewdenesse of hearte, with dangers vnspeakable: so that men are bereaued and robbed of their senses, and are altogether without power of themselues, Who seeth not nowe the miserable estate whereinto men are brought, by these foule filthie monsters, gluttonie and drunkennesse (Proverbs 23.31-35). The body is so much disquieted by them, that as Iesus the sonne of Syrach affirmeth, the vnsatiable feeder neuer sleepeth quietly, such an vnmeasurable heate is kindled, whereof ensueth continuall ache and paine to the whole body (Apoc. Ecclesiastes 31.20). And no lesse truely the minde is also annoyed by surfetting bankettes: for sometimes men are stricken with frensie of minde, and are brought in like manner to meere madnesse, some waxe so brutish and blockish, that they become altogether voyde of vnderstanding. It is an horrible thing that any man should maime himselfe in any member: but for a man of his owne accord to bereaue himselfe of his wittes, is a mischiefe intolerable. The Prophet Osee in the fourth Chapter, saith, that wine and drunkennesse taketh away the heart (Hosea 4.11). Alas then, that any man should yeelde vnto that, whereby hee might bereaue himselfe of the possession of his owne heart. Wine and women leade wise men out of the way, and bring men of vnderstanding to reproofe and shame, sayth Iesus the sonne of Syrach (Apoc. Ecclesiastes 19.2). Yea hee asketh what is the life of man that is ouercome with drunkennesse. Wine drunken with excesse, maketh bitternesse of minde, and causeth brawling and strife (Apoc. Ecclesiastes 31.29). In Magistrates it causeth cruelty in steade of iustice, as that wise Philosopher Plato perceiued right well, when hee affirmed that a drunken man hath a tyrannous heart, and therefore will rule at his pleasure, contrary to right and reason (Plato, *`De Repub.'*, bk. 3). And certainely drunkennesse maketh men forget both law and equitie, which caused King Solomon so straitly to charge that no wine should bee giuen vnto rulers, lest peraduenture by drinking, they forget what the law appointeth them, and so change the iudgement of all the children of the poore (Proverbs 31.4). Therefore among all sortes of men, excessiue drinking is most intolerable in a Magistrate or man of authority, as Plato sayth: For a drunkard knoweth not where hee is himselfe. If then a man of authoritie should bee a drunkard, alasse, how might hee bee a guide vnto other men, standing in neede of a gouernour himselfe (Besides this, a drunken man can keepe nothing secret: manie fonde, foolish and filthie wordes are spoken when men are at their bankets. Drunkennesse (as Seneca affirmeth) discouereth all wickednesse, and bringeth it to light, it remooueth all shamefastnesse, and encreaseth all mischiefe. The proud man being drunken, vttereth his pride, the cruell man his crueltie, and the enuious man his enuie, so that no vice canne lie hid in a drunkard. Moreouer, in that hee knoweth not himselfe, hee fumbleth and stammereth in his speach, staggereth to and fro in his going, beholding nothing stedfastly with his staring eyes, beleeueth that the house runneth round about him. It is euident that the minde is brought cleane out of frame by excessiue drinking, so that whosoeuer is deceiued by wine or strong drinke, becommeth as Solomon saith, a mocker, or a madde man, so that hee can neuer be wise (Proverbs 20.1). If his wittes, hee may aswell suppose, as Seneca saith, that when hee hath drunken poyson, hee shall not die. For wheresoeuer excessiue drinking is, there must needes followe perturbation of minde, and where the belley is stuffed with daintie fare, there the minde is oppressed with slothfull sluggishnesse. A full belly, maketh a grosse vnderstanding, saith Saint Bernard, and much meate maketh a weary minde (Saint Bernard, *`Ad sororem ser.'*, 24). But alasse, now a dayes men passe little either for body or minde: so they haue worldly wealth and riches aboundant to satisfie their vnmeasurable lustes, they care not what they doe. They are not ashamed to shew their drunken faces, and to play the madde man openly. They thinke themselues in good case, and that all is well with them, if they be not pinched by lacke and pouerty. Lest any of vs therefore might take occasion to flatter himselfe in this beastly kinde of excesse, by the aboundance of riches, let vs call to minde what Solomon writeth in the xxi. of his Prouerbs, Hee that loueth wine and fatte fare, shall neuer bee rich, saith he (Proverbs 21.17). And in the xxiii. Chapter, he maketh a vehement exhortation, on this wise, Keepe not company with drunkards and gluttons, for the glutton and drunkard shall come to pouerty (Proverbs 23.20-21).

He that draweth his patrimony through his throat, and eateth and drinketh more in one houre or in one day, then hee is able to earne in a whole weeke, must needes be an vnthrift, and come to beggerie. But some will say, what need any to finde fault with this? He hurteth no man but himselfe, hee is no mans foe but his owne. Indeed I know this is commonly spoken in defence of these beastly belly gods but it is easie to see how hurtfull they are, not only to themselues, but also to the common wealth, by their example. Euery one that meeteth them is troubled with brawling and contentious language, and oft times raging in beastly lusts, like high fed horses, they ney on their neighbours wiues, as Ieremy sayth, and defile their children and daughters. Their example is euill to them among whom they dwell, they are an occasion of offence to many, and whiles they waste their substance in banquetting, their owne household is not prouided of things necessary, their wiues and their children are euill intreated, they haue not wherewith to releeue their poore neighbours in time of necessity, as they might haue, if they liued soberly. They are vnprofitable to the common wealth. For a drunkard is neither fit to rule, nor to be ruled. They are a slander to the Church or congregation of Christ, and therefore Saint Paul doeth excommunicate them among whoremongers, idolaters, couetous persons, and extortioners, forbidding Christians to eat with any such (1 Corinthians 5.11). Let vs therefore, good people, eschew every one of vs, all intemperancy, let vs loue sobriety and moderate diet, oft giue our selues to abstinency and fasting, whereby the minde of man is more lift vp to GOD, more ready to all godly exercises, as prayer, hearing and reading of GODS word, to his spirituall comfort. Finally, whosoeuer regardeth the health and safety of his owne body, or wisheth alwayes to be well in his wits, or desireth quietnesse of minde, and abhorreth fury and madnesse, he that would be rich, and escape pouerty, he that is willing to liue without the hurt of his neighbour, a profitable member of the common wealth, a Christian without slander of Christ and his Church: let him auoyd all riotous and excessiue banquetting, let him learne to keepe such measure as behoueth him that professeth true godlinesse, let him follow S. Pauls rule, and so eat and drink, to the glory and prayse of GOD, who hath created all things to be soberly vsed with thanksgiuing, to whom be all honour and glory for euer. Amen.

HOMILY AGAINST EXCESS OF APPAREL

AN HOMILIE AGAINST
excesse of Apparrell.

WHERE ye haue heeretofore beene excited & stirred to vse temperance of meates and drinkes, and to auoyd the excesse thereof, many wayes hurtfull to the state of the common wealth, and so odious before Almighty GOD, being the authour and giuer of such creatures, to comfort and stablish our frayle nature with thankes vnto him, and not by abusing of them to prouoke his liberality to seuere punishing of that disorder. In like maner it is conuenient, that yee bee admonished of another soule & chargeable excesse: I meane, of apparell, at these dayes so gorgeous, that neither Almighty GOD by his word can stay our proud curiosity in the same, neither yet godly and necessary lawes, made of our Princes, and oft repeated with the penalties, can bridle this detestable abuse, whereby both GOD is openly contemned, and the Princes Lawes manifestly disobeyed, to the great perill of the Realme. Wherefore, that sobriety also in this excesse may bee espied among vs, I shall declare vnto you, both the moderate vse of apparell, approoued by GOD in his holy word, and also the abuses therof, which he forbiddeth and disalloweth, as it may appeare by the inconueniences which dayly encrease, by the iust iudgement of GOD, where that measure is not kept, which he himselfe hath appointed. If we consider the end and purpose whereunto Almighty GOD hath ordayned his creatures, we shall easily perceiue that he alloweth vs apparell, not only for necessities sake, but also for an honest comelinesse. Euen as in herbes, trees, and sundry fruites, we haue not onely diuers necessary vses, but also the pleasant sight and sweet smell, to delight vs withall, wherein wee may behold the singular loue of GOD towards mankinde, in that hee hath prouided both to releeue our necessities, and also to refresh our senses with an honest and moderate recreation. Therefore Dauid in the hundred and fourth Psalme, confessing GODS carefull prouidence, sheweth that GOD not only prouideth things necessary for men, as hearbs and other meats, but also such things as may reioyce & comfort, as wine to make glad the heart, oyles and oyntments to make the face to shine (Psalms 104.14-15). So that they are altogether past the limites of humanity, who yeelding onely to necessity, forbid the lawfull fruition of GODS benefits. With whose traditions wee may not be ledde, if we giue eare to S. Paul, writing to the Colossians, willing them not to hearken vnto such men as shall say, Touch not, Taste not, Handle not, superstitiously bereauing them of the fruition of GODS creatures (Colossians 2.21). And no lesse truely ought we to beware, lest vnder pretence of Christian liberty, wee take licence to doe what wee list, aduancing our selues in sumptuous apparell, and despising other, preparing ourselues in fine brauery, to wanton, lewde, and vnchaste behauiour.

4 Lessons. To the auoyding whereof, it behouueth vs to be mindefull of foure lessons, taught in holy Scripture, whereby we shall learne to temper our selues, and to restraine our immoderate affections, to that measure which GOD hath appoynted (Romans 13.14). The first is, that we make not prouision for the flesh, to accomplish the lustes thereof, with costly apparell, as that harlot did, of whom Salomon speaketh, Prouerbes the seuenth, which perfumed her bed, and deckt it with costly ornaments of Egypt, to the fulfilling of her lewd lust: but rather ought we by moderate temperance to cut off all occasions, whereby the flesh might get the victorie (Proverbs 7.16-17). The second is written by Saint Paul, in the vii. Chapter of his first Epistle to the Corinthes, where he teacheth vs to vse this world, as though we vsed it not. Whereby he cutteth away not onely all ambition, pride, and vaine pompe in apparell: but also all inordinate care and affection, which withdraweth vs from the contemplation of heauenly things, and consideration of our duetie towards GOD. They that are much occupied in caring for things pertaining to the body, are most commonly negligent and carelesse in matters concerning the soule (1 Corinthians 7.31-33). Therefore our Sauiour Christ willeth vs not to take thought what wee shall eate, or what we shall drinke, or wherewith wee shall bee clothed, but rather to seeke the Kingdome of GOD, and the righteousnesse thereof (Matthew 6.31, 33). Whereby

wee may learne to beware, lest wee vse those things to our hinderance, which GOD hath ordained for our comfort and furtherance, towards his Kingdome. The third is, that we take in good part our estate and condition, and content our selues with that which GOD sendeth, whether it bee much or little. He that is ashamed of base and simple attire, will be proud of gorgious apparell, if hee may get it. Wee must learne therefore of the Apostle S. Paul both to vse plenty, and also to suffer penury (Philippians 4.12), remembring that we must yeeld accounts, of those things which wee haue receiued vnto him who abhorreth all excesse, pride, ostentation, and vanitie, who also vtterly condemneth and disalloweth whatsoeuer draweth vs from our duety toward GOD, or diminisheth our charity towards our neighbours and children, whom we ought to loue as ourselues. The fourth and last rule is, that euery man behold and consider his owne vocation, in as much as GOD hath appointed euery man his degree and office, within the limittes whereof it behoueth him to keepe himselfe. Therefore all may not looke to weare like apparell, but euery one according to his degree, as GOD hath placed him. Which, if it were obserued, many one doubtlesse should bee compelled to weare a ruffet coate, which now ruffeleth in silkes and veluets, spending more by the yeere in sumptuous apparell, then their fathers receiued for the whole reuenue of their lands. But alas now a dayes how many may wee behold occupied wholy in pampering the flesh, taking no care at all, but onely how to decke themselues, setting their affection altogether on worldly brauerie, abusing GODS goodnesse, when he sendeth plenty, to satisfie their wonton lusts, hauing no regard to the degree wherein GOD hath placed them. The Israelites were contented with such apparell as GOD gaue them, although it were base and simple: And GOD so blessed them, that their shooes and clothes lasted them fourtie yeeres (Deuteronomy 29.5), yea, and those clothes which their fathers had worne, their children were contented to vse afterward. But we are neuer contented, and therefore we prosper not, so that most commonly hee that ruffeleth in his Sables, in his fine furred gowne, corked slippers, trime buskinnes, and warme mittons, is more ready to chill for colde, then the poore labouring man, which can abide in the field all the day long, when the North winde blowes, with a few beggerly cloutes about him. Wee are loth to weare such as our fathers haue left vs, we thinke not that sufficient or good ynough for vs. Wee must haue one gowne for the day, another for the night, one long, another shorte, one for Winter, another for Summer, one through furred, another but faced, one for the working day, another for the holie day, one of this colour, another of that colour, one of Cloth, another of Silke or Damaske. We must haue change of apparell, one afore dinner, and another after, one of the Spanish fashion, another Turkie: and to bee briefe, neuer content with sufficient. Our Sauiour Christ bad his disciples they should not haue two coates: but the most men, farre vnlike to his schollers, haue their presses so full of apparell, that many know not how many sorts they haue (Matthew 10.10). Which thing caused Saint Iames to pronounce this terrible curse against such wealthie worldlings, Goe to yee rich men, weepe and howle on your wretchednesse that shall come vpon you, your riches are corrupt, and your garments are moth eaten, ye haue liued in pleasure on the earth, and in wantonnesse, yee haue nourished your hearts, as in the day of slaughter (James 5.1-2, 5). Marke I beseech you, Saint Iames calleth them miserable, notwithstanding their richesse and and plenty of apparell, forasmuch as they pamper their bodies, to their owne destruction. What was the rich glutton the better for his fine fare and costly apparell? Did not he nourish himselfe to bee tormented in hell fire (Luke 16.19-25)? Let vs learne therefore to content our selues, hauing foode and rayment, as Saint Paul teacheth, least desiring to bee enriched with aboundance, wee fall into temptations, snares, and many noysome lustes, which drowne men in perdition and destruction (1 Timothy 6.9). Certainely, such as delight in gorgious apparell, are commonly puffed vp with pride, and filled with diuers vanities. So were the daughters of Sion and people of Ierusalem whom Esai the Prophet threatneth, because they walked with stretched out neckes and wandering eyes, mincing as they went, and nicely treading with their feet, that Almighty GOD would make their heads baulde, and discouer their secret shame. In that day, saith hee, shall the Lord take away the ornament of the slippers, and the caules, and the round attires, and the sweete balles, and the bracelets, and the attires of the head, and the sloppes, and the head bandes, and the tabletes, and the eareringes, the rings, and the mufflers, the costly apparell, and the vailes, and wimples, and the crisping pinne, and the glasses, and the fine linnen, and the hoodes, and the launes (Isaiah 3.16-23). So that almightie GOD would not suffer his benefits to bee vainely and wontonly abused, no not of that people whom he most tenderly loued, and had chosen to himselfe before all other. No lesse truely is the vanitie that is vsed among vs in these dayes. For the proude and haughtie stomacks of the daughters of England, are so maintained with diuers disguised sortes of costly apparell, that as Tertullian an auncient father saith, there is left no difference in apparell betweene an honest matrone and a common strumpet (Tertullian,

'Apolog. Con. Gentes,' chap. 6). Yea many men are become so effeminate, that they care not what they spend in disguising themselues, euer desiring new toyes, and inuenting new fashions. Therefore a certaine man that would picture euery countreyman in his accustomed apparell, when hee had painted other nations, he pictured the English man all naked, and gaue him cloth vnder his arme, and bade him make it himselfe as hee thought best, for hee changed his fashion so often, that he knew not how to make it. Thus with our phantasticall deuises, wee make our selues laughing stockes to other nations, while one spendeth his patrimonie vpon pounces and cuttes, another bestoweth more on a dauncing shirte, then might suffice to buy him honest and comely apparell for his whole bodie. Some hang their reuenues about their neckes, ruffling in their ruffes, and many a one ieopardeth his best ioynt, to maintaine himselfe in sumptuous rayment. And euery man, nothing considering his estate and condition, seeketh to excell other in costly attire. Whereby it commeth to passe, that in abundance and plentie of all things, we yet complaine of want and penurie, while one man spendeth that which might serue a multitude, and no man distributeth of the abundance which hee hath receiued, and all men excessiuely waste that which should serue to supply the necessities of other. There hath beene very good prouision made against such abuses, by diuers good and wholsome lawes, which if they were practised as they ought to bee of all true subiects, they might in some part serue to diminish this raging and riotous excesse in apparell. But alas, there appeareth amongst vs little feare and obedience either of GOD, or man. Therefore must wee needes looke for GODS fearefull vengeance from heauen, to ouerthrowe our presumption and pride, as hee ouerthrew Herode, who in his royall apparell, forgetting GOD, was smitten of an Angell, and eaten vp of wormes (Acts 12.21-23). By which terrible example, GOD hath taught vs that wee are but wormes meate, although we pamper our selues neuer so much in gorgeous apparell.

Here we may learne that which Iesus the sonne of Sirach teacheth, not to be proud of clothing and rayment, neither to exalt our selues in the day of honour, because the workes of the Lord are wonderfull, and glorious, secret, and vnknowen (Apoc. Ecclesiastes 11.4), teaching vs with humblenesse of minde, euery one to be mindfull of the vocation whereunto GOD hath called him. Let Christians therefore endeuour themselues to quench the care of pleasing the flesh, let vs vse the benefits of GOD in this world, in such wise, that we be not too much occupied in prouiding for the body. Let vs content our selues quietly with that which GOD sendeth, bee it neuer so little. And if it please him to send plenty, let vs not waxe proud thereof, but let vs vse it moderately, aswell to our owne comfort, as to the reliefe of such as stand in necessity. He that in abundance and plenty of apparel hideth his face from him that is naked, despiseth his owne flesh, as Esay the Prophet sayth (Isaiah 58.7). Let vs learne to know ourselues, and not to despise other, let vs remember that we stand all before the Maiesty of Almighty GOD, who shall iudge vs by his holy word, wherin he forbiddeth excesse, not onely to men, but also to women. So that none can excuse themselues, of what estate or condition so euer they be. Let vs therefore present our selues before his throne, as Tertullian exhorteth, with the ornaments which the Apostle speaketh of, Ephesians the sixt Chapter, hauing our loynes girt about with the verity, hauing the breast-plate of righteousnesse, and shodde with shoes prepared by the Gospel of peace (Ephesians 6.14-15). Let vs take vnto vs simplicity, chastity, and comelinesse, submitting our neckes to the sweet yoke of Christ (Matthew 11.30). Let women be subiect to their husbands, and they are sufficiently attired, sayth Tertullian. The wife of one Philo an heathen Philosopher, being demanded why she ware no gold: she answered, that she thought her husbands vertues sufficient ornaments. How much more ought Christian women, instructed by the word of GOD, to content themselues in their husbands? yea, how much more ought euery Christian to content himselfe in our Sauiour Christ, thinking himselfe sufficiently garnished with his heauenly vertues. But it wil be here obiected & sayd of some nice & vaine women, that al which we do in painting our faces, in dying our haire, in embalming our bodies, in decking vs with gay apparell, is to please our husbands, to delight his eyes, and to retayne his loue towards vs. O vaine excuse, and most shamefull answer, to the reproch of thy husband. What couldst thou more say to set out his foolishnesse, then to charge him to bee pleased and delighted with the Diuels tire? Who can paint her face and curle her hayre, and change it into an vnnaturall colour, but therein doeth worke reproofe to her maker, who made her? As though shee could make her selfe more comely then GOD hath appointed the measure of her beauty. What doe these women, but goe about to reforme that which GOD hath made? not knowing that all things naturall are the worke of GOD, and things disguised and vnnaturall be the workes of the Diuell. And as though a wise and Christian husband should delight to see his wife in such painted and flourished visages, which common harlots most doe vse, to traine therewith their louers to naughtinesse, or as though an honest woman could delight to be like an harlot for pleasing of her husband. Nay, nay, these be but vaine excuses of such as go about to please rather others then their husbands. And such attires be but to prouoke her to shew her selfe abroad, to entice others: a worthy matter. She must keep debate with her husband to maintaine such apparel, whereby shee is the worse huswife, the seldomer at home to see to her charge, and so neglect his thrift, by giuing great prouocation to her houshold to waste and wantonnesse, while shee must wander abroad to shew her owne vanity, and her husbands foolishnesse. By which her pride, she stirreth vp much enuie of others which bee as vainely delighted as she is. She doeth but deserue mockes and scorns, to set out all her commendation in Iewish and Ethnicke apparell, and yet brag of her Christianity. She doeth but waste superfluously her husbands stocke by such sumptuousnesse, and sometimes shee is the cause of much bribery, extortion, & deceit, in her husbands dealings, that she may be the more gorgiously set out to the sight of the vaine world, to please the Diuels eyes, and not GODS, who giueth to euery creature sufficient and moderate comelines, wherewith we should bee contented if wee were of God. What other thing doest thou by those means, but prouokest other to tempt thee, to deceiue thy soule, by the baite of thy pompe and pride? What else doest thou, but settest out thy pride, and makest of the vndecent apparell of thy body, the deuils net, to catch the soules of them which behold thee? O thou woman, not a Christian, but worse, then a Panim, thou minister of the deuill: Why pamperest thou that carren flesh so high, which sometime doeth stincke and rotte on the earth as thou goest? Howsoeuer thou perfumest thy selfe, yet cannot thy beastlynesse be hidden or ouercome with thy smelles and sauours, which doe rather defourme and misshape thee, then beautifie thee. What meant Solomon to say, of such trimming of vaine women, when hee sayd, A faire woman without good manners and conditions is like a Sowe which hath a ring of golde vpon her snout (Proverbs 11.22)? but that the more thou garnish thy selfe with these outward blasinges, the lesse thou carest for the inward garnishing of thy minde, and so doest but deforme thy selfe by such aray, and not beautifie thy selfe? Heare, heare, what Christes holy Apostles doe write, Let not the outward apparell of women (saith Saint Peter) bee decked with the brayding of haire, with wrapping on of golde, or goodly clothing: but let the minde, and the conscience, which is not seene with the eyes, be pure and cleane, that is, sayth hee, an acceptable and an excellent thing before GOD. For so the olde ancient holy women attired themselues, and were obedient to their husbands (1 Peter 3.3-5). And Saint Paul saith, that women should apparell themselues with shamefastnesse and sobernesse, and not with braydes of their haire, or gold, or pearle, or precious clothes, but as women should doe which will expresse godlinesse by their good outward workes (1 Timothy 2.9-10). If ye will not keepe the Apostles preceptes, at the least let vs heare what pagans, which were ignorant of Christ, haue sayde in this matter. Democrates saith, The ornament of a woman, standeth in scarcitie of speach and apparell. Sophocles saith of such apparell thus, It is not an ornament, O thou foole, but a shame and a manifest shew of thy folly. Socrates saith, that that is a garnishing to a woman, which declareth out her honestie. The Grecians vse it in a prouerbe: It is not gold or pearle which is a beauty to a woman, but good conditions.

And Aristotle biddeth that a woman should vse lesse apparell then the lawe doth suffer. For it is not the goodlinesse of apparell, nor the excellencie of beautie, nor the abundance of gold, that maketh a woman to bee esteemed, but modestie, and diligence to liue honestly in all things. This outragious vanitie is now growen so farre, that there is no shame taken of it. We reade in histories, that when king Dionysius sent to the women of Lacedemon rich robes, they answered and sayd, that they shall doe vs more shame then honour: and therefore refused them. The women in Rome in old time abhorred that gay apparell which king Pyrrhus sent to them, and none were so greedy and vaine to accept them. And a law was openly made of the Senate, and a long time obserued, that no woman should weare ouer halfe an ounce of gold, nor should weare clothes of diuers colours. But perchaunce some daintie dame will say and answere mee, that they must doe some thing to shew their birth and blood, to shew their husbands riches: as though nobility were chiefly seene by these things, which be common to those which bee most vile, as though thy husbands riches were not better bestowed then in such superfluities, as though when thou wast christened, thou diddest not renounce the pride of this world, and the pompe of the flesh. I speake not against conuenient apparell for euery state agreeable: but against the superfluity, against the vaine delight to couet such vanities, to deuise new fashions to feede thy pride with, to spend so much vpon thy carkasse, that thou and thy husband are compelled to robbe the poore, to maintaine thy costlinesse. Heare how that noble holy woman Queene Hester, setteth out these goodly ornaments (as they be called) when (in respect of sauing GODS people) she was compelled to put on such glorious apparell, knowing that it was a fit stable to blinde the eyes of carnall fooles. Thus she prayed, Thou knowest, O Lord, the necessity, which I am driuen to, to put on this apparell, and that I abhorre this signe of pride, and of this glory which I beare on my head, and that I defie it as a filthy cloth, and that I weare it not when I am alone. Againe, by what meanes was Holophernes deceiued, by the glittering shew of apparell, which that holy woman Iudith did put on her, not as delighting in them, nor seeking vaine voluptuous pleasure by them: but shee ware it of pure necessitie by GODS dispensation, vsing this vanitie to ouercome the vaine eyes of GODS enemie. Such desire was in those noble women, being very loth and vnwilling otherwise to weare such sumptuous apparell, by the which others should be caused to forget themselues. These be commended in Scripture for abhorring such vanities, which by constraint and great necessitie, against their hearts desire, they were compelled to weare them for a time. And shall such women bee worthy commendations, which neither bee comparable with these women aforesayd in nobility, nor comparable to them in their good zeale to GOD and his people, whose dayly delight and seeking is to flourish in such gay shifts and changes, neuer satisfied, nor regarding who smarteth for their apparell, so they may come by it? O vaine men, which be subiects to their wittes in these inordinate affections. O vaine women, to procure so much hurt to themselues, by the which they come the sooner to misery in this world and in the meane time be abhorred of GOD, hated and scorned of wise men, and in the end, like to be ioyned with such, who in hell, too late repenting themselues, shall openly complaine with these wordes: What hath our pride profited vs? or what profit hath the pompe of riches brought vs? All these things are passed away like a shadow. As for vertue, we did neuer shew any signe thereof: And thus wee are consumed in our wickednesse. If thou sayest that the custome is to bee followed, and the vse of the world doeth compell thee to such curiosity, then I aske of thee, whose custome should be followed? wise folkes manners, or fooles? If thou sayest the wise: then I say, follow them: For fooles customes, who should follow but fooles? Consider that the consent of wise men, ought to be alleadged for a custome. Now if any lewd custome be vsed, be thou the first to breake it, labour to diminish it and lay it downe: and more laud before GOD, and more commendation shalt thou win by it, then by all the glory of such superfluity.

Thus ye haue heard declared vnto you, what GOD requireth by his word concerning the moderate vse of his creatures. Let vs learne to vse them moderately as he hath appointed. Almighty GOD hath taught vs, to what end and purpose we should vse our apparell. Let vs therefore learne so to behaue our selues in the vse thereof, as becommeth Christians, alwayes shewing our selues thankefull to our heauenly Father for his great and mercifull benefits, who giueth vnto vs our dayly bread, that is to say, all things necessary for this our needy life, vnto whom we shall render accounts for all his benefits, at the glorious appearing of our Sauiour Christ, to whom with the Father and the holy Ghost, bee all honour, prayse, and glory for euer and euer. Amen.

HOMILY ON PRAYER

AN HOMILIE OR
SERmon concerning Prayer.

THere is nothing in all mans life (wellbeloued in our Sauiour Christ) so needfull to be spoken of, and dayly to be called vpon, as hearty, zealous, and deuout prayer, the necessity whereof is so great, that without it nothing may bee well obtayned at GODS hand. For as the Apostle Iames sayth, Euery good and perfect gift commeth from aboue, and proceedeth from the father of lights, who is also sayd to be rich and liberall towards all them that call vpon him (Romans 10.12), not because he either will not, or can not giue without asking, but because hee hath appointed Prayer as an ordinary meanes betweene him and vs. There is no doubt but he alwayes knoweth what wee haue need of (Matthew 6.32), and is alwayes most ready to giue abundance of those things that we lacke.

Yet to the intent wee might acknowledge him to bee the giuer of all good things, and behaue our selues thankefully towards him in that behalfe, louing, fearing, and worshipping him sincerely and truely, as we ought to doe, hee hath profitably and wisely ordeined, that in time of necessitie wee should humble our selues in his sight, powre out the secrets of our heart before him, and craue helpe at his hands, with continuall, earnest, and deuout prayer. By the mouth of his holy Prophet Dauid, hee saith on this wise: Call vpon me in the dayes of thy trouble, and I will deliuer thee (Psalms 50.15). Likewise in the Gospel by the mouth of his welbeloued sonne Christ, hee saith, Aske, and it shall bee giuen you, knocke, and it shall be opened: for whosoeuer asketh, receiueth, whosoeuer seeketh, findeth, and to him that knocketh, it shall bee opened (Matthew 7.7-8). Saint Paul also most agreeably consenting heereunto, willeth men to pray euery where, and to continue therein with thankesgiuing (1 Timothy 2.8, Philippians 4.6, Colossians 4.2). Neither doeth the blessed Apostle Saint Iames in this point any thing dissent, but earnestly exhorting all men to diligent prayer, sayth: If any man lacke wisedome, let him aske it of GOD, which giueth liberally to all men, and reproacheth no man (James 1.5). Also in another place, Pray for one another (sayth he) that ye may be healed: For the righteous mans prayer auayleth much, if it be feruent (James 5.16). What other thing are we taught by these and such other places, but onely this, that Almighty GOD notwithstanding his heauenly wisedome and foreknowledge, will be prayed vnto, that he will be called vpon, that he will haue vs no lesse willing on our part to aske, then hee on his part is willing to giue? Therefore most fonde and foolish is the opinion and reason of those men, which therefore thinke all prayer to bee superfluous and vaine, because GOD searcheth the heart and the raynes, and knoweth the meaning of the spirit before we aske. For if this fleshly and carnall reason were sufficient to disanull prayer: then why did our Sauiour Christ so often cry to his disciples, watch, and pray (Luke 22.46)? Why did he prescribe them a forme of prayer, saying, When yee pray, pray after this sort, Our Father which art in heauen. &c (Matthew 6.9-13). Why did hee pray so often and so earnestly himselfe before his passion? Finally, why did the Apostles immediately after his Ascension, gather themselues together into one seuerall place, and there continue a long time in prayer (Acts 1.14)? Either they must condemne Christ and his Apostles of extreame folly, or else they must needes grant that prayer is a thing most necessary for all men, at all times, and in all places. Sure it is, that there is nothing more expedient or needefull for mankinde in all the world, then prayer. Pray alwayes (sayth Saint Paul) with all manner prayer and supplication, and watch therefore withall diligence (Ephesians 6.18). Also in another place hee willeth vs to pray continually without any intermission or ceasing (1 Thessalonians 5.17), meaning thereby that we ought neuer to slacke or faint in prayer, but to continue therein to our liues end. A number of other such places might here bee alleadged of like effect, I meane, to declare the great necessity and vse of prayer: but what neede many proofes in a plaine matter? seeing there is no man so ignorant but hee knoweth, no man so blinde but hee seeth, that prayer is a thing most needefull in all estates and degrees of men. For onely by the helpe hereof, wee attaine to those heauenly and euerlasting treasures, which GOD our heauenly Father hath reserued and layde vp for his children in his deare and welbeloued Sonne Iesus Christ, with this couenant and promise most assuredly confirmed and sealed vnto vs, that if we aske, we shall receiue (John 16.23-27).

Now the great necessity of prayer being sufficiently knowen, that our mindes and heartes may be the more prouoked and stirred thereunto, let vs briefely consider what wonderfull strength and power it hath to bring strange & mighty things to passe. We reade in the booke of Exodus, that Iosua fighting against the Amalekites, did conquer & ouercome them, not so much by vertue of his owne strength, as by the earnest and continuall prayer of Moses, who, as long as hee helde vp his handes to GOD, so long did Israel preuaile, but when he fainted, & let his hands downe, then did Amalek and his people preuaile: Insomuch that Aaron and Hur, being in the mount with him, were faine to stay vp his handes vntill the going downe of the sunne, otherwise had the people of GOD that day beene vtterly discomfited, and put to flight (Exodus 17.11-12). Also we read in another place of Iosua himselfe, how he at the besieging of Gibeon, making his humble petition to Almighty GOD, caused the Sunne and the Moone to stay their course, and to stand still in the middest of heauen for the space of a whole day, vntill such time as the people were sufficiently auenged vpon their enemies (Joshua 10.12-13).

And was not Iehosophats prayer of great force and strength, when GOD at his request caused his enemies to fall out among themselues, and wilfully to destroy one another (2 Chronicles 20.18, 23)? Who can maruell enough at the effect and vertue of Elias prayer? Hee being a man subiect to affections as we are, prayed to the Lord that it might not raine, and there fell no rain vpon the earth for the space of three yeares and sixe moneths. Againe, he prayed that it might raine, and there fell great plenty, so that the earth brought foorth her increase most abundantly (1 Kings 18.45).

It were too long to tell of Iudith, Esther, Susanna, and of diuers other godly men and women, how greatly they preuayled in all their doings, by giuing their mindes earnestly and deuoutly to prayer (Matthew 21.22). Let it bee sufficient at this time to conclude with the sayings of Augustine and Chrysotome, whereof the one calleth prayer the key of heauen, the other plainly affirmeth, that there is nothing in all the world more strong then a man that giueth himselfe to feruent prayer (Augustine, *'Ser. 26. de temp.'* Chrysostome, *'Sup.'*).

Now then dearely beloued, seeing prayer is so needfull a thing, and of so great strength before GOD, let vs, according as wee are taught by the example of Christ and his Apostles, be earnest and diligent in calling on the Name of the Lord. Let vs neuer faint, neuer slacke, neuer giue ouer, but let vs dayly and hourely, early and late, in season, and out of season, bee occupied in godly meditations and prayers. What if we obtaine not our petitions at the first? yet let vs not be discouraged, but let vs continually crie and call vpon GOD: hee will surely heare vs at length, if for no other cause, yet for very importunities sake. Remember the parable of the vnrighteous iudge, and the poore widowe, how shee by her importunate meanes caused him to doe her iustice against her aduersary, although otherwise hee feared neither GOD nor man (Luke 18.1-7). Shall not GOD much more auenge his elect (saith our Sauiour Christ) which cry vnto him day and night? Thus hee taught his disciples, and in them all other true Christian men, to pray alwayes, and neuer to faint or shrinke. Remember also the example of the woman of Canaan, how shee was reiected of Christ, and called dogge, as one most vnworthy of any benefite at his handes: yet shee gaue not ouer, but followed him still, crying and calling vpon him to bee good and mercifull vnto her daughter. And at length by very importunity, shee obtayned her request (Matthew 15.22-28). O let vs learne by these examples, to bee earnest and feruent in prayer, assuring our selues that whatsoeuer wee aske of GOD the Father in the Name of his Sonne Christ, and according to his will, hee will vndoubtedly grant it (John 16.23). He is trueth it selfe, and as truely as he hath promised it, so truely will he performe it. GOD for his great mercies sake so worke in our heartes by his holy Spirit, that wee may alwayes make our humble prayers vnto him, as wee ought to doe, and alwayes obtaine the thing which wee aske, through Iesus Christ our Lord, to whom with the Father and the holy Ghost, bee all honour and glory, world without end. Amen.

THE SECOND PART OF THE HOMILY CONCERNING PRAYER.

IN the first part of this Sermon, ye heard the great necessitie, and also the great force of deuout and earnest prayer, declared and prooued vnto you, both by diuers weighty testimonies, and also by sundry good examples of holy Scripture. Now shall you learne whom you ought to call vpon, and to whom you ought alwayes to to direct your prayers. Wee are euidently taught in GODS holy Testament, that Almighty GOD is the onely fountaine and welspring of all goodnesse, and that whatsoeuer wee haue in this world, we receiue it onely at his handes. To this effect serueth the place of Saint Iames: euery good and perfect gift, saith hee, commeth from aboue, and proceedeth from the Father of lights (James 1.17). To this effect also serueth the testimonie of Paul, in diuers places of his Epistles, witnessing that the spirit of wisedome, the spirit of knowledge and reuelation, yea euery good and heauenly gift, as faith, hope, charity, grace, and peace, commeth onely and solely of GOD. In consideration whereof, hee bursteth out into a suddaine passion, and sayth: O man, what thing hast thou, which thou hast not receiued (1 Corinthians 4.7)? Therefore, whensoeuer wee need or lacke any thing, pertaining either to the body or to the soule, it behoooueth vs to runne onely vnto GOD, who is the onely giuer of all good things. Our Sauiour Christ in the Gospel, teaching his Disciples how they should pray, sending them to the Father in his Name, saying, Verily, verily I say vnto you, whatsoeuer ye aske the Father in his Name, hee will giue it vnto you (John 16.23). And in an other place, when yee pray, pray after this sort? Our Father which art in heauen &c (Matthew 6.9, Luke 11.2). And doeth not GOD himselfe, by the mouth of his Prophet Dauid, will and command vs to call vpon him (Psalms 50.14-23)? The Apostle wisheth grace and peace to all them that call on the Name of the Lord, and of his Sonne Iesus Christ, as doeth also the Prophet Ioel, saying, And it shall come to passe, that whosoeuer shall call on the Name of the Lord, shall be saued (Joel 2.32, Acts 2.21).

Thus then it is plaine by the infallible word of trueth and life, that in all our necessities wee must flee vnto GOD, direct our prayers vnto him, call vpon his holy Name, desire helpe at his handes, and at none others, whereof if we will yet haue a further reason, marke that which followeth. There are certaine conditions most requisite to bee found in euery such a one that must bee called vpon, which if they bee not found in him vnto whom wee pray, then doeth our prayer auaile vs nothing, but is altogether in vaine.

The first is this, that he to whom wee make our prayers, bee able to helpe vs. The second is, that hee will helpe vs. The third is, that hee bee such a one as may heare our prayers. The fourth is, that he vnderstand better then wee our selues what we lacke, and how farre we haue neede of helpe. If these things bee to be found in any other sauing onely GOD, then may wee lawfully call vpon some other besides GOD. But what man is so grosse, but he well vnderstandeth that these things are onely proper to him which is omnipotent, and knoweth all things, euen the very secrets of the heart, that is to say, onely and to GOD alone, whereof it followeth, that we must call neither vpon Angel, nor yet vpon Saint, but only and solely vpon GOD, as Saint Paul doeth write (Romans 10.14)? How shall men call vpon him in whom they haue not beleeued? So that Inuocation or Prayer, may not be made without Faith in him on whom they call, but that we must first beleeue in him, before wee can make our Prayer vnto him, whereupon wee must onely and solely pray vnto GOD. For to say that we should beleeue either in Angel or Saint or in any other liuing creature, were mere horrible blasphemie against GOD and his holy Word, neither ought this fancie to enter into the heart of any Christian man, because we are expressely taught in the word of the Lord onely to repose our Faith in the blessed Trinitie, in whose only Name we are also Baptized, according to the expresse commandement of our Sauiour Iesus Christ, in the last of S. Matthew (Matthew 28.19).

But that the trueth hereof may the better appeare, euen to them that be most simple and vnlearned, let vs consider what Prayer is. Saint Augustine calleth it a lifting vp of the minde to GOD, that is to say, an humble and lowly powring out of the heart to GOD (Augustine, *`De Spi. & Lit.,'* chap. 50). Isidorus saith, that it is an affection of the heart, and not a labour of the lips (Isidorus, *`De Summo Bono'*, Chap. 8, Bk. 3). So that by these places, true prayer doeth consist not so much in the outward sound and voyce of wordes, as in the inward groning, and crying of the heart to GOD.

Now then, is there any Angel, any Virgine, and Patriarke or Prophet among the dead, that can vnderstand, or know the meaning of the heart? The Scripture saith, It is GOD that searcheth the heart and the raynes (Psalms 7.9, Revelations 2.23), and that hee onely knoweth the heartes of the children of men (Jeremiah 17.10, 2 Chronicles 6.30). As for the Saintes, they haue so little knowledge of the secretes of the heart, that many of the ancient fathers greatly doubt, whether they know any thing at all, that is commonly done on earth. And albeit some thinke they doe, yet Saint Augustine a Doctour of great authority, and also antiquitie, hath this opinion of them: that they knowe no more what wee doe on earth, then wee know what they doe in heauen (Augustine, *`Lib. de Cura pro Mort. Agenda'*, chap. 13, Augustine, *`De Vera Reli.'*, chap. 22). For proofe whereof, he alleageth the wordes of Esay the Prophet, where it is sayd, Abraham is ignorant of vs, and Israel knoweth vs not (Isaiah 63.16). His minde therefore is this, not that wee should put any religion in worshipping of them, or praying vnto them: but that wee should honour them by following their vertuous and godly life. For as hee witnesseth in anotherplace, the Martyrs and holy men in times past, were wont after their death to bee remembred, and named of the Priest at diuine seruice: but neuer to bee inuocated or called vpon (Augustinem *`De Civit. Dei,'* chap. 10). And why so? because the Priest (saith he) is GODS Priest, and not theirs: Whereby he is bound to call vpon GOD, and not vpon them.

Thus you see, that the authority both of the Scripture, and also of Augustine, doeth not permit, that wee should pray vnto them (John 5.44). O that all men would studiously read, and search the Scriptures, then should they not be drowned in ignorance, but should easily perceiue the trueth, as well of this point of doctrine, as of all the rest. For there doeth the holy Ghost plainely teach vs, that Christ is or onely Mediatour and Intercessour with GOD, and that we must not seeke and runne to an other. If any man sinneth, sayth Saint Iohn, we haue an aduocate with the Father, Iesus Christ the righteous, and hee is the propitiation for our sinnes (1 John 2.1-2). Saint Paul also sayth, there is one GOD, and one Mediatour betweene GOD and man, euen the man Iesus Christ (1 Timothy 2.5). Wherevnto agreeth the testimonie of our Sauiour himselfe, witnessing that no man commeth to the Father, but only by him, who is the way, the trueth, the life (John 14.6), yea and the onely doore whereby we must enter into the kingdome of heauen (John 10.9), because GOD is pleased in no other but in him. For which cause also he cryeth, and calleth vnto vs that we should come vnto him, saying: Come vnto me, all ye that labour and be heauy laden, and I shall refresh you (Matthew 11.28). Would Christ haue vs so necessarily come vnto him? and shall we most vnthankefully leaue him, and runne vnto other? This is euen that which GOD so greatly complaineth of by his Prophet Ieremy, saying, My people haue committed two great offences, they haue forsaken mee the fountaine of the waters of life, and haue digged to themselues broken pits that can holde no water. Is not that man thinke you vnwise that will runne for water to a little brooke, when he may aswell goe to the head spring? Euen so may his wisedome bee iustly suspected, that will flee vnto Saints in time of necessity, when hee may boldly and without feare declare his griefe, and direct his prayer vnto the Lord himselfe. If GOD were strange, or dangerous to bee talked withall, then might wee iustly drawe backe and seeke to some other. But the Lord is nigh vnto all them that call vpon him in faith and trueth (Psalms 145.18), and the prayer of the humble and meeke hath alwayes pleased him (Apocrypha. Judith 9.11). What if wee bee sinners, shall wee not therefore pray vnto GOD? or shall wee despaire to obtaine any thing at his handes? Why did Christ then teach vs to aske forgiuenesse of our sinnes, saying, And forgiue vs our trespasses, as wee forgiue them that trespasse against vs? Shall we thinke that the Saints are more mercifull in hearing sinners, then GOD? Dauid sayth, that the Lord is full of compassion and mercy, slow to anger, and of great kindnesse (Psalms 103.8). Saint Paul saith, that hee is rich in mercy toward all them that call vpon him (Ephesians 2.4). And hee himselfe by the mouth of his Prophet Esay sayth, For a little while haue I forsaken thee, but with great compassion will I gather thee: For a moment in mine anger I haue hid my face from thee, but with euerlasting mercy I haue had compassion vpon thee (Isaiah 54.7-8). Therefore the sinnes of any man ought not to withhold him from praying vnto the Lord his GOD But if hee be truely penitent and stedfast in faith, let him assure himselfe that the Lord will be mercifull vnto him, and heare his prayers. O but I dare not (will some man say) trouble GOD at all times with my prayers. We see that in Kings houses and Courts of Princes, men cannot be admitted, vnlesse they first vse the helpe and meane of some speciall Noble man, to come vnto the speach of the King, and to obteine the thing that they would haue. To this reason doeth Saint Ambrose answere very well, writing vpon the first Chapter to the Romanes (Ambrose, *'Super Cap. 1, Romans'*). Therefore (saith he) we vse to goe vnto the King by officers and noble men, because the King is a mortall man, and knoweth not to whom hee may commit the gouernement of the common wealth. But to haue GOD our friend, from whom nothing is hid, we neede not any helper, that should further vs with his good word, but onely a deuout and godly minde. And if it be so, that wee neede one to intreate for vs: why may wee not content our selues with that one Mediatour, which is at the right hand of GOD the Father, and there liueth for euer to make intercession for vs? As the blood of Christ did redeeme vs on the crosse, and cleanse vs from our sinnes: euen so it is now able to saue all them that come vnto GOD by it. For Christ sitting in heauen, hath an euerlasting Priesthood, and alwayes prayeth to his Father for them that bee penitent, obteining by vertue of his wounds, which are euermore in the sight of GOD, not onely perfect remission of our sinnes, but also all other necessaries that wee lacke in this world (Matthew 6.33, James 5.15, Colossians 4.12), so that this onely Mediatour is sufficient in heauen (1 Timothy 2.5), and needeth no others to helpe him (Hebrews 7.25). Why then doe wee pray one for another in this life, some man perchance will heere demaund? Forsooth we are willed so to doe, by the expresse commandement both of Christ and his disciples, to declare therein aswell the faith that wee haue in Christ towardes GOD, as also the mutuall charitie that wee beare one towards another, in that pitie our brothers case, and make our humble petition to GOD for him. But that we should pray vnto Saints, neither haue we any commandement in all the Scripture, nor yet example which wee may safely follow. So that being done without authority of Gods word, it lacketh the ground of faith, & therefore cannot be acceptable before GOD (Hebrews 11.6). For whatsoeuer is not of faith, is sin (Romans 14.23). And as the Apostle saith, that faith commeth by hearing, and hearing by the word of GOD (Romans 10.17). Yet thou wilt obiect further, that the Saints in heauen doe pray for vs, and that their prayer proceedeth of an earnest charity that they haue towards their brethren on earth. Whereto it may be well answered. First, that no man knoweth whether they doe pray for vs, or no. And if any will goe about to prooue it by the nature of charitie, concluding, that because they did pray for men on earth, therefore they doe much more the same now in heauen: Then may it be sayd by the same reason, that as oft as we doe weepe on earth, they doe also weepe in heauen, because while they liued in this world, it is most certaine and sure they did so. And for that place which is written in the Apocalyps, namely that the Angel did offer vp the prayers of the Saints vpon the golden Altar: it is properly meant, and ought properly to bee vnderstood of those Saints that are yet liuing on earth, and not of them that are dead, otherwise what neede were it that the Angel should offer vp their prayers, being now in heauen before the face of Almighty GOD? But admit the Saints doe pray for vs, yet doe we not know how, whether specially for them which call vpon them, or else generally for all men, wishing well to euery man alike. If they pray specially for them which call vpon them, then it is like they heare our prayers, and also know our hearts desire. Which thing to bee false, it is already prooued both by the Scriptures, and also by the authority of Augustine. Let vs not therefore put our trust or confidence in the Saints or Martyrs that be dead. Let vs not call vpon them, nor desire helpe at their hands: but let vs alwayes lift vp our hearts to GOD, in the name of his deare Sonne Christ, for whose sake as GOD hath promised to heare our prayer, so he will truely performe it. Inuocation is a thing proper vnto GOD, which if wee attribute vnto the Saints, it soundeth to their reproach, neither can they well beare it at our hands. When Paul had healed a certaine lame man, which was impotent in his feet, at Lystra, the people would haue done sacrifice to him and Barnabas: who renting their clothes, refused it, and exhorted them to worship the true GOD (Acts 14.8-18). Likewise in the Reuelation, when Saint Iohn fell before the Angels feet to worship him, the Angel would not permit him to doe it, but commanded him that he should worship GOD (Revelations 19.10, 22.8-9). Which examples declare vnto vs, that the Saints and Angels in heauen, will not haue vs to doe any honour vnto them, that is due and proper vnto GOD. Hee onely is our Father, he onely is omnipotent, hee onely knoweth and vnderstandeth all things, hee onely can helpe vs at all times, and in all places, he suffereth the sunne to shine vpon the good and the bad, hee seedeth the yong rauens that crie vnto him, hee saueth both man and beast, he will not that any one hayre of our head shall perish: but is alwayes ready to helpe and preserue all them that put their trust in him, according as he hath promised, saying, Before they call, I will answer, and whiles they speake, I will heare (Isaiah 65.24). Let vs not therefore any thing mistrust his goodnesse, let vs not feare to come before the throne of his mercy, let vs not seeke the ayd and helpe of Saints, but let vs come boldly our selues, nothing doubting but GOD for Christs sake, in whom hee is well pleased, will heare vs without a spokes-man, and accomplish our desire in all such things as shall be agreeable to his most holy will. So sayth Chrysostome, an ancient Doctour of the Church (Chrysostome, `*6 Hom. de Profectu. Evang.*'), and so must wee stedfastly beleeue, not because he sayth it, but much more because it is the doctrine of our Sauiour Christ himselfe, who hath promised that if wee pray to the Father in his name, we shall certainely be heard, both to the reliefe of our necessities, and also to the saluation of our soules, which he hath purchased vnto vs, not with gold or siluer, but with his pretious bloud, shed once for all vpon the Crosse.

To him therefore, with the Father and the Holy Ghost, three persons and one GOD, be all honour, prayse, & glory, for euer & euer. Amen.

THE THIRD PART OF THE HOMILIE CONCERNING PRAYER.

YE were taught in the other part of this Sermon, vnto whom ye ought to direct your prayers in time of need and necessity, that is to wit, not vnto Angels or Saints, but vnto the eternall and euerliuing GOD, who because hee is mercifull, is alwayes ready to heare vs, when we call vpon him in true and perfect fayth. And because hee is omnipotent, he can easily performe and bring to passe, the thing that we request to haue at his hands. To doubt of his power, it were a plaine point of infidelity, and cleane against the doctrine of the holy Ghost, which teacheth that hee is all in all. And as touching his good will in this behalfe, we haue expresse testimonies in Scripture, how that he will helpe vs, and also deliuer vs, if wee call vpon him in time of trouble (Psalms 50.15). So that in both these respects, we ought rather to call vpon him then vpon any other. Neither ought any man therefore to doubt to come boldly vnto GOD, because he is a sinner (1 Timothy 1.15-16). For the Lord (as the Prophet Dauid sayth) is gracious and mercifull, yea, his mercy and goodnesse endureth for euer (Psalms 107.1). He that sent his owne sonne into the world to saue sinners, will hee not also heare sinners, if with a true penitent heart and a stedfast fayth they pray vnto him? Yes, if wee acknowledge our sinnes, GOD is faithfull and iust to forgiue vs our sinnes, and to cleanse vs from all vnrighteousnesse (1 John 1.9), as we are plainely taught by the examples of Dauid, Peter, Mary Magdalene, the Publicane, and diuers other. And whereas we must needes vse the helpe of some mediatour and intercessor, let vs content our selues with him, that is the true and onely Mediatour of the new Testament, namely the Lord and Sauiour Iesus Christ.

For as Saint Iohn saith, If any man sinne, we haue an aduocate with the Father, Iesus Christ, the righteous, who is the propitiation for our sinnes (1 John 2.1-2). And Saint Paul in his first Epistle to Timothie, saith, There is one GOD, and one mediatour betweene GOD and man, euen the man Iesus Christ, who gaue himselfe a ransome for all men, to be a testimonie in due time (1 Timothy 2.5-6).

Now after this doctrine established, you shall bee instructed for what kinde of things, and what kinde of persons ye ought to make your prayers vnto GOD. It greatly behoueth all men, when they pray, to consider well and diligently with themselues what they aske and require at Gods hands, lest if they desire that thing which they ought not, their petitions be made voyd, and of none effect. There came on a time vnto Agesilaus the King, a certaine importunate suter, who requested him in a matter earnestly, saying, Sir, and it please your Grace, you did once promise me. Trueth quoth the king, if it be iust that thou requirest, then I promised thee, otherwise I did onely speake it, and not promise it. The man would not bee so answered at the kings hand, but still vrging him more and more, said: It becommeth a king to performe the least word hee hath spoken, yea if hee should onely becke with his head. No more saith the king, then it behoueth one that commeth to a king, to speake and aske those things which are rightfull and honest. Thus the king cast off this vnreasonable and importunate suter.

Now if so great consideration be to be had, when we kneele before an earthly king: how much more ought to be had, when we kneele before the heauenly King, who is onely delighted with iustice and equitie, neither will admit any vaine, foolish, or vniust petition? Therefore it shall bee good and profitable, throughly to consider and determine with our selues, what things we may lawfully aske of GOD, without feare of repulse, and also what kinde of persons wee are bound to commend vnto GOD in our dayly prayers. Two things are chiefly to bee respected in euery good and godly mans prayer: His owne necessitie, and the glory of almighty GOD. Necessitie belongeth either outwardly to the body, or else inwardly to the soule. Which part of man, because it is much more precious and excellent then the other, therefore wee ought first of all, to craue such things as properly belong to the saluation thereof: as the gift of repentance, the gift of faith, the gift of charitie and good workes, remission and forgiuenesse of sinnes patience in aduersitie, lowlinesse in prosperity, & such other like fruits of the spirit, as hope, loue, ioy, peace, long suffering, gentlenesse, goodnesse, meekenesse, and temperancie, which things GOD requireth of all them that professe themselues to be his children (Galatians 5.22-23), saying vnto them in this wise., Let your light so shine before men, that they may see your good workes, and glorifie your Father which is in heauen (Matthew 5.16), And in another place also hee saith, Seeke first the Kingdome of GOD, and his righteousnesse, and then all other things shall bee giuen vnto you (Matthew 6.33). Wherein he putteth vs in minde, that our chiefe and greatest care ought to bee for those things which pertaine to the health and safegard of the soule, because we haue here (as the Apostle saith) no continuing citie, but doe seeke after another in the world to come (Hebrews 13.14).

Now when wee haue sufficiently prayed for things belonging to the soule, then may wee lawfully and with safe conscience, pray also for our bodily necessities, as meate, drinke, clothing, health of body, deliuerance out of prison, good lucke in our dayly affaires, and so forth, according as wee shall haue neede. Whereof, what better example can wee desire to haue, then of Christ himselfe, who taught his disciples, and all other Christian men, first to pray for heauenly things, and afterward for earthly things, as is to bee seene in that prayer which hee left vnto his Church, commonly called the Lords prayer (Matthew 6.9-13, Luke 11.2-4)? In the third booke of Kings and third Chapter it is written, that GOD appeared by night in a dreame vnto Salomon the King, saying, Aske of me whatsoeuer thou wilt, and I will giue it thee. Salomon made his humble prayer, and asked a wise and prudent heart, that might iudge and vnderstand what were good, and what were ill, what were godly, and what were vngodly, what were righteous, and what were vnrighteous in the sight of the Lord. It pleased GOD wonderously that he had asked this thing. And GOD said vnto him, Because thou hast requested this word, and hast not desired many dayes and long yeeres vpon the earth, neither abundance of riches and goods, nor yet the life of thine enemies which hate thee, but hast desired wisedome to sit in iudgement: Behold, I haue done vnto thee according to thy wordes, I haue giuen thee a wise heart, full of knowledge and vnderstanding, so that there was neuer any like thee before time, neither shall bee in time to come. Moreouer I haue, besides this, giuen thee that which thou hast not required, namely worldly wealth and riches, princely honour and glory, so that thou shalt therein also passe all kings that euer were. Note this example, how Salomon being put to his choise to aske of GOD, whatsoeuer he would, requested not vaine and transitorie things, but the high and heauenly treasures of wisdome, and that in so doing, hee obtaineth as it were in recompence, both riches and honour. Wherein is giuen vs to vnderstand, that in our dayly prayers, wee should chiefly and principally aske those things which concerne the Kingdome of GOD, and the saluation of our owne soules, nothing doubting but all other things shall (according to the promise of Christ) be giuen vnto vs. But here we must take heede, that wee forget not that other end whereof mention was made before, namely the glory of GOD. Which vnlesse we minde, and set before our eyes in making our prayers, we may not looke to be heard, or to receiue any thing of the Lord. In the xx. Chapter of Matthew, the mother of the two sonnes of Zebedee came vnto Iesus, worshipping him, and saying, Grant that my two sonnes may sit in thy Kingdome, the one on thy right hand, and the other at thy left hand. In this petition she did not respect the glory of GOD, but plainely declared the ambition and vaine glory of her owne minde, for which cause she was also most worthily repelled, and rebuked at the Lords hand. In like manner wee reade in the Actes, of one Simon Magus a Sorcerer, how that hee perceiuing that through laying on of the Apostles hands the holy Ghost was giuen, offered them money, saying: Giue mee also this power, that on whomsoeuer I lay my hands, hee may receiue the holy ghost (Acts 8.18-19). In making this request, hee sought not the honour and glory of GOD, but his owne priuate gaine and lucre, thinking to get great store of money by this feate, and therefore it was iustly sayd vnto him: Thy money perish with thee, because thou thinkest that the gift of GOD may be obteined with money. By these and such other examples wee are taught, whensoeuer we make our prayers vnto GOD, chiefly to respect the honour, and glory of his Name. Whereof we haue this generall precept in the Apostle Paul, Whether ye eate or drinke, or whatsoeuer ye doe, looke that ye doe it to the glory of GOD (1 Corinthians 10.31, Colossians 3.17). Which thing we shall best of all doe, if wee follow the example of our Sauiour Christ, who praying that the bitter cup of death might passe from him, would not therein haue his owne will fulfilled, but referred the whole matter to the good will and pleasure of his Father (Matthew 26.39, Luke 22.42).

And hitherto concerning those things, that we may lawfully and boldly aske of GOD. Now it followeth, that wee declare what kinde of persons wee are bound in conscience to pray for. Saint Paul writing to Timothie, exhorteth him to make prayers and supplications for all men, exempting none, of what degree or state soeuer they bee (1

Timothy 2.1-2). In which place he maketh mention by name of Kings and Rulers which are in authority, putting vs thereby to knowledge how greatly it concerneth the profit of the common wealth, to pray diligently for the higher powers. Neither is it without good cause, that hee doeth so often in all his Epistls craue the prayers of GODS people for himselfe (Colossians 4.3, Romans 15.30, 2 Thessalonians 3.1, Ephesians 6.19). For in so doing, he declareth to the world, how expedient and needefull it is dayly to call vpon GOD for the ministers of his holy Word and Sacraments, that they may haue the doore of vtterance opened vnto them, that they may truely vnderstand the Scriptures, that they may effectually preach the same vnto the people, and bring foorth the true fruits thereof, to the example of all other.

After this sort did the congregation continually pray for Peter at Ierusalem (Acts 12.5), and for Paul among the Gentiles, to the great encrease and furtherance of Christs Gospel. And if we, following their good example herein, will studie to doe the like, doubtlesse it cannot be expressed, how greatly we shall both helpe our selues, and also please GOD.

To discourse and run through all degrees of persons, it were too long. Therefore yee shall briefly take this one conclusion for all: Whomsoeuer we are bound by expresse commandement to loue, for those also are wee bound in conscience to pray. But wee are bound by expresse commandement to loue all men as our selues: therefore wee are also bound to pray for all men, euen as well as if it were for our selues, notwithstanding we know them to bee our extreme and deadly enemies. For so doeth our Sauiour Christ plainely teach vs in his Gospel, saying, Loue your enemies, blesse them that curse you, doe good to them that hate you, pray for them that persecute you, that yee may bee the children of your Father which is in heauen (Matthew 5.44). And as hee taught his disciples, so did hee practise himselfe in his life time praying for his enemies vpon the crosse, and desiring his Father to forgiue them, because they knew not what they did (Luke 23.34): As did also that holy and blessed Martyr Steuen, when hee was cruelly stoned to death of the stubburne and stifnecked Iewes (Acts 7.60): to the example of all them that will truely and vnfainedly follow their Lord and Master Christ in this miserable and mortall life.

Now to entreate of that question, whether we ought to pray for them that are departed out of this world, or no. Wherein, if wee will cleaue onely vnto the word of GOD, then must we needes graunt, that we haue no commandement so to doe. For the Scripture doeth acknowledge but two places after this life. The one proper to the elect and blessed of GOD; the other to the reprobate and damned soules, as may be well gathered, by the parable of Lazarus and the rich man (Luke 16.19-26), which place Saint Augustine expounding, saith in this wise: That which Abraham speaketh vnto the rich man in Lukes Gospel, namely that the iust cannot goe into those places where the wicked are tormented: what other things doeth it signifie, but onely this, that the iust, by reason of GODS iudgement, which may not be reuoked, can shew no deede of mercy in helping them which after this life are cast into prison, vntill they pay the vttermost farthing (Augustine, *`Evange.', bk. 2, quest. 1, cap. 38*)? These words, as they confound the opinion of helping the dead by prayer, so they doe cleane confute and take away the vaine errour of Purgatory, which is grounded vpon the saying of the Gospel: Thou shalt not depart thence, vntill thou hast payed the vttermost farthing. Now doeth S. Augustine say, that those men which are cast into prison after this life, on that condition, may in no wise bee holpen, though wee would helpe them neuer so much. And why? Because the sentence of GOD is vnchangeable, and cannot be reuoked againe. Therefore let vs not deceiue our selues, thinking that either we may helpe other, or other may helpe vs by their good and charitable prayers in time to come.

For as the Preacher saith: When the tree falleth, whether it bee toward the South, or toward the North, in what place soeuer the tree falleth, there it lieth (Ecclesiastes 11.3): meaning thereby, that euery mortall man dieth either in the state of saluation or damnation, according as the words of the Euangelist Iohn doe also plainely import, saying: He that beleeueth on the Sonne of GOD, hath eternall life: But he that beleeueth not on the Sonne, shall neuer see life, but the wrath of GOD abideth vpon him (John 3.36). Where is then the third place which they call Purgatory? or where shall our prayers helpe and profit the dead? S. Augustine doth onely acknowledge two places after this life, heauen & hell: As for the third place, he doth plainly denie that there is any such to be found in all Scripture (Augustine, *`Hypogno.'*, bk. 5). Chrysostome likewise is of this minde, that vnlesse wee wash away our sinnes in this present world, we shall finde no comfort afterward (Chrysostome, *`Hib.'*, 2). And S. Cyprian saith, that after death, repentance and sorrow of paine shall bee without fruit, weeping also shalbe in vaine, and prayer shall be to no purpose (Cyprian, `Homil. 5' in *'Contra Demetrianum'*). Therefore he counselleth all men to make prouision for themselues while they may, because when they are once departed out of this life, there is no place for repentance, nor yet for satisfaction.

Let these and such other places be sufficient to take away the grosse errour of Purgatory out of our heads, neither let vs dreame any more, that the soules of the dead are any thing at all holpen by our prayers: But as the Scripture teacheth vs, let vs thinke that the soule of man passing out of the body, goeth straight wayes either to heauen, or else to hell, whereof the one needeth no prayer, and the other is without redemption. The only Purgatory wherein we must trust to be saued, is the death and bloud of Christ, which if we apprehend with a true and stedfast faith, it purgeth and cleanseth vs from all our sinnes (1 John 1.7), euen as well as if hee were now hanging vpon the Crosse. The bloud of Christ, sayth Saint Iohn, hath cleansed vs from all sinne. The bloud of Christ, sayth Saint Paul, hath purged our consciences from dead workes, to serue the liuing GOD (Hebrews 9.14). Also in another place hee sayth, Wee bee sanctified and made holy by the offering vp of the body of Iesus Christ done once for all (Hebrews 10.10). Yea hee addeth more, saying, With the one oblation of his blessed body & pretious bloud, he hath made perfect for euer and euer all them that are sanctified (Hebrews 10.14 *Ibidem.*). This then is that Purgatory, wherein all Christian men put their whole trust and confidence, nothing doubting, but if they truely repent them of their sinnes, and die in perfect fayth, that then they shall foorthwith passe from death to life. If this kinde of purgation will not serue them, let them neuer hope to be released by other mens prayers, though they should continue therein vnto the worlds end. He that cannot be saued by fayth in Christs bloud, how shall he looke to bee deliuered by mans intercessions? Hath GOD more respect to man on earth, then hee hath to Christ in heauen? If any man sinne (sayth Saint Iohn) we haue an aduocate with the Father, euen Iesus Christ the righteous, and hee is the propitiation for our sinnes (1 John 2.1). But we must take heed that wee call vpon this aduocate while wee haue space giuen vs in this life, lest when wee are once dead, there bee no hope of saluation left vnto vs. For as euery man sleepeth with his owne cause, so euery man shall rise againe with his owne cause. And looke in what state he dieth, in the same state he shall bee also iudged, whether it bee to salutation or damnation. Let vs not therefore dreame either of Purgatory, or of prayer for the soules of them that be dead: but let vs earnestly and diligently pray for them which are expresly commanded in holy Scripture, namely for Kings and Rulers, for Ministers of GODS holy word and Sacraments, for the Saints of this world, otherwise called the faythfull: to be short, for all men liuing, be they neuer so great enemies to GOD and his people, as Iewes, Turkes, Pagans, Infidels, Heretikes, &c. Then shall we truely fulfill the commandement of GOD in that behalfe, and plainely declare our selues to bee the true children of our heauenly Father, who suffereth the Sunne to shine vpon the good and the bad, and the raine to fall vpon the iust and the vniust: For which and all other benefits most abundantly bestowed vpon mankind from the beginning, let vs giue him hearty thankes, as we are most bound, and prayse his Name for euer and euer. Amen.

HOMILY ON THE PLACE AND TIME OF PRAYER

AN HOMILIE OF THE
place and time of Prayer.

GOD through his Almighty power, wisedome, and goodnesse, created in the beginning, heauen and earth, the sun, the moone, the starres, the foules of the ayre, the beastes of the earth, the fishes in the sea, and all other creatures, for the vse and commodity of man, whom also he had created to his owne image and likenesse, and giuen him the vse and gouernment ouer them all, to the end he should vse them in such sort as he had giuen him in charge and commandement, and also that hee should declare himselfe thankefull and kinde for all those benefits, so liberally and so gratiously bestowed vpon him, vtterly without any deseruing on his behalfe. And although we ought at all times, and in all places, to haue in remembrance, and to be thankefull to our gratious Lord, according as it is written, I will magnifie the Lord at all times. And againe, Wheresoeuer the Lord beareth rule, O my soule prayse the Lord (Psalm 103.22): Yet it appeareth to be GODS good will and pleasure, that wee should at speciall times, and in speciall places, gather our selues together, to the intent his name might bee renowned, and his glory set foorth in the congregation and assemblie of his Saints. As concerning the time which Almighty GOD hath appointed his people to assemble together solemnely, it doeth appeare by the fourth commandement of GOD: Remember, sayth GOD, that thou keepe holy the Sabbath day. Upon the which day, as is plaine in the Actes of the Apostles, the people accustomably resorted together, and heard diligently the Law and the Prophets read among them (Acts

13.14). And albeit this commandement of GOD doeth not binde Christian people so straitely to obserue and keepe the vtter ceremonies of the Sabbath day, as it was giuen vnto the Iewes, as touching the forbearing of worke and labour in time of great necessity, and as touching the precise keeping of the seuenth day, after the manner of the Iewes. For wee keepe now the first day, which is our Sunday, and make that our Sabbath, that is our day of rest, in the honour of our Sauiour Christ, who as vpon that day rose from death, conquering the same most triumphantly: Yet notwithstanding, whatsoeuer is found in the commandement appertaining to the law of nature, as a thing most godly, most iust, and needefull for the setting foorth of GODS glory, it ought to bee retained and kept of all good Christian people. And therefore by this commandement, wee ought to haue a time, as one day in the weeke, wherein wee ought to rest, yea from our lawfull and needefull workes. For like as it appeareth by this commandement, that no man in the sixe dayes ought to bee slothfull or idle, but diligently to labour in that state wherein GOD hath set him: Euen so, GOD hath giuen expresse charge to all men, that vpon the Sabboth day, which is now our Sunday, they should cease from all weekely and workeday labour, to the intent, that like as GOD himselfe wrought sixe dayes, and rested the seuenth, and blessed, and sanctified it, and consecrated it to quietnesse and rest from labour: euen so GODS obedient people should vse the Sunday holily, and rest from their common and dayly businesse, and also giue themselues wholly to heauenly exercises of GODS true religion and seruice. So that GOD doeth not onely command the obseruation of this holy day, but also by his owne example doeth stirre and prouoke vs to the diligent keeping of the same. Good naturall children will not onely become obedient to the commandement of their parents, but also haue a diligent eye to their doings, and gladly follow the same. So if we will be the children of our heauenly Father, wee must be carefull to keepe the Christian Sabboth day, which is the Sunday, not onely for that it is GODS expresse commandement, but also to declare ourselues to be louing children, in following the example of our gratious Lord and Father.

Thus it may plainely appeare, that Gods will and commandement was to haue a solemne time and standing day in the weeke, wherein the people should come together, and haue in remembrance his wonderfull benefits, and to render him thankes for them, as appertaineth to louing, kinde, and obedient people. This example and commandement of GOD the godly Christian people beganne to follow immediatly after the assension of our Lord Christ, and began to chuse them a standing day of the weeke to come together in: Yet not the seuenth day, which the Iewes kept: but the Lords day, the day of the Lords resurrection, the day after the seuenth day, which is the first day of the weeke. Of the which day mention is made by Saint Paul on this wise, In the first day of the Sabboth, let euery man lay vp what hee thinketh good: meaning for the poore (1 Corinthians 16.2). By the first day of the Sabboth, is meant our Sunday, which is the first day after the Iewes seuenth day. And in the Apocalyps it is more plaine, where as Saint Iohn sayth, I was in the Spirit vpon the Lords day (Revelations 1.10). Sithence which time GODS people hath alwayes in all ages, without any gainesaying, vsed to come together vpon the Sunday, to celebrate and honor the Lords blessed Name, and carefully to keepe that day in holy rest and quietnesse, both man, woman, childe, seruant, and stranger. For the transgression and breach of which day, GOD hath declared himselfe much to bee grieued, as it may appeare by him, who for gathering of stickes on the Sabboth day was stoned to death (Numbers 15.32-36). But alasse, all these notwithstanding, it is lamentable to see the wicked boldnesse of those that will bee counted GODS people, who passe nothing at all of keeping and halowing the Sunday. And these people are of two sorts. The one sort if they haue any businesse to doe, though there bee no extreme neede, they must not spare for the Sunday, they must ride and iourney on the Sunday, they must driue and carry on the Sunday, they must rowe and ferry on the Sunday, they must buy and sell on the Sunday, they must keepe markets and fayres on the Sunday: finally, they vse all dayes alike, workedayes and holydayes all are one. The other sort is worse. For although they will not trauell nor labour on the Sunday as they doe on the weeke day, yet they will not rest in holinesse, as GOD commandeth: but they rest in vngodlinesse and filthinesse, prancing in their pride, pranking and pricking, pointing and painting themselues to bee gorgious and gay: they rest in excesse and superfluitie, in gluttony and drunkennesse, like rattes and swine: they rest in brawling and rayling, in quarrelling and fighting: they rest in wantonnesse, in toyish talking, in filthie fleshlinesse, so that it it doeth too euidently appeare that God is more dishonoured, and the deuill better serued on the Sunday, then vpon all the dayes in the weeke besides. And I assure you, the beasts which are commanded to rest on the Sunday, honour GOD better then this kinde of people: For they offend not GOD, they breake not their holy dayes. Wherefore, O yee people of GOD, lay your hands vpon your hearts, repent and amend this grieuous and dangerous wickednesse, stand in awe of the Commandement of GOD, gladly follow the example of GOD himselfe, be not disobedient to the godly order of Christs Church, vsed and kept from the Apostles time, vntill this day. Feare the displeasure and iust plagues of Almightie GOD, if ye be negligent and forbeare not labouring and trauailing on the Sabbath day or Sunday, and doe not resort together to celebrate and magnifie GODS blessed Name, in quiet holinesse and godly reuerence.

Now concerning the place where the people of GOD ought to resort together, and where especially they ought to celebrate and sanctifie the Sabboth day, that is the Sunday, the day of holy rest: That place is called GODS Temple or the Church, because the company and congregation of GODS people (which is properly called the Church) doeth there assemble themselues on the dayes appointed for such assemblies and meetings. And forasmuch as Almightie GOD hath appointed a speciall time to be honoured in, it is very meete, godly, and also necessarie, that there should be a place appointed where these people should meete and resort, to serue their gracious GOD and mercifull Father. Trueth it is, the holy Patriarchs for a great number of yeeres had neither Temple nor Church to resort vnto. The cause was, they were not stayed in any place, but were in a continuall peregrination and wandering, that they could not conueniently build any Church. But so soone as GOD had deliuered his people from their enemies, and set them in some libertie in the wildernesse, he set them vp a costly and curious Tabernacle, which was as it were the Parish Church, a place to resort vnto of the whole multitude, a place to haue his sacrifices made in, and other obseruances and rites to be vsed in. Furthermore, after that GOD according to the trueth of his promise, had placed and quietly setled his people in the land of Canaan, now called Iurie, hee commanded a great and magnificent Temple to be builded by King Solomon, as seldome the like hath beene seene: a Temple so decked and adorned, so gorgeously garnished, as was meete and expedient for people of that time, which would be allured and stirred with nothing so much, as with such outward goodly gay things. This was now the Temple of GOD, endued also with many giftes and sundry promises. This was the publike Church, and the mother Church of all Iurie. Here was God honoured and serued. Hither was the whole Realme of all the Israelites bound to come at three solemne feasts in the yeere, to serue their Lord GOD heere. But let vs proceed further. In the time of Christ and his Apostles, there were yet no Temples nor Churches for Christian men. For why? they were alwayes for the most part in persecution, vexation and trouble, so that there could be no liberty nor licence obtayned for that purpose. Yet GOD delighted much that they should often resort together in a place, and therefore after his ascension they remayned together in an vpper chamber, sometime they entred into the Temple, sometime into the Synagogues, sometimes they were in prison, sometimes in their houses, sometimes in the fields, &c. And this continued so long till the fayth of Christ Iesus began to multiply in a great part of the world. Now when diuers Realmes were established in GODS true Religion, and GOD had giuen them peace and quietnesse: then began Kings, Noble men, and the people also, stirred vp with a godly zeale and feruentnesse, to build vp Temples and Churches, whither the people might resort, the better to doe their dutie towards GOD, and to keepe holy their Sabboth day, the day of rest. And to these Temples haue the Christians customably vsed to resort from time to time, as vnto meet places where they might with common consent prayse and magnifie GODS name, yeelding him thankes for the benefits that he dayly powreth vpon them, both mercifully and abundantly, where they might also heare his holy word read, expounded, and preached syncerely, and receiue his holy Sacraments ministred vnto them duely and purely. True it is that the chiefe and speciall Temples of GOD, wherein he hath greatest pleasure, and most delighteth to dwell, are the bodies and mindes of true Christians, and the chosen people of GOD, according to the doctrine of holy Scriptures, declared by Saint Paul. Know ye not (sayth hee) that yee bee the temple of GOD, and that the spirit of GOD doeth dwell in you? The Temple of GOD is holy, which ye are (1 Corinthians 3.16-17). And againe in the same Epistle: Know ye not that your body is the temple of the holy Ghost dwelling in you, whom you haue giuen you of GOD, and that yee bee not your owne (1 Corinthians 6.19)? Yet this notwithstanding, GOD doeth allow the materiall Temple made with lime and stone (so oft as his people come together into it, to prayse his holy name) to be his house, and the place where hee hath promised to be present, and where he will heare the prayers of them that call vpon him. The which thing both Christ and his Apostles, with all the rest of the holy Fathers, doe sufficiently declare by this: That albeit they certainely knew that their prayers were heard in what place soeuer they made them, though it were in caues, in woodes, and in deserts, yet (so oft as they could conueniently) they resorted to the materiall Temples, there with the rest of the congregation, to ioyne in prayer and true worship.

Wherefore (dearely beloued) you that professe your selues to be Christians, and glory in that name, disdaine not to follow the example of your master Christ, whose schollers you say you bee, shew you to bee like them whose schoolemates you take vpon you to bee, that is, the Apostles and Disciples of Christ. Lift vp pure hands, with cleane hearts, in all places and at all times. But doe the same in the Temples and Churches vpon the Sabbath dayes also. Our godly predecessours, and the ancient Fathers of the Primitiue Church, spared not their goods to build Churches, no they spared not their liues in time of persecution, and to hazard their blood, that they might assemble themselues together in Churches. And shall we spare a little labour to come to Churches? Shall neither their example, nor our duety, nor the commodities (that thereby should come vnto vs) moue vs? If wee will declare our selues to haue the feare of GOD, if we will shew our selues true Christians, if wee will bee the followers of Christ our master, and of those godly Fathers that haue liued before vs, and now haue receiued the reward of true and faithfull Christians, we must both willingly, earnestly, and reuerently come vnto the material Churches and Temples to pray, as vnto fit places appointed for that vse, and that vpon the Sabboth day, as at most conuenient time for GODS people, to cease from bodily and worldly businesse, to giue themselues to holy rest, and godly contemplation pertayning to the seruice of Almighty GOD: Whereby wee may reconcile our selues to GOD, be partakers of his holy Sacraments, and be deuout hearers of his holy word, so to be established in faith to Godward, in hope against all aduersity, and in charity toward our neighbours. And thus running our course as good Christian people, wee may at the last attaine the reward of euerlasting glory, through the merits of our Sauiour Iesus Christ, to whom with the Father and the holy Ghost, be all honour and glory. Amen.

THE SECOND PART OF THE HOMILIE OF THE PLACE AND TIME OF PRAYER.

IT hath beene declared vnto you (good Christian people) in the former Sermon read vnto you, at what time and into what place ye shall come together to prayse GOD. Now I intend to set before your eyes, first how zealous and desirous ye ought to be to come to your Church. Secondly, how sore GOD is grieued with them that doe despise or little regard to come to the Church vpon the holy restfull day. It may well appeare by the Scriptures, that many of the godly Israelites, being now in captiuity for their sinnes among the Babylonians, full often wished and desired to bee againe at Hierusalem. And at their returne, through GODS goodnesse (though many of the people were negligent) yet the fathers were maruellous deuout to build vp the Temple, that GODS people might repayre thither, to honour him. And king Dauid when he was a banished man out of his countrey, out of Hierusalem the holy city, from the Sanctuary, from the holy place and from the Tabernacle of GOD: What desire, what feruentnesse was in him toward that holy place? what wishings and prayers made hee to GOD to be a dweller in the house of the Lord? One thing (sayth hee) haue I asked of the Lord, and this will I still craue, that I may resort and haue my dwelling in the house of the Lord, so long as I liue. Again, Oh how I ioyed when I heard these words, Wee shall goe into the Lords house (Psalms 122.1, 9). And in other places of the Psalmes hee declareth for what intent and purpose he hath such a feruent desire to enter into the Temple and Church of the Lord: I will fall downe (sayth he) and worship in the holy Temple of the Lord. Againe, I haue appeared in thy holy place, that I might behold thy might and power, that I might behold thy glory and magnificence (Psalms 63.1-2). Finally he sayth: I will shew foorth thy name to my brethren, I will prayse thee in the middest of the congregation. Why then had Dauid such an earnest desire to the house of GOD? First because there he would worship and honour GOD. Secondly, there he would haue a contemplation and a sight of the power and glory of GOD. Thirdly, there he would prayse the name of GOD, with all the congregation and company of the people. These considerations of this blessed Prophet of GOD ought to stirre vp, and kindle in vs the like earnest desire to resort to the Church, especially vpon the holy restfull dayes, there to doe our duties, and to serue GOD, there to call to remembrance how GOD euen of his meere mercy, and for the glory of his name sake, worketh mightily to conserue vs in health, wealth and godlinesse, and mightily preserueth vs from the assault and rages of our fierce and cruell enemies, and there ioyfully in the number of his faithfull people to praise and magnifie the Lords holy Name.

Set before your eyes also that ancient father Simeon, of whom the Scripture speaketh thus, to his great commendation, and an encouragement for vs to doe the like. There was a man at Hierusalem named Simeon, a iust man, fearing GOD: he came by the Spirit of GOD into the Temple, and was told by the same Spirit that hee should not dye before hee saw the Annointed of the Lord. In the Temple his promise was fulfilled, in the Temple hee saw Christ, and tooke him in his armes, in the Temple hee brake out into the mighty prayse of GOD his Lord. Anna a prophetesse, an olde widdow departed out of the Temple, giuing herselfe to prayer and fasting day and night: And she, comming about the same time, was likewise inspired, and confessed, and spake of the Lord, to all them that looked for the redemption of Israel (Luke 2.25-38). This blessed man, and this blessed woman, were not disappointed of wonderfull fruit, commodity and comfort, which GOD sent them, by their diligent resorting to GODS holy Temple. Now yee shall heare how grieuously GOD hath beene offended with his people, for that they passed so little vpon his holy Temple, and foulely either despised or abused the same. Which thing may plainely appeare by the notable plagues and punishments which GOD hath layd vpon his people, especially in this, that he stirred vp their aduersaries horribly to beate downe, and vtterly to destroy his holy Temple with a perpetuall desolation. Alasse, how many Churches, Countreys, and Kingdomes of Christian people, haue of late yeeres beene plucked downe, and ouerrunne, and left waste, with grieuous and intolerable tyranny and cruelty of the enemie of our Lord Christ the great Turke, who hath so vniuersally scourged the Christians, that neuer the like was heard or read of? Aboue thirtie yeeres past, the great Turke had ouerrunne, conquered, and brought into his dominion and subiection, twenty Christian kingdomes, turning away the people from the faith of Christ, poysoning them with the diuelish religion of wicked Mahomet, and either destroying their Churches vtterly, or filthily abusing them with their wicked & detestable errours. And now this great Turke, this bitter and sharpe scourge of GODS vengeance, is euen at hand in this part of Christendome, in Europe, at the borders of Italy, at the borders of Germanie, greedily gaping to deuoure vs, to ouerrunne our countrey, to destroy our Churches also, vnlesse wee repent our sinfull life, and resort more diligently to the Church to honour GOD, to learne his blessed will, and to fulfill the same. The Iewes in their time prouoked iustly the vengeance of GOD, for that partly they abused his holy Temple with the detestable idolatry of the heathen, and superstitious vanities of their own inuentions contrary to GODS commandement, partly they resorted vnto it as hypocrites, spotted, imbrewed, and fouly defiled with all kinde of wickednesse and sinfull life, partly many of them passed little vpon the holy Temple, and cared not whether they came thither, or no. And haue not the Christians of late dayes, and euen in our dayes also, in like maner prouoked the displeasure and indignation of Almighty GOD? partly because they haue prophaned and defiled their Churches with heathenish and Iewish abuses, with images and idoles, with numbers of Altars, too too superstitiously and intolerably abused, with grosse abusing and filthy corrupting of the Lords holy supper, the blessed Sacrament of his body and blood, with an infinite number of toyes and trifles of their owne deuises, to make a goodly outward shew, and to deface the plaine, simple, and sincere religion of Christ Iesus, partly they resort to the Church like hypocrites, full of all iniquity and sinfull life, hauing a vaine and dangerous fansie and perswasion, that if they come to the Church, besprinckle them with holy water, heare a masse, and bee blessed with the chalice, though they vnderstand not one word of the whole seruice, nor feele one motion of repentance in their hearts, all is well, all is sure. Fie vpon such mocking and blaspheming of GODS holy ordinance. Churches were made for another purpose, that is, to resort thither, and to serue GOD truely, there to learne his blessed will, there to call vpon his mighty Name, there to vse the holy Sacraments, there to trauaile how to bee in charitie with thy neighbour, there to haue thy poore and needy neighbour in remembrance, from thence to depart better and more godly then thou camest thither. Finally GODS vengeance hath beene, and is dayly prouoked, because much wicked people passe nothing to resort to the Church, either for that they are so sore blinded that they vnderstand nothing of GOD and godlinesse, and care not with diuilish example to offend their neighbours, or else for that they see the Church altogether scoured of such gay gazing sights, as their grosse phantasie was greatly delighted with, because they see the false religion abandoned, and the true restored, which seemeth an vnsauory thing to their vnsauory taste, as may appeare by this that a woman said to her neighbour: Alas gossip, what shall wee now doe at Church, since all the Saints are taken away, since all the goodly sights wee were wont to haue, are gone, since wee cannot heare the like piping, singing, chaunting, and playing vpon the organes that we could before. But (dearely beloued) we ought greatly to reioyce and giue GOD thankes, that our Churches are deliuered out of all those things which displeased GOD so sore, and filthily defiled his holy house and his place of prayer, for the which hee hath iustly destroyed many nations, according, to the saying of S. Paul: If any man defile the Temple of GOD, GOD will him destroy (1 Corinthians 3.17). And this ought we greatly to praise GOD for, that such superstitious & idolatrous maners as were vtterly nought and defaced GODS glory, are vtterly abolished, as they most iustly deserued: and yet those things that either GOD was honoured with, or his people edified, are decently retained, and in our Churches comely practised. But nowe forasmuch as yee perceiue it is GODS determinate pleasure ye should resort vnto your Churches vpon the day of holy rest, seeing yee heare what displeasure GOD conceiueth, what plagues hee powreth vpon his disobedient people, seeing yee vnderstand what blessings GOD are giuen, what heauenly commodities come to such people as desirously and zealously vse to resort vnto their Churches, seeing also ye are now friendly bidden and ioyntly called, beware that ye slacke not your duetie, take haede that you suffer nothing to let you hereafter to come to the Church at such times as you are ordinarily appoynted and commanded. Our Sauiour Christ telleth in a parable, that a great supper was prepared, gestes were bidden, many excused themselues and would not come: I tell you (sayth Christ) none of them that were called shall tast of my supper. This great Supper, is the true religion of Almighty GOD, wherewith hee will bee worshipped in the due receiuing of his Sacraments, and sincere preaching and hearing of his holy word, and practising the same by godly conuersation. This feast is now prepared in GODS banqueting house the Church, you are thereunto called and ioyntly bidden: if you refuse to come, and make your excuses, the same will bee answered to you that was vnto them. Now come therefore (dearely beloued) without delay, and chearefully enter into GODS feasting house, and become pertakers of the Benefites prouided and prepared for you. But see that yee come thither with your holyday garment, not like hypocrites, not of a custome and for manners sake, not with lothsomenesse, as though ye had rather not come then come, if ye were at your liberty. For GOD hateth and punisheth such counterfet hypocrites, as appeareth by Christes former parable. My friend (saith GOD) how camest thou in without a wedding garment? And therefore commanded his seruants to binde him hand and foote, and to cast him into vtter darkenesse, where shall bee weeping, and wayling, and gnashing of teeth. To the intent that yee may auoyd the like danger at GODS hand, come to the Church on the holy day, and come in your holy day garment, that is to say, come with a chearefull and a godly minde, come to seeke GODS glory, and to bee thankefull vnto him, come to bee at one with thy neighbour, and to enter in frendship and charity with him. Consider that all thy doings stincke before the face of GOD, if thou bee not in charity with thy neighbour. Come with an heart sifted and cleansed from worldely and carnall affections and desires, shake off all vaine thoughtes which may hinder thee from GODS true seruice. The bird when she will flee, shaketh her wings: Shake and prepare thy selfe to flee higher then all the birdes in the ayre, that after thy duety duelie done in this earthly Temple and Church, thou mayest flee vp, and be receiued into the glorious Temple of GOD in heauen through Christ Iesus our Lord, to whom with the Father and the holy Ghost bee all glorie and honour. Amen.

HOMILY ON COMMON PRAYER AND SACRAMENTS

AN HOMILIE WHERE-
in is declared that Common Prayer and Sacraments ought to bee ministred in a tongue
that is vnderstood of the
hearers.

AMong the manifold exercises of GODS people (deare Christians) there is none more necessary for all estates, and at all times, then is publike prayer, and the due vse of Sacraments. For in the first, wee beg at GODS hands all such things, as otherwise we can not obtain. And in the other, hee imbraceth vs, and offereth himselfe to bee embraced of vs. Knowing therefore that these two exercises are so necessary for vs, let vs not thinke it vnmeet to consider, first what prayer is, and what a Sacrament is, and then how many sorts of prayers there bee, and how many Sacraments, so shall wee the better vnderstand how to vse them aright. To know what they be, Saint Augustine, teacheth vs in his booke entituled, "Of the spirite and the soule" (Augustine, *`De Spiritu et anima'*). He sayth thus of prayer: Prayer is (saith hee) the deuotion of the minde, that is to say, the returning to GOD, through a godly and humble affection, which affection is certaine willing and sweete inclining of the minde it selfe towards GOD. And in the second booke against the aduersary of the Law and the Prophets, hee calleth Sacraments, holy signes (Augustinem *`Contra Adversarios et Proph.'*, bk. 2). And writing to Bonifacius of the Baptisme of infants, he saith, If Sacraments had not a certaine similitude of those things whereof they bee Sacraments, they should bee no Sacraments at all. And of this similitude they doe for the most part receiue the names of the selfe things they signifie. By these wordes of Saint Augustine it appeareth, that hee alloweth the common description of a Sacrament, which is, that it is a visible signe of an inuisible grace, that is to say, that setteth out to the eyes and other outward senses, the inward working of GODS free mercy, and doeth (as it were) seale in our hearts the promises of GOD (Augustine, *`Ad Boniface'*). And so was circumcision a Sacrament, which preached vnto the outward senses the inward cutting away of the foreskin of the heart, and sealed and made sure in the hearts of the Circumcised the promise of GOD touching the promised seede that they looked for. Nowe let vs see how many sorts of prayer, and howe many Sacraments there bee.

In the scriptures wee reade of three sorts of prayer, whereof two are priuate, and the thirde is common. The first is that which Saint Paul speaketh of in his Epistle to Timothie, sayinge, I will that men pray in euery place, lifting vp pure handes, with out wrath or striuing (1 Timothy 2.8). And it is the deuout lifting vp of the mind to GOD without the vtteringe of the hearts griefe or desire by open voyce. Of this prayer wee haue example in the first booke of the Kinges in Anna the mother of Samuel, when in the heauinesse of her heart shee prayed in the Temple, desiring to be made fruiteful. Shee prayed in her heart (saith the text) but there was no voyce hearde (1 Samuel 1.13). After this sort must all Christians pray, not once in a weeke , or once in a day onely: but as Saint Paul writeth to the Thessalonians, without ceasing (1 Thessalonians 5.17). And as Saint Iames writeth, The continuall prayer of a iust man is of much force (James 5.16). The second sort of prayer is spoken of in the Gospel of Matthew, where it is sayd, when thou prayest, enter into thy secret closet, and when thou hast shutte the doore to thee, pray vnto thy Father in secret, and thy Father which seeth in secret shall reward thee (Matthew 6.6). Of this sort of prayer there bee sundry examples in the Scriptures, but it shall suffice to rehearse one, which is written in the actes of the Apostles.

Cornelius, a deuoute man, a captaine of the Italian army, sayth to Peter: that being in his house in prayer at the ninth houre, there appeared vnto him one in a white garment &c (Acts 10.1, 3, 30-31). This man prayed vnto GOD in secret, and was rewarded openly. These bee the two priuate sorts of prayer. The one mentall, that is to say, the deuout lifting vp of the minde to GOD: And the other vocall, that is to say, the secret vttering of the griefes and desires of the heart with wordes, but yet in a secret closet, or some solitary place. The third sort of prayer is publike or common. Of this prayer speaketh our Sauiour Christ, when he sayth, If two of you shall agree vpon earth vpon any thing, whatsoeuer ye shall aske, my Father which is in heauen shall doe it for you, for wheresoeeuer two or three bee gathered together in my name, there am I in the middest of them (Matthew 18.19-20). Although GOD hath promised to heare vs when we pray priuately, so it be done faithfully and deuoutly (for he saith, Call vpon me in the day of thy trouble, and I will heare thee (Psalms 50.15). And Elias being but a mortall man, saith Saint Iames, prayed, and heauen was shut three yeeres and sixe moneths, and againe he prayed, and the heauen gaue raine (James 5.17-18):) Yet by the histories of the Bible it appeareth, that publike and common prayer is most auaileable before GOD, and therefore is much to be lamented that it is no better esteemed among vs which professe to be but one body in Christ. When the city of Niniue was threatned to be destroyed within fortie dayes, the Prince and the people ioyned themselues together in publike prayer and fasting, and were preserued (Jonah 3.4-10). In the Prophet Ioel, GOD commanded a fasting to be proclaimed, and the people to be gathered together, young and olde, man and woman, and are taught to say with one voyce: Spare vs, O Lord, spare thy people, and let not thine inheritance bee brought to confusion (Joel 2.15-17). When the Iewes should haue beene destroyed all in one day through the malice of Haman, at the commaundement of Hester they fasted and prayed, and were preserued (Esther 4.16). When Holophernes besieged Bethulia by the aduice of Iudith they fasted and prayed, and were deliuered (Apocrypha. Judith 8.17). When Peter was in prison, the congregation ioyned themselues together in prayer, and Peter was wonderfully deliuered (Acts 12.5). By these histories it appeareth, that common or publike prayer is of great force to obteine mercy, & deliuerance at our heauenly Fathers hand.

Therefore brethren, I beseech you, euen for the tender mercies of GOD, let vs no longer bee negligent in this behalfe: but as the people willing to receiue at GODS hand such good things as in the common prayer of the Church are craued, let vs ioyne our selues together in the place of common prayer, and with one voyce and one heart, begge at our heauenly father all those things, which hee knoweth to bee necessary for vs. I forbid you not priuate prayer, but I exhort you to esteeme common prayer as it is worthy. And before all things, bee sure, that in all these three sortes of prayer, your mindes bee deuoutly lifted vp to GOD, else are your prayers to no purpose, and this saying shalbe verified in you: This people honoureth me with their lips, but their heart is farre from mee (Isaiah 29.13, Matthew 15.8). Thus much for the three sortes of prayer, whereof we reade in the Scriptures. Now with like, or rather more breuitie, you shall heare how many Sacraments there be, that were instituted by our Sauiour Christ, and are to bee continued, and receiued of euery Christian in due time and order, and for such purpose as our Sauiour Christ willed them to be receiued. And as for the number of them, if they should be considered according to the exact signification of a Sacrament, namely, for the visible signes, expresly commanded in the new Testament, whereunto is annexed the promise of free forgiuenesse of our sinne, and of our holinesse and ioyning in Christ, there bee but two: namely Baptisme, and the Supper of the Lord. For although absolution hath the promise of forgiuenesse of sinne, yet by the expresse worde of the new Testament it hath not this promise annexed and tyed to the visible signe, which is imposition of hands. For this visible signe (I meane laying on of hands) is not expresly commanded in the new Testament to be vsed in absolution, as the visible signes in Baptisme and the Lords Supper are: and therefore absolution is no such Sacrament as Baptisme and the Communion are. And though the ordering of ministers hath his visible signe and promise: yet it lackes the promise of remission of sinne, as all other sacraments besides the two aboue named doe. Therefore neither it, nor any other sacrament else, bee such Sacraments as Baptisme and the Communion are. But in a generall acception, the mane of a Sacrament may be attributed to any thing whereby an holy thing is signified. In which vnderstanding of the word, the ancient writers haue giuen this name, not only to the other fiue, commonly of late yeres taken and vsed for supplying the number of the seuen Sacraments: but also to diuers and sundry other ceremonies, as to oyle, washing of feete, and such like, not meaning thereby to repute them as Sacraments, in the same signification that the two forenamed Sacraments are (Dionysius, Bernard, '*De Coena Domini, Dionysius, et Abluti pedum*'). And therefore Saint Augustine, weighing the true signification and exact meaning of the word, writing to Ianuarius, and also in the third booke of Christian doctrine, affirmeth that the Sacraments of the Christians, as they are most excellent in signification, so are they most few in number, and in both places maketh mention expresly of two, the sacrament of baptisme, and the supper of the Lord. And although there are retained by the order of the Church of England, besides these two, certaine other Rites and Ceremonies about the institution of Ministers in the Church, Matrimony, Confirmation of the children, by examining them of their knowledge in the articles of the faith, and ioyning thereto the prayers of the Church for them, and likewise for the visitation of the sicke: yet no man ought to take these for Sacraments, in such signification and meaning, as the Sacrament of Baptisme. and the Lords Supper are: but either for godly states of life, necessary in Christes Church, and therefore worthie to bee set foorth by publike action and solemnity by the ministery of the Church, or else iudged to bee such ordinances, as may make for the instruction, comfort, and edification of Christes Church.

Now vnderstanding sufficiently what prayer is, and what a Sacrament is also, and how many sortes of prayers there bee, and how many Sacraments of our Sauiour Christs institution: let vs see whether the Scriptures and examples of the Primatiue Church will alow any vocall prayer, that is, when the mouth vttereth the petitions with voyce, or any maner of Sacrament, or other publike or common rite or action, pertaining to the profite and edifying of the vnlearned, to bee ministred in a tongue vnknowne, or not vnderstood of the Minister or people: yea, and whether any person may priuately vse any vocall prayer, in a language that hee himselfe vnderstandeth not. To this question we must answere, no. And first of Common prayer and administration of Sacraments. Although reason, if it might rule, would soone perswade vs to haue our common prayer and administration of the Sacraments in a knowne tongue, both for that to pray commonly, is for a multitude to aske one and the selfe thing with one voyce, and one consent of minde, and to administer a Sacrament, is by the outward word and element, to preach to the receiuer the inward and inuisible grace of GOD, and also for that both these exercises were first instituted, and are still continued to the end that the congregation of Christ might from time to time bee put in remembrance of their vnity in Christ, and that as members all of one body, they ought both in prayers and otherwise to seeke and desire one anothers commodity, & not their owne without others: Yet shall wee not neede to flee to reasons and proofes in this matter, sith wee haue both the plaine and manifest wordes of the Scripture, and also the consent of the most learned and ancient writers, to commend the prayers of the Congregation in a knowne tongue. First, Paul to the Corinthians saith: Let all things be done to edifying (1 Corinthians 14.26). Which cannot be, vnlesse common prayers and administration of Sacraments bee in a tongue knowen to the people. For where the prayers spoken by the minister, and the wordes in the administration of the Sacraments, bee not vnderstood of them that bee present, they cannot thereby bee edified. For as when the trumpet that is blowne in the field giueth an vncertaine sound, no man is thereby stirred vp to prepare himselfe to the fight. And as when an instrument of musicke maketh no distinct sound, no man can tell what is piped: Euen so when prayers or administration of Sacraments shall bee in a tongue vnknowen to the hearers, which of them shall bee thereby stirred vp to lift vp his minde to GOD, and to begge with the minister at GODS hand, those things which in the wordes of his prayers the minister asketh? Or who shall in the ministration of the Sacraments vnderstand what inuisible grace, is to be craued of the hearer, to bee wrought in the inward man? Truely no man at all. For (saith Saint Paul) hee that speaketh in a tongue vnknowne, shall be to the hearer an aliant, which in a Christian Congregation is a great absurditie.

For wee are not strangers one to another, but wee are the citizens of the Saints, and of the houshold of GOD (Ephesians 2.19), yea, and members of one body (1 Corinthians 10.17, 12.12). And therefore whiles our minister is in rehearsing the prayer that is made in the name of vs all, wee must giue diligent eares to the words spoken by him, and in heart begge at GODS hand those things that hee beggeth in wordes. And to signifie that wee doe so, wee say Amen, at the end of the prayer that hee maketh in the name of vs all. And this thing can wee not doe for edification, vnlesse wee vnderstand what is spoken. Therefore it is required of necessity, that the Common prayer bee had in a tongue that the hearers doe vnderstand. If euer it had bin tolerable to vse strange tongues in the congregations, the same might haue beene in the time of Paul and the other Apostles, when they were miraculously endued with gifts of tongues. For it might then haue perswaded some to imbrace the Gospel, when they had heard men that were Hebrewes borne and vnlearned, speake the Greeke, the Latine, and other languages. But Paul thought it not tolerable then: And shall wee vse it now, when no man commeth by that knowledge of tongues, otherwise then by diligent and earnest study? GOD forbid. For wee should by that meanes bring all our Church exercises to friuolous superstition, and make them altogether vnfruitfull. Luke writeth that when Peter and Iohn were discharged by the Princes and high Priestes of Hierusalem, they came to their fellowes, and tolde them all that the Princes of the Priestes and Elders had spoken to them. Which when they heard, they lifted vp their voyce together to GOD with one assent, and sayd, Lord, thou art he that hast made heauen and earth, the sea, and all things that are in them. &c (Acts 4.23-24). Thus could they not haue done, if they had prayed in a strange tongue, that they had not vnderstood. And no doubt of it, they did not all speake with seuerall voyce: but some one of them spake in the name of them all, and the rest giuing diligent eare to his wordes consented thereunto, and therefore it is sayd, that they lifted vp their voyce together. Saint Luke saith not, Their voyces, as many: but, their voice, as one. That one voyce therefore was in such language as they all vnderstood, otherwise they could not haue lifted it vp with the consent of their heartes. For no man canne giue consent of the thing that he knoweth not. As touching the times before the comming of Christ there was neuer man yet that would affirme, that either the people of GOD or other, had their prayers or administrations of the Sacraments, or sacrifices, in a tongue that they themselues vnderstood not. As for the time since Christ, till that vsurped power of Rome began to spreade it selfe, and to inforce all the nations of Europe to haue the Romish language in admiration, it appeareth by the consent of the most ancient and learned writers, that there was no strange or vnknowne tongue vsed in the congregation of Christians. Iustinus Martyr, who liued about 160 yeeres after Christ, sayth thus of the administration of the Lords Supper in his time (Justinus, `*Apol.,'* 2): Upon the Sunday assemblies are made both of them that dwell in Cities, and of them that dwell in the Countrey also. Amongst whom, as much as may bee, the writings of the Apostles & Prophets are read. Afterwards when the Reader doth cease, the chiefe Minister maketh an exhortation, exhorting them to follow honest things. After this, wee rise altogether and offer prayers, which being ended (as wee haue sayd) bread and wine and water are brought foorth: Then the head Minister offereth prayers and thankesgiuing with all his power, and the people answer, Amen. These words, with their circumstances being duely considered, do declare plainly, that not onely the Scriptures were read in a knowne tongue: but also that prayer was made in the same in the congregations of Iustines time. Basilius Magnus, and Iohannes Chrysostomus did in their time prescribe publike orders of publike administration, which they call Liturgies, and in them they appointed the people to answer to the prayers of the Minister, sometime, Amen, sometime, Lord haue mercy vpon vs, sometime, and with thy spirit, and we haue our hearts lifted vp vnto the Lord, &c. Which answers the people could not haue made in due time, if the prayers had not beene in a tongue that they vnderstood. The same Basil writing to the Clergie of Neoc'sarea, sayth thus of his vsage in common prayer (Basil, epistle 63), appoynting one to begin the song, the rest follow: And so with diuers songs and prayers, passing ouer the night, at the dawning of the day, altogether (euen as it were with one mouth and one heart) they sing vnto the Lord a song of confession, euery man framing vnto himselfe meete wordes of repentance. In another place he sayth, If the Sea bee fayre, how is not the assembly of the congregation much more fayre, in which a ioyned sound of men, women, and children (as it were of the waues beating on the shore) is sent foorth in our prayers vnto our GOD? Marke his words (Basil, Homily 4?): A ioyned sound (sayth he) of men, women, and children. Which cannot be, vnlesse they all vnderstand the tongue wherein the prayer is sayd. And Chrysostome vpon the words of Paul sayth, So soone as the people heare these words, world without end, they all doe foorthwith answer, Amen. This could they not doe, vnlesse they vnderstood the word spoken by the Priest (1 Corinthians 14.16). Dionysius sayth, that hymnes were sayd of the whole multitude of people in the administration of the Communion. Cyprian sayth (Cyprian, *'Ser. 6 de Ora. dominica'*), The Priest doth prepare the mindes of the brethren, with a preface before the prayer, saying, Lift vp your hearts: That whiles the people doth answer, We haue our hearts lifted vp to the Lord, they be admonished that they ought to thinke on none other thing then the Lord. Saint Ambrose writing vpon the words of Saint Paul sayth, This is it that hee sayth, because hee which speaketh in an vnknowne tongue, speaketh to GOD, for hee knoweth all things: but men know not, and therefore there is no profit of this thing (1 Corinthians 14.2). And againe vpon these wordes: If thou blesse, or giue thankes with the spirit, how shall hee that occupieth the roome of the vnlearned, say Amen, at thy giuing of thankes, seeing hee vnderstandeth not what thou sayest? This is (sayth Ambrose) if thou speake the prayse of GOD in a tongue vnknowen to the hearers. For the vnlearned hearing that which he vnderstandeth not, knoweth not the end of the prayer, and answereth not Amen: which word is as much to say, as trueth, that the blessing or thankesgiuing may bee confirmed. For the confirmation of the prayer is fulfilled by them that doe answere, Amen, that all things spoken might be confirmed in the mindes of the hearers, through the testimony of the truth. And after many weighty wordes, to the same end he sayth: The conclusion is this, that nothing should bee done in the Church in vaine, and that this thing ought chiefly to bee laboured for, that the vnlearned also might take profit, lest any part of the body should be darke through ignorance. And lest any man should thinke all this to be meant of preaching, and not of prayer, he taketh occasion of these words of Saint Paul (If there be not an interpreter, let him keepe silence in the Church) to say, as followeth: Let him pray secretly, or speake to GOD, who heareth all things that be dumbe: For in the Church must he speake that may profit all persons. Saint Hierome writing vpon these words of Saint Paul, How shall hee that supplieth the place of the vnlearned, &c. (1 Corinthians 14.16), sayth, It is the Lay man whom Paul vnderstandeth heere to bee in the place of the ignorant man, which hath no Ecclesiasticall office. How shall he answer, Amen, to the prayer of that he vnderstandeth not? And a little after, vpon the words of Saint Paul, For if I should pray in a tongue &c. he sayth thus: Thus is Pauls meaning: If any man speake in strange and vnknowen tongues, his minde is made vnfruitfull, not to himselfe, but to the hearer: For whatsoeuer is spoken, hee knoweth it not. Saint Augustine writing vpon the xviii. Psalme, sayth: What this should bee wee ought to vnderstand, that we may sing with reason of man, and not with chattering of birds. For Owles, Popingayes, Rauens, Pyes, and other such like birds, are taught by men to prate they know not what: but to sing with vnderstanding, is giuen by GODS holy will to the nature of man. Againe, the same Augustine sayth (Augustine, `*De Magist.*'), There needeth no speech when we pray, sauing perhaps as the Priests doe, for to declare their meaning, not that GOD, but that men may heare them. And so being put in remembrance by consenting with the Priest, they may hang vpon GOD.

Thus are we taught by the Scripture and ancient Doctours, that in the administration of Common prayer and Sacraments, no tongue vnknowne to the hearers ought to be vsed. So that for the satisfying of a Christian mans conscience wee need to spend no more time in this matter. But yet to stop the mouthes of the aduersaries, which stay themselues much vpon generall decrees, it shall bee good to adde to these testimonies of Scriptures and Doctours, one Constitution made by Iustinian the Emperour (`*Novel. Consti.,*' 23), who liued fiue hundred twenty and seuen yeeres after Christ, and was Emperour of Rome. The Constitution is this: We command that all Bishops and Priests doe celebrate the holy oblation and the prayers vsed in holy Baptisme, not speaking low, but with a cleare or loud voyce, which may be heard of the people, that thereby the minde of the hearers may be stirred vp with great deuotion, in vttering the prayers of the Lord

GOD, for so the holy Apostle teacheth in his first Epistle to the Corinthians, saying, Truely, if thou onely blesse or giue thankes in spirit, how doeth hee that occupieth the place of the vnlearned, say Amen at that thy giuing thankes vnto GOD, for he vnderstandeth not what thou sayest? Thou verely giuest thankes well, but the other is not edified. And againe in the Epistle to the Romanes, he saith: With the heart a man beleeueth vnto righteousnesse, and with the mouth confession is made vnto saluation. Therefore for these causes it is conuenient that among other prayers, those things also which are spoken in the holy oblation, be vttered and spoken of the most religious Bishops & priestes, vnto our Lord Iesus Christ our GOD, with the Father and the holy Ghost, with a loud voyce. And let the most religious Priestes know this, that if they neglect any of these things, that they shall giue an account for them in the dreadfull iudgement of the great GOD and our Sauiour Iesus Christ. Neither will wee, when we know it, rest and leaue it vnreuenged.

This Emperour (as Sabellicus writeth) fauoured the Bishop of Rome, and yet wee see how plaine a decree hee maketh, for praying and administring of Sacraments in a knowne tongue, that the deuotion of the hearers might be stirred vp by knowledge, contrary to the iudgement of them that would haue ignorance to make deuotion. Hee maketh it also a matter of damnation, to doe these things in a tongue that the hearers vnderstand not. Let vs therefore conclude with GOD and all good mens assent, that no common prayer or Sacraments ought to bee ministred in a tongue that is not vnderstood of the hearers. Now a word or two of priuate prayer in an vnknowne tongue. Wee tooke in hand where we beganne to speake of this matter, not onely to prooue that no common prayer or administration of Sacraments, ought to bee in a tongue vnknowne to the hearers: but also, that no person ought to pray priuately in that tongue that he himselfe vnderstandeth not. Which thing shall not be heard to prooue, if we forget not what prayer is. For if prayer be that deuotion of the minde which enforceth &the; heart to lift vp it selfe to GOD: how should it be said, that that person prayeth, that vnderstandeth not the words that his tongue speaketh in prayer? Yea, how can it be said that he speaketh? For to speake is by voice to vtter &the; thought of the mind. And the voyce that a man vttereth in speaking, is nothing els but the messenger of the minde, to bring abroad the knowledge of that which otherwise lyeth secret in the heart, and cannot be knowen according to that which Saint Paul writeth: What man (sayth hee) knoweth the things that appertaine to man, sauing onely the spirite of man, which is in man (1 Corinthians 2.11)? Hee therefore that doeth not vnderstand the voyces that his tongue doeth vtter, cannot properly be sayd to speake, but rather to counterfait, as Parattes, and such other birdes vse to counterfait mens voyces. No man therefore that feareth to prouoke the wrath of GOD against himselfe, will bee so bolde to speake of GOD vnaduisedly, without regard of reuerent vnderstanding, in his presence, but he will prepare his heart before he presume to speake vnto GOD. And therefore in our common prayer the minister doeth often times say, Let vs pray, meaning thereby to admonish the people that they should prepare their eares to heare, what he should craue at GODS hand, and their hearts to consent to the same, and their tongues to say, Amen, at the ende thereof. On this sort did the Prophet Dauid prepare his heart, when he said, My heart is ready (O GOD) my heart is ready, I will sing and declare a Psalme (Psalms 57.7, 108.1). The Iewes also, when in the time of Iudith they did with all their heart pray GOD to visite his people of Israel had so prepared their hearts before they began to pray. After this sort had Manasses prepared his heart before he prayed, and said, And now (O Lord) doe I bow the knees of my heart, asking of thee part of thy mercifull kindnes (2 Chronicles 33.12?). When the heart is thus prepared, the voyce vttered from the heart, is harmonious in the eares of GOD: otherwise he regardeth it not, to accept it. But forasmuch as the person that so babbleth his words without sense in the presence of GOD sheweth himselfe not to regard the maiestie of him that he speaketh to: He taketh him as a contemner of his Almighty maiestie, and giueth him his reward among hypocrites, which make an outward shew of holinesse, but their hearts are full of abominable thoughts, euen in the time of their prayers. For it is the heart that the Lord looketh vpon, as it is written in the historie of Kings (1 Samuel 16.7). If wee therefore will that our prayers bee not abominable before GOD, let vs so prepare our hearts before wee pray, and so vnderstand the things that wee aske when wee pray, that both our hearts and voyces may together sound in the eares of GODS maiestie, and then we shall not faile to receiue at his hand the things that we aske, as good men which haue beene before vs did, and so haue from time to time receiued that which for their soules health they did at any time desire. S. Augustine seemeth to beare in this matter (Augustine, '*De Catechizandis rudibus*'): For he saith thus of them, which being brought vp in Grammar and Rhetoricke, are conuerted to Christ, and so must be instructed in Christian religion: Let them know also (saith hee) that it is not the voyce, but the affection of the minde that commeth to the eares of God. And so shall it come to passe, that if happily they shall marke that some Bishops or ministers in the Church do call vpon GOD, either with barbarous wordes, or with wordes disordered, or that they vnderstand not, or doe disorderly diuide the wordes that they pronounce, they shall not laugh them to scorne. Hitherto he seemeth to heare with praying in an vnknowen tongue. But in the next sentence hee openeth his minde thus: Not for that these things ought not to be amended, that the people may say Amen, to that which they doe plainely vnderstand: But yet these godly things must bee borne withall of these Catechistes or instructors of the fayth, that they may learne, that as in the common place where matters are pleaded, the goodnes of an oration consisteth in sound: so in the Church it consisteth in deuotion. So that hee alloweth not the praying in a tongue not vnderstood of him that prayeth: But hee instructeth the skilfull Oratour, to beare with the rude tongue of the deuout simple Minister. To conclude, if the lacke of vnderstanding the words that are spoken in the Congregation, doe make them vnfruitfull to the hearers: how should not the same make the words read , vnfruitfull to the Reader? The mercifull goodnesse of GOD, grant vs his grace to call vpon him as we ought to doe, to his glory and our endlesse felicity, which we shall doe, if we humble our selues in his sight, and in all our prayers both common and priuate, haue our mindes fully fixed vpon him. For the prayer of them that humble themselues, shall pearce through the clouds, and till it draw nigh vnto GOD, it will not be answered, and till the most High doe regard it, it will not depart. And the Lord will not be slack, but hee will deliuer the iust, and execute iudgement (Apoc. Ecclesiasticus 35.17-18). To him therefore be all honour and glory, for euer and euer, Amen.

OF THEM WHICH TAKE OFFENCE AT CERTAIN PLACES OF HOLY SCRIPTURE

AN INFORMATION FOR THEM WHICH TAKE OFFENCE AT CERTAINE PLACES OF THE HOLY SCRIPTURE.

The first part.

THE great vtility and profit that Christian men and women may take (if they will) by hearing and reading the holy Scriptures (dearely beloued) no heart can sufficiently conceiue, much lesse is my tongue able with wordes to expresse. Wherefore Satan our enemy, seeing the Scriptures to bee the very meane and right way to bring the people to the true knowledge of GOD, and that Christian Religion is greatly furthered by diligent hearing and reading of them, he also perceiuing what an hinderance and let they bee to him and his kingdome, doth what hee can to driue the reading of them out of GODS Church. And for that end hee hath alwayes stirred vp, in one place or other, cruell tyrants, sharpe persecutors, and extreme enemies vnto GOD, and his infallible trueth, to pull with violence the holy Bibles out of the peoples hands, and haue most spitefully destroyed and consumed the same to ashes in the fire, pretending most vntruely, that the much hearing and reading of GODS word is an occasion of heresie and carnall liberty, and the ouerthrow of all good order in all well ordered common weales. If to know GOD aright be an occasion of euill, then we must needs grant, that the hearing and reading of the holy Scriptures, is the cause of heresie, carnall liberty, and the subuersion of all good orders. But the knowledge of GOD and of ourselues, is so farre from being an occasion of euill, that it is the readiest, yea the onely meane to bridle carnall liberty, and to kill all our fleshly affections. And the ordinary way to attaine this knowledge, is with diligence to heare and read the holy Scriptures. For the whole Scriptures (sayth Saint Paul) were giuen by the inspiration of GOD (2 Timothy 3.16). And shall we Christian men thinke to learne the knowledge of GOD and of ourselues, in any earthly mans worke of writing, sooner or better then in the holy Scriptures, written by the inspiration of the holy Ghost? The Scriptures were not brought vnto vs by the will of man: but holy men of GOD (as witnesseth Saint Peter) spake as they were mooued by the holy spirit of GOD (2 Peter 1.21). The holy ghost is the Schoolemaster of trueth, which leadeth his Schollers (as our Sauiour Christ sayth of him) into all trueth (John 16.13). And whoso is not ledde and taught by his Schoolemaster, cannot but fall into deepe errour, how godly soeuer his pretence is, what knowledge and learning soeuer he hath of all other works and writings, or how fayre soeuer a shew or face of trueth he hath in the estimation and iudgement of the world. If some man will say, I would haue a true patterne and a perfect description of an vpright life, approoued in the sight of GOD: can wee finde (thinke ye) any better or any such againe, as Christ Iesus is, and his doctrine? whose vertuous conuersation and godly life, the Scripture so liuely painteth and setteth foorth before our eyes, that we beholding that patterne, might shape and frame our liues, as nigh as may bee, agreeable to the perfection of the same. Follow you me (sayth Saint Paul) as I follow Christ (1 Corinthians 11.1). And Saint Iohn in his Epistle sayth: Whoso abideth in Christ, must walke euen so as he hath walked before him (1 John 2.6). And where shall wee learne the order of Christs life, but in the Scripture? Another would haue a medicine to heale all diseases and maladies of the minde. Can this be found or gotten other where then out of GODS own booke, his sacred Scriptures? Christ taught so much when he sayd to the obstinate Iewes, Search the Scriptures, for in them ye thinke to haue eternall life (John 5.39). If the Scriptures containe in them euerlasting life, it must needes follow, that they haue also present remedy against all that is an hinderance and let vnto eternall life. If wee desire the knowledge of heauenly wisedome: why had wee rather learne the same of man, then of GOD himselfe, who (as Saint Iames sayth) is the giuer of wisedome (James 1.5)? Yea, why will we not learne it at Christs owne mouth, who promising to be present with his Church till the worlds end (Matthew 28.20) doeth performe his promise, in that hee is not onely with vs by his grace and tender pity: but also in this, that he speaketh presently vnto vs in the holy Scriptures, to the great and endlesse comfort of all them that haue any feeling of GOD at all in them? Yea, he speaketh now in the Scriptures more profitably to vs, then hee did by the word of mouth to the carnall Iewes when he liued with them heere vpon earth. For they (I mean the Iewes) could neither heare nor see those things which we may now both heare and see, if wee will bring with vs those eares and eyes that Christ is heard and seene with, that is, diligence to heare and reade his holy Scriptures, and true faith to beleeue his most comfortable promises. If one could shew but the print of Christs foot, a great number I thinke would fall downe and worship it: But to the holy Scriptures, where we may see daily (if we will) I will not say the print of his feet only, but the whole shape and liuely image of him, alas, we giue little reuerence or none at all.

If any could let vs see Christs coate, a sort of vs would make hard shift except we might come nigh to gaze vpon it, yea and kisse it too. And yet all the clothes that euer hee did weare, can nothing so truely nor so liuely expresse him vnto vs, as doe the Scriptures. Christes images made in wood, stone, or metall, some men for the loue they beare to Christ, doe garnish and beautifie the same with pearle, golde, and precious stone: And should wee not (good brethren) much rather embrace and reuerence GODS holy bookes, the sacred Bible, which doe represent Christ vnto vs, more truely then can any image. The image can but expresse the forme or shape of his body, if it can doe so much: But the Scriptures doeth in such sort set foorth Christ, that wee may see both GOD and man, we may see him (I say) speaking vnto vs, healing our infirmities, dying for our sinnes, rising from death for our iustification. And to be short, wee may in the Scriptures so perfectly see whole Christ with the eye of faith, as wee, lacking faith, could not with these bodily eyes see him, though hee stood now present here before vs. Let euery man, woman, and childe, therefore with all their heart thirst and desire GODS holy Scriptures, loue them, embrace them, haue their delight and pleasure in hearing and reading them, so as at length we may bee transformed and changed into them. For the holy Scriptures are Gods treasure house, wherein are found all things needefull for vs to see, to heare, to learne, and to beleeue, necessary for the attaining of eternall life. Thus much is spoken, onely to giue you a taste of some of the commodities which ye may take by hearing and reading the holy Scriptures. For as I sayd in the beginning, no tongue is able to declare and vtter all. And although it is more cleare then the noone day, that to bee ignorant of the Scriptures, is the cause of errour, as Christ saith to the Sadduces, Ye erre, not knowing the Scriptures (Matthew 22.29), and that errour doth hold backe, and plucke men away from the knowledge of GOD. And as S.

Ierome saith, Not to know the Scriptures, is to be ignorant of Christ. Yet this notwithstanding, some there bee that thinke it not meete for all sortes of men to reade the Scriptures, because they are, as they thinke, in sundry places stumbling blockes to the vnlearned. First, for that the phrase of the Scripture is sometime so simple, grosse, and playne, that it of fendeth the fine and delicate wittes of some courtiers. Furthermore, for that the Scripture also reporteth, euen of them that haue their commendation to be the children of GOD, that they did diuers acts, where of some are contrary to the law of nature, some repugnant to the Law written, and other some seeme to fight manifestly against publique honestie. All which things (say they) are vnto the simple an occasion of great offence, and cause many to thinke euill of the Scriptures, and to discredite their authority. Some are offended at the hearing and reading of the diuersity of the rites and ceremonies of the sacrifices and oblations of the Law. And some worldly witted men, thinke it a great decay to the quiet and prudent gouerning of their common weales, to giue eare to the simple and plaine rules and precepts of our Sauiour Christ in his Gospel, as being offered that a man should bee ready to turne his right eare, to him that strake him on the left, and to him which would take away his coate, to offer him also his cloke, with such other sayings of perfection in Christs meaning. For carnall reason, being alway an enemie to GOD, and not perceiuing the things of GODS spirit, doth abhorre such precepts, which yet rightly vnderstood, infringeth no iudiciall policies, nor Christian mens gouernements. And some there be, which hearing the Scriptures to bid vs to liue without carefulnesse, without studie or forecasting, doe deride the simplicities of them. Therefore to remoue and put away occasions of offence so much as may bee, I will answere orderly to these obiections. First I shall rehearse some of those places that men are offended at, for the simplicity & grossenesse of speach, and will shew the meaning of them. In the booke of Deuteronomie it is written, that almighty GOD made a law, if a man died with out issue, his brother or next kinseman should marrie his widow, and the childe that was first borne betweene them, should be called his childe that was dead, that the dead mans name might not be put out in Israel: And if the brother or next kinseman would not marrie the widow, then shee before the Magistrates of the Citie should pull off his shoe and spit in his face, saying, So bee it done to that man that will not build his brothers house. Here (dearely beloued) the pulling off his shoe, and spitting in his face, were ceremonies, to signifie vnto all the people of that Citie, that the woman was not now in fault that GODS law in that poynt was broken, but the whole shame and blame thereof did now redound to that man, which openly before the Magistrates refused to marrie her. And it was not a reproch to him alone, but to all his posteritie also: For they were called euer after, The house of him whose shoe is pulled off. Another place out of the Psalmes: I wil breake (saith Dauid) the hornes of the vngodly, and the hornes of the righteous shall be exalted (Psalms 75.10). By an horne, in the Scripture, is vnderstood power, might, strength, and sometime rule and gouernment. The Prophet then saying, I will breake the hornes of the vngodly, meaneth, that all the power, strength, and might of GODS enemy, shall not onely be weakened and made feeble, but shall at length also be cleane broken & destroyed, though for a time for the better triall of his people, GOD suffereth the enemies to preuaile and haue the vpper hand. In the Psalme, it is sayd, I will make Dauids horne to florish (Psalms 132.17). Here Dauids horne signifieth his kingdome. Almighty GOD therefore by this manner of speaking, promiseth to giue Dauid victory ouer all his enemies, and to stablish him in his kingdome, spite of all his enemies. And in the threescore Psalme it is written: Moab is my washpot, and ouer Edom will I cast my shoe, &c (Psalms 60.8). In that place the Prophet sheweth how graciously GOD hath dealt with his people the children of Israel, giuing them great victories vpon their enemies on euery side. For the Moabites & Idumeans, being two great nations, proud people, stout and mighty, GOD brought them vnder, and made them seruants to the Israelites, seruants I say, to stoope downe, to pull off their shoes, and wash their feete. Then Moab is my washpot, and ouer Edom will I cast out my shoe, is, as if hee had sayd, The Moabites and the Idumeans, for all their stoutnesse, against vs in the wildernesse, are now made our subiects, our seruants, yea vnderlings to pull off our shoes, and wash our feete. Now I pray you, what vncomely manner of speech is this, so vsed in common phrase among the Hebrewes? It is a shame that Christian men should bee so light headed, to toy as ruffians doe with such manner speaches, vttered in good graue signification by the holy Ghost. More reasonable it were for vaine men to learne to reuerence the fourme of GODS wordes, then to sport at them to their damnation. Some againe are offended to heare that the godly fathers had many wiues and concubines, although after the phrase of the Scripture, a concubine is an honest name, for euery concubine is a lawfull wife, but euery wife is not a concubine. And that ye may the better vnderstand this to be true, ye shall note that it was permitted to the fathers of the old Testament, to haue at one time moe wiues then one, for what purpose yee shall afterward heare. Of which wiues some were free women born, some were bond-women & seruants. She that was free born, had a prerogatiue aboue those that were seruants & bond-women. The free-born woman was by mariage made the ruler of the house vnder her husband, & is called the mother of the housholde, the masters or the dame of the house, after our manner of speaking, & had by her mariage an interest, a right, and an ownershippe of his goods vnto whom shee was maried. Other seruants and bonde-women were giuen by the owners of them, as the manner was then, I will not say alwayes, but for the most part, vnto their daughters at that day of their mariage, to bee handmaydens vnto them. After such a sort did Pharao King of Egypt giue vnto Sara Abrahams wife Agar the Egyptian to bee her maide. So did Laban giue vnto his daughter Lea, at the day of her mariage, Zilpha, to bee her handmaide (Genesis 29.24). And to his other daughter Rachel, he gaue another bondmaid, named Bilha. And the wiues that were the owners of their handmaydens, gaue them in mariage to their husbands, vpon diuers occasions. Sara gaue her mayde Agar in mariage to Abraham (Genesis 16.3). Lea gaue in like manner her mayde Zilpha to her husband Iacob (Genesis 30.9). So did Rachel his other wife giue him Bilha her mayde, saying vnto him, Goe in vnto her, and shee shall beare vpon my knees: which is, as if she had said, Take her to wife, and the children that she shall beare, will I take vpon my lappe, and make of them as if they were mine owne. These hand-maydens or bondwomen, although by mariage they were made wiues, yet they had not this prerogatiue to rule in the house, but were still vnderlings, and in such subiection to their masters, and were neuer called mothers of the houshold, mistresses, or dames of the house, but are called sometimes wiues, sometime concubines. The plurality of wiues, was by a speciall prerogatiue suffered to the fathers of the olde Testament, not for satisfying their carnall and fleshly lustes, but to haue many children, because euery one of them hoped, and begged oft times of GOD in their prayers, that that blessed seede, which GOD promised should come into the world to breake the serpents head, might come and be borne of his stocke and kinred.

Now of those which take occasion of carnality and euill life, by hearing and reading in GODS booke, what GOD had suffered, euen in those men whose commendation is praysed in the Scripture: As that Noe, whom Saint Peter calleth the eight preacher of righteousnesse (2 Peter 2.5), was so drunke with wine, that in his sleepe he vncouered his owne priuities (Genesis 9.21). The iust man Lot was in like manner drunken, and in his drunkennesse lay with his owne daughters, contrary to the law of nature (Genesis 19.32). Abraham, whose faith was so great, that for the same hee deserued to bee called of GODS owne mouth a father of many nations, the father of all beleeuers (Genesis 17.4-5, Romans 4.17), besides with Sara his wife, had also carnall company with Agar, Saraes handmaide. The Patriarch Iacob had to his wiues two sisters at one time (Genesis 29.30). The Prophet Dauid and king Solomon his sonne, had many wiues and concubines &c. Which things wee see plainely to bee forbidden vs by the law of GOD, and are now repugnant to all publike honestie. These and such like in GODS booke (good people) are not written that we should or may doe the like following their examples, or that wee ought to thinke that GOD did allow euery of these things in those men: But wee ought rather to beleeue and to iudge that Noe in his drunkennesse offended GOD highly. Lot lying with his daughters, committed horrible incest. Wee ought then to learne by them this profitable lesson, that if so godly men as they were, which otherwise felt inwardly GODS holy Spirit inflaming in their hearts, with the feare and loue of GOD, could not by their owne strength keepe themselues from committing horrible sin, but did so grieuously fall, that without GODS great mercy they had perished euerlastingly: How much more ought wee then, miserable wretches, which haue no feeling of GOD within vs at all, continually to feare, not onely that we may fall as they did, but also be ouercome and drowned in sinne, which they were not? And so by considering their fall, take the better occasion to acknowledge our owne infirmitie and weakenes, and therefore more earnestly to call vnto Almighty GOD with hearty prayer incessantly, for his grace, to strengthen vs, and to defend vs from all euill. And though through infirmity wee chaunce at any time to fall, yet wee may by hear ty repentance, and true faith, speedily rise againe, and not sleepe and continue in sinne, as the wicked doeth.

Thus good people, should we vnderstand such matters expressed in the diuine Scriptures, that this holy table of GODS word be not turned to vs to be a snare, a trappe, and a stumbling stone, to take hurt by the abuse of our vnderstanding: But let vs esteeme them in a reuerent humilitie, that we may find our necessary food therein, to strengthen vs, to comfort vs, to instruct vs (as GOD of his great mercy hath appoynted them) in all necessary workes, so that wee may be perfect before him in the whole course of our life: Which hee grant vs, who hath redeemed vs, our Lord and Sauiour Iesus Christ, to whom with the Father, & the holy Ghost, bee all honour & glory for euermore, Amen.

THE SECOND PART OF THE INFORMATION FOR THEM WHICH TAKE OFFENCE AT CERTAINE PLACES OF THE HOLY SCRIPTURE.

YEe haue heard (good people) in the Homilie last read vnto you, the great commoditie of holy Scriptures, yee haue heard how ignorant men, voyde of godly vnderstanding, seeke quarrels to discredite them: Some of their reasons haue yee heard answered. Now wee will proceede and speake of such politique wise men which bee offended, for that Christes precepts should seeme to destroy all order in gouernance, as they doe alleadge for example, such as these bee. If any man strike thee on the right cheeke, turne the other vnto him also. If any man will contend to take thy coate from thee, let him haue cloke and all (Matthew 5.39-40). Let not thy left hand know what thy right hand doeth. If thine eye, thine hand, or thy foote offend thee, pull out thine eye, cut off thine hand, thy foote, and cast it from thee (Matthew 18.8-9). If thine enemie (saith Saint Paul) be an hungred, giue him meate, if hee bee thirstie, giue him drinke: so doing, thou shalt heape hote burning coales vpon his head (Romans 12.20). These sentences (good people) vnto a naturall man seeme meere absurdities, contrary to all reason. For a naturall man (as Saint Paul saith) vnderstandeth not the things that belong to GOD (1 Corinthians 2.14), neither can he, so long as old Adam dwelleth in him. Christ therefore meaneth, that he would haue his faith full seruants so farre from vengeance and resisting wrong, that he would rather haue him ready to suffer another wrong, then by resisting to breake charitie, and to bee out of patience. Hee would haue our good deedes so farre from all carnall respects, that he would not haue our nighest friends know of our well doing, to winne vaine glory. And though our friends and kinsefolkes be as deare as our right eyes and our right hands: yet if they would plucke vs from GOD, wee ought to renounce them, and forsake them.

Thus if yee will bee profitable hearers and readers of the holy Scriptures, ye must first denie your selues, and keepe vnder your carnall senses, taken by the outward wordes, and search the inward meaning: reason must giue place to GODS holy spirite, you must submit your worldly wisedome and iudgement, vnto his diuine wisedome and iudgement. Consider that the Scripture, in what strange fourme soeuer it bee pronounced, is the word of the liuing GOD. Let that alwayes come to your remembrance, which is so oft repeated of the Prophet Esaias: The mouth of the Lord (saith he) hath spoken it, and Almighty and euerlasting GOD, who with his onely word created heauen and earth, hath decreed it, the Lord of hostes, whose wayes are in the Seas, whose paths are in the deepe waters, that Lorde and GOD by whose worde all things in heauen and in earth are created, gouerned, and preserued, hath so prouided it. The GOD of gods, and Lord of all lordes, yea, GOD that is GOD alone, incomprehensible, almighty, and euerlasting, hee hath spoken it, it is his word. It cannot therefore be but trueth, which proceedeth from the GOD of all trueth: it cannot be but wisely and prudently commaunded, what Almighty GOD hath deuised, how vainely soeuer, through want of grace, wee miserable wretches doe imagine and iudge of his most holy word. The Prophet Dauid, describing an happy man, sayth: Blessed is the man that hath not walked after the counsaile of the vngodly, nor stand in the way of sinners, nor sit in the seate of the scornefull (Psalms 1.1). There are three sortes of people, whose company the Prophet would haue him to flee and auoyde, which shall be an happy man, and partaker of GODS blessing. First, he may not walke after the counsaile of the vngodly. Secondly, he may not stand in the way of sinners. Thirdly, he must not sit in the seate of the scornefull. By these three sortes of people, vngodly men, sinners, and scorners, all impietie is signified, and fully expressed. By the vngodly, hee vnderstandeth those which haue no regard of almighty GOD, being voyde of all faith, whose hearts and mindes are so set vpon the world, that they studie onely how to accomplish their worldly practises, their carnall imaginations, their filthy lust and desire, without any feare of GOD. The second sort hee calleth sinners, not such as doe fall through ignorance, or of frailenesse, for then who should be found free? What man euer liued vpon earth (Christ onely excepted) but he hath sinned? The iust man falleth seuen times, and riseth againe (Proverbs 24.16). Though the godly do fall, yet they walke not on purposely in sinne, they stand not still to continue and tarry in sinne, they sit not downe like carelesse men, without all feare of GODS iust punishment for sinne: but defying sinne, through GODS great grace and infinite mercie, they rise againe, and fight against sinne. The Prophet then calleth them sinners, whose heartes are cleane turned from GOD, and whose whole conuersation of life is nothing but sinne, they delight so much in the same, that they chuse continually to abide and dwell in sinne. The third sort hee calleth scorners, that is, a sorte of men whose heartes are so stuffed with malice, that they are not contented to dwell in sinne, and to leade their liues in all kinde of wickednesse: but also they doe contemne and scorne in other all godlinesse, true religion, all honesty and vertue. Of the two first sortes of men, I will not say but they may take repentance, and bee conuerted vnto GOD. Of the third sort, I thinke I may without danger of GODS iudgement pronounce, that neuer any yet conuerted vnto GOD by repentance, but continued still in their abominable wickednesse, heaping vp to themselues damnation, against the day of GODS ineuitable iudgement. Examples of such scorners, we reade in the second booke of Chronicles: When the good king Ezechias, in the beginning of his reigne, had destroyed Idolatrie, purged the Temple, and reformed Religion in his Realme, he sent messengers into euery Citie, to gather the people vnto Ierusalem, to solemnize the feast of Easter, in such sort as GOD had appointed . The postes went from citie to citie, through the land of Ephraim and Manassas, euen vnto Zabulon (2 Chronicles 30.1-6). And what did the people, thinke yee? Did they laude and prayse the Name of the Lord which had giuen them so good a King, so zealous a Prince to abolish idolatry, and to restore againe GODS true religion? No, no. The Scripture sayth, The people laughed them to scorne, and mocked the Kinges messengers. And in the last Chapter of the same booke it is written, that Almighty GOD, hauing compassion vpon his people, sent his messengers the Prophets vnto them, to call them from their abominable idolatrie and wicked kinde of liuing. But they mocked his messengers, they despised his words, and misused his Prophets, vntill the wrath of the Lord arose against his people, and till there was no remedy: For hee gaue them vp into the handes of their enemies, euen vnto Nabuchodonozer King of Babylon, who spoyled them of their goods, burnt their citie, and led them, their wiues, and their children, captiues vnto Babylon. The wicked people that were in the dayes of Noe, made but a mocke at the worde of GOD, when Noe tolde them that GOD would take vengeance vpon them for their sinnes. The flood therefore came sodainely vpon them, and drowned them with the whole world. Lot preached to the Sodomites, that except they repented, both they and their Citie should be destroyed. They thought his sayings impossible to bee true, they scorned and mocked his admonition, and reputed him as an olde doating foole. But when GOD by his holy Angels had taken Lot, his wife, and two daughters from among them, hee rained downe fire and brimstone from heauen, and burnt vp those scorners and mockers of his holy word. And what estimation had Christes doctrine among the

Scribes and Pharisees? What reward had hee among them? The Gospel reporteth thus: The Pharisees which were couetous, did scorne him in his doctrine. O then yee see that worldly rich men scorne the doctrine of their saluation. The worldly wise men scorne the doctrine of Christ, as foolishnesse to their vnderstanding. These scorners haue euer beene, and euer shall bee to the worldes end. For Saint Peter prophesied, that such scorners should be in the world before the latter day (2 Peter 3.3). Take heede therefore (my brethren) take heede, be yee not scorners of GODS most holy word, prouoke him not to powre out his wrath now vpon you, as hee did then vpon those gybers and mockers. Be not wilfull murderers of your owne soules. Turne vnto GOD while there is yet time of mercy, yee shall else repent it in the world to come, when it shall be too late, for there shall bee iudgement without mercie. This might suffice to admonish vs, and cause vs henceforth to reuerence GODS holy Scriptures, but all men haue not faith. This therefore shall not satisfie & content all mens minds: but as some are carnall, so they will still continue, and abuse the Scriptures carnally, to their greater damnation. The vnlearned and vnstable (saith S. Peter) peruert the holy Scriptures to their owne destruction (2 Peter 3.16). Iesus Christ (as S. Paul saith) is to the Iewes an offence, to the Gentiles foolishnesse: But to Gods children, as well of the Iewes as of the Gentiles he is the power & wisedome of GOD (1 Corinthians 1.23-24). The holy man Simeon saith, that he is set forth for the fall and rising againe of many in Israel (Luke 2.34). As Christ Iesus is a fall to the reprobate, which yet perish through their owne default: so is his word, yea the whole booke of GOD, a cause of damnation vnto them, through their incredulity. And as hee is a rising vp to none other then those which are GODS children by adoption: so is his word, yea the whole Scripture, the power of GOD to saluation to them onely that doe beleeue it. Christ himselfe, the Prophets before him, the Apostles after him, all the true Ministers of GODS holy word, yea euery word in GODS Booke, is vnto the reprobate, the sauour of death vnto death.

Christ Iesus, the Prophets, the Apostles, and all the true Ministers of his word, yea euery iot and tittle in the holy Scripture, haue beene, is, and shalbe for euermore, the sauour of life vnto eternall life, vnto all those whose hearts GOD hath purified by true fayth. Let vs earnestly take heed, that we make no iesting stocke of the bookes of holy Scriptures. The more obscure and darke the sayings be to our vnderstanding, the further let vs thinke our selues to bee from GOD, and his holy spirit, who was the authour of them. Let vs with more reuerence endeuour our selues to search out the wisedome hidden in the outward barke of the Scripture. If we can not vnderstand the sense and the reason of the saying, yet let vs not be scorners, iesters, and deriders, for that is the vttermost token and shew of a reprobate, of a plaine enemie to GOD and his wisedome. They be not idle fables to iest at, which GOD doeth seriously pronounce, and for serious matters let vs esteeme them. And though in sundry places of the Scriptures, bee set out diuers Rites and Ceremonies, oblations and sacrifices: let vs not thinke strange of them, but referre them to the times and people for whom they serued, although yet to learned men they be not vnprofitable to be considered, but to be expounded as figures and shadowes of things and persons, afterward openly reuealed in the new Testament. Though the rehearsall of the genealogies and pedegrees of the Fathers bee not to much edification of the plaine ignorant people: yet is there nothing so impertinently vttered in all the whole Booke of the Bible, but may serue to spirituall purpose in some respect, to all such as will bestow their labours to search out the meanings. These may not be condemned, because they serue not to our vnderstanding, nor make to our edification. But let vs turne our labour to vnderstand, and to cary away such sentences and stories as bee more fit for our capacity and instruction.

And whereas we read in diuers Psalmes, how Dauid did wish to the aduersaries of GOD sometimes shame, rebuke, and confusion, sometime the decay of their ofspring and issue, sometime that they might perish and come suddenly to destruction, as he did wish to the Captaines of the Philistines. Cast foorth (sayth he) thy lightning, and teare them, shoot out thine arrowes and consume them (Psalms 144.6), with such other maner of imprecations: Yet ought we not to be offended at such prayers of Dauid, being a Prophet as he was, singularly beloued of GOD, and rapt in spirit, with an ardent zeale to GODS glory. Hee spake not of a priuate hatred and in a stomacke against their persons: but wished spiritually the destruction of such corrupt errours and vices, which raigned in all diuellish persons, set against GOD. He was of like minde as S. Paul was when he did deliuer Himeneus and Alexander, with the notorious fornicatour, to Satan, to their temporall confusion, that their spirit might bee saued against the day of the Lord. And when Dauid did professe in some places that he hated the wicked: yet in other places of his Psalmes he professeth, that he hated them with a perfect hate, not with a malicious hate, to the hurt of the soule. Which perfection of spirit, because it cannot be performed in vs, so corrupted in affections as wee bee, wee ought not to vse in our priuate causes the like wordes in forme, for that we cannot fulfill the like words in sense. Let vs not therefore be offended, but search out the reason of such words before we be offended, that wee may the more reuerently iudge of such sayings, though strange to our carnall vnderstandings, yet to them that be spiritually minded, iudged to be zealously and godly pronounced. GOD therefore for his mercies sake, vouchsafe to purifie our mindes through fayth in his sonne Iesus Christ, and to instill the heauenly droppes of his grace into our hard stony hearts, to supple the same, that wee bee not contemners and deriders of his infallible word: but that with all humblenesse of minde and Christian reuerence we may indeuour our selues to heare and to read his sacred Scriptures, and inwardly so to digest them, as shalbe to the comfort of our soules, sanctification of his holy Name, to whom with the Sonne and the holy Ghost, three persons and one liuing GOD, be all laud, honour, and prayse for euer and euer, Amen.

HOMILY ON ALMS DEEDS

AN HOMILIE OF
Almes deedes, and mercifulnesse toward
the poore and needy.

AMongst the manifold dueties that Almighty GOD requireth of his faithfull seruants the true Christians, by the which hee would that both his name should bee glorified, and the certaintie of their vocation declared, there is none that is either more acceptable vnto him, or more profitable for them, then are the workes of mercy and pity shewed vpon the poore, which bee afflicted with any kinde of misery. And yet this notwithstanding (such is the slothfull sluggishnesse of our dull nature, to that which is good and godly) that wee are almost in nothing more negligent and lesse carefull then we are therein. It is therefore a very necessary thing, that GODS people should awake their sleepie mindes, and consider their duty on this behalfe. And meet it is, that all true Christians should desirously seeke and learne what GOD by his holy word doeth heerein require of them: that first knowing their duty (whereof many by their slackenesse seeme to be very ignorant) they may afterwards diligently endeuour to performe the same. By the which both the godly charitable persons may be encouraged to goe forwards and continue in their mercifull deedes of almes giuing to the poore, and also such as hitherto haue either neglected, or contemned it, may yet now at length (when they shall heare how much it appertayneth to them) aduisedly consider it, and vertuously apply themselues thereunto.

And to the intent that euery one of you may the better vnderstand that which is taught, and also easilier beare away, and so take more fruite of that shall be sayd, when seuerall matters are seuerally handled: I minde particularly, and in this order, to speake and intreat of these points.

First I will shew how earnestly Almighty GOD in his holy word, doth exact the doing of almes deeds of vs, and how acceptable they bee vnto him.

Secondly, of almes deeds. Secondly how profitable it is for vs to vse them, and what commodity and fruite they will bring vnto vs.

Thirdly and lastly, I will shew out of GODS word, that who so is liberall to the poore, and relieueth them plenteously, shall notwithstanding haue sufficient for himselfe and euermore bee without danger of penury and scarcitie.

Concerning the first, which is the acceptation and dignity, or price of almes deedes before GOD: Know this, that to helpe and succour the poore in their neede and misery, pleaseth GOD so much, that as the holy Scripture in sundry places recordeth, nothing can bee more thankefully taken or accepted of GOD. For first wee reade, that Almighty GOD doth account that to be giuen and to bee bestowed vpon himselfe, that is bestowed vpon the poore: For so doeth the holy Ghost testifie vnto vs by the wise man, saying, Hee that hath pitie vpon the poore, lendeth vnto the Lord himselfe (Proverbs 19.17). And Christ in the Gospel auoucheth, and as a most certaine trueth, bindeth it with an oath, that the almes bestowed vpon the poore, was bestowed vpon him, and so shall be reckoned at the last day. For thus he saith to the charitable almes giuers, when he sitteth as iudge in the doome, to giue sentence of euery man according to his deserts: Verily I say vnto you, whatsoeuer good and mercifull deede you did vpon any of the least of these my brethren, ye did the same vnto me (Matthew 25.40). In releeuing their hunger, yee releeued mine, in quenching their thirst, yee quenched mine, in clothing them, yee clothed mee, and when yee harboured them, yee lodged me also, when yee visited them being sicke in prison, yee visited mee. For as hee that hath receiued a Princes embassadours, and entertaineth them well, doth honour the prince from whom those embassadours doe come: So he that receiueth the poore and needy, and helpeth them in their affliction and distresse, doeth thereby receiue & honour Christ their Master, who as he was poore and needie himselfe whilest hee liued here amongst vs, to worke the mysterie of our saluation, at his departure hence he promised in his steed to send vnto vs those that were poore, by whose meanes his absence should bee supplied: and therefore that we would doe vnto him, wee must doe vnto them. And for this cause doth the Almighty GOD say vnto Moses, The land wherein you dwell, shall neuer bee without poore men: because he would haue continuall triall of his people (Deuteronomy 15.11), whether they loued him or no, that in shewing themselues obedient vnto his will, they might certainely assure themselues of his loue and fauour towards them, and nothing doubt, but that as his lawe and ordinance (wherein hee commanded them that they should open their hand vnto their brethren that were poore and needy in the land) were accepted of them and willingly performed: So hee would on his part louingly accept them, and truely performe his promises that he had made vnto them.

The holy Apostles and Disciples of Christ, who by reason of his dayly conuersation, saw by his deedes, and heard in his doctrine how much he tendered the poore: the godly Fathers also, that were both before and since Christ, indued without doubt with the holy Ghost, and most certainly certified of GODS holy will: they both do most earnestly exhort vs, and in all their writings almost continually admonish vs, that wee would remember the poore, and bestow our charitable almes vpon them.

Saint Paul crieth vnto vs after this sort, Comfort the feeble minded, lift vp the weake, and be charitable towards all men (1 Thessalonians 5.14). And againe, To doe good to the poore, and to distribute almes gladly, see that thou doe not forget, for with such sacrifices GOD is pleased (Hebrews 13.16). Esay the Prophet teacheth on this wise, Deale thy bread to the hungrie, and bring the poore wandering, home to thy house. When thou seest the naked, see thou cloth him, and hide not thy face from thy poore neighbour, neither despise thou thine owne flesh (Isaiah 58.7). And the holy Father Tobie giueth this counsell, Giue almes (sayth hee) of thine owne goodes, and turne neuer thy face from the poore, eat thy bread with the hungry, and couer the naked with thy clothes (Tobit 4.7, 16). And the learned and godly Doctour Chrysostome giueth this admonition, Let mercifull almes be alwayes with vs as a garment, that is, as mindefull as we will be to put our garments vpon vs, to couer our nakednesse, to defend vs from the cold, and to shew our selues comely (Chrysostome, `Ad Pop. Antio. hom.'): So mindefull let vs be at all times and seasons, that wee giue almes to the poore, and shew our selues mercifull towards them. But what meane these often admonitions and earnest exhortations of the Prophets. Apostles, Fathers, and holy Doctours? Surely, as they were faythfull to Godward, and therefore discharged their duty truly, in telling vs what was GODS will: so of a singular loue to vs: ward, they laboured not only to informe vs, but also to perswade with vs, that to giue almes, and to succour the poore and needy, was a very acceptable thing, and an high sacrifice to GOD, wherein he greatly delighted, and had a singular pleasure. For so doeth the Wise man the sonne of Sirach teach vs, saying, Who so is mercifull and giueth almes, hee offereth the right thanke-offering (Wisdom of Sirach 35.1, 4, 6-7). And he addeth thereunto: The right thanke-offering, maketh the Altar fat, & a sweet smell it is before the Highest, it is acceptable before GOD, and shall neuer be forgotten.

And the truth of this doctrine is verified by the example of those holy and charitable Fathers, of whom wee reade in the Scriptures, that they were giuen to mercifull compassion towardes the poore, and charitable releeuing of their necessities. Such a one was Abraham, in whom GOD had so great pleasure, that he vouchsafed to come vnto him in forme of an Angel, and to be intertayned of him at his house. Such was his kinseman Lot, whom GOD so fauoured for receiuing his messengers into his house, which otherwise should haue lien in the street, that hee saued him, with his whole family, from the destruction of Sodome and Gomorrha. Such were the holy Fathers, Iob and Tobie, with many others, who felt most sensible proofes of GODS speciall loue towards them. And as all these by their mercifulnesse and tender compassion which they shewed to the miserable afflicted members of Christ, in the relieuing, helping and succouring them with their temporall goodes in this life, obtayned GODS fauour, and were deare, acceptable and pleasant in his sight: so now they themselues take pleasure in the fruition of GOD, in the pleasant ioyes of heauen, and are also in GODS eternall word set before vs, as perfect examples euer before our eyes, both how wee shall please GOD in this mortall life, and also how wee may come to liue in ioy with them in euerlasting pleasure and felicitie. For most true is that saying which Augustine hath, that the giuing of almes and releeuing of the poore, is the right way to heauen, *Via c_li pauper*, The poore man (sayth hee) is the way to heauen, . They vsed in times past, to set in hye wayes sides the picture of Mercurie, poynting with his finger which was the right way to the Towne. And we vse in crosse wayes to set vp a wodden or stone crosse, to admonish the trauayling man which way he must turne when hee commeth thither, to directe his iourney aright. But GODS word (as Saint Augustine sayth) hath set in the way to heauen the poore man and his house, so that whoso will goe aright thither, and not turne out of the way, must goe by the poore. The poore man is that Mercurie that shall set vs the ready way: and if wee looke well to this marke, we shall not wander much out of the right path. The maner of wise worldly men amongst vs is, that if they know a man of a meaner estate then themselues to be in fauour with the Prince, or any other noble man, whom they either feare or loue, such a one they will be glad to benefite and pleasure, that when they haue neede they may become their spokes man, either to obteine a commoditie, or to escape a displeasure. Now surely it ought to be a shame to vs, that worldly men for temporall things that last but for a season, should be more wise and prouident in procuring them, then wee in heauenly. Our sauiour Christ testifieth of poore men, that they are deare vnto him, and that hee loueth them especially: For hee calleth them his little ones, by a name of tender loue, he sayth they be his brethren. And Saint Iames saith, that GOD hath chosen them to be the heyres of his kingdome. Hath not GOD (sayth he) chosen the poore of this world to himselfe, to make them hereafter the rich heires of that kingdome which hee hath promised to them that loue him (James 2.5)? And wee know that the prayer which they make for vs, shalbe acceptable and regarded of GOD, their complaint shalbe heard also. Thereof doeth Iesus the sonne of Syrach certainely assure vs, saying: If the poore complaine of thee in the bitternesse of his soule, his prayer shalbe heard, euen hee that made him shall heare him (Ecclesiasticus [Wisdom of Sirach] 4.5-6). Bee courteous therefore vnto the poore. We know also, that hee who acknowledgeth himselfe to bee their master and patrone, and refuseth not to take them for his seruants, is both able to pleasure and displeasure vs, and that we stand euery houre in neede of his helpe. Why should wee then bee either negligent or vnwilling to procure their friendship and fauour, by the which also we may bee assured to get his fauour that is both able and willing to doe vs all pleasures that are for our commoditie and wealth? Christ doth declare by this, how much he accepteth our charitable affection toward the poore, in that he promiseth a reward vnto them that giue but a cup of cold water in his name to them that haue neede thereof, and that reward is the kingdome of heauen. No doubt is it therefore that GOD regardeth highly, that which he rewardeth so liberally. For he that promiseth a Princely recompence, for a beggarly beneuolence, declareth that he is more delighted with the giuing, then with the gift, and that he as much esteemeth the doing of the thing, as the fruit and commodity that commeth of it. Whoso therefore hath hitherto neglected to giue Almes, let him know that GOD now requireth it of him, and he that hath beene liberall to the poore, let him know that his godly doings are accepted, and thankefully taken at GODS hands, which he will requite with double and treble. For so sayth the Wise man: Hee which sheweth mercy to the poore, doeth lay his money in banke to the Lord, for a large interest and gaine: the gaine being chiefly the possession of the life euerlasting, through the merits of our Sauiour Iesus Christ, to whom with the Father and the Holy Ghost, bee all honour and glory for euer, AMEN.

The second part of the Sermon of Almes deedes.

YE haue heard before (dearely beloued) that to giue almes vnto the poore, and to helpe them in time of necessity, is so acceptable vnto our Sauiour Christ, that he counteth that to bee done to himselfe, that we doe for his sake vnto them. Yee haue heard also how earnestly both the Apostles, Prophets, holy Fathers, and Doctours, doe exhort vs vnto the same. And ye see how welbeloued and deare vnto GOD they were, whom the Scriptures report vnto vs to haue bin good almes men. Wherfore if either their good examples, or the wholsome counsell of godly Fathers, or the loue of Christ, whose especiall fauour wee may be assured by this meanes to obtaine may mooue vs, or doe any thing at all with vs: let vs prouide vs that from hencefoorth wee shew vnto GODward this thankefull seruice, to bee mindfull and ready to helpe them that bee poore and in misery.

Now will I this second time that I entreat of almes deedes, shew vnto you how profitable it is for vs to exercise them, and what fruit therby shall arise vnto vs, if we doe them faithfully, Our Sauiour Christ in the Gospel teacheth vs, that it profiteth a man nothing to haue in possession all the riches of the whole world, and the wealth or glory thereof, if in the meane season hee lose his soule, or doe that thing whereby it should become captiue vnto death, sin, and hell fire. By the which saying, hee not onely instructeth vs how much the soules health is to bee preferred before worldly c&omacron;modities: but it also serueth to stirre vp our minds, and to pricke vs forwards to seeke diligently, and learne by what meanes we may preserue and keepe our soules euer in safety: that is, how we may recouer our health, if it bee lost or impaired, and how it may be defended and maintained, if once we haue it. Yea, he teacheth vs also thereby to esteeme that as a precious medicine and an inestimable iewell, that hath such strength and vertue in it, that can either procure or preserue so incomparable a treasure. For if we greatly regard that medicine or salue that is able to heale sundry and grieuous diseases of the body: much more will wee esteeme that which hath like power ouer the soule. And because wee might be better assured both to know and to haue in readines that so profitable a remedy: he, as a most faithfull & louing teacher, sheweth himselfe both what it is, and where we may finde it, and how we may vse and apply it. For when both he & his disciples were grieuously accused of the Pharisees, to haue defiled their soules in breaking the constitutions of the Elders, because they went to meate, & washed not their hands before, according to the custome of the Iewes: Christ answering their superstitious complaint, teacheth them an especiall remedy how to keepe cleane their soules, notwithstanding the breach of such superstitious orders: Giue almes (saith hee) and behold all things are cleane vnto you (Luke 11.41). He teacheth them, that to bee mercifull and charitable in helping the poore, is the meanes to keepe the soule pure and cleane in the sight of GOD. Wee are taught therefore by this, that mercifull almes dealing, is profitable to purge the soule from the infection and filthie spottes or sinne. The same lesson doeth the holy Ghost also teach in sundry places of the Scripture, saying, Mercifulnesse and almes giuing purgeth from all sinnes, and deliuereth from death, and suffereth not the soule to come into darkenes (Tobit 4.10). A great confidence may they haue before the high GOD, that shewe mercie and compassion to them that are afflicted. The wise preacher the sonne of Sirach confirmeth the same, when hee saith, That as water quencheth burning fire, euen so mercie and almes resisteth and reconcileth sinnes (Ecclesiasticus 3.30). And sure it is, that mercifulnesse quaileth the heate of sinne so much, that they shall not take holde vpon man to hurte him, or if yee haue by any infirmitie or weakenesse beene touched and annoyed with them, straightwayes shall mercifulnesse wipe and wash away, as salues and remedies to heale their sores and grieuous diseases. And thereupon that holy father Cyprian taketh good occasion to exhort earnestly to the mercifull worke of giuing almes and helping the poore, and there he admonisheth to consider how wholsome and profitable it is to releeue the needy, and helpe the afflicted, by the which wee may purge our sinnes, and heale our wounded soules.

But yet some will say vnto mee, If almes giuing, and our charitable workes towards the poore, be able to wash away sinnes, to reconcile vs to GOD, to deliuer vs from the perill of damnation, and make vs the sonnes and heires of GODS kingdome: then are Christes merits defaced, and his blood shed in vaine, then are we iustified by workes and by our deeds may we merite heauen, then do we in vaine beleeue that Christ dyed for to put away our sinnes, and that he rose for our iustification, as Saint Paul teacheth. But yee shall vnderstand (dearely beloued) that neither those places of the Scripture before alledged, neither the doctrine of the blessed martyr Cyprian, neither any other godly and learned man, when they, in extolling the dignity, profite, fruit, and effect of vertuous and liberall almes, doe say that it washeth away sinnes, and bringeth vs to the fauour of GOD, doe meane, that our worke and charitable deede, is the originall cause of our acception before GOD, or that for the dignity or worthines therof, our sinnes may be washed away, and we purged and cleansed of all the spottes of our iniquitie: for that were indeede to deface Christ, and to defraude him of his glory. But they meane this, and this is the vnderstanding of those and such like sayinges: that GOD of his mercy and speciall fauour towards them whom he hath appointed to euerlasting saluation, hath so offered his grace especially, and they haue so receiued it fruitfully, that although by reason of their sinfull liuing outwardly, they seemed before to haue beene the children of wrath and perdition, yet now the Spirit of GOD mightily working in them, vnto obedience to GODS will and commandements, they declare by their outward deeds and life, in the shewing of mercy, and charity (which cannot come but of the spirit of GOD, and his especiall grace) that they are the vndoubted children of GOD, appointed to euerlasting life. And so, as by their wickednesse and vngodly liuing, they shewed themselues according to the iudgement of men, which follow the outward appearance, to be reprobates and castawayes: So now by their obedience vnto GODS holy will, and by their mercifulnesse and tender pity (wherin they shew themselues to be like vnto GOD, who is the fountaine and spring of all mercy) they declare openly and manifestly vnto the sight of men, that they are the sonnes of GOD, and elect of him vnto saluation. For as the good fruit is not the cause that the tree is good, but the tree must first be good before it can bring foorth good fruite: so the good deeds of man are not the cause that maketh men good, but he is first made good, by the spirit and grace of GOD that effectually worketh in him, and afterward he bringeth foorth good fruites. And then as the good fruite doeth argue the goodnesse of the tree, so doeth the good and mercifull deed of the man, argue and certainely prooue the goodnesse of him that doeth it, according to Christes sayings: Yee shall know them by their fruites. And if any man will obiect, that euill and noughty men doe sometimes by their deeds appeare to bee verie godly and vertuous: I will answere, so doeth the crab and choke peare seeme outwardly to haue sometime as faire a redde, and as mellowe a colour, as the fruite that is good indeede. But hee that will bite and take a taste, shall easily iudge betwixt the sower bitternesse of the one, and the sweete sauorinesse of the other. And as the true Christian man, in thankefulnesse of his heart, for the redemption of his soule purchased by Christes death, sheweth kindly by the fruite of his faith, his obedience to GOD: so the other as a merchant with GOD, doth all for his owne gaine, thinking to win heauen by the merite of his workes, and so defaceth and obscureth the price of Christs blood, who onely wrought our purgation. The meaning then of these sayings in the Scriptures and other holy writings: "Almes deedes doe washe away our sinnes," and, "mercie to the poore doth blot out our offences", is, that we doing these things according to GODS will and our duetie, haue our sinnes indeede washed away, and our offences blotted out: not for the worthinesse of them, but by the grace of GOD which worketh all in all, and that for the promise that GOD hath made to them that are obedient vnto his commandement, that hee which is the trueth, might be iustified in performing the trueth, due to his true promise. Almes deedes do wash away our sinnes, because GOD doeth vouchsafe then to repute vs as cleane and pure, when we doe them for his sake, and not because they deserue or merit our purging, or for that they haue any such strength and vertue in themselues. I know that some men, too much addict to the aduancing of their workes, will not be contented with this answere, and no maruaile, for such men can no answere content or suffice. Wherefore leauing them to their owne wilfull sense, we will rather haue regarde to the reasonable and godly, who as they most certainely know and perswade themselues, that all goodnesse, all bountie, all mercie, all benefites, all forgiuenesse of sinnes, and whatsoeuer can bee named good and profitable, either for the body or for the soule, do come onely of GODS mercie and meere fauoure, and not of themselues: So though they doe neuer so many and so excellent good deedes, yet are they neuer puft vp with the vaine confidence of them. And though they heare and read in GODS word, and other where in godly mens works, that almes deedes, mercie, and charitablenesse doth wash away sinne, and blot out iniquitie: yet doe they not arrogantly and proudly sticke and trust vnto them, or brag themselues of them, as the proud Pharisee did, lest with the Pharisee they should bee condemned: but rather, with the humble and poore Publicane confesse themselues sinfull wretches, vnworthy to looke vp to heauen, calling and crauing for mercie, that with the Publicane they may bee pronounced of Christ to bee iustified. The godly doe learne that when the Scriptures say, that by good and mercifull works, wee are reconciled to GODS fauour: wee are taught then to know what Christ by his intercession and mediation obtaineth for vs of his Father, when we be obedient to his will, yea, they learne in such maner of speaking a comfortable argument of GODS singular fauour and loue, that attributeth that vnto vs and to our doings, that hee by his spirit worketh in vs, and through his grace procureth for vs. And yet this notwithstanding, they cry out with Saint Paul, Oh wretches that wee are: and acknowledge (as Christ teacheth) that when they haue all done, they are but vnprofitable seruants: and with the blessed king Dauid, in respect of the iust iudgements of GOD, they doe tremble, and say: Who shall be able to abide it, Lord, if thou wilt giue sentence according to our deserts? Thus they humble themselues, and are exalted of GOD: they count themselues vile, and of GOD are counted pure and cleane: they condemne themselues, and are iustified of GOD: they thinke themselues, vnworthy of the earth, and of GOD are thought worthy of heauen. Thus by GODS word are they truely taught how to thinke rightly of mercifull dealing of almes, and of GODS especiall mercy and goodnesse are made pertakers of those fruites that his word hath promised. Let vs then follow their examples, and both shew obediently in our life those workes of mercy that wee are commanded, and haue that right opinion and iudgement of them that we are taught, and we shall in like maner, as they, be made partakers, and feele the fruites and rewards that follow such godly liuing, so shall we know by proofe what profit and commodity doth come of giuing of almes, & succouring of the poore.

THE THIRD PART OF THE HOMILY OF ALMES DEEDES.

YEe haue already heard two parts of this treatise of almes deedes. The first, how pleasant and acceptable before GOD the doing of them is, the second, how much it behoooueth vs, and how profitable it is to apply our selues vnto them. Now in the third part will I take away that let that hindereth many from doing them. There be many that when they heare how acceptable a thing in the sight of GOD the giuing of almes is, and how much GOD extendeth his fauour towards them that are mercifull, and what fruites and commodities doeth come to them by it, they wish very gladly with themselues that they also might obteine these benefites, and be counted such of GOD as whom he would loue or doe for. But yet these men are with greedie couetousnesse so puld backe, that they will not bestow one halfepeny or one peece of bread, that they might be thought worthy of GODS benefites, and so to come into his fauour. For they are euermore fearefull, and doubting, lest by often giuing, although it were but a little at a time, they should consume their goods, and so impouerish themselues, that euen themselues at the length should not be able to liue, but should be driuen to begge, and liue of other mens almes. And thus they seeke excuses to withhold themselues from the fauour of GOD, and chuse with pinching couetousnesse, rather to leane vnto the deuill, then by charitable mercifulnesse, either to come vnto Christ, or to suffer Christ to come vnto them. Oh that wee had some cunning and skilfull Physition that were able to purge them of this so pestilent an humour, that so sore infecteth, not their bodies, but their mindes, and so by corrupting their soules, bringeth their bodies and soules into danger of hell fire. Now lest there bee any such among vs (dearely beloued) let vs diligently search for that Physition, which is Iesus Christ, and earnestly labour that of his mercy hee will truely instruct vs, and giue vs a present remedy against so perillous a disease. Hearken then, whosoeuer thou art that fearest lest by giuing to the poore thou shouldest bring thy selfe to beggery. That which thou takest from thy selfe to bestow vpon Christ, can neuer be consumed and wasted away. Wherein thou shalt not beleeue me, but if thou haue faith, and be a true Christian, beleeue the holy Ghost, giue credite to the authoritie of GODS word that thus teacheth. For thus sayth the holy Ghost by Salomon: He that giueth vnto the poore, shall neuer want. Men suppose that by hoording and laying vp still, they shall at length be rich, and that by distributing and laying out, although it be for most necessary and godly vses, they shalbe brought to pouerty. But the holy Ghost, which knoweth all trueth, teacheth vs another lesson, contrary to this. Hee teacheth vs that there is a kinde of dispending that shall neuer diminish the stocke, and a kinde of sauing that shall bring a man to extreme pouertie. For where he sayth, that the good almes-man shall neuer haue scarsitie, hee addeth: But he that turneth away his eyes from such as be in necessity, shall suffer great pouerty himselfe. How farre different then is the iudgement of man, from the iudgement of the holy Ghost? The holy Apostle Paul, a man full of the holy Ghost, and made priuie euen of the secret will of GOD teacheth: that the liberall almes-giuer shall not thereby bee impouerished. He that ministreth (saith he) seede vnto the sower, will minister also bread vnto you for foode, yea, he will multiply your seede, and encrease the fruits of your righteousnesse (2 Corinthians 9.10). He is not content to aduertise them that they shall not lacke, but he sheweth them also in what sort GOD wil prouide for them. Euen as he prouided seed for the sower in multiplying it, and giuing great increase: so he wil multiply their goods, and increase them, that there shall be great abundance. And lest we should thinke his sayings to be but words and not trueth, we haue an example thereof in the third booke of Kings, which doth confirme and seale it vp as a most certaine trueth. The poore widow that receiued the banished Prophet of GOD, Elias, when as she had but a handfull of meale in a vessel, and a little oyle in a cruse, whereof she would make a cake for her selfe and her sonne, that after they had eaten that, they might die, because in that great famine there was no more foode to bee gotten: yet when she gaue part thereof to Elias, and defrauded her owne hungry belly mercifully to relieue him, she was so blessed of GOD, that neither the meale nor the oyle was consumed all the time while that famine did last, but thereof both the Prophet Elias, shee, and her sonne, were sufficiently nourished and had enough.

Oh consider this example yee vnbeleeuing and faithlesse couetous persons, who discredite GODS worde, and thinke his power diminished! This poore woman, in the time of an extreme and long dearth had but one handefull of meale and a little cruse of oyle, her onely sonne was readie to perish before her face for hunger, and shee her selfe like to pine away: and yet when the poore Prophet came and asked part, she was so mindefull of mercifulnesse, that she forgate her owne miserie, and rather then shee would omit the occasion giuen to giue almes, and worke a worke of righteousnesse, shee was content presently to hazard her owne and her sonnes life. And you, who haue great plenty of meates and drinkes, great store of motheaten apparel, yea, many of you great heapes of gold and siluer, and he that hath least, hath more then sufficient, now in this time, when (thankes bee to GOD) no great famine doeth oppresse you, your children being well clothed and well fed, and no danger of death for famine to bee feared, will rather cast doubts and perils of vnlikely penury, then you will part with any peece of your superfluities, to helpe and succour the poore, hungry, and naked Christ, that commeth to your doores a begging.

This poore & seely widow neuer cast doubts in all her miserie what wants she her selfe should haue, shee neuer distrusted the promise that GOD made to her by the Prophet, but straightway went about to relieue the hungry Prophet of GOD, yea, preferring his necessity before her owne. But we, like vnbeleeuing wretches, before we will giue one mite, wee will cast a thousand doubtes of danger, whether that will stand vs in any stead, that we giue to the poore, whether we should not haue need of it at any other time, & whether heere it would not haue been more profitably bestowed. So that it is more hard to wrench a strong nayle (as the prouerbe sayth) out of a poste, then to wring a farthing out of our fingers. There is neither the feare nor the loue of GOD before our eyes, we will more esteeme a mite, then we either desire GODS kingdome, or feare the Diuels dungeon. Hearken therefore ye mercilesse misers, what will bee the end of this your vnmercifull dealing. As certainely as GOD nourished this poore widow in the time of famine, and increased her little store, so that shee had enough, and felt no penury when other pined away: so certainely shall GOD plague you with pouerty in the middest of plenty. Then when other haue abundance and be fed at full, you shall vtterly waste and consume away your selues, your store shall bee destroyed, your goods pluckt from you, all your glory and wealth shall perish: and that which when you had, you might haue enioyed your selfe in peace, and might haue bestowed vpon other most godly, yee shall seeke with sorrow and sighes, and no where shall finde it. For your vnmercifulnesse towards other, ye shall finde no man that will shew mercy towards you. You that had stony hearts towards other, shall finde all the creatures of GOD, to youward as hard as brasse and yron. Alas, what fury and madnesse doth possesse our mindes, that in a matter of trueth and certainety, wee will not giue credit to the trueth, testifying vnto that which is most certaine. Christ sayth, that if wee will first seeke the kingdome of GOD, and doe the workes of righteousnesse thereof, we shall not be left destitute, all other things shalbe giuen to vs plenteously. Nay say we, I will first looke that I be able to liue my selfe, and bee sure that I haue enough for mee and mine, and if I haue any thing ouer, I will bestow it to get GODS fauour, and the poore shall then haue part with me.

See I pray you the peruerse iudgement of men, we haue more care to nourish the carcasse, then wee haue feare to see our soule perish. And as Cyprian sayth, whilest we stand in doubt lest our goods fayle, in being ouer liberall, we put it out of doubt, that our life and health fayleth, in not being liberall at all (Cyprian, `Sermon. de Eleemosina'">Sermon.). Whilest wee are carefull for diminishing of our stocke, we are altogether carelesse to diminish our selues. We loue Mammon, and loose our soules. Wee feare least our patrimony should perish from vs, but we feare not lest we should perish for it. Thus doe wee peruersly loue that, which we should hate, and hate that we should loue, we be negligent where we should bee carefull, and carefull where wee neede not. Thus vaine feare to lacke our selues if we giue to the poore, is much like the feare of children and fooles, which when they see the bright glimmering of a glasse, they doe imagine straightway that it is the lightning and yet the brightnesse of a glasse neuer was the lightning. Euen so, when we imagine that by spending vpon the poore, a man may come to pouerty, we are cast into a vaine feare, for we neuer heard or knew, that by that meanes any man came to misery, and was left destitute, and not considered of GOD. Nay we read to the contrary in the Scripture (as I haue before shewed, and as by infinite testimonies and examples may bee prooued) that whosoeuer serueth GOD faithfully and vnfeinedly in any vocation, GOD will not suffer him to decay, much lesse to perish. The holy Ghost teacheth vs by Salomon, that the Lord will not suffer the soule of the righteous to perish for hunger (Proverbs 10.3). And therefore Dauid sayth vnto all them that are mercifull: O feare the Lord yee that bee his Saints, for they that feare him lacke nothing (Psalms 34.1). The Lions doe lack and suffer hunger, but they which seeke the Lord shall want no manner of thing that is good. When Elias was in the desert, GOD fed him by the ministery of a Rauen, that euening and morning brought him sufficient victualles (1 Kings 17.4-6). When Daniel was shut vp in the Lions denne, GOD prepared meat for him, and sent it thither to him: And there was the saying of Dauid fulfilled, The Lions doe lacke and suffer hunger, but they which seeke the Lord, shall want no good thing (Psalms 34.10). For while the Lions, which should haue beene fed with his flesh, roared for hunger and desire of their pray, whereof they had no power, although it were present before them, he in the meane time was fresh fed from GOD, that should with his flesh haue filled the Lions. So mightily doth GOD worke to preserue and maintaine those whom he loueth, so carefull is hee also to feede them who in any state or vocation doe vnfeinedly serue him. And shall we now thinke that he will be vnmindfull of vs, if wee bee obedient to his word, and according to his will haue pity on the poore? He giueth vs all wealth before we doe any seruice for it: and will he see vs lacke necessaries when we doe him true seruice? Can a man thinke that he that feedeth

Christ, can be forsaken of Christ, and left without food? Or will Christ denie earthly things vnto them whom he promiseth heauenly things for his true seruice? It cannot be therefore (deare brethren) that by giuing of almes, we should at any time want our selues, or that we which releeue other mens need, should our selues bee oppressed with penury. It is contrary to GODS word, it repugneth with his promise, it is against Christs property and nature to suffer it, it is the crafty surmise of the Diuell to perswade vs it. Wherefore sticke not to giue almes freely, and trust notwithstanding, that GODS goodnesse will minister vnto vs sufficiency and plenty, so long as we shall liue in this transitory life, and after our dayes heere well spent in his seruice, and the loue of our brethren, we shalbe crowned with euerlasting glory, to raigne with Christ our Sauiour in heauen, to whom with the Father and the holy Ghost, be all honour and glory for euer. Amen.

HOMILY ON THE NATIVITY

AN HOMILIE OR SERMON
concerning the Natiuity and birth of our
Sauiour Iesus Christ

AMong all the creatures that GOD made in the beginning of the world most excellent and wonderfull in their kinde, there was none (as the Scripture beareth witnesse) to bee compared almost in any point vnto man, who aswell in body and soule exceeded all other no lesse, then the Sunne in brightnesse and light exceedeth euery small and little star in the firmament. Hee was made according to the image and similitude of GOD, hee was indued with all kinde of heauenly gifts, hee had no spot of vncleannesse in him, he was found and perfect in all parts, both outwardly and inwardly, his reason was vncorrupt, his vnderstanding was pure and good, his will was obedient and godly, he was made altogether like vnto GOD, in righteousnesse, in holinesse, in wisedome, in trueth, to bee short in all kinde of perfection.

When he was thus created and made, Almighty GOD, in token of his great loue towards him, chose out a speciall place of the earth for him, namely Paradise, where he liued in all tranquility and pleasure, hauing great abundance of worldly goodes, and lacking nothing that he might iustly require or desire to haue. For as it is sayde, GOD made him Lord and ruler ouer all the workes of his handes, that he should haue vnder his feete all sheepe and oxen, all beastes of the fielde, all soules of the ayre, all fishes of the sea (Psalms 8.6-8), and vse them alwayes at his owne pleasure, according as he should haue neede. Was not this a mirrour of perfection? Was not this a full perfect and blessed estate? Could any thing else bee well added hereunto, or greater felicity desired in this world? But as the common nature of all men is, in time of prosperity and wealth, to forget not onely themselues, but also GOD: Euen so did this first man Adam, who hauing but one commandement at GODS hand, namely that hee should not eate of the fruite of knowledge of good and ill, did notwithstanding, most vnmindefully, or rather most wilfully breake it, in forgetting the straite charge of his maker, and giuing eare to the craftie suggestion of that wicked serpent the deuill. Whereby it came to passe, that as before he was blessed, so now he was accursed, as before hee was loued, so now hee was abhorred, as before hee was most beautifull and pretious, so now hee was most vile and wretched in the sight of his Lord and maker. In stead of the Image of GOD, he was now become the Image of the deuill. In steade of the citizen of heauen, he was become the bond-slaue of hell, hauing in himselfe no one part of his former purity and cleannesse, but being altogether spotted and defiled, insomuch that now hee seemed to bee nothing else but a lumpe of sinne, and therefore by the iust iudgement of GOD, was condemned to euerlasting death. This so great and miserable a plague, if it had onely rested on Adam, who first offended, it had beene so much the easier, and might the better haue beene borne. But it fell not onely on him, but also on his posterity and children for euer, so that the whole broode of Adams flesh should sustaine the selfe same fall and punishment, which their forefather by his offence most iustly had deserued. Saint Paul in the fifth Chapter to the Romanes sayth, By the offence of onely Adam, the fault came vpon all men to condemnation, and by one mans disobedience many were made sinners. By which wordes wee are taught, that as in Adam all men vniuersally sinned: so in Adam all men vniuersally receiued the reward of sinne, that is to say, became mortall, and subiect vnto death, hauing in themselues nothing but euerlasting damnation both of body and soule. They became (as Dauid sayth) corrupt and abominable, they went all out of the way, there was none that did good, no not one. O what a miserable and wofull state was this, that the sinne of one man should destroy and condemne all men, that nothing in all the world might bee looked for, but onely panges of death, and paines of hell? Had it beene any maruaile if mankinde had beene vtterly driuen to desparation, being thus fallen from life to death, from saluation to destruction, from heauen to hell? But behold the great goodnesse and tender mercy of GOD in his behalfe: albeit mans wickednesse and sinfull behauiour was such, that it deserued not in any part to be forgiuen, yet to the intent he might not bee cleane destitute of all hope and comfort in time to come, hee ordained a new Couenant, and made a sure promise thereof, namely, that hee would send a Messias or Mediatour into the world, which should make intercession, and put himselfe as a stay betweene both parties, to pacifie the wrath and indignation conceiued against sinne, and to deliuer man out of the miserable curse and cursed misery, whereinto he was fallen headlong by disobeying the will and commandement of the onely Lord and maker. This couenant and promise was first made vnto Adam himselfe immediatly after his fall, as wee reade in the 3. of Genesis, where GOD said to the serpent on this wise: I will put enmity betweene thee and the woman, betweene thy seed and her seede. He shall breake thine head, and thou shalt bruise his heele.

Afterward, the selfe same couenant was also more amply and plainely renewed vnto Abraham, where GOD promised him, that in his seede all Nations and families of the earth should be blessed (Genesis 12.3, 22.18). Againe, it was continued and confirmed vnto Isahac, in the same fourme of wordes, as it was before vnto his father (Genesis 26.4). And to the intent that mankinde might not despayre, but alwayes liue in hope, Almighty GOD neuer ceased to publish, repeate, confirme, and continue the same, by diuers and sundry testimonies of his Prophets, who for the better perswasion of the thing, prophesied the time, the place, the manner and circumstance of his birth, the affliction of his life, the kinde of his death, the glory of his resurrection, the receiuing of his kingdome, the deliuerance of his people, with all other circumstances belonging thereunto. Esaias prophesied that he should be borne of a virgine, and called Emanuel. Micheas prophesied that he should bee borne in Bethlehem, a place of Iurie. Ezechiel prophesied that he should come of the stocke and linage of Dauid. Daniel prophesied that all Nations and languages should serue him. Zacharie prophesied that hee should come in pouertie, riding vpon an Asse. Malachie prophesied that hee should send Elias before him, which was Iohn the Baptist. Ieremie prophesied that he should bee solde for thirtie pieces of siluer &c. And all this was done, that the promise and couenant of GOD, made vnto Abraham and his posteritie concerning the redemption of the worlde, might bee credited and fully beleeued. Now as the Apostle Paul saith, when the fulnesse of time was come, that is, the perfection and course of yeeres, appoynted from the beginning, then GOD according to his former couenant and promise, sent a Messias, otherwise called a Mediatour, vnto the world, not such a one as Moses was, not such a one as Iosua, Saul, or Dauid was:

but such a one as should deliuer mankinde from the bitter curse of the Law, and make perfect satisfaction by his death, for the sinnes of all people, namely he sent his deare and onely Sonne Iesus Christ, borne (as the Apostle saith) of a woman, and made vnder the Law, that he might redeeme them that were in bondage of the law, and make them the children of GOD by adoption. Was not this a wonderfull great loue towards vs that were his professed and open enemies, towards vs that were by nature the children of wrath, and firebrands of hell fire? In this (saith Saint Iohn) appeared the great loue of GOD, that he sent his onely begotten Sonne into the world to saue vs, when we were his extreme enemies. Herein is loue, not that we loued him, but that he loued vs, and sent his Sonne to be a reconciliation for our sinnes. S. Paul also saith, Christ, when we were yet of no strength, dyed for vs being vngodly. Doubtlesse a man wil scarse dye for a righteous man. Peraduenture some one durst dye for him of whom they haue receiued good But GOD setteth out his loue towards vs, in that he sent Christ to die for vs, when we were yet void of all goodnesse (Rom 5.6-8). This and such other comparisons doeth the Apostle vse, to amplifie and set forth the tender mercy and great goodnesse of GOD, declared towards mankinde, in sending downe a Sauiour from heauen, euen Christ the Lord. Which one benefite among all other is so great and wonderfull, that neither tongue can well expresse it, neither heart thinke it, much lesse giue sufficient thanks to GOD for it. But here is a great controuersie betweene vs and the Iewes, whether the same Iesus which was borne of the virgine Mary, be the true Messias, and true Sauiour of the world, so long promised and prophesied of before. They, as they are, and haue bene alwayes proud and stiffe necked, would neuer acknowledge him vntill this day, but haue looked and waited for another to come. They haue this fond imagination in their heads, that & the; Messias shall come, not as Christ did, like a poore pilgrime & meeke soule riding vpon an Asse: but like a valiant and mighty King in great royalty and honour. Not as Christ did, with a few fishermen, and men of small estimation in the world: but with a great army of strong men, with a great traine of wise & noble men, as Knights, Lords, Earles, Dukes, Princes and so forth. Neither doe they thinke that their Messias shall slanderously suffer death, as Christ did: but that he shal stoutly conquer and manfully subdue all his enemies, and finally obteine such a kingdome on earth, as neuer was seene from the beginning. While they faine vnto themselues after this sorte a Messias of their owne brayne, they deceiue themselues, and account Christ as an abiect and scorne of the world. Therefore Christ crucified (as S. Paul saith) is vnto the Iewes a stumbling blocke, and to the Gentiles foolishnes, because they thinke it an absurd thing, and contrary to all reason, that a redeemer and Sauiour of the whole world, should be handled after such a sort as he was, namely scorned, reuiled, scourged, condemned, and last of all cruelly hanged. This, I say, seemed in their eyes strange, and most absurd, and therefore neither they would at that time, neither will they as yet, acknowledge Christ to be their Messias and Sauiour. But we (dearely beloued) that hope and looke to be saued, must both stedfastly beleeue, and also boldly confesse, that the same Iesus, which was borne of the virgin Mary, was the true Messias and Mediatiour betweene GOD and man, promised & prophesied of so long before. For as the Apostle writeth: With the heart man beleeueth vnto righteousnesse, and with the mouth confession is made vnto saluation. Againe in the same place: Whosoeuer beleeueth in him, shall neuer be ashamed nor confounded (Rom.10.10-11). Whereto agreeeth also the testimony of S. Iohn, written in the fourth Chapter of his first generall Epistle, on this wise: Whosoeuer confesseth that Iesus is the Sonne of GOD, he dwelleth in GOD, and GOD in him.

There is no doubt, but in this poynt all Christian men are fully and perfectly perswaded. Yet shall it not be a lost labour to instruct and furnish you with a few places concerning this matter, that ye may be able to stoppe the blasphemous mouthes of all them, that most Iewishly, or rather deuilishly, shall at any time goe about to teach or maintaine the contrary. First, ye haue the witnesse and testimony of the Angel Gabriel, declared aswell to Zacharie the high Priest, as also to the blessed virgin. Secondly, ye haue the witnesse and testimony of Iohn the Baptist, poynting vnto Christ, and saying, Behold the Lambe of GOD that taketh away the sinnes of the world. Thirdly, ye haue the witnesse and testimonie of GOD the Father, who thundred from heauen, and said, This is my dearely beloued Sonne, in whom I am well pleased, heare him. Fourthly, yee haue the witnesse and testimony of the holy Ghost, which came downe from heauen in manner of a doue, and lighted vpon him in time of his Baptisme. To these might bee added a great number more, namely the witnesse and testimony of the wise men that came to Herod, the witnesse and testimony of Simeon and Anna, the witnesse and testimonie of Andrew and Philip, Nathanael, and Peter, Nicodemus, and Martha, with diuers other: But it were too long to repeate all, and a few places are sufficient in so plaine a matter, specially among them that are already perswaded. Therefore if the priuy impes of Antichrist, and craftie instruments of the deuill, shall attempt or goe about to withdraw you from this true Messias, and perswade you to looke for another that is not yet come: let them not in any case seduce you, but confirme your selues with these and such other testimonies of holy Scripture, which are so sure and certaine, that all the deuils in hell shall neuer be able to withstand them. For as truely as GOD liueth, so truely was Iesus Christ the true Messias and Sauiour of the world, euen the same Iesus which as this day was borne of the Virgine Mary, without all helpe of man, only by the power and operation of the holy Ghost.

Concerning whose nature and substance, because diuers and sundry heresies are risen in these our dayes, through the motion and suggestion of Satan: therefore it shall bee needefull and profitable for your instruction, to speake a word or two also of this part. We are euidently taught in the Scripture, that our Lord and Sauiour Christ consisteth of two seuerall natures, of his manhood, being thereby perfect man, and of his Godhead, being thereby perfect GOD. It is written, The word, that is to say, the second Person in Trinity, became flesh (John 1.14). GOD sending his owne Sonne in the similitude of sinfull flesh, fulfilled those things which the law could not (Romans 8.3-4). Christ being in forme of GOD, tooke on him the forme of a seruant, and was made like vnto man, being found in shape as a man (Philippians 2.6-8). GOD was shewed in flesh, iustified in spirit, seene of Angels, preached to the Gentiles, beleeued on in the world, and receiued vp in glory (1 Timothy 3.16). Also in another place: There is one GOD, and one mediatour betweene GOD and man, euen the man Iesus Christ. These be plaine places for the proofe and declaration of both natures, vnited and knitte together, in one Christ. Let vs diligently consider and waigh the workes that hee did whiles he liued on earth, and wee shall thereby also perceiue the selfe same thing to bee most true. In that hee did hunger and thirst, eate and drinke, sleepe and wake, in that hee preached his Gospel to the people, in that he wept and sorrowed for Ierusalem, in that he payed tribute for himselfe and Peter, in that hee died and suffered death, what other thing did he else declare, but only this, that he was perfect man as wee are? For which cause hee is called in holy Scripture, sometime the sonne of Dauid, sometime the sonne of man, sometime the sonne of Mary, sometime the sonne of Ioseph, and so foorth. Now in that hee forgaue sinnes, in that hee wrought miracles, in that he did cast out deuils, in that he healed men with his onely word, in that hee knew the thoughts of mens heartes, in that hee had the Seas at his commandement, in that hee walked on the water, in that hee rose from death to life, in that he ascended into heauen, and so forth: What other thing did he shew therin, but onely that hee was perfect GOD, coequall with the Father as touching his deitie? Therefore hee sayth, The Father and I are all one, which is to bee vnderstood of his Godhead. For as touching his manhood, he sayth, The Father is greater then I am. Where are now those Marcionites, that denie Christ to haue beene borne in the flesh, or to haue bin perfect man? Where are now those Arians, which deny Christ to haue beene perfect GOD, of equall substance with the Father? If there bee any such, we may easily reprooue them with these testimonies of GODS word, and such other. Whereunto, I am most sure, they shall neuer bee able to answere. For the necessity of our saluation did require such a mediatour & Sauiour, as vnder one person should be a partaker of both natures: It was requisite he should be man, it was also requisit he should be GOD. For as the transgression came by man, so was it meete the satisfaction should bee made by man. And because death, according to S. Paul, is the iust stipende and reward of sinne, therefore to appease the wrath of GOD, and to satisfie his Iustice, it was expedient that our Mediatour should be such a one, as might take vpon him the sins of mankinde and sustaine the due punishment thereof, namely death. Moreouer, hee came in flesh, and in the selfe same flesh ascended into heauen, to declare and testifie vnto vs, that all faithfull people which stedfastly beleeue in him, shall likewise come vnto the same mansion place, whereunto he being our chiefe captaine, is gone before. Last of all, he became man, that wee thereby might receiue the greater comfort, aswell in our prayers, as also in our aduersity, considering with our selues, that we haue a Mediatour that is true man as we are, who also is touched with our infirmities and was tempted euen in like sort as we are. For these and sundry other causes, it was most needfull he should come, as he did, in the flesh.

But because no creature, in that he is onely a creature, hath or may haue power to destroy death, and giue life, to ouercome hell, and purchase heauen, to remit sins, and giue righteousnesse: therefore it was needfull, that our Messias, whose proper duety and office that was, should bee not onely full and perfect man, but also full and perfect GOD, to the intent he might more fully and perfectly make satisfaction for mankinde. GOD sayth, This is my welbeloued Sonne in whom I am well pleased (Matthew 3.17). By which place we learne, that Christ appeased and quenched the wrath of his Father, not in that he was onely the sonne of man: But much more in that he was the Sonne of GOD.

Thus ye haue heard declared out of the Scriptures, that Iesus Christ was the true Messias & Sauiour of the world, that he was by nature & substance perfect GOD, & perfect man, & for what cause it was expedient he should be so. Now that wee may bee the more mindfull and thankefull vnto GOD in this behalfe, let vs briefly consider, and call to minde, the manifold and great benefits that wee haue receiued by the Natiuitie and birth of this our Messias and Sauiour.

Before Christes comming into the worlde, all men vniuersally in Adam, were nothing else but a wicked and crooked generation, rotten and corrupt trees, stony ground, full of brambles and bryers, lost sheepe, prodigall sonnes, naughty vnprofitable seruantes, vnrighteous stewardes, workers of iniquity, the broode of Adders, blinde guides, sitting in darkenesse and in the shadow of death: to bee short nothing else but children of perdition, and inheritours of hell fire. To this doeth Saint Paul beare witnesse in diuers places of his Epistle, and Christ also himselfe in sundry places of his Gospel. But after hee was once come downe from heauen, and had taken our frayle nature vpon him, he made all them that would receiue him truely, and beleeue his word, good trees, and good ground, fruitfull and pleasant branches, children of light, citizens of heauen, sheepe of his folde, members of his body, heyres of his Kingdome, his true friendes and brethren, sweet and liuely bread, the elect and chosen people of GOD. For as S. Peter sayeth in his first Epistle and second Chapter: Hee bare our sinnes in his body vpon the Crosse, hee healed vs, and made vs whole by his stripes: and whereas before we were sheepe going astray, he by his comming brought vs home againe to the true Shepheard and Bishop of our soules, making vs a chosen generation, a royall Priesthood, an holy Nation, a particular people of GOD, in that he died for our offences, and rose for our iustification. Saint Paul to Timothie the third Chapter: Wee were (sayth he) in times past, vnwise, disobedient, deceiued, seruing diuers lustes and pleasures, liuing in hatred, enuie, malitiousnesse, and so foorth.

But after the louing kindnesse of GOD our Sauiour appeared towardes mankinde, not according to the righteousnesse that we had done, but according to his great mercy, hee saued vs by the fountaine of the newe birth, and by the renewing of the holy Ghost, which he powred vpon vs abundantly, through Iesus Christ our Sauiour, that wee being once iustified by his grace, should bee heires of eternall life, through hope and faith in his blood.

In these and such other places, is set out before our eyes, as it were in a glasse, the abundant grace of GOD (Matthew 1.21, Matthew 5.17, John 18.37, Luke 4.18-19, John 8.12, Matthew 9.13, Matthew 11.28, John 12.31, Colossians 1.21-22, Hebrews 10, Romans 3.25), receiued in Christ Iesu, which is so much the more wonderfull, because it came not of any desert of ours, but of his meere and tender mercy, euen then when wee were his extreme enemies: But for the better vnderstanding and consideration of this thing, let vs behold the end of his comming, so shall wee perceiue what great commodity and profit his Natiuity hath brought vnto vs miserable and sinfull creatures. The end of his comming, was to saue and deliuer his people, to fulfill the Law for vs, to beare witnesse vnto the trueth, to teach and preach the wordes of his Father, to giue light vnto the world, to call sinners to repentance, to refresh them that labour and bee heauie laden, to cast out the prince of this world, to reconcile vs in the body of his flesh, to dissolue the workes of the deuill, last of all, to become a propitiation for our sinnes, and not for ours onely, but also for the sinnes of the whole world.

These were the chiefe ends wherefore Christ became man, not for any profit that should come to himselfe thereby, but onely for our sakes, that we might vnderstand the will of GOD, be pertakers of his heauenly light, be deliuered out of the deuils clawes: released from the burden of sinne, iustified through faith in his blood, and finally, receiued vp into euerlasting glory, there to raigne with him for euer. Was not this a great and singular loue of Christ towards mankind, that being the expresse and liuely image of GOD, he would notwithstanding humble himselfe, and take vpon him the forme of a seruant, and that onely to saue and redeeme vs? O how much are wee bound to the goodnesse of GOD in this behalfe? how many thankes and praises doe wee owe vnto him for this our saluation wrought by his deare and onely Sonne Christ? who became a pilgrime in earth to make vs citizens in heauen, who became the sonne of man, to make vs the sonnes of GOD, who became obedient to the Law, to deliuer vs from the curse of the Law, who became poore, to make vs rich; vile, to make vs pretious; subiect to death, to make vs liue for euer. What greater loue could we seely creatures desire or wish to haue at GODS hands?

Therefore dearely beloued, let vs not forget this exceeding loue of our Lord and Sauiour, let vs not shew our selues vnmindfull or vnthankfull toward him: but let vs loue him, feare him, obey him, and serue him. Let vs confesse him with our mouthes, prayse him with our tongues, beleeue on him with our hearts, and glorifie him with our good workes. Christ is the light, let vs receiue the light. Christ is the trueth, let vs beleeue the trueth. Christ is the way, let vs follow the way. And because he is our onely master, our onely teacher, our onely shepheard and chiefe captaine: therefore let vs become his seruants, his schollers, his sheepe, and his souldiers. As for sinne, the flesh, the world, and the Diuel, whose seruants and bondslaues, we were before Christs comming, let vs vtterly cast them off, and defie them, as the chiefe and onely enemies of our soule. And seeing wee are once deliuered from their cruell tyranny by Christ, let vs neuer fall into their hands againe, lest we chance to be in a worse case then euer we were before. Happy are they, sayth the Scripture, that continue to the end. Be faythfull (sayth GOD) vntill death, and I will giue thee a crowne of life. Againe he sayth in another place, He that putteth his hand vnto the plough, and looketh backe, is not meet for the kingdome of GOD. Therefore let vs be strong, stedfast, and vnmooueable, abounding alwayes in the workes of the Lord. Let vs receiue Christ, not for a time, but for euer, let vs beleeue his word, not for a time, but for euer, let vs become his seruants, not for a time, but for euer, in consideration that he hath redeemed and saued vs, not for a time, but for euer, and will receiue vs into his heauenly kingdome, there to raigne with him, not for a time, but for euer. To him therefore with the Father and the holy Ghost, be all honour, prayse, and glory, for euer and euer, Amen.

HOMILY ON THE PASSION FOR GOOD FRIDAY

AN HOMILIE FOR
good Friday, concerning the death and passion
of our Sauiour Iesus Christ.

IT should not become vs (welbeloued in Christ) being that people which he redeemed from the Diuell, from sin and death, and from euerlasting damnation, by Christ, to suffer this time to passe foorth without any meditation, and remembrance of that excellent worke of our redemption, wrought as about this time, through the great mercy and charity of our Sauiour Iesus Christ, for vs wretched sinners, and his mortall enemies. For if a mortall mans deed, done to the behoofe of the common wealth, bee had in remembrance of vs, with thankes for the benefit and profit which we receiue thereby: how much more readily should wee haue in memory this excellent act and benefite of Christs death? whereby hee hath purchased for vs the vndoubted pardon and forgiuenesse of our sinnes, whereby hee made at one the Father of heauen with vs, in such wise, that he taketh vs now for his louing children, and for the true inheritours, with Christ his naturall sonne, of the kingdome of heauen? And verily so much more doeth Christs kindnesse appeare vnto vs, in that it pleased him to deliuer himselfe of all his goodly honour, which hee was equally in with his Father in heauen, and to come downe into this vale of misery, to bee made mortall man, and to be in the state of a most low seruant, seruing vs for our wealth and profit, vs, I say, which were his sworne enemies, which had renounced his holy Law and Commandements, and followed the lustes and sinfull pleasures of our corrupt nature. And yet, I say, did Christ put himselfe betweene GODS deserued wrath, and our sinne, and rent that obligation wherein we were in danger to GOD, and payd our debt (Colossians 2.14). Our debt was a great deale too great for vs to haue payd. And without payment, GOD the Father could neuer bee at one with vs. Neither was it possible to bee losed from this debt by our owne ability. It pleased him therefore to be the payer thereof, and to discharge vs quite.

Who can now consider the grieuous debt of sinne, which could none otherwise be payd but by the death of an innocent, and will not hate sinne in his heart? If GOD hateth sinne so much, that hee would allow neither man nor Angel for the redemption thereof, but onely the death of his onely and welbeloued Sonne: who will not stand in feare thereof? If we (my friends) consider this, that for our sinnes this most innocent Lambe was driuen to death, we shall haue much more cause to bewaile our selues that we were the cause of his death, then to cry out of the malice and cruelty of the Iewes, which pursued him to his death. We did the deedes wherefore he was thus stricken and wounded, they were onely the ministers of our wickednesse. It is meete then wee should steppe low downe into our hearts, and bewaile our owne wretchednesse and sinfull liuing. Let vs know for a certaintie, that if the most dearely beloued Sonne of GOD was thus punished and stricken for the sinne which he had not done himselfe: how much more ought wee sore to be stricken for our dayly and manifold sinnes which wee commit against GOD, if wee earnestly repent vs not, and be not sorie for them? No man can loue sinne, which GOD hateth so much, and be in his fauour. No man can say that hee loueth Christ truely, and haue his great enemie (sinne I meane, the authour of his death) familiar and in friendship with him. So much doe we loue GOD and Christ, as we hate sinne. Wee ought therefore to take great heede, that we be not fauourers thereof, lest we be found enemies to GOD, and traytours to Christ. For not onely they which nayled Christ vpon the crosse, are his tormentours and crucifiers: but all they (sayth Saint Paul) crucifie againe the Sonne of GOD (Hebrews 6.6), as much as is in them, who doe commit vice and sinne, which brought him to his death. If the wages of sinne be death, and death euerlasting (Romans 6.23): surely it is no small danger to be in seruice thereof. If we liue after the flesh, and after the sinfull lustes thereof, Saint Paul threatneth, yea Almighty GOD in Saint Paul threatneth, that we shall surely die (Romans 8.13). We can none otherwise liue to GOD, but by dying to sinne. If Christ be in vs, then is sinne dead in vs: and if the spirit of GOD bee in vs, which raysed Christ from death to life, so shall the same spirit raise vs to the resurrection of euerlasting life (Romans 8.10-11). But if sinne rule and reigne in vs, then is GOD, which is the fountaine of all grace and vertue, departed from vs: then hath the Deuill, and his vngracious spirite, rule and dominion in vs (Romans 1). And surely if in such miserable state wee die, we shall not rise to life, but fall downe to death and damnation, and that without ende.

Christ hath not redeemed vs from sinne, that we should liue in sinne. For Christ hath not so redeemed vs from sinne, that wee may safely returne thereto againe: but hee hath redeemed vs, that wee should forsake the motions thereof, and liue to righteousnesse. Yea, wee bee therefore washed in our Baptisme from the filthinesse of sinne, that we should liue afterward in the purenesse of life. In Baptisme we promised to renounce the deuill and his suggestions, we promised to bee (as obedient children) alwayes following GODS will and pleasure. Then if he be our Father indeede, let vs giue him his due honour. If we be his children, let vs shew him our obedience, like as Christ openly declared his obedience to his Father, which (as Saint Paul writeth) was obedient euen to the very death, the death of the Crosse (Philippians 2.8). And this he did for vs all that beleeue in him. For himselfe he was not pun ished, for he was pure, and vndefiled of all maner of sinne. He was wounded (sayth Esay) for our wickednesse, and stripped for our sinnes (Isaiah 53.4): he suffered the penalty of them himselfe, to deliuer vs from danger: he bare (sayth Esay) all our sores and infirmities vpon his owne backe. No paine did he refuse to suffer in his owne body, that he might deliuer vs from paine euerlasting. His pleasure it was thus to doe for vs, we deserued it not. Wherefore the more we see our selues bound vnto him, the more he ought to be thanked of vs, yea, and the more hope may we take, that we shall receiue all other good things of his hand, in that we haue receiued the gift of his onely Sonne, through his liberality. For if GOD (sayth Saint Paul) hath not spared his owne Sonne from paine and punishment, but deliuered him for vs all vnto the death: how should he not giue vs all other things with him (Romans 8.32)? If we want any thing, either for body or soule, we may lawfully and boldly approch to GOD, as to our mercifull Father, to aske that we desire, and we shall obteine it. For such power is giuen to vs, to be the children of GOD, so many as beleeue in Christes Name (John 1.12). In his Name whatsoeuer wee aske, wee shall haue it granted vs (Matthew 21.22). For so well pleased is the Father almighty GOD, with Christ his Sonne, that for his sake he fauoureth vs, and will denie vs nothing. So pleasant was this sacrifice and oblation of his Sonnes death, which hee so obediently and innocently suffered, that wee should take it for the onely and full amendes for all the sinnes of the world. And such fauour did he purchase by his death, of his heauenly Father for vs, that for the merite thereof (if we be true Christians indeede, and not in word onely) we be now fully in GODS grace againe, and clearely discharged from our sinne. No tongue surely is able to expresse the worthinesse of this so precious a death. For in this standeth the continuall pardon of our dayly offences, in this resteth our iustification, in this we be allowed, in this is purchased the euerlasting health of all our soules. Yea, there is none other thing that can be named vnder heauen to saue our soules, but this onely worke of Christs precious offering of his body vpon the altar of the crosse (Acts 4.12). Certes there can be no worke of any mortall man (bee hee neuer so holy) that shall bee coupled in merites with Christes most holy act. For no doubt, all our thoughts and deedes were of no value, if they were not allowed in the merites of Christs death. All our righteousnesse is farre vnperfect, if it be compared with Christs righteousnesse. For in his acts and deedes, there was no spot of sinne, or of any vnperfectnesse.

Our deedes be full of imperfection. And for this cause they were the more able to bee the true amends of our righteousnesse, where our acts and deedes be full of imperfection, and infirmities, and therefore nothing worthy of themselues to stirre GOD to any fauour, much lesse to challenge that glory that is due to Christs act and merit. For not to vs (saith Dauid) not to vs, but to thy Name giue the glory, O Lord (Psalms 115.1). Let vs therefore (good friends) with all reuerence glorifie his Name, let vs magnifie and prayse him for euer. For he hath dealt with vs according to his great mercy, by himselfe hath he purchased our redemption (Hebrews 1.3). Hee thought it not ynough to spare himselfe, and to send his Angel to doe this deede, but he would doe it himselfe, that hee might doe it the better, and make it the more perfect redemption. He was nothing moued with the intolerable paines that he suffered in the whole course of his long passion, to repent him thus to doe good to his enemies: but he opened his hart for vs, and bestowed himselfe wholly for the ransomming of vs. Let vs therefore now open our heartes againe to him, and studie in our liues to bee thankefull to such a Lord, and euermore to bee mindfull of so great a benefice, yea let vs take vp our crosse with Christ, and follow him. His passion is not onely the ransome and whole amendes for our sinne, but it is also a most perfect example of all patience and sufferance. For if it behoued Christ thus to suffer, and to enter into the glory of his Father (Acts 17.3): why should it not become vs to beare patiently our small crosses of aduersitie, and the troubles of this world? For surely (as saith S. Peter) Christ therefore suffered, to leaue vs an example to follow his steps (1 Peter 2.21). And if wee suffer with him, wee shall be sure also to raigne with him in heauen (2 Timothy 2.12). Not that the sufferance of this transitorie life should bee worthie of that glorie to come (Romans 8.18), but gladly should wee be contented to suffer, to bee like Christ in our life, that so by our workes we may glorifie our Father which is in heauen (Matthew 5.16). And as it is painefull and grieuous to beare the Crosse of Christ in the griefes and displeasures of this life: so it bringeth foorth the ioyfull fruit of hope, in all them that bee exercised therewith (Hebrews 12.11). Let vs not so much behold the paine, as the reward that shall follow that labour (James 5.11). Nay, let vs rather endeuour our selues in our sufferance, to endure innocently and guiltles, as our Sauiour Christ did. For if we suffer for our deseruings, then hath not patience his perfect worke in vs: but if vndeseruedly we suffer losse of goods and life, if we suffer to be euill spoken of for the loue of Christ, this is thankefull afore GOD, for so did Christ suffer (1 Peter 2.20).

The patience of Christ. Hee neuer did sinne, neither was any guile found in his mouth. Yea when hee was reuiled with taunts, hee reuiled not againe. When hee was wrongfully dealt with, he threatned not againe, nor reuenged his quarrell, but deliuered his cause to him that iudgeth rightly.

Perfect patience. Perfect patience careth not what nor how much it suffereth, nor of whom it suffereth, whether of friend or foe: but studieth to suffer innocently, and without deseruing.

The meeknesse of Christ. Yea, he in whom perfect charity is, careth so little to reuenge, that he rather studieth to doe good for euill, to blesse and say well of them that curse him, to pray for them that pursue him (Matthew 5.44), according to the example of our Sauiour Christ, who is the most perfect example & paterne of all meeknes and sufferance, which hanging vpon his Crosse, in most feruent anguish bleeding in euery part of his blessed Body, being set in the middest of his enemies and crucifiers: and hee, notwithstanding the intolerable paines which they sawe him in, being of them mocked and scorned dispitefully without all fauour and compassion, had yet towards them such compassion in heart, that hee prayed to his Father of heauen for them, and sayd, O Father, forgiue them, for they wote not what they doe (Luke 23.34). What patience was it also which he shewed, when one of his owne Apostles and Seruants which was put in trust of him, came to betray him vnto his enemies to the death? Hee sayde nothing worse to him, but, Friend, wherefore art thou come (Matthew 26.50)? Thus (good people) should we call to minde the great examples of charitie which Christ shewed in his passion, if wee will fruitfully remember his passion. Such charity and loue should wee beare one to an other, if wee will be the true seruants of Christ. For if we loue but them, which loue and say well by vs, what great thing is it that we doe saith Christ? Doe not the Panims and open sinners so (Matthew 5.46-47)? Wee must bee more perfect in our charitie then thus, euen as our Father in heauen is perfect, which maketh the light of his Sunne to rise vpon the good and the bad, and sendeth his raine vpon the kinde and vnkinde. After this maner should we shew our charity indifferently, aswell to one as to another aswell to friend, as foe, like obedient children, after the example of our Father in heauen. For if Christ was obedient to his Father euen to the death, and that the most shamefull death (as the Iewes esteemed it) the death of the Crosse: Why should wee not bee obedient to GOD in lower poyntes of charitie and patience? Let vs forgiue then our neighbors their small faultes, as GOD for Christes sake hath forgiuen vs our great (Sirach 28.2).

It is not meete that wee should craue forgiuenesse of our great offences at GODS handes, and yet will not forgiue the small trespasses of our neighbours against vs. We doe call for mercy in vaine, if wee will not shew mercy to our neighbours (Matthew 18.35). For if we will not put wrath and displeasure foorth of our hearts to our Christian brother, no more will GOD forgiue the displeasure and wrath that our sinnes haue deserued afore him. For vnder this condition doeth GOD forgiue vs, if we forgiue other. It becommeth not Christian men to bee hard one to another, nor yet to thinke their neighbour vnworthy to bee forgiuen. For howsoeuer vnworthie he is, yet is Christ worthie to haue thee doe thus much for his sack, hee hath deserued it of thee, that thou shouldest forgiue thy neighbour. And GOD is also to bee obeyed, which commandeth vs to forgiue, if wee will haue any part of the pardon which our Sauiour Christ purchased once of GOD the Father, by shedding of his precious blood. Nothing becommeth Christes seruantes so much, as mercie and compassion. Let vs then bee fauourable one to another, and pray we one for another, that wee may bee healed from all frailties of our life (James 5.16), the lesse to offend one the other, and that wee may bee of one minde and one spirit, agreeing together in brotherly loue and concord, euen like the deare children of GOD (Ephesians 5.1-2). By these meanes shall wee mooue GOD to bee mercifull vnto our sinnes, yea, & we shall be hereby the more ready to receiue our Sauiour and maker in his blessed Sacrament, to our euerlasting comfort, and health of soule. Christ delighteth to enter and dwell in that soule where loue and charitie ruleth, and where peace & concord is seene. For thus writeth S. Iohn, GOD is charity, hee that abideth in charitie, abideth in GOD, and GOD in him (1 John 4.16). And by this (saith he) we shall know that we be of GOD, if we loue our brethren. Yea, & by this shall we know, that we bee deliuered from death to life, if we loue one another. But hee which hateth his brother (sayth the same Apostle) abideth in death, euen in the danger of euerlasting death, and is moreouer the childe of damnation and of the Diuel, cursed of GOD, and hated (so long as he so remayneth) of GOD and all his heauenly company (1 John 2.11). For as peace and charity make vs the blessed children of Almighty GOD: so doth hatred and enuie make vs the cursed children of the Diuel. GOD giue vs all grace to follow Christs examples in peace and in charity, in patience and sufferance, that wee now may haue him our ghest to enter and dwell within vs, so as we may be in full surety, hauing such a pledge of our saluation. If we haue him and his fauour, we may be sure that we haue the fauour of GOD by his means. For he sitteth on the right hand of GOD his Father, as our proctour and atturney, pleading and suing for vs in all our needes and necessities (Romans 8.34). Wherefore, if wee want any gift of godly wisedome, wee may aske it of GOD for Christs sake, and we shall haue it. Let vs consider and examine our selues, in what want we be concerning this vertue of charity and patience. If we see that our hearts bee nothing inclined thereunto, in forgiuing them that haue offended against vs, then let vs knowledge our want, and wish to GOD to haue it. But if we want it, and see in our selues no desire thereunto, verily wee bee in a dangerous case before GOD, and haue neede to make much earnest prayer to GOD, that we may haue such an heart changed, to the grafting in of a new. For vnlesse we forgiue other, we shall neuer be forgiuen of GOD. No, not all the prayers and good workes of other, can pacifie GOD vnto vs, vnlesse we be at peace, and at one with our neighbour. Nor all our deedes and good workes can mooue GOD to forgiue vs our debts to him, except wee forgiue to other. He setteth more by mercy, then by sacrifice. Mercy moued our Sauiour Christ to suffer for his enemies: it becommeth vs then to follow his example. For it shall little auayle vs to haue in meditation the fruites and price of his passion, to magnifie them, and to delight or trust in them, except we haue in minde his examples in passion to follow them. If we thus therefore consider Christs death, and will sticke thereto with fast fayth for the merit and deseruing thereof, and will also frame our selues in such wise to bestow our selues, and all that we haue by charity, to the behoofe of our neighbour, as Christ spent himselfe wholly for our profit, then doe we truely remember Christs death: and being thus followers of Christs steps, we shall be sure to follow him thither where he sitteth now with the Father and the holy Ghost, to whom bee all honour and glory, Amen.

THE SECOND HOMILIE CONCERNING THE DEATH AND PASSION OF OUR SAUIOUR CHRIST.

THAT wee may the better conceiue the great mercy and goodnesse of our Sauiour Christ, in suffering death vniuersally for all men, it behoueth vs to descend into the bottome of our conscience, and deepely to consider the first and principall cause wherefore he was compelled so to doe. When our great grandfather Adam had broken GODS commandement, in eating the apple forbidden him in Paradise, at the motion and suggestion of his wife, he purchased thereby, not only to himselfe, but also to his posterity for euer, the iust wrath and indignation of GOD, who according to his former sentence pronounced at the giuing of the commandement, condemned both him and all his to euerlasting death, both of body and soule (Genesis 3.17). For it was sayd vnto him, Thou shalt eat freely of euery tree in the Garden: but as touching the tree of knowledge of good and ill, thou shalt in no wise eat of it: For in what houre soeuer thou eatest thereof, thou shalt die the death (Genesis 2.16-17). Now as the Lord had spoken, so it came to passe. Adam tooke vpon him to eat thereof, and in so doing he died the death, that is to say, he became mortall, he lost the fauour of GOD, hee was cast out of Paradise, he was no longer a citizen of heauen: but a firebrand of hell, and a bondslaue to the Diuell. To this doth our Sauiour beare witnesse in the Gospel, calling vs lost sheepe, which haue gone astray, and wandered from the true shepheard of our soules (Luke 15.4-7). To this also doth Saint Paul beare witnesse, saying, That by the offence of onely Adam, death came vpon all men to condemnation (Romans 5.18). So that now neither hee, or any of his, had any right or interest at all in the kingdome of heauen, but were become plaine reprobates and castawayes, being perpetually damned to the euerlasting paynes of hell fire. In this so great misery and wretchednesse, if mankinde could haue recouered himselfe againe, and obtayned forgiuenesse at GODS handes, then had his case beene somewhat tolerable, because hee might haue attempted some way how to deliuer himselfe from eternall death. But there was no way left vnto him, hee could doe nothing that might pacifie GODS wrath, he was altogether vnprofitable in that behalfe. There was not one that did good, no not one. And how then could he worke his owne saluation? Should he goe about to pacifie GODS heauy displeasure by offering vp burnt sacrifices, according as it was ordained in the olde Lawe? by offering vp the blood of oxen, the blood of calues, the blood of goats, the blood of lambes, and so foorth (Hebrews 9.12-13)? O these things were of no force nor strength to take away sinnes, they could not put away the anger of GOD, they coulde not coole the heate of his wrath, nor yet bring mankind into fauour againe, they were but onely figures and shadowes of things to come, and nothing else. Read the Epistle to the Hebrewes, there shall you finde this matter largely discussed, there shall you learne in most plaine wordes, that the bloodie sacrifice of the olde Law was vnperfect, and not able to deliuer man from the state of damnation by any meanes (Hebrews 10.3-4, 8): so that mankinde in trusting thereunto, should trust to a broken staffe, and in the end deceiue himselfe. What should he then doe? Should he goe about to serue and keepe the Law of GOD diuided into two tables, and so purchase to himselfe eternall life? In deede, if Adam and his posterity had beene able to satisfie and fulfill the Law perfectly, in louing GOD aboue all things and their neighbour as themselues: then should they haue easily quenched the Lordes wrath, and escaped the terrible sentence of eternall death pronounced against them by the mouth of Almighty GOD. For it is written, Doe thus, and thou shalt liue; that is to say, fulfill my commandements, keepe thy selfe vpright and perfect in them according to my will, then shalt thou liue, and not die. Here is eternall life promised with this condition, and so that they keepe and obserue the Law (Luke 10.28). But such was the frailty of mankind after his fall, such was his weakenesse & imbecility, that hee could not walke vprightly in GODS commandements though he would neuer so faine, but dayly & hourely fell from his bounden duety, offending the Lord his GOD diuers wayes, to the great increase of his condemnation, insomuch that the Prophet Dauid crieth out on this wise: All haue gone astray, all are become vnprofitable, there is none that doeth good, no not one (Psalms 14.3). In this case what profit could hee haue by the Law? None at all. For as S. Iames saith, Hee that shall obserue the whole Law, and yet fayleth in one poynt, is become guiltie of all (James 2.10). And in the booke of Deuteronomy it is written, Cursed bee hee (saith GOD) which abideth not in all things that are written in the booke of the Law, to doe them (Deuteronomy 27.26).

Behold, the Law bringeth a curse with it, and maketh it guiltie, not because it is of it selfe naught or vnholy, (GOD forbid wee should so thinke) but because the frailty of our sinfull flesh is such, that wee canne neuer fulfill it, according to the perfection that the Lord requireth. Coulde Adam then (thinke you) hope or trust to bee saued by the Law? No hee could not. But the more hee looked on the Law, the more hee sawe his owne damnation set before his eyes, as it were in a cleare glasse. So that now of himselfe hee was most wretched and miserable, destitute of all hope, and neuer able to pacifie GODS heauie displeasure, nor yet to escape the terrible iudgement of GOD, whereunto hee and all his posteritie were fallen, by disobeying the strait commandement of the Lord their GOD. But O the abundant riches of GODS great mercie. O the vnspeakeable goodnesse of his heauenly wisedome (Romans 11.33). When all hope of righteousnesse was past on our part, when wee had nothing in our selues, whereby wee might quench his burning wrath, and worke the saluation of our owne soules, and rise out of the miserable estate wherein we lay: Then, euen then did Christ the Sonne of GOD, by the appoyntment of his Father, come downe from heauen, to bee wounded for our sakes, to bee reputed with the wicked, to be condemned vnto death, to take vpon him the reward of our sinnes, and to giue his Body to bee broken on the Crosse for our offences. Hee (sayth the Prophet Esay, meaning Christ) hath borne our infirmities, and hath caried our sorrowes, the chastisement of our peace was vpon him, and by his stripes we were made whole (Isaiah 53.4-5). Saint Paul likewise saith, GOD made him a sacrifice for our sinnes, which knew not sinne, that wee should bee made the righteousnesse of GOD by him (2 Corinthians 5.21). And Saint Peter most agreeably writing in this behalfe, saith, Christ hath once died and suffered for our sinnes, the iust for the vniust. &c. To these might bee added an infinite number of other places to the same effect: but these fewe shall bee sufficient for this time.

Now then (as it was sayd at the beginning) let vs ponder and weigh the cause of his death, that thereby we may bee the more mooued to glorifie him in our whole life. Which if you will haue comprehended briefly in one word, it was nothing else on our part, but onely the transgression and sinne of mankinde. When the Angel came to warne Ioseph, that hee should not feare to take Marie to his wife:

Did hee not therefore will the childes name to bee called Iesus, because hee should saue his people from their sinnes? When Iohn the Baptist preached Christ , and shewed him to the people with his finger: Did hee not plainely say vnto them, Beholde the Lambe of GOD which taketh away the sinnes of the worlde (John 1.29)? when the Woman of Canaan besought Christ to helpe her daughter which was possest with a Deuill: did hee not openly confesse that hee was sent to saue the lost sheepe of the house of Israel, by giuing his life for their sinnes (Matthew 15.22, 24)? It was sinne then, O man, euen thy sinne that caused Christ the onely Sonne of GOD to bee crucified in the flesh, and to suffer the most vile and slaunderous death of the Crosse. If thou haddest kept thy selfe vpright, if thou haddest obserued the commandements, if thou haddest not presumed to transgresse the will of GOD in thy first father Adam: then Christ , being in forme of GOD, needed not to haue taken vpon him the shape of a seruant (Romans 5.19): being immortall in heauen, he needed not to become mortall on earth: being the true bread of the soule, hee needed not to hunger: being the healthfull water of life hee needed not to thirst: being life it selfe, he needed not to haue suffered death. But to these and many other such extremities, was hee driuen by thy sinne, which was so manifolde and great, that GOD could bee onely pleased in him, and none other. Canst thou thinke of this O sinfull man, and not tremble within thy selfe? Canst thou heare it quietly without remorse of conscience, and sorrow of heart? Did Christ suffer his passion for thee, and wilt thou shew no compassion towards him? While Christ was yet hanging on the Crosse, and yeelding vp the Ghost, the Scripture witnesseth that the vayle of the Temple did rent in twaine and the earth did quake, that the stones claue asunder, that the graues did open, and the dead bodies rise (Matthew 27.51-52). And shall the heart of man be nothing mooued to remember how grieuously and cruelly he was handled of the Iewes for our sinnes? Shall man shew himselfe to bee more hard harted then stones, to haue lesse compassion then dead bodies? Call to mind, O sinfull creature, and set before thine eyes Christ crucified. Thinke thou seest his Body stretched out in length vpon the Crosse, his head crowned with sharpe thornes, and his handes and his feete pearced with nayles, his heart opened with a long speare, his flesh rent and torne with whippes, his browes sweating water and blood. Thinke thou hearest him now crying in an intolerable agony to his Father and saying, My GOD, my GOD, why hast thou forsaken mee? Couldest thou beholde this wofull sight, or heare this mournefull voyce, without teares, considering that hee suffered all this, not for any desert of his owne, but onely for the grieuousnesse of thy sinnes? O that mankinde should put the euerlasting Sonne of GOD to such paines. O that wee should bee the occasion of his death, and the onely cause of his condemnation. May wee not iustly cry, woe worth the time that euer wee sinned? O my brethren, let this Image of Christ crucified, bee alwayes printed in our heartes, let it stirre vs vp to the hatred of sinne, and prouoke our mindes to the earnest loue of Almighty GOD. For why? Is not sinne, thinke you, a greeuous thing in his sight, seeing for the transgressing of GODS precept in eating of one apple, he condemned all the world to perpetuall death, & would not be pacified, but only with the blood of his owne Sonne? True, yea most true is that saying of Dauid: Thou, O Lord, hatest all them that worke iniquitie, neither shall the wicked and euill man dwell with thee (Psalms 5.4). By the mouth of his holy Prophet Esay, he cryed mainely out against sinners, & saith: Wo be vnto you that draw iniquity with cords of vanity, & sin as it were with cartropes (Isaiah 5.18).

Did not he giue a plaine token how greatly he hated and abhorred sin, when he drowned all the world saue only eight persons (Genesis 7.23), when he destroy Sodome and Gomorrhe with fire and brimstone (Genesis 19.24), when in three dayes space hee killed with pestilence threescore and tenne thousand for Dauids offence (2 Sam. 24.15), when hee drowned Pharao and all his hoste in the red sea (Exodus 14.28), when hee turned Nabuchodonosor the king into the forme of a bruit beast, creeping vpon all foure (Daniel 4.33), when he suffered Achitophel and Iudas to hang themselues vpon the remorse of sinne, which was so terrible to their eyes (2 Sam. 17.23, Acts 1.18)? A thousand such examples are to bee found in Scripture, if a man would stand to seeke them out. But what neede we? This one example which wee haue now in hande, is of more force, and ought more to mooue vs, then all the rest. Christ being the Sonne of GOD, and perfect GOD himselfe, who neuer comitted sinne, was compelled to come downe from heauen, to giue his body to bee bruised and broken on the crosse for ouer sinnes. Was not this a manifest token of GODS great wrath and displeasure towards sinne, that he could be pacified by no other meanes, but onely by the sweete and precious blood of his deare Sonne? O sinne, sinne, that euer thou shouldest driue Christ to such extremity! Woe worth the time that euer thou camest into the world. But what booteth it now to bewaile? Sinne is come, and so come that it cannot be auoyded. There is no man liuing, no not the iustest man on the earth, but he falleth seuen times a day, as Salomon sayth (Proverbs 24.16). And our Sauiour Christ, although he hath deliuered vs from sinne: yet not so that we shalbe free from committing sinne: But so that it shall not be imputed to our condemnation. He hath taken vpon him the iust reward of sinne, which was death, and by death hath ouerthrowen death, that wee beleeuing in him, might liue for euer and not dye (Romans 6.9, 23). Ought not this to engender extreme hatred of sinne in vs, to consider that it did violently, as it were, plucke GOD out of heauen, to make him feele the horrours and paines of death? O that we would sometimes consider this in the middest of our pompes and pleasures, it would bridle the outragiousnesse of the flesh, it would abate and asswage our carnall affections, it would restraine our fleshly appetites, that wee should not run at random as wee commonly doe. To commit sinne wilfully and desperately without feare of GOD, is nothing els but to crucifie Christ anew, as we are expresly taught in the Epistle to the Hebrewes (Hebrews 6.6). Which thing if it were deepely printed in all mens hearts, then should not sinne reigne euery where so much as it doth, to the great griefe and torment of Christ now sitting in heauen.

Let vs therefore remember, and alwayes beare in minde Christ crucified, that thereby wee may bee inwardly mooued both to abhorre sinne throughly, and also with an earnest and zealous heart to loue GOD. For this is another fruit which the memoriall of Christes death ought to worke in vs, an earnest and vnfained loue towardes GOD. So GOD loued the world (sayth Saint Iohn) that hee gaue his onely begotten Sonne, that whosoeuer beleeueth in him, should not perish, but haue life euerlasting (John 3.16). If GOD declared so great loue towards vs his seely creatures: how can wee of right but loue him againe? Was not this a sure pledge of his loue, to giue vs his owne Sonne from heauen? Hee might haue giuen vs an Angel if he would, or some other creature, and yet should his loue haue beene farre aboue our deserts. Now hee gaue vs not an Angel, but his Sonne. And what Sonne? His onely Sonne, his naturall Sonne, his welbeloued Sonne, euen that Sonne whom he had made Lord and ruler of all things. Was not this a singular token of great loue? But to whom did he giue him? Hee gaue him to the whole world, that is to say, to Adam, and all that should come after him. O Lord, what had Adam, or any other man deserued at GODS handes, that he should giue vs his owne Sonne? Wee are all miserable persons, sinfull persons, damnable persons, iustly driuen out of Paradise, iustly excluded from heauen, iustly condemned to hell fire: And yet (see a wonderful token of GODS loue) he gaue vs his only begotten Sonne, vs I say, that were his extreme and deadly enemies, that we by vertue of his blood shedde vpon the Crosse, might be cleane purged from our sinnes, and made righteous againe in his sight. Who can chuse but maruell, to heare that GOD should shew such vnspeakable loue towardes vs, that were his deadly enemies? Indeede, O mortall man, thou oughtest of right to maruell at it, and to acknowledge therein GODS great goodnesse and mercy towards mankinde, which is so wonderfull, that no flesh, bee it neuer so worldly wise, may well conceiue it, or expresse it. For as Saint Paul testifieth, GOD greatly commendeth and setteth out his loue towards vs, in that he sent his Sonne Christ to die for vs, when we were yet sinners, and open enemies of his Name (Romans 5.8). If we had in any manner of wise deserued it at his handes, then had it beene no maruell at all, but there was no desert on our part wherefore hee should doe it. Therefore thou sinnefull creature, when thou hearest that GOD gaue his Sonne to die for the sinnes of the world, thinke not he did it for any desert or goodnesse that was in thee, for thou wast then the bondslaue of the Deuill: But fall downe vpon thy knees, and cry with the Prophet Dauid, O Lord, what is man, that thou art so mindefull of him? or the sonne of man, that thou so regardest him (Psalms 8.4)? And seeing he hath so greatly loued thee, endeuour thy selfe to loue him againe, with all thy heart, with all thy soule, and with all thy strength, that therein thou mayest appeare not to be vnworthy of his loue. I report me to thine owne conscience, whether thou wouldest not thinke thy loue ill bestowed vpon him, that could not finde in his heart to loue thee againe? If this be true, (as it is most true) then thinke how greatly it behoueth thee in duetie to loue GOD, which hath so greatly loued thee, that he hath not spared his owne onely Sonne from so cruell and shamefull a death for thy sake. And hitherto concerning the cause of Christs death and passion, which as it was on our part most horrible and grieuous sinne, so on the other side it was the free gift of GOD, proceeding of his meere and tender loue towards mankinde, without any merite or desert of our part. The Lord for his mercies sake graunt that we neuer forget this great benefite of our saluation in Christ Iesu, but that wee alwayes shew our selues thankefull for it, abhorring all kinde of wickednesse and sinne, and applying our mindes wholy to the seruice of GOD, and the diligent keeping of his commandements.

Now it remayneth that I shew vnto you, how to apply Christs death and passion to our comfort, as a medicine to our woundes, so that it may worke the same effect in vs wherefore it was giuen, namely, the health and saluation of our soules. For as it profiteth a man nothing to haue salue, vnlesse it be wel applyed to the part infected: So the death of Christ shall stand vs in nor force, vnlesse wee apply it to our selues in such sort as GOD hath appoynted. Almighty GOD commonly worketh by meanes, and in this thing he hath also ordained a certaine meane, whereby we may take fruit and profite to our soules health.

What meane is that? forsooth it is faith. Not an vnconstant or wauering faith: but a sure, stedfast, grounded, and vnfained faith. GOD sent his sonne into the world (sayth Saint Iohn) To what end? That whosoeuer beleeueth in him should not perish, but haue life euerlasting. Marke these words: that whosoeuer beleeueth in him (John 3.16). Heere is the mean whereby we must apply the fruites of Christs death vnto our deadly wound. Heere is the meane whereby we must obtaine eternall life, namely fayth. For (as Saint Paul teacheth in his Epistle to the Romanes) With the heart man beleeueth vnto righteousnesse, and with the mouth confession is made vnto saluation (Romans 10.10). Paul being demanded of the keeper of the prison, what he should doe to be saued? made this answer: Beleeue in the Lord Iesus , so shalt thou and thine house both be saued (Acts 16.30-31). After the Euangelist had described and set foorth vnto vs at large, the life and the death of the Lord Iesus, in the end he concludeth with these words: These things are written, that we may beleeue Iesus Christ to be the sonne of GOD, and through fayth obtayne eternall life (John 20.31). To conclude with the wordes of Saint Paul, which are these: Christ is the end of the Law vnto saluation, for euery one that doeth beleeue (Romans 10.4). By this then, you may well perceiue, that the onely meane and instrument of saluation required of our parts, is fayth, that is to say, a sure trust and confidence in the mercies of GOD: whereby we perswade our selues, that GOD, both hath, and will forgiue our sinnes, that he hath accepted vs againe into his fauour, that he hath released vs from the bonds of damnation, and receiued vs againe into the number of his elect people, not for our merits or deserts, but onely and solely for the merits of Christs death and passion, who became man for our sakes, and humbled himselfe to sustaine the reproach of the Crosse, that we thereby might be saued, and made inheritours of the kingdome of heauen. This fayth is required at our hands. And this if we keepe stedfastly at our hearts, there is no doubt, but we shall obtayne saluation at GODS hands, as did Abraham, Isaac, and Iacob, of whom the Scripture sayth, that they beleeued, and it was imputed vnto them for righteousnesse (Genesis 15.6, Romans 4.3). Was it imputed vnto them onely? and shall it not bee imputed vnto vs also? Yes, if wee haue the same fayth as they had, it shall be as truely imputed vnto vs for righteousnes, as it was vnto them. For it is one fayth that must saue both vs and them, euen a sure and stedfast fayth in Christ Iesus, who as ye haue heard, came into the world for this end, that whosoeuer beleeue in him, should not perish, but haue life euerlasting (John 3.15). But heere wee must take heed, that wee doe not halt with GOD through an vnconstant and wauering fayth, but that it bee strong and stedfast to our liues end. Hee that wauereth (sayth Saint Iames) is like a waue of the sea, neither let that man thinke that he shall obtayne any thing at GODS hands (James 1.6-7). Peter comming to Christ vpon the water, because he fainted in fayth, was in danger of drowning. So we, if we beginne to wauer or doubt, it is to be feared lest wee shall sinke as Peter did (Matthew 14.29-30), not into the water, but into the bottomlesse pit of hell fire. Therefore I say vnto you, that we must apprehend the merits of Christes death and passion by fayth, and that with a strong and stedfast fayth, nothing doubting, but that Christ by his owne oblation, and once offering of himselfe vpon the Crosse, hath taken away our sinnes, and hath restored vs againe into GODS fauour, so fully and perfectly, that no other sacrifice for sinne, shall heereafter be requisite or needfull in all the world.

Thus haue you heard in few words, the meane whereby wee must apply the fruites and merits of Christs death vnto vs, so that it may worke the saluation of our soules, namely a sure, stedfast, perfect, and grounded fayth. For as all they which beheld stedfastly the brasen serpent, were healed and deliuered at the very sight thereof, from their corporall diseases, and bodily stings (Numbers 21.9): euen so all they which behold Christ crucified with a true and liuely fayth (John 3.14-15), shall vndoubtedly be deliuered from the grieuous wound of the soule, be they neuer so deadly or many in number. Therefore (dearely beloued) if we chance at any time through frailty of the flesh, to fall into sinne (as it cannot be chosen, but wee must needes fall often) and if we feele the heauy burden thereof to presse our soules, tormenting vs with the feare of death, hell, and damnation, let vs then vse that mean which GOD hath appoynted in his word, to wit, the meane of fayth, which is the onely instrument of saluation now left vnto vs. Let vs stedfastly behold Christ crucified, with the eyes of our heart Let vs only trust to be saued by his death and passion, and to haue our sinnes cleane washed away through his most pretious bloud, that in the end of the world, when he shall come againe to iudge both the quicke and the dead, he may receiue vs into his heauenly kingdome, and place vs in the number of his elect and chosen people, there to be partakers of that immortall and euerlasting life, which he hath purchased vnto vs by vertue of his bloudy woundes: To him therefore, with the Father, and the holy Ghost, be all honour and glory, world without end, Amen.

HOMILY ON THE RESURRECTION FOR EASTER DAY

AN HOMILIE OF THE
Resurrection of our Sauiour Iesus
Christ.
For Easter Day.

IF euer at any time the greatnesse or excellency of any matter spirituall or temporall hath stirred vp your mindes to giue diligent care (good Christian people, and welbeloued in our Lord and Sauiour Iesus Christ) I doubt not but that I shall haue you now at this present season most diligent and ready hearers, of the matter which I haue at this time to open vnto you. For I come to declare that great and most comfortable Article of our Christian Religion and fayth, the Resurrection of our Lord Iesus. So great surely is the matter of this Article, and of so great wayght and importance, that it was thought worthy to keepe our sayd Sauiour still on earth forty dayes after hee was risen from death to life, to the confirmation and establishment thereof in the hearts of his Disciples. So that (as Luke clearely testifieth in the first Chapter Actes of the Apostles) he was conuersant with his Disciples by the space of forty dayes continually together, to the intent he would in his person, being now glorified, teach and instruct them, which should bee the teachers of other, fully and in most absolute and perfect wise, the trueth of this most Christian Article, which is the ground and foundation of our whole Religion, before he would ascend vp to his father into the heauens, there to receiue the glory of his most triumphant conquest and victory. Assuredly, so highly comfortable is this Article to our consciences, that it is euen the very locke and key of all our Christian Religion and fayth. If it were not true (sayth the holy Apostle Paul) that Christ rose againe: then our preaching were in vaine, your fayth which you haue receiued were but voyd, ye were yet in the danger of your sinnes. If Christ be not risen againe (sayth the Apostle) then are they in very euill case, and vtterly perished, that be entred their sleepe in Christ, then are wee the most miserable of all men, which haue our hope fixed in Christ, if he be yet vnder the power of death, and as yet not restored to his blisse againe. But now hee is risen againe from death (sayth the Apostle Paul) to be the first fruites of them that be asleepe, to the intent to rayse them to euerlasting life again (1 Corinthians 15.14-20): Yea if it were not true that Christ is risen againe, then were it neither true that he is ascended vp to heauen, nor that hee sent downe from heauen vnto vs the holy Ghost, nor that hee sitteth on the right hand of his heauenly Father, hauing the rule of heauen and earth, raigning (as the Prophet sayth) from sea to sea (Psalms 72.8), nor that he should after this world, be the Iudge aswell of the liuing as of the dead, to giue reward to the good, and iudgement to the euill. That these linkes therefore of our fayth should all hang together in stedfast establishment and confirmation, it pleased our Sauiour not straightway to withdraw himselfe from the bodily presence and sight of his Disciples, but he chose out forty dayes, wherein he would declare vnto them, by manifold and most strong arguments and tokens, that he had conquered death, and that he was also truly risen again to life. He began (sayth Luke) at Moses & all the Prophets, and expounded vnto them the Prophesies that were written in all the Scriptures of him (Luke 24.27), to the intent to confirme the trueth of his resurrection, long before spoken of: which he verified indeed, as it is declared very apparantly and manifestly, by his oft appearance to sundry persons at sundry times. First, he sent his Angels to the Sepulchre, who did shew vnto certaine women the empty graue, sauing that the buriall linnen remayned therein (Matthew 28.5-6). And by these signes were these women fully instructed, that hee was risen againe, and so did they testifie it openly. After this, Iesus himselfe appeared to Mary Magdalene (John 20.16), and after that to certaine other women, & straight afterward he appeared to Peter, then to the two Disciples, which were going to Emaus (Luke 24.13-15). He appeared to the Disciples also, as they were gathered together, for feare of the Iewes, the doore shut. At another time hee was seene at the sea of Tiberias of Peter and Thomas, and of other Disciples, when they were fishing (John 21.1, 4). Hee was seene of more th en fiue hundred brethren in the mount of Galile, where Iesus appoynted them to bee by his Angel, when he sayd, Behold, he shall go before you into Galile, there shall ye see him as he hath sayd vnto you. After this hee appeared vnto Iames, and last of all he was visiblie seene of all the Apostles, at such time as he was taken vp into heauen (1 Corinthians 15.6-7, Acts 1.9). Thus at sundry times he shewed himselfe after he was risen againe, to confirme and stablish this Article. And in these reuelations sometime he shewed them his hands, his feet, and his side, and bade them touch him, that they should not take him for a ghost or a spirit. Sometime he also did eat with them, but euer hee was talking with them of the euerlasting kingdome of GOD, to assure the trueth of his resurrection. For then he opened their vnderstanding, that they might perceiue the Scriptures, and sayd vnto them: Thus it is written, and thus it behooued Christ to suffer, and to rise from death the third day, and that there should be preached openly in his name pardon and remission of sinnes to all the Nations of the world (Luke 24.45-47). Yee see (good Christian people) how necessary this Article of our faith is, seeing it was prooued of Christ himselfe by such euident reasons and tokens, by so long time and space. Now therefore as our Sauiour was diligent for our comfort and instruction to declare it: so let vs be as ready in our beliefe to receiue it to our comfort and instruction. As he died not for himselfe, no more did he rise againe for himselfe. He was dead (sayth Saint Paul) for our sinnes, and rose againe for our iustification (1 Corinthians 15.3-4). O most comfortable word, euermore to be borne in remembrance. He died (saith he) to put away sinne, hee rose againe to endow vs with righteousnesse. His death tooke away sinne and malediction, his death was the ransome of them both, his death destroyed death, and ouercame the deuill, which had the power of death in his subiection, his death destroyed hell, with all the damnation thereof. Thus is death swallowed vp by Christs victory, thus is hell spoyled for euer. If any man doubt of this victory, let Christs glorious resurrection declare him the thing. If death could not keepe Christ vnder his dominion and power, but that he arose againe, it is manifest that his power was ouercome. If death bee conquered, then must it follow that sinne, wherefore death was appoynted as the wages, must bee also destroyed. If death and sinne be vanished away, then is the deuils tyranny vanished, which had the power of death, and was the author and brewer of sinne, and the ruler of hell. If Christ had the victory of them all by the power of his death, and openly prooued it by his most victorious and valiant resurrection (as it was not possible for his great might to bee subdued of them) and it is true, that Christ dyed for our sinnes, and rose againe for our iustification: Why may not wee, that bee his members by true faith, reioyce and boldly say with the

Prophet Osee, and the Apostle Paul, Where is thy dart, O death? Where is thy victory, O hell? Thankes be vnto GOD, say they, which hath giuen vs the victory by our Lord Christ Iesus.

This mighty conquest of his resurrection, was not onely signified before by diuers figures of the olde Testament, as by Sampson when hee slew the Lion, out of whose mouth came sweetenesse and hony, and as Dauid bare his figure when hee deliuered the lambe out of the Lyons mouth, and when he ouercame and slew the great Gyant Goliah (1 Samuel 17.35, 49), and as when Ionas was swallowed vp in the Whales mouth, and cast vp againe on land aliue (Jonas 1.17): but was also most clearely prophesied by the Prophets of the old Testament, and in the new also confirmed by the Apostles. He hath spoyled, saith Saint Paul, rule and power, and all the dominion of our spirituall enemies. Hee hath made a shew of them openly, and hath triumphed ouer them in his owne person (Colossians 2.15). This is the mighty power of the Lord, whom we beleeue on. By his death, hath hee wrought for vs this victory, and by his resurrection, hath hee purchased euerlasting life and righteousnes for vs. It had not beene enough to bee deliuered by his death from sinne, except by his resurrection wee had beene endowed with righteousnesse. And it should not auaile vs to be deliuered from death, except he had risen againe, to open for vs the gates of heauen, to enter into life euerlasting. And therefore Saint Peter thanketh GOD the Father of our Lord Iesus Christ for his aboundant mercy, because hee hath begotten vs (sayth hee) vnto a liuely hope by the resurrection of Iesus Christ from death, to enioy an inheritance immortall, that neuer shall perish, which is layd vp in heauen for them that bee kept by the power of GOD through faith (1 Peter 1:3-5). Thus hath his resurrection wrought for vs life and righteousnes. He passed through death & hell, to the intent to put vs in good hope, that by his strength we shall doe the same. He payd the ransome of sinne, that it should not be laid to our charge. He destroyed the deuill and all his tyranny, and openly triumphed ouer him, and tooke away from him all his captiues, and hath raised and set them with himselfe among the heauenly Citizens aboue (Ephesians 2.6). He dyed, to destroy the rule of the deuill in vs: and he rose againe, to send downe his holy Spirit to rule in our hearts, to endow vs with perfect righteousnesse. Thus it is true that Dauid sung, *Veritas de terra orta est, & iustitia de caelo prospexit (*Psalms 85.11*)*. The trueth of GODS promise is in earth to man declared, or from the earth is the euerlasting veritie GODS Sonne risen to life, and the true righteousnesse of the holy Ghost looking out of heauen, and in most liberall larges dealt vpon all the world (*Captiuam duxit captiuitatem.*, Ephesians 4.8). Thus is glory and prayse rebounded vpwards to GOD aboue, for his mercy & trueth. And thus is peace come downe from heauen to men of good and faithfull hearts (Luke 2.14). Thus is mercy and trueth as Dauid writeth, together mette, thus is peace and righteousnesse imbracing and kissing ech other (*Misericordia & veritas obuiauerunt sibi.*, Psalms 85.10). If thou doubtest of so great wealth and felicity that is wrought for thee, O man, call to thy minde that therefore hast thou receiued into thine owne possession the euerlasting veritie our Sauiour Iesus Christ, to confirme to thy conscience the trueth of all this matter. Thou hast receiued him, if in true faith and repentance of heart thou hast receiued him: If in purpose of amendment, thou hast receiued him for an euerlasting gage or pledge of thy saluation. Thou hast receiued his body which was once broken, and his blood which was shedde for the remission of thy sinne. Thou hast receiued his body, to haue within thee the Father, the Sonne, and the holy Ghost, for to dwell with thee, to endow thee with grace, to strength thee against thine enemies, and to comfort thee with their presence. Thou hast receiued his body to endow thee with euerlasting righteousnesse, to assure thee of euerlasting blisse, and life of thy soule. For with Christ by true faith art thou quickened againe (saith Saint Paul, Ephesians 2.1-2) from death of sinne, to life of grace, and in hope translated from corporall and euerlasting death, to the euerlasting life of glory in heauen, where now thy conuersation should bee, and thy heart and desire set. Doubt not of the trueth of this matter, how great and high soeuer these things be. It becommeth GOD to doe no small deedes, how impossible soeuer they seeme to thee (Luke 18.27). Pray to GOD that thou mayest haue faith to perceiue this great mysterie of Christs resurrection: that by faith thou mayest certainely beleeue nothing to bee impossible with GOD. Onely bring thou faith to Christs holy word and Sacrament. Let thy repentance shew thy faith, let thy purpose of amendment & obedience of thy heart to GODS law, hereafter declare thy true beleefe. Endeuour thy selfe to say with Saint Paul, From hencefoorth our conuersation is in heauen, from whence wee looke for a Sauiour, euen the Lord Iesus Christ, which shall change our vile bodies, that they may be fashioned like his glorious body, which hee shall doe by the same power whereby he rose from death, and whereby he shall bee able to subdue all things vnto himselfe (Philippians 3.20-21). Thus (good Christian people) forasmuch as yee haue heard these so great and excellent benefites of Christes mighty and glorious resurrection, as how that hee hath ransomed sinne, ouercome the diuell, death, and hell, and hath victoriously gotten the better hand of them all, to make vs free and safe from them, and knowing that we bee by this benefite of his resurrection risen with him by our faith, vnto life euerlasting, being in full surety of our hope, that wee shall haue our bodies likewise raised againe from death, to haue them glorified in immortalitie, and ioyned to his glorious body, hauing in the meane while this holy spirit within our heartes as a seale and pledge of our euerlasting inheritance. By whose assistance we be replenished with all righteousnesse, by whose power we shall bee able to subdue all our euill affections, rising against the pleasure of GOD. These things, I say, well considered, let vs now in the rest of our life declare our faith that we haue in this most fruitfull article, by framing our selues thereunto, in rising dayly from sinne, to righteousnesse and holinesse of life. For what shall it auaile vs (saith Saint Peter) to bee escaped and deliuered from the filthinesse of the world, through the knowledge of the Lord and Sauiour Iesus Christ, if wee be intangled againe therewith, and bee ouercome againe? Certainely it had beene better (saith hee) neuer to haue knowne the way of righteousnesse, then after it is knowne and receiued, to turne backe againe from the holy Commandement of GOD giuen vnto vs. For so shall the prouerbe haue place in vs, where it is said: The dogge is returned to his vomit againe, and the Sowe that was washed, to her wallowing in the mire againe (2 Peter 2.20-22). What a shame were it for vs, being thus so clearely and freely washed from our sinne, to returne to the filthinesse thereof againe? What a follie were it, thus endowed with righteousnesse, to loose it againe? What madnesse were it to loose the inheritance that wee bee now set in, for the vile and transitorie pleasure of sinne? And what an vnkindnesse should it bee, where our Sauiour Christ of his mercie is come to vs, to dwell with vs as our ghest, to driue him from vs, and to banish him violently out of our soules, and in stead of him in whom is all grace and vertue, to receiue the vngracious spirit of the diuell, the founder of all naughtinesse and mischiefe. How can wee finde in our heartes to shew such extreme vnkindnesse to Christ, which hath now entred within vs? yea, how dare wee be so bold to renounce the presence of the Father, the Sonne and the holy Ghost? (For where one is, there is GOD all whole in Maiestie, together with all his power, wisedome, and goodnesse) and feare not I say the danger and perill of so traiterous a defiance and departure? Good Christian brethren and sisters, aduise your selues, consider the dignity that yee bee now set in, let no folly loose the thing that grace hath so preciously offered and purchased, let not wilfulnesse and blindnesse put out so great light that is now shewed vnto you. Onely take good heartes vnto you, and put vpon you all the armour of GOD, that yee may stand against your enemies, which would againe subdue you, and bring you into their thraldome (Ephesians 6.11). Remember ye bee bought from your vaine conuersation, and that your freedome is purchased neither with gold nor siluer, but with the price of the precious Blood of that innocent Lambe Iesus Christ, which was ordained to the same purpose before the world was made. But hee was so declared in the latter time of grace, for your sakes which by him haue your faith in GOD, who hath raised him from death, and hath giuen him glory, that you should haue your faith and hope towards GOD (1 Peter 1.18-20). Therefore as you haue hitherto followed the vaine lustes of your mindes, and so displeased GOD, to the danger of our soules: So now, like obedient children thus purified by faith, giue your selues to walke that way which GOD mooueth you to, that ye may receiue the end of your faith, the saluation of your soules (1 Peter 1.9). And as yee haue giuen your bodies to vnrighteousnesse, to sinne after sinne: so now giue your selues to righteousnesse, to bee sanctified therein (Romans 6.19). If yee delight in this Article of our faith, that Christ is risen againe from the death to life: then follow you the example of his resurrection, as Saint Paul exhorteth vs, saying: As we be buried with Christ by our Baptisme into death, so let vs dayly die to sinne, mortifying and killing the euill desires and motions thereof (Romans 6.4). And as Christ was raysed vp from death by the glory of the Father, so let vs rise to a new life, and walke continually therein, that wee may likewise as naturall children liue a conuersation to mooue men to glorifie our Father which is in heauen (Matthew 5.16). If wee then be risen with Christ by our faith to the hope of euerlasting life: let vs rise also with Christ, after his example, to a new life, & leaue our olde. We shall then be truely risen, if we seeke for things that be heauenly, if we haue our affection on things that be aboue, and not on things that bee on the earth. If yee desire to know what these earthly things bee which yee should put off, and what bee the heauenly thinges aboue, that yee should seeke and ensue, Saint Paul in the Epistle to the Colossians declareth, when he exhorteth vs thus. Mortifie your earthly members and old affection of sinne, as fornication, vncleannesse, vnnaturall lust, euill concupiscence, and couetousnes, which is worshipping of idolles, for the which thinges, the wrath of GOD is wont to fall on the children of vnbeliefe, in which things once yee walked, when yee liued in them (Colossians 3.1-2, 5-9). But now put yee also away from you, wrath fiercenesse, maliciousnesse, cursed speaking, filthy speaking, out of your mouthes. Lye not one to another, that the olde man with his workes be put off, and the new bee put on. These bee the earthly thinges which Saint Paul mooued you to cast from you, and to plucke your heartes from them. For in following these, yee declare your selues earthly and worldly. These bee the fruites of the earthly Adam. These should you dayly kill, by good diligence, in withstanding the desires of them, that yee might rise to righteousnesse. Let your affection from hencefoorth bee set on heauenly things, sue and search for mercie, kindenesse, meekenesse, patience, forbearing one another, and forgiuing one another. If any man haue a quarell to another, as Christ forgaue you, euen so doe yee. If these and such other heauenly vertues ye ensue in the residue of your life, ye shal shew plainely that yee bee risen with Christ, and that ye bee the heauenly children of your Father in heauen, from whom, as from the giuer, commeth these graces and giftes (James 1.17). Yee shall prooue by this maner, that your conuersation is in heauen, where your hope is: and not on earth, following the beastly appetites of the flesh (Philippians 3.20). Yee must consider that yee be therefore cleansed and renued, that ye should from hencefoorth serue GOD in holinesse and righteousnesse all the dayes of your liues, that yee may raigne with them in euerlasting life (Luke 1.74-75). If ye refuse so great grace, whereto ye bee called, what other thing doe ye, then heape to you damnation more and more, and so prouoke GOD to cast his displeasure vnto you, and to reuenge this mockage of his holy Sacraments in so great abusing of them? Apply your selues (good friendes) to liue in Christ, that Christ may still liue in you, whose fauour and assistance if ye haue, then haue yee euerlasting life already within you, then can nothing hurt you (John 5.24). Whatsoeuer is hitherto done and committed, Christ yee see hath offered you pardon, and clearely receiued you to his fauour againe, in full suretie whereof, yee haue him now inhabiting and dwelling within you. Onely shew your selues thankeful in your liues, determine with your selues to refuse and auoyde all such thinges in your conuersations as should offend his eyes of mercy (Colossians 3.5). Endeuour your selues that way to rise vp againe, which way ye fell into the well or pitte of sinne. If by your tongue you haue offended, now thereby rise againe, and glorifie GOD therewith, accustome it to laude and prayse the Name of GOD, as ye haue therewith dishonoured it.

Restitution. And as yee haue hurt the name of your neighbour, or otherwise hindered him, so now intend to restore it to him againe. For without restitution, GOD accepteth not your confession, nor yet your repentance. It is not enough to forsake euill, except you set your courage to doe good. By what occasion soeuer you haue offended, turne now the occasion to the honouring of GOD, and profite of your neighbour. Trueth it is that sinne is strong, and affections vnruly. Hard it is to subdue and resist our nature, so corrupt and leauened with the sower bitternesse of the poyson which we receiued by the inheritance of our old father Adam (Psalms 36.1). But yet take good courage, saith our Sauiour Christ, for I haue ouercome the world, and all other enemies for you (John 16.33). Sinne shall not haue power ouer you, for yee bee now vnder grace, saith Saint Paul. Though your power bee weake, yet Christ is risen againe to strengthen you in your battaile, his holy Spirit shall helpe your infirmities (Romans 6.9, Romans 8.26). In trust of his mercy, take you in hand to purge this olde leauen of sinne, that corrupteth and sowreth the sweetenesse of our life before GOD, that yee may bee as newe and fresh dow, voyde of all sower leauen of wickednesse, so shall yee shew your selues to bee sweete bread to GOD, that hee may haue his delight in you (1 Corinthians 5.7). I say kill & offer you vp the worldly and earthly affections of your bodies. For Christ our Easter Lambe is offered vp for vs, to slay the power of sinne, to deliuer vs from the danger thereof, and to giue vs example to die to sinne in our liues. As the Iewes did eate their Easter Lambe, and keepe their feast in remembrance of their deliuerance out of Egypt: Euen so let vs keepe our Easter feast in the thankefull remembrance of Christes benefites, which he hath plentifully wrought for vs by his resurrection and passing to his Father, whereby we are deliuered from the captiuity and thraldome of all our enemies. Let vs in like maner passe ouer the affections of our olde conuersation, that we may be deliuered from the bondage thereof, and rise with Christ. The Iewes kept their feast in abstaining from leauened bread, by the space of seuen dayes (Exodus 12.15). Let vs Christian folke keepe our holy day in spirituall maner, that is, in absteining, not from materiall leauened bread, but from the olde leauen of sinne, the leauen of malitiousnesse and wickednesse. Let vs cast from vs the leauen of corrupt doctrine, that will infect our soules. Let vs kepe our feast the whole terme of our life, with eating the bread of purenesse of godly life, and trueth of Christes doctrine. Thus shall wee declare that Christes giftes and graces haue their effect in vs, and that wee haue the right beliefe and knowledge of his holy resurrection:

where truely if wee apply our faith to the vertue thereof in our life, and conforme vs to the example and signification meant thereby, wee shall be sure to rise hereafter to euerlasting glory, by the goodnesse and mercy of our Lord Iesus Christ, to whom with the Father and the holy Ghost bee all glorie, thankesgiuing, and prayse, *in infinita seculorum secula*, Amen.

HOMILY ON THE WORTHY RECEIVING OF THE SACRAMENT

AN HOMILIE OF THE
worthy receiuing and reuerend esteeming of
the Sacrament of the body and blood
of Christ

THE great loue of our Sauiour Christ towards mankinde (good Christian people) doth not onely appeare in that deare bought benefit of our redemption and saluation by his death and passion, but also in that he so kindely prouided, that the same most mercifull worke might be had in continuall remembrance, to take some place in vs, and not bee frustrate of his end and purpose. For as tender parents are not content to procure for their children costly possessions and liuelyhood, but take order that the same may be conserued and come to their vse: So our Lord and Sauiour thought it not sufficient to purchase for vs his Fathers fauour againe (which is that deepe fountaine of all goodnesse and eternall life) but also inuented the wayes most wisely, whereby they might redound to our commodity and profit. Amongst the which means, is the publike celebration of the memory of his pretious death at the Lords table. Which although it seeme of small vertue to some, yet being rightly done by the faythfull, it doeth not onely helpe their weakenesse (who be by their poysoned nature readier to remember iniuries then benefits) but strengtheneth & comforteth their inward man with peace and gladnesse, and maketh them thankefull to their redeemer, with diligent care and godly conuersation. And as of olde time GOD decreed his wonderous benefits of the deliuerance of his people, to be kept in memory by the eating of the Passeouer, with his

Rites and Ceremonies (Exodus 12.14): So our louing Sauiour hath ordeyned and established the remembrance of his great mercy expressed in his passion, in the institution of his heauenly Supper (Matthew 26.26-28), where euery one of vs must be ghestes, and not gazers, eaters, and not lookers, feeding our selues, and not hiring other to feed for vs, that we may liue by our owne meat, and not to perish for hunger, whiles other deuour all (1 Corinthians 11.21). To this, his commandement forceth vs, saying, Do ye this, drinke yee all of this (Luke 22.17). To this, his promise entiseth, This is my body which is giuen for you (1 Corinthians 11.24-25), this is my blood which is shed for you (Matthew 26.28). So then of necessity we must be our selues partakers of this table, and not beholders of other: So wee must addresse our selues to frequent the same in reuerent and comely maner, lest as Physicke prouided for the body, being misused, more hurteth then profiteth: so this comfortable medicine of the soule vndecently receiued, tendeth to our greater harme and sorrow. And Saint Paul sayth: He that eateth and drinketh vnworthily, eateth and drinketh his owne damnation (1 Corinthians 11.29). Wherefore, that it be not sayd to vs, as it was to the ghest of that great Supper, "Friend, how camest thou in, not hauing the mariage garment? (Matthew 22.12)" And that wee may fruitfully vse Saint Pauls counsell, "Let a man prooue himselfe, and so eate of that bread, and drinke of that cuppe: (1 Corinthians 11.28)" We must certainely know, that three things bee requisite in him which would seemely, as becommeth such high mysteries, resort to the Lordes table. That is: First, a right and worthy estimation and vnderstanding of this mysterie. Secondly, to come in a sure faith. And thirdly, to haue newnesse or purenesse of life to succeede the receiuing of the same.

But before all other things, this we must bee sure of especially, that this Supper be in such wise done and ministred, as our Lord and Sauiour did, and commanded to bee done, as his holy Apostles vsed it, and the good Fathers in the Primitiue Church frequented it. For (as that worthy man Saint Ambrose sayth) he is vnworthy of the Lord, that otherwise doeth celebrate that mystery, then it was deliuered by him. Neither can he be deuout, that otherwise doth presume then it was giuen by the authour. We must then take heed, lest of the memory, it be made a sacrifice, lest of a communion, it be made a priuate eating, lest of two partes, we haue but one, lest applying it for the dead, we lose the fruit that be aliue. Let vs rather in these matters follow the aduice of Cyprian in the like cases, that is, cleaue fast to the first beginning, hold fast the Lords tradition, doe that in the Lords commemoration which he himselfe did, he himselfe commanded, and his Apostles confirmed. This caution or foresight if we vse, then may we see those things that be requisite in the worthy receiuer, whereof this was the first, that we haue a right vnderstanding of the thing it selfe. As concerning which thing, this we may assuredly perswade our selues, that the ignorant man can neither worthily esteeme, nor effectually vse those marueylous graces and benefits offered and exhibited in that Supper: but either will lightly regard them, to no small offence, or vtterly condemne them, to his vtter destruction. So that by his negligence he deserueth the plagues of GOD to fall vpon him, and by contempt hee deserueth euerlasting perdition. To auoyde then these harmes, vse the aduice of the Wise man, who willeth thee when thou sittest at an earthly Kings Table, to take diligent heede what things are set before thee (Proverbs 23.1). So now much more at the King of Kings Table, thou must carefully search and know what daynties are prouided for thy soule, whither thou art come, not to feede thy senses and belly to corruption, but thy inward man to immortalitie and life, nor to consider the earthly creatures which thou seest, but the heauenly graces which thy faith beholdeth. For this Table is not (sayth Chrysostome) for chattering Iayes, but for Eagles, who flee thither where the dead bodie lyeth. And if this aduertisement of man cannot perswade vs to resort to the Lords Table with vnderstanding: see the counsell of GOD in the like matter, who charged his people to teach their posteritie, not only the rites and Ceremonies of the Passeouer, but the cause and end thereof: Whence we may learne, that both more perfect knowledge is required at this time at our hands, and that the ignorant cannot with fruit and profit exercise himselfe in the Lords Sacraments.

But to come nigher to the matter: Saint Paul blaming the Corinthians for the prophaning of the Lords Supper, concludeth that ignorance both of the thing it selfe, and the signification thereof, was the cause of their abuse: for they came thither vnreuerently, not discerning the Lords Body. Ought not we then by the monition of the wise man, by the wisedome of GOD, by the fearefull example of the Corinthians, to take aduised heed, that we thrust not our selues to this Table, with rude and vnreuerent ignorance, the smart whereof Christs Church hath rued and lamented these many dayes & yeres? For what hath bin the cause of the ruine of GODS religion, but the ignorance hereof? What hath bin the cause of this grosse Idolatrie, but the ignorance hereof? What hath beene the cause of this mummish Massing, but the ignorance hereof? Yea, what hath beene, and what is at this day the cause of this want of loue and charitie, but the ignorance hereof? Let vs therefore so trauaile to vnderstand the Lords Supper, that we be no cause of the decay of GODS worship, of no Idolatry, of no dumbe Massing, of no hate and malice: so may we the boldlier haue accesse thither to our comfort. Neither need wee to thinke that such exact knowledge is required of euery man, that hee be able to discusse all high points in the doctrine thereof: But thus much we must be sure to hold, that in the Supper of the Lord, there is no vaine Ceremonie, no bare signe, no vntrue figure of a thing absent (Matthew 26.26): But (as the Scripture saith) the Table of the Lord, the Bread and Cup of the Lord, the memorie of Christ, the Annuntiation of his death, yea the Communion of the Body and Blood of the Lord, in a marueilous incorporation, which by the operation of the holy Ghost (the very bond of our coniunction with Christ) is through faith wrought in the soules of the faithfull, whereby not onely their soules liue to eternall life, but they surely trust to win their bodies a resurrection to immortalitie (1 Corinthians 10.16-17). The true vnderstanding of this fruition and vnion, which is betwixt the body & the head betwixt the true beleeuers and Christ, the ancient Catholike Fathers, both perceiuing themselues, and commending to their people, were not afraid to call this Supper, some of them, the salue of immortalitie and soueraigne preseruatiue against death: other, a deificall Communion: other, the sweet dainties of our Sauiour, the pledge of eternall health, the defence of Faith, the hope of the Resurrection: other, the food of immortalitie, the healthfull grace, and the conseruatorie to euerlasting life (Irenaeus, Bk. 4, Chap. 34; Ignatius, Epis. ad Ephes.; Dionysius?; Origen, Optat. Cyp. de Cana Domini; Athanasius, De Pec. in Spir. Sanct.). All which sayings both of the holy Scripture and godly men, truely attributed to this celestiall banket and feast, if we would often call to minde, O how would they inflame our hearts to desire the participation of these mysteries, and oftentimes to couet after this bread, continually to thirste for this food? Not as specially regarding the terrene and earthly creatures which remaine: but alwayes holding fast, and cleauing by Faith to the rocke whence wee may sucke the sweetnesse of euerlasting saluation? And to be briefe, thus much more the faithfull see, heare, and know the fauourable mercies of GOD sealed, the satisfaction by Christ towards vs confirmed, and the remission of sinne established. Here they may feele wrought the tranquilitie of conscience, the increase of Faith, the strengthening of hope, the large spreading abroad of brotherly kindnesse, with many other sundry graces of GOD. The taste whereof they cannot attaine vnto, who be drowned in the deepe durtie lake of blindnesse and ignorance. From the which (O beloued) wash your selues with the liuing waters of GODS word, whence you may perceiue and know, both the spirituall food of this costly Supper, and the happy trustings and effects that the same doth bring with it.

Now it followeth to haue with this knowledge a sure and constant faith, not onely that the death of Christ is auaileable for the redemption of all the world, for the remission of sins, and reconciliation with GOD the Father: but also that he hath made vpon his Crosse a full and sufficient sacrifice the thee, a perfect cleansing of thy sins, so that thou acknowledgest no other Sauiour, Redeemer, Mediatour, Aduocate, Intercessour, but Christ onely, and that thou mayest say with the Apostle, that he loued thee, and gaue himselfe for thee. For this is to sticke fast to Christs promise made in his Institution, to make Christ thine owne, and to apply his merits vnto thy selfe. Herein thou needest no other mans helpe, no other Sacrifice, or oblation, no sacrificing Priest, no Masse, no meanes established by mans inuention. That Faith is a necessary instrument in all these holy Ceremonies, wee may thus assure our selues, for that as Saint Paul saith, without Faith it is vnpossible to please GOD (Hebrews 11.6). When a great number of the Israelites were ouerthrowne in the wildernesse, Moses, Aaron and Phinees did eat Manna, and pleased GOD, for that they vnderstood (saith Saint Augustine) the visible meat Spiritually (Augustine, In Johan. Hom. 6). Spiritually they hungred it, spiritually they tasted it, that they might be spiritually satisfied. And truely as the bodily meat cannot feede the outward man, vnlesse it be let into a stomacke to bee digested, which is healthsome and sound: No more can the inward man be fed, except his meate bee receiued into his soule and heart, sound and whole in Faith. Therefore (saith Cyprian) when we doe these things, we need not to whet our teeth: but with syncere faith we breake and diuide that whole bread (Cyprian, De cana Domini). It is well knowne that the meat we seeke for in this Supper, is Spirituall food, the nourishment of our soule, a heauenly refection, and not earthly, an inuisible meat, and not bodily, a ghostly substance, and not carnall, so that to thinke that without Faith wee may enioy the eating and drinking thereof, or that that is the fruition of it, is but to dreame a grosse carnall feeding, basely obiecting and binding our selues to the elements and creatures. Whereas by the aduice of the Councell of Nicene, we ought to lift vp our mindes by fayth, and leauing these inferiour and earthly things, there seeke it, where the sunne of righteousnesse euer shineth (Council of Nicene, Concilium). Take then this lesson (O thou that art desirous of this Table) of Emissenus a godly Father, that when thou goest vp to the reuerend Communion, to be satisfied with spirituall meates, thou looke vp with fayth vpon the holy body and blood of thy GOD, thou maruayle with reuerence, thou touch it with the minde, thou receiue it with the hand of thy heart, and thou take it fully with thy inward man (Eusebius Emissenus, Serm. de Euchar.).

Thus we see (beloued) that resorting to this table, we must plucke vp all the rootes of infidelity, all distrust in GODS promises, that we make our selues liuing members of Christs body. For the vnbeleeuers and faithlesse, cannot feed vpon that precious body: whereas the faythfull haue their life, their abiding in him, their vnion, and as it were their incorporation with him. Wherefore let vs prooue and trie our selues vnfaynedly, without flattering our selues, whether we bee plants of the fruitfull Oliue, liuing branches of the true vine, members indeed of Christs mysticall body, whether GOD hath purified our hearts by fayth, to the sincere acknowledging of his Gospel, and imbracing of his mercies in Christ Iesus, so that at this his table we receiue not only the outward Sacrament, but the spirituall thing also: not the figure, but the trueth: not the shadow only, but the body: not to death, but to life: not to destruction, but to saluation: which GOD grant vs to doe through the merits of our Lord and Sauiour, to whom bee all honour and glory for euer, Amen.

The second part of the Homilie, of the worthie receiuing and reuerend esteeming of the Sacrament of the Body and Blood of Christ.

IN the Homilie of late rehearsed vnto you, yee haue heard (good people) why it pleased our Sauiour Christ to institute that heauenly memorie of his death and passion, and that euery one of vs ought to celebrate the same at his Table, in our owne persons, and not by other. You haue heard also with what estimation and knowledge of so high mysteries, wee ought to resort thither. You haue heard with what constant faith wee should clothe and decke our selues, that wee might be fit and decent partakers of that celestiall foode.

Now followeth the third thing necessarie in him that would not eate of this bread, nor drinke of this cup vnworthily, which is, newnesse of life, and godlinesse of conuersation. For newnesse of life, as fruits of faith are required in the partakers of this Table. We may learne by eating of the typicall lambe, whereunto no man was admitted, but hee that was a Iewe, that was circumcised, that was before sanctified. Yea Saint Paul testifieth, that although the people were partakers of the Sacramentes vnder Moses, yet for that some of them were still worshippers of images, whoremongers, tempters of Christ, murmurers, and coueting after euill things: GOD ouerthrew those in the wildernesse, and that for our example, that is, that wee Christians should take heede wee resort vnto our Sacramentes with holinesse of life, not trusting in the outward receiuing of them, and infected with corrupt and vncharitable maners (1 Corinthians 10.1-11). For this sentence of GOD must alwayes be iustified: I will haue mercie and not sacrifice. Wherefore (saith Basil) it behoueth him that commeth to the body and blood of Christ, in commemoration of him that died and rose againe, not onely to bee pure from all filthinesse of the flesh and spirit, lest hee eate and drinke his owne condemnation: but also to shew out euidently, a memorie of him that died and rose againe for vs, in this point, that yee be mortified to sinne and the world, to liue now to GOD in Christ Iesu our Lord (Basil, De Bapt., Bk. 1, chap. 3). So then we must shew outward testimony, in following the signification of Christes death, amongst the which this is not esteemed least, to render thanks to Almighty GOD for all his benefites, briefly comprised in the death, passion, and resurrection of his dearely beloued Sonne. The which thing, because we ought chiefly at this table to solemnise, the godly fathers named it Eucharistia, that is, thankesgiuing. As if they should haue said, Now aboue all other times ye ought to land and praise GOD. Now may you behold the mater, the cause, the beginning and the end of all thankesgiuing. Now if you slacke, ye shewe your selues most vnthankefull, and that no other benefite can euer stirre you to thanke GOD, who so little regard here so many, so wonderfull, and so profitable benefites. Seeing then that the name and thing it selfe doth monish vs of thankes, let vs (as S. Paul saith) offer alwayes to GOD, the host or sacrifice of praise by Christ, that is, the fruite of the lippes which confesse his Name (Hebrews 13.15). For as Dauid singeth: Hee that offereth to GOD thankes and prayse, honoureth him (Psalms 50.23). But how few be there of thankefull persons, in comparison to the vnthankefull? Loe ten Lepers in the Gospel were healed, and but one onely returned to giue thanks for his health (Luke 17.17). Yea happy it were, if among fourtie communicants, we could see two vnfainedly giue thankes. So vnkinde wee bee, so obliuious wee be, so proud beggers wee be, that partly wee care not for our owne commoditie, partly wee knowe not our duety to GOD, and chiefly we will not confesse all that wee receiue. Yea, and if wee be forced by GODS power to doe it: yet wee handle it so coldly, so dryly, that our lippes praise him, but our hearts dispraise him, our tongues blesse him, but our life curseth him, our wordes worship him, but our workes dishonour him. O let vs therefore learne to giue GOD here thankes aright, and so to agnise his exceeding graces powred vpon vs, that they being shut vp in the treasure house of our heart, may in due time and season in our life and conuersation, appeare to the glorifying of his holy Name.

Furthermore, for newnesse of lift, it is to bee noted that Saint Paul writeth: that we being many, are one bread and one body: For all bee partakers of one bread. Declaring thereby, not onely our Communion with Christ, but that vnity also, wherein they that eate at this table, should bee knitte together. For by dissension, vaine glorie, ambition, strife, enuying, contempt, hatred, or malice, they should not bee disseuered: but so ioyned by the bond of loue, in one mysticall bodie, as the cornes of that bread in one loafe. In respect of which straite knotte of charitie, the true Christians in the Primitiue Church, called this supper, loue. As if they should say, none ought to sitte downe there, that were out of loue and charitie, who bare grudge and vengeance in his heart, who also did not professe his kinde affection by some charitable reliefe, for some parte of the congregation. And this was their practise. O heauenly banket then so vsed. O godly ghestes, who so esteemed this feast.

But O wretched creatures that wee bee at these dayes, who bee without reconciliation of our brethren whom we haue offended, without satisfying them whom wee haue caused to fall, without any kinde of thought or compassion toward them whom we might easily relieue, without any conscience of slander, disdaine, misreport, diuision, rancor, or inward bitternesse. Yea, being accombred with the cloked hatred of Cain (Genesis 4.8), with the long coloured malice of Esau (Genesis 27.41), with the dissembled falshood of Ioab (2 Samuel 3.27), dare ye presume to come vp to these sacred and fearefull mysteries? O man, whither rushest thou vnaduisedly? It is a table of peace, and thou art ready to fight. It is a table of singlenesse, and thou art imagining mischiefe. It is a table of quietnesse, and thou art giuen to debate. It is a table of pitie, and thou art vnmercifull. Doest thou neither feare GOD the maker of this feast, nor reuerence his Christ the refection and meate, nor regardest his spouse his welbeloued ghest, nor weighest thine owne conscience, which is sometime thine inward accuser? Wherefore (O man) tender thine owne saluation, examine and try thy good will and loue towards the children of GOD, the members of Christ, the heires of the heauenly heritage: yea, towards the image of GOD, the excellent creature thine owne soule. If thou haue offended, now be reconciled. If thou haue caused any to stumble in the way of GOD, now set them vp againe. If thou haue disquieted thy brother, now pacifie him. If thou haue wronged him, now relieue him. If thou haue defrauded him, now restore to him. If thou haue nourished spite, now imbrace friendship. If thou haue fostered hatred and malice, now openly shew thy loue and charitie, yea be prest and ready to procure thy neighbours health of soule, wealth, commoditie, and pleasures, as thine owne. Deserue not the heauie and dreadfull burden of GODS displeasure for thine euill will towards thy neighbour, so vnreuerently to approch to this table of the Lord. Last of all, as there is here the mysterie of peace, and the Sacrament of Christian societie, whereby wee vnderstand what sincere loue ought to be betwixt the true communicants (Chrysostome, Ad Popu. Ant. Homil. 6): So heere be the tokens of purnesse and innocencie of life, whereby we may perceiue that we ought to purge our owne soule from all vncleannesse, iniquitie, and wickednesse, lest when we receiue the mysticall bread (as Origen saith) we eate it in an vncleane place, that is, in a soule defiled and polluted with sinne (Origen, In Levit. Cap.). In Moses law, the man that did eate of the sacrifice of thankesgiuing, with his vncleannesse vpon him, should bee destroyed from his people. And shall we thinke that the wicked and sinfull person shall bee excusable at the table of the Lord? We both reade in Saint Paul, that the Church of Corinth was scourged of the Lord, for misusing the Lords Supper (1 Corinthians 11.29), and wee may plainely see Christs Church these many yeeres miserably vexed and oppressed, for the horrible prophanation of the same (Luke 17.1, Chrysostome? Homil. 14). Wherefore let vs all vniuersall and singular, behold our owne maners and liues, to amend them. Yea now at the least, let vs call our selues to an accompt, that it may grieue vs of our former euill conuersation, that wee may hate sinne, that wee may sorrow and mourne for our offences, that we may with teares powre them out before GOD, that we may with sure trust desire and craue the salue of his mercy, bought and purchased with the blood of his dearely beloued Sonne Iesus Christ, to heale our deadly wounds withall. For surely, if wee doe not with earnest repentance cleanse the filthie stomacke of our soule, it must needes come to passe, that as wholesome meate receiued into a raw stomacke corrupteth and marreth all, and is the cause of further sickenesse: so shall we eat this wholesome bread, and drinke this cup to our eternall destruction. Thus we and not other, must thorowly examine, and not lightly looke ouer our selues, not other men, our owne conscience, not other mens liues, which wee ought to doe vprightly, truely, and with iust correction. O (saith Chrysostome) let no Iudas resort to this Table, let no couetous person approach (Chrysostome, ad popul. Ant. Homil. 6). If any be a Disciple, let him be present. For Christ saith, With my Disciples I make my Passeouer (Matthew 26.18). Why cryed the Deacon in the Primitiue Church, If any bee holy, let him draw neere? Why did they celebrate these mysteries, the quier doore being shut? Why were the publique penitents and learners in Religion commanded at this time to auoid? was it not because this Table receiued no vnholy, vncleane, or sinfull ghests? Wherefore, if seruants dare not to presume to an earthly masters table, whom they haue offended: Let vs take heed we come not with our sinnes vnexamined, into this presence of our Lord and Iudge. If they bee worthy blame which kisse the Princes hand with a filthy & vncleane mouth: shalt thou be blamelesse which with a stinking soule, full of couetousnesse, fornication, drunkennes, pride, ful of wretched cogitations and thoughts, doest breathe out iniquity and vncleannesse on the Bread and Cup of the Lord?

Thus haue you heard, how you should come reuerently and decently to the Table of the Lord, hauing the knowledge of his word, of the thing it selfe, and the fruits thereof, bringing a true and constant Faith, the roote and welspring of all newnesse of life, aswell in praising GOD, and louing our neighbour, as purging our owne conscience from filthinesse. So that neither the ignorance of the thing shall cause vs to contemne it, nor vnfaithfulnesse make vs voide of fruit, nor sinne and iniquitie procure vs GODS plagues: but shall by Faith, in knowledge and amendment of life in Faith be here so vnited to Christ our Head in his mysteries, to our comfort, that after wee shall haue full fruition of him indeede, to our euerlasting ioy and eternall life, to the which he bring vs, that dyed for vs and Redeemed vs, Iesus Christ the righteous, to whom with the Father, and the holy Ghost, one true and eternall GOD, be all praise, honour and dominion for euer, Amen.

HOMILY ON THE COMING DOWN OF THE HOLY GHOST FOR WHITSUNDAY

AN HOMILIE CONcerning the comming downe of the holy Ghost, and the manifold gifts of the same.
For Whitsunday.

BEfore wee come to the declaration of the great & manifold gifts, of the holy Ghost, wherewith the Church of GOD hath beene euermore replenished, it shall first be needfull, briefly to expound vnto you, whereof this feast of Pentecost or Whitsuntide had his first beginning. You shall therefore vnderstand, that the Feast of Pentecost, was alwayes kept the fiftieth day after Easter, a great and solemne feast among the Iewes, wherein they did celebrate the memoriall of their deliuerance out of Egypt, and also the memorial of the publishing of the Law, which was giuen vnto them in the Mount Sinai vpon that day. It was first ordained and commanded to be kept holy, not by any mortall man, but by the mouth of the Lord himselfe, as wee read in Leuit.23. & Deut.16. The place appointed for the obseruation thereof, was Hierusalem, where was great recourse of people from all parts of the world, as may well appeare in the second Chapter of the Actes, wherein mention is made of Parthians, Medes, Elamites, inhabitours of Mesopotamia, inhabitours if Iurie, Capadocia, Pontus, Asia, Phrygia, Pamphilia, and diuers other such places, whereby we may also partly gather, what great and royall solemnitie was commonly vsed in that Feast. Now as this was giuen in commandement to the Iewes in the olde law (1 Corinthians 10), so did our Sauiour Christ, as it were, confirme the same in the time of the Gospel, ordaining (after a sort) a new Pentecost for his Disciples, namely when he sent downe the holy Ghost visibly in forme of clouen tongues like fire, and gaue them power to speake in such sort, that euery one might heare them, & also vnderstand them in his own language. Which miracle, that it might bee had in perpetuall remembrance, the Church hath thought good to solemnize and keepe holy this day, commonly called Whitsunday. And here is to be noted, that as the Law was giuen to the Iewes in the mount Sinai, the fiftieth day after Easter: so was the preaching of the Gospel, through the mighty power of the holy Ghost, giuen to the Apostles in the mount Sion, the fiftieth day after Easter.

And hereof this feast hath his name, to be called Pentecost, euen of the number of the dayes. For (as Saint Luke writeth in the Actes of the Apostles) When fiftie dayes were come to an end, the Disciples being all together with one accord in one place, the holy Ghost came suddenly among them, and sate vpon eche of them, like as it had bene clouen tongues of fire. Which thing was vndoubtedly done, to teach the Apostles and all other men, that it is he which giueth eloquence and vtterance in preaching the Gospel, that it is hee which openeth the mouth to declare the mighty workes of GOD, that it is he which ingendreth a burning zeale towards GODS word, and giueth all men a tongue, yea a fierie tongue, so that they may boldly and cheare-fully professe the trueth in the face of the whole world, as Esay was indued with this spirit. The Lord (saith Esay) gaue mee a learned and a skilfull tongue, so that I might know to rayse vp them, that are fallen, with the word (Isaiah 50.4). The Prophet Dauid cryeth to haue this gift, saying, Open thou my lippes, O Lord, and my mouth shall shew foorth thy prayse (Psalms 51.15). For our Sauiour Christ also in the Gospel saith to his Disciples, It is not you that speake, but the spirite of your Father which is within you (Matthew 10.20). All which testi-monies of holy Scripture, doe sufficiently declare, that the mysterie in the tongues, betokeneth the preaching of the Gospel, and the open con-fession of the Christian faith, in all them that are possessed with the holy Ghost. So that if any man bee a dumbe Christian, not professing his faith openly, but cloking and colouring himselfe for feare of danger in time to come, he giueth men occasion, iustly, and with good con-science to doubt, lest he haue not the grace of the holy Ghost within him, because hee is tongue-tyed, and doth not speake. Thus then haue ye heard the first institution of this feast of Pentecost or Whitsuntide, aswell in the olde Law, among the Iewes, as also in the time of the Gospel among the Christians.

Now let vs consider what the holy Ghost is, and how consequently he worketh his miraculous workes towards mankinde. The holy Ghost is a spirituall and diuine substance, the third person in the deitie, distinct from the Father and the Sonne, and yet proceeding from them both, which thing to bee true, both the Creede of Athanasius beareth witnesse, and may bee also easily prooued by most plaine testimonies of GODS holy word. When Christ was baptized of Iohn in the riuer, we reade that the holy Ghost came downe in forme of a Doue, and that the Father thundered from heauen, saying, This is my deare and welbeloued Sonne, in whom I am well pleased (Matthew 3.17). Where note three diuers and distinct persons, the Father, the Sonne, and the holy Ghost, which all notwithstanding are not three GODS, but one GOD. Likewise, when Christ did first institute and ordaine the Sacrament of Baptisme, hee sent his Disciples into the whole world, willing them to baptize all Nations, in the Name of the Father, the Sonne, and the holy Ghost (Matthew 28.19). And in another place he saith: I will pray vnto my Father, and hee shall giue you another comforter (John 14.16). Againe, when the comforter shall come, whom I will send from my Father, &c (John 15.26). These and such other places of the new Testament, doe so plainely and euidently confirme the distinction of the holy Ghost, from the other persons in the Trinitie, that no man possibly can doubt thereof, vnlesse hee will blaspheme the euerlasting trueth of GODS word. As for his proper nature and substance, it is altogether one with GOD the Father, and GOD the Sonne, that is to say, Spirituall, Eternall, Vncreated, Incomprehensible, Almightie, to be short, he is euen GOD and Lord euerlasting. Therefore hee is called the Spirit of the Father, therefore he is said to proceed from the Father, and the Sonne, and therefore hee was equally ioyned with them in the Commission that the Apostles had to Baptize all Nations. But that this may appeare more sensibly to the eyes of all men, it shalbe requisite to come to the other part, namely to the wonderfull and heauenly workes of the holy Ghost, which plainely declare vnto the world his mighty and diuine power. First it is euident, that he did wonderfully gouerne & direct the hearts of the Patriarkes, and Prophets, in olde time, illuminating their mindes with the knowledge of the true Messias, and giuing them vtterance to prophesie of things that should come to passe long time after. For as Saint Peter witnesseth, the prophesie came not in old time by the will of man: But the holy men of GOD spake, as they were mooued inwardly by the holy Ghost (2 Peter 1.21). And of Zacharie the high Priest, it is sayd in the Gospel, that hee being full of the holy Ghost, prophesied and praysed GOD (Luke 1.67). So did also Simeon, Anna, Marie, and diuers other, to the great wonder and admiration of all men. Moreouer, was not the holy Ghost a mightie worker in the Conception and the Natiuitie of Christ our Sauiour? Saint Matthew saith, that the blessed virgin was found with child of the holy Ghost, before Ioseph and she came together (Matthew 1.18). And the Angell Gabriel did expressely tell her, that it should come to passe, saying: The holy Ghost shall come vpon thee, and the power of the most high shall ouershadow thee (Luke 1.35). A merueilous matter, that a woman should conceiue and beare a childe, without the knowledge of man. But where the holy Ghost worketh, there nothing is vnpossible, as may further also appeare by the inward regeneration and sanctification of mankind. When Christ sayd to Nicodemus, vnlesse a man be borne anew, of water and the spirit, he can not enter into the kingdome of GOD: he was greatly amazed in his mind, and began to reason with Christ, demanding how a man might bee borne which was olde? Can he enter (saith hee) into his mothers wombe againe, and so be borne a new (John 3.4-6)? Beholde a liuely patterne of a fleshly and carnall man. He had little or no intelligence of the holy Ghost, and therefore he goeth bluntly to worke, and asketh how this thing were possible to be true. Whereas otherwise if he had knowen the great power of the holy Ghost in this behalfe, that it is hee which inwardly worketh the regeneration and new birth of mankinde, he would neuer haue meruailed at Christs words, but would rather take occasion thereby to praise and glorifie GOD. For as there are three seuerall and sundry persons in the Dietie: So haue they three seuerall and sundry offices proper vnto each of them.

The Father to create, the Sonne to redeeme, the holy Ghost to sanctifie and regenerate. Whereof the last, the more it is hidde from our vnderstanding, the more it ought to mooue all men to wonder at the secret and mightie working of GODS holy Spirit which is within vs. For it is the holy Ghost, and no other thing, that doth quicken the minds of men, stirring vp good and godly motions in their hearts, which are agreeable to the will and commandement of GOD, such as otherwise of their owne crooked and peruerse nature they should neuer haue. That which is borne of the Spirit, is Spirit (John 3.6). As who should say: Man of his owne nature is fleshly and carnall, corrupt and naught, sinfull and disobedient to GOD, without any sparke of goodnesse in him, without any vertuous or godly motion, onely giuen to euill thoughts and wicked deedes. As for the workes of the Spirit, the fruits of Faith, charitable and godly motions, if he haue any at all in him, they proceed onely of the holy Ghost, who is the onely worker of our Sanctification, and maketh vs new men in Christ Iesus. Did not GODS holy Spirit miraculously worke in the child Dauid, when of a poore Shepheard, he became a Princely Prophet (1 Samuel 17.12)? Did not GODS holy Spirit miraculously worke in Matthew, sitting at the receit of custome, when of a proude Publicane, he became an humble and lowly Euangelist (Matthew 9.9)? And who can choose but marueile to consider, that Peter should become of a simple fisher, a chiefe and mightie Apostle? Paul of a cruell and bloodie persecutour, a faithfull Disciple of Christ, to teach the Gentiles. Such is the power of the holy Ghost, to regenerate men, and as it were to bring them foorth a new, so that they shall be nothing like the men that they were before. Neither doeth he thinke it sufficient inwardly to worke the spirituall and new birth of man, vnlesse hee doe also dwell and abide in him. Know ye not (saith Saint Paul) that ye are the Temple of GOD, and that his Spirit dwelleth in you (1 Corinthians 3.16)? Know yee not that your bodies are the Temples of the holy Ghost, which is within you (1 Corinthians 6.19)? Againe he saith, You are not in the flesh, but in the spirit (Romans 8.9). For why? The Spirit of GOD dwelleth in you. To this agreeth the doctrine of S. Iohn, writing on this wise, The annointing which ye haue receiued (he meaneth the holy Ghost) dwelleth in you (1 John 2.27). And the doctrine of Peter saith the same, who hath these words: The spirit of glory, and of GOD, resteth vpon you (1 Peter 4.14). O what comfort is this to the heart of a true Christian, to thinke that the holy Ghost dwelleth within him? If GOD be with vs (as the Apostle saith) who can be against vs (Romans 8.31)? O but how shal I know that the holy Ghost is within me! Some man perchance will say, forsooth, as the tree is knowen by his fruit, so is also the holy Ghost. The fruits of the holy Ghost (according to the mind of S. Paul) are these: Loue, ioy, peace, long suffring, gentlenes, goodnes, faithfulnes, meekenes, temperance, &c. Contrariwise, the deeds of the flesh are these: Adultery, fornication, vncleannesse, wantonnes, idolatry, witchcraft, hatred, debate, emulation, wrath, contention, sedition, heresie, enuy, murder, drunkennes, gluttonie, and such like (Galatians 5.19-23).

Heere is now that glasse, wherein thou must behold thy selfe, and discerne whether thou haue the holy Ghost within thee, or the spirit of the flesh. If thou see that thy workes bee vertuous and good, consonant to the prescript rule of GODS word, sauouring and tasting not of the flesh, but of the spirit, then assure thy selfe that thou art endued with the holy Ghost: Otherwise in thinking well of thy selfe, thou doest nothing els but deceiue thy selfe. The holy Ghost doeth alwayes declare himselfe by his fruitfull and gracious giftes, namely, by the worde of wisedome, by the worde of knowledge, which is the vnderstanding of the Scriptures, by faith, in doing of miracles, by healing them that are diseased, by prophesie, which is the declaration of GODS mysteries, by discerning of spirits, diuersities of tongues, interpretation of tongues, and so foorth. All which giftes, as they proceede from one spirit, and are seuerally giuen to man according to the measurable distribution of the holy Ghost: Euen so doe they bring men, and not without good cause, into a wonderfull admiration of GODS diuine power (1 Corinthians 12.7-11). Who wil not maruaile at that which is written in the Actes of the Apostles, to heare their bolde confession before the Counsell at Ierusalem? And to consider that they went away with ioy and gladnesse, reioycing that they were counted worthy to suffer rebukes and checkes for the Name and faith of Christ Iesus (Acts 5.29, 41)? This was the mighty worke of the holy Ghost, who because he giueth patience and ioyfulnesse of heart in temptation and affliction, hath therefore worthily obteined this name in holy Scripture, to be called a comforter. Who will not also maruaile to reade the learned and heauenly Sermons of Peter, and the disciples, considering that they were neuer brought vp in schoole of learning, but called euen from their nets, to supply roomes of Apostles? This was likewise the mighty worke of the holy Ghost, who because he doeth instruct the hearts of the simple in the true knowledge of GOD and his worde, is most iustly tearmed by this name and title, to bee the spirit of trueth (John 14.17). Eusebius in his Ecclesiasticall historie, telleth a strange storie of a certaine learned and subtill Philosopher, who being an extreme aduersary to Christ and his doctrine, could by no kinde of learning bee conuerted to the faith, but was able to withstand all the arguments that could bee brought against him, with little, or no labour (Eusebius, Ecclesiastical History, Bk. 11, Chap. 3). At length there started vp a poore simple man of small wit, and lesse knowledge, one that was reputed among the learned as an ideote: And he on GODS name would needes take in hand to dispute with this proud Philosopher. The Bishops and other learned men standing by, were marueilously abashed at the matter, thinking that by his doings they should bee all confounded and put to open shame. Hee notwithstanding goeth on, and beginning in the Name of the Lord Iesus, brought the Philosopher to such point in the ende, contrary to all mens expectation, that hee could not chuse but acknowledge the power of GOD in his wordes, and to giue place to the trueth. Was not this a miraculous worke, that one seely soule of no learning, should doe that which many Bishops of great knowledge and vnderstanding were neuer able to bring to passe? So true is the saying of Bede: Where the holy Ghost doth instruct and teach, there is no delay at all in learning. Much more might here be spoken of the manifold giftes and graces of the holy Ghost, most excellent and wonderfull in our eyes, but to make a long discourse through all, the shortnesse of time will not serue. And seeing yee haue heard the chiefest, ye may easily conceiue and iudge of the rest. Now were it expedient to discusse this question: Whether all they which boast and bragge that they haue the holy Ghost, doe truely chalenge this vnto themselues, or no? Which doubt, because it is necessary and profitable, shall (GOD willing) be dissolued in the next part of this Homilie. In the meane season, let vs (as we are most bound) giue heartie thankes to GOD the Father, and his Sonne Iesus Christ, for sending downe his comforter, into the world, humbly beseeching him, so to worke in our hearts by the power of this holy Spirit, that wee being regenerate and newly borne againe in all goodnesse, righteousnesse, sobrietie and trueth, may in the end be made partakers of euerlasting life in his heauenly kingdome, through Iesus Christ our LORD and Sauiour, Amen.

THE SECOND PART OF THE HOMILY CONCERNING THE HOLY GHOST, DISSOLUING THIS DOUBT: WHETHER ALL MEN RIGHTLY CHALLENGE TO THEMSELUES THE HOLY GHOST, OR NO

OUR Sauiour Christ departing out of the world vnto his Father, promised his Disciples to send downe another comforter, that should continue with them for euer, and direct them into all trueth (John 14.16, John 15.26). Which thing to bee faythfully and truly performed, the Scriptures doe sufficiently beare witnesse. Neither must wee thinke that this comforter was either promised, or else giuen, onely to the Apostles, but also to the vniuersall Church of Christ, dispersed through the whole world. For vnlesse the holy Ghost had beene alwayes present, gouerning and preseruing the Church from the beginning, it could neuer haue sustayned so many and great brunts of affliction and persecution, with so little damage & harme as it hath.

And the words of Christ are most plaine in this behalfe, saying, that the spirit of truth should abide with them for euer, that he would be with them alwayes (he meaneth by grace, vertue, and power) euen to the worlds end (John 14.17, Matthew 28.20).

Also in the prayer that he made to his Father a little before his death, he maketh intercession, not onely for himselfe and his Apostles, but indifferently for all them that should beleeue in him through their words, that is to wit, for his whole Church (John 17.20-21). Againe, Saint Paul sayth: If any man haue not the spirit of Christ, the same is not his (Romans 8.9). Also in the words following, we haue receiued the spirit of adoption, whereby we cry Abba, Father (Romans 8.15). Heereby then it is euident and plaine to all men, that the holy Ghost was giuen, not only to the Apostles, but also to the whole body of Christs congregation, although not in like forme and maiestie as hee came downe at the feast of Pentecost. But now heerein standeth the controuersie: Whether all men doe iustly arrogate to themselues the holy Ghost, or no? The Bishops of Rome haue for a long time made a sore challenge thereunto, reasoning for themselues after this sort. The holy Ghost (say they) was promised to the Church, & neuer forsaketh the Church. But we are the chiefe heads, & the principal part of the Church, therefore we haue the holy Ghost for euer, and whatsoeuer things we decree, are vndoubted verities, & oracles of the holy Ghost. That ye may perceiue the weakenesse of this argument. It is needefull to teach you, first what the true Church of Christ is, & then to conferre the Church of Rome therewith, to discerne how well they agree together. The true Church is an vniuersall congregation or fellowshippe of GODS faithfull and elect people, built vpon the foundation of the Apostles and Prophets, Iesus Christ himselfe being the head corner stone (Ephesians 2.20). And it hath alwayes three notes or markes whereby it is knowen. Pure and sound doctrine, the Sacraments ministred according to Christs holy institution, and the right vse of Ecclesiasticall discipline. This discription of the Church is agreeable both to the Scriptures of God, and also to the doctrine of the auncient fathers, so that none may iustly finde fault therewith. Now if ye will compare this with the Church of Rome, not as it was in the beginning, but as it is presently, and hath beene for the space of nine hundred yeeres and odde: you shall well perceiue the state thereof to bee so farre wide from the nature of the true Church, that nothing canne bee more. For neither are they built vpon the foundation of the Apostles and Prophets, retaining the sound and pure doctrine of Christ Iesu, neither yet doe they order the Sacraments, or els the Ecclesiasticall keyes, in such sort as hee did first institute and ordaine them: But haue so intermingled their owne traditions and inuentions, by chopping and changing, by adding and plucking away, that now they may seeme to be conuerted into a new guise. Christ commended to his Church a Sacrament of his Body and Blood: They haue changed it into a Sacrifice for the quicke and the dead. Christ did minister to his Apostles, and the Apostles to other men indifferently vnder both kindes: They haue robbed the lay people of the cup, saying, that for them one kinde is sufficient. Christ ordained no other element to bee vsed in Baptisme, but onely Water, whereunto when the word is ioyned, it is made (as S. Augustine saith) a full and perfect Sacrament. They being wiser in their owne conceite then Christ, thinke it is not well nor orderly done, vnlesse they vse coniuration, vnlesse they hallow the water, vnlesse there be oile, salt, spittle, tapers, and such other dumbe Ceremonies, seruing to no vse, contrary to the plaine rule of Saint Paul, who willeth all things to bee done in the Church vnto edification (1 Corinthians 14.5). Christ ordeyned the authoritie of the keyes to excommunicate notorious sinners, and to absolue them which are truely penitent: They abuse this power at their owne pleasure, aswell in cursing the godly, with bell, booke and candles, as also in absoluing the reprobate, which are knowen to bee vnworthy of any Christian societie: Whereof they that lust to see examples, let them search their liues. To be short, looke what our Sauiour Christ pronounced of the Scribes and Pharisees, in the Gospell, the same may bee boldly and with safe conscience pronounced of the Bishops of Rome, namely that they haue forsaken, and dayly doe forsake the Commandements of GOD, to erect and set vp their owne constitutions. Which thing being true, as all they which haue any light of GODS word must needes confesse, wee may well conclude according to the rule of Augustine: That the Bishoppes of Rome and their adherents, are not the true Church of Christ, much lesse then to bee taken as chiefe Heads and Rulers of the same. Whosoeuer (saith he) do dissent from the Scriptures concerning the head, although they be found in all places where the Church is appoynted, yet are they not in the Church: a plaine place, concluding directly against the Church of Rome (Augustine, Contra Petiliani Donatist Epi., Chap. 4). Where is now the holy Ghost which they so stoutly doe claime to themselues? Where is now the spirit of trueth, that will not suffer them in any wise to erre? If it bee possible to bee there, where the true Church is not, then is it at Rome: otherwise it is but a vaine bragge, and nothing else. Saint Paul (as ye haue heard before) sayth: If any man haue not the spirit of Christ, the same is not his. And by turning the wordes, it may bee truely said: If any man be not of Christ, the same hath not the spirit. Now to discerne who are truely his, and who not, wee haue this rule giuen vs, that his sheepe doe alwayes heare his voyce (John 10.3). And Saint Iohn saith, He that is of GOD, heareth GODS worde (John 8.47). Whereof it followeth, that the Popes in not hearing Christes voyce, as they ought to doe, but preferring their owne decrees before the expresse word of GOD, doe plainely argue to the world, that they are not of Christ, nor yet possessed with his spirit. But here they will alledge for themselues, that there are diuers necessary points not expressed in holy Scripture, which were left to the reuelation of the holy Ghost. Who being giuen to the Church, according to Christs promise, hath taught many things from time to time, which the Apostles could not then beare (John 16.7). To this wee may easily answere by the plaine wordes of Christ, teaching vs that the proper office of the holy Ghost is, not to institute and bring in new ordinances, contrary to his doctrine before taught: but shall come and declare those things which he had before taught: so that it might be well and truely vnderstood. When the holy Ghost (saith he) shal come, he shall leade you into all trueth (John 16.13). What trueth doth he meane? Any other then hee himselfe had before expressed in his word? No. For he saith, He shall take of mine, and shew vnto you. Againe, he shall bring you in remembrance of all things that I haue tolde you (John 16.15). It is not then the duetie and part of any Christian, vnder pretence of the holy Ghost, to bring in his owne dreames and phantasies into the Church: but hee must diligently prouide that his doctrine and decrees bee agreeable to Christes holy Testament. Otherwise in making the holy Ghost the authour thereof, hee doeth blaspheme and belye the holy Ghost, to his owne condemnation.

Now to leaue their doctrine, and come to other points. What shall wee thinke or iudge of the Popes intolerable pride? The Scripture sayth, that GOD resisteth the proud, and sheweth grace to the humble. Also it pronounceth them blessed, which are poore in spirit, promising that they which humble themselues, shall be exalted (Matthew 5.3). And Christ our Sauiour willeth all his to learne of him, because he is humble and meeke (Matthew 11.29). As for pride, Saint Gregorie saith, it is the roote of all mischiefe. And Saint Augustines iudgement is this, that it maketh men deuils. Can any man then, which either hath or shall reade the Popes liues, iustly say that they had the holy Ghost within them? First, as touching that they will bee tearmed vniuersall Bishops and heads of all Christian Churches through the world, wee haue the iudgement of Gregorie expresly against them, who writing to Mauricius the Emperour, condemneth Iohn, Bishop of Constantinople, in that behalfe, calling him the prince of pride, Lucifers successour, and the fore-runner of Antichrist (Gregory, Bk. 3, Epistle 76.78). Saint Bernard also agreeing thereunto, sayth, What greater pride can there bee, then that one man should preferre his owne iudgement before the whole congregation, as though he onely had the spirit of GOD (Bernard, Serm. 3, De Resurrect. Domini)? And Chrysostome pronounceth a terrible sentence against them, affirming plainely, that whosoeuer seeketh to be chiefe in earth, shall finde confusion in heauen, and that hee which striueth for the supremacy, shall not bee reputed among the seruants of Christ (Chrysostome, Dialogorum, Bk. 3). Againe hee sayth: To desire a good worke, it is good, but to couet the chiefe degree of honour, it is meere vanitie (Chrysostome, Super Matt.). Doe not these places sufficiently conuince their outragious pride, in vsurping to themselues a superiority aboue all other, aswell ministers and Bishops, as Kings also and Emperours? But as the Lion is knowen by his clawes, so let vs learne to know these men by their deedes. What shall we say of him that made the noble King Dandalus to bee tyed by the necke with a chayne, and to lye flat downe before his table, there to gnaw bones like a Dogge (Sabelli, Ennead. 9. Bk. 7)? Shall wee thinke that hee had GODS holy spirit within him, and not rather the spririt of the deuill? Such a tyrant was Pope Clement the sixt. What shall wee say of him that proudly and contemptuously trode Fredericke the Emperour vnder his feete, applying the verse of the Psalme vnto himselfe: Thou shalt goe vpon the Lyon and the Adder, the yong Lyon and the Dragon thou shalt tread vnder thy foote (Psalms 91.13)? shall wee say that he had GODS holy spirit within him, and not rather the spirit of the deuill? Such a tyrant was Pope Alexander the third. What shall we say of him that armed and animated the sonne against the father, causing him to bee taken, and to be cruelly famished to death, contrary to the law both of GOD, and also of nature? Shall we say that he had GODS holy spirit within him, and not rather the spirit of the deuill? Such a tyrant was Pope Pascal the second. What shall we say of him that came into his Popedome like a Foxe, that reigned like a Lyon, and died like a Dogge? Shall we say that he had GODS holy spirit within him, and not rather the spirit of the deuill? Such a tyrant was Pope Boniface the eight. What shall we say of him that made Henry the Emperour, with his wife and his yong childe, to stand at the gates of the Citie in the rough winter, bare footed and bare legged, onely clothed in Lincie wolcie, eating nothing from morning to night, and that for the space of three dayes? Shall wee say that he had GODS holy spirit within him, and not rather the spirit of the deuill? Such a tyrant was Pope Hildebrand, most worthy to bee called a firebrand, if wee shall tearme him as he hath best deserued. Many other examples might here be alledged. As of Pope Ione the harlot, that was deliuered of a Childe in the high streete, going solemnely in procession. Of Pope Iulius the second, that wilfully cast S. Peters keyes into the riuer Tiberis. Of Pope Vrban the sixt, that caused fiue Cardinals to bee put in sacks, and cruelly drowned. Of Pope Sergius the third, that persecuted the dead body of Formosus his predecessour, when it had beene buried eight yeeres. Of Pope Iohn the xiiii. of that name, who hauing his enemie deliuered into his hands, caused him first to bee stripped starke naked, his beard to bee shauen, and to bee hanged vp a whole day by the hayre, then to bee set vpon an Asse with his face backward toward the tayle, to bee caried round about the citie in despite, to bee miserably beaten with rods, last of all, to bee thrust out of his countrey, and to bee banished for euer. But to conclude & make an ende, yee shall briefly take this short lesson, wheresoeuer yee finde the spirit of arrogancie and pride, the spirit of enuie, hatred, contention, crueltie, murder, extortion, witchcraft, necromancie, &c. assure your selues that there is the spirit of the deuill, and not of GOD, albeit they pretend outwardly to the world neuer so much holinesse. For as the Gospel teacheth vs, the spirit of Iesus is a good spirit, an holy spirit, a sweete spirit, a lowly spirit, a mercifull spirit, full of charitie and loue, full of forgiuenesse and pitie, not rendring euill for euill, extremitie for extremitie, but ouercomming euill with good, and remitting all offence euen from the heart. According to which rule, if any man liue vprightly, of him it may be safely pronounced, that hee hath the holy Ghost within him: If not, then it is a plaine token that hee doeth vsurpe the name of the holy Ghost in vaine. Therefore (dearely beloued) according to the good counsell of Saint Iohn, beleeue not euery spirit, but first try them whether they bee of GOD, or no (1 John 4.1). Many shall come in my Name (sayth Christ) and shall transforme themselues into Angels of light, deceiuing (if it bee possible) the very elect. They shall come vnto you in sheepes clothing, being inwardly cruell and rauening Wolues (Matthew 24.5, 24). They shall haue an outward shew of great holinesse and innocencie of life, so that ye shall hardly or not at all discerne them. But the rule that yee must follow, is this, to iudge them by their fruits (Matthew 7.20). Which if they be wicked and naught, then is it vnpossible that the tree of whom they proceede should bee good. Such were all the Popes and Prelates of Rome for the most part, as doeth well appeare in the storie of their liues, and therefore they are worthily accounted among the number of false Prophets, and false Christs, which deceiued the world a long while (Luke 21.8). The Lord of heauen and earth defend vs from their tyrannie and pride, that they neuer enter into his vineyard againe, to the disturbance of his seely poore flocke: but that they may be vtterly confounded and put to flight in all partes of the world: and he of his great mercy so worke in all mens hearts, by the mighty power of the holy Ghost, that the comfortable Gospel of his Sonne Christ may be truely preached, truely receiued, and truely followed in all places, to the beating downe of sinne, death, the Pope, the Deuill, and all the kingdome of Antichrist, that like scattered and dispersed sheepe being at length gathered into one folde, wee may in the ende rest all together in the bosome of Abraham, Isahac, and Iacob, there to be partakers of eternall and euerlasting life through the merits and death of Iesus Christ our Sauiour. AMEN.

HOMILY FOR ROGATION WEEK

AN HOMILIE FOR THE
dayes of Rogation Weeke.
That all good things commeth from God.

I Am purposed this day (good deuout Christian people) to declare vnto you the most deserued praise and commendation of Almightie GOD, not onely in the consideration of the marueilous creation of this world, or for conuersation and gouernance thereof, wherein his great power and wisedome might excellently appeare, to mooue vs to honour and dread him: but most specially in consideration of his liberall and large goodnesse, which hee dayly bestoweth on vs his reasonable creatures, for whose sake hee made the whole vniuersall world, with all the commodities and goods therein. Which his singular goodnesse well and diligently remembred on our part, should mooue vs (as duety is) againe with hartie affection to loue him, and with word and deede to praise him, and serue him all the dayes of our life. And to this matter, being so worthie to entreate of, and so profitable for you to heare, I trust I shall not neede with much circumstance of wordes to stirre you to giue your attendance to heare what shall bee sayde. Onely I would wish your affection inflamed in secret wise within your selfe, to rayse vp some motion of thankesgiuing to the goodnesse of Almighty GOD, in euery such poynt as shall bee opened by my declaration particularly vnto you. For else what shall it auayle vs to heare and know the great goodnesse of GOD towardes vs, to know that whatsoeuer is good, proceedeth from him, as from the principall fountaine and the onely authour, or to know that whatsoeuer is sent from him, must needes be good and wholsome: if the hearing of such matter moueth vs no further but to know it only? What auaileth it the wise men of the worlde to haue knowledge of the power and diuinity of GOD, by the secret inspiration of him: where they did not honour and glorifie him in their knowledges as GOD? What prayse was it to them, by the consideration of the creation of the world, to beholde his goodnes: and not to be thankefull to him againe for his creatures? What other thing deserued this blindnes & forgetfulnes of them at GODS handes, but vtter forsaking of him? and so forsaken of GOD, they could not but fall into extreame ignorance and errour. And although they much esteemed themselues in their wits and knowledge, and gloried in their wisedome: yet vanished they away blindly, in their thoughts became fooles, and perished in their folly. There can bee none other end of such as draweth nigh to GOD by knowledge, and yet depart from him in vnthankefulnesse, but vtter destruction. This experience saw Dauid in his dayes. For in his Psalme he saith, Behold, they which withdraw themselues from thee, shall perish, for thou hast destroyed them all that are strayed from thee (Psalms 73.27).

This experience was perceiued to be true, of that holy Prophet Ieremie: O Lord (saith he) whatsoeuer they be that forsake thee, shall be confounded, they that depart from thee, shall be written in the earth, and soone forgotten (Jeremiah 17.13). It profiteth not (good people) to heare the goodnes of GOD declared vnto vs, if our hearts bee not inflamed thereby to honour and thanke him. It profited not the Iewes which were GODS elect people, to heare much of GOD, seeing that hee was not receiued in their hearts by Faith, nor thanked for his benefits bestowed vpon them: their vnthankefulnesse was the cause of their destruction. Let vs eschew the maner of these before rehearsed, and follow rather the example of that holy Apostle Saint Paul, who when in a deepe meditation he did behold the marueilous proceedings of Almightie GOD, and considered his infinite goodnesse in the ordering of his creatures, hee burst out into this conclusion: Surely (saith he) of him, by him, and in him, be all things. And this once pronounced, he stucke not still at this point, but foorthwith thereupon ioyned to these words, To him bee glorie and praise for euer, Amen (Romans 11.36).

Vpon the ground of which words of Saint Paul (good audience) I purpose to build my exhortation of this day vnto you. Wherein I shall doe my endeuour, first to prooue vnto you that all good things come downe vnto vs from aboue from the Father of light. Secondly, that Iesus Christ his Sonne and our Sauiour, is the meane by whom wee receiue his liberall goodnesse. Thirdly, that in the power and vertue of the holy Ghost, wee be made meete and able to receiue his gifts and graces. Which things distinctly and aduisedly considered in our mindes, must needs compell vs in most low reuerence, after our bounden duetie, alwayes to render him thankes againe, in some testification of our good hearts for his deserts vnto vs. And that the entreating of this matter in hand may be to the glorie of Almightie GOD, let vs, in one Faith and Charitie call vpon the Father of mercie, from whom commeth euery good gift, and euery perfect gift, by the mediation of his welbeloued Sonne our Sauiour, that we may be assisted with the presence of his holy Spirit, and profitably on both parts, to demeane our selues in speaking and hearkening ot the saluation of our soules.

In the beginning of my speaking vnto you, (good Christian people) suppose not that I doe take vpon mee to declare vnto you the excellent power, or the incomparable wisedome of Almightie GOD, as though I would haue you beleeue that it might be expressed vnto you by words. Nay it may not be thought, that that thing may bee comprehended by mans words, that is incomprehensible. And too much arrogancie it were for dust and ashes, to thinke that he can worthily declare his maker. It passeth far the darke vnderstanding and wisedome of a mortall man, to speake sufficiently of that diuine Maiestie, which the Angels cannot vnderstand. Wee shall therefore lay apart to speake of the profound and vnsearchable nature of Almightie GOD, rather acknowledging our weakenesse, then rashly to attempt that is aboue all mans capacitie to compasse. It shall better suffice vs in lowe humilitie to reuerence and dread his Maiestie, which wee can not comprise, then by ouermuch curious searching to be ouercharged with the glorie. We shall rather turne our whole contemplation to answere a while his goodnesse towards vs, wherein we shall be much more profitably occupied, and more may we be bold to search. To consider the great power hee is of, can but make vs dread and feare. To consider his high wisedome might vtterly discomfort our frailtie to haue any thing to doe with him. But in consideration of his inestimable goodnesse, we take good heart againe to trust well vnto him. By his goodnesse wee be assured to take him for our refuge, our hope and comfort, our mercifull Father, in all the course of our liues. His power and wisedome, compelleth vs to take him for GOD omnipotent, inuisible, hauing rule in heauen and earth, hauing all things in his subiection, and will haue none in counsell with him, nor any to aske the reason of his doing. For he may do what liketh him, and none can resist him (Daniel 4.35, 11.16). For he worketh all things in his secret iudgement to his own pleasure, yea euen the wicked to damnation saith Salomon (Proverbs 16.4). By the reason of this nature, he is called in Scripture, consuming fire (Hebrews 12.29), hee is called a terrible and fearefull GOD. Of this behalfe therefore, we haue no familiaritie, no accesse vnto him, but his goodnesse againe tempereth the rigour of his high power, and maketh vs bold, and putteth vs in hope that hee will be conuersant with vs, and easie vnto vs.

It is his goodnesse that mooueth him to say in Scripture: It is my delight to be with the children of men (Prouerbs 8.31). It is his goodnesse that mooueth him to call vs vnto him, to offer vs his friendship and presence. It is his goodnesse that patiently suffereth our straying from him, and suffereth vs long, to winne vs to repentance. It is of his goodnes that wee bee created reasonable creatures, where else hee might haue made vs bruite beastes. It was his mercie to haue vs borne among the number of Christian people, and thereby in a much more nighnesse to saluation, where we might haue beene borne (if his goodnesse had not beene) among the Panims, cleane void from GOD, and the hope of euerlasting life. And what other thing doth his louing and gentle voice spoken in his Word, where hee calleth vs to his presence and friendship, but declare his goodnesse, onely without regard of our worthinesse? And what other thing doeth stirre him to call vs to him, when wee be strayed from him, to suffer vs patiently, to winne vs to repentance, but onely his singular goodnesse, no whitte of our deseruing? Let them all come together that bee now glorified in heauen, and let vs heare what answere they will make in these poyntes afore rehearsed, whether their first creation was in GODS goodnesse, or of themselues. Forsooth Dauid would make answere for them all, and say, Know yee for suretie, euen the Lord is GOD, he hath made vs, and not we our selues. If they were asked againe, who should bee thanked for their regeneration? for their iustification? and for their saluation? whether their desertes, or GODS goodnesse onely? Although in this point, euery one confesse sufficiently the trueth of this matter in his owne person: yet let Dauid answere by the mouth of them all at this time, who cannot chuse but say, Not to vs, O Lord, not to vs, but to thy Name giue all the thanke, for thy louing mercie, and for thy trueths sake. If we should aske againe, from whence came their glorious workes and deedes, which they wrought in their liues, wherewith GOD was so highly pleased and worshipped by them? Let some other witnesse bee brought in, to testifie this matter, that in the mouth of two or three may the trueth bee knowen.

Verily that holy Prophet Esay beareth record, and sayth, O Lord, it is thou of thy goodnesse that hast wrought all our workes in vs, not wee our selues (Isaiah 26.12). And to vphold the trueth of this matter, against all iusticiaries and hypocrites, which robbe Almighty GOD of his honour, and ascribe it to themselues, Saint Paul bringeth in his beliefe: Wee be not (saith he) sufficient of our selues, as of our selues once to thinke any thing: but all our ablenesse is of GODS goodnesse (2 Corinthians 3.5). For hee it is in whom wee haue all our being, our liuing, and moouing (Acts 17.28). If yee will know furthermore, where they had their gifts and sacrifices, which they offered continually in their liues to Almighty GOD, they cannot but agree with Dauid, where hee saith: Of thy liberall hand, O Lord, we haue receiued that we gaue vnto thee. If this holy company therefore confesse so constantly, that all the goods and graces wherewith they were indued in soule, came of the goodnesse of GOD onely: what more can be said to prooue that all that is good, commeth from Almighty GOD? Is it meete to thinke that all spirituall goodnes commeth from GOD aboue onely: and that other good things, either of nature or of fortune (as we call them) commeth of any other cause? Doeth GOD of his goodnesse adorne the soule, with all the powers thereof, as it is: and commeth the gifts of the body, wherewith it is indued, from any other? If he doth the more, cannot he doe the lesse? To iustifie a sinner, to new create him from a wicked person to a righteous man, is a greater act (saith S. Augustine) then to make such a new heauen & earth as is already made. Wee must needes agree, that whatsoeuer good thing is in vs, of grace, of nature or of fortune, is of GOD only, as the only authour and worker.

And yet it is not to be thought, that GOD hath created all this whole vniuersall world as it is, and thus once made, hath giuen it vp to be ruled and vsed after our owne with and deuice, and so taketh no more charge therefore. As we see the shipwright, after he hath brought his shippe to a perfect end, then deliuereth it to the Mariners, and taketh no more care thereof. Nay GOD hath not so created the world, that hee is carelesse of it: but hee still preserueth it by his goodnesse, hee still stayeth it in his creation. For els without his speciall goodnesse, it could not stand long in his condition. And therefore Saint Paul saith, that he preserueth all things, and beareth them vp still in his word (Hebrews 1.3), lest they should fall without him to their nothing againe, whereof they were made. If his especiall goodnesse were not euery where present, euery creature should be out of order, and no creature should haue his propertie wherein hee was first created. Hee is therefore inuisible euery where, and in euery creature, and fulfilleth both heauen and earth with his presence. In the fire, to giue heat, in the water to giue moisture, in the earth to giue fruit, in the heart to giue his strength, yea in our bread and drinke is hee, to giue vs nourishment, where without him the bread and drinke cannot giue sustenance, nor the hearbe health, as the wise man plainely confesseth it, saying, It is not the increase of fruits that feedeth men, but it is thy word (O Lord) which preserueth them that trust in thee (Apocrypha. Wisdom 16.26). And Moses agreeth to the same, when he saith, Mans life resteth not in bread onely, but in euery word which proceedeth out of GODS mouth (Deuteronomy 8.3). It is neither the hearbe nor the plaister, that giueth health of themselues, but thy word, O Lord (saith the wiseman) which healeth all things (Apocrypha. Wisdom 16.12). It is not therefore the power of the creatures which worketh their effects, but the goodnesse of GOD which worketh in them. In his word truely doeth all things consist. By that same word that heauen and earth were made, by the same are they vpholden, mainteined, and kept in order (saith S. Peter) and shall be till Almightie GOD shall withdraw his power from them, and speake their dissolution (2 Peter 3.7). If it were not thus, that the goodnesse of GOD were effectually in his creatures to rule them, how could it bee that the maine sea, so raging and labouring to ouerflow the earth, could bee kept within his bounds and bankes as it is? That holy man Iob euidently spied the goodnesse of GOD in this point, and confessed, that if hee had not a speciall goodnesse to the preseruation of the earth, it could not but shortly be ouerflowed of the sea. How could it be that the elements, so diuers and contrary as they be among themselues, should yet agree and abide together in a concord, without destruction one of another to serue our vse, if it came not onely of GODS goodnesse so to temper them? How could the fire not burne and consume all things, if it were let loose to goe whither it would, and not stayed in his sphere by the goodnesse of GOD, measurably to heat these inferiour creatures to their riping? Consider the huge substance of the earth, so heauie and great as it is: How could it so stand stably in the space as it doth, if GODS goodnesse reserued it not so for vs to trauell on? It is thou O Lord (saith Dauid) which hast founded the earth in his stabilitie, and during thy word, it shall neuer reele or fall downe (Psalms 104.5). Consider the great strong beasts and fishes, farre passing the strength of man, how fierce soeuer they be and strong, yet by the goodnes of GOD they preuaile not against vs, but are vnder our subiection, and serue our vse. Of whom came the inuention thus to subdue them, and make them fit for our commodities? Was it by mans braine- nay rather this inuention came by the goodnesse of GOD, which inspired mans vnderstanding to haue his purpose of euery creature. Who was it (saith Iob) that put will and wisedome in mans head, but GOD onely his goodnesse (Job 38.36)? And as the same saith againe, I perceiue that euery man hath a minde, but it is the inspiration of the Almighty that giueth vnderstanding. It could not be verily (good Christian people) that man of his own wit vpholden, should inuent so many and diuerse deuises in all crafts and sciences, except the goodnesse of Almighty GOD had beene present with men, and had stirred their wits and studies of purpose to know the natures and disposition of all his creatures, to serue vs sufficiently in our needes and necessities. Yea, not only to serue our necessities, but to serue our pleasures and delight, more then necessitie requireth. So liberall is GODS goodnesse to vs, to prouoke vs to thanke him, if any hearts we haue. The wise man in his contemplation by himselfe, could not but graunt this thing to bee true that I reason vnto you. In his hands (saith he) be we, and our words, and all our wisedome, and all our sciences and workes of knowledge (Apocrypha. Wisdom 7.16). For it is hee that gaue mee the true instruction of his creatures, both to know the disposition of the world, and the vertues of the elements, the beginning and end of times, the change and diuersities of them, the course of the yeere, the order of the starres, the natures of beasts, and the powers of them, the power of the windes, and thoughts of men, the differences of planets, the vertue of rootes, and whatsoeuer is hid and secret in nature, I learned it. The artificer of all these taught me this wisedome (Apocrypha. Wisdom 9.13-17). And further hee saith, Who can search out the things that bee in heauen? for it is hard for vs to search such things as be on earth, and in daily sight afore vs. For our wittes and thoughts (saith he) be imperfect, and our policies vncertaine. No man can therefore search out the meaning in these things, except thou giuest wisedome, and sendest thy Spirit from aboue. If the wise man thus confesseth all things to be of GOD, why should not we acknowledge it? and by the knowledge of it, consider our duety to GOD-ward, and giue him thankes for his goodnes? I perceiue that I am far heere ouercharged with the plentie and coppy of matter, that might be brought in for the proofe of this cause. If I should enter to shew how the goodnesse of Almighty GOD appeared euery where in the creatures of the world, how marueilous they be in their creation, how beautifull in their order, how necessary they bee to our vse: all with one voyce must needes graunt their Authour to be none other but Almighty GOD, his goodnesse must they needs extoll and magnifie euery where, to whom bee all honour and glorie for euermore.

THE SECOND PART OF THE HOMILY FOR ROGATION WEEKE.

IN the former part of this Homilie (good Christian people) I haue declared to your contemplation, the great goodnesse of Almighty GOD, in the creation of this world, with all the furniture thereof, for the vse and comfort of man, whereby wee might rather bee moued to acknowledge our dutie againe to his maiestie. And I trust it hath wrought not only beliefe in you, but also it hath mooued you to render your thanks secretly in your hearts to Almighty GOD for his louing kindnes. But yet peraduenture some will say, that they canne agree to this, that all that is good partayning to the soule, or whatsoeuer is created with vs in body, should come from GOD, as from the authour of all goodnesse and from none other. But of such things as bee without them both, I meane such good things which wee call goods of fortune, as richesse, authoritie, promotion, and honour some men may thinke, that they should come of our industry and diligence, of our labour and trauaile, rather then supernaturally. Now then consider, good people, if any authour there bee of such things concurrant of mans labour and endeuour, were it meete to ascribe them to any other then to GOD? as the Panimes Philosophers and Poets did erre,, which tooke Fortune, and made her a goddesse to be honoured, for such things? GOD forbid (good Christian people) that this imagination should earnestly bee receiued of vs that bee worshippers of the true GOD, whose workes and proceedings bee expressed manifestly in his word. These bee the opinions and sayings of infidels, not of true GOD, whose workes and proceedings bee expressed manifestly in his word. These bee the opinions and sayings of infidels, not of true Christians. For they indeede (as Iob maketh mention) beleeue and say, that GOD hath his residence and resting place in the cloudes, and considereth nothing of our matters (Job 22.14). Epicures they bee that imagine that he walketh about the coastes of the heauens, & hath no respect of these inferiour things, but that all these things should proceede either by chance or at aduenture, or else by disposition of fortune, and GOD to haue no stroke in them. What other thing is this to say, then as the foole supposeth in his heart, there is no GOD (Psalms 14.1)? Whom we shall none otherwise reprooue, then with GODS owne wordes by the mouth of Dauid. Heare my people (saith he) for I am thy GOD, thy very GOD. All the beastes of the wood are mine. Sheepe and oxen that wander in the mountaines. I haue the knowledge of all the fowles of the ayre, the beauty of the fielde is my handy worke, mine is the whole circuite of the world, and all the plenty that is in it (Psalms 50.7-12). And againe the Prophet Ieremie: Thinkest thou that I am a GOD of the place nigh me (saith the Lord) and not a GOD farre of? Can a man hide himselfe in so secret a corner, that I shall not see him? Do not I fulfill and replenish both heauen and earth, saith the Lord (Jeremiah 23.23-24)? Which of these two should be most beleeued? Fortune whom they paint to bee blinde of both eyes, euer vnstable and vnconstant in her wheele, in whose handes they say these things bee? Or GOD, in whose hand and power these things bee indeed, who for his trueth and constancie was yet neuer reproued? For his sight looketh thorow heauen and earth, and seeth all things presently with his eyes. Nothing is too darke or hidden from his knowledge, not the priuie thoughts of mens mindes. Trueth it is, that GOD is all riches, all power, all authoritie, all health, wealth, and prosperity, of the which wee should haue no part without his liberall distribution, and except it came from him aboue. Dauid first testifieth of riches and possessions: If thou giuest good lucke, they shall gather, and if thou openest thy hand, they shalbe full of goodnesse: but if thou turnest thy face they shall be troubled (Psalms 104.28-29). And Solomon saith, It is the blessing of the Lord that maketh rich men (Proverbs 10.22). To this agreeth that holy woman Anne, where shee saith in her song: It is the Lord that maketh the poore, and maketh the rich, it is hee that promoteth and pulleth downe, hee can raise a needy man from his miserie and from the dunghill, hee can lift vp a poore personage to sit with princes, and haue the seate of glory: for all the coastes of the earth be his (1 Samuel 2.7-8). Now if any man will aske, What shall it auaile vs to know that euery good gift, as of nature and fortune (so called) and euery perfect gift, as of grace, concerning the soule to be of GOD, and that it is his gift only? Forsoth for many causes it is conuenient for vs to know it. For so shall we know (if wee confesse the trueth) who ought iustly to bee thanked for them. Our pride shall be thereby abated, perceiuing naught to come of our selues but sinne and vice: if any goodnesse bee in vs, to referre all laude and prayse for the same to Almighty GOD. It shall make vs to aduance our selues before our neighbour, to dispise him for that hee hath fewer giftes, seeing GOD giueth his giftes where hee will. It shall make vs by the consideration of our giftes, not to extoll our selues before our neighboures. It shall make the wise man not to glory of his wisedome, nor the strong man in his strength, nor the rich to glory in his riches (Jeremiah 9.23), but in the liuing GOD, which is the authour of all these: lest if we should doe so, wee might be rebuked with the wordes of Saint Paul, What hast thou, that thou hast not receiued? & if thou hast receiued it, why gloriest thou in thy selfe, as though thou haddest not receiued it (1 Corinthians 4.7)? To confesse that all good things commeth from Almighty GOD, is a great poynt of wisedome, my friendes: For so confessing, we know whither to resort for to haue them, if wee want, as Saint Iames biddeth vs, saying, If any man wanteth the gift of wisedome, let him aske it of GOD that giues it, and it shall bee giuen him (James 1.5). As the wise man in the want of such a like gifte, made his recourse to GOD for it, as hee testifieth in his booke: After I knew (saith hee) that otherwise I could not be chaste, except GOD granted it, (and this was as hee there writeth, hie wisedome to know whose gifte it was) I made haste to the Lord, and earnestly besought him, euen from the rootes of my heart, to haue it (Apocrypha. Wisdom 8.21). I would to GOD (my friendes) that in our wants and necessities, we would goe to GOD, as Saint Iames biddeth, and as the wise man teacheth vs that hee did. I would wee beleeued stedfastly that GOD only giues them: If wee did, wee shoulde not seeke our want and necessitie of the deuill and his ministers so oft as wee doe, as dayly experience declareth it. For if wee stand in necessitie of corporall health, whither goe the common people, but to charmes, witchcraftes and other delusions of the Deuill? If wee knewe that GOD were the authour of this gift, wee woulde only vse his meanes appoynted, and bide his leysure, till hee thought it good for vs to haue it giuen, If the Merchaunt and worldly occupier knew that GOD is the giuer of riches, hee woulde content himselfe with so much as by iust meanes approued of GOD, hee coulde get to his liuing, and would be no richer then trueth would suffer him, hee woulde neuer procure his gaine and aske his goods at the Deuils hand. GOD forbid ye will say, that any man should take his riches of the Deuill. Verily so many as increase them selues by vsurie, by extortion, by periury by stealth, by deceits and crafte, they haue their goods of the Deuills gift. And all they that giue themselues to such meanes, and haue renounced the true meanes that GOD hath appoynted, haue forsaken him, and are become worshippers of the Deuill, to haue their lukers and aduantages. They be such as kneele downe to the deuill at his bidding, and worship him: For he promiseth them for so doing, that he will giue them the world, and the goods therein. They cannot otherwise better serue the deuill, then to doe his pleasure and commandement: And his motion and will it is, to haue vs forsake the trueth, and betake vs to falsehood, to lyes and periuries. They therefore which beleeue perfectly in their heart that GOD is to be honoured, and requested for the gift of all things necessary, would vse none other meanes to relieue their necessities but trueth and verity, and would serue GOD to haue competencie of all things necessary. The man in his neede would not releeue his want by stealth. The woman would not relieue her necessity and pouerty by giuing her body to other in adulterie for gaine. If GOD be the authour indeede of life, health, riches, and welfare, let vs make our recourse to him, as the authour, and we shall haue it, saith Saint Iames. Yea it is hie wisedome by the wise man therefore to know whose gift it is, for many other skilles it is wisedome to know and beleeue that all goodnesse and graces be of GOD, as the authour. Which thing well considered, must needes make vs thinke that we shall make account for that which GOD giueth vs to possesse, and therefore shall make vs to be more diligent well to spend them to GODS glory, and to the profite of our neighbour, that we may make a good account at the last, and be praysed for good stewards, that we may heare these wordes of our Iudge: Well done good seruant and faithfull, thou hast beene faithfull in little, I will make thee ruler ouer much, goe in into they Master ioy (Matthew 25.21). Besides, to beleeue certainely GOD to bee the authour of all the giftes that we haue, shall make vs to bee in silence and patience when they bee taken againe from vs: For as GOD of his mercy doeth grant vs them to vse: So other whiles he doeth iustly take them againe from vs, to prooue our patience, to exercise our faith, and by the meanes of the taking away of a fewe, to bestow the more warily those that remaine, to teach vs to vse them the more to his glorie, after hee giueth them to vs againe. Many there be that with mouth can say that they beleeue that GOD is the authour of euery good gift that they haue: but in the time of temptation they goe backe from this beliefe. They say it in worde, but deny it in deede. Consider the custome of the world, and see whether it bee not true. Behold the rich man that is indued with substance, if by any aduersitie his goodes bee taken from him, how fumeth and fretteth he? How murmureth hee and dispayreth? He that hath the gift of good reputation, if his name bee any thing touched by the detractour, how vnquiet is he? how busie to reuenge his dispite? If a man hath the gifte of wisedome, and fortune to bee taken of some euill willer for a foole, and is so reported: how much doeth it grieue him to bee so esteemed? Thinke yee that these belieue constantly that GOD is the authour of these giftes? If they belieue it verely, why should they not patiently suffer GOD to take away his giftes againe, which hee gaue them freely, and lent for a time? But ye will say, I could bee content to resigne to GOD such giftes, if hee tooke them againe from me: But now are they taken from mee by euill chances and false shrewes, by naughtie wretches, how should I take this thing patiently? To this may be answered, that Almighty GOD is of his nature inuisible, and commeth to no man visible after the manner of man, to take away his giftes that hee lent. But in this point whatsoeuer GOD doeth, hee bringeth it about by his instrumentes ordained thereto. Hee hath good Angels, hee hath euill angels, hee hath good men, and hee hath euill men, hee hath haile and raine, hee hath wind and thunder, hee hath heate and cold. Innumerable instruments hath hee, and messengers, by whom againe hee asketh such giftes as he committeth to our trust, as the wise man confesseth, The creature must needes waite to serue his maker, to bee fierce against vniust men to their punishment (Apocrypha. Wisdom 16.9). For as the same authour saith, He armeth the creature, to reuenge his enemies, and other whiles to the probation of our faith, stirreth hee vp such stormes. And therefore by what meane and instrument soeuer GOD takes from vs his giftes, we must patiently take GODS iudgement in worth, and acknowledge him to bee the taker and giuer, as Iob saith: The Lord gaue, and the Lord tooke (Job 1.21), when yet his enemies draue his cattell away, and when the deuill slewe his children, and afflicted his body with grieuous sickenesse. Such meekenesse was in that holy King and Prophet Dauid, when hee was reuiled of Semei in the presence of all his hoste, hee tooke it patiently, and reuiled not againe, but as confessing GOD to be the authour of his innocency and good name, and offering it to bee at his pleasure: Let him alone (saith hee to one of his seruants that would haue reuenged such dispite) for GOD hath commanded him to curse Dauid, and peraduenture GOD intendeth thereby to render mee some good turne for this curse of him to day (2 Samuel 16.10-12). And though the minister other whiles doeth euill in his acte, proceeding of malice, yet forasmuch as GOD turneth his euill act to a proofe of our patience, wee shoulde rather submit our selfe in patience, then to haue indignation at GODS rodde, which peraduenture when hee hath corrected vs to our nurture, he will cast it into the fire, as it deserueth. Let vs in like maner truely acknowledge all our gifts and prerogatiues, to be so GODS gifts, that wee shall bee ready to resigne them vp at his will and pleasure againe. Let vs throughout our whole liues confesse all good thinges to come of GOD, of what name or nature soeuer they bee, not of these corruptible things only, whereof I haue now last spoken, but much more of all spirituall graces behoueable for our soule, without whose goodnesse no man is called to faith, or staied therein, as I shall hereafter in the next part of this Homilie declare to you. In the meane season forget not what hath already beene spoken to you, forget not to bee comfortable in your iudgementes to the trueth of his doctrine, and forgette not to practise the same in the whole state of your life, whereby yee shall obtaine the blessing promised by our Sauiour Christ: Blessed bee they which heare the word of GOD, and fulfill it in life. Which blessing hee grant to vs all, who raigneth ouer all, one GOD in Trinitie, the Father, the Sonne, and the holy Ghost, to whom bee all honour and glorie for euer. Amen.

The third part of the Homilie for Rogation Weeke. I Promised to you to declare that all spirituall giftes and graces come specially from GOD. Let vs consider the trueth of this matter, and heare what is testified first of the gift of faith, the first entry into the Christian life, without &the; which no man can please GOD. For Saint Paul confesseth it plainely to be GODS gift, saying, Faith is the gift of GOD (Ephesians 2.8). And againe Saint Peter sayth, It is of GODS power that yee be kept through faith to saluation (1 Peter 1.5). It is of the goodnesse of GOD that we falter not in our hope vnto him. It is verily GODS worke in vs, the charitie wherewith wee loue our brethren. If after our fall wee repent, it is by him that we repent, which reacheth forth his mercifull hand to rayse vs vp. If any will we haue to rise, it is he that preuenteth our wil, and disposeth vs thereto. If after contrition wee feele our conscience at peace with GOD through remission of our sinne, and so bee reconciled againe to his fauour, and hope to be his children and inheritors of euerlasting life: who worketh these great miracles in vs? our worthinesse, our deseruings and indeuours, our wits, and vertue? Nay verily: Saint Paul will not suffer flesh and clay to presume to such arrogancie, and therefore sayth, All is of GOD which hath reconciled vs to himselfe by Iesus Christ. For GOD was in Christ when he reconciled the world vnto himselfe. GOD the Father of all mercy, wrought this high benefite vnto vs, not by his owne person: but by a meane, by no lesse meane then his onely beloued Sonne, whom he spared not from any paine and trauaile that might doe vs good. For vpon him he put our sinnes, vpon him he made our ransome, him he made the meane betwixt vs and himselfe, whose mediamediation was so acceptable to GOD the Father, through his absolute and perfect obedience, that he tooke his act for a full satisfaction of all our disobedience and rebellion, whose righteousnesse he tooke to weigh against our sinnes, whose redemption hee would haue stand against our damnation. In this poynt, what haue wee to muse within our selues good friends? I thinke no lesse then that which S. Paul sayd, in the remembrance of this wonderfull goodnesse of GOD. Thankes be to Almighty GOD, through Christ Iesus our Lord: for it is hee for whose sake wee receiued this high gift of grace (Romans 7.25). For as by him (being the euerlasting wisedome) hee wrought all the world and that is contained therein: So by him onely and wholy, would hee haue all things restored againe in heauen and in earth. By this our heauenly Mediatour therefore doe we know the fauour and mercy of GOD the Father, by him know we his will and pleasure towards vs, for he is the brightnesse of his Fathers glory, and a very cleare image and paterne of his substance. It is hee whom the Father in heauen delighteth to haue for his welbeloued Sonne (Matthew 3.17), whom he authorised to be our teacher, whom he charged vs to heare, saying, Heare him. It is hee by whom the Father of heauen doeth blesse vs with all spirituall and heauenly gifts (Ephesians 1.3), for whose sake and fauour (writeth Saint Iohn) we haue receiued grace and fauour (John 1.16). To this our Sauiour and Mediatour, hath GOD the Father giuen the power of heauen and earth, and the whole iurisdiction and authority, to distribute his goods and gifts committed to him: for so writeth the Apostle, To euery one of vs is grace giuen, according to the measure of Christes giuing (Ephesians 4.7). And thereupon to execute his authority committed, after that he had brought sinne and the Deuill to captiuitie, to bee no more hurtfull to his members, hee ascended vp to his Father againe, and from thence sent liberall giftes to his welbeloued seruants, and hath still the power to the worldes ende to distribute his Fathers giftes continually in his Church, to the establishment and comfort thereof. And by him hath Almighty GOD decreed to dissolue the world, to call all before him, to iudge both the quicke and the dead, and finally by him shall he condemne the wicked to eternall fire in hell, and giue the good eternall life, and set them assuredly in presence with him in heauen for euermore. Thus yee see how all is of GOD, by his Sonne Christ our Lord and Sauiour. Remember I say once againe your duetie of thankes, let them be neuer to want, still inioyne your selfe to continue in thankesgiuing, yee can offer to GOD no better sacrifice: For hee sayth himselfe, It is the sacrifice of prayse and thanks that shall honour me (Psalms 50.14). Which thing was well perceiued of that holy Prophet Dauid, when hee so earnestly spake to himselfe thus, O my soule, blesse thou the Lord, and all that is within me blesse his holy Name. I say once againe: O my soule blesse thou the Lord, and neuer forget his manifold rewardes (Psalms 103.1-2). GOD giue vs grace (good people) to know these things, and to feele them in our hearts. This knowledge and feeling is not in our selfe, by our selfe it is not possible to come by it, a great pitie it were &that; we should lose so profitable knowledge. Let vs therefore meekely call vpon that bountifull spirit the holy Ghost, which proceedeth from our Father of mercy, and from our Mediatour Christ, that he would assist vs, and inspire vs with his presence, that in him we may be able to heare the goodnesse of GOD declared vnto vs to our saluation. For without his liuely and secret inspiration, can we not once so much as speake the Name of our Mediatour, as S. Paul plainely testifieth: No man can once name our Lord Iesus Christ, but in the holy Ghost (1 Corinthians 12.3). Much lesse should we be able to beleeue and know these great mysteries that be opened to vs by Christ. Saint Paul saith, that no man can know what is of GOD, but the spirit of GOD. As for vs (saith he) we haue receiued not the spirit of the world, but the spirit which is of GOD, for this purpose: that in that holy spirit we might know the things that bee giuen vs by Christ (1 Corinthians 2.11-12). The wise man saith, that in the power and vertue of the holy Ghost, resteth all wisedome, and all ability to know GOD, and to please him. For he writeth thus, We know that it is not in mans power to guide his goings. No man can know thy pleasure except thou giuest wisedome, and sendest thy holy Spirit from aboue. Send him downe therefore (prayeth he to GOD) from the holy heauens, and from the throne of thy Maiestie, that he may be with me, and labour with me, that so I may know what is acceptable before thee (Wisdom 9.10, 13). Let vs with so good heart pray, as he did, and we shall not faile but to haue his assistance. For he is soone seene of them that loue him, he will be found of them that seeke him: For very liberall and gentle is the spirit of wisedome. In his power shall we haue sufficient abilitie to know our duety to GOD, in him shall we be comforted and couraged to walke in our duetie, in him shall we bee meete vessels to receiue the grace of Almighty GOD: for it is he that purgeth and purifieth the minde by his secret working. And hee onely is present euery where by his inuisible power, and conteineth all things in his dominion. Hee lighteneth the heart to conceiue worthy thoughts to Almighty GOD, he sitteth in the tongue of man to stirre him to speake his honour, no language is hid from him, for he hath the knowledge of all speach, he onely ministreth spirituall strength to the powers of our soule and body. To hold the way which GOD had prepared for vs, to walke rightly in our iourney, wee must acknowledge that it is in the power of his spirit which helpeth our infirmitie. That wee may boldly come in prayer, and call vpon Almighty GOD as our Father, it is by this holy spirit, which maketh intercession for vs with continuall sighes (Galatians 4.6, Romans 8.26). If any gift we haue wherewith we may worke to the glory of GOD, and profite of our neighbour, all is wrought by his owne and selfe same spirit, which maketh his distributions peculiarly to euery man as hee will (1 Corinthians 12.8-11). If any wisdome wee haue, it is not of our selues, we cannot glory therein as begun of our selues, but we ought to glory in GOD from whom it came to vs, as the Prophet Ieremie writeth: Let him that reioyceth, reioyce in this, that hee vnderstandeth and knoweth mee, for I am the Lord which shew mercy, iudgement, and righteousnesse in the earth, for in these things I delight, saith the Lord (Jeremiah 9.24). This wisedome cannot bee atteined, but by the direction of the spirit of GOD, and therefore it is called spirituall wisedome. And no where can we more certainely search for the knowledge of this will of GOD (by the which wee must direct all our workes and deedes) but in the holy Scriptures, for they be they that testifie of him, sayth our Sauiour Christ (John 5.39). It may bee called knowledge and learning that is otherwhere gotten without the word: but the wise man plainely testifieth, that they all bee but vayne which haue not in them the wisedome of GOD (Apocrypha. Wisdom 13.1). Wee see to what vanitie the olde Philosophers came, who were destitute of this science, gotten and searched for in his word. Wee see what vanitie the schoole doctrine is mixed with, for that in this word they sought not the will of GOD, but rather the will of reason, the trade of custome, the path of &the; fathers, the practise of the Church. Let vs therefore reade and reuolue the holy Scripture both day and night, for blessed is hee that hath his whole meditation therein (Psalms 1.2). It is that that giueth light to our feete to walke by (Psalms 119.105). It is that which giueth wisedome to the simple & ignorant (Psalms 19.7). In it may we finde eternall life (John 5.24).

In the holy Scriptures finde wee Christ, in Christ finde wee GOD: for hee it is that is the expresse Image of the Father. He that seeth Christ, seeth the Father. And contrariwise, as Saint Ierome sayth, the ignorance of Scripture, is the ignorance of Christ. Not to know Christ, is to bee in darkenesse, in the middes of our worldly and carnall light of reason and philosophie (Hebrews 1.3, John 14.9). To bee without Christ, is to be in foolishnesse: For hee is the onely wisedome of the Father, in whom it pleased him that all fulnesse and perfection should dwell (Colossians 1.19). With whom whosoeuer is indued in heart by faith, and rooted fast in charity hath layde a sure foundation to build on, whereby hee may bee able to comprehend with all Saints what is the breadth, length, and depth, and to know the loue of Christ (Ephesians 3.18). This vniuersall and absolute knowledge, is that wisedome which S. Paul wisheth these Ephesians to haue, as vnder heauen the greatest treasure that can bee obtained. For of this wisedome the wise man writeth thus of his experience, All good things came to mee together with her, and innumerable riches through her handes (Apocrypha. Wisdom 7.11). And addeth moreouer in that same place. She is the mother of all these things: For shee is an infinite treasure vnto men, which whoso vse, become partakers of the loue of GOD. I might with many words moue some of this audience to search for this wisedome, to sequester their reason, to followe GODS commaundement, to cast from them the witts of their braines, to fauoure this wisedome, to renounce the wisedome and policie of this fond world, to tast and sauoure that whereunto the fauour and will of GOD hath called them, and willeth vs finally to enioy by his fauour, if wee would giue eare: But I will haste to the third part of my text, wherein is expressed further in sapience, how GOD giueth his elect vnderstanding of the motions of the heauens, of the alterations and circumstances of time. Which as it followeth in words more plentifull in the text which I haue last cited vnto you: so it must needes follow in them that bee indued with this spirituall wisedome. For as they can search where to ende this wisedome, and know of whom to aske it: So know they againe that in time it is founde, and can therefore attemper themselues to the occasion of the time, to suffer no time to passe away, wherein they may labour for this wisedome. And to encrease therein, they know how GOD of his infinite mercie and lenitie giueth all men heere time and place of repentance. And they see how the wicked (as Iob writeth) abuse the same to their pride, and therefore doe the godly take the better holde of the time, to redeeme it out of such vse as it is spoiled in by the wicked (Job 24.1). They which haue this wisedome of GOD, can gather by the diligent and earnest studie of the worldlings of this present life, how they waite their times, and applie themselues to euery occasion of time and to get riches, to encrease their lands and patrimonie. They see the time passe away, and therefore take hold on it, in such wise, that other whiles they will with losse of their sleepe and ease, with suffering many paines, catch the offer of their time, knowing that that which is past can not bee returned againe, repentance may follow, but remedy in none, Why should not they then that be spirituall wise in their generation, waite their time to encrease as fast in their state, to winne and gayne euerlastingly? They reason what a bruite forgetfulnesse it were in man indued with reason, to be ignorant of their times and tides, when they see the Turtle doue, the Storke, and the Swalow to waite their times, as Ieremie saith: The Storke in the ayre knoweth her appointed times, the Turtle, the Crane, and the Swallow obserue the time of their comming: but my people knoweth not the iudgement of the Lord (Jeremiah 8.7). S. Paul willeth vs to redeeme the time, because the dayes are euill (Ephesians 5.16). It is not the counsell of Saint Paul onely, but of all other that euer gaue precepts of wisedome.

There is no precept more seriously giuen and commanded, then to know the time. Yea Christian men for that they heare how grieuously GOD complaineth, and threatneth in the Scriptures them which will not know the time of his visitations are learned thereby, the rather earnestly to apply themselues thereunto (Luke 19.44). After our Sauiour Christ had prophesied with weeping teares of the destruction of Ierusalem at the last hee putteth the cause: For that thou hast not knowen the time of thy visitation. O Englande, ponder the time of GODS mercifull visitation which is shewed thee from day to day, and yet wilt not regard it, neither wilt thou with his punishment bee driuen to thy duety, nor with his benefites bee prouoked to thanks! If thou knewest what may fall vpon thee for thine vnthankefulnesse, thou wouldest prouide for thy peace. Brethren, howsoeuer the world in generalitie is forgetfull of GOD, let vs particularly attend to our time, and winne the time with diligence, and applye our selues to that light and grace that is offered vs, let vs, if GODS fauour and iudgements which hee worketh in our time, cannot stir vs to call home to our selfe to doe that belonging to our saluation: At the leaste way, let the malice of the diuel, the naughtines of the worlde, which wee see exercised in these perilous and last times, wherein wee see our daies so dangerously set, prouoke vs to watch diligently to our vocation, to walke and goe forwarde therein.

Let the miserie and short transitorie ioyes spied in the casualtie of our dayes, moue vs while wee haue them in our handes, and seriously stirre vs to be wise, and to expend the gratious good will of GOD to vs-ward, which all the day long stretcheth out his handes (as the prophet saith) vnto vs (Isaiah 65.2), for the most part his mercifull handes, sometime his heauie handes, that wee, beeinge learned thereby, may escape the danger that must needes fall on the vniust, who leade their daies in felicitie and pleasure, without the knowinge of GODS will towarde them, but sodenly they goe downe into hell. Let vs bee founde watchers, founde in the peace of the Lorde, that at the laste day wee may bee found without spot, & blamelesse: yea let vs endeuoure our selues (good Christian people) diligently to keep the presence of his holy spirit. (Apocrypha. Wisdom 1.5) Let vs renounce all vncleannes, for he is the spirit of puritie. Let vs auoyd all hypocricsie, for this holy spirit will flee from that which is faigned. Cast we off all malice & all euill will, for this spirit will neuer enter into an euill willing soule. Let vs cast away all the whole lumpe of sin that standeth about vs, for he will neuer dwell in that body that is subdued to sin (Hebrews 12.1). Wee cannot be seene thankfull to Almighty GOD, and worke such despite to the spirit of grace, by whom we be sanctified (Hebrews 10.29). If we do our endeuour, we shall not neede to feare. We shall bee able to ouercome all our enemies that fight against vs. Onely let vs apply our selues to accept that grace that is offered vs. Of almighty GOD wee haue comfort by his goodnesse, of our sauiour Christs mediation wee may bee sure. And this holy spirit will suggest vnto vs that shall bee wholsome, and confirme vs in all things. Therefore it cannot bee but true that Saint Paul affirmeth: Of him, by him and in him be all thinges, and in him (after this transitory life well passed) shall we haue all thinges. For Saint Paul saith: when the sonne of GOD shall subdue all thinges vnto him, then shall GOD bee all in all (1 Corinthians 15.28). If ye will know how GOD shall be all in all, verely after this sense may ye vnderstand it: In this world yee see that we bee faine to borrow many things to our necessitie, of many creatures: there is no one thing that sufficeth all our necessities. If wee bee an hungred, wee lust for bread. If we be a thirst, wee seeke to bee refreshed with ale or wine. If wee bee colde, wee seeke for cloth. If we bee sicke, we seeke to the Phisition. If wee be in heauinesse, we seeke for comfort of our friendes, or of company: so that there is no one creature by it selfe that can content all our wants and desires. But in the world to come, in that euerlasting felicitie, wee shall no more begge and seeke our particular comforts and commodities of diuers creatures: but wee shall possesse all that wee can aske and desire, in GOD, and GOD shall bee to vs all things. He shall be to vs both father and mother, he shall bee bread and drinke, cloth, physitions comfort, he shall bee all things to vs, and that of much more blessed fashion, and more sufficient contentation, then euer these creatures were vnto vs, with much more declaration then euer mans declaration then euer mans reason is able to conceiue. The eye of man is not able to behold, nor his eare can heare, nor it can bee compassed in the heart of man, what ioy it is that GOD hath prepared for them that loue him (1 Corinthians 2.9).

Let vs all conclude then with one voice with the wordes of Saint Paul: To him which is able to doe aboundantly beyond our desires and thoughtes, according to the power working in vs, bee glorie and praise in his Church, by Christ Iesus for euer, world without end (Ephesians 3.20). Amen.

AN EXHORTATION TO be spoken to such Parishes where they vse their Preambulation in Rogation weeke, for the ouersight of the boundes and limits of their Towne.

ALthough wee be now assembled together (good Christian people) most principally to laud and thanke Almightie GOD for his great benefits, by beholding the fields replenished with all maner of fruit, to the maintenance of our corporall necessities, for our food and sustenance, and partly also to make our humble suits in prayers to his Fatherly prouidence, to conserue the same fruits in sending vs seasonable weather, whereby we may gather in the said fruits, to that end for which his Fatherly goodnesse hath prouided them: Yet haue we occasion secondarily giuen vs in our walkes on those dayes, to consider the olde ancient bounds and limits belonging to our owne Towneship, and to other our neighbours bordering about vs, to the intent that wee should be content with our owne, and not contentiously striue for others, to the breach of charitie, by any incroching one vpon another, for claiming one of the other, further then that in ancient right and custome our forefathers haue peaceably laid out vnto vs for our commoditie and comfort. Surely a great ouersight it were in vs, which be Christian men in one profession of Faith, daily looking for that heauenly inheritance which is bought for euery one of vs by the bloodshedding of our Sauiour Iesus Christ, to striue and fall to variance for the earthly bounds of our townes, to the disquiet of our life betwixt our selues, to the wasting of our goods by vaine expences and costes in the law. We ought to remember, that our habitation is but transitorie and short in this mortall life. The more shame it were to fall out into immortall hatred among our selues, for so brittle possessions, and so to loose our eternall inheritance in heauen. It may stand well with Charitie, for a Christian man quietly to maintaine his right and iust title. And it is the part of euery good Townes man, to preserue as much as lieth in him, the liberties, franchises, boundes, and limites of his towne and countrey: But yet to striue for our very rightes and dueties with the breach of loue and charitie, which is the onely liuery of a Christian man, or with the hurt of godly peace and quiet, by the which wee bee knitte together in one generall fellowship of Christes familie, in one common houshold of GOD, that is vtterly forbidden. That doeth GOD abhorre and detest, which prouoketh Almighty GODS wrath otherwhile to depriue vs quite of our commodities and liberties, because wee doe so abuse them, for matters of strife, discord, and dissension. Saint Paul blamed the Corinthians for such contentious suing among themselues, to the slaunder of their profession before the enemies of Christes religion, saying, thus vnto them. Now there is vtterly a falt among you, because yee goe to lawe one with another. Why rather suffer yee not wrong? Why rather suffer ye not harme (1 Corinthians 6.7)? If S. Paul blameth the Christian men, whereof some of them, for their owne right, went contentiously so to law, commending thereby the profession of patience in a Christian man: If Christ our Sauiour would haue vs rather to suffer wrong, and to turne our left cheeke to him which hath smitten the right, to suffer one wrong after another, rather then by breach of charitie to defend our owne (Matthew 5.39): In what state be they before GOD who doe the wrong? What curses do they fall into, who be false witnesse defraud either their neighbour, or towneship of his due right and iust possession? which will not let to take an oath by the holy Name of GOD, the authour of all trueth, to set out falshood and a wrong? Know yee not (saith Saint Paul) that the vnrighteous shall not inherite the kingdome of GOD (1 Corinthians 6.9)? what shall we then winne to increase a little the boundes and possessions of the earth, and loose the possessions of the inheritance euerlasting? Let vs therefore take such heed in maintaining of our bounds and possessions, that we commit not wrong by encroching vpon other. Let vs beware of suddaine verdite in things of doubt. Let vs well aduise our selues to aduouch that certainely, whereof either we haue no good knowledge or remembrance, or to claime that wee haue no iust title to. Thou shalt not (commandeth Almighty GOD in his Law) remoue thy neighbours marke, which they of olde time haue set in their inheritance (Deuteronomy 19.14). Thou shalt not (saith Solomon) remooue the ancient boundes which thy fathers haue layde (Proverbs 22.28). And lest wee should esteeme it to bee but a light offence so to doe, we shall vnderstand, that it is reckoned among the curses of GOD pronounced vpon sinners. Accursed be hee (saith Almighty GOD by Moses) who remooueth his neighbours doles and markes, and all the people shall say, answering Amen thereto, as ratifying that curse vpon whom it doth light (Deuteronomy 27.17). They doe much prouoke the wrath of GOD vpon themselues, which vse to grinde vp the doles and markes, which of ancient time were layd for the diuision of meeres and balkes in the fieldes, to bring the owners to their right. They do wickedly which do turne vp the ancient terries of the fieldes, that old men before times with great paines did tread out, whereby the Lordes recordes (which bee the tenantes euidences) bee peruerted and translated sometime to the disheriting of the right owner, to the oppression of the poore fatherlesse, or the poore widow. These couetous men know not what inconueniences they be the authours of. Sometime by such craft and deceit be committed great disorders and riottes in the challenge of their lands, yea sometimes murders and bloodshed, whereof thou art guiltie whosoeuer thou bee that giuest the occasion thereof. This couetous practising therefore with thy neighbours landes and goods, is hatefull to Almighty GOD. Let no man subtily compasse or defraud his neighbour (biddeth Saint Paul) in any maner of cause. For GOD (saith hee) is a reuenger of all such (1 Thessalonians 4.6). GOD is the GOD of all equity and righteousnesse, and therefore forbiddeth all such deceit and subtiltie in his Law, by these wordes, Yee shall not deale vniustly in iudgement, in line, in weight, or measure. Ye shall haue iust ballances, true weightes, and true measures (Levit. 19.35-36). False balance (saith Solomon) are an abomination vnto the Lord (Proverbs 20.23). Remember what Saint Paul saith, GOD is the reuenger of all wrong and iniustice, as wee see by dayly experience, how euer it thriueth vngraciously which is gotten by falshood and craft. Wee bee taught by experience, how Almighty GOD neuer suffereth the third heire to enioy his fathers wrong possessions, yea many a time they are taken from himselfe in his owne life time. GOD is not bound to defend such possessions as are gotten by the diuell and his counsell. GOD will defende all such mens goods and possessions, which by him are obtained and possessed, and will defend them against the violent oppressour. So witnesseth Solomon, The Lord will destroy the house of the proude man: But hee will stablish the borders of the widow (Proverbs 15.25). No doubt of it (saith Dauid) better is a little truely gotten to the righteous man, then the innumerable riches of the wrongfull man (Psalms 37.16). Let vs flee therefore (good people) all wrong practises in getting, maintaining and defending our possessions, lands, and liuelords, our bounds and liberties, remembring that such possessions bee all vnder GODS reuengeance. But what doe wee speake of house and land? Nay it is sayd in the Scripture, that GOD in his yre doeth roote vp whole kingdomes for wronges and oppressions, and doeth translate kingdomes from one nation to another, for vnrighteous dealing, for wrongs and riches gotten by deceit. This is the practise of the holy One (saith Daniel) to the intent that liuing men may know, that the most High hath power ouer the kingdomes of men, and giueth them to whomsoeuer hee will (Daniel 4.17). Furthermore, what is the cause of penurie and scarcenesse, of dearth and famine? Is it any other thing but a token of GODS yre, reuenging our wrongs and iniuries done one to another? Yee haue sowne much, (obraydeth GOD by his Prophet Aggei) and yet bring in little, yee eate, but yee be not satisfied, yee drinke, but yee bee not filled, yee cloth your selues, but yee bee not warme, and hee that earneth his wages, putteth it in a bottomlesse purse: yee looked for much increase, but loe, it came to little, and when yee brought it home (into your barnes) I did blow it away, sayth the the Lord (Haggai 1.6-9). O consider therefore the yre of GOD against gleaners, gatherers, and incrochers vpon other mens landes, and possessions! It is lamentable to see in some places, how greedy men vse to plowe and grate vpon their neighbors land that lieth next them, how couetous men now adayes plow vp so nigh the common balkes and walkes, which good men before time made the greater & broader, partly for the commodious walke of his neighbor, partly for the better shacke in haruest time, to the more comfort of his poore neighbours cattell? It is a shame to behold the insatiablenesse of some couetous persons in their doings: that where their ancestours left of their land a broade and sufficient beere balke, to carry the corps to the Christian sepulture, how men pinch at such beere balkes, which by long vse and custome ought to bee inuiolably kept for that purpose, And now they either quite ere them vp, and turne the dead body to be borne farther about in the high streets, or els if they leaue any such meere, it is too strait for two to walke on.

These strange encrochments (good neighbours) should be looked vpon. These should bee considered in these dayes of our Perambulations. And afterwards the parties admonished, and charitably reformed, who be the doers of such priuate gaining, to the slander of the towneship, and the hinderance of the poore. Your high wayes should be considered in your walkes, to vnderstand where to bestow your dayes workes, according to the good Statutes prouided for the same. It is a good deed of mercie, to amend the dangerous and noisome wayes, whereby thy poore neighbour sitting on his silly weake beast foundereth not in the deepe thereof, and so the Market the worse serued, for discouraging of poore vittailers to resort thither for the same cause. If now therefore yee will haue your prayers heard before Almightie GOD, for the increase of your corne and cattell, and for the defence thereof from vnseasonable mistes and blastes, from haile and other such tempestes, loue, equitie, and righteousnesse, ensue mercie and charitie, which GOD most requireth at our hands. Which Almightie GOD respecting chiefly, in making his ciuill lawes for his people the Israelites, in charging the owners not to gather vp their corne too nigh at haruest season, nor the grapes and Oliues in gathering time, but to leaue behind some eares of corne for the poore gleaners (Leviticus 19.9-10, Deuteronomy 24.19-21). By this he meant to induce them to pittie the poore, to relieue the needie, to shew mercie and kindnesse. It cannot be lost, which for his sake is distributed to the poore. (1 Corinthians 9.9-10) For he which ministreth seed to the sower, and bread to the hungry, which sendeth downe the early and latter raine vpon your fields, so to fill vp the barnes with corne, and the wine presses with wine and oyle (Joel 2.23-24), he I say who recompenseth all kind of benefits in the resurrection of the iust, he will assuredly recompence all mercifull deedes shewed to the needie, howsoeuer vnable the poore is, vpon whom it is bestowed. O (saith Salomon) let not mercie and trueth forsake thee. Binde them about thy necke (saith hee) and write them on the table of thy heart, so shalt thou find fauour at GODS hand (Proverbs 3.3-4).

Thus honour thou the Lord with thy riches, and with the first fruites of thine increase: So shall thy barnes be filled with abundance, and thy presses in all burst with new wine. Nay, GOD hath promised to open the windowes of heauen, vpon the liberall righteous man, that hee shall want nothing. He will represse the deuouring Caterpiller, which should deuour your fruits. Hee will giue you peace and quiet to gather in your prouision, that ye may sit euery man vnder his owne vine quietly, without feare of the forreine enemies to inuade you. Hee will giue you not onely food to feed on, but stomackes and good appetites to take comfort of your fruites, whereby in all things yee may haue sufficiencie. Finally, he will blesse you with all maner abundance in this transitorie life,and endue you with all manner of benediction in the next world, in the kingdome of heauen, through the merits of our Lord and Sauiour, to whom with the Father, and the holy Ghost, be all honor euerlasting. Amen.

HOMILY ON THE STATE OF MATRIMONY

AN HOMILIE OF
the state of Matrimonie

THE word of Almightie GOD doth testifie and declare, whence the originall beginning of Matrimony commeth, and why it is ordained. It is instituted of GOD, to the intent that man and woman should liue lawfully in a perpetuall friendship, to bring foorth fruite, and to auoide Fornication. By which meane a good conscience might bee preserued on both parties, in brideling the corrupt inclinations of the flesh, within the limites of honestie. For GOD hath straitly forbidden all whoredome and vncleannesse, and hath from time to time taken grieuous punishment of this inordinate lust, as all stories and ages haue declared. Furthermore it is also ordained, that the Church of GOD and his kingdome might by this kinde of life be conserued and enlarged, not onely in that GOD giueth children by his blessing, but also in that: they be brought vp by the Parents godly, in the knowledge of GODS word, that thus the knowledge of GOD and true Religion might bee deliuered by succession from one to another that finally many might enioy that euerlasting immortalitie. Wherefore, forasmuch as Matrimonie serueth vs as well to auoide sinne and offence, as to encrease the kingdome of GOD: you, as all other which enter the state, must acknowledge this benefit of GOD, with pure and thankefull minds, for that he hath so ruled your hearts, that yee follow not the example of the wicked world, who set their delight in filthinesse of sinne, but both of you stand in the feare of GOD, and abhorre all filthinesse. For that is surely the singular gift of GOD, where the common example of the world declareth how the diuell hath their hearts bound and entangled in diuers snares, so that they in their wiuelesse state runne into open abominations, without any grudge of their conscience. Which sort of men that liue so desperately, and filthy, what damnation tarieth for them, Saint Paul describeth it to them, saying: Neither whoremonger, neither adulterers, shall inherite the kingdome of GOD (1 Corinthians 6.9). This horrible iudgement of GOD yee bee escaped through his mercie, if so bee that yee liue inseparately, according to GODS ordinance. But yet I would not haue you carelesse without watching. For the deuill will assay to attempt all things to interrupt and hinder your hearts and godly purpose, if ye will giue him any entry. For hee will either labour to breake this godly knot once begun betwixt you, or else at the least hee will labour to encumber it with diuers griefes and displeasures.

And this is the principall craft, to worke dissension of hearts of the one from the other: That whereas now there is pleasant and sweet loue betwixt you, he will in the stead thereof, bring in most bitter & vnpleasant discord, And surely that same aduersarie of ours, doeth, as it were from aboue, assault mans nature and condition. For this folly is euer from our tender age growne vp with vs, to haue a desire to rule, to thinke highly of our selfe, so that none thinketh it meet to giue place to another. That wicked vice of stubborne will and selfe loue, is more meet to breake and to disseuer the loue of heart, then to preserue concord. Wherefore married persons must apply their minds in most earnest wise to concorde, and must craue continually of GOD the helpe of his holy Spirit, so to rule their hearts, and to knit their minds together, that they be not disseuered by any diuision of discord. This necessitie of prayer, must be oft in the practise and vsing of married persons, that oft times the one should pray for the other, lest hate and debate doe arise betwixt them. And because few doe consider this thing, but more few doe performe it (I say to pray diligently) we see how wonderfull the diuell deludeth and scorneth this state, how few Matrimonies there be without chidings, brawlings, tauntings, repentings, bitter cursings, and fightings. Which things whosoeuer doth commit, they doe not consider that it is the instigation of the ghostly enemie, who taketh great delight therein: For else they would with all earnest endeauour, striue against these mischiefes, not onely with prayer, but also with all possible diligence. Yea they would not giue place to the prouocation of wrath, which stirreth them either to such rough and sharpe words, or stripes, which is surely compassed by the diuell, whose temptation, if it be followed, must needs beginne and weaue the web of all miseries, and sorrowes. For this is most certainely true, that of such beginnings must needs ensue the breach of true concord in heart, whereby all loue must needes shortly be banished. Then can it not be but a miserable thing to behold, that yet they are of necessity compelled to liue together, which yet can not bee in quiet together. And this is most customably euery where to bee seene. But what is the cause thereof? Forsooth because they will not consider the craftie traines of the diuell, and therefore giue not themselues to pray to GOD, that hee would vouchsafe to represse his power. Moreouer, they doe not consider how they promote the purpose of the diuell, in that they follow the wrath of their hearts, while they threat one another, while they in their folly turne all vpside downe, while they will neuer giue ouer their right as they esteeme it, yea, while many times they will not giue ouer the wrong part in deed. Learne thou therefore, if thou desirest to be void of all these miseries, if thou desirest to liue peaceably and comfortably in wedlocke, how to make thy earnest prayer to GOD, that he would gouerne both your heartes by the holy Spirit, to restraine the Diuels power, whereby your concorde may remaine perpetually. But to this prayer must bee ioyned a singular diligence, whereof Saint Peter giueth this precept, saying, You husbands, deale with your weaker vessell, and as vnto them that are heires also of the grace of life, that your prayers bee not hindered (1 Peter 3.7). This precept doth particularly pertaine to the husband: for hee ought to be the leader and authour of loue, in cherishing and increasing concord, which then shall take place, if hee will vse moderation and not tyranny, and if he yeelde some thing to the woman. For the woman is a weake creature, not indued with like strength and constancie of minde, therefore they be the sooner disquieted, and they be the more prone to all weake affections & dispositions of mind, more then men bee, & lighter they bee, and more vaine in their fantasies & opinions. These things must bee considered of the man, that hee be not too stiffe, so that he ought to winke at some thinges, and must gently expounde all things, and to forbeare. Howbeit the common sort of men doeth iudge, that such moderation should not become a man: For they say that it is a token of womanish cowardnesse, and therefore they thinke that it is a mans part to fume in anger, to fight with fiste and staffe. Howbeit, howsoeuer they imagine, vndoubtedly Saint Peter doth better iudge what should be seeming to a man, and what he should most reasonably performe. For he saith, reasoning should be vsed, and not fighting. Yea hee saith more, that the woman ought to haue a certaine honour attributed to her, that is to say, shee must bee spared and borne with, the rather for that she is the weaker vessell, of a fraile heart, inconstant, and with a word soone stirred to wrath. And therefore considering these her frailties, shee is to be the rather spared. By this meanes, thou shalt not onely nourish concord: but shalt haue her heart in thy power and will. For honest natures will sooner bee reteined to doe their dueties, rather by gentle words, then by stripes. But hee which will doe all things with extremitie and seueritie, and doeth vse alwayes rigor in words and stripes, what will that auaile in the conclusion? Verely nothing, but that hee thereby setteth forward the diuels worke, hee banisheth away concord, charitie, and sweete amity, and bringeth in dissension, hatred, & yrkesomnesse, the greatest griefes that can be in the mutuall loue and felowship of mans life. Beyond all this, it bringeth another euill therewith, for it is the destruction and interruption of prayer: For in the time that the minde is occupied with dissention and discord, there can bee no true prayer vsed. For the Lords prayer hath not onely a respect to particular persons, but to the whole vniuersall, in the which wee openly pronounce, that we will forgiue them which haue offended against vs, euen as we aske forgiuenesse of our sinnes of GOD, Which thing how canne it be done rightly, when their hearts be at dissension? How can they pray each for other, when they bee at hate betwixt themselues? Now, if the ayde of prayer bee taken away, by what meanes can they sustaine themselues in any comfort? For they cannot otherwise either resist the deuill, or yet haue their heartes staide in stable comfort in all perills and necessities, but by prayer. Thus all discommodities, as well worldly as ghostly, follow this froward testines, and cumbrous fiercenesse, in maners, which bee more meete for bruite beastes, then for reasonable creatures. Saint Peter doeth not allow these things, but the diuell desireth them gladly. Wherefore take the more heede. And yet a man may be a man, although hee doeth not vse such extremitie, yea although hee should dissemble some things in his wiues manners. And this is the part of a Christian man, which both pleaseth GOD, and serueth also in good vse to the comfort of their mariage state. Now as concerning the wiues duety. What shall become her? shall she abuse the gentlenesse and humanity of her husband and, at her pleasure, turne all things vpside downe? No surely. For that is far repugnant against GODS commandement, For thus doeth Saint Peter preach to them, Yee wiues, be ye in subiection to obey your owne husbands (1 Peter 3.1). To obey, is another thing then to controle or command, which yet they may doe, to their children, and to their family: But as for their husbands, them must they obey, and cease from commanding, and performe subiection. For this surely doth nourish concord very much, when the wife is ready at hand at her husbands commandement, when she will apply her selfe to his will, when shee endeuoureth her selfe to seeke his contentation, and to doe him pleasure, when shee will eschewe all things that might offend him: For thus will most truely bee verified the saying of the Poet, A good wife by obeying her husband, shall beare the rule, so that he shall haue a delight and a gladnesse, the sooner at all times to returne home to her. But on the contrary part, when the wiues bee stubborne, froward, and malipert, their husbands are compelled therby to abhorre and flee from their owne houses, euen as they should haue battaile with their enemies. Howbeit, it can skantly be, but that some offences shall sometime chance betwixt them: For no man doth liue without fault, specially for that the woman is the more fraile partie. Therefore let them beware that they stand not in their faultes and wilfullnesse: but rather let them acknowledge their follies, and say, My husband, so it is, that by my anger I was compelled to doe this or that forgiue it me, and hereafter I will take better heede. Thus ought the woman more readily to doe, the more they be ready to offend. And they shall not doe this onely to auoyd strife and debate: but rather in the respect of the commandement of GOD, as Saint Paul expresseth it in this forme of words, Let women bee subiect to their husbands as to the Lorde: for the husband is the head of the woman, as Christ is the head of the Church (Ephesians 5.22-23). Here you vnderstand, that GOD hath commanded that ye should acknowledge the authoritie of the husband, and referre to him the honour of obedience. And Saint Peter saith in that place before rehearsed, that holy matrons did in former time decke themselues, not with gold and siluer, but in putting their whole hope in GOD, and in obeying their husbands, as Sara obeyed Abraham, calling him lord, whose daughters ye bee (saith he) if yee follow her example. This sentence is very meete for women to print in their remembrance. Trueth it is, that they must specially feele the griefe and paines of their Matrimonie, in that they relinquish the liberty of their owne rule, in the paine of their trauailing, in the bringing vp of their children. In which offices they be in great perils, and be grieued with great afflictions, which they might bee without if they liued out of Matrimonie. But S. Peter sayth, that this is the chiefe ornament of holy matrons, in that they set their hope and trust in GOD, that is to say, in that they refused not from mariage for the businesse thereof, for the giftes and perils thereof: but committed all such aduentures to GOD, in most sure trust of helpe, after that they haue called vpon his ayde. O woman, doe thou the like, and so shalt thou be most excellently beautified before GOD and all his Angels & Saints, and thou needest not to seeke further for doing any better workes. For, obey thy husband, take regard of his requests, and giue heede vnto him in perceiue what he requireth of thee, and so shalt thou honour GOD and liue peaceably in thy house. And beyond all this, GOD shall follow thee with his benediction, that all things shall well prosper, both to thee and to thy husband, as the Psalme saith: Blessed is the man which feareth GOD, and walketh in his wayes, thou shalt haue the fruit of thine owne hands, happy shalt thou be, and well it shall goe with thee. Thy wife shal be as a vine, plentifully spreading about thy house. Thy children shalbe as the young springs of the Oliues about thy table. Loe thus shall that man be blessed (saith Dauid) that feareth the Lord. This let the wife haue euer in minde, the rather admonished thereto by the apparell of her head. whereby is signified, that she is vnder couert or obedience of her husband. And as that apparell is of nature so appointed, to declare her subiection: So biddeth Saint Paul that all other of her rayment should expresse both shamefastnesse and sobriety. For if it be not lawfull for the woman to haue her head bare, but to beare thereon the signe of her power, wheresoeuer she goeth: more is it required that she declare the thing that is ment therby. And therefore these ancient women of the old world called their husbands lords, and shewed them reuerence in obeying them. But peraduenture shee will say, that those men loued their wiues indeede. I know that well ynough, & beare it well in minde. But when I doe admonish you of your dueties, then call not to consideration what their dueties be. For when we our selues doe teach our children to obey vs as their parents, or when we reforme our seruants, and tell them that they should obey their masters, not only at the eye, but as the Lord: If they should tell vs againe our dueties, we should not thinke it well done. For when we be admonished of our dueties and faults, wee ought not then to seeke what other mens dueties be. For though a man had a companion in his fault, yet should he not thereby be without his fault. But this must be onely looked on, by what meanes thou mayest make thy selfe without blame. For Adam did lay the blame vpon the woman, and she turned it vnto the serpent: but yet neither of them was thus excused. And therefore bring not such excuses to me at this time: but apply all thy diligence to heare thine obedience to thine husband. For when I take in hand to admonish thy husband to loue thee, and to cherish thee: yet will I not cease to set out the law that is appointed for the woman, aswell as I would require of the man what is written for his law. Goe thou therefore about such things as becommeth thee only, & shew thy selfe tractable to thy husband. Or rather if thou wilt obey thy husband for GODS precept, then alledge such things as be in his duty to doe, but performe thou diligently those things which the lawmaker hath charged thee to doe: For thus is it most reasonable to obey GOD, if thou wilt not suffer thy selfe to transgresse his law. He that loueth his friend, seemeth to doe no great thing: but he that honoureth that is hurtfull & hatefull to him, this man is worthy most commendation: Euen so think you, if thou canst suffer an extreme husband, thou shalt haue a great reward therefore: But if thou louest him only because he is gentle & courteous, what reward will GOD giue thee therefore? Yet I speake not these things that I would wish the husbands to bee sharpe towards their wiues: But I exhort the women that they would patiently beare the sharpnesse of their husbands. For when either partes doe their best to performe their duties the one to the other, then followeth thereon great profite to their neighbours for their examples sake. For when the woman is ready to suffer a sharpe husband, & the man will not extremely intreate his stubborne & troublesome wife, then be all things in quiet, as in a most sure hauen. Euen thus was it done in old time, that euery one did their owne duety and office, and was not busie to require the duetie of their neighbours. Consider I pray thee that Abraham tooke to him his brothers sonne, his wife did not blame him therefore. He commanded him to goe with him a long iourney, she did not gainesay it, but obeyed his precept.

Againe, after all those great miseries, labours and paines of that iourney, when Abraham was made as lord ouer all, yet did he giue place to Lot of his superioritie: which matter Sara tooke so little to griefe, that she neuer once suffered her tongue to speake such wordes as the common manner of women is woont to doe in these dayes, when they see their husbands in such roomes, to bee made vnderlings, and to bee put vnder their yongers, then they vpbrayd them with combrous talke, and call them fooles, dastards, and cowards for so doing. But Sara was so farre from speaking any such thing, that it came neuer into her minde and thought so to say, but allowed the wisedome & will of her husband. Yea, besides all this, after the said Lot had thus his will, and left to his vncle the lesse portion of land, hee chanced to fall into extreme perill: Which chance when it came to the knowledge of this said Patriarch, he incontinently put all his men in harnesse, and prepared himselfe with all his familie & friends, against the host of the Persians. In which case, Sara did not counsaile him to the contrary, nor did say, as then might haue beene said: My husband, whither goest thou so vnaduisedly? Why runnest thou thus on head? Why doest thou offer thy selfe to so great perilles, and art thus ready to ieopard thine owne life, and to perill the liues of all thine, for such a man as hath done thee such wrong? At the least way, if thou regardest not thy selfe, yet haue compassion on me, which for thy loue haue forsaken my kinred & my countrey, and haue the want both of my friends and kinsesfolkes, and am thus come into so farre countreys with thee, haue pitie on mee, and make me not here a widow, to cast mee into such cares and troubles. Thus might she haue said: but Sara neither said nor thought such words, but she kept herselfe in silence in all things. Furthermore, all that time when she was barren, and tooke no paines, as other women did, by bringing foorth fruit in his house? What did he? He complained not to his wife, but to Almighty GOD. And consider how either of them did their duties as became them: for neither did hee dispise Sara, because shee was barren, nor neuer did cast it in her teeth. Consider againe how Abraham expelled the handmaid out of the house, when she required it: So that by this I may truely prooue, that the one was pleased and contented with the other in all things: But yet set not your eyes onely on this matter, but looke further what was done before this, that Agar vsed her mistresse dispitefully, and that Abraham himselfe was somewhat prouoked against her, which must needes bee an intolerable matter, and a painfull, to a free hearted woman & a chaste. Let not therefore the woman be too busie to call for the duty of her husband, where shee should be ready to performe her owne, for that is not worthy any great commendations. And euen so againe, let not the man only consider what belongeth to the woman, and to stand too earnestly gazing thereon, for that is not his part or duty. But as I haue said, let either party be ready and willing to performe that which belongeth especially to themselues. For if wee be bound to hold out our left cheeke to strangers which will smite vs on the right cheeke: how much more ought wee to suffer an extreme and vnkind husband? But yet I meane not that a man should beat his wife, GOD forbid that, for that is the greatest shame that can be, not so much to her that is beaten, as to him that doth the deed. But if by such fortune thou chancest vpon such an husband, take it not too heauily, but suppose thou, that thereby is laid vp no small reward hereafter, & in this life time no small commendation to thee, if thou canst be quiet. But yet to you that be men, thus I speake, Let there bee none so grieuous fault to compell you to beat your wiues. But what say I, your wiues? no, it is not to be borne with, that an honest man should lay hands on his maide seruant to beat her. Wherefore if it be a great shame for a man to beat his bondseruant, much more rebuke it is, to lay violent hands vpon his freewoman. And this thing may be well vnderstood by the lawes which the Panims haue made, which doth discharge her any longer to dwell with such an husband, as vnworthy to haue any further company with her that doeth smite her. For it is an extreme point, thus so vilely to entreat her like a slaue, that is fellow to thee of thy life, and so ioyned vnto thee before time in the necessary matters of thy liuing. And therfore a man may well liken such a man (if he may be called a man, rather then a wild beast) to a killer of his father or his mother. And whereas wee be commanded to forsake our father and mother, for our wiues sake, and yet thereby doe worke them none iniurie, but doe fulfill the Law of GOD: How can it not appeare then to bee a point of extreame madnesse, to entreate her dispitefully, for whose sake GOD hath commaunded thee to leaue parents? Yea, who can suffer such despite? Who can worthily expresse the inconuenience that is, to see what weepings and waylings bee made in the open streetes, when neighbours runne together to the house of so vnruly an husband, as to a Bedlem man, who goeth about to ouerturne all that hee hath at home? Who would not thinke that it were better for such a man to wish the ground to open, and swallow him in, then once euer after to bee seene in the market? But peraduenture thou wilt obiect, that the woman prouoketh thee to this point. But consider thou againe that the woman is a fraile vessel, and thou art therefore made the ruler and head ouer her, to beare the weakenesse of her in this her subiection. And therefore studie thou to declare the honest commendation of thine authoritie, which thou canst no way better doe, then to forbeare to vrge her in her weakenesse and subiection. For euen as the King appeareth so much the more noble, the more excellent and noble hee maketh his officers and lieuetenants, whom if hee should dishonour, and despise the authoritie of their dignitie, he should depriue himselfe of a great part of his owne honour: Euen so, if thou doest despise her that is set in the next roome beside thee, thou doest much derogate and decay the excellencie and vertue of thine owne authoritie. Recount all these things in thy minde, and be gentle and quiet. Vnderstand that GOD hath giuen thee children with her, and art made a father, and by such reason appease thy selfe. Doest thou not see the husbandmen what diligence they vse to till that ground which once they haue taken to farme, though it be neuer so full of faults? As for an example, though it be dry, though it bringeth forth weedes, though the soyle cannot beare too much wette, yet he tilleth it, and so winneth fruit thereof: Euen in like manner, if thou wouldest vse like diligence to instruct and order the minde of thy spouse, if thou wouldest diligently apply thy selfe to weede out by little and little the noysome weedes of vncomely maners out of her minde, with wholesome precepts, it could not bee, but in time thou shouldest feele the pleasant fruit thereof to both your comforts. Therefore that this thing chance not so, performe this thing that I doe here counsaile thee: Whensoeuer any displeasant matter riseth at home, if thy wife hath done ought amisse, comfort her, & increase not the heauines. For though thou shouldest be grieued with neuer so many things, yet shalt thou finde nothing more grieuous then to want the beneuolence of thy wife at home. What offence soeuer thou canst name, yet shalt thou finde none more intolerable, then to be at debate with thy wife. And for this cause most of all oughtest thou to haue this loue in reuerence. And if reason moueth thee to beare any burden at any other mens hands, much more at thy wiues. For if she be poore, vpbraid her not, if she be simple, taunt her not, but be the more curteous: for she is thy body, and made one flesh with thee. But thou peraduenture wilt say that she is a wrathfull woman, a drunkard, and beastly, without wit and reason. For this cause bewayle her the more. Chafe not in anger, but pray vnto Almighty GOD. Let her bee admonished and helped with good counsaile, and doe thou thy best endeuour, that she may be deliuered of all these affections. But if thou shouldest beate her, thou shalt encrease her euill affections: For frowardnesse and sharpnesse, is not amended with frowardnesse, but with softnesse and gentlenesse. Furthermore, consider what reward thou shalt haue at GODS hand: For where thou mightest beate her, and yet, for the respect of the feare of GOD, thou wilt absteine and beare patiently her great offences, the rather in respect of that Law which forbiddeth that a man should cast out his wife what fault soeuer shee bee made the combred with, thou shalt haue a very great reward, and before the receit of that reward, thou shalt feele many commodities. For by this meanes she shall bee more obedient, and thou for her sake shalt be made the more meeke. It is written in a storie of a certaine strange Philosopher, which had a cursed wife, a froward and a drunkard. When he was asked for what consideration hee did so beare her euill manners? He made answere, By this meanes (sayd hee) I haue at home a Schoolemaster, and an example how I should behaue my selfe abroad: For I shall (saith hee) bee the more quiet with others, being thus dayly exercised and taught in the forbearing of her. Surely it is a shame that Panims should be wiser then we, we I say, that be commanded to resemble angels, or rather GOD himselfe through meekenesse. And for the loue of vertue, this sayd Philosopher Socrates would not expell his wife out of his house. Yea, some say that hee did therefore mary his wife, to learne this vertue by that occasion. Wherefore, seeing many men bee farre behinde the wisedome of this man, my counsell is, that first and before all things, a man doe his best endeuour to get him a good wife, endued with all honestie and vertue: But if it so chaunce that he is deceiued, that hee hath chosen such a wife as is neither good nor tolerable, then let the husband follow this Philosopher, and let him instruct his wife in euery condition, and neuer lay these matters to sight. For the Marchant man, except hee first bee at composition with his factour to vse his interfayres quietly, hee will neither stirre his shippe to sayle, nor yet will lay handes vpon his marchandize: Euen so, let vs doe all things, that we may haue the fellowship of our wiues, which is the factour of all our doings at home, in great quiet and rest. And by these meanes all things shall prosper quietly, and so shall we passe through the dangers of the troublous sea of this world. For this state of life will bee more honourable and comfortable then our houses, then seruants, then money, then landes and possessions, then all things that can bee told. As all these with sedition and discord, can neuer worke vs any comfort: So shall all things turne to our commoditie and pleasure, if wee draw this yoke in one concord of heart and minde. Whereupon doe your best endeuour, that after this sort ye vse your Matrimony, and so shall yee be armed on euery side. Yee haue escaped the snares of the deuill, and the vnlawfull lustes of the flesh, yee haue the quietnesse of conscience by this institution of Matrimony ordeined by GOD: therefore vse oft prayer to him, that hee would bee present by you, that hee would continue concord and charitie betwixt you. Doe the best yee can of your partes, to custome your selues to softnesse and meekenesse, and beare well in worth such ouersights as chaunce: and thus shall your conuersation bee most pleasant and comfortable. And although (which can no otherwise bee) some aduersities shall follow, and otherwhiles now one discommodity, now another shall appeare: yet in this common trouble and aduersity, lift vp both your hands vnto heauen, call vpon the helpe and assistance of GOD, the authour of your mariage, and surely the promise of releefe is at hand. For Christ affirmeth in his Gospel, Where two or three be gathered together in my name, and bee agreed, what matter soeuer they pray for, it shalbe granted them of my heauenly father. Why therefore shouldest thou be afrayd of the danger, where thou hast so ready a promise, and so nigh an helpe? Furthermore, you must vnderstand how necessary it is for

Christian folke to beare Christs crosse: for else we shall neuer feele how comfortable GODS helpe is vnto vs. Therefore giue thanks to GOD for his great benefit, in that yee haue taken vpon you this state of wedlocke, and pray you instantly, that Almighty GOD may luckily defend and maintaine you therein, that neither yee bee ouercome with any temptations, nor with any aduersity. But before all things, take good heede that yee giue no occasion to the diuell to let and hinder your prayers by discord and dissension : for there is no stronger defence and stay in all our life, then is prayer, in the which wee may call for the helpe of GOD and obtayne it, whereby we may win his blessing, his grace, his defence, and protection, so to continue therein to a better life to come: Which grant vs he that died for vs all, to whom bee all honour and prayse, for euer and euer, Amen.

HOMILY AGAINST IDLENESS

AN HOMILIE AGAINST IDLENESSE.

FOrasmuch as man, being not borne to ease and rest, but to labour and trauaile, is by corruption of nature through sinne, so farre degenerated and growne out of kinde, that hee taketh Idlenesse to bee no euill at all, but rather a commendable thing, seemely for those that be wealthy, and therefore is greedily imbraced of most part of men, as agreeable to their sensuall affection, and all labour and trauaile is diligently auoyded, as a thing painefull and repugnant to the pleasure of the flesh: It is necessary to bee declared vnto you, that by the ordinance of GOD, which hee hath set in the nature of man, euery one ought, in his lawfull vocation and calling, to giue himselfe to labour: and that idlenesse, being repugnant to the same ordinance, is a grieuous sinne, and also, for the great inconueniences and mischiefes which spring thereof, an intolerable euill: to the intent that when ye vnderstand the same, ye may diligently flee from it, and on the other part earnestly apply your selues, euery man in his vocation, to honest labour and businesse, which as it is enioyned vnto man by GODS appointment, so it wanteth not his manifold blessings and sundry benefits.

Almighty GOD, after that he had created man, put him into Paradise, that hee might dresse and keepe it: But when hee had transgressed GODS commandement, eating the fruit of the tree which was forbidden him, Almighty GOD foorthwith did cast him out of Paradise into this wofull vale of miserie, enioyning him to labour the ground that hee was taken out of, and to eat his bread in the sweat of his face all the dayes of his life (Genesis 3.23). It is the appointment and will of GOD, that euery man, during the time of this mortall and transitorie life, should giue himselfe to such honest and godly exercise and labour, and euery one follow his owne busines, & to walke vprightly in his owne calling. Man (saith Iob) is borne to labor (Job 5.7). And we are commanded by Iesus Sirach, not to hate painefull workes, neither husbandry, or other such mysteries of trauell, which the hiest hath created (Ecclesiasticus 7.15). The wiseman also exhorteth vs to drinke the waters of our owne cesterne, and of the riuers that runne out of the middes of our owne well: meaning thereby, that wee should liue of our owne labours, and not deuoure the labours of other. S. Paul hearing that among the Thessalonians, there were certaine that liued dissolutely and out of order, that is to say, which did not worke, but were busibodies: not getting their owne liuing with their owne trauaile, but eating other mens bread of free cost, did command the said Thessalonians, not onely to withdraw themselues, and abstaine from the familiar company of such inordinate persons, but also that if there were any such among them that would not labour, the same should not eate, nor haue any liuing at other mens hands (2 Thessalonians 3.11-12). Which doctrine of Saint Paul (no doubt) is grounded vpon the generall ordinance of GOD, which is, that euery man should labour; And therefore it is to be obeyed of all men, and no man can iustly exempt himselfe from the same. But when it is said, all men should labour: it is not so straitly meant, that all men should vse handy labour. But as there be diuers sorts of labours, some of the minde, and some of the body, and some of both: So euery one (except by reason of age, debilitie of body, or want of health, he be vnapt to labor at all) ought both for the getting of his owne liuing honestly, and for to profite others, in some kind of labour to exercise himselfe, according as the vocation whereunto GOD hath called him shall require. So that whosoeuer doeth good to the common weale and societie of men with his industrie and labour, whether it be by gouerning the common weale publikely, or by bearing publike office or ministery, or by doing any common necessary affaires of his countrey, or by giuing counsell, or by teaching and instructing others, or by what other meanes soeuer hee bee occupyed, so that a profit and benefit redound thereof vnto others, the same person is not to be accounted idle, though he worke no bodily labour, nor is to be denyed his liuing (if hee attend his vocation) though hee worke not with his hands.

Bodily labour is not required of them which by reason of their vocation and office are occupied in the labour of the mind, to the succour and helpe of others. Saint Paul exhorteth Timothie to eschew and refuse idle widowes, which goe about from house to house, because they are not only idle, but pratlers also, and busibodies, speaking things which are not comely (1 Timothy 5.13). The Prophet Ezechiel declaring what the sinnes of the citie of Sodome were, reckoneth idlenesse to be one of the principall (Ezechiel 16.49). The sinnes (saith he) of Sodome were these, Pride, fulnesse of meat, abundance, and idlenesse: These things had Sodome and her daughters, meaning the cities subiect to her. The horrible and strange kind of destruction of that citie, and all the countrey about the same, (which was fire and brymstone rayning from heauen) most manifestly declareth, what a grieuous sinne Idlenesse is, and ought to admonish vs to flee from the same, and embrace honest and godly labour. But if wee giue our selues to Idlenesse and slouth, to lurking and loytering, to wilfull wandering, and wastefull spending, neuer setling our selues to honest labour, but liuing like drone bees by the labours of other men, then do we breake the Lords Commandement, we goe astray from our vocation, and incur the danger of GODS wrath and heauy displeasure, to our endlesse destruction, except by repentance we turne againe vnfaignedly vnto GOD. The inconueniences and mischiefes that come of idlenesse, aswell to mans body, as to his soule, are more then can in short time be well rehearsed. Some we shall declare and open vnto you, that by considering them, yee may the better with your selues gather the rest. An idle hand (sayth Solomon) maketh poore, but a quicke labouring hand maketh rich (Proverbs 10.4). Againe, he that tilleth his land, shall haue plenteousnesse of bread, but hee that floweth in idlenesse is a very foole, and shall haue pouerty ynough (Proverbs 12.11, 28.19). Againe, A slothfull body will not goe to plowe for cold of the winter, therefore shall he goe a begging in summer, and haue nothing (Proverbs 20.4).

But what shall wee neede to stand much about the proouing of this, that pouerty followeth idlenesse? We haue too much experience thereof (the thing is the more to bee lamented) in this Realme. For a great part of the beggery that is among the poore, can bee imputed to nothing so much, as to idlenesse, and to the negligence of parents, which do not bring vp their children, either in good learning, honest labour, or some commendable occupation or trade, whereby when they come to age, they might get their liuing. Dayly experience also teacheth, that nothing is more enemy or pernicious to the health of mans body, then is idlenes, too much ease and sleepe, and want of exercise. But these and such like incommodities, albeit they bee great and noysome, yet because they concerne chiefly the body and externall goodes, they are not to bee compared with the mischiefes and inconueniences, which thorow idlenesse happen to the soule, whereof wee will recite some. Idlenesse is neuer alone, but hath alwayes a long tayle of other vices hanging on, which corrupt and infect the whole man, after such sort, that he is made at length nothing else but a lumpe of sinne. Idlenesse (saith Iesus Syrach) bringeth much euill and mischiefe (Ecclesiasticus 33.27-29). Saint Bernard calleth it the mother of all euilles, and stepdame of all vertues, adding moreouer, that it doeth prepare and (as it were) treade the way to hell fire. Where idlenesse is once receiued, there the deuill is ready to set in his foote, and to plant all kinde of wickednesse and sinne, to the euerlasting destruction of mans soule. Which thing to bee most true, we are plainely taught in the xiii. of Matthew, where it is sayd, that the enemy came while men were asleepe, and sowed naughtie tares among the good wheate (Matthew 13.25). In very deede the best time that the diuell can haue to worke his feate, is when men bee asleepe, that is to say, idle: Then is hee most busie in his worke, then doeth hee soonest catch men in the snare of perdition, then doeth hee fill them with all iniquitie, to bring them (without GODS speciall fauour) vnto vtter destruction. Hereof wee haue two notable examples, most liuely set before our eyes. The one in king Dauid, who tarying at home idlely (as the Scripture sayth) at such times as other Kinges goe foorth to battell, was quickly seduced of Satan to forsake the Lord his GOD, and to commit two grieuous and abominable sinnes in his sight: adulterie, and murder (2 Sam. 11.1, 2 Sam. 12.9).

The plagues that ensued these offences were horrible and grieuous, as it may easily appeare to them that will reade the storie. Another example of Sampson, who so long as hee warred with the Philistines, enemies to the people of GOD, could neuer bee taken or ouercome: But after that hee gaue himselfe to ease and idlenesse, he not onely committed fornication with the strumpet Dalila, but also was taken of his enemies, and had his eyes miserably put out, was put in prison, and compelled to grinde in a Mill, and at length was made the laughing stocke of his enemies (Judges 16.1-25). If these two, who were so excellent men, so welbeloued of GOD, so endued with singular and diuine gifts, the one namely of prophesie, and the other of strength, and such men as neuer could by vexation, labour, or trouble, be ouercome, were ouerthrowen and fell into grieuous sinnes, by giuing themselues for a short time to ease and idlenesse, and so consequently incurred miserable plagues at the hands of GOD: what sinne, what mischiefe, what inconuenience and plague is not to bee feared, of them which all their life long giue themselues wholy to idlenesse and ease? Let vs not deceiue our selues, thinking little hurt to come of doing nothing: For it is a true saying, When one doeth nothing, hee learneth to doe euill. Let vs therefore alwayes bee doing of some honest worke, that the deuill may finde vs occupied. He himselfe is euer occupied, neuer idle, but walketh continually seeking to deuoure vs. Let vs resist him with our diligent watching, in labour, and in well doing. For hee that diligently exerciseth himselfe in honest businesse, is not easily catched in the deuils snare. When man through idlenesse, or for default of some honest occupation or trade to liue vpon, is brought to pouertie, and want of things necessary, wee see how easily such a man is induced for his gaine, to lye, to practise how he may deceiue his neighbour, to forsweare himselfe, to beare false witnesse, and oftentimes to steale and murder, or to vse some other vngodly meane to liue withall. Whereby not onely his good name, honest reputation, and a good conscience, yea his life is vtterly lost, but also the great displeasure and wrath of GOD, with diuers and sundry grieuous plagues, are procured. Loe heere the ende of the idle and sluggish bodies, whose hands cannot away with honest labour: losse of name, fame, reputation, and life, here in this world, and without the great mercy of GOD, the purchasing of euerlasting destruction in the world to come. Haue not all men then good cause to beware and take heede of idlenesse, seeing they that imbrace and follow it, haue commonly of their pleasant idlenesse, sharpe and sowre displeasures? Doubtlesse good and godly men, weighing the great and manifold harmes that come by idlenesse to a Common weale, haue from time to time prouided with all diligence, that sharpe and seuere lawes might bee made for the correction and amendment of this euill. The Egyptians had a law, that euery man should weekely bring his name to the chiefe rulers of the Prouince, and therewithall declare what trade of life hee vsed, to the intent that idlenesse might bee worthily punished, and diligent labour duely rewarded. The Athenians did chastice sluggish and slothfull people, no lesse then they did hainous and grieuous offenders, considering (as the trueth is) that idlenesse causeth much mischiefe. The Areopagites called euery man to a straite accompt how he liued: And if they found any loyterers that did not profite the common weale by one meanes or other, they were driuen out, and banished, as vnprofitable members, that did onely hurt and corrupt the body. And in this Realme of England, good and godly lawes haue bin diuers times made, that no idle vagabonds and loitering runnagates, should be suffered to goe from Towne to Towne, from Place to Place, without punishment, which neither serue GOD nor their Prince, but deuoure the sweet fruits of other mens labour, being common lyers, drunkardes, swearers, theeues, whooremasters, and murderers, refusing all honest labour, and giue themselues to nothing else, but to inuent and doe mischiefe, whereof they are more desirous and greedie, then is any Lyon of his pray. To remedy this inconuenience, let all parents and others, which haue the care and gouernance of youth so bring them vp either in good learning, labour, or some honest occupation or trade, whereby they may be able in time to come, not onely to susteine themselues competently, but also to releeue and supplie the necessitie and want of others. And Saint Paul saith, Let him that hath stolen, steale no more, and he that hath deceiued others, or vsed vnlawfull waies to get his liuing, leaue off the same, and labour rather, working with his hands that thing which is good, that he may haue that which is necessary for himselfe, and also be able to giue vnto others that stand in need of his helpe (Ephesians 4.28). The Prophet Dauid thinketh him happy that liueth vpon his labour, saying, When thou eatest the labours of thine hands, happy art thou, and well is thee (Psalms 128.2). This happinesse or blessing consisteth in these and such like points.

First it is the gift of GOD (as Salomon saith) when one eateth and drinketh, and receiueth good of his labour (Ecclesiastes 3.13). Secondly, when one liueth of his owne labour (so it be honest and good) he liueth of it with a good conscience: and an vpright conscience is a treasure inestimable. Thirdly, he eateth his bread not with brawling and chiding, but with peace and quietnesse: when he quietly laboureth for the same, according to Saint Pauls admonition. Fourthly, he is no mans bondman for his meat sake, nor needeth not for that, to hang vpon the good will of other men: but so liueth of his owne, that hee is able to giue part to others. And to conclude, the labouring man and his family, whyles they are busily occupied in their labour, bee free from many temptations and occasions of sinne, which they that liue in idlenesse are subiect vnto. And here ought Artificers and labouring men, who bee at wages for their worke and labour, to consider their conscience to GOD, and their duety to their neighbour, lest they abuse their time in idlenesse, so defrauding them which be at charge both with great wages, and deare commons. They be worse then idle men indeede, for that they seeke to haue wages for their loytering. It is lesse daunger to GOD to be idle for no gayne, then by idlenesse to win out to their neighbours purses wages for that which is not deserued. It is true that Almighty GOD is angry with such as doe defraud the hired man of his wages: the cry of that iniury ascendeth vp to GODS eare for vengeance. And as true it is, that the hired man, who vseth deceit in his labour, is a theefe before GOD. Let no man (saith S. Paul to the Thessalonians) subtilly beguile his brother, let him not defraud him in his businesse: For the Lord is a reuenger of such deceits (1 Thessalonians 4.6). Whereupon he that will haue a good conscience to GOD, that labouring man, I say, which dependeth wholly vpon GODS benediction, ministring all things sufficient for his liuing, let him vie his time in a faithfull labour, and when his labour by sickenesse or other misfortune doeth cease, yet let him thinke for that in his health he serued GOD and his neighbour truely, he shall not want in time of necessitie. GOD vpon respect of his fidelitie in health, will recompence his indigence, to mooue the hearts of good men, to relieue such decayed men in sickenesse. Where otherwise, whatsoeuer is gotten by idlenesse shall haue no meanes to helpe in time of need.

Let the labouring man therefore eschew for his part this vice of idlenesse and deceit, remembring that Saint Paul exhorteth euery man to lay away all deceit, dissimulation and lying, and to vse trueth and plainenesse to his neighbour, because (saith he) we be members together in one body, vnder one head Christ our Sauiour (Ephesians 4.15). And here might bee charged the seruing men of this Realme, who spend their time in much idlenesse of life, nothing regarding the opportunitie of their time, forgetting how seruice is no heritage, how age will creepe vpon them: where wisedome were they should expend their idle time in some good businesse, whereby they might increase in knowledge, and so the more worthy to be readie for euery mans seruice. It is a great rebuke to them, that they studie not either to write faire, to keepe a booke of account, to studie the tongues, and so to get wisedome and knowledge in such bookes and workes, as bee now plentifully set out in print of all manner of languages, Let young men consider the precious value of their time, and waste it not in idlenesse, in iollitie, in gaming, in banquetting, in ruffians company. Youth is but vanitie, and must bee accounted for before GOD. How merrie and glad soeuer thou be in thy youth, O yong man (saith the Preacher) how glad soeuer thy heart be in thy yong dayes, how fast and freely soeuer thou follow the wayes of thine owne heart, and the lust of thine owne eyes, yet be thou sure that GOD shall bring thee into iudgement for all these things (Ecclesiastes 11.9). GOD of his mercie put it into the hearts and minds of all them that haue the sword of punishment in their hands, or haue families vnder their gouernance, to labour to redresse this great enormitie, of all such as liue idlely and vnprofitably in the common weale, to the great dishonour of GOD, and the grieuous plague of his seely people. To leaue sinne vnpunished, and to neglect the good bringing vp of youth, is nothing els but to kindle the Lords wrath against vs, and to heape plagues vpon our owne heads. As long as the adulterous people were suffered to liue licenciously without reformation: so long did the plague continue and increase in Israel, as ye may see in the booke of Numbers (Numbers 25.8).

But when due correction was done vpon them, the Lords anger was straight way pacified, and the plague ceased. Let all officers therefore looke straitly to their charge. Let all masters of housholds reforme this abuse in their families, let them vse the authority that GOD hath giuen them, let them not maintaine vagabonds and idle persons, but deliuer the Realme and their housholds from such noysome loyterers, that idlenesse, the mother of all mischiefe, being cleane taken away, Almighty GOD may turne his dreadfull anger away from vs, and confirm the couenant of peace vpon vs, for euer, through the merites of Iesus Christ our onely Lord and Sauiour, to whom with the Father and the holy Ghost, be all honour and glory, world without end, AMEN.

HOMILY ON REPENTANCE AND TRUE RECONCILIATION UNTO GOD

AN HOMILIE OF
Repentance, and of true reconciliation
vnto GOD

THere is nothing that the holy Ghost doth so much labour in all the Scriptures to beat into mens heads, as repentance, amendment of life, and speedy returning vnto the Lord GOD of hostes. And no maruell why. For wee doe dayly and hourely by our wickednesse and stubborne disobedience, horribly fall away from GOD, thereby purchasing vnto our selues (if hee should deale with vs according to his iustice) eternall damnation.

The doctrine of repentance is most necessary. So that no doctrine is so necessary in the Church of GOD, as is the doctrine of repentance and amendment of life. And verily the true preachers of the Gospel of the kingdome of heauen, and of the glad and ioyfull tidings of saluation, haue alwayes in their godly Sermons and Preachings vnto the people, ioyned these two together, I meane repentance and forgiuenesse of sinnes, euen as our Sauiour Iesus Christ did appoint himselfe, saying, So it behoued Christ to suffer, and to rise againe the third day, and that repentance and forgiuenesse of sinnes should bee preached in his Name among all Nations. And therefore the holy Apostle doeth in the Actes speake after this manner: I haue witnessed both to the Iewes and to the Gentiles, the repentance towards GOD, and fayth towardes our Lord Iesus Christ. Did not Iohn Baptist, Zacharias sonne, begin his ministery with the doctrine of repentance, saying, Repent, for the kingdome of GOD is at hand? The like doctrine did our Sauiour Iesus Christ preach himselfe, and commanded his Apostles to preach the same.

I might heere alledge very many places out of the Prophets, in the which this most wholesome doctrine of repentance is very earnestly vrged, as most needfull for all degrees and orders of men, but one shall bee sufficient at this present time.

These are the wordes of Ioel the Prophet. Therefore also now the Lord sayth, Returne vnto mee with all your heart, with fasting, weeping, and mourning, rent your hearts and not your clothes, and returne vnto the Lord your GOD, for hee is gracious and mercifull, slow to anger, and of great compassion, and ready to pardon wickednesse (Joel 2.12-13).

A perpetuall rule which all must follow. Whereby it is giuen vs to vnderstand, that wee haue here a perpetuall rule appointed vnto vs, which ought to bee obserued and kept at all times, and that there is none other way whereby the wrath of GOD may be pacified, and his anger asswaged, that the fiercenesse of his furie, and the plagues of destruction, which by his righteous iudgement hee had determined to bring vpon vs, may depart, be remooued and taken away. Where hee saith, But now therefore, saith the Lord, returne vnto mee: It is not without great importance, that the Prophet speaketh so. For hee had afore set foorth at large vnto them, the horrible vengeance of GOD, which no man was able to abide, and therefore he doeth mooue them to repentance, to obtaine mercie, as if hee should say, I will not haue these things to be so taken, as though there were no hope of grace left. For although yee doe by your sinnes deserue to be vtterly destroyed, & GOD by his righteous iudgements hath determined to bring no small destruction vpon you, yet know that yee are in a maner on the very edge of the sword, if yee will speedily returne vnto him, he will most gently and most mercifully receiue you into fauour againe. Whereby wee are admonished, that repentance is neuer too late, so that it be true and earnest. For sith that GOD in the Scriptures will bee called our Father, doubtlesse hee doeth follow the nature and property of gentle and mercifull fathers, which seeke nothing so much, as the returning againe, and amendment of their children, as Christ doeth aboundantly teach in the parable of the prodigall sonne (Luke 15.11-32). Doeth not the Lord himselfe say by the Prophet, I will not the death of the wicked, but that he turne from his wicked wayes and liue (Ezechiel

18.23, Isaiah 1.16)? And in another place, If wee confesse our sinne, GOD is faithfull and righteous to forgiue vs our sinnes, and to make vs cleane from all wickednesse (1 John 1.9). Which most comfortable promises are confirmed by many examples of the Scriptures. When the Iewes did willingly receiue and imbrace the wholesome counsell of the Prophet Esay, GOD by and by did reach his helping hand vnto them, and by his Angel, did in one night slay the most worthy and valiant souldiers of Sennacheribs campe (Isaiah 37.6, 36). Whereunto may King Manastes be added, who after all manner of damnable wickednesse, returned vnto the Lord, and therefore was heard of him, and restored againe into his kingdome (2 Chron. 33.12-13). The same grace and fauour did the sinfull woman Magdalene, Zacheus, the poore thiefe, and many other feele (Luke 7.48). All which things ought to serue for our comfort against the temptations of our consciences, whereby the deuill goeth about to shake, or rather to ouerthrow our faith. For euery one of vs ought to apply the same vnto himselfe, and say, Yet now returne vnto the Lord: neither let the remembrance of thy former life discourage thee, yea the more wicked that it hath beene, the more feruent and earnest let thy repentance or returning be, and foorthwith thou shalt feele the eares of the Lord wide open vnto thy prayers. But let vs more narrowly looke vpon the commandement of the Lord touching this matter. Turne vnto mee (saith hee by the holy Prophet Ioel) with all your hearts, with fasting, weeping, and mourning. Rent your hearts, and not your garments &c. In which wordes, hee comprehendeth all manner of things that can bee spoken of repentance, which is a returning againe of the whole man vnto GOD, from whom wee be fallen away by sinne. But that the whole discourse thereof may the better bee borne away, we shall first consider in order foure principall points, that is, from what wee must returne, to whom wee must returne, by whom wee may bee able to conuert, and the maner how to turne to GOD.

From whence we must returne. First, from whence, or from what things wee must returne. Truely wee must returne from those things, whereby wee haue beene withdrawen, pluckt, and led away from GOD. And these generally are our sinnes, which as the holy Prophet Esay doeth testifie, doe separate GOD and vs, and hide his face, that hee will not heare vs. But vnder the name of sinne, not onely those grosse wordes and deedes, which by the common iudgement of men, are counted to bee filthy and vnlawfull, and so consequently abominable sinnes: but also the filthie lustes and inward concupiscences of the flesh, which (as S. Paul testifieth) doe resist the will and Spirit of GOD, and therefore ought earnestly to bee bridled and kept vnder (Galatians 5.17). We must repent of the false and erronious opinions that wee haue had of GOD, and the wicked superstition that doth breede of the same, the vnlawfull worshipping and seruice of GOD, and other like. All these things must they forsake, that will truely turne vnto the Lord and repent aright. For sith that for such things the wrath of GOD commeth vpon the children of disobedience (Ephesians 5.6), no end of punishment ought to bee looked for, as long as wee continue in such things. Therefore they be here condemned, which will seeme to bee repentant sinners, and yet will not forsake their Idolatrie and superstition.

Vnto whom wee ought to returne. Secondly, wee must see vnto whom we ought to returne. *Reuertimini vsque ad me,* saith the Lord: that is, Returne as farre as vnto me. Wee must then returne vnto the Lord, yea we must returne vnto him alone: For he alone is the trueth, and the fountaine of all goodnesse: But wee must labour that wee doe returne as farre as vnto him, and that wee doe neuer cease nor rest till wee haue apprehended and taken hold vpon him.

But this must bee done by faith. For sith that GOD is a Spirit, he can by no other meanes be apprehended and taken hold vpon. Wherefore, first they doe greatly erre, which doe not turne vnto GOD, but vnto the creatures, or vnto the inuentions of men, or vnto their owne merites.

By whom we must returne vnto GOD. Secondly, they that doe beginne to returne vnto the Lord, and doe faint in the mid way, before they come to the marke that is appointed vnto them. Thirdly, because wee haue of our owne selues nothing to present vs to GOD, and doe no lesse flee from him, after our fall, then our first parent Adam did, who when hee had sinned, did seeke to hide himselfe from the sight of GOD, wee haue neede of a mediatour for to bring and reconcile vs vnto him, who for our sinnes is angry with vs. The same is Iesus Christ, who being true and naturall GOD, equall and of one substance with the Father, did at the time appointed take vpon him our fraile nature, in the blessed Virgins wombe, and that of her vndefiled substance, that so he might be a mediatour betweene GOD and vs, and pacifie his wrath. Of him doeth the Father himselfe speake from heauen, saying, This is my welbeloued Son, in whom I am well pleased (Matthew

3.17). And hee himselfe in his Gospel doeth cry out and say, I am the way, the trueth, and the life, no man commeth vnto the Father but by mee (John 14.6). For hee alone did with the sacrifice of his Body and Blood, make satisfaction vnto the Iustice of GOD for our sinnes (John 1, 1 Peter 1.19, John 15). The Apostles doe testifie, that hee was exalted, for to giue repentance and remission of sinnes vnto Israel (Acts 5.31). Both which things hee himselfe did commaund to be preached in his Name (Luke 24.47). Therefore they are greatly deceiued that preach repentance without Christ, and teach the simple and ignorant that it consisteth onely in the workes of men. They may indeede speake many things of good workes, and of amendment of life and manners: but without Christ they bee all vaine and vnprofitable. They that thinke that they haue done much of themselues towards repentance, are so much more the farther from GOD, because they doe seeke those things in their owne workes and merites, which ought onely to bee sought in our Sauiour Iesus Christ, and in the merites of his death, and passion, and bloodshedding.

The manner of our turning. Fourthly, this holy Prophet Ioel doeth liuely expresse the manner of this our returning or repentance, comprehending all the inward and outward things that may bee here obserued. First hee will haue vs to returne vnto GOD with our whole heart, whereby he doeth remooue and put away all hypocrisie, lest the same might iustly be said vnto vs: This people draweth neere vnto me with their mouth, and worshippe mee with their lippes, but their heart is farre from me (Isaiah 29.13, Matthew 15.8-9).

Secondly, hee requireth a sincere and pure loue of godlinesse, and of the true worshipping and seruice of GOD, that is to say, that forsaking all maner of things that are repugnant and contrary vnto GODS will, wee doe giue our heartes vnto him, and the whole strength of our bodies and soules, according to that which is written in the Law: Thou shalt loue the Lord thy GOD with all thy heart, with all thy soule, and with all thy strength (Deuteronomy 6.5). Here therefore nothing is left vnto vs, that wee may giue vnto the worlde, and vnto the lustes of the flesh. For sith that the heart is the fountaine of all our workes, as manie as doe with whole heart turne vnto the Lord, doe liue vnto him onely.

Halting on both sides. Neyther doe they yet repent truely, that halting on both sides, doe otherwhiles obey GOD, but by and by doe thinke, that laying him aside, it is lawfull for them to serue the world and the flesh. And because that wee are letted by the naturall corruption of our owne flesh, and the wicked affections of the same, hee doeth bidde vs also to returne with fasting: not thereby vnderstanding a superstitious abstinence and choosing of meates but a true discipline or taming of the flesh, whereby the nourishments of filthie lustes, and of stubborne contumacie and pride, may be withdrawen and pluckt away from it. Whereunto hee doeth adde weeping and mourning, which doe conteine an outward profession of repentance, which is very needefull and necessary, that so wee may partly set foorth the righteousnesse of GOD, when by such meanes wee doe testifie that wee deserued punishments at his hands, and partly stoppe the offence that was openly giuen vnto the weake.

This did Dauid see, who being not content to haue bewept and bewayled his sinnes priuately, would publikely in his Psalmes declare and set foorth the righteousnesse of GOD, in punishing sinne, and also stay them that might haue abused his example to sinne the more boldly (Psalms 25, 32, 51, 103, 142). Therefore they are farthest from true repentance, that will not confesse and acknowledge their sinnes, nor yet bewayle them, but rather doe most vngodly glorie and reioyce in them.

Hypocrites doe counterfait all manner of things. Now lest any man should thinke that repentance doeth consist in outwarde weeping and mourning onely (Psalms 52), hee doeth rehearse that wherein the chiefe of the whole matter doeth lye, when hee sayth: Rent your hearts, and not your garments, and turne vnto the Lord your GOD (Joel 2.13). For the people of the East part of the world were woont to rent their garments, if any thing happened vnto them that seemed intolerable. This thing did hypocrites sometime counterfaite and follow, as though the whole repentance did stand in such outward gesture. Hee teacheth then, that another manner of thing is required, that is, that they must be contrite in their heartes, that they must vtterly detest and abhorre sinnes, and being at defiance with them, returne vnto the Lord their GOD, from whome they went away before. For GOD hath no pleasure in the outward ceremonie, but requireth a contrite and humble heart, which he will neuer despise, as Dauid doeth testifie (Psalms 51.17). There is therefore none other vse to these outward ceremonies, but as farre forth as we are stirred vp by them, and doe serue to the glory of GOD, and to the edifying of other.

How repentance is not vnprofitable. Now doeth hee adde vnto this doctrine or exhortation, certaine godly reasons, which hee doeth ground vpon the nature and propertie of GOD, and whereby hee doeth teach, that true repentance can neuer be vnprofitable or vnfruitfull. For as in all other things mens hearts doe quaile and faint, if they once perceiue that they trauell in vaine: Euen so most specially in this matter, must we take heede and beware that we suffer not our selues to bee perswaded that all that wee doe is but labour lost: For thereof either sudden desperation doeth arise, or a licencious boldnesse to sinne, which at length bringeth vnto desperation. Lest any such thing then should happen vnto them, he doeth certifie them of the grace and goodnesse of GOD, who is alwayes most ready to receiue them into fauour againe, that turne speedily vnto him. Which thing hee doeth prooue with the same titles wherewith GOD doeth describe and set foorth himselfe vnto Moyses, speaking on this maner: For hee is gracious and mercifull, slowe to anger, of great kindenesse, and repenteth him of the euill, that is, such a one as is sorie for your afflictions (Exodus 34.6). First he calleth him gentle and gracious, as hee who of his owne nature is more prompt and ready to doe good, then to punish. Whereunto this saying of Esaias the Prophet seemeth to pertaine, where he saith, Let the wicked forsake his way, and the vnrighteous his owne imaginations, and returne vnto the Lord, and hee will haue pittie on him, and to our GOD, for he is very ready to forgiue (Isaiah 55.7). Secondly, he doth attribute vnto him mercy, or rather (according to the Hebrew word) the bowels of mercies: Whereby hee signified the naturall affections of Parents towards their children. Which thing Dauid doeth set foorth goodly, saying, As a father hath compassion on his children, so hath the Lord compassion on them that feare him, for he knoweth whereof we be made, he remembreth that we are but dust (Psalms 103.13-14). Thirdly, hee saith, that hee is slow to anger, that is to say, long suffering, and which is not lightly prouoked to wrath. Fourthly, that he is of much kindnesse, for hee is that bottomlesse well of all goodnesse, who reioyceth to doe good vnto vs: therefore did he create and make men, that he might haue whom hee should doe good vnto, and make partakers of his heauenly riches. Fiftly, he repenteth of the euill, that is to say, hee doth call backe againe, and reuoke the punishment which he had threatned, when he seeth men repent, turne, and amend.

Against the Nouatians. Whereupon we doe not without a iust cause detest and abhorre the damnable opinion of them which doe most wickedly goe about to perswade the simple and ignorant people, that if wee chance after wee be once come to GOD, and grafted in his Sonne Iesus Christ, to fall into some horrible sinne, shall be vnprofitable vnto vs, there is no more hope of reconciliation, or to be receiued againe into the fauour and mercy of GOD.

The sinne against the holy Ghost. And that they may giue the better colour vnto their pestilent and pernicious errour, they doe commonly bring in the sixth and tenth Chapters of the Epistle to the Hebrewes, and the second Chapter, of the second Epistle of Peter, not considering that in those places the holy Apostles doe not speake of the daily falles, that we (as long as wee carrie about this bodie of sinne, are subiect vnto: but of the finall falling away from Christ and his Gospell, which is a sinne against the holy Ghost that shall neuer bee forgiuen, because that they doe vtterly forsake the knowen trueth, doe hate Christ and his word, they doe crucifie and mocke him (but to their vtter destruction) and therefore fall into desperation, and cannot repent (Matthew 12.31, Mark 3.29). And that this is the true meaning of the holy Spirit of GOD, it appeareth by many other places of the Scriptures, which promiseth vnto all true repentant sinners, and to them that with their whole heart doe turne vnto the Lord their GOD, free pardon and remission of their sinnes. For the probation hereof, we read this: O Israel (saith the holy Prophet Hieremie) if thou returne, returne vnto me saith the Lord, and if thou put away thine abominations out of my sight, then shalt thou not be remooued (Jer. 4.1). Againe, these are Esaias words: Let the wicked forsake his owne wayes, and the vnrighteous his owne imaginations, and turne againe vnto the Lord, and hee will haue mercie vpon him, and to our GOD, for hee is ready to forgiue (Isaiah 55.7). And the Prophet Osee, the godly doe exhort one another after this maner, Come and let vs turne againe vnto the Lord, for hee hath smitten vs, and hee will heale vs, hee hath wounded vs, and hee will binde vs vp againe (Hosea 6.1). It is most euident and plaine, that these things ought to be vnderstood of them that were with the Lord afore, and by their sinnes and wickednesses were gone away from him.

For wee doe not turne againe vnto him with whom wee were neuer before, but we come vnto him (Ecclesiastes 7.1-3, 1 John 1.8-9). Now, vnto all them that will returne vnfainedly vnto the Lord their

GOD, the fauour and mercy of GOD vnto forgiuenesse of sinnes is liberally offered. Whereby it followeth necessarily, that although wee doe, after wee bee once come to GOD and grafted in his Sonne Iesus Christ, fall into great sinnes (for there is no righteous man vpon the earth that sinneth not, and if wee say wee haue no sinne, wee deceiue our selues, and the trueth is not in vs) yet if wee rise againe by repentance, and with a full purpose of amendment of life doe flee vnto the mercie of GOD, taking sure holde thereupon, through faith in his Sonne Iesu Christ, there is an assured and infallible hope of pardon and remission of the same, and that wee shall bee receiued againe into the fauour of our heauenly Father. It is written of Dauid: I haue found a man according to mine owne heart, or, I haue found Dauid the sonne of Iesse, a man according to mine owne heart, who will doe all things that I will (Acts 13.22, 1 Sam. 13-14). This is a great commendation of Dauid. It is also most certaine, that hee did stedfastly beleeue the promise that was made him touching the Messias; who should come of him touching the flesh, and that by the same faith hee was iustified, and grafted in our Sauiour Iesu Christ to come, and yet afterwardes hee fell horribly, committing most detestable adulterie and damnable murder (2 Samuel 11.4, 15, 17), and yet as soone as hee cryed *Peccaui*, I haue sinned, vnto the Lord, his sinne being forgiuen, he was receiued into fauour againe (2 Samuel 12.13). Now will wee come vnto Peter, of whom no man can doubt but that hee was grafted in our Sauiour Iesus Christ, long afore his denyall. Which thing may easily bee prooued by the answere which hee did in his name, and in the name of his fellow Apostles make vnto our Sauiour Iesu Christ, when he sayd vnto them, Will yee also goe away? Master (sayth he) to whom shall wee goe? Thou hast the wordes of eternall life, and wee beleeue and knowe that thou art that Christ the Sonne of the liuing GOD (John 6.67-69). Whereunto may bee added the like confession of Peter, where Christ doeth giue vs most infallible testimonie: Thou art blessed Simon the sonne of Ionas, for neyther flesh nor blood hath reueyled this vnto thee, but my Father which is in heauen. These wordes are sufficient to prooue that Peter was already iustified, through this his liuely faith in the onely begotten Sonne of GOD, whereof he made so notable and so solemne a confession. But did not hee afterwards most cowardly denie his Master (Matthew 26.69-75), although he had heard of him, Whosoeuer denieth me before men, I wil denie him before my Father (Matthew 10.33)? Neuerthelesse, assoone as with weeping eyes, and with a sobbing heart he did acknowledge his offence, and with an earnest repentance did flee vnto the mercy of

GOD, taking sure hold thereupon, through faith in him whom he had so shamefully denyed, his sinne was forgiuen him, and for a certificate and assurance thereof, the roome of his Apostleship was not denyed vnto him. But now marke what doth follow. After the same holy Apostle had on Whitsunday with the rest of the Disciples receiued the gift of the holy Ghost most abundantly (Acts 2.1-4), he committed no small offence in Antiochia, by bringing the consciences of the faithfull into doubt by his example, so that Paul was faine to rebuke him to his face, because that hee walked not vprightly, or went not the right way in the Gospel (Galatians 2.11). Shall we now say, that after this grieuous offence, hee was vtterly excluded and shut out from the grace and mercy of GOD, & that this his trespasse, whereby he was a stumbling blocke vnto many, was vnpardonable? GOD defend we should say so.

What we must beware of. But as these examples are not brought in, to the ende that wee should thereby take a boldnesse to sinne, presuming on the mercy and goodnesse of GOD, but to the ende that if through the frailenesse of our owne flesh, and the temptation of the Deuill, we fall into like sinnes, we should in no wise despaire of the mercy and goodnesse of GOD: Euen so must wee beware and take heede, that wee doe in no wise thinke in our hearts, imagine, or beleeue that we are able to repent aright, or to turne effectually vnto the Lord by our owne might and strength. For this must bee verified in all men, Without me ye can doe nothing (John 15.5). Againe, Of our selues wee are not able as much as to thinke a good thought (2 Corinthians 3.5). And in another place, It is GOD that worketh in vs both the will and the deede (Philippians 2.13). For this cause, although Hieremie had sayd before, If thou returne, O Israel, returne vnto me, saith the Lord (Jeremiah 4.1): Yet afterwards he saith, Turne thou me, O Lord, and I shall bee turned, for thou art the Lord my GOD. And therefore that holy writer and ancient father Ambrose doeth plainely affirme (Ambrose, De vocat. Gent., Bk. 8, Chap. 9), that the turning of the heart vnto GOD, is of GOD, as the Lord himselfe doeth testifie by his Prophet, saying, And I will giue thee an heart to know mee, that I am the Lord, and they shall bee my people, and I will bee their GOD, for they shall returne vnto mee with their whole heart. These things being considered, let vs earnestly pray vnto the liuing GOD our heauenly Father, that hee will vouchsafe by his holy Spirit, to worke a true and vnfained repentance in vs, that after the painefull labours and trauels of this life, may liue eternally with his Sonne Iesus Christ, to whom bee all prayse and glory for euer and euer. Amen.

THE SECOND PART OF THE HOMILY OF REPENTANCE.

HItherto haue ye heard (welbeloued) how needfull and necessary the doctrine of repentance is, and how earnestly it is thorowout all the Scriptures of GOD vrged and set foorth, both by the ancient Prophets, by our Sauiour Iesus Christ, and his Apostles, and that forasmuch as it is the conuersion or turning againe of the whole man vnto GOD, from whom we go away by sinne: these foure points ought to be obserued, that is, from whence or from what things we must returne, vnto whom this our returning must be made, by whose meanes it ought to be done, that it may be effectuall, and last of all, after what sort we ought to behaue our selues in the same, that it may be profitable vnto vs, and atteine vnto the thing that we doe seeke by it. Ye haue also learned, that as the opinion of them that denie the benefit of repentance, vnto those that after they bee come to GOD and grafted in our Sauiour Iesus Christ, doe through the frailenesse of their flesh, and the temptation of the diuell fall into some grieuous and detestable sinne, is most pestilent and pernicious: So wee must beware, that wee doe in no wise thinke that we are able of our owne selues, and of our own strength, to returne vnto the Lord our GOD, from whom we are gone away by our wickednesse and sinne. Now it shall be declared vnto you, what bee the true parts of repentance, and what things ought to mooue vs to repent, and to returne vnto the Lord our GOD with all speed. Repentance (as it is sayd before) is a true returning vnto GOD, whereby men forsaking vtterly their idolatrie and wickednesse, doe with a liuely fayth embrace, loue, and worship the true liuing GOD onely, and giue themselues to all manner of good workes, which by GODS word they know to be acceptable vnto him.

There bee foure parts of repentance. Now there bee foure parts of repentance, which being set together, may bee likened to an easie and short ladder, whereby we may climbe from the bottomlesse pit of perdition, that wee cast our selues into by our dayly offences and greeuous sinnes, vp into the castle or towre of eternall and endlesse saluation.

The first, is the contrition of the heart. For we must be earnestly sorry for our sinnes, and vnfeignedly lament and bewayle that wee haue by them so greeuously offended our most bounteous and mercifull GOD, who so tenderly loued vs, that he gaue his onely begotten sonne to die a most bitter death, and to shedde his deare heart blood for our redemption and deliuerance. And verily this inward sorrow and griefe being conceiued in the heart for the heynousnesse of sin, if it be earnest and vnfeigned, is as a sacrifice to GOD, as the holy Prophet Dauid doth testifie, saying, A sacrifice to GOD is a troubled spirit, a contrite and broken heart, O Lord, thou wilt not despise (Psalms 51.17).

But that this may take place in vs, we must bee diligent to reade and heare the Scriptures and the worde of GOD, which most liuely doe paint out before our eyes our naturall vncleannesse, and the enormitie of our sinfull life. For vnlesse wee haue a thorow feeling of our sinnes, how can it bee that wee should earnestly bee sorie for them? Afore Dauid did heare the worde of the Lord by the mouth of the Prophet Nathan, what heauinesse I pray you was in him for the adulterie and the murder that hee had committed (2 Samuel 12.13)? So that it might bee sayd right well, that hee slept in his owne sinne. Wee reade in the Actes of the Apostles, that when the people had heard the Sermon of Peter, they were compunct and pricked in their hearts (Acts 2.37). Which thing would neuer haue beene, if they had not heard that wholesome Sermon of Peter. They therefore that haue no minde at all neyther to reade, nor yet to heare GODS word, there is but small hope of them that they will as much as once set their feete, or take hold vpon the first staffe or step of this ladder: but rather wil sinke deeper and deeper into the bottomlesse pit of perdition. For if at any time through the remorse of their conscience, which accuseth them, they feele any inward griefe, sorrow, or heauinesse for their sinnes, forasmuch as they want the salue and comfort of GODS word, which they doe despise, it will be vnto them rather a meane to bring them to vtter desperation, then otherwise. The second is, an vnfained confession and acknowledging of our sinnes vnto GOD, whom by them we haue so grieuously offended, that if he should deale with vs according to his iustice, wee doe deserue a thousand helles, if there could bee so many. Yet if wee will with a sorrowfull and contrite heart make an vnfained confession of them vnto GOD, hee will freely and frankely forgiue them, and so put all our wickednesse out of remembrance before the sight of his Maiestie, that they shall no more bee thought vpon (Ezechiel 18.27). Hereunto doeth pertaine the golden saying of the holy Prophet Dauid, where he saith on this maner: Then I acknowledged my sinne vnto thee, neither did I hide mine iniquitie: I sayd, I will confesse against my selfe my wickednesse vnto the Lorde, and thou forgauest the vngodlinesse of my sinne (Psalms 32.5). These are also the wordes of Iohn the Euangelist If we confesse our sinnes, GOD is faithfull and righteous, to forgiue vs our sinnes, and to make vs cleane from all our wickednes (1 John 1.9). Which ought to be vnderstood of the confession that is made vnto GOD. For these are Saint Augustines wordes (Augustine, Epist. ad Julian Comitem, 30): That confession which is made vnto GOD, is required by GODS Law, whereof Iohn the Apostle speaketh, saying, If we confesse our sinnes, GOD is faithfull and righteous to forgiue vs our sinnes, and to make vs cleane from all our wickednesse. For without this confession, sinne is not forgiuen. This is then the chiefest and most principall confession that in the Scriptures and worde of GOD wee are bidden to make, and without the which wee shall neuer obtaine pardon and forgiuenesse of our sinnes. Indeede, besides this there is another kinde of confession, which is needefull and necessary.

And of the same doeth Saint Iames speake, after this maner, saying: Acknowledge your faults one to another, and pray one for another, that yee may bee saued. As if hee should say: Open that which grieueth you, that a remedie maye be found. And this is commanded both for him that complayneth, and for him that heareth, that the one should shew his griefe to the other. The true meaning of it is, that the faithfull ought to acknowledge their offences, whereby some hatred, rancour, ground, or malice, hauing risen or growen among them one to another, that a brotherly reconciliation may be had, without the which nothing that wee doe can bee acceptable vnto GOD, as our Sauiour Iesus Christ doeth witnesse himselfe, saying, When thou offerest thine offering at the altar, if thou remembrest that thy brother hath ought against thee, leaue there thine offering, and goe and bee reconciled, and when thou art reconciled, come and offer thine offering (Matthew 5.23-24). It may also be thus taken, that we ought to confesse our weaknesse and infirmities one to another, to the end that knowing each others frailenesse, wee may the more earnestly pray together vnto Almighty GOD our heauenly Father, that he will vouchsafe to pardon vs our infirmities, for his Sonne Iesus Christs sake, and not to impute them vnto vs, when he shall render to euery man according to his workes.

Answere to the aduersaries which maintaine auricular confession. And whereas the aduersaries goe about to wrest this place, for to maintaine their auricular confession withall, they are greatly deceiued themselues, and doe shamefully deceiue others: For if this text ought to bee vnderstood of auricular confession: then the Priestes are as much bound to confesse themselues vnto the lay people, as the lay people are bound to confesse themselues to them. And if to pray, is to absolue: then the laytie by this place hath as great authoritie to absolue the Priestes, as the Priestes haue to absolue the laytie. This did Iohannes Scotus, otherwise called Duns well perceiue, who vpon this place writeth on this maner (Johannes Scotus, Senten. Distinct. 17, quaest.1).

Neither doeth it seeme vnto mee that Iames did giue this commandment, or that he did set it foorth as being receiued of Christ. For first and foremost, whence had he authoritie to binde the whole Church, sith that hee was onely Bishop of the Church of Ierusalem? except thou wilt say, that the same Church was at the beginning the head Church, and consequently that hee was the head Bishop, which thing the Sea of Rome will neuer graunt. The vnderstanding of it then, is as in these wordes: Confesse your sinnes one to another. A perswasion to humilitie, whereby he willeth vs to confesse our selues generally vnto our neighbours, that wee are sinners, according to this saying: if wee say wee haue no sinne, wee deceiue our selues, and the trueth is not in vs. And where that they do alledge this saying of our Sauiour Iesus Christ vnto the Leper, to prooue auricular confession to stand on GODS word Goe thy way and shew thy selfe vnto the Priest: Doe they not see that the Leper was cleansed from his leprosie, afore he was by Christ sent vnto the Priest for to shew himselfe vnto him (Matthew 8.4)? By the same reason wee must bee cleansed from our spirituall leprosie, I meane, our sinnes must be forgiuen vs afore that wee come to confession. What neede wee then to tell forth our sinnes into the eare of the Priest, sith that they bee already taken away? Therefore holy Ambrose in his second Sermon vpon the hundred and ninetienth Psalme, doth say full well, Goe shew thy selfe vnto the Priest. Who is the true Priest, but he which is the Priest for euer, after the order of Melchisedech? Whereby this holy Father doeth vnderstand, that both the Priesthoode and the Law being changed we ought to acknowledge none other Priest for deliuerance from our sinnes, but our Sauiour Iesus Christ, who being soueraigne Byshoppe, doeth with the

Sacrifice of his Body and Blood, offered once for euer vpon the Altar of the Crosse most effectually cleanse the spirituall leprosie, and wash away the sinnes of all those that with true confession of the same doe flee vnto him. It is most euident and playne, that this auricular confession hath not his warrant of GODS word, els it had not beene lawfull for Nectarius Bishoppe of Constantinople, vpon a iust occasion to haue put it downe(Nectarius Sozomen, Ecclesiast. Hist., Bk. 7, Chap. 16). For when any thing ordayned of GOD, is by the lewdnesse of men abused, the abuse ought to be taken away, and the thing it selfe suffered to remaine. Moreouer, these are S. Augustines wordes (Augustine, Confessions, Bk. 10, Chap. 3), What haue I to doe with men, that they should heare my confession, as though they were able to heale my diseases? A curious sort of men to know another mans life, & slothfully to correct & amend their owne. Why do they seeke to heare of me what I am, which will not heare of thee what they are? And how can they tell when they heare by me of my selfe, whether I tell the trueth or not, sith no mortall man knoweth what is in man, but the spirit of man which is in him? Augustine would not haue written thus, if auricular confession had beene vsed in his time. Being therefore not ledde with the conscience thereof, let vs with feare and trembling, and with a true contrite heart, vse that kinde of confession, that GOD doeth commaund in his worde, and then doubtlesse, as hee is faithfull and righteous, hee will forgiue vs our sinnes, and make vs cleane from all wickednesse. I doe not say, but that if any doe finde themselues troubled in conscience, they may repayre to their learned Curate or Pastour, or to some other godly learned man, and shew the trouble and doubt of their conscience to them, that they may receiue at their hand the comfortable salue of GODS word: but it is against the true Christian libertie, that any man should bee bound to the numbring of his sinnes, as it hath beene vsed heretofore in the time of blindnesse and ignorance.

The third part of repentance, is fayth, whereby wee doe apprehend and take hold vpon the promises of GOD, touching the free pardon and forgiuenesse of our sinnes. Which promises are sealed vp vnto vs, with the death and blood-shedding of his Sonne Iesu Christ. For what should auayle and profite vs to bee sorrie for our sinnes, to lament and bewayle that wee haue offended our most bounteous and mercifull Father, or to confesse and acknowledge our offences and trespasses, though it be done neuer so earnestly, vnlesse we doe stedfastly beleeue, and bee fully perswaded, that GOD for his Sonne Iesus

Christs sake, will forgiue vs all our sinnes, and put them out of remembrance, and from his sight?

The repentance of the Schoolemen. Therefore they that teach repentance without a liuely faith in our Sauiour Iesus Christ, doe teach none other but Iudas repentance as all the Schoole-men doe, which doe only allow these three parts of repentance: the contrition of the heart, the confession of the mouth, and the satisfaction of the worke.

Iudas & his repentance. But all these things we finde in Iudas repentance: which in outward appearance did farre exceede and passe the repentance of Peter. For first and foremost wee reade in the Gospel, that Iudas was so sorrowfull and heauy, yea, that hee was filled with such anguish and vexation of minde, for that which hee had done, that hee could not abide to liue any longer (Matthew 27). Did not hee also afore hee hanged himselfe make an open confession of his fault, when hee sayde, I haue sinned, betraying the innocent blood? And verely this was a very bold confession, which might haue brought him to great trouble. For by it he did lay to the high Priests and Elders charge, the shedding of innocent blood, and that they were most abominable murderers. Hee did also make a certaine kinde of satisfaction, when hee did cast their money vnto them againe.

Peter and his repentance. No such thing doe wee read of Peter although hee had committed a very heinous sinne, and most grieuous offence, in denying of his Master. We find that he went out and wept bitterly, whereof Ambrose speaketh on this manner (Ambrose, De penitentia distin., 1 Chap.): Peter was sory and wept, because he erred as a man. I doe not finde what hee said, I know that hee wept. I read of his teares, but not of his satisfaction. But how chaunce that the one was receiued into fauour againe with GOD, and the other cast away, but because that the one did by a liuely Faith in him whom he had denyed take holde vpon the mercy of GOD, and the other wanted Faith, whereby hee did dispayre of the goodnesse and mercie of GOD? It is euident and plaine then, that although wee be neuer so earnestly sorie for our sinnes, acknowledge and confesse them: yet all these things shall bee but meanes to bring vs to vtter desperation, except wee doe stedfastly beleeue, that GOD our heauenly Father will for his Sonne Iesus Christs sake, pardon and forgiue vs our offences and trespasses, and vtterly put them out of remembrance in his sight. Therefore, as wee sayd before, they that teach repentance without Christ, and a liuely Faith in the mercy of GOD, doe onely teach Caines or Iudas repentance. The fourth is, an amendment of life, or a new life, in bringing foorth fruits worthy of repentance. For they that doe truely repent, must bee cleane altered and changed, they must become new creatures, they must be no more the same that they were before. And therefore thus said Iohn Baptist vnto the Pharisees and Sadduces that came vnto his Baptisme: O generation of vipers, who hath forewarned you to flee from the anger to come? bring foorth therefore fruits worthy of repentance (Matthew 3.7-8). Whereby wee doe learne, that if wee will haue the wrath of GOD to bee pacified, wee must in no wise dissemble, but turne vnto him againe with a true and sound repentance, which may bee knowen and declared by good fruits, as by most sure and fallible signes thereof.

They that doe from the bottome of their hearts acknowledge their sinnes, and are vnfaignedly sory for their offences, will cast off all hypocrisie, and put on true humility, and lowlinesse of heart. They will not only receiue the Physition of the soule, but also with a most feruent desire long for him. They will not onely absteine from the sinnes of their former life, and from all other filthy vices, but also flee, eschew, and abhorre all the occasions of them. And as they did before giue themselues to vncleannesse of life, so will they from henceforwardes with all diligence giue themselues to innocency, purenesse of life, and true godlinesse. Wee haue the Nineuites for an example, which at the preaching of Ionas did not onely proclaime a generall fast, and that they should euery one put on sackecloth: but they all did turne from their euill wayes, and from the wickednesse that was in their hands (Jonas 3.5, 10). But aboue all other, the historie of Zacheus is most notable: For being come vnto our Sauiour Iesu Christ, hee did say, Behold Lord, the halfe of my goods I giue to the poore, and if I haue defrauded any man, or taken ought away be extortion or fraude, I doe restore him foure fold (Luke 19.8).

Here we see that after his repentance, hee was no more the man that hee was before, but was cleane chaunged and altered. It was so farre of, that hee would continue and bide still in his vnsatiable couetousnes, or take ought away fraudulently from any man, that rather hee was most willing and ready to giue away his owne, and to make satisfaction vnto all them that hee had done iniury and wrong vnto. Here may wee right well adde the sinfull woman, which when shee came to our Sauiour Iesus Christ did powre downe such abundance of teares out of those wanton eyes of hers, wherewith she had allured many vnto folly, that shee did with them wash his feete, wiping them with the haires of her head, which she was wont most gloriously to set out, making of them a nette of the deuill (Luke 7.37). Hereby we doe learne, what is the satisfaction that GOD doeth require of vs, which is, that we cease from euill, and doe good, and if wee haue done any man wrong, to endeuour our selues to make him true amends to the vttermost of our power (Isaiah 1.16-17), following in this the example of Zacheus, and of this sinfull woman, and also that goodly lesson that Iohn Baptist Zacharies sonne did giue vnto them that came to aske counsayle of him. This was commonly the penaunce that Christ enioyned sinners: Goe thy way, and sinne no more (John 8.11). Which penance wee shall neuer be able to fulfill, without the speciall grace of him that doeth say, Without me ye can doe nothing. It is therefore our parts, if at least we be desirous of the health and saluation of our owne selues, most earnestly to pray vnto our heauenly Father, to assiste vs with his Holy spirit, that we may be able to hearken vnto the voyce of the true shepheard, and with due obedience to follow the same.

Let vs hearken to the voyce of Almighty GOD, when he calleth vs to repentance, let vs not harden our hearts, as such Infidels doe, who abuse the time giuen them of GOD to repent, and turne it to continue their pride and contempt against GOD and man, which know not how much they heape GODS wrath vpon themselues, for the hardnesse of their hearts, which cannot repent at the day of vengeance. Where wee haue offended the Law of GOD, let vs repent vs of our straying from so good a Lord. Let vs confesse our vnworthynesse before him, but yet let vs trust in GODS free mercy, for Christs sake, for the pardon of the same. And from hencefoorth let vs endeuour our selues to walke in a new life, as new borne babes, whereby we may glorifie our Father which is heauen, and thereby to beare in our consciences a good testimony of our fayth. So that at the last, to obtaine the fruition of euerlasting life, through the merites of our Sauiour, to whom be all prayse and honour for euer, AMEN.

THE THIRD PART OF THE HOMILIE OF REPENTANCE.

IN the Homilie last spoken vnto you (right welbeloued people in our Sauiour Christ) ye heard of the true parts and tokens of Repentance, that is, heartie contrition and sorrowfulnesse of our hearts, vnfained confession in word of mouth for our vnworthy liuing before GOD, a stedfast faith to the merites of our Sauiour Christ for pardon, and a purpose of our selues by GODS grace to renounce our former wicked life, and a full conuersion to GOD in a new life to glorifie his Name, and to liue orderly and charitably, to the comfort of our neighbour, in all righteousnesse, and to liue soberly and modestly to our selues, by vsing abstinence, and temperance in word and in deede, in mortifying our earthly members heere vpon earth: Now for a further perswasion to mooue you to those partes of repentance, I will declare vnto you some causes, which should the rather mooue you to repentance.

The causes that should mooue vs to repent. First, the commandement of GOD, who in so many places of the holy and sacred Scriptures, doeth bid vs returne vnto him. O yee children of Israel (sayth he) turne againe from your infidelitie, wherein ye drowned your selues (Isaiah 31.6). Againe, Turne you, turne you from your euill wayes: For why will ye die, O ye house of Israel (Ezechiel 33.11)? And in another place, thus doth he speake by his holy Prophet Osee: O Israel, returne vnto the Lord thy GOD: For thou hast taken a great fall by thine iniquitie. Take vnto you these wordes with you, when you turne vnto the Lord and say vnto him, Take away all iniquitie, and receiue vs graciously, so will we offer the calues of our lippes vnto thee (Hosea 14.2). In all these places wee haue an expresse commandement giuen vnto vs of GOD for to returne vnto him. Therefore we must take good heede vnto ourselues, lest whereas wee haue already by our manifold sinnes and transgressions, prouoked and kindled the wrath of GOD against vs, wee doe by breaking this his commandement, double our offences, and so heape still damnation vpon our owne heads by our dayly offences and trespasses, whereby we prouoke the eyes of his Maiestie, wee doe well deserue (if hee should deale with vs according to his iustice) to be put away for euer from the fruition of his glory. How much more then are wee worthy of the endlesse torments of hell, if when wee bee so gently called againe after our rebellion, and commanded to returne, wee will in no wise hearken vnto the voyce of our heauenly Father, but walke still after the stubbornnesse of our owne hearts.

Secondly, the most comfortable and sweet promise, that the Lord our GOD did of his meere mercy and goodnesse ioyne vnto his commandement. For he doeth not onely say, Returne vnto me, O Israel: but also, If thou wilt returne, and put away all thine abominations out of my sight, thou shalt neuer bee mooued (Jeremiah 4.1). These words also haue wee in the Prophet Ezechiel: At what time soeuer a sinner doth repent him of his sinne, from the bottome of his heart, I will put all his wickednesse out of my remembrance (saith the Lord) so that they shall bee no more thought vpon (Ezechiel 18.21-22). Thus are we sufficiently instructed, that GOD will according to his promise, freely pardon, forgiue, and forget all our sinnes, so that we shall neuer be cast in the teeth with them, if, obeying his commandement, and allured by his sweet promises, wee will vnfainedly returne vnto him.

Thirdly, the filthinesse of sinne, which is such, that as long as wee doe abide in it, GOD cannot but detest and abhorre vs, neither can there be any hope, that we shall enter into the heauenly Ierusalem, except wee be first made cleane and purged from it. But this will neuer be, vnlesse forsaking our former life, wee doe with our whole heart returne vnto the Lord our GOD, and with a full purpose of amendment of life, flee vnto his mercy, taking sure hold thereupon through Faith in the blood of his Sonne Iesus Christ.

<u>Similitude.</u> If we should suspect any vncleannesse to be in vs, wherefore the earthly Prince should lothe and abhorre the sight of vs, what paines would wee take to remooue and put it away? How much more ought wee with all diligence and speed that may be, to put away that vncleane filthinesse that doeth separate and make a diuision betwixt vs and our GOD, and that hideth his face from vs, that hee will not heare vs (Isaiah 59.2)? And verily herein doth appeare how filthy a thing sinne is, sith that it can by no other meanes be washed away, but by the blood of the onely begotten Sonne of GOD. And shall wee not from the bottome of our hearts detest and abhorre, and with all earnestnesse flee from it, sith that it did cost the deare heart blood of the onely begotten Sonne of GOD our Sauiour and Redeemer, to purge vs from it? Plato doeth in a certaine place write, that if vertue could

bee seene with bodily eyes, all men would wonderfully be inflamed and kindled with the loue of it: Euen so on the contrary, if we might with our bodily eyes behold the filthinesse of sinne, and the vncleannesse thereof, wee could in no wise abide it, but as most present and deadly poyson, hate and eschew it. Wee haue a common experience of the same in them, which when they haue committed any heinous offence, or some filthy and abominable sinne, if it once come to light, or if they chance to haue a through feeling of it, they bee so ashamed (their owne conscience putting before their eyes the filthinesse of their acte) that they dare looke no man in the face, much lesse that they should be able to stand in the sight of GOD.

Fourthly, the vncertaintie and brittlenesse of our owne liues, which is such, that we cannot assure our selues, that we shall liue one houre, or one halfe quarter of it. Which by experience we doe find daily to be true, in them that being now merrie and lustie, and sometimes feasting and banquetting with their friends, doe fall suddainely dead in the streetes, and other-whiles vnder the board when they are at meat. These daily examples, as they are most terrible and dreadfull, so ought they to mooue vs to seeke for to be at one with our heauenly iudge, that we may with a good conscience appeare before him, whensoeuer it shall please him for to call vs, whether it be suddenly or otherwise, for wee haue no more charter of our life, then they haue. But as wee are most certaine that wee shall die, so are wee most vncertaine when wee shall die. For our life doeth lie in the hand of GOD, who will take it away when it pleaseth him.

Death the Lords Summer. And verily when the highest Summer of all, which is death, shall come, hee will not bee said nay: but wee must foorth with be packing, to be present before the iudgement seat of GOD, as hee doth find vs, according as it is written: Whereas the tree falleth, whether it bee toward the South, or toward the North, there it shall lie (Ecclesiastes 11.3). Whereunto agreeth the saying of the holy Martyr of GOD Saint Cyprian, saying: As GOD doeth find thee when hee doth call, so doth hee iudge thee (Cyprian, Contra Demetrianum). Let vs therefore follow the counsell of the wise man, where he saith: Make no tarying to turne vnto the Lord, and put not off from day to day (Ecclesiastes 5.7). For suddainely shall the wrath of the Lord breake foorth, and in thy securitie shalt thou be destroyed and shalt perish in the time of vengeance. Which words I desire you to marke diligently, because they doe most liuely put before our eyes, the fondnesse of many men, who abusing the long suffering and goodnesse of GOD, doe neuer thinke on repentance or amendment of life. Follow not (saith he) thine owne mind, and thy strength, to walke in the wayes of thy heart, neither say thou, who will bring me vnder for my workes: For GOD the reuenger, will reuenge the wrong done by thee. And say not, I haue sinned, and what euill hath come vnto me? For the Almightie is a patient rewarder, but he will not leaue thee vnpunished. Because thy sinnes are forgiuen thee, be not without feare to heape sinne vpon sinne. Say not neither, The mercie of GOD is great, he will forgiue my manifold sinnes. For mercie and wrath come from him and his indignation commeth vpon vnrepentant sinners. As if yee should say: Art thou strong and mightie? Art thou lustie and young? Hast thou the wealth and riches of the world? Or when thou hast sinned, hast thou receiued no punishment for it? Let none of all these things make thee to be the slower to repent, and to returne with speed vnto the Lord. For in the day of punishment and of his suddaine vengeance, they shall not be able to helpe thee. And specially when thou art either by the preaching of GODS word, or by some inward motion of his holy spirit, or els by some other meanes called vnto repentance, neglect not the good occasion that is ministred vnto thee, lest when thou wouldest repent, thou hast not the grace for to doe it. For to repent, is a good gift, of GOD, which he will neuer grant vnto them, who liuing in carnall securitie, doe make a mocke of his threatnings, or seeke to rule his spirit as they list, as though his working and gifts were tyed vnto their will. Fiftly, the auoyding of the plagues of GOD, and the vtter destruction that by his righteous iudgement doth hang ouer the heads of them all that will in no wise returne vnto the Lord: I will (saith the Lord) giue them for a terrible plague to all the kingdomes of the earth, and for a reproach, and for a prouerbe, and for a curse in all places where I shall cast them, and will send the sword of famine, and the pestilence among them, till they be consumed out of the land (Jeremiah 24.9). And wherefore is this? Because they hardened their hearts, and would in no wise returne from their euill wayes, nor yet forsake the wickednesse that was in their owne hands, that the fiercenesse of the Lords fury might depart from them (Romans 2.5). But yet this is nothing in comparison of the intolerable and endlesse torments of hell fire, which they shall bee faine to suffer, who after their hardnesse of heart that cannot repent, doe heape vnto themselues wrath against the day of anger, and of the declaration of the iust iudgement of GOD: Whereas if we will repent, and bee earnestly sorry for our sinne, and with a full purpose and amendment of life flee vnto the mercy of our GOD, and taking sure hold thereupon through fayth in our Sauiour Iesus Christ doe bring foorth fruits worthy of repentance: hee will not onely powre his manifold blessings vpon vs heere in this world, but also at the last, after the painefull trauels of this life, reward vs with the inheritance of his children, which is the kingdome of heauen, purchased vnto vs with the death of his sonne Iesu Christ our Lord, to whom with the Father and the holy Ghost, be all praise, glory, and honour, world without end. Amen.

AGAINST DISOBEDIENCE AND WILFUL REBELLION

AN HOMILIE AGAINST disobedience and wilfull rebellion

The first part. AS GOD the Creatour and Lord of all things appointed his Angels and heauenly creatures in all obedience to serue and to honour his maiesty: so was it his will that man, his chiefe creature vpon the earth, should liue vnder the obedience of his Creatour and Lord: and for that cause, GOD, as soone as hee had created man, gaue vnto him a certaine precept and law, which hee (being yet in the state of innocency, and remayning in Paradise) should obserue as a pledge and token of his due and bounden obedience, with denunciation of death if hee did transgresse and breake the sayd Law and commandement. And as GOD would haue man to be his obedient subiect, so did he make all earthly creatures subiect vnto man, who kept their due obedience vnto man, so long as man remayned in his obedience vnto GOD: in the which obedience if man had continued still, there had beene no pouerty, no diseases, no sickenesse, no death, nor other miseries wherewith mankinde is now infinitely and most miserably afflicted and oppressed. So heere appeareth the originall kingdome of GOD ouer Angels and man, and vniuersally ouer all things, and of man ouer earthly creatures which GOD had made subiect vnto him, and with all the felicity and blessed state, which Angels, man, and all creatures had remayned in, had they continued in due obedience vnto GOD their King. For as long as in this first kingdome the subiects continued in due obedience to GOD their king, so long did GOD embrace all his subiects with his loue, fauour, and grace, which to enioy, is perfect felicity, whereby it is euident, that obedience is the principall vertue of all vertues, and indeed the very root of all vertues, and the cause of all felicitie. But as all felicitie and blessednesse should haue continued with the continuance of obedience, so with the breach of obedience, and breaking in of rebellion, al vices and miseries did withall breake in, and ouerwhelme the world. The first authour of which rebellion, the root of all vices, and mother of all mischiefes, was Lucifer, first GODS most excellent creature, and most bounden subiect, who by rebelling against the Maiestie of GOD (Matthew 4.9, Matthew 25.41), of the brightest and most glorious Angel, is become the blackest and most foulest fiend and deuill: and from the height of heauen, is fallen into the pit and bottome of hell (John 8.44, 2 Peter 2.4, Jude 6, Revelation 12.7-9).

Here you may see the first authour and founder of rebellion (Genesis 3.1, Apocrypha. Wisdom 2.24), and the reward thereof, here you may see the graund captaine and father of rebels, who perswading the following of his rebellion against GOD their Creatour and Lord (Genesis 3.8, 17.23-24), vnto our first Parents Adam and Eue brought them in high displeasure with GOD, wrought their exile and banishment out of Paradise, a place of all pleasure and goodnesse, into this wretched earth and vale of misery: procured vnto them, sorrowes of their mindes, mischiefes, sickenesse, diseases, death of their bodies, and which is farre more horrible then all worldly and bodily mischiefes, he had wrought thereby their eternall and euerlasting death and damnation, had not GOD by the obedience of his Sonne Iesus Christ repaired that, which man by disobedience and rebellion had destroyed, and so of his mercy had pardoned and forgiuen him: of which all and singular the premises, the holy Scriptures doe beare record in sundry places (Romans 5.12, 19).

Thus doe you see, that neither heauen nor paradise could suffer any rebellion in them, neither be places for any rebels to remaine in. Thus became rebellion, as you see, both the first and the greatest, and the very foot of all other sinnes, and the first and principall cause, both of all worldly and bodily miseries, sorrowes, diseases, sickenesses, and deathes, and which is infinitely worse then all these, as is said, the very cause of death and damnation eternall also (Genesis 3.17). After this breach of obedience to GOD, and rebellion against his Maiestie, all mischiefes and miseries breaking in therewith, and ouerflowing the world, lest all things should come vnto confusion and vtter ruine, GOD foorthwith by lawes giuen vnto mankind, repaired againe the rule and order of obedience thus by rebellion ouerthrowne, and besides the obedience due vnto his Maiesty, hee not onely ordained that in families and housholds, the wife should be obedient vnto her husband (Genesis 3.16), the children vnto their parents, the seruants vnto their masters: but also, when mankind increased, and spread it selfe more largely ouer the world, hee by his holy word did constitute and ordaine in Cities and Countreys seuerall and speciall gouernours and rulers (Job 34.30, 36.7, Ecclesiastes 8.2, 10.16-17, 20), vnto whom the residue of his people should be obedient.

As in reading of the holy Scriptures, we shall finde in very many and almost infinite places, as well of the olde Testament, as of the new, that Kings and Princes, as well the euill as the good, doe raigne by Gods ordinance, and that subiects are bounden to obey them (Psalms 18.50, 20.6, 21.2, Proverbs 8.15-16): that GOD doth giue Princes wisedome, great power, and authority: that GOD defendeth them against their enemies, and destroyeth their enemies horribly: that the anger and displeasure of the Prince, is as the roaring of a Lyon, and the very messenger of death: and that the subiect that prouoketh him to displeasure, sinneth against his own soule: With many other things, concerning both the authority of Princes, and the duetie of subiects. But heere let vs rehearse two speciall places out of the new Testament, which may stand in stead of all other. The first out of Saint Pauls Epistle to the Romanes and the thirteenth Chapter, where hee writeth thus vnto all subiects, Let euery soule be subiect vnto the higher powers, for there is no power but of GOD, and the powers that be, are ordeined of GOD (Romans 13.1). Whosoeuer therefore resisteth the power, resisteth the ordinance of GOD, and they that resist, shall receiue to themselues damnation. For Princes are not to be feared for good works, but for euill. Wilt thou then be without feare of the power? Doe well, so shalt thou haue praise of the same: For he is the minister of GOD for thy wealth: But if thou doe euill, feare: for he beareth not the sword for nought, for he is the minister of GOD to take vengeance vpon him that doth euil. Wherefore ye must be subiect, not because of wrath onely, but also for conscience sake: for, for this cause ye pay also tribute, for they are GODS ministers, seruing for the same purpose. Giue to euery man therfore his duty: tribute, to whom tribute belongeth: custome, to whom custome is due: feare, to whom feare belongeth: honour, to whom ye owe honour. Thus far are S. Pauls words. The second place is in S. Peters Epistle, and the second Chapter, whose words are these, Submit your selues vnto all maner of ordinances of man for the Lords sake, whether it bee vnto the King, as vnto the chiefe head, either vnto rulers, as vnto them that are sent of him for the punishment of euil doers, but for the cherishing of them that doe well (1 Peter 2.13-14). For so is the will of GOD, that with well doing ye may stoppe the mouthes of ignorant & foolish men: as free, and not as hauing the libertie for a cloake of maliciousnesse, but euen as the seruants of GOD. Honour all men, loue brotherly fellowship, feare GOD, honour the King. Seruants, obey your masters with feare, not onely if they be good and courteous, but also though they be froward. Thus farre out of Saint Peter.

By these two places of the holy Scriptures, it is most euident that Kings, Queenes, and other Princes (for hee speaketh of authoritie and power, be it in men or women) are ordeined of GOD, are to bee obeyed and honoured of their subiects: that such subiects, as are disobedient or rebellious against their Princes, disobey GOD, and procure their owne damnation: that the gouernment of Princes is a great blessing of GOD, giuen for the common wealth, specially of the good and godly: For the comfort and cherishing of whom GOD giueth and setteth vp princes: and on the contrary part, to the feare and for the punishment of the euill and wicked. Finally, that if seruants ought to obey their masters, not onely being gentle, but such as be froward: as well and much more ought subiects to be obedient, not only to their good and courteous, but also to their sharpe and rigorous Princes. It commeth therefore neither of chance and fortune (as they terme it) nor of the ambition of mortal men and women climing vp of their owne accord to dominion, that there bee Kings, Queenes, Princes, and other gouernours ouer men being their subiects: but all Kings, Queenes, and other gouernours are specially appoynted by the ordinance of GOD. And as GOD himselfe, being of an infinite Maiestie, power, and wisedome, ruleth and gouerneth all things in heauen and earth, as the vniuersall Monarch and onely King and Emperour ouer all, as being onely able to take and beare the charge of all (Psalms 10.16, 45.6, 47.2): so hath hee constituted, ordeyned, and set earthly Princes ouer particular Kingdomes and Dominions in earth (Ecclesiasticus 17), both for the auoyding of all confusion, which els would be in the world, if it should be without gouernours, and for the great quiet and benefite of earthly men their subiects, and also that the Princes themselues, in authoritie, power, wisedome, prouidence, and righteousnesse in gouernement of people and countreys committed to their charge, should resemble his heauenly gouernance, as the maiestie of heauenly things may by the basenesse of earthly things bee shadowed and resembled. And for that similitude, that is betweene the heauenly Monarchie, and earthly Kingdomes well gouerned, our Sauiour Christ in sundry parables saith, that the Kingdom of heauen is resembled vnto a man, a king (Matthew 18.23, 22.2): and as the name of the king, is very often attributed and giuen vnto GOD in the holy Scriptures (Psalms 10.16, 45.6, 47.2), so doeth GOD himselfe in the same Scriptures sometime vouchsafe to communicate his Name with earthly Princes, terming them gods (Psalms 82.6): doubtlesse for that similitude of gouernement which they haue or should haue, not vnlike vnto GOD their King (Matthew 22.13, 25.34). Vnto the which similitude of heauenly gouernement, the neerer and neerer that an earthly Prince doth come in his regiment, the greater blessing of GODS mercy is he vnto that countrey and people ouer whom he reigneth: and the further and further that an earthly prince doth swarue from the example of the heauenly gouernment, the greater plague is he of GODS wrath, and punishment by GODS iustice, vnto that countrey and people, ouer whom GOD for their sinnes hath places such a Prince and gouernour. For it is indeede euident, both by the Scriptures, and dayly by experience, that the maintenance of all vertue and godlinesse, and consequently of the wealth and prosperity of a kingdome and people, doeth stand & rest more in a wise and good Prince on the one part, then in great multitudes of other men being subiects: and on the contrary part, the ouerthrow of all vertue and godlinesse, and consequently the decay and vtter ruine of a Realme and people doth grow and come more by an vndiscreete and euill gouernour, then by many thousands of other men being subiects. Thus say the holy Scriptures, Well is thee, O thou land (saith the Preacher) whose King is come of Nobles, and whose princes eate in due season, for necessity, and not for lust (Ecclesiastes 10.17, Proverbs 16.29). Againe, a wise and righteous King maketh his Realme and people wealthy: and a good, mercifull, and gracious Prince, is as a shadow in heate, as a defence in stormes, as deaw, as sweete showres, as fresh water springs in great droughts (Ecclesiasticus 10, Isaiah 22.1-2).

Againe the Scriptures, of vndiscreet and euill Princes, speake thus, Woe be to thee (O thou land) whose King is but a child, and whose Princes are early at their bankets (Ecclesiastes 10.16). Againe, when the wicked doe raigne, then men goe to ruine. And againe, A foolish Prince destroyeth the people, and a couetous King vndoeth his

Subiects (Proverbs 28.15-16, 29.2,4). Thus speake the Scriptures, thus experience testifieth of good and euill Princes.

What shall Subiects doe then? shall they obey valiant, stout, wise, and good Princes, and contemne, disobey, and rebell against children being their Princes, or against vndiscreet and euill gouernours? God forbid: For first what a perilous thing were it to commit vnto the Subiects the iudgement which Prince is wise and godly, and his gouernement good, and which is otherwise: as though the foot must iudge of the head: an enterprise very heinous, and must needs breed rebellion. For who else be they that are most inclined to rebellion, but such haughtie spirits? From whom springeth such foule ruine of Realmes? Is not rebellion the greatest of all mischiefes? And who are most ready to the greatest mischiefes, but the worst men? Rebels therefore the worst of all Subiects are most ready to rebellion, as being the worst of all vices, and farthest from the duetie of a good Subiect: as on the contrary part the best Subiects are most firme and constant in obedience, as in the speciall and peculiar vertue of good Subiects. What an vnworthy matter were it then to make the naughtiest Subiects, and most inclined to rebellion and all euill, iudges ouer their Princes, ouer their gouernment, and ouer their counsellers, to determine which of them be good or tolerable, and which be euill, and so intolerable, that they must needs be remooued by rebels, being euer ready as the naughtiest subiects, soonest to rebell against the best Princes, specially if they be yong in age, women in sexe, or gentle and curteous in gouernment, as trusting by their wicked boldnesse, easily to ouerthrow their weakenesse and gentlenesse, or at the least so to feare the mindes of such Princes, that they may haue impunitie of their mischieuous doings.

But whereas indeede a rebell is worse then the worst prince, and rebellion worse then the worst gouernement of the worst prince that hitherto hath beene: both rebels are vnmeete ministers, and rebellion an vnfit and vnwholsome medicine to reforme any small lackes in a prince, or to cure any little griefes in gouernment, such lewd remedies being far worse then any other maladies and disorders that can bee in the body of a common wealth. But whatsoeuer the prince bee, or his gouernement, it is euident that for the most part, those princes whom some subiectes doe thinke to bee very godly, and vnder whose gouernement they reioyce to liue: some other subiects doe take the same to bee euill and vngodly, and doe wish for a change. If therefore all subiects that mislike of their prince, should rebell, no Realme should euer bee without rebellion. It were more meete that rebels should heare the aduise of wise men, and giue place vnto their iudgement, and follow the example of obedient subiectes, as reason is that they whose vnderstanding is blinded with so euill an affection, should giue place to them that bee of sound iudgement, and that the worst should giue place to the better: and so might Realmes continue in long obedience, peace, and quietnesse. But what if the Prince be vndiscreete, and euill indeed, and is also euident to all mens eyes, that hee so is? I aske againe, what if it be long of the wickednesse of the Subiects, that the Prince is vndiscreete and euill? Shall the Subiects both by their wickednesse prouoke GOD for their deserued punishment, to giue them an vndiscreet or euill Prince, and also rebell against him, and withall against GOD, who for the punishment of their sinnes did giue them such a Prince? Will you heare the Scriptures concerning this point? GOD (say the holy Scriptures) maketh a wicked man to raigne for the sinnes of the people (Isaiah 19.4). Againe, GOD giueth a Prince in his anger, meaning an euill one, and taketh away a Prince in his displeasure (Hosea 13.11), meaning specially when hee taketh away a good Prince for the sinnes of the people: as in our memorie hee tooke away our good Iosias (2 Chronicles 34.1) king Edward in his yong and good yeeres for our wickednesse. And contrarily the Scriptures doe teach, that GOD giueth wisedome vnto Princes, and maketh a wise and good King to raigne ouer that people whom he loueth, and who loueth him (Proverbs 8.15-17). Againe, if the people obey GOD, both they and their king shal prosper and be safe, els both shall perish, saith GOD by the mouth of Samuel (1 Sam. 12.14).

Here you see, that GOD placeth as well euill Princes as good, and for what cause he doth both. If wee therefore will haue a good Prince, either to be giuen vs, or to continue: now we haue such a one, let vs by our obedience to GOD and to our Prince moue GOD thereunto. If we will haue an euill Prince (when GOD shall send such a one) taken away, and a good in his place, let vs take away our wickednesse which prouoketh GOD to place such a one ouer vs, and GOD will either displace him, or of an euill Prince make him a good Prince, so that wee first will change our euill into good. For will you heare the Scriptures? The heart of the Prince is in GODS hand, which way soeuer it shall please him, he turneth it (Proverbs 21.1). Thus say the Scriptures. Wherefore let vs turne from our sinnes vnto the Lord with all our hearts, and he will turne the heart of the Prince, vnto our quiet and wealth? Els for Subiects to deserue through their sinnes to haue an euill Prince, and then to rebell against him, were double and treble euill, by prouoking GOD more to plague them. Nay let vs either deserue to haue a good Prince, or let vs patiently suffer and obey such as wee deserue. And whether the Prince be good or euill, let vs according to the counsell of the holy Scriptures, pray for the Prince, for his continuance and increase in goodnesse, if he be good, and for his amendment if he be euill.

Well you heare the Scriptures concerning this most necessary point? I exhort therefore (saith S. Paul) that aboue all things, Prayers, Supplications, Intercessions, and giuing of thankes bee had for all men, for Kings, and all that are in authority, that wee may liue a quiet and peaceable life with all godlines: for that is good and acceptable in the sight of GOD our Sauiour, &c (1 Timothy 2.1-3). This is S. Pauls counsell. And who I pray you, was Prince ouer the most part of the Christians, when GODS holy spirit by Saint Pauls pen gaue them this lesson? Forsooth, Caligula, Claudius or Nero: who were not onely no Christians, but Pagans, and also either foolish rulers, or most cruell tyrants. Will you yet heare the word of GOD to the Iewes, when they were prisoners vnder Nabuchodonosor King of Babylon, after he had slaine their king, nobles, parents, children, and kinsefolkes, burned their countrey, cities, yea Hierusalem it selfe, and the holy Temple, and had caried the residue remaining aliue captiues with him vnto Babylon? Will you heare yet what the Prophet Baruch sayth vnto GODS people being in this captiuity? Pray you, saith the Prophet, for the life of Nabuchodonosor king of Babylon, and for the life of Balthasar his sonne, that their dayes may bee as the dayes of heauen vpon the earth, that GOD also may giue vs strength, and lighten our eyes, that wee may liue vnder the defence of Nabuchodonosor king of Babylon, and vnder the protection of Balthasar his sonne, that we may long doe them seruice, and finde fauour in their sight. Pray for vs also vnto the Lord our GOD, for we haue sinned against the Lord our GOD (Apocrypha. Baruch 1.11-13).

Thus farre the Prophet Baruch his wordes: which are spoken by him vnto the people of GOD, of that king who was an Heathen, a tyrant, and cruell oppressour of them, and had beene a murtherer of many thousands of their nation, and a destroyer of their countrey, with a confession that their sinnes had deserued such a prince to raigne ouer them. And shall the old Christians, by Saint Pauls exhortation, pray for Caligula, Claudius, or Nero? Shall the Iewes pray for Nabuchodonosor? these Emperours and Kings being strangers vnto them, being pagans and infidels being murtherers, tyrantes, and cruell oppressours of them, and destroyers of their countrey, countreymen, and kinsemen, the burners of their villages, townes, cities, and temples? And shall not wee pray for the long, prosperous, and godly raigne of our naturall Prince? No stranger (which is obserued as a great blessing in the Scriptures) of our Christian, our most gratious Soueraigne, no Heathen, nor Pagan Prince? Shall wee not pray for the health of our most mercifull, most louing Soueraigne, the preseruer of vs and our countrey, in so long peace, quietnesse, and securitie, no cruell person, no tyrant, no spoyler of our goods, no shedder of bloodes, no burner and destroyer of our townes, cities, and countreys, as were those, for whom yet as yee haue heard, Christians being their subiectes ought to pray? Let vs not commit so great ingratitude against GOD and our Soueraigne, as not continually to thanke GOD for his gouernement, and for his great and continuall benefites and blessings powred vpon vs by such gouernement. Let vs not commit so great a sinne against GOD, against our selues, and our countrey, as not to pray continually vnto GOD for the long continuance of so gratious a Ruler vnto vs, and our countrey. Else shall we be vnworthy any longer to enioy those benefites and blessings of GOD, which hitherto wee haue had by her shalbe most worthy to fall into all those mischiefes & miseries, which wee & our countrey haue by GODS grace through her gouernment hitherto escaped.

What shall wee say of those Subiects? may wee call them by the name of Subiects? Who neither bee thankefull, nor make any prayer to GOD for so gracious a Soueraigne: but also themselues take armour wickedly, assemble companies and bands of rebels, to breake the publique peace so long continued, and to make, not warre, but rebellion, to endanger the person of such a gracious Soueraigne, to hazard the estate of their countrey, (for whose defence they should bee ready to spend their liues) and being Englishmen, to robbe, spoyle, destroy and burne in England Englishmen, to kill and murther their owne neighbours and kinsefolke, their owne countreymen, to doe all euill and mischiefe, yea and more to, then forreigne enemies would, or could doe? What shall wee say of these men, who vse themselues thus rebelliously against their gracious Soueraigne? Who if GOD for their wickednesse had giuen them an Heathen tyrant to reigne ouer them, were by GODS word bound to obey him, and to pray for him? What may bee spoken of them? so farre doeth their vnkindenesse, vnnaturalnesse, wickednesse, mischieuousnesse in their doings, passe and excell any thing, and all things that can bee expressed and vttered by wordes. Onely let vs wish vnto all such most speedie repentance, and with so grieuous sorrow of heart, as such so horrible sinnes against the Maiestie of GOD doe require, who in most extreme vnthankefulnesse doe rise, not onely against their gracious Prince, against their naturall countrey, but against all their countreymen, women, and children, against themselues, their wiues, children & kinsefolkes, and by so wicked an example against all Christendome, and against whole mankinde of all maner of people throughout the wide world, such repentance, I say, such sorrow of heart GOD graunt vnto all such, whosoeuer rise of priuate and malicious purpose, as is meete for such mischiefes attempted, and wrought by them. And vnto vs and all other Subiectes, GOD of his mercie graunt, that wee may bee most vnlike to all such, and most like to good, naturall, louing, and obedient Subiects: nay, that wee may be such indeede, not onely shewing all obedience our selues, but as many of vs as bee able, to the vttermost of our power, abilitie and vnderstanding, to stay and represse all rebels, and rebellions against GOD, our gracious Prince, and naturall countrey, at euery occasion that is offered vnto vs. And that which wee all are able to doe, vnlesse wee doe it, wee shall bee most wicked, and most worthy to feele in the ende such extreme plagues, as GOD hath euer powred vpon rebels.

Let vs make continuall prayers vnto Almighty GOD, euen from the bottome of our hearts, that hee will giue his grace, power and strength vnto our gracious Queene Elizabeth, to vanquish and subdue all, aswell rebels at home, as forreigne enemies, that all domesticall rebellions being suppressed and pacified, and all outward inuasions repulsed and abandoned, wee may not onely be sure, and long continue in all obedience vnto our gracious Soueraigne, and in that peaceable and quiet life which hitherto wee haue ledde vnder her Maiestie, with all securitie: but also that both our gracious Queene Elizabeth, and we her subiects, may altogether in all obedience vnto GOD the King of Kings, and vnto his holy Lawes, leade our liues so in this world, in all vertue and godlinesse, that in the world to come, wee may enioy his euerlasting kingdome: which I beseech GOD to grant, aswell to our gracious Soueraigne, as vnto vs all, for his Sonne our Sauiour Iesus Christes sake, to whom with the Father and the holy Ghost, one GOD and King immortall bee all glory, prayse, and thankesgiuing world without end, Amen.

Thus haue you heard the first part of this Homilie, now good people let vs pray.

The Prayer as in that time it was published.

O Most mighty GOD, the Lord of hostes, the Gouernour of all creatures, the only giuer of all victories, Who alone art able to strengthen the weake against the mighty, and to vanquish infinite multitudes of thine enemies with the countenance of a few of thy seruants calling vpon thy Name, and trusting in thee: Defend O Lord, thy seruant & our Gouernour vnder thee, our Queene Elizabeth and all thy people committed to her charge, O Lord withstand the crueltie of all those which be common enemies as well to the trueth of thy eternall Word, as to their owne naturall Prince and countrey, and manifestly to this Crowne and Realme of England, which thou hast of thy diuine prouidence assigned in these our dayes to the gouernment of thy seruant, our Soueraigne & gracious Queene. O most mercifull Father, (if it be thy holy will) make soft and tender the stonie hearts of all those that exalt themselues against thy Trueth, and seeke either to trouble the quiet of this Realme of England, or to oppresse the Crowne of the same, and conuert them to the knowledge of thy Sonne the onely Sauiour of the world, Iesus Christ that we and they may ioyntly glorifie thy mercies. Lighten we beseech thee their ignorant hearts, to imbrace the truth of thy Word, or els so abate their cruelty (O most mighty Lord) that this our Christian Realm, with others that confesse thy holy Gospel, may obtaine by thine aide and strength, suretie from all enemies, without shedding of Christian blood, whereby all they which bee oppressed with their tyrannie, may be relieued, and they which bee in feare of their crueltie may bee comforted: and finally that all Christian Realmes, and specially this Realme of England, may by thy defence and protection continue in the trueth of the Gospel, and enioy perfect peace, quietnesse, and securitie: and that we for these thy mercies, ioyntly altogether with one consonant heart and voice, may thankefully render to thee all laud and praise, that we knit in one godly concord and vnitie amongst our selues, may continually magnifie thy glorious Name, who with thy son our Sauiour Iesus Christ, and the holy Ghost, art one Eternall, Almightie, and most mercifull GOD: To whom be all laud, and praise world without end, Amen.

THE SECOND PART OF THE HOMILY AGAINST DISOBEDIENCE AND WILFULL REBELLION.

AS in the first part of this treatie of obedience of subiects to their princes, and against disobedience and rebellion, I haue alledged diuers sentences out of the holy Scriptures for proofe: so shall it be good for the better declaration and confirmation of the sayd wholesome doctrine, to alledge one example or two out of the holy Scriptures of the obedience of subiects, not only vnto their good and gracious gouernours, but also vnto their euill and vnkinde princes. As king Saul was not of the best, but rather of the worst sort of Princes, as being out of GODS fauour for his disobedience against GOD in sparing (in a wrong pity) the king Agag, whom Almighty GOD commanded to be slaine, according to the iustice of GOD against his sworn enemy: and although Saul of a deuotion meant to sacrifice such things as he spared of the Amalechites to the honour and seruice of GOD: yet Saul was reprooued for his wrong mercy and deuotion, and was told that obedience would haue more pleased him then such lenity, which sinfull humanity (sayth holy Chrysostome) is more cruell before GOD, then any murther or shedding of blood when it is commanded of GOD. But yet how euill soeuer Saul the King was, and out of GODS fauour, yet was he obeyed of his subiect Dauid, the very best of all subiects, and most valiant in the seruice of his Prince and Country in the warres, the most obedient and louing in peace, and alwayes most true and faythfull to his Soueraigne and Lord, and furthest off from all manner of rebellion. For the which his most painefull, true, and faythfull seruice, King Saul yet rewarded him not onely with great vnkindnesse, but also sought his destruction and death by all meanes possible: so that Dauid was faine to saue his life, not by rebellion, or any resistance, but by flight and hiding himselfe from the Kings sight. Which notwithstanding, when king Saul vpon a time came alone into the caue where Dauid was, so that Dauid might easily haue slaine him, yet would he neither hurt him himselfe, neither suffer any of his men to lay hands vpon him. Another time also Dauid entring by night with one Abisai a valiant and fierce man, into the tent where King Saul did lie a sleepe, where also he might yet more easily haue slaine him, yet would he neither hurt him himselfe, nor suffer Abisai (who was willing and ready to slay King Saul) once to touch him. Thus did Dauid deale with Saul his Prince, notwithstanding that King Saul continually sought his death and destruction. It shall not be amisse vnto these deedes of Dauid to adde his words, and to shew you what he spake vnto such as encouraged him to take his opportunity and aduantage to slay King Saul, as his mortall enemie, when hee might. The Lord keepe me, saith Dauid, from doing that thing, and from laying hands vpon my lord, GODS anoynted (1 Sam. 24.7-10). For who can lay his hand vpon the Lords anoynted, and be guiltlesse (1 Sam. 26.9-10)? As truely as the Lord liueth, except that the Lord doe smite him, or his dayes shall come to die, or that hee goe downe to warre, and be slaine in battell: the Lord be mercifull vnto me, that I lay not my hand vpon the Lords anoynted. These bee Dauids words spoken at sundry times to diuers his seruants prouoking him to slay king Saul, when opportunitie serued him thereunto. Neyther is it to bee omitted and left out, how when an Amalechite had slaine king Saul, euen at Sauls owne bidding, and commandement (for hee would liue no longer now, for that hee had lost the field against his enemies the Philistims) the said Amalechite making great haste to bring first word & newes thereof vnto Dauid, as ioyous vnto him for the death of his mortall enemie, bringing withall the crowne that was vpon king Sauls head, and the bracelet that was about his arme, both as a proofe of the trueth of his newes, and also as fit and pleasant presents vnto Dauid, being by GOD appoynted to be King, Saul his successour in the kingdome: Yet was that faithfull and godly Dauid so farre from reioycing at these newes, that he rent his clothes, wept, and mourned, and fasted: and so farre off from thankesgiuing to the messenger, eyther for his deede in killing the king, though his deadly enemie, or for his message and newes, or for his presents that he brought, that he said vnto him, How happened it that thou wast not afraid to lay thy hands vpon the Lords anoynted, to slay him? Whereupon, immediatly he commanded one of his seruants to kill the messenger, and said, Thy blood be vpon thine owne head, for thine owne mouth hath witnessed against thy selfe, in confessing that thou hast slaine the Lords anoynted (2 Samuel 1.1-15).

This example dearely beloued is notable, and the circumstances thereof are well to bee considered, for the better instruction of all Subiects in their bounden duetie of obedience, and perpetuall fearing of them from attempting of any rebellion, or hurt against their

Prince. On the one part, Dauid was not onely a good and true Subiect, but also such a Subiect, as both in peace and warre had serued and saued his Princes honour and life, and deliuered his countrey and countreymen from great danger of Infidels, forraigne and most cruell enemies, horribly inuading the king, and his countrey: for the which Dauid was in a singular fauour with all the people, so that hee might haue had great numbers of them at his commandement, if hee would haue attempted any thing (1 Sam. 18.6-7). Besides this, Dauid was no common or absolute subiect but heire apparant to the crowne and kingdome (1 Sam. 16.12), by GOD appoynted to reigne after Saul: which as it increased the fauour of the people that knew it, towards Dauid, so did it make Dauids cause and case much differing from the case of common and absolute subiects. And which is most of all, Dauid was highly and singularly in the fauour of GOD (1 Sam. 18.10, 12): On the contrary part, king Saul was out of GODS fauour (1 Sam. 15.11), (for that cause which is before rehearsed) and he as it were GODS enemie (1 Sam. 15.10-11), and therefore like in warre and peace to bee hurtfull and pernitious vnto the common wealth, and that was knowen to many of his subiects, for that hee was openly rebuked of Samuel for his disobedience vnto GOD, which might make the people the lesse to esteeme him. King Saul was also vnto Dauid a mortall and deadly enemie (1 Sam. 18.8-9), though without Dauids deseruing, who by his faithfull, painefull, profitable, yea most necessary seruice, had well deserued, as of his countrey, so of his Prince, but King Saul farre otherwise: the more was his vnkindnesse, hatred, and crueltie towardes such a good subiect, both odious and detestable (1 Sam. 22.11-19, 26.7-9). Yet would Dauid neither himselfe slay nor hurt such an enemie, for that hee was his Prince and Lord, noe would suffer any other to kill, hurt, or lay hand vpon him, when he might haue beene slaine without any stirre, tumult, or danger of any mans life.

The demande. Now let Dauid answer to such demands, as men desirous of rebellion, doe vse to make. Shall not we, specially being so good men as we are, rise and rebell against a Prince, hated of GOD, and GODS enemy, and therefore like not to prosper either in warre or peace, but to be hurtfull and pernicious to the common wealth?

The answer. No saith good and godly Dauid, GODS and such a kings faythfull subiect: and so conuicting such subiects as attempt any rebellion against such a king, to be neither good subiects nor good men.

The demande. But say they, Shall we not rise and rebell against so vnkinde a Prince, nothing considering or regarding our true, faythfull, and painefull seruice, or the safegard of our posterity?

The answer. No sayth good Dauid, whom no such vnkindnesse could cause to forsake his due obedience to his soueraigne.

The demande. Shall we not, say they, rise and rebell against our knowen, mortall, and deadly enemy, that seeketh our liues?

The answer. No sayth godly Dauid, who had learned the lesson that our Sauiour afterward plainely taught, that wee should doe no hurt to our fellow subiects, though they hate vs, and be our enemies: much lesse vnto our prince, though he were our enemy.

The demande. Shall we not assemble an army of such good fellowes as we are, and by hazarding of our liues, and the liues of such as shall withstand vs, and withall hazarding the whole estate of our countrey, remooue so naughty a Prince?

The answer. No saith godly Dauid, for I, when I might without assembling force, or number of men, without tumult or hazard of any mans life, or shedding of any droppe of blood, haue deliuered my selfe and my countrey of an euill Prince, yet would I not doe it.

The demande. Are not they (say some) lustie and couragious captaines, valiant men of stomacke, and good mens bodies, that doe venture by force to kill and depose their King, being a naughtie Prince, and their mortall enemy?

The answer. They may be as lusty and couragious as they list, yet saith godly Dauid, they can be no good nor godly men that so doe: for I not onely haue rebuked, but also commanded him to be slaine as a wicked man, which slew king Saul mine enemy, though hee being weary of his life for the losse of the victorie against his enemies, desired that man to slay him.

The demande. What shall we then doe to an euill, to an vnkinde Prince, an enemy to vs, hated of GOD, hurtfull to the common wealth, &c.

The answer. Lay no violent hand vpon him, saith good Dauid, but let him liue vntill GOD appoint and worke his end, either by naturall death, or in warre by lawfull enemies, not by traiterous subiects.

Thus would godly Dauid make answer: And S. Paul as ye heard before, willeth vs also to pray for such a Prince.

An vnnaturall and wicked question. If king Dauid would make these answeres, as by his deedes and words recorded in the holy Scriptures, indeed he doth make vnto all such demands concerning rebelling against euill princes, vnkinde princes, cruell princes, princes that bee to their good subiects mortall enemies, princes that are out of GODS fauour, and so hurtfull, or like to be hurtfull to the common wealth: what answere thinke you, would he make to those that demand, whether they (being noughty and vnkinde subiects) may not, to the great hazarde of the life of many thousands, and the vtter danger of the state of the common wealth, and whole Realme, assemble a sort of rebels, either to depose, to put in feare, or to destroy their naturall and louing princes, enemy to none, good to all, euen to them the worst of all other, the maintayner of perpetuall peace, quietnesse, and security, most beneficiall to the common wealth, most necessary for the safegard of the whole Realme? what answere would Dauid make to their demand, whether they may not attempt cruelly and vnnaturally to destroy so peaceable and mercifull a Prince, what I say would Dauid, so reuerently speaking of Saul, and so patiently suffering so euill a king, what would he answere and say to such demandes? What would he say, nay what would hee doe to such high attempters, whoso sayd and did as you before haue heard, vnto him that slew the king his master, though a most wicked prince? If hee punished with death as a wicked doer, such a man: With what reproches of wordes would he reuile such, yea with what torments of most shamefull deaths would he destroy such hell hounds rather then euill men, such rebels I meane, as I last spake of? For if they who doe disobey an euill and vnkinde prince, bee most vnlike vnto Dauid that good subiect: what bee they, who doe rebell against a most naturall and louing prince? And if Dauid being so good a Subiect, that he obeyed so euill a king, was worthy of a subiect to be made a king himselfe: What bee they, which are so euill subiects that they will rebell against their gratious prince, worthy of? Surely no mortall man can expresse with wordes, nor conceiue in minde the horrible and most dreadfull damnation that such be worthy of: who disdayning to be the quiet and happy subiects of their good prince, are most worthy to be the miserable captiues and vile slaues of that infernall tyrant Satan, with him to suffer eternall slauery and torments. This one example of the good subiect Dauid out of the old Testament may suffice, and for the notablenesse of it serue for all.

In the New Testament the excellent example of the blessed Virgin Mary the mother of our Sauiour Christ, doeth at the first offer it selfe. When proclamation or commandement was sent into Iurie from Augustus the Emperour of Rome, that the people there should repayre vnto their owne Cities and dwelling places, there to be taxed (Luke 2.1): neither did the blessed Virgin, though both highly in GODS fauour, and also being of the royall blood of the ancient naturall Kings of Iurie, disdayne to obey the commandement of an Heathen and forreigne prince, when GOD had placed such a one ouer them: Neither did shee alleage for an excuse, that shee was great with child, and most neere her time of deliuerance: Neither grudged shee at the length and tedious iourney from Nazareth to Bethlehem, from whence and whither she must goe to bee taxed: Neither repined shee at the sharpenesse of the dead time of Winter, being the latter end of December, an vnfit time to trauaile in, specially a longe iourney for a woman beeing in her case: but all excuses set apart, shee obeyed, and came to the appointed place, whereat her comming she found such great resort and throng of people, that finding no place in any Inne, shee was faine after her long painefull and tedious iourney, to take vp her lodging in a stable, where also shee was deliuered of her blessed Childe (Luke 2.7): and this also declareth how neere her time shee tooke that iourney. This obedience of this most noble, and most vertuous Lady, to a forraigne and pagan Prince, doth well teach vs (who in comparison of her are most base and vile) what ready obedience wee doe owe to our naturall and gratious Soueraigne. Howbeit, in this case the obedience of the whole Iewish nation (beeing otherwise a stubborne people) vnto the commandement of the same forraigne heathen Prince (Luke 2.3), doeth prooue, that such Christians as doe not most readily obey their naturall gratious Soueraigne, are far worse then the stubborne Iewes, whom we yet account as the worst of all people. But no example ought to bee of more force with vs Christians, then the example of Christ our Master and Sauiour, who though hee were the Sonne of GOD (Matthew

17.25, Luke 20.25), yet did alwayes behaue himselfe most reuerently to such men as were in authority in the world in his time, and hee not rebelliously behaued himselfe, but openly did teach the Iewes to pay tribute vnto the Romane Emperour (Mark 12.17), though a forraigne and a pagan Prince, yea himselfe with his Apostles payd tribute vnto him: and finally, being brought before Pontius Pilate (Luke 23.1, Matthew 27.1), a stranger borne, and an heathen man, being Lord president of Iurie, he acknowledged his authority and power to bee giuen him from GOD, and obeyed patiently the sentence of most painefull and shamefull death, which the sayd Iudge pronounced and gaue most vniustly against him, without any grudge, murmuring, or euill word once giuing (Luke 23.24).

There bee many and diuers other examples of the obedience to Princes, euen such as bee euill, in the new Testament, to the vtter confusion of disobedient and rebellious people, but this one may be an eternall example, which the Sonne of GOD, and so the Lord of all, Iesus Christ hath giuen to vs his Christians and seruants, and such as may serue for all, to teach vs to obey Princes, though strangers, wicked, and wrongfull, when GOD for our sinnes shall place such ouer vs. Whereby it followeth vnauoidably, that such as doe disobey or rebell against their owne naturall gratious Soueraignes, howsoeuer they call themselues, or be named of others, yet are they indeede no true Christians, but worse then Iewes, worse then Heathens, and such as shall neuer enioy the Kingdome of heauen, which Christ by his obedience purchased for true Christians, being obedient to him the King of all kings, and to their Prince whom he hath placed ouer them: The which kingdome the peculiar place of all such obedient subiectes, I beseech GOD our heauenly Father, for the same our Sauiour Iesus Christes sake to grant vnto vs, to whom with the holy Ghost be all laude, honour, and glory, now and for euer. Amen.

Thus haue you heard the second part of this Homily, now good people let vs pray.

The Prayer as in that time it was published.

O Most mighty GOD, the Lord of hostes, the Gouernour of all creatures, the only giuer of all victories, who alone art able to strengthen the weake against the mighty, and to vanquish infinite multitudes of thine enemies with the countenance of a few of thy seruants calling vpon thy Name, and trusting in thee: Defend O Lord, thy seruant & our Gouernour vnder thee, our Queene Elizabeth and all thy people committed to her charge, O Lord withstand the crueltie of all those which be common enemies as well to the trueth of thy eternall Word, as to their owne naturall Prince and countrey, and manifestly to this Crowne and Realme of England , which thou hast of thy diuine prouidence assigned in these our dayes to the gouernment of thy seruant, our Soueraigne & gracious Queene. O most mercifull Father, (if it be thy holy will) make soft and tender the stonie hearts of all those that exalt themselues against thy Trueth, and seeke either to trouble the quiet of this Realme of England, or to oppresse the Crowne of the same, and conuert them to the knowledge of thy Sonne the onely Sauiour of the world, Iesus Christ, that we and they may ioyntly glorifie thy mercies. Lighten we beseech thee their ignorant hearts to imbrace the truth of thy Word, or els so abate their cruelty (O most mighty Lord) that this our Christian Realm, with others that confesse thy holy Gospel, may obtaine by thine aide and strength, suretie from all enemies, without shedding of Christian blood, whereby all they which bee oppressed with their tyrannie, may be relieued, and they which bee in feare of their crueltie, may bee comforted: and finally that all Christian Realmes, and specially this Realme of England, may by thy defence and protection continue in the trueth of the Gospel, and enioy perfect peace, quietnesse, and securitie: and that we for these thy mercies, ioyntly altogether with one consonant heart and voice, may thankefully render to thee all laud and praise, that we knit in one godly concord and vnitie amongst our selues, may continually magnifie thy glorious Name, who with thy son our Sauiour Iesus Christ, and the holy Ghost, art one Eternall, Almightie, and most mercifull GOD: To whom be all laud, and praise world without end, Amen.

THE THIRD PART OF THE HOMILY AGAINST DISOBEDIENCE AND WILFULL REBELLION.

AS I haue in the first part of this treatise shewed vnto you the doctrine of the holy Scriptures, as concerning the obedience of true subiects to their princes, euen as well to such as be euill, as vnto the good, and in the second part of the same treaty confirmed the same doctrine by notable examples, likewise taken out of the holy Scriptures: so remayneth it now that I partly doe declare vnto you in this third part, what an abominable sin against GOD and man rebellion is, and how dreadfully the wrath of GOD is kindled and inflamed against all rebels, and what horrible plagues, punishments, and deaths, and finally eternall damnation doeth hang ouer their heads: as how on the contrary part, good and obedient subiects are in GODS fauour, and be partakers of peace, quietnesse, and security, with other GODS manifold blessings in this world, and by his mercies through our Sauiour Christ, of life euerlasting also in the world to come. How horrible a sinne against GOD and man rebellion is, cannot possibly bee expressed according vnto the greatnesse thereof. For he that nameth rebellion, nameth not a singular or one onely sinne, as is theft, robbery, murder, and such like, but he nameth the whole puddle and sinke of all sinnes against GOD and man, against his Prince, his country, his countrymen, his parents, his children, his kins folkes, his friends, and against all men vniuersally, all sinnes I say against GOD and all men heaped together nameth he, that nameth rebellion. For concerning the offence of GODS Maiesty, who seeth not that rebellion riseth first by contempt of GOD and of his holy ordinances and lawes, wherein hee so straitely commandeth obedience, forbiddeth disobedience and rebellion? And besides the dishonour done by rebels vnto GODS holy Name, by their breaking of their oath made to their Prince, with the attestation of GODS name, and calling of his Maiesty to witnesse: Who heareth not the horrible oathes and blasphemies of GODS holy name, that are vsed dayly amongst rebels, that is either amongst them, or heareth the trueth of their behauiour? Who knoweth not that rebels doe not onely themselues leaue all workes necessary to be done vpon workedayes, vndone, whiles they accomplish their abominable worste of rebellion, and to compell others that would gladly be well occupied, to doe the same: but also how rebels doe not onely leaue the Sabboth day of the Lord vnsanctified, the Temple and Church of the Lord vnresorted vnto, but also doe by their workes of wickednesse most horribly prophane and pollute the Sabboth day, seruing Satan, and by doing of his worke, making it the deuils day, in steede of the Lords day? Besides that, they compell good men that would gladly serue the Lord assembling in his Temple and Church vpon his day, as becommeth the Lords seruants, to assemble and meete armed in the field, to resist the furie of such rebels. Yea, & many rebels, lest they should leaue any part of GODS commandements in the first table of his Law vnbroken, or any sinne against GOD vndone, doe make rebellion for the maintenance of their Images and Idols, and of their idolatrie committed, or to bee committed by them: and in dispite of GOD, cut and teare in sunder his holy word, and treade it vnder their feete, as of late yee know was done.

The fifth commandement. As concerning the second table of GODS Law, and all sinnes that may bee committed against man, who seeth not that they bee contained in rebellion? For first the rebels doe not onely dishonour their Prince, the parent of their countrey, but also do dishonour and shame their naturall parents, if they haue any, doe shame their kinred and friendes, doedisinherite & vndoe for euer their children and heyres.

The sixt and eight commandement. Theftes, robberies, and murders, which of all sinnes are most lothed of most men, are in no men so much nor so pernitiously and mischieuously, as in rebels. For the most arrant theeues, cruellest murderers that euer were, so long as they refraine from rebellion, as they are not many in number, so spreadeth their wickednesse and damnation vnto a few, they spoyle but a few, they shed the blood but of a few in comparison. But rebels are the cause of infinite robberies, and murders of great multitudes, and of those also whom they should defend from the spoyle and violence of other: and as rebels are many in number, so doeth their wickednesse and damnation spread it selfe vnto many.

The seuenth commandement. And if whoredome and adulterie amongst such persons as are agreeable to such wickednesse, are (as they indeede bee most damnable:) what are the forceable oppressions of matrons and mens wiues, and the violating and deflowring of virgins and maides, which are most rife with rebels? How horrible and damnable thinke you are they?

The ninth commandement. Now besides that, rebels by breach of their faith giuen, and the oath made to their Prince, bee guiltie of most damnable periurie: it is wonderous to see what false colors and fained causes, by slanderous lies made vpon their Prince, and the councellers, rebels will deuise to cloke their rebellion withall, which is the worst and most damnable of all false witnesse bearing that may be possible.

The tenth commandement. For what should I speake of coueting or desiring of other mens wiues, houses, landes, goods and seruants in rebels, who by their willes would leaue vnto no man anie thing of his owne?

Thus you see that all good lawes are by rebels violated and broken, and that all sinnes possible to bee committed against GOD or man, bee contained in rebellion: which sinnes if a man list to name by the accustomed names of the seuen capitall or deadly sinnes, as pride, enuy, wrath, couetousnesse, sloth, gluttonie, and lecherie, he shall finde them all in rebellion, and amongst rebels. For first, as ambition and desire to be aloft, which is &that; property of pride, stirreth vp many mens minds to rebellion, so commeth it of a Luciferian pride and presumption, that a few rebellious subiects should set themselues vp against the Maiesty of their Prince, against the wisedome of the counsellers, against the power and force of all Nobility, and the faithfull subiects and people of the whole Realme. As for enuie, wrath, murder, and desire of blood, and couetousnesse of other mens goodes, landes and liuings, they are the inseparable accidents of all rebels, and peculiar properties that doe vsually stirre vp wicked men vnto rebellion.

Now such as by riotousnesse, gluttony, drunkennesse, excesse of apparell, and vnthrifty games, haue wasted their owne goodes vnthriftitily, the same are most apt vnto, and most desirous of rebellion, whereby they trust to come by other mens goodes vnlawfully and violently. And where other gluttons and drunkardes take too much of such meats and drinkes as are serued to tables, rebels waste and consume in short space, all corne in barnes, fieldes, or elsewhere, whole garners, whole storehouses, whole cellers, deuoure whole flockes of sheepe, whole droues of Oxen and Kine. And as rebels that are married, leauing their owne wiues at home, doe most vngraciously: so much more do vnmarried men, worse then any stallands or horses (being now by rebellion set at liberty from correction of Lawes which brideled them before) abuse by force other mens wiues, and daughters, and rauish virgins and maydens, most shamefully, abominably, and damnably.

Thus all sinnes, by all names that sinnes may be named, and by all meanes that sinnes may be committed and wrought, doe all wholly vpon heapes follow rebellion, and are to bee found altogether amongst rebels. Now whereas pestilence, famine, and warre, are by the holy Scriptures declared to bee the greatest worldly plagues and miseries that likely can be (2 Sam. 24.14), it is euident, that all the miseries that all these plagues haue in them, doe wholly altogether follow rebellion, wherein, as all their miseries bee, so is there much more mischiefe then in them all.

For it is knowen that in the resorting of great companies of men together, which in rebellion happeneth both vpon the part of true subiectes, and of the rebels, by their close lying together, and corruption of the ayre and place where they doe lie, with ordure and much filth, in the hot weather, and by vnwholesome lodging, and lying often vpon the ground, specially in colde and wet weather in Winter, by their vnwholesome diet, and feeding at all times, and often by famine and lacke of meate and drinke in due time, and againe by taking too much at other times: It is well knowen, I say, that aswell plagues and pestilences, as all other kindes of sickenesses and maladies by these meanes growe vp and spring amongst men, whereby moe men are consumed at the length, then are by dint of sword sodainely slaine in the field. So that not onely pestilences, but also all other sickenesses, diseases, and maladies, doe follow rebellion, which are much more horrible then plagues, pestilences, and diseases sent directly from GOD, as hereafter shall appeare more plainely.

And as for hunger and famine, they are the peculiar companions of rebellion: for while rebels doe in short time spoile and consume all corne and necessary prouision, which men with their labours had gotten and appointed vpon, for their finding the whole yeere after, and also doe let all other men, husbandmen and others, from their husbandry, and other necessary workes, whereby prouision should bee made for times to come, who seeth not that extreame famine and hunger must needes shortly ensue and follow rebellion? Now whereas the wise King & godly Prophet Dauid iudged warre to be worse then either famine or pestilence (2 Sam. 24.14), for that these two are often suffered by GOD, for mans amendement, and be not sinnes of themselues: but warres haue alwayes the sins and mischiefes of men vpon the one side or other ioyned with them, and therefore is war the greatest of these worldly mischiefes: but of all warres, ciuill warre is the worst, and farre more abominable yet is rebellion then any ciuill warre, being vnworthy the name of any warre, so farre it exceedeth all warres in all naughtinesse, in all mischiefe, and in all abomination. And therefore our Sauiour Christ denounceth desolation and destruction to that Realme, that by sedition and rebellion is diuided in it selfe (Matthew 12.25).

Now as I haue shewed before, that pestilence and famine, so is it yet more euident that all the calamities, miseries, and mischiefes of warre, be more grieuous and doe more follow rebellion, then any other warre, as being farre worse then all other warres. For not onely those ordinarie and vsuall mischiefes and miseries of other warres, doe follow rebellion, as corne, and other things, necessary to mans vse to be spoiled, Houses, Villages, Townes, Cities, to be taken, sacked, burned, and destroyed, not onely many very wealthy men, but whole countreys to be impouerished, and vtterly beggered, many thousands of men to be slaine and murdered, women and maides to be violated and deflowred: which things when they are done by forraine enemies, we doe much mourne, as wee haue great causes, yet are all these miseries without any wickednesse wrought by any of our owne countreymen. But when these mischiefes are wrought in rebellion by them that should be friends, by countreymen, by kinsemen, by those that should defend their countrey, and countreymen from such miseries, the misery is nothing so great, as is the mischiefe and wickednes when the Subiects vnnaturally doe rebell against their Prince, whose honour and life they should defend, though it were with the losse of their owne liues: countreymen to disturbe the publique peace and quietnesse of their countrey, for defence of whose quietnesse they should spend their liues: the brother to seeke, and often to worke the death of his brother, the sonne of the father, the father to seeke or procure the death of his sons, being at mans age, and by their faults to disinherite their innocent children and kinsemen their heires for euer, for whom they might purchase liuings and lands, as naturall Parents doe take care and paines, and to be at great costes and charges: and vniuersally in stead of all quietnesse, ioy, and felicitie, which doe follow blessed peace & due obedience, to bring in all trouble, sorrow, disquietnes of minds & bodies & all mischiefe & calamitie, to turne all good order vpside downe, to bring all good lawes in contempt, and to treade them vnder feete, to oppresse all vertue and honestie, and all vertuous and honest persons, and to set all vice and wickednesse, and all vicious and wicked men at libertie, to worke their wicked willes, which were before bridled by wholsome Lawes, to weaken, to ouerthrow, and to consume the strength of the Realme their naturall Countrey, as well by the spending and wasting of monie and treasure of the Prince and Realme, as by murdering the people of the same, their owne countrimen, who should defend the honour of their Prince, and libertie of their Countrie (Proverbs 14.28), against the inuasion of forraigne enemies: and so finally, to make their countrie thus by their mischeefe weakened, ready to bee a pray and spoyle to all outwarde enemies that will inuade it, to the vtter and perpetuall captiuitie, slauerie, and destruction of all their countriemen, their children, their friendes, their kinsefolkes left aliue, whom by their wicked rebellion they procure to bee deliuered into the hands of the forraigne enemies, as much as in them doeth lie.

In forraigne warres our countriemen in obtaining the victorie win the prayse of valiantnesse, yea and though they were ouercommed and slaine, yet winne they an honest commendation in this world, and die in a good conscience for seruing GOD, their Prince, and their countrie, and bee children of eternall saluation: But the rebellion how desperate and strong soeuer they bee, yet winne they shame here in fighting against GOD, their Prince and Countrie, and therefore iustly doe fall headlong into hell if they die, and liue in shame and fearefull conscience, though they escape.

But commonly they be rewarded with shamefull deathes, their hands and carkases set vpon poles, and hanged in chaines, eaten with kytes and crowes, iudged vnworthy the honour of buriall, and so their soules, if they repent not (as commonly they doe not) the deuill hurrieth them into hell, in the middest of their mischiefe. For which dreadfull execution Saint Paul sheweth the cause of obedience, not onely for feare of death, but also in conscience to GOD-ward, for feare of eternall damnation in the world to come (Romans 13.2).

Wherefore good people, let vs, as the children of obedience, feare, the dreadfull execution of GOD, and liue in quiet obedience, to bee the children of euerlasting Saluation. For as heauen is the place of good obedient subiectes, and hell the prison and dungeon of rebels against GOD and their Prince: so is that Realme happy where most obedience of subiects doth appeare, being the verie figure of heauen: and contrariwise where most rebellions and rebelles bee, there is the expresse similitude of hell, and the rebelles themselues are the verie figures of fiendes and deuils, and their captaine the vngratious patterne of Lucifer and Satan, the prince of darkenesse, of whose rebellion as they bee followers, so shall they of his damnation in hell vndoubtedly bee partakers, and as vndoubtedly children of peace the inheritours of heauen with GOD the Father, GOD the Sonne, and GOD the holy Ghost: To whom bee all honour and glory for euer and euer, Amen.

Thus haue you heard the third part of this Homilie, now good people let vs pray.

The Prayer as in that time it was published.

O Most mighty GOD, the Lord of hostes, the Gouernour of al creatures, the only giuer of all victories, & who alone art able to strengthen the weak against the mighty, and to vanquish infinite multitudes of thine enemies with the countenance of a few of thy seruants calling vpon thy Name, & trusting in thee: Defend, O Lord, thy seruant and our Gouernour vnder thee, our Queene ELIZABETH, & all thy people committed to her charge: O Lord withstand the cruelty of all those which be common enemies aswell to the trueth of thy eternall Word, as to their owne naturall Prince and countrey, and manifestly to this Crowne & Realme of England which thou hast of thy diuine prouidence assigned in these our dayes to the gouernement of thy seruant, our Soueraigne and gracious Queene, O most mercifull Father, (if it be thy holy will) make soft and tender the stony hearts of all those that exalt themselues against thy Trueth and seeke either to trouble the quiet of this Realme of England, or to oppresse the Crowne of the same, and conuert them to the knowledge of thy Sonne the onely Sauiour of the world, Iesus Christ, that we and they may ioyntly glorifie thy mercies. Lighten we beseech thee their ignorant hearts, to imbrace the truth of thy word, or els so abate their cruelty (O most mighty Lord) that this our Christian Realme with others that confesse thy holy Gospel, may obtaine by thine ayde and strength, surety from all enemies, without shedding of Christian blood, whereby all they which bee oppressed with their tyranny, may bee relieued, and they which bee in feare of their cruelty, may bee comforted: and finally that all Christian Realmes, and specially this Realme of England, may by thy defence and protection continue in the trueth of the Gospel and enioy perfect peace, quietnesse, and security: and that wee for these thy mercies, iointly altogether with one consonant heart and voyce, may thankfully render to thee all laud and prayse, that we knit in one godly concord and vni-

ty amongst our selues, may continually magnifie thy glorious Name, who with thy son our Sauiour Iesus Christ and the holy Ghost, art one Eternall, Almighty, and most mercifull GOD: To whom be all laud and prayse world without end. Amen.

THE FOURTH PART OF THE HOMILY AGAINST DISOBEDIENCE AND WILFULL REBELLION.

FOr your further instruction (good people) to shew vnto you how much Almighty GOD doeth abhore disobedience and wilfull rebellion, specially when rebelles aduance themselues so high, that they arme themselues with weapon, and stand in fielde to fight against GOD, their Prince, and their countrie: it shall not bee out of the way to shew some examples set out in Scriptures, written for our eternall erudition. Wee may soone know (good people) how heinous offence the trecherie of rebellion is, if we call to remembrance the heauie wrath and dreadfull indignation of Almighty GOD against subiectes as doe onely but inwardly grudge, mutter, and murmure against their gouernours though their inward treason so priuily hatched in their breastes, come not to open declaration of their doings, as harde it is whom the deuill hath so farre entised against GODS word to keepe themselues there: no hee meaneth still to blowe the coale, to kindle their rebellious hearts to flame into open deedes, if he be not with grace speedily withstood.

Some of the children of Israel, beeing murmurers against their Magistrates appoynted ouer them by GOD, were stricken with foule leprosie: many were burnt vp with fire sodainely sent from the Lord: sometime a great sort of thousandes were consumed with the pestilence (Numbers 11.1, 33, 12.10, 16.32-33, 35, Psalms 78.30-31, 50): sometime they were stinged to death with a strange kinde of firie Serpents: & (which is most horrible) some of the Captaines with their band of murmurers not dying by any vsuall or naturall death of men, but the earth opening, they with their wiues, children, and families, were swallowed quicke downe into hell (Numbers 16.31-32). Which horrible destructions of such Israelites as were murmurers against Moses, appointed by GOD, to bee their heade and chiefe Magistrate, are recorded in the booke of Numbers, and other places of the scriptures, for perpetuall memorie and warninge to all subiects, how highly GOD is displeased with the murmuringe and euill speaking of subiectes against their princes, for that as the Scripture recordeth, their murmure was not against their prince onely, beeing a mortall creature, but against GOD himselfe also (Exodus 16.7-8). Now if such strange and horrible plagues, did fall vpon such subiects as did only murmure and speake euill against their heads: what shall become of those most wicked impes of the deuill that doe conspire, arme themselues, assemble great numbers of armed rebels, and leade them with them against their Prince and countrey, spoyling and robbing, killing, and murdering all good subiectes that doe withstand them, as many as they may preuaile against? But those examples are written to stay vs, not onely from such mischiefes, but also from murmuring, and speaking once an euill word against our Prince, which though any should doe neuer so secretly, yet doe the holy Scriptures shew that the verie birdes of the ayre will bewray them (Ecclesiasticus 10.20): and these so many examples before noted out of the holy Scriptures doe declare, that they shall not escape horrible punishment therefore. Now concerning actuall rebellion, amongst many examples thereof set foorth in the holy Scriptures, the example of Absolon is notable (2 Sam. 15.12, 17.1, 12, 18.7, 18): who entring into conspiracie against King Dauid his father, both vsed the aduise of very wittie men, and assembled a very great and huge company of rebelles: the which Absolon though hee were most goodly of person, of great nobilitie, beeing the Kinges sonne, in great fauour of the people, and so dearely beloued of the king himselfe, so much that hee gaue commandement that (notwithstanding his rebellion) his life should bee saued (2 Sam. 18.5): when for these considerations, most men were afraide to lay handes vpon him, a great tree stretching out his arme, as it were for that purpose, caught him by the great and long bush of his goodly haire, lapping about it as hee fledde hastilie bare-headed vnder the saide tree, and so hanged him vp by the haire of his head in the ayre (2 Sam. 18.9), to giue an eternall document, that neither comelinesse of personage, neither nobilitie, nor fauour of the people, no nor the fauour of the king himselfe, can saue a rebell from due punishment: GOD the King of all kings beeing so offended with him, that rather then hee should lacke due execution for his treason, euery tree by the way will be a gallous or gibbet vnto him, and the haire of his owne head will bee vnto him in stead of an halter to hang him vp with, rather then he should lacke one.

Achitophel. A fearefull example of GODS punishment (good people) to consider. Now Achitophel (2 Sam. 15.12, 16.21, 23, 17.23), though otherwise an exceding wise man, yet the mischeeuous counceller of Absolon, in this wicked rebellion, for lacke of an hangman, a conuenient seruitour for such a traytour, went and hanged vp himselfe. A worthy end of all false rebels, who rather then they should lacke due execution, will by GODS iust iudgement, become hangmen vnto themselues. Thus happened it to the captaines of that rebellion: beside fourtie thousand of rascall rebels slaine in the field, and in the chase (2 Sam. 18.7-9).

Likewise is it to bee seene in the holy Scriptures show that great rebellion which the traytour Seba moued in Israel, was suddenly appeased, the head of the captaine traytour (by the meanes of a seely woman) being cut off (2 Sam. 20.22). And as the holy Scriptures doe shew, so doeth dayly experience prooue, that the counsels, conspiracies, and attempts of rebels, neuer tooke effect, neither came to good, but to most horrible ende (Psalms 21.12). For though GOD doth oftentimes prosper iust and lawfull enemies, which bee no subiects against their forreigne enemies: yet did hee neuer long prosper rebellious subiects against their Prince, were they neuer so great in authoritie, or so many in number. Fiue Princes or Kings (for so the Scripture tearmeth them) with all their multitudes, could not preuaile against Chodorlaomer (Genesis 14.4, 10, 14), vnto whom they had promised loyaltie and obedience, and had continued in the same certaine yeeres, but they were all ouerthrowen and taken prisoners by him: but Abraham with his familie and kinsefolkes, an handfull of men in respect, owing no subiection vnto Chodorlaomer, ouerthrew him and all his hoste in battell, and recouered the prisoners, and deliuered them. So that though warre bee so dreadfull and cruell a thing, as it is, yet doeth GOD often prosper a few in lawfull warres with forreigne enemies against many thousands: but neuer yet prospered hee subiects being rebels against their naturall Soueraine, were they neuer so great or noble, so many, so stout, so wittie, and politike, but alwayes they came by the ouerthrow, and to a shameful ende: so much doeth GOD abhorre rebellion, more then other warres, though otherwise being so dreadfull, and so great a destruction to mankinde. Though not onely great multitudes of the rude and rascall commons, but sometime also men of great wit, nobilitie, and authoritie, haue mooued rebellions against their lawfull Princes whereas true nobility should most abhorre such villanous, and true wisedome should most detest such franticke rebellion) though they should pretend sundry causes, as the redresse of the common wealth (which rebellion of all other mischiefes doeth most destroy) or reformation of religion (whereas rebellion is most against all true religion) though they haue made a great shew of holy meaning by beginning their rebellions with a counterfeit seruice of GOD, (as did wicked Absolon begin his rebellion with sacrificing vnto GOD, 2 Sam. 15.12) though they display, and beare about ensignes, and banners, which are acceptable vnto the rude ignorant common people, great multitudes of whom by such false pretences and shewes they doe deceiue, and draw vnto them: yet were the multitudes of the rebels neuer so huge and great, the captaines neuer so noble, politike and wittie, the pretences fained to bee neuer so good and holy, yet the speedie ouerthrow of all rebels, of what number, state, or condition soeuer they were, or what colour or cause soeuer they pretended, is, and euer hath beene such, that GOD thereby doeth shew that hee alloweth neither the dignitie of any person, nor the multitude of any people, nor the weight of any cause, as sufficient for the which the subiectes may mooue rebellion against their Princes.

Turne ouer and reade the histories of all Nations, looke ouer the Chronicles of our owne countrey, call to minde so many rebellions of old time, and some yet fresh in memorie, yee shall not finde that GOD euer prospered any rebellion against their naturall and lawfull Prince, but contrariwise that the rebels were ouerthrowen and slaine, and such as were taken prisoners dreadfully executed. Consider the great and noble families of Dukes, Marquesses, Earles, and other Lords, whose names yee shall reade in our Chronicles, now cleane extinguished and gone, and seeke out the causes of the decay, you shall finde, that not lacke of issue and heires male hath so much wrought that decay, and waste of noble bloods and houses, as hath rebellion.

And for so much as the redresse of the common wealth hath of old bene the vsuall fained pretence of rebels, and religion now of late beginneth to bee a colour of rebellion: let all godly and discreete subiects consider well of both, and first concerning religion. If peaceable King Salomon was iudged of GOD to bee more meete to build his Temple (whereby the ordering of religion is meant) then his father King Dauid, though otherwise a most godly King, for that Dauid was a great warriour, and had shedde much blood, though it were in his warres against the enemies of GOD: of this may all godly and reasonable subiects consider, that a peaceable Prince, specially our most peaceable and mercifull Queene, who hath hitherto shed no blood at all, no not of her most deadly enemies, is more like and farre meeter either to set vp, or to maintaine true religion, then are bloody rebels, who haue not shed the blood of GODS enemies, as king Dauid had done, but doe seeke to shed the blood of GODS friends, of their owne countreymen, and of their owne most deare friends and kinsefolke, yea the destruction of their most gracious Prince and naturall countrey, for defence of whom they ought to bee ready to shedde their blood, if neede should so require. What a religion it is that such men by such meanes would restore, may easily bee iudged: euen as good a religion surely, as rebels bee good men and obedient subiects, and as rebellion is a good meane of redresse and reformation, being it selfe the greatest deformation of all that may possible bee. But as the trueth of the Gospel of our Sauiour Christ, being quietly and soberly taught, though it doe cost them their liues that doe teach it, is able to maintaine the true Religion: so hath a franticke religion neede of such furious maintenances as is rebellion, and of such patrons as are rebels, being ready not to die for the true Religion, but to kill all that shall or dare speake against their false superstition and wicked idolatrie. Now concerning pretences of any redresse of the common wealth, made by rebels, euery man that hath but halfe an eye, may see how vaine they bee, rebellion being as I haue before declared, the greatest ruine and destruction of all common wealths that may bee possible. And who so looketh on the one part vpon the persons and gouernement of the Queenes most honourable Counsellers, by the experiment of so many yeeres prooued honourable to her Maiestie, and most profitable and beneficiall vnto our countrey and countreymen, and on the other part, considereth the persons, state and conditions of the rebels themselues, the reformers, as they take vpon them, of the present gouernement, hee shall finde that the most rash and hairebrained men, the greatest vnthriftes, that haue most lewdly wasted their owne goods and landes, those that are ouer the eares in debt, and such as for their theftes, robberies, and murders, dare not in any well gouerned common wealth, where good Lawes are in force, shew their faces, such as are of most lewd and wicked behauiour and life, and all such as will not, or cannot liue in peace, are alwayes most ready to mooue rebellion, or take part with rebels. And are not these meete men, trow you, to restore the common wealth decayed, who haue so spoyled and consumed all their owne wealth and thrift? and very like to amend other mens maners, who haue so vile vices, and abominable conditions themselues? Surely that which they falsely call reformation, is indeede not onely a defacing or a deformation, but also an vtter destruction of all common wealth, as would well appeare, might the rebels haue their wils, and doth right well and too well appeare by their doing in such places of the countrey where rebels doe rout, where though they tary but a very little while, they make such reformation that they destroy all places, and vndoe all men where they come, that the childe yet vnborne may rue it, and shall many yeeres hereafter curse them.

Let no good and discreete subiectes therefore follow the flagge or banner displayed to rebellion, and borne by rebels, though it haue the image of the plough painted therein, with God speede the plough, written vnder in great letters, knowing that none hinder the plough more then rebels, who will neyther goe to the plough themselues, nor suffer other that would goe vnto it. And though some rebels beare the picture of the fiue wounds paynted, against those who put their onely hope of saluation in the wounds of Christ, not those wounds which are painted in a clout by some lewd paynter, but in those wounds which Christ himselfe bare in his precious body: though they, little knowing what the crosse of Christ meaneth, which neither caruer nor paynter can make, doe beare the image of the crosse painted in a ragge, against those that haue the crosse of Christ painted in their hearts, yea though they paint withall in their flagges, *Hoc signo vinces*, By this signe thou shalt get the victorie, by a most fonde imitation of the posie of Constantinus Magnus, that noble Christian Emperour, and great conquerour of GODS enemies, a most vnmeete ensigne for rebels, the enemies of GOD, their Prince, and countrey, or what other banner soeuer they shall beare: yet let no good and godly subiect, vpon any hope of victorie or good successe, follow such standerd bearers of rebellion.

For as examples of such practises are to bee found aswell in the histories of olde, as also of latter rebellions, in our fathers, and our fresh memorie: so notwithstanding these pretences made and banners borne, are recorded withall to perpetuall memorie, the great and horrible murders of infinite multitudes and thousands of the common people slaine in rebellion, dreadfull executions of the authours and captaines, the pitifull vndoing of their wiues & children, and disinheriting of the heyres of the rebels for euer, the spoyling, wasting, and destruction of the people and countrey where rebellion was first begun, that the childe then yet vnborne might rue and lament it, with the finall ouerthrow, and shamefull deaths of all rebels, set foorth aswell in the histories of forreigne nations, as in the Chronicles of our owne countrey, some thereof being yet in fresh memorie, which if they were collected together, would make many volumes and bookes: But on the contrary part all good lucke, successe and prosperitie that euer happened vnto any rebelles of any age, time or countrey, may bee conteyned in a very few lines, or wordes.

Wherefore to conclude, let all good subiects, considering how horrible a sinne against GOD, their Prince, their country, and countrimen, against all GODS and mans lawes rebellion is, being indeed not one seuerall sinne, but all sinnes against GOD and man heaped together, considering the mischieuous life and deeds, & the shamefull ends & deaths of all rebels hitherto, and the pitifull vndoing of their wiues, children, and families, and disinheriting of their heires for euer, and aboue all things considering the eternall damnation that is prepared for all impenitent rebels in hell with Satan the first founder of rebellion, and grand captaine of all rebels, let all good Subiects I say, considering these things, auoide and flee all rebellion, as the greatest of all mischiefes, and imbrace due obedience to GOD and our Prince, as the greatest of all vertues, that wee may both escape all euils and miseries that doe follow rebellion in this world, and eternall damnation in the world to come, and enioy peace, quietnesse, and securitie, with all other GODS benefits and blessings which follow obedience in this life, and finally may enioy the kingdome of heauen, the peculiar place of all obedient Subiects to GOD and their Prince in the world to come: which I beseech GOD the King of all kings, graunt vnto vs for the obedience of his Sonne our Sauiour Iesus Christ, vnto whom with the Father and the holy Ghost, one GOD and King immortall, al honour, seruice, and obedience of all his creatures is due for euer and euer, Amen.

Thus haue you heard the fourth part of this Homilie, now good people let vs pray.

The Prayer as in that time it was published.

O Most mighty GOD, the Lord of hostes, the Gouernour of al creatures, the only giuer of all victories, & who alone art able to strengthen the weak against the mighty, and to vanquish infinite multitudes of thine enemies with the countenance of a few of thy seruants calling vpon thy Name, & trusting in thee: Defend, O Lord, thy seruant and our Gouernour vnder thee, our Queene Elizabeth, & all thy people committed to her charge: O Lord withstand the cruelty of all those which be common enemies aswell to the trueth of thy eternall Word, as to their owne naturall Prince and countrey, and manifestly to this Crowne & Realme of England which thou hast of thy diuine prouidence assigned in these our dayes to the gouernement of thy seruant, our Soueraigne and gracious Queene, O most mercifull Father, (if it be thy holy will) make soft and tender the stony hearts of all those that exalt themselues against thy Trueth and seeke either to trouble the quiet of this Realme of England, or to oppresse the Crowne of the same, and conuert them to the knowledge of thy Sonne the onely Sauiour of the world, Iesus Christ, that we and they may ioyntly glorifie thy mercies. Lighten we beseech thee their ignorant hearts, to imbrace the truth of thy word, or els so abate their cruelty (O most mighty Lord) that this our Christian Realme with others that confesse thy holy Gospel, may obtaine by thine aide and strength, suretie from all enemies, without shedding of Christian blood, whereby all they which bee oppressed with their tyrannie, may be relieued, and they which bee in feare of their crueltie, may bee comforted: and finally that all Christian Realmes, and specially this Realme of England, may by thy defence and protection continue in the trueth of the Gospel and enioy perfect peace, quietnesse, and security: and that wee for these thy mercies, iointly altogether with one consonant heart and voyce, may thankfully render to thee all laud and prayse, that we knit in one godly concord and vnity amongst our selues, may continually magnifie thy glorious Name, who with thy son our Sauiour Iesus Christ, and the holy Ghost, art one Eternall, Almighty, and most mercifull GOD: To whom be all laud and prayse world without end. Amen.

THE FIFTH PART OF THE HOMILY AGAINST DISOBEDIENCE AND WILFULL REBELLION.

WHereas after both doctrine and examples of due obedience of subictes to their Princes, I declared lastly vnto you what an abominable sinne against GOD and man rebellion is, and what horrible plagues, punishments, and deathes, with death euerlasting, finally doeth hang ouer the heades of all rebels: it shall not bee either impertinent, or vnprofitable now to declare who they bee, whom the deuill, the first authour and founder of rebellion, doeth chiefely vse to the stirring vp of subiects to rebell against their lawfull Princes: that knowing them, ye may flee them, and their damnable suggestions, auoid all rebellion, and to escape the horrible plagues, and dreadfull death, and damnation eternall finally due to all rebels.

Though many causes of rebellion may bee reckoned, and almost as many as there be vices in men and women, as hath beene before noted: yet in this place I will onely touch the principall and most vsuall causes as specially ambition and ignorance. By ambition, I meane the vnlawfull and restlesse desire in men, to bee of higher estate then GOD hath giuen or appointed vnto them. By ignorance, I meane no vnskilfulnesse in artes or sciences, but the lacke of knowledge of GODS blessed will declared in his holy word, which teacheth both extreamely to abhorre all rebellion, as beeing the roote of all mischiefe, and specially to delight in obedience, as the beginning and foundation of all goodnesse, as hath beene also before specified. And as these are the two chiefe causes of rebellion: so are there specially two sortes of men in whom these vices doe raigne, by whom the deuill, the authour of all euill, doeth chiefly stirre vp all disobedience and rebellion.

The restlesse ambitious hauing once determined by one meanes or other to atchieue to their intended purpose, when they cannot by lawfull and peaceable meanes clime so high as they doe desire, they attempt the same by force and violence: wherein when they cannot preuaile against the ordinarie authoritie and power of lawfull Princes and gouernours themselues alone, they doe seeke the ayde and helpe of the ignorant multitude, abusing them to their wicked purpose. Wherefore seeing a few ambitious and malitious are the authours and heads, and multituds of ignorant men are the ministers and furtherers of rebellion, the chiefe point of this part shall bee aswell to notifie to the simple and ignorant men who they bee, that haue beene and be vsuall authours of rebellion, that they may know them: and also to admonish them to beware of the subtill suggestions of such restlesse ambitious persons, and so to flee them: that rebellions (though attempted by a few ambitious) through the lacke of maintenance by any multitudes, may speedily and easily without any great labour, danger or domage be repressed and clearely extinguished.

It is well knowen aswell by all histories, as by dayly experience, that none haue either more ambitiously aspired aboue

Emperours, Kings and Princes: nor haue more pernitiously mooued the ignorant people to rebellion against their Princes, then certaine persons which falsely chalenge to themselues to bee onely counted and called spirituall. I must therefore heere yet once againe briefly put you (good people) in remembrance out of GODS holy worde, how our Sauiour Iesus Christ, and his holy Apostles, the heads and chiefe of all true Spirituall and Ecclesiasticall men, behaued themselues towards the Princes and Rulers of their time (Matthew 17.25), though not the best gouernours that euer were, that you bee not ignorant whether they be the true disciples and followers of Christ and his Apostles, and so true spirituall men, that either by ambition doe so highly aspire, or doe most maliciously teach, or most pernitiously doe execute rebellion against their lawfull Princes, being the worst of all carnall workes, and mischieuous deedes.

The holy Scriptures doe teach most expresly, that our Sauiour Christ himselfe, and his Apostles Saint Paul, Saint Peter, with others, were vnto the Magistrates and higher powers, which ruled at their being vpon the earth, both obedient themselues, and did also diligently and earnestly exhort all other Christians to the like obedience vnto their Princes and Gouernours (Mark 12.17, Luke 20.25): whereby it is euident that men of the Cleargie, and Ecclesiasticall ministers, as their successours ought both themselues specially, and before other, to bee obedient vnto their Princes, and also to exhort all others vnto the same (Romans 13.1, 1 Timothy 2.1-2, 1 Peter 2.13). Our Sauiour Christ likewise teaching by his doctrine that his Kingdome was not of this world (Matthew 27.11, Luke 23.3), did by his example in fleeing from those that would haue made him king, confirme the same (John 6.15, 18, 36): expresly also forbidding his Apostles, and by them the whole Cleargie, all princely dominion ouer people and Nations, and hee and his holy Apostles likewise, namely Peter and Paul, did forbid vnto all Ecclesiasticall ministers, dominion ouer the Church of Christ (Matthew 20.25, Mark 10.42, Luke 22.25). And indeede whiles the Ecclesiasticall ministers continued in Christes Church in that order that is in Christes word prescribed vnto them, and in Christian kingdoms kept themselues obedient to their owne Princes, as the holy Scripture doeth teach them: both was Christs Church more cleare from ambitious emulations and contentions (Matthew 23.8, Luke 9.46, 2 Corinthians 1.24), and the state of Christian kingdomes, lesse subiect vnto tumults and rebellions. But after that ambition and desire of dominion entred once into Ecclesiasticall ministers, whose greatnesse after the doctrine and example of our Sauiour, should chiefly stand in humbling themselues (1 Peter 5.3, Matthew 18.4, 20.28, Luke 9.48, 22.27): and that the Bishop of Rome being by the order of GODS word none other then the Bishop of that one See and Diocesse, and neuer yet well able to gouerne the same, did by intolerable ambition chalenge, not onely to bee the head of all the Church dispersed throughout the world, but also to bee Lord of all Kingdomes of the world, as is expresly set foorth in the booke of his owne Canon lawes (*Sex Decre. Bk. 3, tit. 16, chap. unic., Bk. 5, tit. 9, Chap. 5 in glossa*), most contrary to the doctrine and example of our Sauiour Christ, whose Vicar, and of his Apostles, namely Peter, whose successour hee pretendeth to bee: after his ambition entred, and this chalenge once made by the Bishop of Rome, hee became at once the spoyler and destroyer both of the Church, which is the kingdome of our Sauiour Christ, and of the Christian Empire, and all Christian kingdomes, as an vniuersall tyrant ouer all.

And whereas before that chalenge made, there was great amitie and loue amongst the Christians of all countreys, hereupon began emulation, and much hatred betweene the Bishop of Rome and his Cleargie and friendes on the one part, and the Grecian Cleargie and Christians of the East on the other part, for that they refused to acknowledg any such supreme authoritie of the Bishop of Rome ouer them: the Bishoppe of Rome for this cause amongst other, not onely naming them, and taking them for Schismatikes, but also neuer ceasing to persecute them, and the Emperours who had their See and continuance in Greece, by stirring of the subiectes to rebellion against their soueraigne Lords, and by raysing deadly hatred and most cruell warres betweene them and other Christian Princes. And when the Bishoppes of Rome had translated the title of the Emperour, and as much as in them did lie, the Empire it selfe from their Lord the Emperour of Greece, and of Rome also by right vnto the Christian Princes of the West, they became in short space no better vnto the West Emperours, then they were before vnto the Emperours of Greece: for the vsuall discharging of subiectes from their oath of fidelitie made vnto the Emperours of the West their soueraigne Lords, by the Bishoppes of Rome: the vnnaturall stirring vp of the subiectes vnto rebellion against their Princes, yea of the sonne against the father, by the Bishoppe of Rome: the most cruell and bloodie warres raysed amongst Christian Princes of all kingdomes: the horrible murder of infinite thousandes of Christian men beeing slaine by Christians: and which ensued thereupon, the pitifull losses, of so manie goodly Cities, Countreys, Dominions, and Kingdomes, sometime possessed by Christians in Asia, Africa, Europa: the miserable fall of the Empire and Church of Greece, sometime the most flourishing parte of Christendome, into the handes of the Turkes: the lamentable diminishing, decaye, and ruine of Christian religion: the dreadfull increase of paganisme, and power of the infidels and miscreants, and all by the practise and procurement of the Bishop of Rome chiefly, is in the histories and chronicles written by the Bishop of Romes own fauourers and friendes to bee seene, and aswell knowen vnto all such as are acquainted with the said histories. The ambitious intent and most subtile driftes of the Bishops of Rome in these their practises, appeared euidently by their bold attempt in spoyling and robbing the Emperours, of their townes, cities, dominions, and kingdomes, in Italie, Lombardie,Italie, Lombardie, and Sicilie, of ancient right belonging vnto the Empire, and by ioyning of them vnto their Bishopricke of Rome, or else giuing them vnto strangers, to hold them of the Church and Bishop of Rome as in *capite*, and as of the chiefe Lordes thereof, in which tenure they hold the most part thereof, euen at this day. But these ambitious and indeede traiterous meanes and spoyling of their soueraigne Lords, the Bishops of Rome, of Priestes, and none other by right then the Bishops of one citie and diocesse, are by false vsurpation become great Lordes of many dominions, mightie Princes, yea or Emperours rather, as claiming to haue diuerse Princes and Kings to their vassals, liege men, and subiects: as in the same histories written by their owne familiars and courtiers is to bee seene. And indeede since the time that the Bishops of Rome by ambition, treason, and vsurpation atchieued and attained to this height and greatnesse, they behaued themselues more like Princes, Kinges, and Emperours in all things, then reamined like Princes, Bishoppes, and ecclesiasticall, or (as they would bee called) spirituall persons, in any one thing at all. For after this rate they haue handled other Kings and Princes of other Realmes throughout Christendome, as well as their Soueraigne Lords the Emperours, vsually discharging their subiects of their oath of fidelity, & so stirring them vp to rebellion against their naturall Princes, whereof some examples shall in the last part hereof be notified vnto you.

Wherefore let all good subiectes, knowing these the speciall instruments, and ministers of the deuill, to the stirring vp of all rebellions, auoyde and flee them, and the pestilent suggestions of such forraigne vsurpers, and their adherentes, and embrace all obedience to

GOD, and their naturall Princes and Soueraignes, that they may enioy GODS blessings, and their Princes fauour, all peace, quietnesse, securitie in this world, and finally attaine through Christ our Sauiour, life euerlasting in the world to come: which GOD the Father for the same our Sauiour Iesus Christ his sake grant vnto vs all, to whom with the holy Ghost, be all honour and glory, world without end, Amen.

Thus haue you heard the fifth part of this Homilie, now good people let vs pray.

The Prayer as in the time it was published.

O Most mighty GOD, the Lord of hostes, the Gouernour of all creatures, the only giuer of all victories, who alone art able to strengthen the weake against the mighty, and to vanquish infinite multitudes of thine enemies with the countenance of a few of thy seruants calling vpon thy Name, and trusting in thee: Defend O Lord, thy seruant & our Gouernour vnder thee, our Queene Elizabeth and all thy people committed to her charge, O Lord withstand the crueltie of all those which be common enemies as well to the trueth of thy eternall Word, as to their owne naturall Prince and countrey, and manifestly to this Crowne and Realme of England, which thou hast of thy diuine prouidence assigned in these our dayes to the gouernment of thy seruant, our Soueraigne & gracious Queene. O most mercifull Father, (if it be thy holy will) make soft and tender the stonie hearts of all those that exalt themselues against thy Trueth, and seeke either to trouble the quiet of this Realme of England, or to oppresse the Crowne of the same, and conuert them to the knowledge of thy Sonne the onely Sauiour of the world, Iesus Christ that we and they may ioyntly glorifie thy mercies. Lighten we beseech thee their ignorant hearts, to imbrace the truth of thy Word, or els so abate their cruelty (O most mighty Lord) that this our Christian Realm, with others that confesse thy holy Gospel, may obtaine by thine ayde and strength, surety from all enemies, without shedding of Christian blood, whereby all they which bee oppressed with their tyranny, may bee relieued, and they which bee in feare of their cruelty, may bee comforted: and finally that all Christian Realmes, and specially this Realme of England, may by thy defence and protection continue in the trueth of the Gospel, and enioy perfect peace, quietnesse, and security: and that wee for these thy mercies, ioyntly altogether with one consonant heart and voyce, may thankfully render to thee all laud and prayse, that we knit in one godly concord and vnity amongst our selues, may continually magnifie thy glorious Name, who with thy son our Sauiour Iesus Christ, and the holy Ghost, art one Eternall, Almighty, and most mercifull GOD: To whom be all laud and prayse world without end. Amen.

THE SIXTH AND LAST PART OF THE HOMILY AGAINST DISOBEDIENCE AND WILFULL REBELLION.

NOW whereas the iniuries, oppressions, rauenie, and tyranny of the Bishop of Rome, vsurping aswell against their naturall Lords the Emperours, as against all other Christian Kings, and Kingdomes, and their continuall stirring of subiects vnto rebellions against their Soueraigne Lords, whereof I haue partly admonished you before, were intolerable: and it may seeme more then maruayle, that any subiects would after such sort hold with vnnaturall forraine vsurpers against their owne soueraigne Lords, and naturall countrey: It remayneth that I doe declare the meane whereby they compassed these matters, and so to conclude this whole treaty of due obedience, and against disobedience, and wilfull rebellion.

Of ignorance of the simple people the latter part. You shall vnderstand, that by ignorance of GODS word, wherein they kept all men, specially the common people, they wrought and brought to passe all these things, making them beleeue that all that they sayd was true, all that they did was good and godly: and that to hold with them in all things, against father, mother, prince, countrey, and all men, was most meritorious. And indeed what mischiefe will not blinde ignorance leade simple men vnto?

By ignorance the Iewish Clergie induced the common people to aske the deliuery of Barabbas the seditious murderer, and to sue for the cruell crucifying of our Sauiour Christ, for that he rebuked the ambition, superstition, and other vices of the high Priests and Clergie. For as our Sauiour Christ testifieth, that those who crucified him wist not what they did: so doeth the holy Apostle Saint Paul say, If they had knowen, if they had not beene ignorant, they would neuer haue crucified the Lord of glory: but they knew not what they did. Our Sauiour Christ himselfe also foreshewed that it should come to passe by ignorance, that those who should persecute and murder his true Apostles and Disciples, should thinke they did GOD acceptable sacrifice, and good seruice: as it is also verified euen at this day.

And in this ignorance haue the Bishops of Rome kept the people of GOD, specially the common sort, by no meanes so much, as by withdrawing of the word of GOD from them, and by keeping it vnder the vayle of an vnknowen strange tongue. For as it serued the ambitious humour of the Bishops of Rome, to compell all nations to vse the naturall language of the city of Rome, where they were Bishops, which shewed a certain acknowledging of subiection vnto them: so yet serued it much more their craftie purpose, thereby to keepe all people so blind, that they not knowing what they prayed, what they beleeued, what they were commanded by GOD, might take all their commandements for GODS. For as they would not suffer the holy Scriptures or Church seruice to bee vsed or had in any other language then the Latine: so were very fewe, euen of the most simple people taught the Lords prayer, the articles of the faith, and the tenne commandements, otherwise then in Latine, which they vnderstood not: by which vniuersall ignorance, all men were ready to beleeue whatsoeuer they sayde, and to doe whatsoeuer they commanded.

Sicognouissent. For to imitate the Apostles phrase: If the Emperours subiectes had knowne out of GODS word their dutie to their prince, they would not haue suffered the Bishop of Rome to perswade them to forsake their Soueraigne lord the Emperour against their oath of fidelitie, and to rebel against him, onely for that he cast images (vnto the which idolatrie was committed) out of the churches (Gregorius 2. and 3. Anno Do. 726 &c. In the second commandement), which the Bishoppe of Rome bare them in hand to bee heresie. If they had knowen of GODS worde but as much as the tenne commaundements, they should haue founde that the Bishop of Rome, was not onely a traytour to the Emperour his liege Lord, but to GOD also, and an horrible blasphemer of his maiesty, in calling his holy word and commaundement heresie: and that which the Byshoppe of Rome tooke for a iust cause to rebell against his lawfull prince, they might haue knowen to bee a doublinge and triplinge of his most heynous wickednesse, heaped with horrible impiety and blasphemy.

But lest the poore people should know too much, he would not let them haue as much of GODS word, as the tenne commaundements wholy and perfectly, withdrawinge from them the second commaundement, that bewrayeth his impietie, by a subtill sacrilege. Had the Emperours subiects likewise knowen, and beene of any vnderstanding in GODS (Henrie 4. Gregor.7. Anno Domini 176. Paschal.2. Anno 199.) word, would they at other times haue rebelled against their Soueraigne Lord, and by their rebellion haue holpen to depose him, onely for that the Byshop of Rome did beare them in hand, that it was symonie and heresie to, for the Emperour to giue any ecclesiasticall dignities, or promotions to his learned Chaplaines, or other of his learned Clergie, which al Christian Emperours before him had done without controulement? woulde they, I say, for that the Bishop of Rome bare them so in hand, haue rebelled by the space of more then fourtie yeeres together against him, with so much shedding of Christian bloud, and murther of so many thousandes of Christians, and finally haue deposed their Soueraigne Lorde, had they knowen and had in GODS word any vnderstanding at all? Specially had they knowen that they did all this to plucke from their Soueraigne Lord, and his successours for euer, their auncient right of the Empire, to giue it vnto the Romish Clergie, and to the Bishop of Rome, that hee might for the confirmation of one Archbishop, and for the Romish ragge, which he calleth a Paul, scarce worth twelue pence, receiue many thousand crownes of gold, and of other Bishops, likewise great summes of money for their bulles, which is symonie indede: Would, I say, Christian men and subiectes by rebellion haue spent so much Christian blood, and haue desposed their naturall, most noble, and most valiant Prince, to bring the matter finally to this passe, had they knowen what they did, or had any vnderstanding in GODS word at all? And as these ambitious vsurpers the Bishops of Rome haue ouerflowed all Italie and Germanie with streames of Christian blood, shed by the rebellions of ignorant subiects against their naturall Lords and Emperours, whom they haue stirred thereunto by such false pretences: so is there no countrey in Christendome, which by their like meanes and false pretences, hath not beene ouersprinkled with the blood of subiectes by rebellion against their naturall Soueraigns stirred vp by &the; same Bishops of Rome.

King Iohn. And to vse one example of our owne countrey: The Bishoppe of Rome did picke a quarrell to King Iohn of England, about the election of Steuen Langton to the Bishopricke of Canterburie, wherein the King had ancient right, being vsed by his progenitors, all Christian Kinges of England before him, the Bishops of Rome hauing no right, but had begunne then to vsurpe vpon the Kinges of Englande, and all other Christian Kinges, as they had before done against their Soueraigne Lordes the Emperours: proceeding euen by the same waies & meanes, & likewise cursing King Iohn, and discharginge his subiects of their oath of fidelitie vnto their Soueraigne Lord. Now had Englishmen at that time knowen their duetie to their prince set forth in GODS worde, would a great many of nobles, and other Englishmen naturall subiectes, for this forraigne and vnnaturall vsurper his vayne curse of the King, and for his faigned discharginge of them of their oath and fidelitie to their naturall Lord, vpon so slender or no grounde at all, haue rebelled against their soueraigne Lorde the Kinge (*Innocencini.3.*)? Would Englishe subiects haue taken part against the King of England, and against Englishemen, with the French King and Frenchmen, beeing incensed against this Realme by the Bishoppe of Rome?

Philip French King. Lewes Dolphine of France. Would they haue sent for, and receiued the Dolphine of Fraunce with a great armie of Frenchmen into the Realme of England? Would they haue sworne fidelitie to the Dolphine of Fraunce, breaking their oath of fidelitie to their naturall Lord the Kinge of England, and haue stood vnder the Dolphins banner displayed against the King of England? Would they haue expelled their soueraigne Lorde the Kinge of England out of London, the chiefe cittie of England, and out of the greatest part of England, vpon the Southside of Trent, euen vnto Lincolne, and out of Lincolne it selfe also, and haue deliuered the possession thereof vnto the Dolphin of Fraunce, wherof he kept &the; possession a great while? Would they beeing Englishmen haue procured so great shedding of English bloud, and other infinite mischiefes and miseries vnto England their natural countrie, as did follow those cruell warres and trayterous rebellion, the fruits of the Bishop of Romes blessings? Would they haue driuen their naturall soueraigne Lord the King of England to such extremitie, that he was inforced to submit himselfe vnto that forraigne false vsurper the Bishop of Rome, who compelled him to surrender vp the crowne of England into the handes of his Legate, who in token of possession kept it in his handes diuers dayes, and then deliuered it againe to King Iohn, vpon that condition that the King and his Successours, Kings of England, should hold the Crowne, and Kingdome of England of the Bishop of Rome and his successours, as the vassals of the sayd Bishops of Rome for euer: in token whereof, the Kings of England should also pay a yeerely tribute to the sayd Bishoppe of Rome as his vassals and liege men? Would Englishmen haue brought their Soueraigne lord, and naturall countrey into this thraldome and subiection to a false forraigne vsurper, had they knowen and had any vnderstanding in GODS word at all?

See the Acts of Parliament in king Edward the third his dayes.

Out of the which most lamentable case, and miserable tyrannie, rauenie, and spoyle of the most greedie Romish wolues ensuing hereupon, the Kings and Realme of England could not rid themselues by the space of many yeeres after: the Bishop of Rome by his ministers continually not onely spoyling the Realme and Kings of England of infinite treasure, but also with the same money hiring and maintaining forreigne enemies against the Realme and Kings of England, to keepe them in such his subiection, that they should not refuse to pay whatsoeuer those vnsatiable wolues did greedily gape for, and suffer whatsoeuer those most cruell tyrants would lay vpon them. Would Englishmen haue suffered this? would they by rebellion haue caused this trow you, and all for the Bishop of Romes causelesse curse, had they in those dayes knowen and vnderstood, that GOD doeth curse the blessings, and blesse the cursings of such wicked vsurping Bishops and tyrants? as it appeared afterward in King Henry the eight his dayes, and King Edward the sixt, and in our gracious Soueraignes dayes that now is, where neither the Popes curses, nor GODS manifold blessings are wanting (Malachi 2.2). But in King Iohns time, the Bishop of Rome vnderstanding the bruit blindnesse, ignorance of GODS word, and superstition of Englishmen, and how much they were enclined to worship the Babylonicall beast of Rome, and to feare all his threatnings, and causelesse curses, hee abused them thus, and by their rebellion brought this noble Realme, and Kings of England vnder his most cruell tyrannie, and to bee a spoyle of his most vile and vnsatiable couetousnesse and rauenie, for a long and a great deale too long a time. And to ioyne vnto the reportes of Histories, matters of later memorie, could the Bishop of Rome haue raised the late rebellions in the North and West countreys in the times of King Henry, and King Edward, our gracious Soueraignes father and brother, but by abusing of the ignorant people? Or is it not most euident that the Bishop of Rome hath of late attempted by his Irish Patriarkes and Bishops, sent from Rome with his Bulles, (whereof some were apprehended) to breake downe the barres and hedges of the publique peace in Ireland, onely vpon confidence easily to abuse the ignorance of the wilde Irish men? Or who seeth not that vpon like confidence, yet more lately hee hath likewise procured the breach of the publique peace in England, (with the long and blessed continuance whereof hee is sore grieued) by the ministery of his disguised Chaplaynes, creeping in Lay mens apparell into the houses, and whispering in the eares of certaine Northern borderers, being then most ignorant of their duetie to GOD and to their Prince of all people of the Realme, whom therefore as most meete and ready to execute his intended purpose, hee hath by the said ignorant Masse priests, as blinde guides leading the blinde, brought those seely blinde subiects into the deepe ditch of horrible rebellion, damnable to themselues, and very dangerous to the state of the Realme, had not GOD of his mercy miraculously calmed that raging tempest, not onely without any ship wracke of the Common wealth, but almost without any shedding of Christian and English blood at all.

And it is yet much more to be lamented, that not onely common people, but some other youthfull or vnskilfull Princes also, suffer themselues to bee abused by the Bishop of Rome, his Cardinals and Bishops, to oppressing of Christian men their faithfull subiects, eyther themselues, or els by procuring the force and strength of Christian men, to bee conueyed out of one countrey, to oppresse true Christians in another countrey, and by these meanes open an entry vnto Moores and Infidels, into the possession of Christian Realmes countries: other Christian Princes in the meane time, by the Bishop of Romes procuring also, being so occupied in ciuill warres, or troubled with rebellions, that they haue neither leisure nor abilitie to conferre their common forces, to the defence of their fellow Christians, against such inuasions of the common enemies of Christendome, the Infidels and miscreants. Would to GOD we might onely reade and heare out of the histories of olde, and not also see and feele these new and present oppressions of Christians, rebellions of subiects, effusion of Christian blood, destruction of Christian men, decay and ruine of Christendome, increase of Paganisme, most lamentable and pitifull to behold, being procured in these our dayes, aswell as in times past, by the Bishop of Rome and his ministers, abusing the ignorance of GODS word, yet remayning in some Christian Princes and people. By which sorrow and bitter fruites of ignorance, all men ought to bee mooued to giue eare and credite to GODS worde, shewing as most truely, so most plainely how great a mischiefe ignorance is, and againe how great and how good a gift of GOD knowledge in GODS word is. And to beginne with the Romish Cleargie, who though they doe bragge now, as did sometime the Iewish Cleargie, that they cannot lacke knowledge (Jeremiah 18.18): yet doeth GOD by his holy Prophets both charge them with ignorance (Ezechiel 7.26), and threaten them also, for that they haue repelled the knowledge of GODS word and Law (Hosea 4.6), from themselues, and from his people, that hee will repell them, that they shall bee no more his Priests (Psalms 2.5). GOD likewise chargeth Princes aswell as Priests, that they should indeuour themselues to get vnderstanding and knowledge in his word, threatning his heauie wrath and destruction vnto them, if they faile thereof. And the wise man saith to all men vniuersally, Princes, priests, and people: Where is no knowledge, there is no good nor health to the soule: and that all men be vaine in whom is not the knowledge of GOD, and his holy word (Proverbs 19.2): That they who walke in darknesse, wote not whither they goe (Apocrypha. Wisdom 13.1, Proverbs 17.24): and that the people that will not learne, shall fall into great mischiefes (Ephesians 4.18, John 12.35, Isaiah 5.13), as did the people of Israel, who for their ignorance in GODS word, were first led into captiuitie, and when by ignorance afterward they would not know the time of their visitation (Luke 19.44, 23.34), but crucified Christ our Sauiour, persecuted his holy Apostles, and were so ignorant and blinde, that when they did most wickedly and cruelly, they thought they did GOD good and acceptable seruice (as doe many by ignorance thinke euen at this day: John 16.2) finally, through their ignorance and blindenesse (Isaiah 27.11, Hosea 4.6), their countrey, townes, cities, Hierusalem it selfe, and the Temple of GOD, were all most horribly destroyed, the most chiefest part of their people slaine, and the rest ledde into most miserable captiuitie (*Acts passim multis locis.*). For hee that made them, had no pitie vpon them, neither would spare them, and all for their ignorance (Apocrypha. Baruch 3.28).

And the holy Scriptures doe teach, that the people that will not see with their eyes, nor heare with their eares, to learne, and to vnderstand with their heartes, cannot bee conuerted, and saued (Isaiah 6.9, Matthew 13.14, 15, John 12.40). And the wicked themselues, beeing damned in hell (Apocrypha. Wisdom 5), shall confesse ignorance in GODS worde to haue brought them thereunto, saying, Wee haue erred from the way of the trueth, and the light of righteousnesse hath not shined vnto vs, and the sunne of vnderstanding hath not risen vnto vs (Matthew 13.19), wee haue wearied our selues in the way of wickednesse and perdition, and haue walked cumberous and crooked wayes: but the way of the Lord haue we not knowen.

And as well our Sauiour himselfe, as his Apostle Saint Paul doth teach, that the ignorance of GODS worde commeth of the deuill, is the cause of all errour, and misiudging (as falleth out with ignorant subiects (2 Corinthians 4.2-4), who can rather espie a little mote in the eye of the Prince (Matthew 7.3-5), or a Counsellour, then a great beame in their owne) and vniuersally it is the cause of all euill, and finally of eternall damnation, GODS iudgement being seuere towards those, who when the light of Christes Gospel is come into the world, doe delight more in darkenesse of ignorance, then in the light of knowledge in GODS worde (John 3.19). For all are commanded to reade or heare (Matthew 11.15, 13.9, 43, Luke 8.8, Luke 16.30-31), to search and studie the holy Scriptures (John 5.39), and are promised vnderstanding to bee giuen them from GOD (Matthew 7.7, Luke 11.9), if they so doe (Psalms 1.2): all are charged not to beleeue eyther any dead man, nor if an Angel should speake from heauen (Galatians 1.8), much lesse if the Pope doe speake from Rome against or contrary to the word of GOD, from the which we may not decline, neither to the right hand nor to the left (Deuteronomy 5.32).

In GODS worde Princes must learne how to obey GOD, and to gouerne men (Deuteronomy 17.14-15, Psalms 18, 118.8-9): in GODS worde subiects must learne obedience, both to GOD and their Princes (Romans 13.2, 1 Peter 2.13). Olde men and young, rich and poore, all men and women, all estates, sexes and ages, are taught their seuerall dueties in the worde of GOD. For the word of GOD is bright, giuing light vnto all mens eyes, the shining lampe directing all mens pathes, and steppes. Let vs therefore awake from the sleepe and darkenesse of ignorance (Ephesians 5.14), and open our eyes that wee may see the light, let vs rise from the workes of darkenesse, that we may escape eternall darkenesse, the due reward thereof, and let vs walke in the light of GODS word (1 Thessalonians 5.4, 5), whiles we haue light (John 12.35-36), as becommeth the children of light (James 1.17, 1 Timothy 6.16, John 3.19), so directing the steppes of our liues in that way which leadeth to light and life euerlasting, that wee may finally obtayne and enioy the same: which GOD the father of lights, who dwelleth in light incomprehensible, and inaccessable, grant vnto vs, through the light of the world our Sauiour Iesus Christ, vnto whom with the holy Ghost, one most glorious GOD, be all honour, prayse, and thankesgiuing for euer and euer. Amen.

Thus haue you heard the sixth part of this Homily, now good people let vs pray.

The Prayer as in that time it was published.

O Most mighty GOD, the Lord of hostes, the Gouernour of all creatures, the only giuer of all victories, who alone art able to strengthen the Weake against the mighty, and to vanquish infinite multitudes of thine enemies with the countenance of a few of thy seruants calling vpon thy Name, and trusting in thee: Defend O Lord, thy seruant & our Gouernour vnder thee, our Queene Elizabeth and all thy people committed to her charge, O Lord withstand the crueltie of all those which be common enemies as well to the trueth of thy eternall Word, as to their owne naturall Prince and countrey, and manifestly to this Crowne and Realme of England, which thou hast of thy diuine prouidence assigned in these our dayes to the gouernment of thy seruant, our Soueraigne & gracious Queene. O most mercifull Father, (if it be thy holy will) make soft and tender the stonie hearts of all those that exalt themselues against thy Trueth, and seeke either to trouble the quiet of this Realme of England, or to oppresse the Crowne of the same, and conuert them to the knowledge of thy Sonne the onely Sauiour of the world, Iesus Christ that we and they may ioyntly glorifie thy mercies. Lighten we beseech thee their ignorant hearts, to imbrace the truth of thy Word, or els so abate their cruelty (O most mighty Lord) that this our Christian Realm, with others that confesse thy holy Gospel, may obtaine by thine ayde and strength, surety from all enemies, without shedding of Christian blood, whereby all they which bee oppressed with their tyranny, may bee relieued, and they which bee in feare of their cruelty, may bee comforted: and finally that all Christian Realmes, and specially this Realme of England, may by thy defence and protection continue in the trueth of the Gospel, and enioy perfect peace, quietnesse, and securitie: and that we for these thy mercies, ioyntly altogether with one consonant heart and voice, may thankefully render to thee all laud and praise, that we knit in one godly concord and vnitie amongst our selues, may continually magnifie thy glorious Name, who with thy son our Sauiour Iesus Christ, and the holy Ghost, art one Eternall, Almightie, and most mercifull GOD: To whom be all laud, and praise world without end, Amen.

A THANKESGIVING FOR THE SUPPRESSION OF THE LAST REBELLION.

O Heauenly and most mercifull Father, the defender of those that put their trust in thee, the sure fortresse of all them that flie to thee for succour: who of thy most iust iudgements for our disobedience and rebellion against thy holy word, and for our sinfull and wicked liuing, nothing answering to our holy profession, wherby we haue giuen an occasion that thy holy name hath beene blasphemed amongst the ignorant, hast of late both sore abashed the whole Realm, and people of England, with the terrour and danger of rebellion, thereby to awake vs out of our dead sleepe of carelesse security: and hast yet by the miseries following the same rebellion more sharpely punished part of our countreymen and Christian brethren, who haue more neerely felt the same: and most dreadfully hast scourged some of the seditious persons with terrible executions, iustly inflicted for their disobedience to thee, and to thy seruant their Soueraigne, to the example of vs all, and to the warning, correction and amendment of thy seruants, of thine accustomed goodnesse, turning alwaies the wickednesse of euill men to the profit of them that feare thee: who in thy iudgements remembring thy mercy, hast by thy assistance giuen the victory to thy seruant our Queene, her true Nobility, and faithfull Subiects, with so little, or rather no effusion of Christian blood, as also might haue iustly ensued, to the exceeding comfort of all sorrowfull Christian hearts, and that of thy fatherly pity, and mercifull goodnesse onely, and euen for thine owne names sake, without any our desert at all.

Wherefore we render vnto thee most humble and hearty thankes for these thy great mercies shewed vnto vs, who had deserued sharper punishment, most humbly beseeching thee to grant vnto all vs that confesse thy holy Name, and professe the true and perfect Religion of thy holy Gospel, thy heauenly grace to shew our selues in our liuing according to our profession: that wee truely knowing thee in they blessed word, may obediently walke in thy holy commandements, and that wee being warned by this thy fatherly correction, doe prouoke thy iust wrath against vs no more: but may enioy the continuance of thy great mercies towards vs, thy right hand, as in this, so in all other inuasions, rebellions, and dangers, continually sauing and defending our Church, our Realme, our Queene, and people of England, that all our posterities ensuing, confessing thy holy Name, professing thy holy Gospel, and leading an holy life, may perpetually prayse and magnifie thee, with thy only Son Iesus Christ our Sauiour and the holy Ghost, to whom bee all laud, prayse, glory, and Empire for euer, and euer, Amen.

Also from Benediction Books ...

Wandering Between Two Worlds: Essays on Faith and Art
Anita Mathias
Benediction Books, 2007
152 pages
ISBN: 0955373700

Available from www.amazon.com, www.amazon.co.uk
www.wanderingbetweentwoworlds.com

In these wide-ranging lyrical essays, Anita Mathias writes, in lush, lovely prose, of her naughty Catholic childhood in Jamshedpur, India; her large, eccentric family in Mangalore, a sea-coast town converted by the Portuguese in the sixteenth century; her rebellion and atheism as a teenager in her Himalayan boarding school, run by German missionary nuns, St. Mary's Convent, Nainital; and her abrupt religious conversion after which she entered Mother Teresa's convent in Calcutta as a novice. Later rich, elegant essays explore the dualities of her life as a writer, mother, and Christian in the United States--Domesticity and Art, Writing and Prayer, and the experience of being "an alien and stranger" as an immigrant in America, sensing the need for roots.

About the Author

Anita Mathias was born in India, has a B.A. and M.A. in English from Somerville College, Oxford University and an M.A. in Creative Writing from the Ohio State University. Her essays have been published in The Washington Post, The London Magazine, The Virginia Quarterly Review, Commonweal, Notre Dame Magazine, America, The Christian Century, Religion Online, The Southwest Review, Contemporary Literary Criticism, New Letters, The Journal, and two of HarperSanFrancisco's The Best Spiritual Writing anthologies. Her non-fiction has won fellowships from The National Endowment for the Arts; The Minnesota State Arts Board; The Jerome Foundation, The Vermont Studio Center; The Virginia Centre for the Creative Arts, and the First Prize for the Best General Interest Article from the Catholic Press Association of the United States and Canada. Anita has taught Creative Writing at the College of William and Mary, and now lives and writes in Oxford, England.

Lightning Source UK Ltd.
Milton Keynes UK
UKHW011330251119
354202UK00004B/1393/P

9 781849 02784